1000
FAVOURITE
FAMILY
RECIPES

1000
FAVOURITE
FAMILY
RECIPES

Recipes by

Sue Cutts, Audrey Ellis, Mary Morris
Elizabeth Pomeroy, Rosemary Wadey
Harold Wilshaw, Jeni Wright

NOTES

1. *Recipes marked with an asterisk are variations. They come after and refer back to the master recipe.

2. † Recipes marked with a dagger are specially designed to be prepared in a pressure cooker.

3. All recipes serve four unless otherwise stated.

4. All spoon measurements are level.

5. All eggs are sizes 3, 4, 5 (standard) unless otherwise stated.

6. Metric and imperial measurements have been calculated separately. Use one set of measurements only as they are not exact equivalents.

7. Cooking times may vary slightly depending on the individual oven. Dishes should be placed in the centre of the oven unless otherwise specified.

8. Always preheat the oven or grill to the specified temperature.

9. Spoon measures can be bought in both imperial and metric sizes to give accurate measurement of small quantities. Use the 5 ml spoon in place of 1 teaspoon and the 15 ml spoon in place of 1 tablespoon.

First published in 1981 by Octopus Books Limited
59 Grosvenor Street, London W.1.
under the title "1,000 Recipe Cookbook"

This edition published in 1987

Printed in Great Britain

ISBN 0 7064 2431 X

CONTENTS

SOUPS & STARTERS

White Stock

approx. 450 g (1 lb) veal, lamb or
   chicken bones
approx. 1¾ litres (3 pints) cold water
1 onion, peeled and sliced
2 carrots, scraped and sliced
1 stalk celery, washed and chopped
bouquet garni
1 teaspoon salt
6–8 peppercorns

This will yield approximately 1¼ litres (2
pints). Ask the butcher to chop large
bones such as knuckle of veal. This will
release the gelatine during cooking and
give "body" to the stock. Remove any
fat from the bones, wash and place them
in a large pan. Cover with water and
bring to the boil. This is called
"blanching".

When water boils and scum rises to
the surface, remove the scum carefully
with a skimmer. Add the prepared vegetables, bouquet garni, salt and peppercorns. Cover and simmer gently for 4 to
6 hours on top of the stove or alternatively, in a slow oven.

Strain the stock through a large sieve
into a cold bowl. Discard the bones and
vegetables and allow the stock to cool.
If meat bones have been used, leave the
stock until it is quite cold as the fat will
solidify into a cake on top of the stock
and can be easily lifted off.

The fat of chicken stock will rise to
the surface as it cools, but will not
harden. Remove it by drawing sheets of
kitchen or tissue paper carefully across
the surface of the stock until it is clear.
Cover the bowl and chill quickly.

Brown Stock

450 g (1 lb) beef or veal bones,
   chopped
2 tablespoons dripping or butter
approx. 1¾ litres (3 pints) water
1 teaspoon salt
6–8 peppercorns
bouquet garni
1 onion, peeled and sliced
2 carrots, scraped and sliced
1 stalk celery, washed and chopped

This will yield approximately 1¼ litres (2
pints).

Ask the butcher to chop any really
large bones. Trim any fat from the
bones. Heat the dripping or butter in a
roasting pan in a preheated oven at
200°C, 400°F, Gas Mark 6 and brown the
bones for 30 to 40 minutes. Drain on
kitchen paper.

Put the bones into a large pan, cover
with water and bring to the boil.
Remove the scum carefully (as described in White Stock above), add salt,
peppercorns, bouquet garni and vegetables. Cover and simmer gently for 4 to
6 hours.

Strain, cool until the fat is set and
remove it. Cover the stock and chill.

* Game Stock

Follow the recipe for Brown Stock (above), with this change: use the carcass and giblets of game birds, or the bones of hare or venison.

Court Bouillon (Fish Stock)

$\frac{1}{2}$–$\frac{3}{4}$ kg (1–1$\frac{1}{2}$ lb) fish trimmings, bones, skin, head etc.
1 medium onion, peeled and sliced
1 carrot, scraped and sliced
1 small stalk celery
bouquet garni
1 teaspoon salt
10 peppercorns
approx. 1$\frac{3}{4}$ litres (3 pints) water
1 wineglass white wine
or
1 tablespoon white wine vinegar

This will yield approximately 1$\frac{1}{2}$ litres (2$\frac{1}{2}$ pints).

Rinse the fish trimmings in cold water and put them in a large pan with the vegetables, bouquet garni, salt and peppercorns. Cover with the cold water and add the wine or vinegar. Bring to the boil and skim off the scum. Simmer for 20 to 30 minutes.

Strain the stock through a large sieve with a fine mesh to catch any small bones. Use the stock for poaching fish or return it to the pan and reduce it by rapid boiling if it is required for a sauce.

Giblet Stock

giblets (see recipe)
cold water
bay leaf
sprig of parsley
1 shallot
8 peppercorns
$\frac{1}{2}$ teaspoon salt

The giblets consist of the bird's neck, gizzard (crop), heart and liver.

The liver can be reserved for stuffing. Any liver which has been stained yellow by the gall bladder (if this was broken when the bird was drawn) should be cut out and discarded as it will be bitter.

The gizzard should be cut in half, thoroughly washed and all fat removed. Squeeze any blood clots out of the heart and wash under running cold water.

Put the clean giblets in a small saucepan, cover with cold water, add the bay leaf, sprig of parsley, shallot, peppercorns and salt. Bring to the boil and remove the scum (as described in White Stock, above). Cover and simmer for 20 minutes or until required. Strain and use as required.

Gazpacho

1 × 400 g (14 oz) can tomatoes
2 slices of bread, crusts removed
$\frac{1}{2}$ small Spanish onion, peeled and very finely chopped
2 green peppers, cored, seeded and very finely chopped
2 garlic cloves, peeled and crushed
3 tablespoons olive oil
3 tablespoons wine vinegar
300 ml ($\frac{1}{2}$ pint) water
$\frac{1}{2}$ teaspoon sugar
salt
freshly ground black pepper
$\frac{1}{2}$ cucumber, very finely chopped, to garnish

Work the canned tomatoes through a fine wire sieve into a bowl or use a mouli-légume. Grate or crumble the bread into the bowl, then stir in the remaining ingredients, except the cucumber, with salt and pepper to taste. Chill for several hours, stirring occasionally, then taste and adjust the seasoning. Sprinkle the cucumber over the soup just before serving and a little more pepper if liked.

Vichyssoise

450 g (1 lb) leeks
450 g (1 lb) potatoes, peeled and sliced
1 medium onion, peeled and sliced
50 g (2 oz) butter or margarine
900 ml (1½ pints) good chicken stock
salt
freshly ground white pepper
150 ml (¼ pint) single cream
snipped chives or chopped parsley, to
  garnish

Trim the roots off the leeks and discard
the coarse outer leaves. Finely slice the
white part and about 5 cm (2 inches) of
the green and wash thoroughly. Fry the
leeks, potatoes and onions gently in the
butter or margarine in a covered pan
until softened. Add the stock and cook
for 40 to 45 minutes. Put through the
medium grid of a mouli-légume or
liquidize in a blender until very smooth.

To serve hot, reheat, sprinkle with
chopped parsley and swirl with cream
just before serving.

To serve cold, chill thoroughly and
adjust the seasoning. Just before serving, swirl in the cream and serve garnished with snipped chives.

Tomato Vichyssoise

50 g (2 oz) butter
3 medium-sized leeks, white part only,
  washed and sliced
1 medium-sized onion, peeled and
  finely chopped
3 medium-sized potatoes, peeled and
  finely sliced
300 ml (½ pint) chicken stock
salt and freshly ground white pepper
pinch of ground mace
1 bay leaf
450 ml (¾ pint) tomato juice
300 ml (½ pint) unsweetened natural
  yogurt
1 tablespoon snipped chives, to
  garnish

Heat the butter in saucepan. Add the
leeks and the finely sliced onion and
potato. Shake the pan over low heat
until the vegetables are well coated
with the butter. Cover the pan and cook
over low heat until tender. Be careful
the vegetables do not brown.

Add the stock, seasoning to taste,
mace and bay leaf. Cover and simmer
for about 20 minutes. Remove the bay
leaf. Allow to cool.

Liquidize the soup in an electric
blender or pass through a sieve, then
pour into a bowl.

Add the tomato juice and yogurt.
Taste and adjust the seasoning if necessary. Place in the refrigerator until
thoroughly chilled and serve sprinkled
with snipped chives.

As an accompaniment, serve brown
bread and butter or melba toast.

Lebanese Cucumber Soup

2 large cucumbers, peeled
salt
pinch of sugar
2 garlic cloves, peeled and crushed
  with ½ teaspoon salt
1 litre (2 pints) natural yogurt
2 teaspoons lemon juice
3 tablespoons finely chopped mint
freshly ground black pepper

Grate the cucumbers coarsely, place in
a sieve, sprinkle with salt and leave to
drain for 30 minutes. Transfer to a
chilled soup tureen or large serving
bowl, add the sugar and stir in the
garlic. Gradually pour in the yogurt,
stirring constantly, then stir in the
lemon juice, two thirds of the mint, and
pepper to taste.

Taste and adjust seasoning, then
sprinkle over the remaining mint as a
garnish and grind a little pepper over
the soup to finish.

Chill in the refrigerator until serving
time.
Serves 8–10

Cold Cucumber and Prawn Soup

1 large cucumber, peeled and halved
6 spring onions, trimmed
900 ml (1½ pints) chicken stock
1 teaspoon dried dill
25 g (1 oz) cornflower
3 tablespoons water
salt and freshly ground black pepper
few drops of green food colouring
50 g (2 oz) peeled prawns
4 tablespoons single cream, to garnish

Deseed the cucumber and slice. Chop the spring onions, including as much of the green parts as possible, and simmer in the stock with the cucumber and dill until quite tender. Liquidize in an electric blender or pass through a sieve.

Reheat the soup. Moisten the cornflour with the water, add to the soup, stir until boiling and simmer gently for 3 minutes. Remove from the heat and add the seasoning to taste. When cool stir in a few drops of food colouring, and the prawns. Chill well

Swirl a spoonful of cream into each portion before serving.

Carrot and Orange Soup

25 g (1 oz) butter
1 clove of garlic, crushed
1 medium-sized onion, peeled and chopped
450 g (1 lb) carrots, peeled and coarsely grated
900 ml (1½ pints) water
2 tablespoons orange juice and finely grated rind of 1 orange
1 teaspoon of tomato purée
1 chicken stock cube, crumbled
salt and freshly ground black pepper
1 teaspoon cornflour
2 tablespoons cold water
150 ml (¼ pint) milk
1 teaspoon chopped parsley, to garnish (optional)

Melt the butter in a saucepan, add the crushed garlic, chopped onion and grated carrot. Stir and cook, covered, for 5 minutes over a low heat. Add the water, orange juice and rind, tomato purée and the stock cube. Season to taste. Simmer, covered, for 30 minutes. Moisten the cornflour with the cold water, stir into the soup and simmer for another 5 minutes. Liquidize the soup in an electric blender or pass through a sieve. Stir in the milk and chill in the refrigerator. Before serving taste and adjust the seasoning and, if liked, sprinkle with the chopped parsley.

Chilled Beetroot Soup

450 g (1 lb) raw beetroot, peeled
900 ml (1½ pints) water
1 beef stock cube, crumbled
½ teaspoon sugar
1 medium sized onion, peeled and chopped
½ teaspoon dried or 1 teaspoon fresh dill
3 cloves
1 tablespoon malt vinegar
salt and freshly ground black pepper
To finish:
1 pickled cucumber, chopped
1 hard-boiled egg, shelled and chopped
150 ml (¼ pint) unsweetened natural yogurt

Finely grate the raw beetroot. Bring the water to the boil, dissolve the crumbled stock cube and sugar in it. Add the beetroot, chopped onion, dill and cloves, and bring back to the boil. Simmer, covered, for 45 minutes.

Allow the soup to cool slightly and strain through a fine sieve. Add the vinegar and seasoning to taste. Chill in the refrigerator.

Before serving, stir the chopped pickled cucumber and hard-boiled egg into the soup and finally swirl with the yogurt.

Cauliflower and Green Pea Soup

1 small cauliflower, trimmed and
    leaves removed.
600 ml (1 pint) water
1 medium-sized onion, peeled and
    grated
salt and freshly ground white pepper
1 teaspoon grated nutmeg
50 g (2 oz) butter
2 tablespoons flour
600 ml (1 pint) milk
100 g (4 oz) frozen green peas
1 egg yolk

Break the cauliflower into florets. Put
them into a saucepan with the water,
grated onion and seasonings. Bring to
the boil and simmer, covered, for about
20 minutes or until the cauliflower is
just tender. Remove the cauliflower
florets with a slotted draining spoon
and mash to make into a purée.

Melt the butter in a clean saucepan,
stir in the flour and cook for 1 minute.
Gradually stir in the water in which
cauliflower florets were cooked, add the
milk and bring to the boil, stirring all
the time. Reduce the heat, add the
cauliflower purée and the frozen green
peas and simmer for 10 minutes.
Remove from the heat, adjust the
seasoning if necessary and stir in
slightly beaten egg yolk. Return to the
heat for 1 minute, stirring constantly,
but do not allow to boil.

Celery Soup

1 head of celery, scrubbed and finely
    chopped, a few young leaves
    reserved
1 small onion, peeled and finely
    chopped
1 tablespoon flour
½ teaspoon celery salt
white pepper to taste
600 ml (1 pint) milk

Put all the ingredients, except the
celery leaves, in an electric blender and
purée until quite smooth. Pour into a
saucepan and bring slowly to the boil,
stirring constantly. Work through a
sieve, return to the rinsed-out pan and
reheat gently. Adjust seasoning. Garnish each bowl with a few celery leaves.

Carrot and Tomato Soup

25 g (1 oz) butter
1 large onion, peeled and finely
    chopped
450 g (1 lb) carrots, scraped and
    chopped
1 × 400 g (14 oz) can tomatoes
1 teaspoon sugar
600 ml (1 pint) chicken stock
finely grated rind and juice of 1
    orange
salt and freshly ground black pepper
3 tablespoons finely chopped parsley,
    to garnish

Melt the butter in a heavy saucepan,
add the onion and cook gently for approximately 5 minutes until soft and
lightly coloured. Stir in the carrots,
cover the vegetables with greaseproof
paper, then cover the pan and cook over
a very low heat for another 5 minutes.

Remove the lid and greaseproof
paper, stir in the tomatoes, sugar, stock,
orange rind and juice and season to
taste with salt and pepper. Bring to the
boil, stirring, then lower the heat, half
cover with the lid and simmer for 10 to
15 minutes until the carrots are tender.
Remove from the heat and leave to cool
a little. Purée in an electric blender or
work through a mouli-légumes until
smooth. Return the soup to the rinsed-
out pan and heat through. If the soup is
too thick, stir in a little chicken stock,
milk or water. Taste and adjust seasoning. Pour into warmed soup bowls and
sprinkle each with a little parsley.
Serve immediately.
Serves 4–6

† Cream of Artichoke Soup

750 g (1½ lb) Jerusalem artichokes
cold water
juice of 1 lemon
50 g (2 oz) butter or margarine
1 small onion, peeled and chopped
900 ml (1½ pints) white stock or water
 and 1 chicken stock cube
1 bay leaf
a few parsley stalks
salt
freshly ground black pepper
To garnish:
¼ pint (150 ml) single cream
a little finely chopped fresh parsley

Peel the artichokes and cut into 2.5 cm
(1 inch) pieces. Place in cold water to
cover and add the strained lemon juice
to prevent discoloration. Heat the
butter or margarine in the cooker and
fry the onion until transparent. Drain
and dry the artichokes then add to the
cooker. Sauté for a few minutes, without colouring. Add the stock or water
and stock cube, bay leaf, parsley stalks
and a little salt and pepper to the
cooker. Close the cooker, bring to H
pressure and cook for 6 minutes. Reduce
pressure quickly and remove the bay
leaf. Blend the soup in a liquidizer or
press through a sieve.

To serve hot: return the soup to the
open cooker and reheat, adjusting
seasoning if necessary. Stir in the
cream just before serving and garnish
with a little chopped parsley.

To serve chilled: after liquidizing,
cool the soup and chill thoroughly in
the refrigerator. Before serving, adjust
seasoning if necessary and stir in the
cream. Garnish with a little chopped
parsley.

Herbed Cream of Chestnuts

40 g (1½ oz) butter
1 large onion, peeled and sliced
2 small carrots, peeled and sliced
1 stalk celery, scrubbed and chopped
450 g (1 lb) fresh peeled chestnuts
1 litre (1¾ pints) beef stock
3–4 sprigs of parsley
pinch of dried thyme
1 bay leaf
salt and freshly ground black pepper
pinch of grated nutmeg
300 ml (½ pint) single cream or milk
To finish:
1 large cooking apple
25 g (1 oz) butter
1 teaspoon sugar
1 tablespoon parsley, chopped

Heat the butter in a saucepan. Add the
sliced onion and carrot and the chopped
celery. Cover and cook for 3 to 4 minutes, shaking the pan occasionally. Add
the chestnuts, cook for a further 3
minutes then add the stock, herbs and
seasonings and simmer for 20 to 30
minutes, or until the chestnuts are
tender. Remove the bay leaf and
liquidize the soup in an electric blender
or pass through a sieve. Return to the
pan, reheat and adjust the seasoning if
necessary. Add the cream or milk just
before serving. If using cream, do not
allow the soup to boil.

Peel, core and slice the apple into
rings. Fry in the butter until golden-
brown on both sides, sprinkling each
side with a little sugar. Float one or two
apple slices in each plate of soup and
sprinkle with chopped parsley.

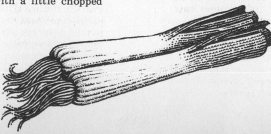

† Cream of Mushroom Soup

450 g (1 lb) mushrooms, cleaned and
   thinly sliced (reserve a few slices
   for garnish)
1 small onion, finely chopped
900 ml (1½ pints) white stock or water
   and 1 chicken stock cube
1 bay leaf
salt
freshly ground black pepper
To garnish:
1 tablespoon cornflour
2 tablespoons water
150 ml (¼ pint) single cream

Put the mushrooms into the cooker and
add the onion, stock or water and stock
cube, bay leaf and a little salt and
pepper. Make sure that the cooker is
not more than half full. Close the
cooker and bring to H pressure, cook for
5 minutes. Reduce the pressure quickly
and remove the bay leaf. Blend the soup
in a liquidizer or if preferred, leave the
soup as it is. Return the soup to the open
cooker, stir in the cornflour blended
with the water. Reheat, stirring continuously, until boiling and thickened.
Just before serving, stir in the cream,
taste and adjust the seasoning as necessary and garnish with slices of raw
mushroom.

†·Beef and Onion Soup

25 g (1 oz) lard or margarine
2 large onions, peeled and coarsely
   chopped
225 g (8 oz) minced beef
900 ml (1½ pints) brown stock or water
   and 1 beef stock cube
1 teaspoon Worcestershire sauce
salt
freshly ground black pepper
To garnish:
25 g (1 oz) butter or margarine
1 onion, peeled and thinly sliced
a little fresh parsley, chopped

Heat the lard or margarine in the
cooker and fry the onions until they
start to colour. Lift the onions out, set
aside and brown the meat. Add the
stock or water and stock cube, Worcestershire sauce, salt, pepper and fried
onion, stir well. Make sure that the
cooker is not more than half full. Close
the cooker and bring to H pressure,
cook for 8 minutes. Reduce the pressure
quickly. Blend soup in a liquidizer or
press through a sieve. Return to the
open cooker to reheat. Taste and adjust
the seasoning as necessary. Heat the
butter or margarine in a frying pan and
fry the onion briskly until well browned. Transfer the soup to a heated
tureen and garnish with the onion rings
and chopped parsley.

† Cream of Onion Soup

25 g (1 oz) butter or margarine
450 g (1 lb) onions, peeled and thinly
   sliced
900 ml (1½ pints) white stock or water
   and 1 chicken stock cube
salt and freshly ground black pepper
To garnish:
1 tablespoon flour
150 ml (¼ pint) milk
2 tablespoons single cream
freshly chopped chives, to garnish

Heat the butter or margarine in the
cooker, fry the onions gently, without
colouring, until they start to soften.
Add the stock or water and stock cube
and a little salt and pepper. Make sure
that the cooker is not more than half
full. Close the cooker, bring to H pressure and cook for 5 minutes. Reduce
the pressure quickly. Blend soup in a
liquidizer or press through a sieve.
Return the soup to the open cooker.
Blend the flour with the milk, add to the
soup and bring to the boil, stirring
constantly. Stir in the cream just before
serving and taste and adjust the seasoning as necessary. Garnish with chives.

† Tomato and Orange Soup

25 g (1 oz) butter or margarine
1 onion, peeled and finely chopped
2 small carrots, scraped and thinly
  sliced
1 large potato, peeled and cut into
  small dice
750 g (1½ lb) tomatoes, quartered
finely grated rind and juice of 2
  oranges
1 bay leaf
600 ml (1 pint) white stock or water
  and ½ chicken stock cube
salt
freshly ground black pepper
1 teaspoon caster sugar
To garnish:
1 tablespoon flour
150 ml (¼ pint) milk
2 tablespoons single cream

Heat the butter or margarine in the
cooker and fry the onion, carrots, and
potato without colouring. Add the tomatoes, grated rind of 1 orange and the
juice of 2 oranges, the bay leaf, stock or
water and stock cube, salt, pepper and
sugar. Make sure that the cooker is not
more than half full. Close the cooker,
bring to H pressure and cook for 5
minutes. Reduce the pressure quickly.
Blend soup in a liquidizer or press
through a sieve and return to the open
cooker. Blend the flour with the milk
and stir into the soup. Return to the
heat and cook, stirring constantly,
until boiling and thickened. Taste and
adjust the seasoning as necessary. Just
before serving pour into a heated
tureen, pour the cream in a swirl over
the centre and sprinkle with the remaining orange rind.

French Onion Soup

450 g (1 lb) Spanish onions
50 g (2 oz) unsalted butter or lard
1¼ litres (2 pints) good brown stock
salt
freshly ground black pepper
For the topping:
4 slices French bread cut 2 cm (¾ in)
  thick
40 g (1½ oz) butter
100 g (4 oz) Gruyère or cheddar
  cheese, grated

Peel and thinly slice the onions. Heat
the butter or lard in a heavy saucepan,
add the onions, stir well and cover with
a lid. Cook over gentle heat, stirring
occasionally, until the onions are
softened. Remove the lid and fry the
onions until turning golden. Pour in the
stock and bring to the simmer. Cover
and cook gently for 30 minutes. Add salt
and pepper to taste.

Spread the bread slices with butter
and cover with grated cheese, reserving
some cheese for serving. Bake in a
preheated oven at 200°C, 400°F, Gas
Mark 6 until the bread is crisp and the
cheese has melted. Alternatively, toast
under the grill.

Place a bread slice (croûte) in each
soup bowl and pour hot soup over it.
Serve immediately and hand the remaining grated cheese in a separate
bowl for sprinkling over the soup.

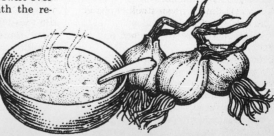

Bone Stock Tomato Soup

25 g (1 oz) butter
450 g (1 lb) onions, peeled and
    chopped
4 medium-sized carrots, peeled and
    chopped
2 medium-sized potatoes, peeled and
    chopped
2 celery stalks, scrubbed and chopped
1 clove of garlic, crushed
pinch of dried basil
2 litres (3½ pints) ham stock
1 tablespoon soft brown sugar
1 × 165 g (5½ oz) can tomato purée
salt and freshly ground black pepper

Melt the butter in a saucepan. Add the
chopped vegetables and crushed garlic
and stir for 3 to 4 minutes until well
coated with the butter. Add the basil
and sufficient of the stock to cover the
vegetables. Bring to the boil, lower
heat, cover and simmer for 20 minutes,
or until the vegetables are tender.
Liquidize in an electric blender or press
through a sieve.

Return the purée to the rinsed-out
pan and add the remaining stock, brown
sugar, tomato purée and seasoning to
taste. Bring the soup back to the boil
and simmer for 20 to 30 minutes. Check
the seasoning and serve hot.

† Lentil and Tomato Soup

100 g (4 oz) lentils
25 g (1 oz) lard or margarine
1 onion, peeled and chopped
2 rashers bacon, rinded and chopped
2 carrots, scraped and sliced
450 g (1 lb) tomatoes, skinned and
    chopped
900 ml (1½ pints) white stock or water
    and 1 chicken stock cube
1 bay leaf
salt and freshly ground black pepper
a little milk (optional)
toasted bread croûtons, to garnish

Cover the lentils with boiling water and
leave to soak for 1 hour. Heat the lard or
margarine in the cooker and fry the
onion, bacon and carrots without
browning. Add the drained lentils,
tomatoes, stock or water and stock
cube, bay leaf and salt and pepper. Close
the cooker, bring to H pressure and
cook for 15 minutes. Reduce the pressure slowly and remove the bay leaf.
Blend the soup in a liquidizer or press
through a sieve. Return the soup to the
open cooker to reheat. Adjust the consistency with a little milk if necessary.
Taste and adjust the seasoning as
necessary. Serve with toasted croûtons.

Minestrone Medley

2 tablespoons vegetable oil
1 onion, peeled and finely chopped
175 g (6 oz) piece garlic sausage, cut
    into thin strips
1 × 400 g (14 oz) can tomatoes
2 handfuls (94 ml) (⅓ cup) macaroni
600 ml (1 pint) water
1 × 25 g (1 oz) packet quick dried
    garden peas
½ teaspoon dried oregano
salt
freshly ground black pepper
1 × 425 g (15 oz) can red kidney beans,
1 × 425 g (15 oz) can cut green beans,
    drained
grated Parmesan cheese, to garnish

Heat the oil in a large saucepan, add the
onion and fry over gentle heat until
soft. Add the garlic sausage and fry for 5
minutes, then add the remaining ingredients except the beans and cheese.
Stir well to mix. Bring to the boil, cover
and simmer over gentle heat for 15
minutes, stirring occasionally. Stir in
the beans and simmer for a further 5
minutes or until the pasta is tender.
Taste and adjust seasoning, adding
plenty of black pepper.

Serve hot with the Parmesan handed
separately.

Mixed Country Vegetable Soup

2 rashers streaky bacon
50 g (2 oz) butter or margarine
1 large onion, peeled and thinly sliced
100 g (4 oz) leeks, white part, washed
  and chopped
2–3 stalks celery, washed and chopped
50 g (2 oz) mushrooms, washed and
  chopped
100 g (4 oz) carrots, scraped and diced
100 g (4 oz) parsnips or swedes, peeled
  and diced
100 g (4 oz) Jerusalem artichokes or
  turnips, peeled and diced
2–3 tablespoons flour
300 ml (½ pint) milk
250 ml (8 fl oz) tomato juice
or
225 g (8 oz) tomatoes, skinned and
  chopped
1 tablespoon chopped fresh parsley
½ teaspoon mixed dried herbs
salt and freshly ground black pepper
approx. 450 ml (¾ pint) white stock or
  water
lemon juice to sharpen
croûtons or grated cheese, to garnish

Remove the rind and gristle from the
bacon and dice the rashers. Melt the
butter or margarine and fry the bacon,
onion, leeks, celery and mushrooms
until softened but do not allow them to
brown. Add the prepared root vegetables and fry gently for 5 minutes.

Remove the pan from the heat and stir
in sufficient flour to absorb the fat.
Blend in the milk and stir over moderate heat until the liquid has thickened. Add tomato juice or tomatoes,
the herbs and salt and pepper to taste.
Bring to the simmer and thin as required with water or stock.

Cover and cook over gentle heat for
about 45 minutes or until the vegetables
are tender. Taste and adjust the seasoning and sharpen to taste with lemon
juice. The soup can be served with a
bowl of croûtons or grated cheese.

* Cream of Vegetable Soup

Follow the recipe for Mixed Country
Vegetable Soup (above), with these
changes: put the soup through a mouli-
légumes or blender. Reheat and thin to
desired consistency with water or white
stock and enrich with 3 to 4 tablespoons
single cream.

Serve sprinkled with chopped fresh
parsley or chives and fried croûtons.

† Red Bean and Pepper Soup

100 g (4 oz) small red kidney beans
900 ml (1½ pints) white stock or water
  and 1 chicken stock cube
2 rashers unsmoked streaky bacon,
  rinded and chopped
1 small onion, peeled and coarsely
  chopped
2 red peppers, cored, seeded and
  chopped
4 tomatoes, skinned and quartered
salt
freshly ground black pepper
1 bay leaf

Put the beans into a basin. Bring 450 ml
(¾ pint) of the stock or water to the boil,
pour over the beans to cover and leave
to stand for 1 hour. Heat the cooker
gently and fry the bacon in its own fat.
Add a little more fat if necessary and fry
the onion and peppers, without colouring. Add the tomatoes, beans with their
soaking liquid, the remaining stock or
water and stock cube, salt, pepper and
bay leaf. Close the cooker, bring to H
pressure and cook for 15 minutes.
Reduce the pressure slowly. Remove the
bay leaf and then blend the soup in
a liquidizer or press through a sieve.
Return to the open cooker to reheat,
taste and adjust the seasoning as
necessary. If this recipe is not prepared
in a pressure cooker, be sure that the red
kidney beans are boiled briskly for at
least 40 minutes at some stage.

† Split Pea and Bacon Soup

100 g (4 oz) unsmoked streaky bacon,
   rinded and chopped
25 g (1 oz) butter or margarine
1 large onion, peeled and chopped
100 g (4 oz) split peas
900 ml (1½ pints) white stock or water
   and 1 chicken stock cube
salt
freshly ground black pepper

Heat the cooker gently, add the bacon
and fry in its own fat until softened. Add
the butter or margarine and fry the
onion without colouring. Add the split
peas, stock or water and stock cube and
a little salt and pepper. Close the
cooker, bring to H pressure and cook for
12 minutes. Reduce the pressure slowly.
Blend the soup in a liquidizer or press
through a sieve. Return to the open
cooker to reheat. Taste and adjust the
seasoning as necessary before serving.

Sweetcorn and Ham Chowder

1 large knob of butter
1 large onion, peeled and finely
   chopped
2 tablespoons flour
300 ml (½ pint) milk
1 chicken stock cube dissolved in
   600 ml (1 pint) hot water
1 × 300 g (11 oz) can sweetcorn,
   drained
1 × 200 g (7 oz) can sweetcure ham,
   diced
1 × 450 g (1 lb) can new potatoes,
   drained and diced
freshly ground black pepper
½ teaspoon paprika
grated Parmesan cheese, to serve

Melt the butter in a pan, add the onion
and fry over gentle heat until golden
brown, stirring occasionally. Add the
flour and cook for 1 minute, stirring
constantly, then gradually stir in the
milk and chicken stock. Bring to the
boil, then add the remaining ingredients except the cheese and half the
paprika. Simmer for 10 minutes until
hot and bubbling. Taste and adjust
seasoning. Dust with the remaining
paprika and serve with Parmesan
cheese handed separately.

Variation:
Prawns can be substituted for the ham.

Scots Broth

750 g (1½ lb) neck of lamb, scrag and
   middle neck
2¼ litres (4 pints) cold water or white
   stock
salt
freshly ground black pepper
2 carrots, scraped and diced
1 turnip, peeled and diced
1 parsnip or small swede, peeled and
   diced
1 large onion, peeled and chopped
2 leeks, washed and thinly sliced
3 tablespoons pearl barley
3 tablespoons chopped parsley, to
   garnish

Ask the butcher to chop the neck of
lamb into joints. Trim off all fat and put
all the meat in a large pan. Cover with
the water and add salt and pepper to
taste. Bring to the boil and skim. Cover
with a lid and simmer gently for 1 hour.
Add the prepared vegetables and barley
and continue cooking gently for a further hour or until the meat and vegetables are tender.
   Lift the lamb from the stock with a
slotted spoon, take the meat off the
bones and cut into small pieces.
Remove the fat from the soup with
kitchen paper or lift off when the stock
is cold and the fat is solid. Add the meat
to the soup and reheat thoroughly.
Serve garnished with chopped parsley
sprinkled on each portion.

† Mulligatawny

25 g (1 oz) dripping or lard
450 g (1 lb) lean scrag of mutton or
  lamb, cut into thin chops
1 large onion, peeled and sliced
1 large carrot, scraped and sliced
1 large cooking apple, peeled, cored
  and chopped
2 teaspoons curry powder
a generous pinch of chilli powder
1¼ litres (2 pints) white stock or
  water and 1 chicken stock cube
a little salt
To garnish:
1 tablespoon flour
150 ml (¼ pint) milk
a little finely chopped green pepper,
  to garnish

Heat the dripping or lard in the cooker,
brown the meat, vegetables and apple.
Stir in the curry and chilli powders and
cook for a few minutes. Add the stock or
water and stock cube with a little salt
and stir well. Make sure that the cooker
is not more than half full. Close the
cooker, bring to H pressure and cook for
15 minutes. Reduce the pressure
quickly. Remove the meat from the
bones, cut into small pieces and set
aside. Blend the vegetables and stock in
a liquidizer or press through a sieve.
Return the soup to the cooker, stir in
the flour blended with the milk and
bring to the boil, stirring constantly.
Put the meat back into the soup to
reheat. Taste and adjust the seasoning
as necessary. Garnish with chopped
green pepper.

  This soup is also delicious served
cold. The consistency may need to be
thinner as it thickens when chilled.
Cover the surface of the soup with a
piece of damp greaseproof paper or foil
to prevent a skin from forming.

Split Pea Soup
with Frankfurters

225 g (8 oz) salt belly of pork, cubed
450 g (1 lb) green split peas, soaked
  overnight in cold water to cover
4 medium-sized carrots, peeled and
  chopped
2 medium-sized leeks, white and pale
  green part, washed and chopped
4 stalks celery, scrubbed and chopped
1 small cooking apple, peeled, cored
  and chopped
1 tablespoon soft brown sugar or
  treacle
sprig of mint
sprig of parsley
salt and freshly ground black pepper
To serve:
25 g (1 oz) butter
2 or 3 frankfurters cut into 1 cm
  (½ inch) lengths

Put the cubes of pork into a large
saucepan. Cover them with water and
bring slowly to the boil. Drain off the
water and cover the meat with 2½ litres
(4½ pints) of fresh cold water.

  Rinse the soaked peas under cold
running water. Add the peas, vegetables, apple, sugar or treacle, herbs
and seasoning to the saucepan and
bring to the boil. Remove any scum with
a slotted draining spoon. Reduce the
heat, cover and simmer gently, stirring
occasionally, for about 2 hours or until
the peas are soft and pulpy. The time
will depend upon the quality and fresh-
ness of the dried peas.

  Taste and adjust the seasoning.
Remove the herbs and stir in the butter
and frankfurters. Reheat and serve very
hot with wholemeal bread.
Serves 8

† Cock-a-leekie Soup

1 small boiling fowl, approx. 1½ kg (3 lb), cleaned and trussed
1 bouquet garni
salt and freshly ground black pepper
1.2 litres (2 pints) water
4 large leeks, washed, sliced lengthways and cut into 2.5 cm (1 inch) pieces
8 prunes, soaked for 10 minutes in boiling water, then drained, stoned and halved

A whole boiling fowl will produce more than sufficient meat for the soup. However, the leftover meat can be used for Savoury Stuffed Pancakes (p. 99).

Put the fowl, bouquet garni, salt, pepper and water into the cooker. Bring to the boil and skim well. Make sure that the cooker is not more than half full. Close the cooker, bring to H pressure and cook for 20 minutes. Reduce the pressure quickly. Add leeks and the prunes. Bring back to H pressure and cook for a further 10 minutes. Reduce the pressure quickly. Lift out the fowl, remove the skin and discard. Cut some of the flesh into large pieces and return to the soup to reheat. Remove the bouquet garni and season to taste.

Game Soup

50 g (2 oz) pickled belly of pork or streaky bacon
50 g (2 oz) butter or lard
1 onion, peeled and chopped
2 stalks celery, washed and chopped
100 g (4 oz) mushrooms, washed and chopped
½ teaspoon mixed dried herbs
50 g (2 oz) flour
2 tablespoons port or sherry
750 ml (1¼ pints) good game stock
salt and freshly ground pepper
lemon juice to taste
French bread croûtons, to garnish

Remove the rind from the pickled pork or bacon rashers and dice the meat. Fry it gently in a heavy pan until the fat runs. Add the butter or lard and fry the onion, celery and mushrooms until they start changing colour. Add the herbs. Remove the pan from the heat and stir in the flour. Return the pan to the heat and fry briskly, stirring continuously, until the vegetables are nicely browned.

Remove the pan from the heat and blend in the port or sherry. Stir in the stock and return the pan to the heat. Bring to the simmer and cook gently for 20 to 30 minutes until the celery is tender. Add salt and pepper and sharpen to taste with lemon juice.

Serve the soup as it is or if a smoother texture is preferred, put it in a blender or through a mouli-légumes. Garnish with croûtons of French bread or Roast Herb Dumplings (p. 364).

Cheese Soup with Dumplings

50 g (2 oz) butter
1 medium-sized onion, peeled and finely chopped
25 g (1 oz) flour
½ teaspoon dry mustard
900 ml (1½ pints) chicken stock
300 ml (½ pint) milk
½ teaspoon salt
¼ teaspoon freshly ground white pepper
¼ teaspoon grated nutmeg
75 g (3 oz) Cheddar cheese, grated
For the dumplings
50 g (2 oz) quick cook oats
25 g (1 oz) shredded beef suet
1 tablespoon grated onion
1 tablespoon chopped parsley
salt and freshly ground white pepper
1 egg

Melt the butter in a fairly large saucepan. Add the onion and fry gently until soft but not brown. Stir in the flour and the dry mustard and cook for 1 minute. Gradually add the stock and milk and bring to the boil, stirring constantly. Add the salt, pepper and grated nutmeg, stir well, cover then simmer for 10 minutes.

Meanwhile, make the dumplings. Place the oats, suet, grated onion and chopped parsley in a bowl and season to taste. Beat the egg until fluffy and use to bind the dry ingredients. Divide the mixture into 16 pieces and roll each one into a ball. Drop the balls into boiling salted water and cook gently for 10 to 15 minutes. Remove with a slotted draining spoon and keep warm.

Liquidize the soup in an electric blender, or pass through a sieve and return to the rinsed-out saucepan. Stir in the cheese and reheat without boiling. Taste and adjust the seasoning, and serve topped with the brown dumplings.

New England Fish Chowder

450 g (1 lb) cod or haddock fillet
600 ml (1 pint) Court bouillon or water
salt to taste
50 g (2 oz) pickled belly of pork or streaky bacon, diced
50 g (2 oz) butter or bacon fat
225 g (8 oz) potatoes, peeled
1 large onion, peeled and chopped
50 g (2 oz) mushrooms, washed and sliced
2 tablespoons flour
300 ml ($\frac{1}{2}$ pint) milk
lemon juice to taste
freshly ground pepper
2 tablespoons chopped parsley
French bread croûtons, to garnish

Wash the fish and cut it into 4 pieces. Bring the court bouillon or water to the boil, add the fish and simmer gently for 10 minutes. Lift the fish out and flake it roughly, discarding any skin and bones. Reserve 450 ml ($\frac{3}{4}$ pint) of the court bouillon. In a thick pan, fry the pickled

pork or bacon gently until the fat runs and the meat crisps, then add the butter or bacon fat.

Cut the potatoes roughly into cubes and add them to the pan with the onion and mushrooms, Fry slowly for 5 minutes. Remove the pan from the heat, blend in the flour and gradually stir in the milk. Return the pan to the heat and cook, stirring continuously until the liquid thickens. Gradually mix in reserved court bouillon and bring to the simmer. Cook until the potatoes are soft, then add the fish and cook gently for 5 minutes. Sharpen with lemon juice and add salt and freshly ground pepper to taste. Stir in the parsley. Serve with croûtons of French bread.

† Chicken Noodle Soup

1 chicken portion, skinned
1 small onion, peeled and chopped
1 carrot, cut into small dice
50 g (2 oz) fine noodles, such as vermicelli or egg noodles
$\frac{1}{2}$ teaspoon dried thyme
900 ml (1$\frac{1}{2}$ pints) poultry stock or water and 1 chicken stock cube
salt
freshly ground black pepper
a little chopped fresh parsley, to garnish

If using a leg portion of chicken, cut into 2 pieces – thigh and drumstick. Place the chicken, vegetables, noodles, thyme, stock or water and stock cube and a little salt and pepper into the cooker. Make sure that the cooker is not more than half full. Close the cooker, bring to H pressure and cook for 4 minutes. Reduce the pressure quickly. Lift out the chicken and remove the meat from the bones. Cut the meat into small pieces and return to the soup. Reheat the soup and taste and adjust the seasoning as necessary. Serve garnished with chopped parsley, sprinkled on each portion.

Fish and Lemon Soup

1 head halibut, turbot or cod
75 g (3 oz) rice
1¼ litres (2 pints) good Court bouillon
3 egg yolks
4 tablespoons lemon juice
salt
freshly ground pepper
shredded lettuce or chopped chives, to
   garnish

Wash the fish head and add it with the rice to the strained hot court bouillon. Bring to the boil, reduce heat and simmer for 20 minutes. Remove the head, flake off the flesh and discard the skin and bones. Crush the flesh with a fork and set it aside. Whisk the egg yolks with the lemon juice in a cup. Mix in 3 to 4 tablespoons of the hot soup and blend the mixture into the soup. Add the flaked fish and reheat, stirring continuously until thickened BUT DO NOT BOIL or the soup will separate. Season with salt and pepper to taste. Serve immediately in soup bowls and garnish with a sprinkling of finely shredded lettuce or chopped chives.

† Artichokes Vinaigrette

4 globe artichokes
300 ml (½ pint) water
a little salt
For the vinaigrette dressing:
150 ml (¼ pint) oil
3 tablespoons wine vinegar
1 garlic clove crushed with ½ teaspoon
   salt
freshly ground black pepper
1 tablespoon freshly chopped thyme
   or parsley

Remove the stem of each artichoke and trim the base leaves so that they will stand upright. Lay the artichokes on their sides and slice 1 cm (½ inch) off the top of the centre cone of leaves. Trim off the points of the rest of the leaves with scissors. Wash well under cold running water.

Put water and the trivet into the cooker and bring to the boil. Stand the artichokes upright on the trivet and sprinkle very lightly with salt. Close the cooker and bring to H pressure, cook for 10 minutes. Reduce the pressure quickly. Lift out the artichokes and cool. Put the oil and vinegar in a bowl and beat with a fork until thick. Beat in the garlic, black pepper and thyme or parsley. Serve the artichokes either with a little dressing spooned over them or plain, with the dressing in a side dish.

Avocado Mousse

1 tablespoon powdered gelatine
150 ml (¼ pint) chicken stock
2 ripe avocados
2 tablespoons lemon juice
150 ml (¼ pint) thick homemade
   mayonnaise (p. 42)
150 ml (¼ pint) double cream
1 teaspoon Worcestershire sauce
dash of Tabasco sauce
salt and freshly ground pepper
To garnish:
1 green pepper, cored, seeded and
   finely chopped
1 red pepper, cored, seeded and finely
   chopped
few tablespoons well-flavoured
   vinaigrette dressing

Do not unmould until just before ready to serve or the avocados will discolour. Sprinkle the gelatine over the stock in a small heatproof bowl and leave to stand until spongy. Put the bowl in a pan of hot water and stir over low heat until the gelatine has dissolved. Remove from the heat and leave to cool. Peel and halve the avocados and discard the stones. Mash the flesh with a fork and stir in the lemon juice immediately to prevent discoloration. Stir in the cooled gelatine stock until well mixed, then fold in the mayonnaise.

Whip the cream until thick, then fold into avocado mixture, mixing in the Worcestershire and Tabasco sauces at the same time. Season to taste.

Pour the mixture into a lightly oiled 900 ml (1½ pint) ring mould and chill in the refrigerator for several hours or overnight until set. Unmould on to a serving plate: hold an inverted plate over the top of the mousse, then turn the mould over.

Fill the centre of the mousse with red and green peppers tossed in the vinaigrette dressing.
Serves 8–10

Smoked Salmon and Avocado Cream

2 large avocado pears, very ripe
2 teaspoons tarragon vinegar
salt
freshly ground black pepper
60 ml (2 fl oz) double cream
100 g (4 oz) smoked salmon pieces
4 tablespoons mayonnaise
2 teaspoons tomato purée
few drops of Tabasco
lemon juice to taste
lettuce heart, rinsed and dried
100 g (4 oz) peeled prawns
To garnish:
twists of lemon
sprigs of watercress

Peel and stone the avocado pears. Mash the flesh with the tarragon vinegar until it is smooth, add salt and pepper to taste. Whip the cream until heavy and fold into the avocados. Trim off any skin, fins and bones from the salmon and dice it. Fold the salmon into the mixture, then chill it.

Mix together the mayonnaise, tomato purée, Tabasco and lemon juice to taste. Line four individual glass dishes with the lettuce leaves, spoon the avocado mixture into them, fold prawns into the mayonnaise mixture and pour over the top. Garnish with the lemon and watercress and serve with brown bread and butter.

Avocado and Cheese Croûtes

4 slices of rye bread
butter
French mustard
1 avocado pear, peeled, stoned and sliced
grated cheese

Spread the slices of rye bread with butter and a little French mustard. Halve the avocado pear, and remove the stone and peel. Cut the avocado into slices and arrange on top of the rye bread. Sprinkle each slice with a generous topping of grated cheese and pop under the grill for a short time until bubbling and golden.

Avocado Maryland

1 avocado pear, stoned
juice of ½ a lemon
grated rind of ½ a lemon
100 g (4 oz) chopped cooked chicken
salt
freshly ground black pepper
2 tablespoons drained sweetcorn
2 tablespoons single cream
grilled chopped bacon, to garnish

Halve the avocado pear and remove the stone. Scoop the flesh into a bowl with a teaspoon. Add the juice and grated rind of half a lemon, the chopped, cooked chicken, and salt and freshly ground black pepper to taste. Beat until well combined, stir in 2 tablespoons of drained sweetcorn and 2 tablespoons single cream. Spoon into small dishes and sprinkle with crisply grilled and chopped bacon.

Italian Starter

100 g (4 oz) Dolcelatte cheese
1 avocado pear, peeled, stoned and
  sliced
French dressing
lettuce leaves

Crumble the Dolcelatte cheese. Halve
the avocado pear, and remove the stone
and peel. Cut the avocado into thin
slices and toss lightly in French dressing. Arrange the cheese and avocado
on a bed of lettuce and spoon over a
little extra French dressing.

Taramavocado

1 avocado pear, stoned
juice of 1 lemon
grated rind of 1 lemon
75 g (3 oz) smoked cod's roe
1 clove of garlic, crushed
salt
freshly ground black pepper
3 tablespoons whipped cream
black olives, to garnish

Halve the avocado pear, and remove the
stone. Scoop the flesh into a bowl with a
teaspoon. Add the juice and grated rind
of half a lemon, the smoked cod's roe,
crushed clove of garlic, and salt and
freshly ground black pepper to taste.
Pound to a smooth creamy paste. Stir in
3 tablespoons whipped cream. Spoon
into small cocotte dishes and garnish
with black olives.

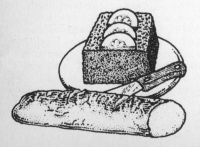

Sardine Eggs

4 eggs, hard-boiled and shelled
1 × 124 g (4¾ oz) can sardines in oil,
  drained
1 teaspoon chopped parsley
2 teaspoons quick cook oats
2 tablespoons single cream
pinch of cayenne pepper
salt
freshly ground black pepper
To garnish:
lettuce leaves
parsley sprigs

Cut each egg in half lengthwise. Using a
teaspoon carefully remove the yolks
and place them in a basin. Add the
sardines to the egg yolks with the parsley, oats, cream and cayenne pepper.
Mash with a fork then beat thoroughly
until smooth and well blended. Season
to taste and divide the mixture equally
among the egg halves.

Place the stuffed eggs on a bed of
lettuce leaves and garnish with parsley
sprigs. Serve with brown bread and
butter.

Eggs In Ramekins
(En Cocotte)

4 to 8 eggs
butter for greasing
2 tablespoons cream or top of the
  milk
salt
freshly ground black pepper

Preheat the oven to 180°C, 350°F, Gas
Mark 4. Butter individual ovenproof
ramekin dishes. Put 1 tablespoon cream
or top of the milk in each ramekin. Drop
in 1 or 2 eggs, season with salt and
pepper and put another spoonful of
cream or butter on top. Place in a
shallow pan with hot water and bake for
8 to 10 minutes until yolks are just set
and whites filmy.

Mushroom and Ham Cocotte

1 egg
4 tablespoons milk
salt
freshly ground black pepper
25 g (1 oz) mushrooms, sliced
25 g (1 oz) lean cooked ham
freshly chopped parsley

Beat together the egg and milk and season to taste with salt and pepper. Stir in the mushrooms, ham and a little parsley. Pour into a lightly greased individual ovenproof dish and bake in a warm oven (160°C, 325°F, Gas Mark 3) for 20 minutes or until set. Garnish with fresh parsley and serve with green salad vegetables.
Serves 1

Savoury Mushroom Toasts

40 g (1½ oz) butter
100 g (4 oz) button mushrooms, wiped and thinly sliced
4 large slices white bread
1 × 75 g (3 oz) jar chicken and bacon spread
2 teaspoons chopped parsley, to garnish

Melt 15 g (½ oz) of the butter in a small frying pan and use to fry the sliced mushrooms until golden. Meanwhile, toast the bread lightly and spread one side of each slice with the remaining butter. Spread the buttered toast fairly thickly with the chicken and bacon spread and arrange the cooked mushrooms on top.

Place the toasts under a hot grill for 2 minutes. Serve hot, scattered with chopped parsley and cut into fingers.

Chilled Ratatouille

2 large aubergines, sliced
salt
olive oil for frying
2 large onions, peeled and finely sliced
2 garlic cloves, peeled and crushed
2 large green or red peppers, cored, seeded and finely sliced
700 g (1½ lb) courgettes, sliced
700 g (1½ lb) tomatoes, skinned, seeded and chopped
2 tablespoons tomato purée
½ teaspoon sugar
freshly ground black pepper

Spread the aubergine slices in a single layer on a large plate or board and sprinkle liberally with salt. Leave to stand for 30 minutes, then rinse under cold running water and pat dry with absorbent kitchen paper. Heat 4 spoons of oil in a large saucepan. Add the onion and garlic and fry gently until soft and lightly coloured. Add peppers and fry for a further 5 minutes, then add the aubergine slices, courgettes and tomatoes. Increase the heat and cook briskly for a few minutes, stirring constantly. Stir in the tomato purée, sugar and black pepper to taste, then lower the heat, cover with a lid and cook gently for approximately 40 minutes, or until the vegetables are soft. Remove from the heat, taste and adjust seasoning, and leave to cool. When cold, chill in the refrigerator until serving time.
Serves 10

Cheese Straws

cheese shortcrust pastry (p. 360)
anchovy paste

Roll the cheese shortcrust pastry out
into a strip 10 cm (4 inches) wide. Trim
the edges. Using an 8 cm (3½ inch) scone
cutter, cut some rounds from the pastry.
With a 6 cm (2½ inch) scone cutter, cut
rounds from the centre of the large
circles and place both on a greased
baking tray. With a sharp knife, cut
strips off the rectangle, place on a
baking tray. Bake in a preheated oven
at 220°C, 425°F, Gas Mark 7 for 5 to 7
minutes. Cool on a wire tray. Arrange
in bundles with straws pushed through
circles. Sandwich the little rounds together with anchovy paste.

Anchovy Plaits and Twists

cheese shortcrust pastry (p. 360)
anchovy fillets

Cut strips of cheese shortcrust pastry as
for cheese straws (above). Lay two
pastry strips side by side. Put an anchovy fillet in the middle and plait the
anchovy fillet with the pastry strips.
Damp the ends of the pastry and then
seal together. Alternatively, twist one
pastry strip with an anchovy fillet,
damp and seal the ends. Bake plaits and
twists in a preheated oven at 220°C,
425°F, Gas Mark 7 for 5 to 7 minutes.
Serve hot or cold.

Crab Crescents

15 g (½ oz) butter
1 shallot, peeled and finely chopped
100 g (4 oz) crab meat
1 tablespoon brandy
2 to 3 tablespoons thick double cream
salt
freshly ground black pepper
pinch of grated nutmeg or ground
    mace
225 g (8 oz) packet frozen puff pastry,
    defrosted
a little beaten egg
sprigs of parsley, to garnish
For the sauce:
150 ml (¼ pint) reduced (Court
    Bouillon) Fish Stock (p. 7)
about 2 tablespoons double cream
medium sweet sherry to taste
squeeze of lemon juice

Melt the butter in a small pan, add the
shallot and cook gently until softened.
Add the crab meat, heat carefully and
stir in the brandy and gradually add
cream, taking care not to make the
mixture too soft. Add salt and pepper to
taste, then the nutmeg or mace. Leave
to cool.

On a floured surface roll out the
pastry 3 mm (⅛ inch) thick and cut out
about 8 × 7.5 cm (3 inch) rounds. Wet the
edges, put a small spoonful of crab
mixture on one side of the circle and
fold over to form a crescent. Press the
edges well together. Brush with beaten
egg and bake on a damp baking sheet in
a preheated hot oven (220°C, 425°F, Gas
Mark 7) for 15 minutes, or until well
risen, golden brown and crisp. Remove
to a serving dish and garnish with
parsley.

To make the sauce bring the fish
stock to the boil, then remove from the
heat. Stir in the cream, flavour with
sherry to taste, lemon juice and taste
and then adjust the seasoning. Serve
separately.

Cod's Roe Spread

1 kg (2 lb) fresh cod's roe
4 peppercorns
1 bay leaf
1 blade of mace
100 g (4 oz) butter
1 teaspoon tarragon vinegar
1 teaspoon lemon juice
½ teaspoon anchovy essence
salt and freshly ground black pepper

Wash the roes well, tie them in muslin and place in a saucepan with the peppercorns, bay leaf and mace. Cover with boiling water. Bring back to the boil, cover and simmer for 20 minutes. Take the roe from the pan. Discard the muslin and the skin from the roe.

Put the roe into a basin and mash with a fork. Beat in the butter, vinegar, lemon juice and anchovy essence. Taste and add seasoning if necessary. Beat well until smooth or use an electric blender to make a smooth paste. Press into a buttered mould. Cover with a weighted plate and allow to cool. Refrigerate until required.

Variation:
Tinned cod's roe may be used if fresh is unavailable.

Stuffed Soused Herrings

5 herrings
salt and freshly ground black pepper
1 small onion, peeled and cut into
  rings
1 small blade mace
3 cloves
8 peppercorns
150 ml (¼ pint) water
150 ml (¼ pint) vinegar
For the stuffing:
50 g (2 oz) quick cook oats
2 teaspoons chopped capers
grated rind of 1 small lemon
salt and freshly ground black pepper
25 g (1 oz) butter, melted
1 egg, beaten

Clean and bone the herrings and lay them flat, skin side down. Sprinkle with salt and pepper.

To make the stuffing, place the oats, chopped capers, lemon rind and seasoning to taste in a bowl. Add the melted butter and the beaten egg and mix thoroughly. The mixture should be stiff but not unmanageable. Add a little milk if necessary. Put equal quantities of the oat stuffing near the tail end of each herring, then roll up from the tail end.

Arrange the stuffed herrings, joins downwards, in a single layer in an ovenproof dish with the onion rings, mace, cloves and peppercorns. Mix together the water and vinegar and pour over the herrings. Bake in a fairly hot oven (190°C, 375°F, Gas Mark 5) for 30 to 35 minutes. Serve hot or cold accompanied by a green salad.

Kipper Mousse

225 g (8 oz) kipper fillets
150 ml (¼ pint) chicken stock
15 g (½ oz) gelatine
4 teaspoons lemon juice
75 g (3 oz) butter, melted
75 g (3 oz) Gouda cheese, grated
freshly ground black pepper
lemon and cucumber slices, to garnish

Grill the kippers, or cook boil-in-the-bag kippers in boiling water. Skin and flake. Place the stock and gelatine in a pan and heat to dissolve the gelatine. Liquidize all the ingredients in a blender.

Pour into a rinsed mould or dish to set. To unmould, dip the dish in hot water and invert on to a plate. Garnish with lemon and cucumber slices.

Can be served as a spread on biscuits or with toast.

Stuffed Lemons

6 fresh lemons
1 × 125 g (4⅜ oz) can sardines in oil, or tuna fish, drained
pinch of paprika
freshly ground black pepper
1 teaspoon French mustard
6 tablespoons mayonnaise
1 egg white, stiffly beaten
To finish:
shredded lettuce
parsley sprigs

Cut the tops off the lemons. Cut a thin slice off the bottom of the lemons carefully, so that they will stand firmly. Ease out the flesh with a knife and teaspoon. Discard the pith, pips and membranes and chop the flesh.

Place the fish in a basin and mash to a smooth paste. Season with the paprika, black pepper and mustard. Stir in the lemon flesh and the mayonnaise. Sharpen to taste with a little of the lemon

juice. Fold in the stiffly beaten egg white. Taste and adjust the seasoning.

Stuff the lemons with the fish mixture, mounding up at the tops. Chill in the refrigerator. Serve in egg cups or small dishes surrounded by shredded lettuce. Decorate with parsley sprigs.
Makes 6

Fish Ramekins

225 g (8 oz) cooked white fish, flaked
300 ml (½ pint) Anchovy Sauce (p. 355)
salt and freshly ground black pepper
1 egg white, stiffly whipped
2 tablespoons fresh white breadcrumbs
1 tablespoon grated Cheddar cheese
4 rolled stuffed anchovy fillets, to garnish

Blend the fish and sauce together and add salt and pepper to taste. Fold the egg white into the mixture, then spoon it into 4 individual ramekin dishes. Combine the breadcrumbs and cheese and sprinkle over the tops. Bake in a preheated moderately hot oven (200°C, 400°F, Gas Mark 6) for 10 to 15 minutes until golden and bubbling. Garnish with stuffed anchovy fillets.

Mackerel Spread

1 × 225 g (8 oz) can mackerel fillets in tomato sauce, drained
juice of ½ lemon
3 tablespoons bottled mayonnaise
2 teaspoons horseradish cream
freshly ground black pepper

Put all the ingredients in a bowl with plenty of pepper and beat together until smooth. Spoon into a polythene container and smooth the top. Cover and chill for at least 1 hour. Serve with crusty French bread and butter, crispbreads or crackers.

Potted Salmon

1 × 200 g (7 oz) can salmon, drained
1 × 225 g (8 oz) carton cottage cheese
  with chives
2 tablespoons bottled mayonnaise
2 tablespoons Worcestershire sauce
freshly ground black pepper

Put all the ingredients in a bowl with
pepper to taste, then beat well to mix.
Spoon the mixture into a polythene
container and smooth the top. Cover
and chill for several hours or overnight
if possible. Serve as a spread with crackers, crispbreads, toast or French bread.
Serves 6 to 8

Liver and Bacon Pâté

275 g (10 oz) streaky bacon rashers,
  derinded
450 g (1 lb) pigs' liver
1 onion, peeled
2 cloves garlic, crushed
salt
freshly ground black pepper
1 egg, beaten
2 tablespoons red wine
stuffed olives, to garnish

Finely mince half the bacon with the
liver, onion and garlic, twice. Season
very well and mix in the egg and wine.
Stretch the remaining bacon with the
back of a knife and use to line a greased
450 g (1 lb) loaf tin. Spoon in the liver
mixture, pressing well down and fold
the ends of the bacon over the filling.
Stand in a baking tin containing 4 cm
(1½ inches) water and cook in a
moderate oven (180°C, 350°F, Gas Mark
4) for 1½ hours. Cool in the tin slightly,
then stand a weight on it and chill
thoroughly.
  Turn out, garnish with stuffed olives
and serve in slices with hot toast and
butter.
Serves 6.

Creamy Liver Pâté

50 g (2 oz) butter
1 small onion, peeled and very finely
  chopped
1–2 cloves garlic, crushed
350 g (12 oz) pigs' liver, chopped
4 tablespoons white wine
salt
freshly ground black pepper
2 tablespoons brandy or wine
2 tablespoons double cream
melted butter
cucumber slices, to garnish

Melt the butter in a pan and fry the
onion and garlic until soft. Add the liver
and cook gently for 10 minutes, stirring
frequently. Add the wine, seasonings,
and brandy (if using), cover and simmer
for about 20 minutes or until tender.
Cool slightly then either blend in a
liquidizer until smooth or mince finely
twice. Stir in the cream, taste and
adjust the seasonings. Spoon into individual dishes or one larger dish and
chill until set. Top with a layer of
melted butter to cover the pâté and chill
again.
  Serve garnished with slices of cucumber, with hot fingers of toast.

Liver Sausage Pâté

225 g (8 oz) liver sausage
100 g (4 oz) cream cheese and chives
50 g (2 oz) butter, softened
2 tablespoons milk
freshly ground black pepper

Put all the ingredients in a bowl with
pepper to taste, then beat well to mix.
Press the mixture into a well buttered
polythene container and smooth the
top. Cover and chill for several hours or
overnight if possible, then turn out to
serve, if liked. Serve with crusty French
bread and butter.
Serves 6

Variation:
If you happen to have a bottle of wine,
sherry or brandy or dry cider open, then
substitute 2 tablespoons for the milk.

Pâté au Citron

350 g (12 oz) piece boned, skinned
    ham shank
6 juniper berries
6 black peppercorns
1 bay leaf
225 g (8 oz) pig's liver, minced
350 g (12 oz) pie (stewing) veal,
    minced
1 small onion, peeled and finely
    chopped
1 garlic clove, peeled and crushed
50 g (2 oz) fresh white breadcrumbs
4 tablespoons lemon juice
1 teaspoon freshly chopped tarragon;
    or $\frac{1}{2}$ teaspoon dried tarragon
1 egg, beaten
salt and freshly ground black pepper
3 lemons, cut into thin slices, pips
    removed
watercress sprigs, to garnish

Put the ham, juniper berries, peppercorns and bay leaf in a saucepan and
cover with water. Bring to the boil, then

lower the heat, half cover with a lid and
simmer gently for approximately 1 hour
or until the ham is tender. Remove from
the heat and leave to cool. Remove the
ham from the cooking liquid and mince
finely into a mixing bowl. Add the
remaining ingredients, except lemon
slices, and stir well until the mixture is
thoroughly combined. Lightly oil the
base and sides of a 1 kg (2 lb) loaf tin or
earthenware pâté or casserole dish and
line with the lemon slices, arranging
them as close together as possible.
Spoon the pâté mixture into the tin or
dish, packing it down well and smoothing with a wooden spoon. Cover with
foil and stand in a bain marie (water
bath) of hot water. Bake in a warm oven
(160°C, 325°F, Gas Mark 3) for approximately 2 hours until the pâté is firm and
has shrunk away from the sides of the
tin or dish. Remove from the bain marie,
put heavy weights on top of pâté and
leave until completely cold. Turn pâté
out on to a serving board or platter and
garnish with sprigs of watercress.

Hummus

350 g (12 oz) dried chick peas, soaked
    overnight
2–3 garlic cloves, according to taste,
    peeled
1 teaspoon salt
about 150 ml ($\frac{1}{4}$ pint) lemon juice
about 150 ml ($\frac{1}{4}$ pint) hot water
about 150 ml ($\frac{1}{4}$ pint) tahini paste
2–3 tablespoons olive oil
2 tablespoons finely chopped mint or
    parsley, to garnish

Drain the chick peas and rinse
thoroughly under cold running water.
Put in a large saucepan with plenty of
cold water, bring to the boil, then lower
the heat, half cover with a lid and
simmer for approximately 1 hour or
until the chick peas are tender. Drain,
rinse under cold running water and set
aside.

Crush the garlic cloves with the salt and put in an electric blender with some of the chick peas, lemon juice, hot water and tahini paste. Blend at high speed until a smooth pureé is obtained. Repeat this blending process until all the chick peas have been pureéd, adding more tahini paste, lemon juice and hot water to obtain a smooth, creamy consistency.

Transfer to a bowl, beat well with a wooden spoon and adjust the consistency of the hummus with more lemon juice or hot water if it is too thick. Taste and add more salt if necessary.

Pour hummus into a shallow serving bowl, spoon over the olive oil and sprinkle with mint or parsley.

Refrigerate until serving time.

Serve this Middle Eastern dip with hot flat Greek or Arab bread known as pita, or, if this is unavailable, substitute crisp French bread. Tahini paste is available at most Middle Eastern shops and health food stores.

Serves 10

Pork and Liver Terrine

350 g (12 oz) lean belly pork, skinned
225 g (8 oz) pigs' or lambs' liver
25 g (1 oz) butter
1 onion, peeled
1–2 cloves garlic, crushed
1 tablespoon capers
25 g (1 oz) fresh breadcrumbs
salt and freshly ground black pepper
1 large egg, beaten
3 tablespoons stock
To garnish:
few cucumber slices
6–8 stuffed olives
150 ml ($\frac{1}{4}$ pint) aspic jelly

Roughly chop the pork and liver and fry in the melted butter for 10 minutes, stirring occasionally. Cool slightly, then mince finely with the onion, garlic and capers. Add the breadcrumbs, seasonings, egg and stock and press into a greased 15 cm (6 inch) round ovenproof dish. Stand in a baking tin containing 4 cm (1$\frac{1}{2}$ inches) water, cover with buttered paper and cook in a warm oven (160°C, 325°F, Gas Mark 3) for 1$\frac{1}{2}$–1$\frac{3}{4}$ hours, until cooked through.

Remove and cool, and then chill thoroughly.

Decorate the top with cucumber and sliced stuffed olives and spoon over a thin layer of aspic. Chill until set.

Serves 4–6

SALADS

Courgette and Anchovy Salad

1 tablespoon vegetable oil
450 g (1 lb) courgettes, trimmed and
thinly sliced
6 spring onions, trimmed and chopped
150 ml ($\frac{1}{4}$ pint) chicken stock
1 × 50 g (2 oz) can anchovy fillets
2 tablespoons white vinegar
1 teaspoon caster sugar
freshly ground black pepper
1 clove of garlic, crushed

Heat the oil in a saucepan. Add the
sliced courgettes and spring onions and
sauté over moderate heat until the vegetables are limp. Add the stock, cover
and simmer for 5 minutes. Remove from
the heat, stir well, cover again and
allow to cool.

Remove the anchovies from the can,
place on a board, and chop finely. Mix
the vinegar, caster sugar, black pepper
to taste and crushed garlic with the
anchovy oil from the can. Stir in the
chopped anchovies. Drain the cooked
courgettes, toss them lightly in the
dressing and serve in a glass dish. (No
salt should be added to the cooking
water for the courgettes or the basic
dressing, as the anchovies are sufficiently salty.)

Carrot, Apple and Nut Salad

1 tablespoon lemon juice
1 red-skinned dessert apple, cored and
thinly sliced
2 large carrots, peeled and grated
100 g (4 oz) white cabbage, core
removed and finely shredded
1 leek, white and pale green part
only, washed and finely sliced
8 walnut halves
For the dressing:
1 tablespoon lemon juice
$\frac{1}{2}$ teaspoon caster sugar
$\frac{1}{2}$ teaspoon salt
pinch of freshly ground black pepper
2 tablespoons vegetable oil
1 tablespoon smooth peanut butter

Pour the lemon juice into a saucer. Dip
the apple slices in the lemon juice and
coat both sides to prevent discoloration. Arrange the grated carrot, shredded cabbage, sliced leek and apple slices
in a salad bowl. Scatter the walnut
halves over the top.

To make the dressing, place the
lemon juice, sugar, salt and pepper in a
small basin and beat vigorously until
blended. Gradually beat in the oil and
peanut butter alternately, until the
dressing is smooth and slightly thickened. To save time, place all the ingredients in a screw-topped jar and
shake briskly until the dressing emulsifies. Pour dressing over salad and toss.

Bean, Sweetcorn and Potato Salad

1 × 450 g (1 lb) packet frozen cut
  green beans
2 × 225 g (8 oz) packets frozen
  sweetcorn and peppers
salt
1 kg (2 lb) small new potatoes,
  scrubbed; or 2 × 538 g (1 lb 3 oz)
  cans new potatoes
2 bunches of spring onions, trimmed,
  washed and roughly chopped
about 175 ml (8 fl oz) thick homemade
  mayonnaise (see p. 42)
1 tablespoon lemon juice
freshly ground black pepper
2 tablespoons finely chopped mint, to
  garnish

Cook the beans and sweetcorn in salted
water according to packet directions,
drain, rinse under cold running water
and leave to cool. Meanwhile, boil the
potatoes for approximately 15 minutes
or until just barely tender. Drain, leave
to cool for a few minutes, then remove
any remaining skin, if liked. Leave to
cool completely. (If using canned potatoes, drain, rinse under cold running
water and drain again.) Slice thickly or
cut into chunks. Put the beans, sweetcorn and potatoes in a large mixing
bowl with the spring onions and fold in
the mayonnaise to coat the vegetables
completely. Add the lemon juice, and
salt and black pepper to taste, then turn
the salad into a serving bowl and chill
in the refrigerator. Sprinkle with the
mint just before serving.
Serves about 15

Beetroot Salad

1 kg (2 lb) cooked beetroot, skinned
  and diced
100 g (4 oz) walnuts, finely chopped
4 tablespoons creamed horseradish
  sauce

4 tablespoons fresh orange juice
salt and freshly ground black pepper
150 ml ($\frac{1}{4}$ pint) soured cream
2 tablespoons snipped chives

Put the beetroot and walnuts in a large
mixing bowl and stir in the horseradish
sauce and orange juice. Mix thoroughly
and season to taste with salt and
pepper. Transfer the salad to a serving
bowl. Beat the soured cream with a fork
until evenly mixed, then trickle over
the beetroot. Sprinkle with chives to
garnish and chill in the refrigerator
until serving time.
Serves 15

Chinese Leaf Salad

$\frac{1}{2}$ head Chinese leaves, washed
225 g (8 oz) cooked broad beans
2 tablespoons mustard sauce from jar
  of piccalilly
4 tablespoons mayonnaise
For the garlic croûtons:
2 tablespoons vegetable oil
1 clove of garlic, very finely chopped
2 slices white bread, trimmed and cut
  into dice

Reserve one large outer leaf from the
Chinese leaves for serving and shred
the remainder finely. Place the shredded vegetable in a bowl with the cooked
broad beans.

Mix together the mustard sauce and
the mayonnaise, pour over the leaves
and beans and toss lightly. Allow to
stand while preparing the garlic
croûtons.

Heat the oil in a frying pan. Add the
garlic and stir well. Drop in the bread
cubes and fry them, stirring frequently,
until crisp and golden-brown, then
drain well.

Spoon the salad on to the reserved
leaf on a serving dish and scatter over
the garlic croûtons.

Coleslaw

450 g (1 lb) cabbage heart
75 ml (⅛ pint) sour cream
75 ml (⅛ pint) mayonnaise (see p. 42)
chopped apple (optional)
chopped peppers (optional)
celery seed (optional)
paprika pepper (optional)

This salad of Dutch-American origin is usually made with the white Dutch cabbage, but red cabbage is also very good. Prepare the cabbage heart and shred it finely. Crisp in cold water and drain thoroughly.

Mix the cabbage with the sour cream mayonnaise, i.e. equal quantities of mayonnaise and soured cream. Add chopped apple, peppers, celery seed and paprika pepper if liked. Season to taste.

Celery and Walnut Salad

2 large heads of celery, trimmed, scrubbed and roughly chopped
50 g (2 oz) walnuts, chopped
4 satsumas or mandarin oranges, peeled, divided into segments and pith removed
6 crisp dessert apples
1 tablespoon lemon juice
300 ml (½ pint) natural yogurt
1 teaspoon caraway seeds
salt and freshly ground black pepper

Put the celery, walnuts and satsumas or mandarins in a mixing bowl and stir to combine. Peel and core the apples, then chop roughly. Sprinkle immediately with the lemon juice to prevent discoloration and stir into the celery and walnut mixture. Stir in the yogurt, caraway seeds, and salt and pepper to taste, then mix well to combine. Taste and adjust seasoning, transfer to a serving bowl and chill in the refrigerator until serving time.
Serves 12–15

Cheese Coleslaw

1 tablespoon unsweetened natural yogurt
vinegar to taste
pinch of salt
pinch of pepper
pinch of sugar
50 g (2 oz) shredded white cabbage
½ small, red eating apple, cored and diced
2 teaspoons lemon juice
1 tablespoon grated onion
50 g (2 oz) diced Edam cheese
parsley, chicory or watercress, to garnish

Put the yogurt, vinegar, salt, pepper and sugar together in a bowl and beat together to form a dressing. Taste and adjust seasoning if necessary.

Mix together the cabbage, apple, lemon juice, grated onion and cheese. Add the dressing and toss well together. Serve garnished with parsley, chicory or watercress.

Rosy Coleslaw

3–4 tablespoons cranberry sauce
4 tablespoons mayonnaise (see p. 42)
1 tablespoon white vinegar
salt
freshly ground black pepper
450 g (1 lb) white cabbage, core removed and finely shredded
chopped chives, to garnish

If using homemade mayonnaise, follow the recipe on p. 42.

Combine the cranberry sauce with mayonnaise and vinegar in a bowl and season to taste.

Add the shredded cabbage gradually, tossing it to coat well with the dressing. Cover and chill in the refrigerator for at least 2 hours.

Spoon the coleslaw into a glass salad bowl and serve sprinkled with chives.

Chicory and Grapefruit Salad

1 large ripe grapefruit
4 large heads chicory, trimmed and
  separated into leaves
For the dressing:
150 ml (¼ pint) soured cream
½ teaspoon French mustard
½ teaspoon salt
good pinch of freshly ground black
  pepper
1 tablespoon white vinegar
1 tablespoon vegetable oil
1 teaspoon clear honey
1 tablespoon chopped parsley, to
  garnish

Grate a little rind from the skin of the
grapefruit. (As it is strongly flavoured,
add it gradually to the finished dressing, tasting to make sure the flavour
does not become too strong.) Peel the
grapefruit, remove all white pith, separate into segments, and cut each of
these in half. Place in a bowl. Reserve
about 16 well-shaped leaves of chicory
to line a salad bowl and chop the rest
roughly and add to the grapefruit. Place
the reserved chicory leaves in a polythene bag to keep them fresh.

To make the dressing, put the soured
cream in a small basin and beat in the
mustard, salt, pepper, vinegar and oil.
Stir in the honey. Add sufficient grated
rind to give a hint of grapefruit to the
flavour. Pour the dressing over the
chopped grapefruit segments and
chicory and toss lightly.

Arrange the chicory leaves to make a
decorative border on a round platter
and pile up the salad in the centre.
Scatter the chopped parsley over the
salad to garnish.

Cucumber and Tomato Salad

½ cucumber
4 tomatoes
3–4 tablespoons French dressing
  (p. 43)
fresh green herbs

Top and tail half a cucumber, wipe it
and peel if preferred. Cut it into thin
slices. Wipe the tomatoes and slice them
across, not downwards. Arrange the
cucumber and tomatoes in overlapping
slices in a round shallow flat dish. Pour
over the well mixed French dressing.
Sprinkle with chopped fresh green
herbs – tarragon, chives, mint, chervil
or parsley, singly or mixed. Leave to
marinate for 30 minutes before serving.

Gingered Cucumber Strips

1 large cucumber, peeled
1 teaspoon salt
1 tablespoon finely chopped preserved
  ginger
1 tablespoon ginger syrup from the
  jar
4 tablespoons white vinegar

Cut the cucumber into finger lengths
and then cut each length into 6 or 8 long
thin strips, like large match sticks.
Spread the strips out on a flat dish and
sprinkle with the salt. Allow to stand
for 30 minutes, then drain off the liquid
and transfer to a bowl.

Mix the chopped ginger with the
syrup and vinegar. Pour over the cucumber strips and toss together lightly.
Serve the salad in a glass dish.

French Bean and Mushroom Salad

3 tablespoons vegetable oil
2 tablespoons lemon juice
1 tablespoon chopped fresh mint
salt and freshly ground black pepper
225 g (8 oz) button mushrooms, wiped and thinly sliced
450 g (1 lb) young French beans, trimmed
To garnish:
lettuce leaves
2 teaspoons snipped chives

To make the dressing, mix together the oil, lemon juice and chopped mint and seasoning to taste.

Place the mushrooms in a small bowl, pour over the dressing, cover and allow to marinate for several hours, or overnight if time permits.

Cook the beans, whole, in boiling lightly salted water for about 4 minutes, or until just tender but still slightly crisp. Drain and cool.

Combine the beans with the mushrooms and stir lightly with a fork to coat the beans with the dressing. Serve on a bed of lettuce leaves in a salad dish and scatter over the snipped chives.

Italian Salad

1½ kg (3 lb) firm, ripe tomatoes, skinned and quartered
½ teaspoon sugar
225 g (8 oz) garlic sausage, rinds removed and thickly sliced
100 g (4 oz) black olives, halved and pitted
225 g (8 oz) mozarella cheese, diced
4 tablespoons olive oil
2 tablespoons lemon juice
1 teaspoon French mustard
salt and freshly ground black pepper
1 large onion, peeled and thinly sliced
2 tablespoons finely chopped basil or parsley

The large continental varieties of tomatoes are ideal for this salad, and are normally available during the summer months. If Italian mozarella is not obtainable, the Danish equivalent can be substituted. If preparing salad ahead of time, do not add dressing, onion and herbs until just before serving.

Put the quartered tomatoes in a large serving bowl and sprinkle with sugar. Cut each slice of garlic sausage into small pieces, add to the bowl with the olives and cheese and stir gently to mix. In a separate bowl whisk together the oil and lemon juice until thick, then whisk in the mustard and salt and pepper to taste. Pour this dressing over the tomato salad, add the onion and basil or parsley and mix gently until the salad is thoroughly coated in dressing and herbs. Taste and adjust seasoning, then cover and chill in the refrigerator until serving time.
Serves 12

Haricot Bean Salad

1 kg (2 lb) dried haricot beans, soaked overnight
2 large onions, peeled and very finely chopped
2 large green peppers, cored, deseeded and finely diced
2 large red peppers, cored, deseeded and finely diced
225 g (8 oz) button mushrooms, cleaned and finely sliced
For the dressing:
150 ml (¼ pint) salad oil
4 tablespoons tarragon vinegar
¼ teaspoon sugar
¼ teaspoon English mustard powder
4 tablespoons finely chopped parsley
salt and freshly ground black pepper

Drain the haricot beans and rinse under cold running water. Put in a large saucepan with plenty of water (without salt), bring to the boil, then lower the heat, half cover with a lid and simmer gently for 1 hour until tender. Check the water level from time to time during cooking and add more boiling water if it is low.

When the beans are cooked, drain and rinse under cold running water until cold. Turn into a large serving bowl, add the onions, peppers and mushrooms and stir well.

Pour the oil and vinegar into the bowl, add the remaining dressing ingredients with plenty of salt and pepper and toss the salad until the dressing coats the beans and vegetables. Chill in the refrigerator until serving time, toss well just before serving and adjust seasoning.
Serves about 25

Mushroom Macédoine Salad

225 g (8 oz) button mushrooms
3 tablespoons vegetable oil
4 tablespoons salad cream
2 tablespoons single cream
350 g (12 oz) frozen mixed vegetables, cooked
1 teaspoon finely chopped onion
salt and freshly ground black pepper
watercress sprigs, to garnish

Wipe the mushrooms, but do not peel. Trim off the stalks level with the caps. Slice the mushrooms. Heat the oil in a frying pan and use to sauté the mushroom stalks and sliced caps for 2 minutes, until pale golden. Drain and cool on absorbent kitchen paper.

Stir together the salad cream and single cream in a large basin. Add the cooked mixed vegetables and chopped onion and mushrooms. Season, stir well, turn into a salad bowl and serve chilled, garnished with watercress sprigs.

To serve hot, cook the mushrooms in a saucepan, add the other ingredients and heat through gently. Serve with crusty French bread.

Melon in Curry Cream

1 medium-sized melon, preferably honeydew, peeled and quartered
For the curry cream:
50 g (2 oz) butter
1 small onion, peeled and finely chopped
2 inner stalks celery, scrubbed and chopped
3 tablespoons flour
1 tablespoon curry powder
1 teaspoon soft brown sugar
$\frac{1}{2}$ teaspoon ground bay leaves
3 tablespoons lemon juice
150 ml ($\frac{1}{4}$ pint) milk
150 ml ($\frac{1}{4}$ pint) chicken stock
4 tablespoons single cream
salt
pinch of curry powder, to garnish (optional)

Place the melon quarters on a large dish and carefully remove the seeds, reserving the juice. Discard the seeds. Dice the melon flesh neatly, and place in a glass serving dish.

To make the curry cream, melt the butter in a saucepan with a heavy base. Add the chopped onion and celery and cook gently until limp. Stir in the flour and curry powder and cook over low heat for 2 minutes, stirring all the time. Add the sugar, ground bay leaves, lemon juice, reserved melon juice, milk and stock and bring to the boil, stirring constantly. Lower the heat, cover and simmer for 15 minutes. Cool, stir in the cream and add salt to taste. Chill well.

Pour the curry cream over the melon dice and, if liked, garnish with a pinch of curry powder. Serve very cold.

Spicy Mushroom Salad

1 tablespoon Worcestershire sauce
$\frac{1}{4}$ teaspoon prepared French mustard
juice of $\frac{1}{2}$ lemon
2 tablespoons oil
225 g (8 oz) button mushrooms, finely
  sliced
freshly ground black pepper

If available, chopped chives or parsley
give colour and flavour to this salad.
  Put the Worcestershire sauce, mustard, lemon juice and oil in a bowl and
beat well to mix. Add the mushrooms
and stir until thoroughly coated in the
dressing, then add pepper to taste.
Leave to stand for about 30 minutes,
stirring occasionally.

Orange, Grapefruit and Date Salad

2 oranges
1 grapefruit
8 fresh dates, stoned and chopped
3 tablespoons clear honey
3 teaspoons French mustard
2 tablespoons lemon juice
salt and freshly ground black pepper

Remove all the peel and pith from the
oranges and the grapefruit. Cut the
fruits into thin slices, and cut each slice
into 3 or 4 sections.
  Mix together the orange and grapefruit pieces in a bowl with the chopped
fresh dates. Combine the honey, French
mustard, lemon juice and seasoning to
taste. Spoon the mustard and honey
dressing over the prepared fruit and
toss lightly. Chill for at least 1 hour.
  Spoon the salad out on 4 small dishes,
and serve with sliced salami, or other
Continental sausage.

Neapolitan Salad

3 large bunches of watercress,
  trimmed and washed
2 large heads of fennel, trimmed and
  finely sliced
1$\frac{1}{2}$ kg (3 lb) firm ripe tomatoes,
  quartered
2 large cucumbers, peeled, seeded and
  cut into julienne strips
2 × 50 g (2 oz) cans anchovies
4 hard-boiled eggs, quartered
100 g (4 oz) black olives, halved,
  stoned and quartered
For the dressing:
2 tablespoons Meaux mustard
3 tablespoons boiling water
150 ml ($\frac{1}{4}$ pint) olive or salad oil
2 tablespoons lemon juice
salt and freshly ground black pepper

Put the watercress in a large serving
bowl, add the fennel, tomatoes and
cucumber and mix all the vegetables
together with salad servers.
  Soak the anchovies in milk for 30
minutes, drain, dry with absorbent kitchen paper and cut each one in half.
Add to the salad bowl with the eggs and
olives.
  To make the dressing: put the mustard in a heatproof bowl and gradually
beat in the boiling water. Add the oil
drop by drop, beating constantly until
the dressing is thick. Beat in the lemon
juice and season to taste with salt and
pepper.
  Add the dressing to the salad bowl
just before serving and toss well. Taste
and adjust seasoning.
Serves about 20

Orange, Cottage Cheese and Ham Salad

2 oranges
225 g (8 oz) cottage cheese
225 g (8 oz) cooked ham, or other
cooked meat, chopped
1 onion, peeled and grated
salt and freshly ground black pepper
25 g (1 oz) preserved stem ginger,
chopped
sprigs of watercress, to garnish

Finely grate the rind from 1 orange. Remove all the peel and pith from both oranges. Cutting between each section membrane, remove the segments from the oranges, discarding the pips.

Mix the cottage cheese with the grated orange rind, the chopped ham, grated onion, salt and pepper to taste, and the chopped ginger.

Spoon the salad into the centres of 4 small dishes or plates, and arrange the orange segments and sprigs of watercress around the edges. Serve with slices of pumpernickel.

Orange, Chicken and Bean Sprout Salad

175 g (6 oz) cooked, boned chicken
2 oranges
175 g (6 oz) fresh bean sprouts
For the dressing:
4 tablespoons orange juice
2 tablespoons lemon juice
150 ml ($\frac{1}{4}$ pint) olive or corn oil
salt and freshly ground black pepper
To garnish:
2 tablespoons chopped parsley
25 g (1 oz) cashew nuts, chopped

Remove any skin from the chicken meat and pull it into shreds. (This is more easily done while the chicken is still warm, and it is best to take any leftovers from the carcass of a chicken as soon after cooking as possible.)

Remove all the peel and white pith from the oranges. Cutting between each section membrane, remove the segments from the oranges, discarding the pips. Put the orange segments into a bowl with the bean sprouts and chicken. To make the dressing, put the orange and lemon juices into a screw topped jar with the oil and a pinch of salt and pepper. Shake vigorously. Taste and adjust seasoning if necessary.

Pour the dressing over the chicken, orange segments and bean sprouts, and toss lightly together.

Spoon the salad out on 4 small dishes or plates, and garnish with a sprinkling of chopped parsley and cashew nuts.

Rice Salad

225 g (8 oz) long-grain rice, boiled and
drained
1 small onion, peeled and finely
chopped
1 green pepper, cored, seeded and
finely chopped
1 red pepper, cored, seeded and finely
chopped
4 tablespoons chopped nuts (almonds,
cashews, peanuts, walnuts)
4 tablespoons bottled mayonnaise
salt
freshly ground black pepper

Put all the ingredients in a bowl with salt and pepper to taste, then stir carefully but thoroughly so that the salad is well mixed.

Variations:
Substitute a 225 g (8 oz) can of sweetcorn and peppers (drained) for the green and red peppers. Or substitute a 50 g (2 oz) packet of nuts and raisins for the mixed nuts.

Add chopped ham or luncheon meat to serve as a main course salad. If preferred, use a French dressing instead of the mayonnaise. (See French Dressing on p. 43.)

Patio Salad

50 g (2 oz) canned tuna
50 g (2 oz) Edam cheese, diced
50 g (2 oz) button mushrooms, wiped
    and cut in quarters
1 large stalk celery, scrubbed and
    chopped
25 g (1 oz) black olives
few lettuce leaves, shredded, to finish
For the dressing:
pinch each of salt, pepper and sugar
good pinch of dry mustard
2 teaspoons vinegar
1 tablespoon salad oil

Prepare the dressing by shaking together the seasonings, vinegar and oil.
Drain the oil from the fish and break
into chunks. Place this and all the other
ingredients, except the lettuce leaves,
in a bowl. Pour over the dressing and
mix well. Allow to stand for at least 30
minutes in a cold place. Serve on a bed
of shredded lettuce.
Serves 2

Pilaf

50 g (2 oz) butter
1 large onion, peeled and finely
    chopped
2 large sticks celery, trimmed,
    scrubbed and finely chopped
450 g (1 lb) long-grain rice
about 750 ml (1¼ pints) hot chicken
    stock
salt and freshly ground black pepper
1 large green pepper, cored, seeded
    and finely chopped
50 g (2 oz) seedless raisins

Cooking rice in larger quantities than
given here can be tricky, therefore if
more is required it is best to make
several casseroles of this size, rather
than attempting to cook all the rice in
one dish.
    Melt the butter in a flameproof
casserole dish. Add the onion and celery
and cook gently until soft and lightly
coloured. Add the rice to the pan and fry
until it begins to turn colour, stirring
occasionally with a wooden spoon.
Pour in 600 ml (1 pint) of the hot stock
all at once, bring to the boil, add salt
and pepper to taste, stir once, then
cover with buttered greaseproof paper
and a lid and transfer to a fairly hot
oven (190°C, 375°F, Gas Mark 5). Cook
for 30 minutes or until the rice is tender
and all the stock has been absorbed.
Check the level of the stock after 20
minutes of cooking time, adding more
hot stock if the rice is becoming dry.
Remove from the oven, leave until cold,
then gently fold in the green pepper and
raisins. Taste and adjust seasoning.
Arrange on a large serving platter and
serve to accompany Chicken Mayonnaise (see p. 100).

Potato Salad

450 g (1 lb) new or small maincrop
    potatoes
2–3 tablespoons French dressing (see
    p. 43) or mayonnaise (see p. 42)
To garnish:
chopped spring onions
fresh herbs
lettuce or curly endive leaves

Wash and boil new or small maincrop
potatoes until just cooked. Peel them,
then slice or cut into dice. Mix in
French dressing carefully while the
potatoes are still warm. Sprinkle with
chopped spring onions and fresh herbs.
Marinate for 30 minutes or longer and
serve in a bowl lined with lettuce or
curly endive leaves. Mayonnaise may
be used instead of French dressing.

Hot New Potato Salad

450 g (1 lb) new potatoes, scrubbed
1 chicken stock cube
150 ml ($\frac{1}{4}$ pint) boiling water
225 g (8 oz) frozen peas
4 tablespoons mayonnaise
2 tablespoons chopped parsley and dill
50 g (2 oz) gherkins, finely sliced, to garnish

Place the potatoes in a saucepan, cover with lightly salted water and bring to the boil. Cover and simmer until tender. Drain well and halve any larger potatoes while still warm. Transfer to a salad bowl.

Meanwhile, crumble the stock cube into the boiling water and stir until dissolved. Rinse out the saucepan in which the potatoes were cooked, pour in the stock, add the frozen peas and bring to the boil, stirring gently to separate the peas. Remove from the heat and transfer the peas from the stock to the potatoes with a slotted draining spoon.

Allow the stock to cool slightly then beat in the mayonnaise and stir in the chopped herbs. Pour this mixture over the potatoes and peas and stir well several times to coat the vegetables evenly with the dressing. Serve warm garnished with the sliced gherkin.

Hot Sausage and Potato Salad

450–675 g (1–1$\frac{1}{2}$ lb) new potatoes, scraped
salt and freshly ground black pepper
450 g (1 lb) fresh chipolatas
1 bunch spring onions, cleaned and trimmed
1 × 350 g (12 oz) can pineapple cubes or rings, diced
1 tablespoon finely chopped parsley
4–6 gherkins, sliced

For the dressing:
3 tablespoons oil
1 tablespoon wine vinegar
large pinch dry mustard
1 clove garlic, crushed
lettuce or curly endive, to garnish

Boil the potatoes in salted water until just tender. Drain, allow to cool slightly, cut into quarters and keep warm. Grill or fry the chipolatas until cooked through and well browned, then drain and cut each one into three slanting slices; keep warm. Slice half the onions and place in a bowl with the drained pineapple, parsley and gherkins. Mix the dressing ingredients, 1 tablespoon pineapple juice and plenty of seasonings together and add to the pineapple mixture with the hot potatoes and chipolatas.

Toss thoroughly and serve at once garnished with the remaining spring onions and placed on a bed of lettuce or endive.

Tuna Fish Salad

2 × 225 g (8 oz) cans tuna, drained and flaked
1 large green pepper, cored, seeded and sliced
$\frac{1}{2}$ large cucumber, peeled and diced
3 firm tomatoes, chopped
juice of $\frac{1}{2}$ lemon
4 tablespoons bottled mayonnaise
salt
freshly ground black pepper

Put the tuna, green pepper, cucumber and tomatoes in a bowl, sprinkle with the lemon juice and stir gently to mix. Fold in the mayonnaise with salt and pepper to taste. Serve on a bed of lettuce and garnish with tomato quarters, if liked.

Variation:
Substitute 150 ml ($\frac{1}{4}$ pint) oil and vinegar dressing for the mayonnaise.

Russian Salad

1 × 225 g (8 oz) packet frozen mixed
   vegetables with sweetcorn
4 small beetroot
1 × 450 g (1 lb) can new potatoes,
   drained and chopped
1 × 150 ml (5 fl oz) carton soured
   cream
3 tablespoons bottled mayonnaise
1 teaspoon creamed horseradish or
   prepared mustard (optional)
salt and freshly ground black pepper

Cook the mixed vegetables according
to the packet directions, then drain
thoroughly and leave to cool. Chop half
the beetroot, then put in a bowl with the
mixed vegetables and potatoes. Add
half the soured cream, the mayonnaise,
horseradish or mustard (if using) and
salt and pepper to taste.

Fold gently until well mixed. Slice
the remaining beetroot and arrange in a
circle on top of the salad. Spoon the
remaining soured cream in the centre.
Serves 6

Salata Inglese

For the dressing:
6 tablespoons olive oil
2 tablespoons red wine vinegar
1 tablespoon Meaux mustard
salt and freshly ground black pepper
For the salad:
2 curly endives, washed and broken
   into sprigs
2 large green peppers, cored, seeded
   and finely sliced
2 heads of fennel, trimmed and finely
   sliced
2 hard-boiled eggs, finely sieved
175 g (6 oz) Stilton cheese

Put the dressing ingredients, with salt
and pepper to taste, in a large salad
bowl and beat well with a fork until
thick. Add the salad vegetables and

eggs to the bowl, crumble over the
cheese, then mix gently together until
salad and cheese are lightly coated in
the dressing. Taste and adjust seasoning and serve immediately.
Serves 10–12

Tossed Green Salad

Webbs Wonder or Cos lettuce
watercress sprigs
3–4 tablespoons French dressing (see
   p. 43)
curly endive or small chicory leaves
   (optional)

With the exception of the cabbage-like
heart of the Webbs, lettuce leaves
should be torn in pieces, not cut with a
knife. Discard any coarse outer leaves,
wash the rest carefully and dry by
swinging in a salad basket or using a
salad spinner. Arrange the lettuce in a
salad bowl with sprigs of watercress,
which is available all year, but tastes
peppery when in flower. Cut off the
coarse watercress stalks, wash and dry
the sprigs.

Tender leaves from the hearts of curly
endive can also be added, or some small
chicory leaves. Just before serving, toss
the salad with a few tablespoons of well
mixed French dressing. Serve with cold
dishes, hot roast poultry and game,
grills, cheese soufflé and pasta dishes.

* Mixed French Salad

Follow the recipe for Tossed Green
Salad (above) with these changes: add
some sliced cucumber, tomato wedges
and crisp radishes which have been
washed, topped and tailed. Trim and
peel a few fresh spring onions, leave
them 6 or 7 cm (2 or 3 inches) long or
chop up the white part and sprinkle it
over the salad. Toss with French
dressing.

Sour Cream Herring Salad

4 × 175 g (6 oz) herrings
1 medium onion, peeled and sliced
2 bay leaves
1 teaspoon pickling spice
salt
freshly ground black pepper
120 ml (4 fl oz) dry white wine
120 ml (4 fl oz) white wine vinegar
4 spring onions, finely chopped
150 ml (¼ pint) soured cream
To garnish:
1 red-skinned eating apple
lemon juice

Cut off the heads and tails of the herring and remove the fillets, keep the soft roes. Rinse the fish and roes, clean them and place them in a shallow ovenproof dish. Cover with the onion slices, add the bay leaves, pickling spice, a little salt and pepper and pour over the wine and vinegar. Poach in a preheated moderate oven (160°C, 325°F, Gas Mark 3) for 30 minutes. Remove from the oven and leave until quite cold.

Stir the spring onions into the soured cream and add salt and pepper to taste. Arrange the fish fillets on a serving dish, strain a little of the fish liquor over them and smother with the soured cream. Core and slice the unpeeled apple, dip in lemon juice to prevent discoloration, then garnish the fish.

Sweet Winter Salad

100 g (4 oz) seedless raisins
50 g (2 oz) shelled walnuts
100 g (4 oz) carrots, peeled
2 stalks celery, scrubbed
1 sweet green pepper
2 small heads endive, trimmed
For the dressing:
2 teaspoons lemon juice
salt and freshly ground black pepper
1 teaspoon clear honey
3 tablespoons salad oil

Mix all the ingredients for the dressing except the oil, and gradually beat in the oil so that it emulsifies and thickens the dressing. Allow to stand for at least 1 hour.

Chop the raisins and shelled walnuts roughly. Grate the carrot. Remove coarse strings from the celery and chop. Remove seeds, core and white pith from the green pepper and cut into thin strips. Separate the endive heads into leaves. Toss all the salad ingredients lightly in the dressing, and serve chilled with assorted cold meats, or with hot roast beef or pork.

Sardine Salad

2 eating apples
juice of ½ lemon
75 g (3 oz) Edam or Gouda cheese, diced
1 handful of broken walnuts, finely chopped
1 × 150 ml (5 fl oz) carton soured cream
salt and freshly ground black pepper
8 lettuce leaves
2 × 100 g (4 oz) cans sardines in oil, drained
sprig of parsley, to garnish

Peel and core the apples, then chop finely. Put in a bowl and sprinkle with a little lemon juice, then add the cheese, walnuts, half the soured cream and salt and pepper to taste. Stir well to mix. Arrange the lettuce leaves in a circle on a large plate or dish, then spoon the apple and cheese mixture on top. Arrange the sardines in a circle and sprinkle with the remaining lemon juice. Spoon the remaining soured cream in the centre of the sardines and garnish with parsley.

Variation:
Any canned fish in oil can be used instead of the sardines – try mackerel, brisling or pilchards.

Salad Niçoise

225 g (8 oz) tomatoes
½ Spanish onion
1 small or ½ large green pepper
1 lettuce heart
1 × 90 g (3½ oz) can tuna fish
6 anchovy fillets
75 ml (3 fl oz) Garlic French dressing
225 g (8 oz) French beans, cooked
6 black olives, stoned
2 hard-boiled eggs

Skin the tomatoes and cut into quarters. Peel and slice the onion and break it into rings. Halve the pepper, remove stem and seeds and finely slice the flesh. Wash and dry the lettuce. Drain the tuna fish and flake it roughly. Split anchovy fillets lengthwise. Shell and quarter the eggs.

Put half the French dressing in a shallow salad bowl and toss in it the prepared lettuce and beans. Arrange the tuna fish on top with the onion rings, peppers and olives, and the hard-boiled eggs topped with anchovy fillets. Sprinkle with the remaining dressing.

Winter Salad

1 firm white cabbage, about 1 kg
  (2 lb), shredded
3 large carrots, peeled and grated
50 g (2 oz) sultanas

100 g (4 oz) dates, pitted and roughly chopped
225 g (8 oz) Edam or Gouda cheese, rind removed and diced
For the dressing:
6 tablespoons corn or vegetable oil
2 tablespoons lemon juice
2 tablespoons clear honey
salt and freshly ground black pepper

Put the cabbage, carrots, sultanas, dates and cheese in a mixing bowl and stir well to combine. Put the ingredients for the dressing in a screw-topped jar and shake well. Pour the dressing over the salad and toss until thoroughly coated. Taste and adjust seasoning, transfer to a serving bowl and toss again before serving.
Serves about 12

Piquant Yogurt Dressing

1 tablespoon corn oil
1 tablespoon lemon juice
1 tablespoon drained capers
150 ml (¼ pint) unsweetened natural yogurt
salt
freshly ground black pepper

Beat together the corn oil, lemon juice and drained capers. Stir in the unsweetened natural yogurt and season to taste with salt and freshly ground black pepper. Use to dress a green salad.

Mayonnaise

2 egg yolks
¼ teaspoon each salt and sugar
freshly ground pepper to taste
½ teaspoon French mustard
150 ml (¼ pint) olive oil
1 tablespoon tarragon vinegar

This quantity makes 150 ml (¼ pint). Stand a small bowl on a teatowel and wrap the towel around the bowl to prevent it sliding about while you are stirring.

Put the egg yolks in the bowl with the salt, sugar, pepper and mustard and mix well with a small wooden spoon.

Put the oil in a jug and add it to the egg yolks trickle by trickle, while stirring steadily, always in the same direction, to avoid curdling.

When the mixture thickens, stir in a little of the vinegar; add the rest when all the oil is used. Taste and adjust the seasoning. To reduce the cost, up to 50 per cent corn oil can be mixed with the olive oil. Wine or cider vinegar can be used but not malt vinegar.

* Lemon Mayonnaise

Follow the recipe for Mayonnaise (above), with this change: use fresh lemon juice instead of the vinegar.

Mustard Mayonnaise

1 tablespoon French mustard
150 ml ($\frac{1}{4}$ pint) mayonnaise
double cream

Mix the French mustard together with mayonnaise, and a little double cream. Season, stir and chill.

Anchovy Mayonnaise

1 small can anchovies
150 ml ($\frac{1}{4}$ pint) mayonnaise
capers
salt
freshly ground black pepper

Drain the anchovies and pound to a paste, mix with the mayonnaise; add capers and seasoning to taste. Chill in the refrigerator until serving time.

French Dressing (Sauce Vinaigrette)

$\frac{1}{2}$ teaspoon salt
$\frac{1}{2}$ teaspoon caster sugar
$\frac{1}{2}$ teaspoon French mustard
$\frac{1}{4}$ teaspoon ground black pepper
75 ml (3 fl oz) wine or cider vinegar
150 ml (6 fl oz) olive oil

Mix all seasonings together and stir in the vinegar. Mix in the oil and whip or put in a screw-top jar and shake well to blend thoroughly. Taste and adjust the seasoning if wished.

Lemon French Dressing

Follow the recipe for French Dressing (above), with this change: use lemon juice instead of vinegar.

Fresh Herb Dressing

Follow the recipe for French Dressing (above), with this change: add 1–2 tablespoons chopped fresh tarragon, chives, chervil or mint.

Sour Cream Dressing

150 ml ($\frac{1}{4}$ pint) soured cream
or
150 ml ($\frac{1}{4}$ pint) thick cream mixed
    with 1 tablespoon lemon juice
1 teaspoon French mustard
1–2 teaspoons caster sugar
salt
freshly ground black pepper
lemon juice

Mix the ingredients thoroughly using either soured cream or thick cream and lemon juice. Season to taste with salt, pepper and lemon juice.

VEGETABLES

Fruited Beetroot Dice

1 tablespoon soft brown sugar
75 ml (3 fl oz) pineapple juice
1 tablespoon white vinegar
1 tablespoon cornflour
15 g ($\frac{1}{2}$ oz) butter
salt and freshly ground black pepper
450 g (1 lb) cooked beetroot, peeled
   and finely diced
1 tablespoon finely chopped spring
   onion, to garnish

Place the sugar, pineapple juice, vinegar and cornflour in a small saucepan. Stir until smooth then bring to the boil, stirring constantly. Reduce the heat and simmer for 2 minutes, stirring occasionally. Beat in the butter and season to taste.
   Fold the beetroot dice into the sauce and reheat carefully to boiling point. Spoon into a warm serving dish and garnish with the chopped spring onions.

Runner Beans Tuscan Style

450 g (1 lb) runner beans
50 g (2 oz) butter
1 tablespoon olive oil
2 tablespoons chopped fresh sage or
   parsley or 1 teaspoon dried sage
1 clove garlic, crushed
salt

freshly ground pepper
$\frac{1}{4}$ teaspoon ground nutmeg
1 tablespoon grated Parmesan cheese

Top and tail the beans and remove the strings from the sides with a small vegetable knife. Cut the beans obliquely into chunks $2\frac{1}{2}$ cm (1 inch) long. Simmer in salted water for 10 minutes or until tender. Drain in a colander. Heat the butter and oil in a saucepan, stir in 1 tablespoon of the sage or parsley and the crushed garlic and fry for 1 minute. Add the cooked beans, season to taste with salt and pepper and add the nutmeg. Stir over gentle heat for 5 minutes. Mix in the grated cheese and serve at once sprinkled with the remaining fresh herbs.

French Beans with Poulette Sauce

450 g (1 lb) French beans
50 g (2 oz) butter
1 tablespoon flour
salt
freshly ground black pepper
pinch of mixed dried herbs
1 egg yolk
lemon juice
2 tablespoons chopped fresh parsley

Top and tail the beans if necessary. Wash and simmer gently in salted water for 10 to 20 minutes, according to age and size. Drain in a colander and keep warm under a cloth. Reserve the bean liquor. Melt the butter in a small saucepan. Withdraw the pan from the heat, stir in the flour and gradually blend in 300 ml (½ pint) of the reserved bean liquor.

Bring to the boil, stirring well. Add salt and pepper to taste and the mixed herbs, reduce the heat and simmer gently for 5 to 10 minutes.

Beat the egg yolk with 1 tablespoon lemon juice and 2 tablespoons of the bean liquor. Remove the sauce from the heat and stir in the egg yolk mixture. Reheat without boiling. Taste and adjust the seasoning, adding more lemon juice if desired. Arrange the beans neatly in a warm serving dish, pour the sauce over them and sprinkle with chopped fresh parsley.

Boston Baked Beans

225–350 g (8–12 oz) haricot beans, soaked overnight
2 medium onions, peeled and chopped
100 g (4 oz) salt pork, diced
2 tablespoons treacle or dark brown sugar
2–3 tablespoons tomato ketchup
1 tablespoon cider vinegar
1 teaspoon dry mustard
1 teaspoon salt
1 tablespoon Worcester sauce (optional)

Drain the soaked beans and simmer them in fresh water for about 1 hour. To test, take out a few beans on a spoon; if when you blow on them the skins burst, they are ready. Drain them, reserving the liquor. Put the beans in a greased casserole. Mix in the other ingredients and just enough liquid to cover them. Put on a lid and bake in a preheated oven at 150°C, 300°F, Gas Mark 2 for 7 to 8 hours. Stir occasionally and leave uncovered for the last hour. If the beans become too dry, add a little more liquid.

Butter Beans with Sauce

225 g (8 oz) butter beans or lentils
salt
dry ingredients for Parsley, Onion or Cheese Sauce (p. 356)
4 tablespoons cream (optional)

Cover the beans or lentils with boiling water and soak overnight. Drain. Cover generously with cold water, bring to the boil, cover and simmer for 1 hour or until tender, adding salt towards the end of cooking. Drain and measure off 300 ml (½ pint) of the bean liquor. Use this to make Parsley, Onion or Cheese sauce and mix in the drained beans. For a rich sauce, reduce amount of bean liquor and add 4 tablespoons cream. These are good with grilled ham or bacon, sausages, lamb or pork chops.

Broccoli à la Crème

75 ml (3 fl oz) single cream
450 g (1 lb) cooked broccoli
lemon juice
salt
freshly ground pepper

Heat 75 ml (3 fl oz) single cream per 450 g (1 lb) broccoli. Season with lemon juice, salt and freshly ground pepper and pour the cream over the cooked broccoli spears. Serve hot.

Broccoli au Gratin

450 g (1 lb) cooked broccoli spears
3–4 tablespoons melted butter
grated cheese

Arrange the cooked broccoli spears in a shallow flameproof dish. Pour over 3–4 tablespoons melted butter, sprinkle with grated cheese and flash under a preheated grill.

Buttered Cabbage

450 g (1 lb) shredded cabbage
salt
25 g (1 oz) butter
freshly ground pepper
pinch of nutmeg

Put shredded cabbage in a large pan
with just enough boiling water to cover
the base. Season with salt, cover and
cook over low heat, shaking occasionally, for about 10 minutes, until tender
but still slightly crisp. Do not overcook.
Drain in a colander.

Melt the butter in the warm empty
saucepan, add the cooked cabbage and
stir well, seasoning with salt, freshly
ground pepper and a pinch of nutmeg.
Serve very hot.

Spicy Red Cabbage

1 kg (2 lb) red cabbage, core removed
  and finely shredded
450 g (1 lb) onions, peeled and finely
  chopped
450 g (1 lb) cooking apples, peeled,
  cored and finely chopped
salt
freshly ground black pepper
good pinch of ground mixed spice
2 tablespoons soft brown sugar
2 tablespoons wine vinegar
25 g (1 oz) butter

Put a layer of shredded cabbage in the
bottom of a casserole. Arrange a layer
of chopped onions and apples over the
top. Season and add a little mixed spice
and a sprinkling of sugar. Fill up the
dish with alternating layers of onion
and apple mixture and cabbage, seasoning each layer and sprinkling with the
spices and sugar. Pour in the wine
vinegar and dot surface with butter.

Cover and bake in a preheated cool
oven (150°C, 300°F, Gas Mark 2) for 2
hours.

Glazed Carrots

450 g (1 lb) carrots, scraped
300 ml ($\frac{1}{2}$ pint) good White stock
  (p. 6)
50 g (2 oz) butter
1 tablespoon granulated sugar
salt
freshly ground pepper
chopped mint or parsley

Cut the carrots into rounds or fingers.
Put them in a sauté pan, cover with the
stock and add the butter and sugar.
Cover the pan, bring quickly to boil and
simmer gently for 20 minutes. Remove
the lid and continue cooking until the
liquid is reduced to a glaze. Stir carefully from time to time to prevent the
carrots catching and burning. When
they are bright and glistening, season
to taste with salt and pepper and place
them in a hot serving dish and sprinkle
with chopped fresh mint or parsley.

Glazed Carrots and Parsnips

50 g (2 oz) butter
4 large carrots, peeled and cut into
  rings
2 large parsnips or turnips, peeled or
  cut into rings
$\frac{1}{2}$ teaspoon ground ginger
$\frac{1}{2}$ teaspoon grated nutmeg
salt and freshly ground black pepper
2 tablespoons lemon juice
2 tablespoons soft brown sugar

Melt half the butter in a heavy
saucepan and use to sauté the sliced
carrots and parsnips gently, turning
frequently, for 2 minutes. Add the
ground ginger, grated nutmeg and
seasoning to taste. Stir well, add the
lemon juice and just sufficient water to
cover the vegetables. Put on the lid and
simmer, covered, for 12 to 15 minutes or
until the vegetables are just tender and

most of the liquid absorbed. Add the soft brown sugar and remaining butter and increase the heat slightly. Toss the vegetables frequently in the pan to glaze them evenly. Taste and adjust the seasoning if necessary.

Austrian Cabbage with Soured Cream

1 small white cabbage weighing
  approx. 450 g (1 lb)
25–50 g (1–2 oz) butter or bacon fat
1 small onion, peeled and chopped
1 teaspoon paprika pepper
salt
freshly ground pepper
100 ml (3 fl oz) soured cream
extra paprika pepper or fried pimento
  strips, to garnish

Remove any discoloured or coarse leaves from the cabbage. Cut the heart into quarters and remove the stalk. Shred finely, wash and drain. Preheat the oven to 160°C, 325°F, Gas Mark 3.

In a flameproof casserole, heat the butter or bacon fat and fry the onion gently until softened. Add the cabbage and sauté lightly until well buttered.

Season with paprika pepper, salt and freshly ground pepper. Stir in the soured cream and mix well.

Cover with a lid and bake in the oven for 20 minutes, or cook over low heat on top of the stove. Do not overheat or the cream will separate. Garnish with paprika pepper or fried pimento strips.

Fried Mexican Beans

225 g (8 oz) red kidney beans, soaked
  overnight
100 g (4 oz) onions, peeled and
  coarsely chopped
1 × 225 g (8 oz) can tomatoes
salt and freshly ground pepper
50 g (2 oz) lard

1 clove garlic, finely chopped
¼ teaspoon chilli powder

Drain the soaked beans and put them in a large thick pan, cover with water, bring to the boil, boil for 10 minutes. Drain, then add 1 tablespoon of the onion, 2 tablespoons of the tomatoes and sufficient fresh water to cover the beans. Bring to the simmer and cook gently for 1 hour or until the beans start to soften. Add salt to taste and a knob of lard. Continue cooking for a further 30 minutes or until the beans are completely soft, stirring from time to time as the liquid is absorbed. Withdraw the pan from the heat. In a large thick frying pan, heat the remaining lard and fry the rest of the onions and the garlic until transparent. Stir in the rest of the tomatoes and simmer for 2 to 3 minutes. Gradually add the cooked beans, mashing them as you go. Add the chilli powder (not too much as it is very hot) and salt and pepper to taste. Cook gently over low heat, stirring steadily until the mixture thickens. Turn the fried beans into a heated bowl and serve with spicy pork sausages.

Spiced Carrots and Swede

4 large carrots, peeled and sliced
450 g (1 lb) swede, peeled and diced
25 g (1 oz) butter, melted
2 tablespoons orange juice
1 teaspoon grated orange rind
good pinch of ground ginger
good pinch of grated nutmeg
salt and freshly ground black pepper

Place the sliced carrots and diced swede in an ovenproof dish.

Combine the melted butter, orange juice, grated orange rind, ground ginger and grated nutmeg and seasoning to taste. Pour over the vegetables.

Lightly cover with foil and bake in a fairly hot oven (190°C, 375°F, Gas Mark 5) for 45 minutes.

† Cauliflower au Gratin

1 medium cauliflower, leaves removed
   and washed
300 ml ($\frac{1}{2}$ pint) hot water
salt
To finish:
25 g (1 oz) butter or margarine
1 tablespoon flour
150 ml ($\frac{1}{4}$ pint) milk
75 g (3 oz) Cheddar cheese, grated
freshly ground black pepper
1 tablespoon fresh white breadcrumbs

Divide the cauliflower into quarters
and remove the thick pieces of stalk.
Put the water into the cooker and add
the trivet, rim side down. Stand the
cauliflower on the trivet and season
lightly with salt. Close the cooker,
bring to H pressure and cook for 4
minutes. Reduce the pressure quickly.
Lift out the cauliflower and transfer to a
lightly greased ovenproof dish. Drain
off the liquid from the cooker, retaining
150 ml ($\frac{1}{4}$ pint) for the sauce.

Melt the butter or margarine in a
small saucepan. Stir in the flour and
cook gently for 1–2 minutes, stirring
constantly. Remove the pan from the
heat and gradually add the reserved
cooking liquid and milk, stirring
vigorously. Return the pan to the heat
and bring to the boil, stirring constantly. Add 50 g (2 oz) of the cheese and
a little pepper, stir until the cheese has
melted. Taste and adjust the seasoning
of the sauce as necessary and pour the
sauce evenly over the cooked cauliflower. Sprinkle the sauce with a mixture of the remaining cheese and breadcrumbs. Brown under a hot grill.

Celery with Sauce

12–16 sticks celery
dry ingredients for Poulette (p. 44)
   Parsley or Cheese Sauce (p. 356)
chopped fresh parsley, to garnish

Cut celery into 5 cm (2 inch) lengths and
cook in boiling salted water for 10 to 20
minutes, until tender. Drain and use the
liquid to make Poulette sauce (p. 44), or
use it with 50 per cent milk for Parsley
or Cheese sauce (p. 356). Mix the celery
in the chosen sauce and garnish with
chopped fresh parsley.

Braised Celery Hearts

4 small or 2 large celery hearts
300 ml ($\frac{1}{2}$ pint) good white stock
   (p. 6) or bouillon
50 g (2 oz) Beurre Manié (p. 352)

Trim and clean the celery. Cut the
hearts and stalks down to 10 cm (4 inch)
lengths. Tie the stalks into small
bundles. Place the celery in a casserole
and add sufficient stock to cover. Cover
with a lid and simmer gently on top of
stove or in a preheated oven at 180°C,
350°F, Gas Mark 4 for 1 hour or until
tender.

When the celery is cooked, place it
neatly in a warm serving dish. Remove
the strings and keep it warm. Add
beurre manié one ball at a time to the
stock in the casserole, stirring steadily
until the sauce is of a creamy consistency. Boil for 3 to 5 minutes to cook
the flour thoroughly. Taste and adjust
the seasoning and pour the sauce over
the celery.

† Braised Celery with Ham

25 g (1 oz) butter
1 head of celery, scrubbed and cut
    into 5 cm (2 inch) pieces
2 carrots, peeled and sliced
300 ml ($\frac{1}{2}$ pint) hot brown stock or
    water and $\frac{1}{2}$ beef stock cube
100 g (4 oz) cooked shoulder of ham,
    cut into 2.5 cm (1 inch) strips
salt
freshly ground black pepper

Heat the butter in the cooker. Sauté the celery and carrots until both are beginning to colour. Remove the cooker from the heat, stir in the stock or water and stock cube with the ham and a little salt and pepper. Close the cooker, bring to H pressure and cook for 5 minutes. Reduce the pressure quickly.

Flemish Chicory with Ham and Cheese Sauce

4 medium chicory heads
4 slices cooked ham
300 ml ($\frac{1}{2}$ pint) Cheese sauce (p. 356)
3 tablespoons grated cheese
1-2 tablespoons crisp breadcrumbs

Roll each blanched chicory head in a slice of ham and place in a buttered shallow ovenproof dish. Pour cheese sauce over the chicory and cover with grated cheese and breadcrumbs. Bake in a preheated oven at 190°C, 375°F, Gas Mark 5 for 20 to 30 minutes, until golden brown and sizzling.

Courgette Neapolitan

450 g (1 lb) fresh tomatoes, skinned,
    or 1 × 400 g (14 oz) can tomatoes
1 small onion, peeled and chopped
salt and freshly ground black pepper
750 g (1$\frac{1}{2}$ lb) courgettes

2 tablespoons flour
25 g (1 oz) butter
225 g (8 oz) Edam cheese, thinly sliced

Chop the tomatoes and heat in a saucepan with the chopped onion and seasoning to taste, for 10 minutes, to make a thick tomato sauce. Slice the courgettes into 1 cm ($\frac{1}{2}$ inch) rings and then into quarters. Shake in a bag with the flour to coat evenly. Melt the butter in a large frying pan and fry the courgettes until brown on both sides. Put alternate layers of courgette, the tomato mixture and the cheese in a shallow baking dish, finishing with a layer of cheese. Bake in a fairly hot oven (190°C, 375°F, Gas Mark 5) for 30 minutes. Serve topped with crispy grilled bacon.

Courgettes au Gratin

4 courgettes, topped, tailed and
    halved
50 g (2 oz) butter
salt
freshly ground pepper
grated cheese
hot cream

Top, tail and wipe the courgettes and cut them in half lengthwise. Heat the butter in a shallow flameproof casserole and fry the courgette halves cut side down until golden.

Turn the courgettes over, season with salt and the freshly ground pepper. Sprinkle with grated cheese, dot with butter. Put on a lid and cook gently on top of the stove for 20 minutes, or in the oven at 180°C, 350°F, Gas Mark 4 for 30 minutes or until tender. Trickle a little hot cream over the courgettes, flash under a hot grill and serve at once.

Sautéed Vegetable Marrow

40 g (1½ oz) butter
1 tablespoon vegetable oil
1 medium-sized vegetable marrow,
  peeled, seeds removed and diced
6 spring onions, trimmed and finely
  chopped
1 tablespoon fresh tarragon, chopped
  or 1 teaspoon dried tarragon
salt and freshly ground black pepper

Melt the butter with the oil in a
saucepan. Add the diced marrow and
finely chopped onions. Sauté for 3 minutes, turning frequently, until the
juices begin to run from the marrow.
Sprinkle in the tarragon and season to
taste. Reduce the heat, cover and cook
for 5 minutes, shaking the covered pan
occasionally. Test one of the marrow
dice with a skewer and if tender serve
immediately in a warm vegetable dish.
If not cooked, add 2 tablespoons water
and replace the pan over moderate heat
until the marrow is tender.

† Stuffed Marrow Rings

25 g (1 oz) lard
1 small onion, peeled and finely
  chopped
450 g (1 lb) sausagemeat
1 hard-boiled egg, chopped
large pinch mixed herbs
salt
freshly ground black pepper
1 marrow, peeled
450 ml (¾ pint) hot brown stock or
  water and ½ beef stock cube
2 teaspoons cornflour
little cold water

Heat the lard in the cooker and gently
fry the onion and sausagemeat until
both are just beginning to colour. Lift
out and drain well. Drain off excess lard
from the cooker. Add the egg, herbs, salt
and pepper to the sausagemeat and

onion and mix well. Cut the marrow
into 5 cm (2 inch) thick rings. Use a
vegetable peeler or grapefruit knife to
remove the seeds carefully without
breaking the flesh. Fill each cavity with
the meat filling, packing it well down.
Put the stock or water and stock cube
into the cooker with the trivet. Stand
the filled marrow rings on the trivet.
Close the cooker, bring to H pressure
and cook for 5 minutes. Reduce the
pressure quickly. Lift out the marrow to
a warmed dish and keep hot. Remove
the trivet and return the open cooker to
the heat. Add the cornflour blended
with a little cold water. Bring to the
boil, stirring constantly. Taste and
adjust the seasoning as necessary and
serve the sauce poured around the
marrow rings.

Skirlie-Mirlie

1 kg (2 lb) mashed swedes
1 kg (2 lb) mashed potatoes
hot milk
bacon fat or butter
salt
freshly ground pepper
chopped parsley, to garnish

Add an equal quantity of mashed potatoes (p. 57) to the mashed swedes. Whip
together with a little hot milk and extra
bacon fat or butter over low heat until
creamy. Season well with salt and freshly ground pepper and serve garnished
with chopped fresh parsley.

Leeks with Sauce

8 small leeks, cooked
Parsley (p. 356) or Poulette Sauce
  (p. 44)

Arrange well drained cooked leeks
lengthwise in a warm serving dish and
coat with Parsley or Poulette sauce.

Cheesy Leeks

8 small leeks, cooked
Cheese sauce (p. 356)
grated cheese

Arrange the leeks in a flameproof dish.
Coat the cooked leeks with Cheese
sauce. Sprinkle generously with grated
cheese and brown under the grill.

Leeks au Gratin

8 small leeks, cooked
grated cheese
butter

Arrange the leeks in a flameproof dish.
Well butter a shallow flameproof dish.
Arrange the cooked leeks neatly on the
dish, sprinkle them thickly with grated
cheese and dot with butter. Cook under
the grill until the cheese is bubbling and
golden.

Leeks à la Niçoise

4 leeks
2 tablespoons olive oil
1 × 225 g (8 oz) can tomatoes
pinch of basil
garlic
salt
freshly ground black pepper
sugar
chopped parsley, to garnish

Prepare the leeks, trimming off all
green leaves. Heat the olive oil in a
flameproof casserole and fry the leeks
until slightly coloured, turning them
once. Add the can of tomatoes. Add a
pinch of basil and flavour to taste with
garlic, salt, freshly ground black pepper
and sugar.

Cook over low heat for 20 minutes or
until tender. Serve sprinkled with chopped parsley.

Leek and Bacon Gratin

8 large leeks, white and pale green
    part washed and sliced into 5 cm (2
    inch) lengths
1 large carrot, peeled and sliced into
    5 cm (2 inch) lengths
12 rashers streaky bacon
For the sauce:
25 g (1 oz) butter
25 g (1 oz) flour
300 ml ($\frac{1}{2}$ pint) milk
salt and freshly ground black pepper
50 g (2 oz) Cheddar cheese, grated
To finish:
50 g (2 oz) Cheddar cheese, grated
50 g (2 oz) fresh white breadcrumbs

Cook the sliced leeks and carrots in
boiling, salted water to cover for 10 to
15 minutes or until tender. Drain, reserving the liquid and turn into a buttered flameproof casserole.

Meanwhile prepare the sauce. Melt
the butter in a pan, stir in the flour and
cook for 2 to 3 minutes, stirring constantly. Remove the pan from the heat
and gradually add the milk and 150 ml ($\frac{1}{4}$
pint) of the liquid from the vegetables,
stirring constantly. Return the pan to
the heat. Bring slowly to the boil stirring all the time. Lower the heat, add
the seasoning to taste and simmer
gently until the sauce thickens. Stir in
the 50 g (2 oz) cheese.

Grill the bacon rashers, arrange on
top of the leeks and carrots and cover
with the sauce. Sprinkle thickly with
the mixed cheese and breadcrumbs.
Pour over the drippings from the grilled
bacon and place the dish under a hot
grill until the surface is golden-brown
and crisp. Serve immediately.

Lentils with Parsley Butter

225 g (8 oz) brown or green lentils,
  soaked for 1 hour
250 ml (8 fl oz) good White or Brown
  stock (p. 6)
40 g (1½ oz) Parsley butter (p. 352)

Drain the soaked lentils, cover with
cold water and simmer for 1 hour or
until they are tender. If the water is not
absorbed, strain the lentils, add the
stock and cook gently until no liquid
remains.

Remove the pan from the heat, stir in
the parsley butter and season to taste
with salt and pepper.

† Onions Provençale

2 tablespoons olive or cooking oil
8 small onions, peeled
1 × 400 g (14 oz) can tomatoes,
  chopped
150 ml (¼ pint) dry white wine
1 tablespoon freshly chopped parsley
salt
freshly ground black pepper
½ teaspoon sweet basil

Heat the oil in the cooker and sauté the
onions until just beginning to colour.
Add all the remaining ingredients.
Close the cooker, bring to H pressure
and cook for 6 minutes. Reduce the
pressure quickly.

Glazed Onions

pickling or button onions
butter
caster sugar
chopped parsley, to garnish

Skin and cook pickling or button
onions in boiling salted water for 20
minutes or until tender. Drain and dry

on absorbent kitchen paper. Heat
enough butter in a sauté pan to cover
the base of the pan, add the onions and
sprinkle them with caster sugar. Cook
over gentle heat, shaking frequently,
until they glaze. Serve with the rest of
the butter and sugar poured over and
sprinkle with chopped parsley.

French Fried Onion Rings

1 large Spanish onion
milk
seasoned flour
fat for frying

Skin a large Spanish onion and cut into
5 mm (¼ inch) slices. Separate the slices
into rings. Dip the rings in milk and toss
them in seasoned flour, shaking off any
surplus. Heat deep fat to 190°C, 375°F.
Put the onion rings in a heated frying
basket and cook for 2 to 3 minutes until
crisp and golden.

Drain on absorbent kitchen paper,
sprinkle with salt and serve at once
with grilled or fried fish or meat.

Fried Parsley

parsley, stalks removed, washed
fat for frying

Remove long stalks from the parsley,
wash and dry the sprigs. Cook in deep
fat at 182°C, 360°F for about 2 minutes.
As soon as the parsley starts sizzling
remove it with a slotted spoon.

Drain on absorbent kitchen paper
and use at once.

Roast Parsnips

parsnips
fat for roasting
salt

Peel and wash the parsnips. Quarter them and remove the core. Boil for 5 to 10 minutes in salted water. Drain and dry and cook in hot fat round a roasting joint for 45 minutes to 1 hour; or roast in a separate tin with hot dripping or lard.

Green Peas à la Française

1 kg (2 lb) peas, shelled
25 g (1 oz) butter
1 rasher streaky bacon, de-rinded and chopped
4 spring onions, chopped
$\frac{1}{4}$ lettuce
1 teaspoon sugar
salt and freshly ground pepper
fresh mint

Melt the butter in a flameproof casserole and fry the bacon and onions gently until transparent. Shred and wash the lettuce and add it to the casserole. Cover and 'sweat' over gentle heat until the lettuce is bright green and juicy.

Tip in the peas, add a sprig of mint, sugar and salt and pepper to taste. Cover and cook over gentle heat on top of the stove for 30 minutes, or in the oven at 150°C, 300°F, Gas Mark 2 for 45 minutes or until tender.

Replace the cooked mint with fresh sprigs to garnish.

Pease Pudding

225 g (8 oz) split peas, soaked overnight
1 ham bone or bacon scraps
1 onion, peeled and spiked with cloves
25 g (1 oz) butter
1 egg, beaten
pinch of sugar
salt
freshly ground pepper
parsley sprigs, to garnish

Drain the soaked peas and tie in a loose muslin cloth allowing room for them to swell. Put them in a saucepan and cover with cold water. Add the ham bone and onion. Simmer for 2 hours or until soft. Lift out the bag, put the peas through a mouli or sieve and add the butter, egg, sugar and salt and pepper to taste. Beat the ingredients together well and tie up tightly in a floured cloth. Return the pudding to the pan and simmer for a further 30 minutes. Turn the pudding into a warm serving bowl and garnish with parsley. Serve very hot.

† Stuffed Peppers

65 g (2$\frac{1}{2}$ oz) long-grain rice
salt
4 green peppers
100 g (4 oz) cooked ham or streaky bacon, chopped
100 g (4 oz) Cheddar cheese, grated
2 teaspoons Worcestershire sauce
freshly ground black pepper
300 ml ($\frac{1}{2}$ pint) water

Cook the rice in plenty of boiling salted water until tender, about 12 to 15 minutes. Drain in a sieve and rinse with hot water. Carefully cut a hole around the stalk end of each pepper and remove the core and seeds. If necessary, cut a thin slice from the base of the pepper so that it will stand upright. Mix together the cooked rice, ham or bacon, cheese, Worcestershire sauce and a little salt and pepper. Pack the stuffing into each pepper, pressing it down well. Put the water and the trivet into the cooker. Stand the peppers upright on the trivet. Close the cooker, bring to H pressure and cook for 5 minutes. Reduce the pressure quickly.

Chipped Potatoes

1 kg (2 lb) medium to large potatoes
fat for frying

To make sure chipped potatoes are
served really crisp and golden they
must be fried twice. The first frying gets
rid of the excess water in the potatoes
and is called blanching; it can be
done well in advance of the meal. The
second frying takes only 1 to 2 minutes
in the hot fat or oil and should be done
just before serving. For general use, cut
the chips about 1 cm ($\frac{1}{2}$ inch) thick with
a knife or wavy cutter; for poultry and
game cut them thinner and shorter,
these are called straws or matchstick
potatoes. The latter cook very quickly
in the second frying.

Peel and wash the potatoes. Cut into
slices 1 cm ($\frac{1}{2}$ inch) thick, then into
strips of the same thickness. Dry the
chips in a clean cloth and keep covered
or they will discolour. If kept in cold
water they tend to lose vitamin C.

Fill a deep frying pan two-thirds full
with oil or fat. Put in the frying basket
and heat it in the oil or the food will
stick to it when frying. Heat the oil or
fat to 182°C, 360°F. Remove basket, put
in a thick layer of chips and slowly
lower it into the pan. Cook for 3 to 4
minutes or until chips are tender but
not brown. Lift out basket, allowing fat
to drain back into pan. Spread chips on
kitchen paper to drain. Reheat oil or fat
between batches.

Just before the chips are required,
reheat the fat to 190°C, 375°F. Put the
first batch of chips in the basket and fry
for 1 to 2 minutes or until crisp and
golden. Remove the basket, drain the
fat back into the pan. Spread the chips
on absorbent kitchen paper to drain,
sprinkle with salt and serve very hot as
soon as possible.

Fried Potato Shapes

1 kg (2 lb) large potatoes, peeled
vegetable oil for frying

Cut the potatoes into even slices and
stamp out shapes with tiny cocktail
cutters. Rinse and drain very well.

Heat the oil in a deep-fat fryer or
large saucepan until it is hot enough to
turn a stale bread cube golden-brown in
30 seconds (190°C/375°F). Add the
potato shapes and fry until crisp and
golden-brown round the edges. Drain
well on absorbent kitchen paper and
serve hot.

Mashed Potato Cakes

mashed potato
minced cooked meat
chopped parsley
grated onion
salt
freshly ground black pepper
seasoned flour
fat for frying

Mix together equal quantities of leftover mashed potato and minced cooked
meat. Season with chopped parsley,
grated onion, salt and freshly ground
black pepper to taste. Shape into round
cakes, coat in seasoned flour and fry in
dripping until golden-brown on both
sides. Serve with tomato slices.

Potato and Onion Cakes

225 g (8 oz) self-raising flour
pinch of salt
1 teaspoon dry mustard
100 g (4 oz) butter
1 small onion, peeled and grated
1 large potato, peeled and grated
2 tablespoons chopped parsley
1 egg

50 g (2 oz) Cheddar cheese, grated
2 tablespoons milk
vegetable oil or fat for greasing the
    griddle

Sift the flour, salt and mustard into a
bowl. Rub in the butter until the mixture resembles fine breadcrumbs. Add
the grated onion, grated potato, chopped parsley and grated cheese and mix
to a fairly stiff dough with the egg and
the milk. Knead lightly on a floured
surface and roll the scone dough to a
circle about 22.5 cm (9 inches) in diameter. Divide the scone round into 8
equal sections.
    Grease and warm a griddle or heavy-
based frying pan. The griddle is hot
enough when a piece of the mixture
placed on it turns golden-brown underneath in 30 seconds.
    Cook the potato and onion cakes for 2
to 3 minutes on each side. Serve hot.
Makes 8

Swiss Potato Cake

1 kg (2 lb) medium potatoes, peeled
    and cut in half
salt
100 g (4 oz) Gruyère cheese
freshly ground black pepper
1 large knob of butter
1 small onion, peeled and finely
    chopped
4 back bacon rashers, de-rinded and
    cut into thin strips

Cook the potatoes in boiling salted
water for 10 minutes, drain and rinse
under cold running water. Leave until
cool enough to handle, then grate into a
bowl. Grate in the cheese, add salt and
pepper to taste and stir gently to mix.
    Melt the butter in a frying pan, add
the onion and bacon and fry over gentle
heat until soft. Add the potato mixture,
flatten it into a cake shape with a
spatula and smooth the top. Fry over
moderate heat for 10 minutes until crisp

and brown underneath. Invert a plate
over the pan and turn the cake out onto
the plate. Slide the cake back into the
pan and fry for a further 10 minutes
until crisp and brown on the underside.
Cut into wedges to serve.

Variation:
For a lighter and less expensive version,
omit the bacon and use Edam or Gouda
cheese.

Sauté Potatoes

$\frac{3}{4}$ kg (1$\frac{1}{2}$ lb) small or medium potatoes
50 g (2 oz) butter or lard
salt
freshly ground pepper
chopped chives or parsley, to garnish

Scrub the potatoes and boil them in well
salted water for 10 minutes or until they
begin to get tender. Do not cook the
potatoes completely or they will fall to
pieces in the sauté pan. Drain in a
colander and cool slightly. Peel them
and cut into 5 mm ($\frac{1}{4}$ inch) thick slices.
    Heat the butter or lard in a large
frying pan with a thick base. Spread the
potatoes in a single layer over the
bottom of the pan and fry until golden
brown underneath. Using a palette
knife, turn slices and fry the other side.
Sauté potatoes in batches if necessary;
do not crowd the pan.
    Spread the potatoes on absorbent
kitchen paper to drain. Sprinkle with
salt and pepper. Keep hot in a warm
oven while frying the next batch. Serve
the sauté potatoes in a hot vegetable
dish. Garnish with chopped parsley or
chives.

† Scalloped Potatoes and Mushrooms

a little butter or margarine for
    greasing
750 g (1½ lb) potatoes, peeled and
    thinly sliced
100 g (4 oz) mushrooms, cleaned and
    thinly sliced
1 small onion, peeled and grated
salt
freshly ground black pepper
1 × 275 g (10½ oz) can condensed
    mushroom soup
2 tablespoons milk
450 ml (¾ pint) water
little lemon juice
a little freshly chopped mint

Lightly grease a 1¼ litre (2 pint) soufflé
dish or other suitable size ovenproof
dish with a little butter or margarine.
Put half the potatoes in the bottom, add
half the mushrooms and onion, a little
salt and pepper, half the can of soup and
1 tablespoon of milk. Add the remaining
ingredients in the same order. Cover
with a piece of greaseproof paper. Put
the water into the cooker with a little
lemon juice.
Stand the dish on the trivet, close
cooker, bring to H pressure and cook for
40 minutes, then reduce the pressure
quickly. Sprinkle with the mint, to garnish before serving.

Layered Casserole

chopped, mixed, cooked vegetables
fresh sliced apple
diced, cooked bacon
cheese sauce (p. 356)

Grease a small casserole, fill with layers
of chopped, mixed cooked vegetables,
fresh sliced apple and diced cooked
bacon. Cover with cheese sauce and
bake for 25 minutes in a fairly hot oven
(190°C, 375°F, Gas Mark 5).

Baked Potatoes

4 medium to large potatoes
oil for brushing
pat of butter
parsley sprig, to garnish

Scrub the potatoes well and prick all
over with a cook's fork. This is to allow
the steam to escape during cooking,
otherwise the potatoes may burst in the
oven. For a crisp skin, brush with oil.
Place on a baking sheet and bake in a
preheated oven (200–220°C, 400–425°F,
Gas Mark 6–7) for 1 hour or until soft.
    When cooked, cut two slits crosswise
in the top and gently squeeze the bottom
of the potato until the cross opens. Push
in a good pat of butter, top with a
parsley sprig and serve piping hot with
salt and pepper.
    Alternatively, when cooked, cut an
oval piece from the top of each potato,
or if a large potato, cut in half lengthwise. Scoop out the pulp into a basin,
beat with butter and seasoning and put
back into shell. Ruffle top with a fork and
reheat in oven or brown under grill.

* Baked Stuffed Potatoes

Follow the recipe for Baked Potatoes
(above), with these changes: mix potato
pulp with cream or soured cream and
chives; or with grated Cheddar cheese
and paprika pepper; or add chopped
cooked mushrooms and parsley; or you
could use up any leftover chopped cooked meat, chicken or ham, or crisp fried
and diced bacon.

Duchesse Potatoes

450 g (1 lb) old potatoes
25 g (1 oz) butter
1 egg yolk
hot milk

Boil and sieve the potatoes as above and beat in the butter, egg yolk and sufficient hot milk to give a creamy consistency. Put into a forcing bag with a large rose nozzle and pipe onto a greased baking tray into pyramids, rings or nests. Bake in a preheated oven (220°C, 425°F, Gas Mark 7) for 20 minutes or until golden. For a shiny glazed finish, remove from the oven when set, brush with beaten egg yolk and return to oven to brown.

† Pommes Maître D'Hôtel

450 g (1 lb) new potatoes
50 g (2 oz) butter
1 shallot, peeled and chopped
2 tablespoons chopped parsley
salt
freshly ground pepper
150 ml (¼ pint) milk or single cream

Scrub the potatoes and boil them in their skins. Peel and slice fairly thinly. Melt the butter in a flameproof dish. Layer the potatoes with the shallot and parsley and season each layer with salt and pepper. Bring the milk or cream nearly to the boil and pour it over the potatoes. Heat gently until well heated through, but do not boil.

French Potato Casserole

about 1½ kg (3 lb) potatoes, peeled
salt
50 g (2 oz) butter, softened
freshly ground black pepper
6 tablespoons milk
6 tablespoons single cream
50 g (2 oz) Gruyère or Emmenthal
   cheese, grated

Blanch the potatoes in boiling salted water for 5 minutes, then drain and leave until cool enough to handle. Slice the potatoes thickly.

Brush the inside of a large casserole dish with some of the butter. Arrange a layer of potato slices in the bottom, sprinkle with salt and pepper and dot with some more of the butter. Pour in 1 tablespoon each of milk and cream. Continue with these layers until all the ingredients are used up, pouring in any remaining milk and cream at the end. Sprinkle the top of casserole with the grated cheese and more salt and pepper.

Bake, uncovered, in a fairly hot oven (190°C, 375°F, Gas Mark 5) for about 1 hour until the top is golden brown and the potatoes are tender when pierced. Serve hot straight from the casserole.

Mashed Potatoes

450 g (1 lb) old potatoes
25–50 g (1–2 oz) butter or margarine
2 tablespoons hot milk
salt
freshly ground pepper
pinch of nutmeg (optional)

Peel the potatoes thinly and cut into chunks of even size. Cover with salted water, bring to the boil and simmer gently for 10 to 20 minutes according to size. Do not over-cook or the mash will be watery. Drain well, dry off in pan over low heat. Mash thoroughly with potato masher or put through a mouli.

Replace the pan over low heat and beat in the butter and hot milk with a kichamajig or wooden spoon until fluffy. Season well with salt, pepper and a pinch of nutmeg if liked. Serve hot.

Risotto Espagnole

50 g (2 oz) butter or 2 tablespoons
  olive oil
1 large onion, peeled and sliced
225 g (8 oz) long-grain rice
225 ml ($\frac{1}{2}$ pint) tomato juice
stock or bouillon (made with a cube)
  as required
75 g (3 oz) grated cheese
1 teaspoon paprika pepper
salt
freshly ground black pepper
lemon juice to taste

Heat the butter or oil and fry the sliced
onion until transparent, stirring
steadily. Do not allow it to colour or it
will burn when you are frying the rice.
Add unwashed rice and stir over moderate heat until it turns a pale biscuit
colour; do not brown.

Add enough tomato juice to float the
rice. Cover and cook over low heat,
adding more juice as it is absorbed. Stir
frequently to prevent rice sticking.
When tomato juice is finished, add
stock as needed until rice is cooked and
liquid absorbed. The rice should still
have a slight bite. If too liquid, cook
uncovered until stock has evaporated.

Remove the pan from the heat, mix in
the grated cheese and stir until it has
melted. Season to taste with paprika
pepper, salt and pepper. Sharpen to
taste with lemon juice. It can now be
served as a side dish; for a main course
continue as follows.

Mix in one of the following: 175–225 g
(6–8 oz) shelled prawns, smoked sausage,
cooked chicken giblets, chopped cooked
ham or poultry meat; 100 g (4 oz) fried
sliced mushroom may also be added.
Garnish with cooked green peas or strips
of blanched green pepper.

* Risotto Milanaise

Follow the recipe for Risotto Espagnole
(above), with these changes: replace the
tomato juice with good chicken stock
(p. 6). When the rice is cooked, mix in $\frac{1}{4}$
teaspoon powdered saffron and add 2–3
tablespoons dry white wine.

Creamed Spinach

700 g ($1\frac{1}{2}$ lb) fresh spinach, washed
salt and freshly ground black pepper
25 g (1 oz) butter
3 tablespoons double cream
$\frac{1}{4}$ teaspoon grated nutmeg

Put the spinach in a saucepan with the
minimum of salted water. Heat gently
until the juices flow from the spinach,
then cover the pan and cook gently for
approximately 5 minutes until the
spinach is tender. Drain well and leave
to cool in a colander, then purée in an
electric blender or work through a
mouli-légumes. Return to the rinsed-out
pan, add the butter and heat through.
Stir in the cream and nutmeg, then
season to taste with salt and pepper.
Stir gently until the spinach is hot and
combined with the cream and seasonings, then transfer to a warmed serving
dish and serve immediately.

Mashed Swedes

1 kg (2 lb) boiled swedes
2 tablespoons bacon fat or butter
salt
freshly ground pepper
chopped parsley, to garnish

Dry 1 kg (2 lb) boiled swedes and mash
them thoroughly. Add 2 tablespoons
bacon fat or butter and season well with
salt and freshly ground pepper. Garnish
with chopped parsley.

Buttered Turnips with Mustard

450 g (1 lb) young white turnips,
  peeled, cut into sticks like chips
50 g (2 oz) unsalted butter
1 teaspoon salt
1-2 tablespoons French mustard
1-2 tablespoons chopped fresh parsley

Drop them into boiling salted water, simmer for 15 minutes or until just tender; be careful not to overcook. Drain and dry them in the colander under a cloth to keep warm. Soften the butter in the hot pan until creamy, but do not allow it to go oily. Add the turnips and then the mustard gradually and stir until the turnips are thoroughly coated.

Mix in the chopped fresh parsley and serve very hot.

Vegetable Curry of Your Choice

1 tablespoon turmeric
1 tablespoon flour
1 kg (2 lb) mixed fresh vegetables,
  prepared and cut into suitable
  pieces, eg. cauliflower sprigs, sliced
  beans, carrots, celery, courgettes,
  green or red peppers, potatoes
4 tablespoons vegetable oil
  or 50 g (2 oz) dripping, for frying
3 medium-sized onions, peeled and
  chopped
2 medium-sized cooking apples,
  peeled, cored and chopped
2 tablespoons curry powder
1 × 400 g (14 oz) can tomatoes
1 teaspoon ground coriander
225 g (8 oz) haricot or red kidney
  beans or chick peas or a
  combination, soaked overnight and
  boiled for 10 minutes
salt
3 hard-boiled eggs, shelled and
  halved, to finish (optional)

Mix the turmeric and flour together in a large bowl. Put in the prepared fresh vegetables and toss to coat lightly with the mixture.

Heat the oil or dripping in a large frying or sauté pan. Add the fresh vegetables and fry for 3 to 4 minutes. Remove from the pan with a slotted draining spoon and set aside.

Add the chopped onion and apple to the fat remaining in the pan and fry gently for 5 minutes. Stir in the curry powder and continue frying for a further 3 minutes. Pour in the tomatoes and their liquid, add the coriander, mixed vegetables and the cooked beans or chick peas. Add salt to taste and bring to the boil. Cover and simmer for 30 minutes or until the vegetables are tender. Stir occasionally to prevent the curry powder from sticking and, if the sauce becomes too thick, add a little water.

Just before serving, taste and adjust seasoning if necessary, add the hard-boiled eggs and heat through.

Mashed 'Neeps'

about 1½–1¾ kg (3–3½ lb) turnips or
  swedes, peeled and diced
salt
50 g (2 oz) butter
4 tablespoons single cream or top of
  the milk
1 teaspoon ground ginger
freshly ground black pepper

Cook the turnips or swedes in boiling salted water for approximately 25 minutes or until quite tender. Drain, then mash thoroughly with a potato masher or purée in an electric blender. Stir or work in the butter, then pour in the cream or top of the milk with the ginger, and salt and pepper to taste.

Return to the rinsed-out pan and reheat gently. Transfer to a hot serving dish and serve.
Serves 6

Turnip and Potato Purée

40 g (1½ oz) butter
350 g (12 oz) young turnips, peeled
  and sliced
350 g (12 oz) potatoes, peeled and
  sliced
1 small onion, peeled and sliced
salt
freshly ground black pepper
300 ml (½ pint) milk
½ teaspoon grated nutmeg
25 g (1 oz) butter to finish

Heat the butter in a saucepan until just melted, add the sliced turnip, potato and onion. Sauté the vegetables, stirring frequently, for 3 minutes. Season to taste, add the milk and sprinkle in the grated nutmeg. Bring to the boil, reduce the heat, cover and cook gently for 10 minutes or until the vegetables are tender. Liquidize in an electric blender or pass through a sieve. Return the purée to the saucepan and reheat.

Spoon on to individual plates, and mound up each serving. Make a dent in the top of each mound with the back of a spoon and put in a knob of butter.

† Vegetable and Cheese Pie

25 g (1 oz) butter or margarine
1 onion, peeled and coarsely chopped
1 green pepper, cored, seeded and
  chopped
4 stalks celery, scrubbed and coarsely
  chopped
100 g (4 oz) frozen or canned
  sweetcorn kernels
1 × 400 g (14 oz) can tomatoes,
  chopped
1 teaspoon yeast extract e.g. Marmite
150 ml (¼ pint) hot brown stock or
  water and ¼ beef stock cube
To finish:
175 g (6 oz) cheese, grated e.g.
  Cheddar, Lancashire
50 g (2 oz) fresh white breadcrumbs

Heat the butter or margarine in the cooker and lightly fry the onion, pepper and celery. Add the sweetcorn, tomatoes with juice, yeast extract and stock or water and stock cube. Stir well. Close the cooker, bring to H pressure and cook for 5 minutes. Reduce the pressure quickly. Spoon half the mixture into a lightly greased ovenproof dish and cover with half the cheese. Add the remaining vegetables and then top with a mixture of the cheese and breadcrumbs. Brown and crisp the top under a hot grill or in the top of a hot oven.

† Vegetable and Nut Pilaf

2 tablespoons cooking oil
1 onion, peeled and coarsely chopped
3 stalks celery, scrubbed and finely
  chopped
1 green pepper, cored, seeded and
  coarsely chopped
225 g (8 oz) long-grain patna rice
600 ml (1 pint) hot poultry stock or
  water and ½ chicken stock cube
salt
freshly ground black pepper
25 g (1 oz) shelled walnuts, coarsely
  chopped
50 g (2 oz) roasted unsalted peanuts

Heat the oil in the cooker, sauté the vegetables for a few moments without colouring. Add the rice and cook until all the oil is absorbed. Add the stock or water and stock cube, salt and pepper and stir well. Close the cooker, bring to H pressure and cook for 5 minutes. Reduce the pressure quickly. Return the open cooker to the heat, add the nuts and stir with a fork to separate the rice grains.

EGGS, CHEESE & QUICHES

Boiling Eggs

Eggs should be at room temperature. If they are very cold, warm them under the hot tap, or prick the rounded end of the shell with a needle to prevent cracking. A teaspoon of salt added to the water will 'set' any escaping white. The water should only simmer, never boil quickly.

Place the eggs in a pan of cold water, bring to boil, turn down to simmer and count the cooking time from then.

SIZE	SOFT	MEDIUM	HARD
Large	3 mins	4 mins	10 mins
Standard	2½ mins	3½ mins	9 mins

Lift the cooked eggs out of the water, tap the shell at one end to allow steam to escape and prevent further cooking. Put hard-boiled eggs in cold water to prevent a grey line forming round the yolk.

Coloured Eggs

Eggs, hard-boiled, with white shells
For decorating:
2 teaspoons food colouring
or
onion skins and 2 teaspoons malt vinegar

If you wish to paint decorative designs on eggs, then you must hard-boil them for 12 minutes before working on them.

Eggs can be left white or coloured by steeping in fabric dyes after hard-boiling. Use fine-nibbed felt tip pens for decorating eggs, etching in the design with a faint pencil beforehand. Allow one area of the egg to dry before working round the egg. Hard-boiled eggs will keep indefinitely if the shells are kept intact, and they make a most attractive Easter decoration.

To colour eggs with food colouring: put 2 teaspoons food colouring – red, cochineal, blue, yellow etc. – into a saucepan of boiling water and stir well. Put in the quantity of white-shelled eggs you wish to colour and boil for 10 minutes or until the egg shells become coloured. The eggs will take on delicate, pale colours which can be improved by rubbing gently with a little oil after the eggs have cooled.

To colour eggs yellow or rust with onion skins: put the skins of several onions in a pan with plenty of cold water (add 2 teaspoons malt vinegar for a rust colour). Bring to the boil, then simmer gently until the water becomes coloured. The longer the skins are simmered, the deeper the colour. Strain into a bowl. Put hard-boiled white eggs into the strained liquid and leave to steep until the desired colour is obtained. Remove from the liquid with a slotted spoon, pat dry with absorbent kitchen paper, then brush lightly with oil and buff with more paper or a duster. Leave plain or decorate as above and keep indefinitely.

* Eggs Mornay

Follow the recipe for Boiling Eggs
(p. 61), shell the eggs and halve them,
then coat the eggs with Cheese sauce (p.
356), top with bread crumbs and grated
cheese and brown under the grill.

* Eggs Mayonnaise

Follow the recipe for hard-boiled eggs
(p. 61), then coat them with Mayonnaise (p. 42) and garnish with lettuce or
watercress.

Coddled Eggs

Put the eggs into boiling water, cover
the pan, remove from the heat and leave
the egg in the pan for 8 to 10 minutes.
The white will be just set and be more
digestible for babies and invalids.

Poaching Eggs

An egg for poaching should be broken
carefully into a cup or saucer. Heat 2.5
cm (1 inch) of water in a shallow pan (a
frying pan is suitable). Do not add salt
or vinegar or the whites will toughen.
Bring the water to a gentle simmer,
with the water barely moving, and slide
in the egg gently. Cook for about 3
minutes or remove the pan from heat,
cover and leave for $3\frac{1}{2}$ to 4 minutes. Lift
out with a perforated spoon – when
poaching more than one, take eggs out
in the order in which they were put in.
Drain over a cloth before serving on hot
toast spread with butter or anchovy
paste or on smoked ham, smoked haddock or spinach purée.

Frying Eggs

Heat a little butter, bacon fat or oil in a
frying pan and slide in the egg just
before the fat starts to sizzle. Fry gently
or the white will be tough. Baste with
the hot fat until the white is set but the
yolk still soft, about 3 minutes. Lift out
carefully with a fish slice and serve with
fried or grilled bacon, sausages, hamburgers or corned beef hash.

Scrambling Eggs

8 eggs
salt
freshly ground black pepper
knob of butter
1 tablespoon cream or top of the milk
sprig of parsley, to garnish

Allow 2 eggs per person. Season the
eggs to taste with salt and pepper and
beat with a fork, not a whisk. Melt a
knob of butter in the top of a double
boiler or thick, non-stick saucepan and
add the eggs. Stir with a wooden spoon
over very gentle heat until thick and
creamy. Remove from the heat and stir
in 1 tablespoon of cream or top of the
milk; this will stop the eggs from over-
cooking. Serve immediately on buttered
toast or fried bread and garnish with a
sprig of parsley; for a first course serve
on asparagus tips.

Variations:
Mix grated cheese, cooked ham or
bacon, flaked cooked or smoked fish,
crab-meat or prawns into the beaten
eggs before cooking. Serve hot or cold
in sandwiches, bread rolls or pastry
cases.

Baked Eggs
(*Sur le plat*)

8 eggs
1 tablespoon melted butter or cream
salt
freshly ground black pepper

Preheat the oven to 220°C, 425°F, Gas Mark 7. Butter and warm individual ovenproof plates in the oven for a minute or two. Break 2 eggs into each plate. Top with 1 tablespoon melted butter or cream, season to taste with salt and pepper and bake for 4 to 5 minutes until the whites are set and the yolks still soft. Serve at once in the dishes.

Variations:
Put a slice of cooked ham, sliced smoked sausages or fried sliced mushrooms on the plate and break the eggs on top. Bake in a preheated oven as before. When cooked, garnish with a sprinkling of fresh parsley sprigs.

Basic Omelette

2 eggs
1 tablespoon cold water
salt
freshly ground black pepper
butter for frying

Beat the eggs lightly together in a small bowl, stir in the water and season to taste.

Melt just sufficient butter in the omelette pan to coat the base well. When the butter starts to foam, pour in the egg mixture all at once and tilt the pan so that it coats the base evenly. If necessary, use a palette knife to lift the edges away from the side and allow any unset mixture to run underneath. (If you use a non-stick pan, stir the egg mixture as it begins to set instead of tilting the pan.) When the top of the omelette is almost set but still creamy, hold the pan over a warm plate and, with the palette knife, turn the omelette over away from the handle on to the plate, folding it in half or into three. Serve at once as the egg continues to cook in its own heat and the omelette may become leathery if it is left standing too long.
Serves 1

* Mushroom Omelette

Follow the recipe for Basic Omelette (above), with these changes: add 50 g (2 oz) sliced, cooked mushrooms to each two-egg omelette mixture and garnish with sprigs of watercress.

* Peasant's Omelette

Follow the recipe for Basic Omelette (above), with these changes: dice a cooked potato and add 2 tablespoons of it to each two-egg omelette, together with a little grated apple, onion, dried mixed herbs and grated nutmeg. Fry the omelette in leftover bacon fat if possible, or in butter, until surface is set.

Omelette with Croûtons

1 slice white bread
1 tablespoon bacon fat
knob of butter
basic omelette mixture (see left)
mixed fresh herbs (parsley, chives, marjoram), to garnish

Trim the slice of white bread and cut into dice. Melt the bacon fat in the omelette pan and use to fry the bread dice until golden-brown. Add a little butter and the omelette mixture and cook as for Basic omelette (above).

Serve sprinkled with chopped herbs.
Serves 1

Omelette with Baked Bean Stuffing

1 small onion
15 g (½ oz) butter
2 tablespoons baked beans in tomato
   sauce
Tabasco sauce
basic omelette mixture (p. 63)

Peel and very finely chop the onion.
Melt the butter in a small saucepan and
use to fry the onion until soft. Stir in the
baked beans in tomato sauce and a few
drops of Tabasco sauce. Leave over
gentle heat while you cook the omelette. Spoon the filling into the centre of
the omelette and fold over on to a warm
plate. Serve at once.
Serves 1

Omelette Fines Herbes

2 or 4 eggs
1 tablespoon chopped fresh herbs
   (parsley, chervil and chives)
1 teaspoon water
salt
freshly ground white pepper
small knob of butter

Beat the eggs with a fork. Mix in the
herbs, water and salt and pepper to
taste. Heat butter until it sizzles but do
not allow it to brown. Pour in beaten
egg mixture.
   With a fork or a palette knife, draw
the mixture from sides to middle of pan
and tilt pan so the uncooked egg runs
underneath and sets.
   When the underneath is set but the
top still slightly runny, fold the omelette in half (if using 4 eggs, fold the
omelette in three).
   Turn a 2-egg omelette upside down
onto a warm plate. If making a 4-egg
omelette, fold it in three and slide it
onto a warm plate. Serve immediately.
Serves 1–2

* Stuffed Savoury Omelettes

Follow the recipe for Omelette Fines
Herbes (above), for the omelettes.
Sliced mushrooms, chopped ham or
bacon, crisp bread croûtons, potato
cubes, asparagus tips, spinach purée
are all good fillings. Fry the filling in
butter and keep warm while you make
the omelette. Spoon the filling on top of
the omelette just before folding it over.
Allow 2–3 tablespoons cooked filling for
each person.

* Cheese Omelette

Follow the recipe for Omelette Fines
Herbes (above), with this change: mix 2
tablespoons grated cheese into the
beaten eggs instead of the herbs.

Tortilla

2 tablespoons vegetable oil
1 large onion, peeled and finely sliced
2 garlic cloves, peeled and crushed
4 medium potatoes, peeled and cut
   into small dice
6 eggs, beaten
salt and freshly ground black pepper
1 × 200 g (7 oz) can sweetcure ham,
   cut into small dice

Heat the oil in a large skillet or frypan,
add the onion and fry over gentle heat
until soft. Add the garlic and potatoes,
cover and cook over gentle heat for 20
minutes or until the potatoes are
tender. Increase the heat, pour in the
eggs and season with salt and pepper to
taste. Cook over high heat for 5 minutes, stirring with a fork and shaking
the pan to allow the uncooked egg to
set. Add the ham, lower the heat, cover
and cook for a further 5 minutes or until
the omelette is set on top. Serve immediately with a tossed mixed salad.

Cheese Soufflé

4 eggs, separated
50 g (2 oz) butter or margarine
50 g (2 oz) flour
300 ml (½ pint) milk
75 g (3 oz) Cheddar cheese, grated
1 tablespoon grated Parmesan cheese
salt
freshly ground black pepper
paprika pepper
1 teaspoon French mustard

Grease an 18 cm (7 inch) soufflé dish. Cut a strip of greaseproof paper long enough to wrap around the dish and overlap by 5 cm (2 inches) and deep enough to extend 7.5 cm (3 inches) above the rim. Secure with string. Pre-heat oven to 190°C, 375°F, Gas Mark 5.

Make a binding sauce with the butter or margarine, flour and milk (p. 355). Remove the pan from the heat and stir in the grated cheeses, salt, pepper and paprika pepper to taste, and the mustard. Gradually beat in the egg yolks. In a wide bowl whisk the egg whites until stiff but not brittle. Pour over the cheese sauce, about a third at a time, and fold it in quickly and lightly with a concave spatula or large cook's spoon.

Pour the mixture into the prepared soufflé dish: to make the soufflé rise evenly with a 'crown' in the centre scoop out a shallow ring round the top about 2.5 cm (1 inch) from the rim of the dish.

Stand the soufflé dish on a baking tray and place it in the centre of the oven. Bake for about 30 minutes until well risen and golden brown. It should still be slightly soft in the centre. Serve immediately: remove paper at last moment or the soufflé may fall.

* Cheese and Meat Soufflé

Follow the recipe for Cheese Soufflé (above), with these changes: mix the following into the binding sauce before adding the egg yolks: 1 tablespoon chopped parsley, 225 g (8 oz) finely minced cooked chicken, turkey or ham, lemon juice and Worcestershire sauce to taste.

* Cheese and Fish Soufflé

Follow the recipe for Cheese Soufflé (above), with these changes: mix the following into the binding sauce before adding the egg yolks: 225 g (8 oz) finely flaked cooked (or canned) salmon, smoked haddock or mackerel, white fish, crab or lobster meat; flavour to taste with finely chopped chervil or parsley, lemon juice and anchovy essence.

* Cheese and Vegetable Soufflé

Follow the recipe for Cheese Soufflé (above), with these changes: mix the following into the binding sauce before adding the egg yolks: 225 g (8 oz) finely chopped cooked mushroom or spinach or potato purée and flavour to taste with fresh herbs and garlic or onion.

Macaroni Cheese

6 large handfuls, about 300 ml ($\frac{1}{2}$ pint)
    quick cooking macaroni
salt
1 knob of butter
1 onion, peeled and finely chopped
4 back bacon rashers, de-rinded and
    chopped
1 × 300 ml ($\frac{1}{2}$ pint) packet cheese sauce
    mix
300 ml ($\frac{1}{2}$ pint) milk
freshly ground black pepper
100 g (4 oz) Cheddar cheese
3 tablespoons golden breadcrumbs
2 tomatoes, quartered

Cook the macaroni in boiling salted
water until tender according to packet
directions. Meanwhile, melt the butter
in a large shallow pan, add the onion
and bacon and fry over gentle heat for 5
minutes, stirring occasionally. Mix the
sauce mix with the milk according to
packet directions, pour into the pan.
Bring to the boil, stirring constantly,
lower the heat and simmer until the
sauce thickens. Remove from the heat
and add salt and pepper to taste.

Drain the macaroni thoroughly and
stir into the pan. Grate the cheese over
the top and sprinkle over the breadcrumbs. Arrange the tomatoes around
the edge of the pan. Put under a hot grill
for about 10 minutes until golden
brown, turning the pan occasionally to
ensure even browning. Serve hot with
frankfurters, sausages or hamburgers.

Variations:
Add 100 g (4 oz) chopped mushrooms to
the cheese sauce, or substitute 100 g (4
oz) chopped garlic or ham sausage for
the bacon.

Tomato Cauliflower Cheese

portion boiled cauliflower
5 tablespoons condensed cream of
    tomato soup
Worcestershire sauce
25 g (1 oz) grated Edam cheese

Cover the cauliflower with a tomato
sauce prepared from the tomato soup
and a dash of Worcestershire sauce.
Sprinkle the grated cheese over the top.
Heat under a hot grill until the cheese
melts and turns golden.
Serves 1

Macaroni Cheese Balls with Spanish Sauce

225 g (8 oz) short-cut macaroni
50 g (2 oz) butter
50 g (2 oz) plain flour
300 ml ($\frac{1}{2}$ pint) milk
$\frac{1}{2}$ teaspoon salt
$\frac{1}{2}$ teaspoon dry mustard
225 g (8 oz) cheese, grated
2 eggs, beaten
vegetable oil for frying
For the coating:
2 eggs, beaten
175 g (6 oz) dry breadcrumbs
For the sauce:
4 tablespoons vegetable oil
1 onion, peeled and finely chopped
2 cloves of garlic, crushed
1 small green pepper, deseeded and
    chopped
1 × 400 g (14 oz) can tomatoes
1 teaspoon dried mixed herbs
salt and freshly ground black pepper
2 teaspoons cornflour

Cook the macaroni in plenty of boiling
lightly salted water. Drain well. Place
the butter, flour, milk, salt and mustard
together in a saucepan and whisk over
moderate heat until the mixture comes
to the boil. Cook for 2 minutes. Remove
from the heat and add the cheese. Stir in

the beaten eggs and the macaroni. Allow to become almost cold and then divide the mixture into 12 to 16 equal portions. With clean wet hands shape each portion into a ball and coat with the beaten eggs and then the bread-crumbs. The balls must be completely coated in crumbs so repeat the process if necessary.

To make the sauce, heat the oil in a saucepan. Add the chopped onion and the crushed garlic and fry until the onion is soft but not browned. Add the chopped pepper, tomatoes and their liquid and the herbs. Season to taste. Moisten the cornflour with a little cold water and stir into the tomato mixture. Bring to the boil, stirring constantly, reduce the heat and simmer for 15 minutes.

To fry the macaroni cheese balls, heat the oil in a deep-fat fryer or saucepan until it is hot enough to turn a stale bread cube golden-brown in 45 seconds (185°C/360°F). Fry the balls, a few at a time, until golden-brown. Pile up on a warm serving dish and hand the sauce separately.

Egg Noodles Milanaise Style

225 g (8 oz) egg noodles (tagliatelle)
50 g (2 oz) melted butter
25 g (1 oz) grated Parmesan cheese
2–3 tablespoons double cream
freshly ground pepper

Cook the noodles and drain well. Mix the butter with the Parmesan cheese. Stir in 2–3 tablespoons double cream and season well with freshly ground pepper. Serve hot.

Swiss Cheese Fondue

1 garlic clove, peeled and cut in half
600 ml (1 pint) dry white wine
2 teaspoons lemon juice
450 g (1 lb) Emmenthal cheese, grated
450 g (1 lb) Cheddar cheese, grated
2 tablespoons cornflour
1 miniature bottle (4 tablespoons) Kirsch
pinch of cayenne pepper
freshly ground black pepper
1–2 long French loaves cut into 2.5 cm (1 inch) cubes

Rub the garlic around the inside of a heavy-based saucepan, then discard. Add the wine and lemon juice and heat gently, then gradually stir in the Em-menthal and Cheddar cheeses, a little at a time. Stir constantly until both cheeses are melted and thoroughly com-bined with the wine. Mix the cornflour to a paste with the Kirsch, then stir slowly into the cheese mixture. Heat gently until the fondue bubbles and thickens, stirring constantly. Add the cayenne, and black pepper to taste. Pour the fondue into a heated fondue pot and keep hot over a low flame, stirring occasionally. Serve with cubes of French bread. (Guests should spear cubes of bread on fondue forks and dip these well into the fondue pot until thoroughly coated in the cheese). Serves 8–10

Cheese and Potato Pasties

225 g (8 oz) flour
pinch of salt
100 g (4 oz) lard, cut into pieces
2–3 tablespoons cold water
For the filling:
2 medium-sized potatoes, peeled and
    chopped
1 teaspoon grated onion
100 g (4 oz) Cheddar cheese, diced
salt and freshly ground black pepper
pinch of dried sage (optional)

Sift the flour and salt into a bowl. Rub in
the lard until the mixture resembles fine
breadcrumbs. Stir in just sufficient
water to hold the mixture together,
then form into a smooth ball. Wrap in
foil or greaseproof paper and chill in the
refrigerator for 30 minutes.

Roll out the pastry on a floured surface and cut out 4 rounds using a
saucer. Mix the filling ingredients together and place an equal amount in the
centre of each circle. Dampen the edges,
draw the opposite edges together over
the centres and pinch firmly together to
seal and hold.

Place the pasties on a greased baking
sheet and bake in a fairly hot oven
(200°C, 400°F, Gas Mark 6) for 30 minutes. Serve hot or cold.

Cheese and Onion Pudding

25 g (1 oz) butter
2 medium-sized onions, peeled and
    finely sliced
600 ml (1 pint) milk
100 g (4 oz) soft white breadcrumbs
100 g (4 oz) Cheddar cheese, grated
salt and freshly ground black pepper
3 large eggs (size 1 or 2), lightly
    beaten

Heat the butter in a pan. Add the onions
and fry gently until golden. Add the
milk and bring just to boiling point.
Pour over the breadcrumbs, stir well.
Fold in the cheese, seasoning and
beaten eggs. Turn into a greased pie
dish and bake in a fairly hot oven
(190°C, 375°F, Gas Mark 5) for 30 minutes or until golden-brown and well
risen. Serve immediately.

Mushroom and Edam Cheese Roast

1 large onion, peeled and chopped
1 large green pepper, deseeded and chopped
25 g (1 oz) butter
175 g (6 oz) mushrooms, sliced
100 g (4 oz) fresh brown breadcrumbs
3 eggs, beaten
salt and freshly ground black pepper
175 g (6 oz) Edam cheese, grated
pinch of dried mixed herbs

Gently fry the chopped onion and green pepper together in the butter until soft but not browned. Add the sliced mushrooms and cook for a further 2 minutes. Remove from the heat and add the remaining ingredients, except the grated cheese and mixed herbs. Mix thoroughly. Grease a 1 kg (2 lb) loaf tin and press the mixture into it. Sprinkle over the grated cheese and mixed herbs. Bake in a moderate oven (180°C, 350°F, Gas Mark 4) for 45 minutes. Serve hot with tomato slices, watercress and tomato sauce.

Toasted Cheese and Pineapple Sandwich

2 thin slices bread
25 g (1 oz) grated Edam cheese
1 tablespoon drained, crushed pineapple

Toast the bread on one side only. Mix together the cheese and pineapple and sandwich between the toasted sides of the bread. Then toast on the outside. Serve hot.
Serves 1

Egg Croquettes

4 hard-boiled eggs, shelled and chopped
1 egg yolk
salt
freshly ground pepper
For the panada:
250 ml (8 fl oz) milk
1 slice of onion
3 peppercorns
1 blade of mace
1 small bay leaf
50 g (2 oz) butter
50 g (2 oz) flour
For coating:
seasoned flour
1 egg, beaten
dry white breadcrumbs
vegetable oil for frying

First make the panada. Put the milk into a saucepan. Add the onion, peppercorns, mace and bay leaf. Bring slowly to the boil then remove from the heat, cover and allow to stand for 10 minutes. Strain the liquid and discard the flavourings.

Melt the butter in a clean saucepan over low heat. Stir in the flour and allow to cook for 3 minutes stirring constantly. Gradually add the flavoured milk and bring to the boil, stirring all the time. The mixture should be very thick. Remove from the heat and add the chopped hard-boiled eggs, egg yolk and seasoning to taste. Turn the mixture out on a plate to cool then chill well.

Shape into 8 croquettes and coat with the seasoned flour. Dip each one into the beaten egg and cover evenly with breadcrumbs.

Heat the oil in a deep-fat fryer or saucepan until it is hot enough to turn a stale bread cube golden-brown in 30 seconds (190°C/375°F). Fry the croquettes, 4 at a time, in the hot oil, until golden-brown and crisp. Drain on absorbent kitchen paper and serve hot with a tomato sauce.
Makes 8

Basic Savoury Fritters

50 g (2 oz) plain flour
$\frac{1}{4}$ teaspoon salt
1 egg
15 g ($\frac{1}{2}$ oz) butter, melted
100 ml (4 fl oz) flat beer
1 egg white
vegetable oil for frying

Sift the flour and salt into a bowl. Beat the egg lightly and stir in the melted butter. Pour this mixture into the flour with the beer and beat until just smooth. Allow the batter to stand at room temperature for 1 hour if you have time. Stiffly whisk the egg white and fold into the batter.

Heat the oil in a deep-fat fryer or saucepan until it is hot enough to turn a stale bread cube golden in 30 seconds (190°C/375°F). Drop tablespoonfuls of the mixture into the hot oil, a few at a time, and fry until crisp and golden-brown. Remove and drain on absorbent kitchen paper. Transfer to a warm serving dish and serve hot, sprinkled with crumbled Danish blue or grated hard cheese.

* Chicken Fritters

Follow the recipe for Basic Savoury Fritters (above), with these changes: very finely chop 100 g (4 oz) cooked chicken. Stir into the basic batter with 1 tablespoon grated mild onion and a little freshly ground black pepper. Drop by spoonfuls and fry as Basic savoury fritters.

* Salami fritters

Follow the recipe for Basic Savoury Fritters (above), with these changes: remove the rind and finely chop 75 g (3 oz) Continental sausage (Salami, Mortadella or Cervelat). Stir this into the basic batter, drop by spoonfuls and fry as Basic savoury fritters.

Cheeseburgers

750 g (1$\frac{1}{2}$ lb) minced beef
1 onion, peeled and very finely chopped
1 teaspoon mixed dried herbs
2 tablespoons Worcestershire sauce
pinch of mustard powder
salt
freshly ground black pepper
1 egg, beaten
4 tablespoons vegetable oil
6 slices Edam cheese
6 baps
butter for spreading

Put the beef in a bowl with the onion, herbs, Worcestershire sauce, mustard and salt and pepper to taste. Mix well, then stir in the egg. Divide the mixture into 6 equal portions and form into hamburger shapes with the hands. Heat the oil in a large frying pan, add the hamburgers and fry for 7 minutes on each side until cooked through. Place a slice of cheese on top of each hamburger and put under a hot grill for 5 minutes until bubbling. Serve between buttered baps with sliced tomato, cucumber, shredded lettuce and potato crisps. Hand ketchup, relish, mustard and mayonnaise separately.
Makes 6 large hamburgers

Variations:
If you have a barbecue, then the burning charcoal will give the hamburgers a superb flavour. Cook them for the same length of time as above, but omit cheese.

Curried Eggs

2 tablespoons vegetable oil
1 onion, peeled and finely chopped
1 eating apple, peeled, cored and
   chopped
2 tablespoons curry paste
1 tablespoon flour
300 ml ($\frac{1}{2}$ pint) water
1 chicken stock cube
1 tablespoon tomato purée
4 hard-boiled eggs, halved
1 × 350 g (12 oz) can pre-cooked pilau
   (savoury fried) rice
salt
freshly ground black pepper

Heat the oil in a pan, add the onion and
apple and fry over gentle heat until
golden. Stir in the curry paste and fry
for 5 minutes, stirring constantly. Stir
in the flour and fry for a further minute,
then stir in the water gradually. Bring
to the boil, add the stock cube and
tomato purée and stir well to dissolve
the stock cube. Lower the heat and cook
gently for 5 minutes, then add the eggs,
cut side uppermost. Spoon the sauce
over the yolks, cover with a lid and set
aside.

Put the pilau rice in a separate stacking pan. Add a little water and heat
through for 3 minutes according to
directions on the can. Break up the rice
with a fork while cooking. Stack the
pan of rice on top of the pan of eggs and
place on the burner. Cover and cook
over the lowest possible heat for 10
minutes. Taste and adjust the seasoning
of the sauce, serve with mango chutney
and a side salad of yogurt and
cucumber.
Serves 2

Eggs in a Nest

600 ml (1 pint) water
2 knobs of butter
3 eggs
1 × 425 g (15 oz) can baked beans
1 × 100 g (4 oz) packet instant mashed
   potato mix
salt
freshly ground black pepper
approx. 75 g (3 oz) Cheddar cheese

You will need a stacking set with an egg
poacher.

Heat the water in the large shallow
pan of the stacking set. Put the egg
poacher on the top and divide 1 knob of
butter equally between the poaching
cups. Crack in the eggs, cover with a lid
and poach over gentle heat for 5
minutes.

Meanwhile, put the baked beans in a
separate pan and heat gently. Remove
the egg poacher with the lid and set
aside. Sprinkle the potato mix over the
water in the bottom pan, beat until
smooth. Add the remaining butter and
salt and pepper to taste.

Spread the potato around the outside
of the pan to make the nest, then pour
the baked beans into the centre. Slide
the eggs on top of the beans and grate
the cheese on top. Put under a hot grill
for 5 minutes until the cheese melts.
Serves 3

Quiche Lorraine

1 × 18 cm (7 inch) cooked flan case,
    made with plain or cheese
    shortcrust (p. 363 or 360)
For the filling:
15 g ($\frac{1}{2}$ oz) butter or margarine
1 tablespoon chopped onion
2 rashers streaky bacon, rinded and
    chopped
225 ml (8 fl oz) single cream or
    evaporated milk
50 g (2 oz) Cheddar cheese, grated
1 egg, beaten
salt
freshly ground pepper
paprika pepper
grilled bacon rolls, to garnish

Heat the butter and fry the onion and
bacon until they begin to change
colour. Add the cream or evaporated
milk and heat until it has a rim of
bubbles, but do not boil. Remove the
pan from the heat and mix in the grated
cheese. Stir until the cheese has melted
then mix in the beaten egg. Season to
taste with salt, pepper and paprika.

Pour the mixture into the prepared
flan case and bake in a preheated oven
(180°C, 350°F, Gas Mark 4) for 20 minutes or until the filling is set and the top
is golden.

Serve hot garnished with small grilled bacon rolls or serve cold with tossed
green salad, which is an excellent combination for picnics.

* Asparagus Quiche

Follow the recipe for Quiche Lorraine
(above), using cream rather than evaporated milk. Cover the base of the flan
case with cooked asparagus tips, fresh
or canned, and pour over the heated
filling. Bake as for Quiche Lorraine and
serve hot garnished with asparagus tips
or watercress sprigs. This makes a de-
lightful first course.

* Mushroom Quiche

Follow the recipe for Quiche Lorraine
(above), with these changes: fry 100 g (4
oz) sliced mushrooms with the bacon
and onion. Serve hot, topped with fried
mushroom caps, turned black side up
and garnished with paprika.

Asparagus Barquettes

plain or shortcrust pastry
asparagus tips
Quiche Lorraine filling (see left)

Bake pastry shells in boat shapes. Put 2
asparagus tips in each one and pour
over the filling. Bake for 15 minutes or
until set, in a preheated oven (180°C,
350°F, Gas Mark 4). Serve hot or cold as
a buffet snack.

Spinach and
Cheese Quiche

100 g (4 oz) plain white flour
pinch of salt
100 g (4 oz) wholemeal flour
100 g (4 oz) butter or margarine
about 4 tablespoons cold water to mix
For the filling:
350 g (12 oz) cottage cheese, sieved
1 whole egg, beaten
3 egg yolks, beaten
150 ml ($\frac{1}{4}$ pint) soured cream
$\frac{1}{2}$ teaspoon grated nutmeg
salt and freshly ground black pepper
3 × 225 g (8 oz) packets frozen chopped
    spinach, thawed
50 g (2 oz) Cheddar cheese, grated
$\frac{1}{2}$ teaspoon cayenne pepper

To make the pastry: sieve the plain
flour and salt into a mixing bowl. Stir
in the wholemeal flour. Add the butter or
margarine in pieces and rub into the
flour until the mixture resembles fine

breadcrumbs. Stir in enough cold water to draw the mixture together. Form into a ball, wrap in foil or greaseproof paper and chill in the refrigerator for at least 30 minutes before using.

Roll out the dough on a floured board and use to line a 28 cm (11 inch) flan tin or flan ring, placed on a baking sheet. Prick the base with a fork. Line the dough with foil, fill with baking beans and bake blind in a fairly hot oven (200°C, 400°F, Gas Mark 6) for 10 minutes, then remove beans and foil and continue baking for a further 5 minutes. Remove from oven and set aside.

To prepare filling: put the cottage cheese, eggs and soured cream in a bowl and mix well to combine. Stir in half the nutmeg and salt and pepper to taste. Put the spinach in the base of the pastry case, sprinkle with salt and pepper and the remaining nutmeg, then pour over the cottage cheese mixture. Mix the grated Cheddar cheese with cayenne pepper and evenly sprinkle over the quiche.

Bake in a fairly hot oven (200°C, 400°F, Gas Mark 6) for approximately 35 minutes until the filling is set and the cheese topping is golden. Remove from the oven and serve warm, cut into wedges.

Cuts into 16 wedges

Smoked Salmon Quiche

225 g (8 oz) flour
pinch of salt
125 g (4 oz) butter
3–4 tablespoons cold water to mix
For the filling:
225 g (8 oz) cream cheese, softened
4 egg yolks, beaten
4 whole eggs, beaten
175 g (6 oz) smoked salmon, slivered
2 tablespoons lemon juice
about 300 ml ($\frac{1}{2}$ pint) milk or single cream
$\frac{1}{2}$ teaspoon cayenne pepper
freshly ground black pepper

To make the pastry: sieve flour and salt into a bowl, add butter in pieces and rub into flour until mixture resembles fine breadcrumbs. Stir in enough cold water to draw mixture together, form into a ball, wrap in foil and chill in the refrigerator for at least 30 minutes. Roll out the dough on a floured board and use to line a 28 cm (11 inch) flan tin. Chill for a further 15 minutes.

Meanwhile, make the filling: put the cream cheese in a large mixing bowl and gradually beat in the eggs a little at a time. Stir in the smoked salmon, then add the lemon juice, and enough milk or cream to give the mixture a soft consistency. Stir in the cayenne, and black pepper to taste. Pour the filling into the chilled flan case, place on a preheated baking sheet and bake in a fairly hot oven (190°C, 375°F, Gas Mark 5) for 35 minutes until the filling is set and the pastry golden. Remove from the oven and leave until cold before cutting into wedges to serve.

Cuts into 16 wedges

FISH

Coquilles au Gratin

4 scallops, opened and cleaned
salt
freshly ground black pepper
150 ml ($\frac{1}{4}$ pint) dry white wine
$\frac{1}{2}$ onion, peeled and sliced
1 shallot, peeled and sliced
bouquet garni
75 g (3 oz) butter
50 g (2 oz) mushrooms, finely sliced
2 tomatoes, skinned, seeded and diced
juice of $\frac{1}{2}$ lemon
25 g (1 oz) flour
a little single cream
1 teaspoon anchovy essence
25 g (1 oz) Gruyère cheese, grated
4 tablespoons fresh white
   breadcrumbs
To garnish:
flaked almonds, toasted
chopped anchovy fillets

Scrub the scallop shells and place on a
baking sheet. Rinse and dry the scallops
and season them lightly with salt and
pepper. Put the wine, onion, shallot and
bouquet garni into a small pan. Bring to
the boil and add the scallops. Reduce
the heat immediately and poach for
about 5 minutes – this should be long
enough, scallops get tougher the longer
you cook them. Remove the scallops
and keep warm. Strain and reserve the
liquor.

Melt 25 g (1 oz) of the butter in a pan,
add the mushrooms, tomatoes and
lemon juice, season to taste and cook
for 3 minutes.

Melt another 25 g (1 oz) of the butter
in a small pan and stir in the flour. Cook
for 2 to 3 minutes, remove from the heat
and blend in the strained liquor from
the scallops, and the mushroom mixture. Return to the heat, and stirring
continuously, add enough cream to give
a good coating consistency. Stir in the
anchovy essence. Taste and adjust the
seasoning and simmer for 5 minutes.

Cut each scallop into 4, mix with half
the sauce and divide equally between
the 4 scallop shells. Mix the cheese into
the remaining sauce and spoon it over
each shell. Sprinkle with the breadcrumbs, flake the remaining butter over
and brown under a hot grill. Garnish
with the almonds and anchovies.

Coquilles St. Jacques 'Patricia'

4×8 cm ($3\frac{1}{4}$ inch) round bread slices
   3.5 cm ($1\frac{1}{2}$ inches) thick
oil for deep frying
8 opened, cleaned scallops
50 g (2 oz) butter
2 shallots, peeled and finely chopped
150 ml ($\frac{1}{4}$ pint) dry white wine
150 ml ($\frac{1}{4}$ pint) double cream
2 eggs, separated
salt
freshly ground black pepper
pinch of cayenne

2 tablespoons grated Parmesan cheese
To garnish:
pinch of paprika
sprigs of watercress

Using a plain 7.5 cm (3 inch) round cutter, cut into the bread to a depth of about 2 cm (¾ inch), leaving an edge of about 5 mm (¼ inch) all round. Remove the centre carefully with a knife, leaving a base and thin wall of bread. Heat the oil to 190°C/375°F and deep fry the bread until golden and crisp. Drain and keep warm.

Rinse and dry the scallops and detach the corals. If very large, cut the white meat in half. Melt the butter in a pan, add the white meat, cook gently for about 5 minutes, add the corals and cook for another minute. Do not overcook the scallops as they get tougher the longer you cook them. Remove to a warm dish.

Add the shallot to the pan and fry gently until softened. Pour in the wine and reduce to half by boiling rapidly. Add the cream, and again reduce to half. Remove the pan from the heat, cool the mixture slightly and stir in the egg yolks. Season to taste with salt and pepper, then cook over very gentle heat until the sauce thickens, do not boil. Remove from the heat. Whisk the egg whites until just stiff, season with salt, pepper and cayenne. Whisk again until very stiff then fold in 1 tablespoon of the cheese. Place the fried bread slices, called croustades, on a baking sheet, arrange the scallops in them and pour over the sauce.

Fill the meringue mixture into a piping bag fitted with a plain 2 cm (¾ inch) nozzle. Pipe the mixture over the tops of the bread to completely cover. Sprinkle with the remaining cheese and bake in a preheated moderately hot oven (200°C, 400°F, Gas Mark 6) for 6 to 8 minutes, or until the meringue is lightly coloured and crisp.

Serve immediately, garnished with a sprinkling of paprika, and a few sprigs of watercress.

Cheesy Yogurt Topped Fish

750 g (1½ lb) fresh or frozen cod or
    haddock fillets, defrosted
300 ml (½ pint) unsweetened natural
    yogurt
1 teaspoon dry mustard
freshly ground black pepper
175 g (6 oz) Edam cheese, grated
parsley sprigs, to garnish

Place the fish in a lightly greased shallow baking dish. Mix together the yogurt, mustard, pepper and 100 g (4 oz) of the cheese. Spread over the fish. Bake in a moderate oven (180°C, 350°F, Gas Mark 4) for 20 to 25 minutes. Sprinkle with the remaining grated cheese. Return to the oven for about 10 minutes until cheese melts. Garnish with sprigs of parsley.

Smoked Cod Jumble

225 g (8 oz) macaroni
75 g (3 oz) butter
350 g (12 oz) smoked cod or haddock
    fillet, skinned and cut into chunks
4 tomatoes, chopped
6 spring onions, trimmed and chopped
salt and freshly ground black pepper

Cook the macaroni in plenty of boiling slightly salted water. Drain well. Melt the butter in a saucepan. Add the fish, cover and cook very gently for 10 minutes, or until the fish is tender. Remove the lid, add the cooked macaroni, chopped tomato and spring onion and season carefully. Stir the mixture lightly to avoid breaking up the fish, and reheat well. Serve with hot buttered toast.

Cod and Bean Pie

175 g (6 oz) haricot beans, soaked
  overnight in cold water
2 medium-sized onions, peeled and
  chopped
1 kg (2 lb) cod or other white fish
  fillet, skinned and cut into small
  pieces
4 rashers streaky bacon, cut into
  strips
salt and freshly ground black pepper
pinch of dried thyme
pinch of dried marjoram
600 ml (1 pint) milk or milk and fish
  stock mixed
450 g (1 lb) potatoes, peeled and very
  thinly sliced
25 g (1 oz) butter
1 tablespoon chopped parsley, to
  garnish

Drain the haricot beans, cover with
fresh cold water, bring to the boil and
simmer for 1½ hours or until tender.
Drain.

Put the onions into a greased
casserole and cover with the fish and
strips of bacon. Season to taste and add
the herbs. Add a layer of cooked beans
and pour in the milk or milk and stock.
Top with the potatoes which should
overlap and be arranged to form an
attractive crust.

Dot the pie with butter and bake in a
moderate oven (180°C, 350°F, Gas Mark
4) for about 40 minutes or until the
potatoes are cooked and golden-brown.
Scatter the chopped parsley over the pie
and serve very hot.
Serves 6

Fried Fillets of Fish

175 g (6 oz) filleted fish *per person*
  (plaice, lemon sole, witches,
  monkfish, whiting, haddock)
flour for coating
1 egg
breadcrumbs
cooking fat
To garnish:
lemon slices
parsley sprigs

Trim and wash the fillets. Dry with
absorbent kitchen paper. Coat evenly
with flour and shake off any surplus.
Beat an egg until liquid and pour it into
a shallow dish. Spread a thick bed of
crumbs on a sheet of greaseproof paper.
Coat the fillets one at a time. Lay each
fillet skinless side down in the egg. Hold
the tail and brush egg over the top side.

Draw the fillet out over the side of the
dish to remove surplus egg, allowing
the egg to drip back into the dish, not
into the crumbs.

Lay the fillet skinless side down on
the bed of crumbs. Use the edges of the
paper to toss more crumbs over the top
of the fish. Sprinkle on more crumbs
when necessary.

Press the fillet down firmly into the
bed of crumbs with the heel of your
hand. Lift it by the tail, shake off loose
crumbs and lay it face upwards to
harden so the coating will remain firm
while frying.

Heat sufficient cooking fat to cover
completely the base of the frying pan.
When the fat hazes or the oil starts to
seeth, carefully put in the fillets, skinless side down first and fry until golden
underneath. Turn carefully with a fish
slice and palette knife and fry the other
side. Drain on absorbent kitchen paper
and keep warm.

Arrange the fillets, best side upwards,
overlapping on a warm serving plate.
Garnish with lemon butterflies and
parsley sprigs. Serve with Tartare
sauce (p. 352) if liked.

Family Fish Pie

1 kg (2 lb) coley or other white fish, skinned
600 ml (1 pint) milk
50 g (2 oz) butter
50 g (2 oz) flour
2 hard-boiled eggs, shelled and roughly chopped
salt and freshly ground black pepper
225 g (8 oz) frozen peas, defrosted
1 kg (2 lb) freshly cooked potatoes, mashed

Place the fish in a saucepan, cover with the milk and poach for 10 minutes. Lift out the fish with a slotted draining spoon, remove the bones and flake the fish. Reserve the milk for the sauce.

Heat the butter in a saucepan, stir in the flour and cook for 2 minutes. Gradually add the milk and bring to the boil stirring constantly. Remove from the heat. Stir in the flaked fish and chopped eggs and season to taste. Pour the mixture into a buttered baking dish. Cover with the defrosted peas and spread the mashed potatoes over the top. Bake in a fairly hot oven (200°C, 400°F, Gas Mark 6) for 30 minutes, or until golden-brown on top.
Serves 6 to 8

Fish in Pastry Envelopes

225 g (8 oz) flour
100 g (4 oz) quick cook oats
pinch of salt
175 g (6 oz) margarine
4–5 tablespoons cold water
1 egg, beaten
quick cook oats for sprinkling
For the filling:
25 g (1 oz) butter
1 tablespoon flour
150 ml ($\frac{1}{4}$ pint) milk
1 tablespoon chopped parsley
350 g (12 oz) white fish fillets
salt and freshly ground black pepper

First make the filling. Melt the butter in a small saucepan. Stir in the flour and cook for 1 minute. Gradually stir in the milk and bring to the boil, stirring constantly. Add the parsley and cook for 2 minutes, stirring all the time.

Cut the fish into bite-sized pieces and place in a bowl with the parsley sauce and seasoning to taste. Mix thoroughly and allow to become cold.

Meanwhile, make the pastry. Mix together the flour, oats and salt in a bowl. Rub in the margarine and bind with cold water to give a stiff consistency. Roll out the pastry on a floured surface to a rectangle about 25×38 cm (10×15 inches) and divide into six 12.5 cm (5 inch) squares. Place equal quantities of the fish mixture in the centre of each pastry square. Brush the edges of the pastry with water and join the edges together to form envelopes. Brush each envelope with beaten egg and sprinkle with extra oats. Place on a lightly greased baking sheet and bake in a fairly hot oven (200°C, 400°F, Gas Mark 6) for 10 minutes, then reduce the heat to cool (150°C, 300°F, Gas Mark 2) and cook a further 20 to 25 minutes.
Makes 6

Rolled Pancakes with Dressed Crab

1 × 50 g ($1\frac{3}{4}$ oz) can dressed crab
knob of butter
150 ml ($\frac{1}{4}$ pint) Béchamel Sauce (p. 356)
1 tablespoon chopped parsley
8 hot cooked pancakes (p. 243)
50 g (2 oz) grated cheese

Mix the dressed crab with the butter and the white sauce until well blended. Stir in the parsley. Divide the mixture among the 8 pancakes and roll them up round the filling. Arrange them, closely packed, in a shallow ovenproof dish, sprinkle with grated cheese and place under a hot grill until the cheese melts.

Oriental Fillets

4 × 175 g (6 oz) white fish fillets
salt
freshly ground pepper
2 tablespoons oil
50 g (2 oz) butter
1 garlic clove, peeled and crushed
12 thin slices of fresh green ginger or
    1 teaspoon ground ginger
1 tablespoon sugar
1 tablespoon cider or wine vinegar
2 tablespoons soy sauce
3 teaspoons cornflour
5 tablespoons water
To garnish:
4 spring onions, chopped
few unpeeled prawns

Rinse and dry the fish, season with salt
and pepper. Heat the oil and butter
together in a frying pan, add the fillets
and fry carefully until they flake easily,
about 5 minutes on each side depending
on the thickness. Arrange the fish on a
hot serving dish and keep warm. Add
the garlic and ginger to the fat in the
pan. Mix the sugar with the vinegar and
soy sauce and add to the pan. Combine
the cornflour and water and stir into the
mixture, stirring continuously over the
heat until it is thick and smooth. Pour
the sauce over the fish, garnish with the
spring onions and prawns and serve
with fried rice.

Spanish Fish

2 tablespoons olive oil
1 small onion, peeled and finely
    chopped
1 garlic clove, peeled and finely
    chopped
2 small green or red peppers, cored,
    seeded and finely chopped
1 × 400 g (14 oz) can tomatoes
$\frac{1}{2}$ teaspoon dried tarragon
salt
freshly ground black pepper
2 knobs of butter
4 large white fish fillets, skinned

Heat the oil in a pan, add the onion,
garlic and peppers and fry over gentle
heat for 10 minutes. Add the tomatoes,
break up with a spoon, then stir in the
tarragon and salt and pepper to taste.
Bring to the boil, lower the heat and
simmer for 20 minutes, stirring
occasionally.
    Meanwhile, melt the butter in a sep-
arate pan, add the fish and fry over
gentle heat for 5 minutes on each side.
Pour the onion and pepper mixture over
the fish, then continue cooking for a
further 10 minutes. Taste and adjust
seasoning. Serve hot with crusty
French bread or mashed potato.

Fish Finger Bake

450 g (1 lb) frozen spinach, thawed
salt
freshly ground black pepper
16 frozen fish fingers
vegetable oil or lard, for frying
1$\frac{1}{2}$ tablespoons cornflour
450 ml ($\frac{3}{4}$ pint) milk
1 large knob of butter
100 g (4 oz) Cheddar cheese

Preheat the oven at low temperature for
5 minutes. Put the spinach in the
bottom of an ovenproof dish, sprinkle
with salt and pepper, then put in the

oven to heat through. Meanwhile, fry the fish fingers in hot oil or lard until crisp on both sides. Mix the cornflour to a paste with a little of the milk. Heat the remaining milk in a pan with the butter, then gradually stir in the cornflour paste. Bring to the boil and cook until the sauce thickens, stirring constantly. Remove from the heat, grate in half the cheese, then stir until melted. Add salt and pepper to taste.

Arrange the fish fingers on top of the spinach, then pour over the cheese sauce. Grate the remaining cheese over the top. Turn the oven up to medium temperature, then bake in the centre of the oven for 15 minutes until golden brown and bubbling. Serve immediately with boiled new potatoes or French bread.

Variations:
Substitute frozen cod or haddock steaks for the fish fingers.

If preferred, cheese sauce mix can be used instead of the milk, cornflour and cheese.

Smoked Haddock Crêpes

300 ml (½ pint) pancake (crêpe) batter
    (see p. 363)
For the filling:
50 g (2 oz) butter
50 g (2 oz) flour
450 ml (¾ pint) hot milk
¼ teaspoon ground mace
75 g (3 oz) Parmesan cheese, grated
freshly ground white pepper
350 g (12 oz) smoked haddock,
    poached in milk, drained, boned
    and flaked

Make 12 crêpes as in the method on p. 00 and keep them warm.

To make the filling: melt the butter in a pan, stir in the flour and cook gently for 1 to 2 minutes, stirring all the time. Remove from the heat and add the hot milk gradually, stirring vigorously.

When all the milk is incorporated, return the pan to the heat and bring to the boil, stirring constantly. Lower the heat, add the mace, two-thirds of the Parmesan cheese, and pepper to taste. Simmer gently until the sauce is thick, stirring constantly. Taste and adjust seasoning.

Remove the pan from the heat and pour approximately half the sauce into a mixing bowl. Fold in the flaked fish. Lay the crêpes flat on a board or working surface and put a spoonful of filling on each one. Roll up the crêpes and place in a single layer in a shallow heatproof serving dish. Pour over the remaining sauce, sprinkle with the remaining Parmesan cheese and put under a preheated hot grill for a few minutes until the top is golden brown. Serve hot straight from the dish.

Jellied Eels

1 kg (2 lb) eels, cleaned, skinned and
    cut into 5 cm (2 inch) lengths
1¼ litres (1 pint) cold water
1 teaspoon whole allspice
1 large Spanish onion, peeled and
    sliced
1 tablespoon vinegar
1 bay leaf
4 tablespoons chopped fresh parsley
salt and freshly ground black pepper

Put the eels into a pan with the water. Tie up the allspice in a piece of muslin and add to the pan with the onion, vinegar, bay leaf and parsley. Add salt and pepper. Bring slowly to the boil, cover and simmer for 1 hour or until the eel is absolutely tender. Remove the bay leaf and allspice. Take out the pieces of eel and place in a serving dish.

Reduce the liquid if necessary, by boiling, uncovered, until there is just enough to cover the fish. Taste and adjust the seasoning. Pour the liquid over the eels and leave to set. Serve with a green salad and boiled potatoes.

Smoked Haddock and Egg Lasagne

1 tablespoon vegetable oil
175 g (6 oz) lasagne verde
450 ml ($\frac{3}{4}$ pint) Savoury white cooking
    sauce (p. 355)
100 g (4 oz) Cheddar cheese, grated
175 g (6 oz) cooked smoked haddock
    fillet, skinned, boned and flaked
4 tablespoons double or single cream
salt and freshly ground black pepper
3 eggs
25 g (1 oz) butter

Bring a large pan of lightly salted water to the boil and add the oil. Now lower lasagne, one sheet at a time, into the pan and cook for 5 minutes. Drain well and lay the sheets of lasagne on a large piece of greased greaseproof paper or foil.

Heat the white sauce in a pan with half the grated cheese, the flaked smoked haddock, cream and seasoning. Layer the lasagne and fish sauce in a greased ovenproof dish, starting and finishing with a layer of sauce. Bake in a fairly hot oven (190°C, 375°F, Gas Mark 5) for 30 minutes.

Meanwhile, beat the eggs with the seasoning to taste. Melt the butter in a frying pan and add the beaten eggs. Cook, stirring, over a gentle heat until the eggs begin to scramble. Remove from the heat and immediately spoon over the lasagne. Sprinkle with the remaining cheese and then return to oven for a further 10 minutes.

Kedgeree

350–450 g (12–16 oz) smoked cod or
    haddock fillet
75 g (3 oz) butter
225 g (8 oz) long-grain rice, boiled
2 hard-boiled eggs
3 tablespoons chopped parsley
lemon juice to taste
salt and freshly ground black pepper
lemon butterflies, to garnish

Poach the fish, remove any skin and bones and flake the flesh. Heat the butter in a large frying pan and stir in the cooked rice and flaked fish. Chop and add one hard-boiled egg and 1$\frac{1}{2}$ tablespoons of the chopped parsley. Sharpen with lemon juice and season well with salt and pepper. Separate the yolk and white of the remaining egg; chop the white and sieve the yolk. Turn the kedgeree into a warm serving dish and decorate with lines of sieved yolk, chopped white and the remaining chopped parsley. Finish by garnishing with lemon butterflies.

Cooked salmon, fresh or canned, also makes an excellent kedgeree.

Crispy Herrings in Oatmeal

4 herrings weighing about 275–350 g
    (10–12 oz) each
milk
medium oatmeal for coating
175 g (6 oz) butter
To garnish:
lemon wedges
parsley sprigs

Scale and clean the herrings slitting the belly right down to the tail. Cut off head, fins and tail. Open out flat and place, skin side uppermost, on a board. Press firmly with knuckles all along backbones to loosen it.

Turn the herring over and with the point of a knife ease out the backbone in one piece, starting at the head end. Remove as many of the small bones as possible. Wash the fish and dry with kitchen paper.

Dip fish in milk, coat with oatmeal following the method for egg and breadcrumbs. Fry in hot butter, skinless side first, until crisp, then turn and fry other side. Drain on kitchen paper. If the herring has roe, coat and fry it separately and place down centre of each fish. Garnish with lemon wedges and parsley sprigs. Serve hot with Gooseberry sauce (p. 350) or Mustard sauce (p. 356) if liked.

Kipper Goujons with Soured Cream Sauce

150 ml (¼ pint) soured cream
1 tablespoon lemon juice
1 teaspoon chopped drained capers
1 tablespoon milk
1 teaspoon chopped parsley
good pinch of cayenne pepper
salt and freshly ground black pepper
For the goujons:
1 × 275 g (10 oz) packet kipper fillets
100 g (4 oz) quick cook oats
25 g (1 oz) grated Parmesan cheese
1 egg, beaten
1 tablespoon milk
vegetable oil for frying

To make the sauce, place the soured cream, lemon juice, capers, milk, parsley and seasonings in a bowl and mix thoroughly. Chill in the refrigerator until required.

Remove the skin from the kipper fillets and cut each fillet into equal strips. Now mix together the oats and Parmesan cheese. Beat the egg with the milk. Dip the kipper strips first in the beaten egg and then in the oat mixture, pressing firmly to ensure the goujons are well coated. Heat the oil in a deep-fat fryer or saucepan until it is hot enough to turn a stale bread cube golden-brown in about 45 seconds (185°C/360°F). Fry the kipper goujons for about 2 minutes, until golden-brown. Drain well, on absorbent kitchen paper, pile up in a serving dish and serve with soured cream sauce.

Pilchard and Potato Cakes

225 g (8 oz) freshly cooked potatoes, mashed
1 × 225 g (8 oz) can pilchards in tomato sauce, boned and flaked
1 teaspoon salt
freshly ground black pepper
½ teaspoon finely grated onion
½ teaspoon lemon juice
For the coating:
1 egg, beaten
75 g (3 oz) dried breadcrumbs
vegetable oil for frying

Dry mash the potatoes (without adding any milk or butter) and place in a bowl with the fish, seasoning, grated onion and lemon juice. Combine gently with a fork until the mixture holds together. Shape into 8 round flat cakes on a floured board. Dip the cakes into the beaten egg, making sure that they are thoroughly and evenly covered, then coat with breadcrumbs.

Heat the oil gently in a deep-fat fryer or saucepan until it is hot enough to turn a stale bread cube golden in 20 to 30 seconds (180–190°C/350–375°F). Lower the cakes, 4 at a time, into the hot oil and fry for 1 to 2 minutes until crisp and golden-brown on all sides. Drain on absorbent kitchen paper.

The fish cakes may also be shallow fried for 2 to 3 minutes on each side or until golden-brown.
Makes 8 cakes

Manor House Smokies

4 small Arbroath smokies, skinned
   and boned
4 ripe tomatoes, skinned and diced
100 g (4 oz) Gruyère cheese, grated
300 ml ($\frac{1}{2}$ pint) double cream
freshly ground black pepper

Flake the flesh of the fish, then divide it
between 4 ovenproof pottery mugs (the
depth prevents the sauce drying up).
Spread the tomato over the fish. Mix
50 g (2 oz) of the cheese into the cream
and season with black pepper. Pour the
mixture into the mugs. Sprinkle the
remaining cheese over the tops. Bake in
a preheated moderate oven (180°C,
350°F, Gas Mark 4) for 20 minutes.
Flash under a hot grill for a few moments to glaze the tops. Serve with crisp
oatcakes or crusty bread, and eat with
teaspoons.

Tomato and
Mackerel Parcels

4 fresh mackerel, about 350 g (12 oz)
   each
salt and freshly ground black pepper
4 spring onions, trimmed and sliced
4 large tomatoes, sliced
1 lemon, quartered
1 bay leaf, quartered
1 teaspoon chopped parsley

Slit the mackerel from head to tail and
clean them thoroughly. Remove the
tails, fins, gills and eyes. The heads may
also be removed if desired. Wash the fish
well and dry on absorbent kitchen
paper. Season the cavities.
   Butter well 4 pieces of foil, each large
enough to completely enclose a fish. Put
on each square a layer of sliced onion
and tomato, one mackerel, a lemon
quarter and a piece of bay leaf. Season
well, sprinkle with a little chopped
parsley and fold up the foil, crimping

the edges well together so that no juices
can escape.
   Place the 4 foil parcels on a baking
sheet and bake in a moderate oven
(180°C, 350°F, Gas Mark 4) for 20 minutes. Serve in the foil parcels.

Grilled Mackerel

4 fresh mackerel weighing about
   275 g (10 oz) each
8 large mushrooms
salt
freshly ground pepper
1 tablespoon butter
lemon and parsley sprigs, to garnish

Scale and clean the mackerel, cutting
off the fins, and vandyke the tail (i.e. cut
a 'V' in the middle). Remove the eyes
from the head.
   Cut 3 diagonal slits on each side of
the fish. Place on a greased grid and
grill under moderate heat for 7 minutes,
then turn carefully. Put seasoned mushroom caps, black side uppermost, on
grid and dot with butter. Cook the fish
until the flesh shrinks from the bone at
the head end.
   Place the fish and mushrooms on a
warm serving dish. Garnish the fish
with lemon wedges and mushroom caps,
black side uppermost, and small parsley
sprigs. Serve with Rich lemon sauce
(p. 357) if liked.

Baked Stuffed Mackerel

1 × 75 g (3 oz) packet parsley and
thyme stuffing mix
about 150 ml (¼ pint) hot water
finely grated rind and juice of 1
lemon
1 bunch of parsley, finely chopped
1 large knob of butter
freshly ground black pepper
4 mackerel, cleaned and filleted

Put the stuffing mix in a bowl, add the
water according to packet directions
and stir well. Add the remaining ingredients except the mackerel and stir
again. Lay the mackerel flat on a board,
skin side down, then put the stuffing
along the centre of each fish and wrap
the fish around the stuffing to enclose it.
Preheat the oven at medium temperature for 5 minutes. Place the fish in an
ovenproof dish with the joins underneath, then cover with a sheet of buttered greaseproof paper or foil. Bake in
the centre of the oven for 30 minutes,
then serve hot with new potatoes and
seasonal vegetables.

Variation:
Stuffed mackerel is also good served
cold with mayonnaise and accompanied
by tomato salad.

Madras Prawns

2 tablespoons vegetable oil
2 large onions, peeled and finely
chopped
2 tablespoons garam masala or
Madras curry powder, or to taste
450 g (1 lb) peeled prawns
salt
freshly ground black pepper
1 × 200 g (7 oz) can tuna fish, drained
and flaked
300 ml (½ pint) thick homemade
mayonnaise (p. 42)
150 ml (¼ pint) soured cream

1 tablespoon lemon juice
1 kg (2 lb) long-grain rice, boiled,
drained and rinsed
4–5 tablespoons well seasoned
vinaigrette dressing (p. 43)
To garnish:
1 large cucumber, peeled and thinly
sliced
2 tablespoons finely chopped mint

This quantity makes two 23 cm (9 inch)
rice rings with a filling of prawns and
tuna in a curried mayonnaise, and it is
enough to serve approximately 25 per-
sons as a starter. If you wish to make
only one rice ring, then halve all the
quantities given above. Serve with chilled dry white wine for a refreshing start
to a buffet party meal.

Heat the oil in a large frying pan, add
the onion and fry until soft and golden.
Stir in the curry powder and cook for a
further 2 minutes, stirring occasionally. Stir in the prawns, with salt and
pepper to taste, and heat through.
Remove the pan from the heat, transfer
curried prawns to a mixing bowl and
fold in the flaked tuna, mayonnaise,
soured cream and lemon juice. Taste
and adjust seasoning if necessary, then
chill in the refrigerator until ready to
serve.

In a separate bowl, mix the rice with
enough vinaigrette dressing to hold it
together, then press into two oiled 23 cm
(9 inch) ring moulds.

If you only have one ring mould,
make one rice ring, refrigerate and turn
out, then oil the mould again and make
the second rice ring.

Chill in the refrigerator for at least 2
hours before serving. It is even better to
refrigerate overnight.

Turn the rice out on to serving platters and carefully spoon the prawn and
tuna mixture into the centres, dividing
it equally between the two. Arrange the
cucumber slices on top of the rice in
overlapping rings and sprinkle the mint
over the prawn and tuna filling in the
middle of each.
Serves about 25

Prawn Savoury

2 tablespoons vegetable oil
1 onion, peeled and finely chopped
4 tomatoes, quartered
$\frac{1}{4}$ teaspoon ground turmeric
1 coffee mug, 300 ml ($\frac{1}{2}$ pint), long-
grain rice
$1\frac{1}{2}$ coffee mugs, 450 ml ($\frac{3}{4}$ pint), water
1 chicken stock cube
freshly ground black pepper
225 g (8 oz) peeled prawns
1 green or red pepper, cored, seeded
and finely chopped

Heat the oil in a pan, add the onion,
tomatoes and turmeric and fry over
gentle heat for 10 minutes until soft,
stirring occasionally. Add the rice and
water, stir once and bring to the boil.
Add the stock cube and stir until dissolved, then add plenty of pepper.
Lower the heat, cover with a tight
fitting lid and cook gently for 20 minutes until the rice is 'al dente'. Stir in
the prawns 5 minutes before the end of
cooking, taste and adjust seasoning.
Sprinkle with the pepper. Serve hot
with a cucumber or tomato salad and
crusty French bread and butter.

Variations:
Substitute 4 chopped frankfurters for
the prawns, or a 200 g (7 oz) can of tuna
fish, flaked.
Serves 2 to 3

Devilled Prawn and Egg Mousse

150 ml ($\frac{1}{4}$ pint) double cream
150 ml ($\frac{1}{4}$ pint) mayonnaise
4 hard-boiled eggs, chopped
3 teaspoons anchovy essence
15 g ($\frac{1}{2}$ oz) (1 envelope) powdered
gelatine
3 tablespoons chicken stock
100 g (4 oz) watercress, chopped
salt

freshly ground black pepper
For the devil sauce:
120 ml (4 fl oz) tomato ketchup
1 teaspoon soft brown sugar
2 teaspoons lemon juice
Worcestershire sauce to taste
Tabasco to taste
175 g (6 oz) peeled prawns
To garnish:
1 unpeeled prawn
sprigs of watercress

Lightly whip the cream and reserve 2
tablespoons for the sauce. Mix together
the mayonnaise, hard-boiled eggs and
anchovy essence. Soak the gelatine in
the stock. Dissolve over a low heat, cool
a little and add to the mayonnaise
mixture, stir well. Fold in the cream and
watercress, and add salt and pepper to
taste. Turn into an 18 cm (7 inch) soufflé
dish and leave in the refrigerator to set,
about 20 minutes.
To prepare the sauce, mix all the
ingredients together, adding the Worcestershire and Tabasco sauces to taste.
Stir in the prawns. When the mousse is
set, turn it out into a shallow serving
dish and pour the devilled prawns
around. Garnish the top with prawn
and watercress sprigs.

Prawn Vol-Au-Vent

225 g (8 oz) Flaky pastry (p. 362)
1 egg, beaten
For the filling:
50 g (2 oz) button mushrooms, sliced
100 g (4 oz) peeled prawns
40 g ($1\frac{1}{2}$ oz) butter
300 ml ($\frac{1}{2}$ pint) Parsley coating sauce
(p. 356)
lemon juice to taste
To garnish:
lemon
watercress sprigs

Preheat the oven to 230°C, 450°F, Gas
Mark 8. Roll out chilled flaky pastry 5
mm ($\frac{1}{4}$ inch) thick. With a floured 7.5 cm

(3 inch) pastry cutter, cut out rounds and place half on a damp baking tray. With a 4.5 cm (1¾ inch) cutter, cut the centre out of the remaining rounds, leaving rings. Place trimmings in a pile on each other (do not knead). Reroll and cut as before.

Prick the large round with a fork and damp the edges lightly. Place a pastry ring on each one and press down. Mark a criss-cross pattern with a knife on top of the rings and brush with beaten egg. Glaze the remaining little rounds with egg and place on a separate tray as they will cook very quickly. They will serve as lids.

Bake the pastry on the upper shelf of the oven for 10 minutes until well risen and set. Remove the tray of lids. Lower the heat to 220°C, 425°F, Gas Mark 7 and cook the cases for a further 10 minutes or until crisp and golden brown. Remove the soft dough from inside cases and from the bottom of the lids. Cool on a wire rack.

Fry the mushrooms and prawns lightly in butter and add them to the hot parsley sauce. Sharpen to taste with lemon juice.

To serve, heat the cases in a pre-heated oven (190°C, 375°F, Gas Mark 5) for about 15 minutes. Place on a warm serving dish. Fill each with hot Prawn filling and put on the lids. Decorate the dish with quarter slices of lemon and watercress sprigs.

Star Gazey

8 × 100 g (4 oz) pilchards, scaled and cleaned
double quantity shortcrust pastry (p. 363), using 450 g (1 lb) flour and 225 g (8 oz) fat
1 onion, peeled and finely chopped
4 streaky bacon rashers, de-rinded and diced
3 tablespoons chopped fresh parsley
salt
freshly ground black pepper
½ teaspoon mixed spice
150 ml (¼ pint) double cream
1 egg, beaten with 1 teaspoon salt

Rinse and dry the fish. Divide the pastry in half. Roll out one piece and line a shallow 25 cm (10 inch) pie plate with it.

Trim the fins off the fish. Mix together the onion, bacon and parsley and season well with salt and pepper. Stuff the fish with this mixture. Arrange the pilchards fanwise on the dish, tails to the centre and heads resting on the rim. Stir the mixed spice into the cream and pour it over the fish.

Roll out the second piece of pastry to cover the dish, leaving the heads sticking out. Press lightly between each fish. Brush with the beaten egg and salt mixture, to give a shiny brown glaze. Bake in a preheated hot oven (220°C, 425°F, Gas Mark 7) for 15 minutes, reduce the heat to moderate (160°C, 325°F, Gas Mark 3) and cook for a further 20 minutes until deep golden brown. Brush again with egg during cooking.

Variation:
Herrings may be substituted for the pilchards.

Sardine Roll

2 × 100 g (4 oz) cans sardines in oil,
    drained
2 tomatoes, finely chopped
1 garlic clove, peeled and crushed
    (optional)
1 tablespoon lemon juice
freshly ground black pepper
1 × 400 g (14 oz) packet frozen puff
    pastry, thawed
1 small egg, beaten

Put the sardines in a bowl with the
tomatoes, garlic (if using), lemon juice
and plenty of black pepper. Mash the
ingredients thoroughly together. Cut
pastry in two, then roll out each piece to
an oblong about 25 × 15 cm (10 × 6
inches). Spread the sardine mixture
over the two pieces of pastry, leaving a 1
cm (½ inch) margin around the edges.

Preheat the oven at high temperature
for 5 minutes. Roll up each piece of
pastry from the long end to form a Swiss
roll shape, then cut each roll into about
10 slices. Stand the slices close together
on a baking sheet, then brush all over
with the egg.

Bake in the centre of the oven for 20
minutes, turning the baking sheet
round half way through cooking. Cover
the slices with foil if they are becoming
too brown. Leave to stand for 5 minutes
before serving with a crisp green salad
or a tomato and onion salad.

Variations:
Substitute a 200 g (7 oz) can salmon,
drained and boned, or a 225 g (8 oz) can
pilchards, drained, for the sardines.

Sardines au Gratin

1 slice wholemeal bread
2 sardines in tomato sauce
lemon juice
grated onion
chopped parsley
25 g (1 oz) grated Edam cheese

Toast the bread on one side. Place the
sardines on the untoasted side, sprinkle
with lemon juice, a little grated onion
and a little chopped parsley. Cover with
the cheese. Melt under a hot grill, and
serve really hot.
Serves 1

Scampi di Napoli

50 g (2 oz) flour
salt
freshly ground pepper
450 g (1 lb) scampi
25 g (1 oz) butter
100 g (4 oz) mushrooms, sliced
225 g (8 oz) ripe tomatoes, skinned,
    seeded and diced
For the sauce:
150 ml (¼ pint) dry white wine
1 small onion, peeled and finely
    chopped
bouquet garni
25 g (1 oz) butter
25 g (1 oz) flour
1 garlic clove, peeled and crushed
2 teaspoons tomato purée
300 ml (½ pint) good chicken stock
salt
freshly ground black pepper
120 ml (4 fl oz) double cream
chopped fresh parsley, to garnish

To make the sauce pour the wine into a
small pan, add the onion and bouquet
garni, bring to the boil, then reduce to
half by boiling rapidly. Set aside.

Melt the butter in a pan, remove from
the heat and stir in the flour. Return the
pan to the heat and cook for 3 minutes.

Remove from the heat, then stir in the garlic, tomato purée, stock and salt and pepper to taste. Bring to the boil and simmer for 15 minutes. Remove the bouquet garni from the wine, then stir the wine and onions into the other pan and simmer for a further 10 minutes.

For the scampi, season the flour with salt and pepper. Coat the fish in the flour, shaking off the surplus. Melt the butter in a sauté pan and fry the scampi gently for about 5 minutes. Remove to a hot serving dish. Add the mushrooms to the pan and cook for a minute or two, stir in the sauce and tomatoes, taste and adjust seasoning, bring to the boil and pour over the fish. Garnish with the parsley and serve very hot.

Koulibiac

700 g (1½ lb) fresh salmon
300 ml (½ pint) dry white wine
1 bay leaf, crushed
1 large parsley sprig
4 black peppercorns
salt
50 g (2 oz) butter
1 large onion, peeled and finely chopped
350 g (12 oz) button mushrooms, cleaned and finely sliced
225 g (8 oz) long-grain rice, boiled and drained
finely grated rind and juice of 1 lemon
3 tablespoons finely chopped parsley
freshly ground black pepper
2 × 368 g (13 oz) packets frozen puff pastry, thawed
3 hard-boiled eggs, shelled and sliced
1 egg, beaten
2 cartons soured cream, to garnish

This is a version of a classic Russian dish which makes a splendid centre piece to a special meal. It is well worth the expense of fresh salmon.

Put the salmon in a fish kettle or large saucepan, pour in the wine and enough water to cover the fish, then add the bay leaf, parsley sprig, peppercorns and salt to taste. Bring slowly to the boil, then lower the heat, cover with a lid and poach gently for approximately 20 minutes until the fish flakes easily with a fork. Remove the salmon from the kettle or pan, leave until cool enough to handle, discard any skin and bones, then flake the fish. Set aside.

Melt the butter in a pan, add the onion and cook gently until soft and lightly coloured. Add the mushrooms and cook for a further 2 minutes. Transfer this mixture to a mixing bowl, add the rice, lemon rind and juice, parsley and salt and pepper to taste. Mix gently.

Divide the dough into two portions, one slightly larger than the other. Roll out the smaller portion thinly on a floured board, transfer to a dampened baking sheet and cut into the shape of a fish, approximately 40 cm (16 inches) long and 25 cm (10 inches) at its widest point.

Divide the rice and mushroom mixture into two and spread one half on the dough, leaving a 2.5 cm (1 inch) margin all round. Divide the salmon in two and lay half on top of the rice. Arrange the sliced hard-boiled eggs in a line down the centre of the salmon, then cover with a second layer of salmon and remaining rice mixture.

Roll out the larger piece of dough on a floured board and cut into the same shape as the first piece, but slightly larger. Lay the dough over the filling, seal the edges with a little water and flute them with the fingers or a fork. Brush all over with the beaten egg, make slits in the top to let the steam escape, then bake in a fairly hot oven (200°C, 400°F, Gas Mark 6) for approximately 45 minutes until the pastry is golden brown. Remove from the oven, transfer to a serving platter and serve warm or cold. Pour the soured cream into a serving jug and hand separately. Serves 10–12

Salmon Suprême

2 × 150 g (5 oz) packets savoury rice
1 packet Parmesan cheese sauce mix
300 ml (½ pint) milk
approx. 50 g (2 oz) Cheddar cheese,
  grated
1 × 200 g (7 oz) can salmon, drained
  and flaked
1 × 200 g (7 oz) can tuna, drained and
  flaked
1 × 200 g (7 oz) can button mushrooms,
  drained
freshly ground black pepper
grated cheese, to garnish

Cook the savoury rice for 20 minutes
according to packet directions. Remove
from the heat, cover tightly with a lid
and set aside. Make the cheese sauce
with the milk according to packet directions, then gently fold in the cheese, fish
and mushrooms. Add plenty of black
pepper and heat through for 5 minutes.
Put the rice on individual plates, pour
over the sauce and sprinkle with
cheese, or hand the cheese separately in
a bowl. Serve immediately.

Poached Salmon

750 g (1½ lb) tail cut of salmon
1.2 litres (2 pints) Fish Stock Court
  Bouillon (p. 7)
bunch of watercress, to garnish

Wipe the fish free of any blood. Do not
wash it unless really necessary. Tie the
salmon up in a piece of muslin if you
have any, this makes it easy to remove
from the pan. Bring the court bouillon
to the boil, then gently lower in the fish.
Reduce the heat at once, then poach for
15 minutes.
  Remove the fish, take off the muslin
(if used) and the skin. Arrange on a hot
serving dish and garnish with sprigs of
watercress. Serve a hollandaise sauce
separately see (p. 351).

Sole Véronique

2 sole, skinned and filleted
juice of 1 lemon
salt
freshly ground pepper
25 g (1 oz) butter
225 g (8 oz) green grapes
100 ml (4 fl oz) dry white wine
2 egg yolks
court bouillon (p. 7)
75 ml (3 fl oz) single cream

Trim and wash the fillets. Rub them
with lemon juice to flavour and whiten
and season with salt and pepper. Roll
each fillet round your index finger,
starting from tail end, with skinned side
outward.
  Spread the bottom of a shallow
baking dish with the butter. Arrange
the turbans (rolled fish fillets) in the
centre of the baking dish, packing them
closely together so they will not unroll
while cooking. Alternatively, tie each
turban with thick thread. Slit and seed
the grapes. Fill the centre of each
turban with grapes and place the remaining grapes in the dish. Pour in the
wine. Add sufficient court bouillon to
come nearly to the top of the turbans,
but not to cover them.
  Lay buttered greaseproof paper over
the top of the dish and poach the fish in
the preheated oven (190°C, 375°F, Gas
Mark 5) for about 20 minutes. When
cooked, a white curd will appear on the
fish. Remove the fish and grapes to a
heated serving dish and keep warm.
Boil the fish liquor until it is reduced by
half and strain it.
  Beat the egg yolks and cream together in a bowl. Gradually stir in 125
ml (5 fl oz) of the reduced liquor.
  Place over a saucepan of boiling
water, taking care water does not touch
the bottom of the bowl. Stir with a
wooden spoon until the sauce coats the
back of the spoon with a thin cream.
Taste and adjust seasoning with lemon
juice, salt and pepper. Pour the sauce

over and around the fish.

For a main course serve with Duchess potatoes (p. 56) and Courgettes (p. 49). For a first course, serve one turban coated with sauce in an individual ramekin for each person.

If reheating the dish, place in a bainmarie, otherwise the direct heat will curdle the sauce.

Goujons de Sole with Tartare Sauce

2–3 small fillets lemon sole, about
   350 g (12 oz) skinned and cut into
   2.5 cm (1 inch) strips
2 tablespoons flour
salt and freshly ground black pepper
2 eggs, beaten
about 100 g (4 oz) dried breadcrumbs
oil for deep frying
To garnish:
2 lemon wedges
parsley sprigs

Coat the fish in the flour seasoned with salt and pepper, then dip in the egg, making sure that the fish is thoroughly coated. Coat evenly with breadcrumbs, then chill in the refrigerator for approximately 30 minutes.

Pour enough oil for deep-fat frying into a deep-fat fryer and heat gently until the oil is hot enough to turn a stale bread cube golden in 20 to 30 seconds. Put in the fish, increase the heat and fry for approximately 3 minutes or until the goujons are crisp. Drain on absorbent kitchen paper, transfer to a hot serving platter and garnish with lemon wedges and parsley sprigs. Serve immediately with Tartare Sauce handed separately.

Variation:
Plaice fillets can be substituted for the sole for a more economical starter.

Filets de Sole Dieppoise

2 × 450 g (1 lb) Dover sole, cleaned,
   skinned and filleted
salt
freshly ground black pepper
150 ml ($\frac{1}{4}$ pint) Fish Stock (p. 7)
150 ml ($\frac{1}{4}$ pint) Coating Sauce (p. 355)
   with 4 tablespoons dry white wine
2 tablespoons double cream
squeeze of lemon juice
12 mussels, cooked
75 g (3 oz) peeled prawns
To garnish:
few unpeeled prawns
few mussels in half shells

Rinse and dry the fillets, fold them into 3 and place in a buttered ovenproof dish. Season lightly with salt and pepper and pour over the stock. Cover with buttered greaseproof paper and poach in a preheated moderate oven (180°C, 350°F, Gas Mark 4) for 15 minutes. Drain the fish, reserving the liquor, and arrange on a heated serving dish. Set aside, keeping warm.

Put the cooking liquor into a small pan and reduce by boiling rapidly to about 1 tablespoon. Add the white wine sauce together with any strained liquor from the mussel shells. Bring to the boil and stir in the cream and lemon juice. Add the mussels and peeled prawns. Heat through carefully, without boiling. Pour the sauce over the fillets and garnish with the whole prawns and opened mussels.

Trout Meunière with Almonds

4 trout, weighing 225–350 g (8–12 oz)
  each
flour for coating
175 g (6 oz) clarified butter (p. 352)
6 tablespoons flaked almonds
4–5 tablespoons lemon juice or dry
  white wine
salt and freshly ground pepper
To garnish:
lemon wedges
parsley sprigs

Scale and gut the trout. Remove the eyes from the head. Dry the fish and coat evenly with flour, shaking off any surplus. Heat 50 g (2 oz) clarified butter in a frying pan until very hot. Put in the trout and fry quickly until golden brown underneath.

Turn the fish carefully, using a fish slice and palette knife, so as not to break the skin, and fry the other side. Cook until the second side is crisp and the flesh shrinks away from the back-bone just below the head. Lift the fish onto a heated serving dish and keep it warm. Add the remaining clarified butter to the pan, heat it and fry the flaked almonds until golden. Add the lemon juice or wine and season with salt and pepper to taste. Bring to the boil and pour the sauce and almonds over the fish. Garnish with lemon wedges and parsley sprigs. Serve im-mediately with new potatoes, boiled and tossed in butter and chopped pars-ley, or Sauté potatoes (p. 55).

* Trout Meunière aux Champignons

Follow the recipe for Trout Meunière with Almonds (above), with this change: in place of the almonds, add 100 g (4 oz) sliced button mushrooms, fried in butter.

Trout Cleopatra

4 × 175 g (6 oz) trout, cleaned
175 g (6 oz) soft herring roes
2 tablespoons oil
50 g (2 oz) butter
salt and freshly ground pepper
50 g (2 oz) flour
175 g (6 oz) peeled shrimps
1 tablespoon drained capers
juice of 1 lemon
1 lemon, peeled, sliced and pips
  removed (optional)

Rinse and dry the trout and herring roes. Heat the oil and 25 g (1 oz) of the butter in a large frying pan. Now season flour with salt and pepper. Coat the trout in the flour, then shake off any surplus. Cook gently in the hot fat until coloured on both sides, about 8 minutes, turning once. Arrange on a heated serv-ing dish and keep warm.

Dip the roes in flour and cook quickly to lightly colour, about 3 to 4 minutes. Drain and arrange on the trout. Toss the shrimps in the hot fat for a moment to heat through, then drain well and lay over the trout and roes. Sprinkle with the capers and lemon juice, then place lemon slices on top, if using. Heat the remaining butter in a clean pan until it is deep golden brown, pour at once over the fish. Serve immediately.

Smoked Trout Mousse

4 fresh smoked trout, about 450 g
  (1 lb), heads removed, skinned,
  boned and flaked
2 teaspoons lemon juice
150 ml ($\frac{1}{4}$ pint) mayonnaise (p. 42)
150 ml ($\frac{1}{4}$ pint) double cream, lightly
  whipped
$\frac{1}{4}$ teaspoon cayenne pepper
  freshly ground white pepper
1 tablespoon powdered gelatine
2 tablespoons cold water
2 egg whites

To garnish:
$\frac{1}{4}$ cucumber, sliced
1 × 40 g ($1\frac{1}{2}$ oz) jar lump fish roe
1 tablespoon aspic jelly powder
150 ml ($\frac{1}{4}$ pint) water

Put the smoked trout in a mixing bowl and sprinkle with the lemon juice. Add the mayonnaise and stir well to combine, then fold in the whipped cream. Season with the peppers.

Sprinkle the gelatine over the water in a small heatproof bowl and leave to stand until spongy. Put the bowl in a pan of hot water and stir over a low heat until the gelatine has dissolved.

Remove from the heat, leave to cool for 5 minutes, then stir into the trout mixture until evenly distributed. Chill in the refrigerator or leave in a cool place for approximately 1 hour until just beginning to set. Beat the egg whites until stiff, then fold into the mousse. Taste and adjust seasoning, then spoon into a 15 cm (6 inch) soufflé dish, flatten top with a palette knife and chill in the refrigerator until set.

Decorate the top of mousse with the cucumber slices and lump fish roe. Make up the aspic jelly with the powder and water according to packet directions, leave to cool, then pour over the mousse. Return to the refrigerator and chill until serving time.
Serves 12–14

Crispy Corned Tuna

25 g (1 oz) butter
25 g (1 oz) flour
300 ml ($\frac{1}{2}$ pint) milk
50 g (2 oz) Cheddar cheese, grated
salt and freshly ground black pepper
1 × 200 g (7 oz) can tuna fish
1 × 326 g ($11\frac{1}{2}$ oz) can sweetcorn
2 large tomatoes, finely sliced
1 × 71 g ($2\frac{1}{2}$ oz) packet potato crisps

Melt the butter in a saucepan. Stir in the flour and cook for 1 minute. Gradu-

ally add the milk and bring to the boil, stirring constantly. Simmer for 2 minutes, stir in the cheese and season to taste. Flake the tuna and add to the sauce with the liquid from the can. Fold in the drained sweetcorn.

Use the tomato slices to line a greased ovenproof dish. Spoon the tuna mixture into the centre of the dish and crumble the potato crisps on top. Place in a moderate oven (180°C, 350°F, Gas Mark 4) for about 20 minutes, until the top is brown and crisp. Serve with thick slices of French bread.

Tuna Italian Style

6 handfuls (good 300 ml, $\frac{1}{2}$ pint) quick-cooking macaroni
salt
$1\frac{1}{2}$ tablespoons cornflour
450 ml ($\frac{3}{4}$ pint) milk
1 large knob of butter
1 large bunch of parsley, finely chopped
2 × 175 g (6 oz) cans tuna fish, drained and flaked
freshly ground black pepper
3 tomatoes, sliced
1 small packet of plain crisps, crushed

Cook the macaroni in boiling salted water until barely tender, according to packet directions. Drain thoroughly, then return to the pan. Mix the cornflour to a paste with a little of the milk. Heat the remaining milk and the butter in the pan with the macaroni, then gradually stir in the cornflour paste. Bring to the boil and cook until the sauce thickens, stirring constantly. Remove from the heat, then gently fold in the parsley and tuna, and season.

Preheat the oven at high temperature for 5 minutes. Pour the mixture into an ovenproof dish and smooth the top. Arrange the tomato slices around the edge, then sprinkle the crisps in the centre. Bake in the centre of the oven for 15 minutes, then serve immediately.

Turbot in Champagne

1 × 1½ kg (3 lb) chicken turbot, or a
    1 kg (2 lb) centre cut from a larger
    one, cleaned
salt
freshly ground black pepper
½ bottle (400 ml, 14 fl oz) dry
    champagne
300 ml (½ pint) rich Béchamel Sauce
    (p. 356)
50 g (2 oz) butter
To garnish:
450 g (1 lb) creamed potato, piped into
    4 halved, seeded tomatoes, and
    browned
chopped fresh parsley

Rinse and dry the fish. Place it, white
skin down, in a buttered baking tin,
season with salt and pepper and pour
over the champagne. Cover the tin with
buttered greaseproof paper or foil and
poach in a preheated moderately hot
oven (190°C, 375°F, Gas Mark 5) for
about 30 minutes. Carefully lift the fish
into a hot serving dish, remove the
black skin and keep the fish warm.

Place the tin over a brisk heat and
reduce the liquor by half. Whisk in the
béchamel sauce, remove from the heat
and flake in the butter. Ladle enough of
the sauce over the fish to just cover,
then flash under a hot grill to glaze.
Garnish with the tomatoes and parsley
and serve the remaining sauce separately. Serve accompanied by plain
boiled potatoes.

Variation:
Dry white sparkling wine may be substituted for the champagne.

Fillets of Whiting Bercy

4 × 225 g (8 oz) whiting, filleted
salt
freshly ground black pepper
50 g (2 oz) shallots or small onions,
    peeled and finely chopped
1 tablespoon chopped fresh parsley
120 ml (4 fl oz) dry white wine
120 ml (4 fl oz) water
15 g (½ oz) butter
15 g (½ oz) flour
To garnish:
4 lemon twists
4 sprigs of parsley

Rinse the fish, then season with salt and
pepper. Place in a buttered ovenproof
dish and sprinkle with the shallots or
onion and parsley. Pour on the wine and
water, cover with buttered greaseproof
paper and poach in a preheated
moderate oven (180°C, 350°F, Gas Mark
4) for 15 minutes. Lift the fillets on to a
warm serving dish reserving the liquid.

Melt the butter in a small pan, stir in
the flour and cook for two minutes.
Remove the pan from the heat and
gradually stir in the fish liquid. Return
to the heat and bring to the boil, stirring, until the sauce is thick and
smooth. Simmer for 2 to 3 minutes and
pour over the fish.

Garnish with the lemon twists and
parsley sprigs.

Variation:
Add a little thick cream to the thickened sauce, then carefully heat
through before pouring over the fish.

POULTRY & GAME

Roast Chicken

1 chicken with giblets (1¼ kg (2½ lb)
    for two people, 1½ kg (3½ lb) for four
    people, 2 kg (4½ lb) for six people)
fat bacon rashers
butter

Clean the giblets and use to make giblet
stock for gravy (p. 7). Preheat the oven
to 200°C, 400°F, Gas Mark 6. The breast
should be protected by covering with fat
bacon rashers and well buttered greaseproof paper or foil during roasting, or
the flesh will become dry. Prepare the
bird and place it in a greased roasting
pan in the centre of the oven. Cook for
20 minutes per 450 g (1 lb). Remove the
bacon and paper 20 minutes before end
of the cooking time to allow the breast
to brown and crisp. Test by inserting
a skewer into the thickest part of the
thigh. When the juices run amber
coloured, the bird is cooked. Place the
chicken on a warm serving dish and
make the gravy.

Spiced Chicken Pot Roast

1½–1¾ kg (3–3½ lb) roasting chicken
    with giblets
1 teaspoon ground coriander
1 teaspoon ground cumin seed
50 g (2 oz) butter
225 g (8 oz) cooked long-grain rice

1 small green pepper, deseeded and
    cut into strips
1 × approx. 100 g (4 oz) can red
    pimientos, drained and chopped
2 large tomatoes, peeled and chopped
salt and freshly ground black pepper
1 large onion, peeled and chopped
1 tablespoon powdered turmeric

Wash the chicken well, wash and drain
the giblets, and cook the giblets in
lightly salted water for about 20 minutes to make stock.

Meanwhile, prick the chicken all
over with a fork. Combine the ground
coriander and cumin seed and rub into
the chicken.

Melt half the butter in a saucepan.
Mix in the cooked rice, strips of green
pepper, chopped pimiento and chopped
tomato and season well. Use the mixture to stuff the chicken.

Heat the remaining butter in a frying
pan. Add the chopped onion and turmeric and cook, stirring constantly,
until golden-brown. Add the stuffed
chicken, turning frequently, until
coated with the mixture. Transfer the
chicken with the onion and spices, to a
casserole which fits it with little space
to spare. Make up the strained giblet
stock to 300 ml (½ pint) with boiling
water and pour into the frying pan. Stir
well and pour over the chicken. Cover
tightly and put the casserole into a
moderate oven (180°C, 350°F, Gas Mark
4) for 1½ hours. Serve with a salad and
potatoes in their jackets.

Boned, Stuffed and Rolled Chicken

1 roasting chicken about 2½ kg (5 lb),
  with the giblets
1 garlic clove, peeled and cut in half
25 g (1 oz) butter, softened
salt and freshly ground black pepper
For the stuffing:
butter for frying
1 large onion, peeled and finely
  chopped
4 large sticks celery, trimmed,
  scrubbed and roughly chopped
225 g (8 oz) mushrooms, cleaned and
  finely sliced
225 g (8 oz) back bacon, rinds
  removed, chopped
100 g (4 oz) pork sausagemeat
liver from chicken giblets, cleaned
  and chopped
    100 g (4 oz) granary bread,
    crumbled
50 g (2 oz) fresh parsley, finely
  chopped
1 teaspoon mixed dried herbs
salt and freshly ground black pepper
1 small egg, beaten
100 g (4 oz) stuffed green olives
watercress sprigs, to garnish

Some butchers will bone a chicken for you; if not, then it is quite simple to bone it yourself by following the instructions given below, and it will be so much easier to carve the bird into neat slices at the buffet.

Remove the giblets from the chicken and reserve the liver for the stuffing. Wash the bird thoroughly and dry inside and out with a clean tea towel or absorbent kitchen paper. Put the bird on a working surface, breast side down. Slit the skin along the centre of the underside with a sharp knife, working from neck to tail end. Ease the flesh away from the carcass on one side of the bird, working down to the ball joint. Repeat this process on the other side.

Twist or cut off the scaly end of the leg, then cut through the legs where they join the carcass. Hold the leg bone and scrape the flesh away until the bones come free. Repeat with the other leg and the wings.

Continue to scrape the flesh away from the carcass on both sides, working round to the breastbone. When the breastbone is reached, carefully remove the flesh, being careful not to cut through the skin which is very thin at this point. Lift out the carcass. Lay the chicken as flat as possible on a board, skin side down. Rub the exposed flesh with the garlic clove and season.

To make the stuffing: melt a little butter in a pan, add the onion and celery and cook gently for approximately 5 minutes until soft and lightly coloured. Add the mushrooms and continue cooking for a further 2 to 3 minutes until the juices flow. Remove the vegetables from the pan with a slotted spoon and set aside in a mixing bowl. Add the bacon, sausagemeat and reserved chicken livers to the pan and cook for 5 minutes or until golden brown. Remove from pan with a slotted spoon and add to the vegetables in the bowl. Stir in the crumbled bread, parsley and mixed herbs, with plenty of salt and pepper, and mix well before binding the mixture with the egg.

Spread half the stuffing on the chicken, place the stuffed olives in a layer on top, then cover with the remaining stuffing. Roll up and tuck in the legs and wings. Overlap the skin on the underside and sew the bird neatly together with trussing string. Weigh the bird and calculate the cooking time, allowing 25 minutes to the ½ kg (1 lb). Place on a rack in a roasting tin. Rub the skin with the garlic clove, then brush with the softened butter and season. Roast in a fairly hot oven (about 190°C, 375°F, Gas Mark 5) for 1¾ hours, according to weight. Baste and turn occasionally during cooking.

Remove from the oven, leave to cool on the rack, then chill in the refrigerator until firm. Remove the trussing strings, slice the chicken neatly and transfer to a large serving platter. Garnish with sprigs of watercress. Alternatively, the whole chicken may be placed on a serving platter with just a few slices cut.

Cuts into about 12 slices

Spit Roasted Chicken with Fresh Herbs

1 × 1½ kg (3½ lb) roasting chicken
a good bunch of fresh tarragon or
    chervil
40 g (1½ oz) butter
1 bay leaf
1 sprig parsley
1 shallot or small onion
salt
black peppercorns
50 ml (2 fl oz) white wine (optional)
2 tablespoons finely chopped tarragon
    or chervil leaves
150 ml (¼ pint) single cream
lemon juice to taste
fresh parsley, tarragon or chervil
    sprigs, to garnish

Truss the chicken, but instead of stuffing it, insert several sprigs of fresh tarragon or chervil in the body cavity with a knob of butter.

Clean the giblets and put on to cook with water, bay leaf, parsley, shallot, salt and a few black peppercorns to make Giblet stock (p. 7).

Heat the grill. Melt the remaining butter and brush it over the chicken. Put the chicken on the spit, with the tray beneath, and grill under high heat for about 20 minutes or until golden. Lower the heat slightly and continue cooking for 50 minutes or until the juice runs amber coloured when tested with a skewer. Baste occasionally with the butter from the drip tray unless the bird is very fatty.

Use only the butter in the drip tray as the juices will stain the chicken if spooned over it. When cooked, place the bird on a warm serving dish. Allow the juices to settle in the drip tray and carefully pour off all the fat. Add the wine (if used) and 150 ml (¼ pint) strained giblet stock. Bring to the boil, scraping up the juices from drip tray. Add the tarragon or chervil and the cream. Stir over gentle heat for 5 to 10 minutes and season to taste with salt, pepper and lemon juice. Pour into a warm gravy boat. Serve the chicken garnished with sprigs of fresh parsley, tarragon or chervil and accompany with chips or sauté potatoes and a tossed green salad.

Chicken and Cheese Grill

4 chicken portions, skinned
2 garlic cloves, peeled and slivered
2 large knobs of butter
150 ml (¼ pint) water
salt
freshly ground black pepper
1 × 300 ml (½ pint) packet cheese sauce
    mix
300 ml (½ pint) milk
75 g (3 oz) Cheddar cheese
2 small packets plain potato crisps,
    crushed

Make several incisions in the chicken flesh and insert the slivers of garlic.

Melt the butter in a large frying pan, add the chicken and fry quickly until golden brown on both sides. Add the water carefully and sprinkle with salt and pepper to taste. Cover with foil and simmer for 40 minutes until the liquid is absorbed, turning the portions once during cooking.

Meanwhile, make the cheese sauce with the milk according to packet directions. Pour over the chicken and grate the cheese over the top. Sprinkle with the crisps, then put under a low preheated grill for 10 minutes until golden brown, turning the pan occasionally to ensure even browning. Serve hot with a mixed salad or seasonal green vegetables and noodles or rice.

† Chicken Pot Roast

75 g (3 oz) fresh white breadcrumbs
4 rashers unsmoked streaky bacon,
   rinded and chopped
1 small onion, peeled and finely
   chopped
1 garlic clove, crushed
1 teaspoon dried thyme
salt
freshly ground black pepper
1 egg, beaten
1 kg (2½ lb) roasting chicken
50 g (2 oz) butter or margarine
2 parsnips, peeled and quartered
3 celery stalks, scrubbed and chopped
4 large carrots, peeled and quartered
450 ml (¾ pint) hot brown stock or
   water and 1 beef stock cube
2 tablespoons flour
little water

Mix together the breadcrumbs, bacon,
onion, garlic, thyme and salt and
pepper. Bind together with the beaten
egg. Stuff the body cavity of the chicken
with this mixture. Tie the chicken securely with fine string. Heat the butter
or margarine in the base of the cooker
and brown the chicken evenly all over.
Remove the chicken and sauté the vegetables until lightly coloured. Transfer
the vegetables to a plate. Add the hot
stock or water and stock cube to the
cooker and add the trivet. Stand the
chicken on the trivet and add a little
salt and pepper. Close the cooker, bring
to H pressure and cook for 20 minutes.
Reduce the pressure quickly.

Place the vegetables around the chick-
en, together with a little salt and
pepper. Close the cooker, bring to H
pressure and cook for 5 minutes. Reduce
the pressure quickly. Lift out the chick-
en and vegetables to a warmed dish and
keep hot. Remove the trivet and return
the open cooker to the heat. Stir in the
flour blended with a little water. Stir
and cook until thickened. Taste and
adjust seasoning as necessary before
serving with the chicken.

Casserole Curry

1 tablespoon corn oil
1 large onion, peeled and finely
   chopped
2 tablespoons curry powder
1 tablespoon cornflour
900 ml (1½ pints) chicken stock
1 medium-sized cooking apple, peeled,
   cored and grated
1 tablespoon apricot jam
2 tablespoons desiccated coconut
2 teaspoons lemon juice
salt to taste
350 g (12 oz) cooked chicken or
   turkey, diced
25 g (1 oz) seedless raisins

Heat the corn oil in a saucepan and
cook the chopped onion in it for a few
minutes until limp and transparent.
Add the curry powder and the cornflour
and cook over low heat for a further 3
minutes. Stir in the stock, grated apple,
apricot jam and coconut. Simmer gently
for at least a further 30 minutes, stirring
occasionally.

Add the lemon juice and adjust
seasoning if necessary. Stir in the diced
chicken or turkey and the raisins and
reheat to make the dish piping hot.

Serve in the traditional way with
boiled long-grain rice and chutney.

† Curried Chicken Drumsticks with Rice

25 g (1 oz) butter or margarine
1 onion, peeled and roughly chopped
2 tablespoons curry powder
1 teaspoon ground ginger
½ teaspoon chilli powder
450 ml (¾ pint) hot white stock or
    water and ½ chicken stock cube
8 chicken drumsticks, skinned
1 garlic clove, crushed
1 eating apple, peeled and chopped
25 g (1 oz) sultanas
grated rind and juice of 1 lemon
225 g (8 oz) long-grain patna rice
450 ml (¾ pint) water
½ teaspoon salt
1 tablespoon cornflour
little water

Heat the butter or margarine in the base of the cooker. Fry the onion until lightly coloured. Stir in the curry powder, ginger and chilli powder. Remove the cooker from the heat and gradually stir in the stock or water and stock cube. Add all the remaining ingredients, except the rice, water, salt and cornflour and stir well. Place the trivet over the chicken. Put the rice, water and salt into an ovenproof dish that will fit easily into the cooker. Cover with a piece of greaseproof paper or foil. Stand the container on the trivet. Close the cooker, bring to H pressure and cook for 5 minutes. Reduce the pressure slowly. Lift out the container, transfer the rice to a strainer and rinse with boiling water. Drain well. Blend the cornflour with a little water and stir into the curry sauce. Return the open cooker to the heat and bring to the boil, stirring constantly. Taste and adjust the seasonings of the curry, as necessary, before serving on the bed of rice.

† Eastern Chicken

25 g (1 oz) butter
2 tablespoons cooking oil
1 large onion, peeled and chopped
4 chicken portions or quarters,
    skinned
150 ml (¼ pint) white stock or water
    and ½ chicken stock cube
150 ml (¼ pint) medium dry sherry
1 × 225 g (8 oz) can tomatoes
2 teaspoons brown sugar
2 teaspoons soy sauce
2 oranges, peeled and segmented
salt
freshly ground black pepper
To garnish:
2 teaspoons cornflour blended with 4
    teaspoons water
orange slices

Heat the butter and oil in the cooker. Fry the onion until it is beginning to soften. Lift out and drain well. Sauté the chicken portions until golden brown and lift out. Drain excess butter and oil from the cooker. Away from the heat add the stock or water and stock cube, sherry and tomatoes. Stir well to remove any residues from the base of the cooker. Return the chicken to the cooker with the onion, sugar, soy sauce, orange segments and a little salt and pepper. Close the cooker, bring to H pressure and cook for 6 minutes. Reduce the pressure quickly.

Lift out the chicken to a warmed serving dish and keep hot. Return the cooker to the heat and add the blended cornflour. Cook, stirring constantly, until the sauce boils and thickens. Taste and adjust the seasoning as necessary. Pour the sauce over the chicken and garnish with orange slices.

Chicken Hot-pot

2–2½ kg (4–5 lb) boiling fowl
25 g (1 oz) butter
salt and freshly ground black pepper
3 large onions, peeled and thickly
   sliced
¾ kg (1½ lb) potatoes, peeled and
   thickly sliced
1 teaspoon ground bay leaves
grated rind and juice of 1 lemon
1 chicken stock cube
450 ml (¾ pint) boiling water
1 tablespoon chopped parsley, to
   garnish

Joint the boiling fowl into 8 pieces so
that there are 2 breasts, 2 wings, 2
thighs and 2 drumsticks.

Grease a deep casserole with a little
of the butter and place half the joints in
the bottom. Season lightly and cover
with a layer of onion slices, then with a
layer of potato slices. Sprinkle with half
the ground bay leaves and lemon rind.
Put the remaining chicken pieces on
top, season and again cover with a layer
of onion slices then potato slices. Dissolve the stock cube in the hot water,
add the lemon juice and pour into the
casserole. Sprinkle with the remaining
lemon rind and bay leaves and dot with
the remainder of the butter. Cover the
casserole with a sheet of foil and put on
the lid.

Bake in a warm oven (160°C, 325°F,
Gas Mark 3) for 2 hours. Remove the foil
cover and lid, and cook for a further 30
minutes to brown the top. (An old boiling fowl may take even longer, so test
with a fork to make sure it is tender
before cooking the dish uncovered for
the last 30 minutes.)

Serve sprinkled with the chopped
parsley.
Serves 6

† Chicken and Tomato Casserole

2 tablespoons oil
4 chicken portions or quarters,
   skinned
salt
freshly ground black pepper
4 rashers unsmoked streaky bacon,
   rinded and chopped
1 onion, peeled and sliced
1 green pepper, cored, seeded and
   sliced
1 × 400 g (14 oz) can tomatoes
150 ml (¼ pint) white stock or water
   and ¼ chicken stock cube
1 bay leaf
finely chopped parsley to garnish

Heat the oil in the cooker. Season the
chicken with salt and pepper. Fry with
the bacon until the chicken is a light
golden brown and the bacon is beginning to colour. Lift out of the cooker
and drain well. Pour off any excess oil
from the cooker. Add all the remaining
ingredients to the cooker and return to
the heat. Stir well to remove any residues from the base of the cooker.
Return the chicken and bacon with a
little more salt and pepper and stir well.
Close the cooker, bring to H pressure
and cook for 6 minutes. Reduce the
pressure quickly. Remove the bay leaf
before serving; taste and adjust seasoning as necessary and sprinkle with
parsley.

† Galantine of Chicken

1½–2 kg (3–4 lb) chicken
For the stuffing:
350 g (12 oz) pork sausagemeat
1 teaspoon chopped fresh parsley
1 teaspoon chopped fresh thyme
1 teaspoon chopped fresh tarragon
1 teaspoon finely grated lemon rind
salt
freshly ground black pepper
100 g (4 oz) button mushrooms,
  washed and sliced
900 ml (1½ pints) poultry stock or
  water and 1 chicken stock cube

Bone the chicken or ask your butcher to
do this for you. Lay the chicken on a
board, skin side down and level the flesh
as much as possible. Mix the sausagemeat with the herbs, lemon rind, salt
and pepper. Spread half the sausagemeat mixture down the centre of the
chicken and sprinkle with a little salt
and pepper. Add a layer of the mushrooms and then spread the remaining
sausagemeat over the mushrooms,
sprinkle with a little salt and pepper.
Fold in the ends of the chicken first then
fold over the longer edges so that the
stuffing is well enclosed. Sew up with
strong thread and weigh the chicken to
calculate the cooking time (it will need
10 minutes per 450 g/1 lb stuffed weight).
Wrap and tie securely into a pudding
cloth or into several thicknesses of
muslin.
  Put the stock into the cooker with the
chicken. Close the cooker, bring to H
pressure and cook for the calculated
time. Reduce the pressure slowly. Lift
out the chicken and reserve 300 ml (½
pint) of the stock. Cool the chicken
quickly and thoroughly. When quite
cold, remove the cloth and thread carefully. Boil the reserved stock in a
saucepan until well reduced and syrupy
then cool. Brush the stock over the
chicken. Transfer carefully to a serving
dish and decorate the galantine with
salad ingredients.

Savoury Stuffed Pancakes

8 thin pancakes (p. 243)
for the filling:
40 g (1½ oz) butter or 40 ml (1½ fl oz)
  olive oil
1 medium onion, peeled and chopped
100 g (4 oz) mushrooms, washed and
  sliced
2 tablespoons chopped celery
1 × 400 g (14 oz) can tomatoes
pinch of mixed herbs
salt
freshly ground pepper
sugar and lemon juice to taste
100–175 g (4–6 oz) frozen prawns or
chopped cooked chicken and/or ham
300 ml (½ pint) Cheese sauce (p. 356)
2 tablespoons grated cheese
celery leaves or parsley sprigs, to
  garnish
or
lemon butterflies, to garnish

Heat the butter or oil and fry the onion,
mushrooms and celery until softened.
Add the tomatoes and herbs. Season to
taste with salt, pepper, sugar and lemon
juice. Simmer, uncovered, until reduced
to a thick purée. Add the prawns or
chopped cooked meat; taste and adjust
the seasoning.
  Spread the pancakes out flat. Put 2
tablespoons of the filling in the centre of
each pancake and fold over the sides to
make an envelope. Arrange the filled
pancakes, side by side, in a shallow
greased gratin dish. Pour hot cheese
sauce over the pancakes and sprinkle
with grated cheese. The dish may be
prepared well in advance up to this
stage, which makes it an ideal choice
for entertaining.
  To finish: place the dish in a preheated oven at 200°C, 400°F, Gas Mark 6
and bake for about 20 minutes or until
heated through and bubbly on top.
Serve garnished with tufts of celery
leaves or parsley sprigs. If using prawn
filling, decorate with lemon 'butterflies'
as well.

Chicken and Mushroom Vol-au-vents

2 × 400 g (14 oz) packets frozen puff
  pastry, thawed
2 eggs, beaten
For the filling:
40 g (1½ oz) butter
225 g (8 oz) button mushrooms,
  cleaned and finely chopped
40 g (1½ oz) flour
450 ml (¾ pint) hot milk
150 ml (¼ pint) double cream
½ teaspoon ground mace
salt and freshly ground black pepper
350 g (12 oz) cooked chicken meat,
  finely diced
parsley sprigs, to garnish

Roll out the dough thinly on a floured
board and stamp into 40 rounds with a
7.5 cm (3 inch) fluted pastry cutter.
Place the rounds on dampened baking
sheets and brush with beaten egg.
Stamp circles on the rounds with a 5 cm
(2 inch) cutter, without cutting right
through the dough. Bake in a fairly hot
oven (200°C, 400°F, Gas Mark 6) for
approximately 15 minutes or until well
risen and golden.

Meanwhile, make the filling: melt the
butter in a pan, add the mushrooms and
cook gently for 2 minutes until the
juices flow. Stir in the flour and cook for
a further 1 to 2 minutes, stirring constantly. Remove the pan from the heat
and gradually add the hot milk, stirring
vigorously with a wooden spoon.
Return the pan to the heat and bring
slowly to the boil, stirring constantly.
Lower the heat and simmer gently until
the sauce thickens. Remove from the
heat and leave to cool for 1 to 2 minutes,
then stir in the double cream, mace and
salt and pepper to taste. Fold in the
chicken meat, return the pan to a very
low heat and cook gently until hot.

Taste and adjust for seasoning.
Remove the pastry cases from the oven,
leave to cool slightly, then remove the
tops with a sharp knife and reserve.

Scoop out any soft pastry with a teaspoon, spoon the filling into each vol-
au-vent and replace reserved tops. Garnish each vol-au-vent with a small sprig
of parsley, transfer to a warmed serving
platter and serve immediately.
Makes 40

Chicken Mayonnaise

1 × 2 kg (4 lb) roasting chicken
1 garlic clove, peeled and cut in half
50 g (2 oz) butter, melted
1 teaspoon dried tarragon
salt and freshly ground black pepper
150 ml (¼ pint) dry white wine
150 ml (¼ pint) thick homemade
  mayonnaise (p. 42)
150 ml (¼ pint) double cream
3 tablespoons sweet mango chutney
2 red dessert apples
1 green dessert apple
1 tablespoon lemon juice
100 g (4 oz) blanched almonds,
  roughly chopped
4 large oranges, peeled and sliced into
  rings, pith and pips removed

Remove the skin from the chicken, rub
the flesh with the garlic, then place
garlic inside the bird. Brush the bird
with butter, sprinkle with tarragon and
season liberally. Put the chicken on its
side in a roasting tin, pour in the wine
and roast in a fairly hot oven (190°C,
375°F, Gas Mark 5) for approximately 1½
hours or until the chicken is tender,
turning it over on to its other side and
its back during the cooking time and
basting occasionally. When the chicken
is cooked, remove from the oven and
leave to cool, then carve into small neat
slices or strips.

Put the chicken in a large mixing
bowl and fold in the mayonnaise, half
the cream and the chutney. Core the
apples, slice thinly into bite-sized pieces
and sprinkle with the lemon juice to
prevent discoloration. Mix into the
chicken and mayonnaise mixture with

half the almonds. Fold gently until all the chicken and apple pieces are coated lightly in the mayonnaise, then taste and adjust seasoning.

Arrange the pilaf on a large serving platter, place the orange slices in a single layer in the centre of the rice and spoon the chicken mayonnaise on to the oranges, leaving a border of oranges around the chicken. Trickle the remaining cream in a line down the centre of the chicken and scatter the remaining almonds on top.
Serves 10

Chicken, Ham and Mushroom Pie

1 knob of butter
100 g (4 oz) button mushrooms, sliced
1 × 300 ml ($\frac{1}{2}$ pint) packet parsley sauce mix
300 ml ($\frac{1}{2}$ pint) milk
2 roasted chicken quarters, skinned, boned and cut into small chunks
1 × 100 g (4 oz) piece boiled ham, fat removed and cut into small chunks
freshly ground black pepper
1 × 225 g (8 oz) packet frozen puff pastry, thawed
1 small egg, beaten

Melt the butter in a pan, add the mushrooms and fry over gentle heat for 5 minutes. Combine the parsley sauce mix and the milk according to packet directions, then add to the pan. Bring to the boil and cook until the sauce thickens, stirring constantly. Stir in the chicken and ham, and pepper to taste, then cook gently for 10 minutes, stirring occasionally. Meanwhile, preheat the oven at high temperature for 5 minutes.

Spoon the filling into a deep ovenproof pie dish. Roll out the pastry for the lid, moisten the rim of the dish and place the pastry over the filling. Seal the edges and brush all over the pastry with the egg. Make a small hole in the

centre for the steam to escape and use any trimmings for decoration. Bake in the centre of the oven for about 25 minutes, turning the dish round half way through cooking. Cover the pastry with foil if it is becoming too brown. Leave to stand for 5 minutes before serving with seasonal vegetables or a fresh salad.

Chicken Parcels

1 large knob of butter
4 boned chicken breasts, skinned
1 × 400 g (14 oz) packet frozen puff pastry, thawed
salt
freshly ground black pepper
50 g (2 oz) liver sausage
1 small egg, beaten

Melt the butter in a frying pan, add the chicken and fry for 20 minutes, turning occasionally. Remove from the pan and leave until cool enough to handle.

Meanwhile, roll out the pastry thinly and cut into 4 squares large enough to wrap up a chicken piece in. Sprinkle the chicken pieces with salt and pepper. Spread the liver sausage on top of each piece, then place the chicken on the squares of pastry, with the liver sausage downwards. Wrap the pastry around the chicken to enclose it completely, then place in a roasting tin with the joins underneath.

Preheat the oven at high temperature for 5 minutes. Brush all over the pastry with the egg, then bake in the centre of the oven for 15 minutes or until golden brown. Serve hot with seasonal vegetables and gravy, or cold with a selection of salads.

Variations:
Substitute chutney, mustard or chopped cooked mushrooms for the liver sausage.

Normandy Chicken with Apple and Cider

1 oven-ready chicken, about 1½ kg (3½ lb)
chicken giblets
1 bay leaf
1 sprig parsley
8 peppercorns
½ teaspoon salt
approx. 50 g (2 oz) flour
50 g (2 oz) unsalted butter or lard
1 large onion, peeled and sliced
1–2 stalks celery, washed and chopped
1 large or 2 small cooking apples, peeled and chopped
150 ml (¼ pint) dry cider
4 tablespoons double cream
salt
freshly ground pepper
To garnish:
1 dessert apple
25 g (1 oz) butter
celery leaves

Joint the chicken. Skin the joints by holding the narrow end firmly with the left hand and drawing the skin upwards and off with the right hand. Use a damp cloth to hold both the joint and the skin as both are greasy and tend to slip. Put the skin, carcass, giblets, herbs and peppercorns and salt in a saucepan, cover with cold water and make Giblet stock (see p. 7).

Coat the chicken joints with flour; pat off surplus and reserve it. Heat the butter or lard in a flameproof casserole and fry the joints until golden brown all over, then remove them from the casserole. Gently fry the onion and celery until they are softened. Add the apple and cook for 5 minutes.

Draw the casserole off the heat, stir in sufficient flour (about 3 tablespoons) to absorb the fat. Gradually stir in the cider and 300 ml (½ pint) strained giblet stock. Bring to the simmer, replace the chicken joints in the casserole and add more giblet stock if necessary to cover the chicken. Put the lid on the casserole and cook over gentle heat for 30 minutes or until the chicken legs are tender. Remove the chicken and boil the sauce briskly without a lid until it has thickened slightly. Mix 3 tablespoons of the sauce into the cream and stir the mixture into the casserole. Taste and adjust the seasoning. Replace the chicken.

Core the unpeeled dessert apple and cut it into rings. Fry the rings in the butter until golden brown on each side and arrange them on top of the chicken with little tufts of fresh celery leaves. Serve with boiled or creamed potatoes and buttered peas, green beans or broccoli.

Farmer's Style Noodles

2 tablespoons vegetable oil
1 large onion, peeled and finely chopped
100 g (4 oz) button mushrooms, wiped and chopped
1 × 400 g (14 oz) can tomatoes
1 tablespoon tomato purée
1 clove of garlic, crushed
1 teaspoon dried rosemary
salt and freshly ground black pepper
100 g (4 oz) cooked boned chicken, or other meat, chopped
100 g (4 oz) ham, chopped
350 g (12 oz) noodles

Heat the oil in a saucepan. Add the chopped onion and fry gently for 5 minutes. Add the chopped mushrooms and cook for a further few minutes. Add the canned tomatoes and their juice, tomato purée, crushed garlic, rosemary, and seasoning to taste. Bring to the boil and simmer for 20 minutes. Add the chopped chicken and ham and reheat.

Meanwhile, cook the noodles in a pan of rapidly boiling salted water. Drain the noodles thoroughly, place on a serving dish and spoon over the chicken and ham sauce. For easy eating serve in deep soup bowls.

Chicken Paprikash

1 large knob of butter
1 onion, peeled and finely chopped
1–2 teaspoons paprika pepper
1 tablespoon flour
4 chicken portions, skinned
4 large tomatoes, quartered
150 ml ($\frac{1}{4}$ pint) water
1 chicken stock cube
pinch of sugar
salt
freshly ground black pepper
1 × 150 ml ($\frac{1}{4}$ pint) carton soured
    cream or plain unsweetened yogurt,
    to finish

Melt the butter in a large frying pan,
add the onion and paprika and fry over
gentle heat for 5 minutes, stirring occasionally. Push the onions to one side.
Sprinkle the flour over the chicken, add
to the pan and fry until browned on both
sides. Add the tomatoes and water,
bring to the boil, add the stock cube and
stir to dissolve. Add the sugar and salt
and pepper to taste. Cover and cook
over low heat for 20 minutes on each
side, spooning the sauce over the chick-
en occasionally.

Remove the chicken from the pan, stir
in the soured cream or yogurt. Heat
through gently, stirring constantly.
Taste and adjust seasoning and pour
over the chicken. Serve with boiled rice
or noodles and a seasonal green vegetable or a tossed salad.

Oven-baked Pilaf

350 g (12 oz) boneless raw chicken,
    finely diced
600 ml (1 pint) chicken stock
25 g (1 oz) butter
1 tablespoon vegetable oil
25 g (1 oz) flaked almonds
1 tablespoon pine nuts (optional)
225 g (8 oz) long-grain rice
$\frac{1}{2}$ teaspoon ground ginger
$\frac{1}{4}$ teaspoon ground cinnamon
salt and freshly ground black pepper
2 bay leaves

Place the chicken meat in a saucepan
and pour over the chicken stock. Bring
to the boil, reduce the heat, cover and
simmer for 5 minutes. Heat the butter
and oil in a clean saucepan and use to
fry the flaked almonds and pine nuts,
then the rice, stirring until the rice is
transparent. Sprinkle in the ground
ginger and cinnamon and stir for 1
minute. Add the strained stock from
cooking the chicken and bring to the
boil. Remove from the heat, then stir in
chicken meat, season, and pour the
mixture into a greased, shallow casserole. Lay the bay leaves on top.

Cover and cook in a fairly hot oven
(190°C, 375°F, Gas Mark 5) for 35 minutes, or until all the liquid is absorbed.
Remove the bay leaves and fork round
lightly before serving.

Sweet and Sour Chicken

1 large knob of butter
4 boned chicken breasts, skinned and
    thinly sliced
1 × 225 g (8 oz) can sliced pineapple
1 green pepper, cored, seeded and
    finely chopped
1 tablespoon brown sugar
1 tablespoon vinegar
2 tablespoons soy sauce
1 tablespoon cornflour
100 g (4 oz) button mushrooms, sliced
    if large
salt
freshly ground black pepper

Melt the butter in a large frying pan,
add the chicken and fry over brisk heat
until lightly coloured. Drain the pineapple and make up the juice to 220 ml (7
fl oz) with water. Chop the pineapple
slices roughly. Stir the green pepper,
sugar, vinegar and soy sauce into the
pineapple juice and add to the pan.
Bring to the boil, stirring constantly,
lower the heat, cover with foil and
simmer for 15 to 20 minutes until the
chicken is tender.

Mix the cornflour to a paste with a
little water. Add to the pan and stir in
well, then cook until the sauce thickens, stirring constantly. Add the chopped pineapple and the mushrooms and
heat through for 5 minutes, stirring
occasionally to prevent the sauce from
sticking. Taste and adjust seasoning.
Serve hot with freshly boiled noodles.

† Chicken with
Tarragon Cream Sauce

300 ml (½ pint) white stock
150 ml (¼ pint) dry white wine
4 chicken breast portions, skinned
salt
freshly ground black pepper
1 teaspoon chopped tarragon or ½
    teaspoon dried

To garnish:
beurre manié made with 40 g (1½ oz)
    butter mixed with 1½ tablespoons
    flour (p. 352)
150 ml (¼ pint) single cream
a little chopped fresh tarragon to
    garnish, if available

Put the stock and wine into the cooker.
Add the chicken with a little salt and
pepper and the tarragon. Close the
cooker, bring to H pressure and cook for
5 minutes. Reduce the pressure quickly.
Lift out the chicken to a warmed serving dish, keep hot. Return the open
cooker to the heat, add the beurre
manié in small pieces, stirring constantly. Simmer until the sauce thickens. Taste and adjust seasoning as
necessary. Remove the cooker from the
heat, stir in the cream and pour the
sauce over the chicken pieces. Sprinkle
over chopped fresh tarragon, if
available.

Tandoori Chicken

2 × 5 cm (2 in) pieces fresh root
    ginger, peeled and chopped
3 garlic cloves, peeled and chopped
3 black peppercorns
2 teaspoons chilli powder
2 teaspoons ground coriander seeds
1 teaspoon ground cumin seeds
½ teaspoon salt
finely grated rind and juice of 1
    lemon
1–2 drops of bright red food colouring
10 chicken breasts or drumsticks,
    skinned
10 tablespoons natural yogurt
To garnish:
1–2 lettuces, washed and separated
    into leaves
3 tomatoes, quartered
1 cucumber, sliced
salt and freshly ground black pepper

Pound the root ginger, garlic and peppercorns in a pestle and mortar. Mix

with the chilli powder, ground coriander and cumin, salt, lemon rind and juice and food colouring. Score the chicken flesh with the point of a very sharp knife, then rub the pounded mixture into the skin. Brush each chicken portion with 1 tablespoon yogurt, then chill in the refrigerator for 24 hours. Let stand at room temperature for 1 to 2 hours before cooking.

When the barbecue charcoals are hot, place the chicken on the grid and cook for approximately 20 minutes until the outside of the chicken is charred and the meat is cooked through, turning the portions frequently.

Arrange lettuce leaves, tomato quarters and slices of cucumber on a serving platter and sprinkle liberally with salt and pepper. Place tandoori chicken on top of salad; serve immediately with yogurt handed separately.
Serves 10

Chicken Tetrazzini

1 large knob of butter
1 onion, peeled and finely chopped
4 chicken portions, skinned
2 tablespoons flour
1 × 400 g (14 oz) can tomatoes
450 ml ($\frac{3}{4}$ pint) water
1 chicken stock cube
4 medium carrots, peeled and very finely sliced
$\frac{1}{2}$ teaspoon dried tarragon
salt
freshly ground black pepper
300 ml ($\frac{1}{2}$ pint) finely broken spaghetti
To garnish:
175 g (6 oz) mushrooms, sliced
Parmesan cheese, grated

Melt the butter in a large saucepan, add the onion and fry over gentle heat until soft. Add the chicken, sprinkle over the flour, then fry until browned on both sides. Stir in the tomatoes and water. Bring to the boil, stirring constantly, add the stock cube and stir to dissolve.

Add the carrots, tarragon and salt and pepper to taste, then cover and simmer for 25 minutes, stirring occasionally. Add the spaghetti and simmer for a further 15 minutes, then add the mushrooms. Stir well to mix, simmer for a further 5 minutes or until the chicken is cooked and the spaghetti is tender.

Taste and adjust seasoning. Serve immediately with a tossed green salad and the Parmesan handed separately.

† Braised Fowl

1 thick slice unsmoked bacon, rinded and chopped
25 g (1 oz) butter or margarine (optional)
2 onions, peeled and sliced
2 carrots, scraped and sliced
3 celery stalks, scrubbed and chopped
1 boiling fowl, jointed and skinned (if liked)
450 ml ($\frac{3}{4}$ pint) hot brown stock or water and $\frac{1}{2}$ chicken stock cube
1 tablespoon tomato purée
salt
freshly ground black pepper
1 bouquet garni
grilled bacon rolls, to garnish

Heat the cooker gently. Heat the bacon rind gently to release the fat. Add the bacon to the cooker and fry until beginning to colour. If necessary add the butter or margarine to the cooker and sauté the vegetables. Lift them out and drain well, discard the bacon rind. Brown the pieces of fowl well on both sides. Lift out the fowl and drain off the excess fat. Add the stock and tomato purée to the cooker, stir well. Replace the vegetables and bacon. Put the pieces of fowl on top. Add salt and pepper and the bouquet garni. Close the cooker, bring to H pressure and cook for 15 minutes. Reduce the pressure quickly. Discard the bouquet garni. Skim off any excess fat. Taste and adjust seasoning. Garnish with bacon rolls.

† Coq au Vin

2 tablespoons cooking oil
25 g (1 oz) butter
4 rashers unsmoked streaky bacon,
    rinded and chopped
12 pickling onions, peeled
100 g (4 oz) button mushrooms,
    cleaned
4 chicken portions or quarters,
    skinned
2 tablespoons brandy
300 ml (½ pint) red wine (Burgundy-
    type)
150 ml (¼ pint) white stock or water
    and ½ chicken stock cube
1 garlic clove, crushed
1 bouquet garni
salt
freshly ground black pepper
To garnish:
beurre manié made with 25 g (1 oz)
    butter mixed with 2 tablespoons
    flour (p. 352)

Heat the oil and butter in the cooker.
Fry the bacon, onions and mushrooms
until just beginning to colour. Lift out
and drain well. Add the chicken and
brown on both sides.

Warm the brandy gently in a small
saucepan, pour over the chicken and set
alight. When the flames have died down
return the bacon, onions and mushrooms to the cooker together with the
wine, stock or water and stock cube,
garlic, bouquet garni, salt and pepper.
Stir well to remove any residues from
the base of the cooker. Close the cooker,
bring to H pressure and cook for 6
minutes.

Reduce the pressure quickly. Lift out
the chicken and vegetables and keep
hot. Remove the bouquet garni. Return
the open cooker to the heat. Add the
beurre manié in small pieces, stirring
constantly, simmer until the sauce thickens. Taste and adjust the seasoning as
necessary and serve the sauce poured
over the chicken and accompany with
new potatoes and green peas.

Roast Duck

1 oven ready duck (about 1¾ kg (4 lb)
    for four people)

Ducks have a layer of fat beneath the
skin of the breast so they do not need
covering with bacon or protecting with
greaseproof paper or foil. To make the
skin crisp, prick the breast all over
about 20 minutes before the end of the
cooking time. This allows the extra fat
to escape into the pan. Fatty birds are
best cooked on a grid in the roasting
pan with the surplus fat syphoned off
from the base of the pan during cooking.
Cook for about 20 minutes per 450 g/
1 lb at 200°C, 400°F, Gas Mark 6. Make
gravy as for turkey (p. 109).

Serve with Apple sauce (p. 350) or
roast apples, if liked.

Caneton aux Cerises

1 duck (about 2 kg (4 lb)), with the
    giblets
25 g (1 oz) butter, softened
salt and freshly ground black pepper
For the cherry sauce:
25 g (1 oz) butter
1 × 240 g (8½ oz) can red cherries,
    drained, stoned and chopped
2 tablespoons brandy (optional)
2 tablespoons redcurrant jelly
finely grated rind and juice of 1
    orange
150 ml (¼ pint) duck stock (made with
    the giblets)
1½ teaspoons arrowroot
1 tablespoon water
To garnish:
1 bunch of watercress
potato crisps

Wash the duck and dry thoroughly with
a clean tea-towel or absorbent kitchen
paper. Brush the duck with the butter
and sprinkle liberally with salt and
pepper. Prick all over with a fork and

place on a rack in a roasting tin. Roast in a fairly hot oven (200°C, 400°F, Gas Mark 6) for 1½–2 hours, turning over occasionally.

Meanwhile, make the cherry sauce: melt the butter in a small pan, add the cherries and heat through. Pour in the brandy, if using, and set alight. Stir in the redcurrant jelly and orange rind and juice, then pour in the stock. Season to taste with salt and pepper. Blend the arrowroot and water together, then stir into the pan. Bring slowly to the boil, stirring constantly, then lower the heat to simmer gently for a few minutes until the sauce thickens. Taste and adjust seasoning.

Transfer the roasted duck to a carving dish and garnish with sprigs of watercress and a few potato crisps. Serve the cherry sauce separately in a sauce boat.

Serves 2

† Boiling Fowl with Parsley Sauce

1 boiling fowl, jointed if very large
cold water
a few black peppercorns
1 small onion, peeled and quartered
1 bay leaf
bunch of mixed fresh herbs
For the sauce:
25 g (1 oz) butter or margarine
25 g (1 oz) flour
150 ml (¼ pint) milk
1 tablespoon finely chopped fresh
  parsley
salt
white pepper
finely chopped parsley, to garnish

Weigh the fowl to calculate the cooking time and wash and dry thoroughly. Truss with string for ease of handling. Put the fowl into the cooker, without the trivet, and add the water to half fill the cooker. Bring to the boil and skim well. Place the peppercorns in a bag and crush lightly with a rolling pin. Add the onion, herbs and crushed peppercorns. Close the cooker, bring to H pressure and then cook for the calculated time (approx. 12 minutes per 450 g/1 lb). Reduce the pressure quickly. Lift out the fowl, drain well and remove the string. Cut the fowl into serving portions, place on a warmed dish and keep hot. Strain the liquid, reserve 300 ml (½ pint) and rinse and dry the cooker.

Melt the butter or margarine in the cooker, add the flour and cook gently for 1 minute, stirring well. Remove from the heat and gradually stir in the reserved cooking liquid and the milk. Return to the heat and bring to the boil, stirring constantly. Add the parsley and salt and pepper to taste. Pour over the fowl and garnish with chopped parsley. Serve with plain boiled rice or buttered boiled potatoes.

Guinea Fowl in Red Wine

50 g (2 oz) butter
1 × 1½ kg (3 lb) guinea fowl, jointed
100 g (4 oz) unsmoked streaky bacon
  rashers, rinds removed, finely diced
2 large onions, peeled and finely diced
40 g (1½ oz) plain flour
600 ml (1 pint) dry red wine
300 ml (½ pint) game or chicken stock
100 g (4 oz) mushrooms, sliced
1 teaspoon dried tarragon
salt
pepper

Melt the butter in a flameproof casserole. Add the guinea fowl and bacon and fry until lightly coloured. Add the onions. Sprinkle over the flour and cook, stirring, for 1 minute. Stir in the red wine and stock. Add the mushrooms, tarragon and salt and pepper to taste. Cover and simmer for about 1 hour or until tender.

* Casserole of Guinea Fowl

Follow the recipe for Guinea Fowl in Red Wine (p. 107), with these changes: add 2 crushed garlic cloves and fry with the guinea fowl. Substitute 600 ml (1 pint) game or chicken stock for the wine as a more economical dish.

Roast Guinea Fowl

1 × 1½ kg (3 lb) guinea fowl
3 streaky bacon rashers
50 g (2 oz) butter
salt
pepper

Truss the bird and tie the bacon over the breast. Melt the butter in a roasting tin and brown the bird on all sides. Season with salt and pepper and roast in a preheated moderately hot oven (200°C, 400°F, Gas Mark 6) for about 1 hour, basting frequently.

Roast Grouse

4 streaky bacon rashers
2 large young grouse
50 g (2 oz) butter
100 ml (3 fl oz) red wine
4 thick slices of toast
watercress, to garnish

Tie the bacon slices onto the breasts of the grouse and truss the birds, leaving the feet on. Melt the butter in a roasting tin and fry the birds until they have a good colour. Transfer to a preheated moderately hot oven (200°C, 400°F, Gas Mark 6) and roast for 30 to 45 minutes, depending on size.

Ten minutes before they are cooked, baste them with wine. When cooked transfer to a warmed dish and serve on the toast with pan juices poured over, garnished with watercress.

Casserole of Grouse

50 g (2 oz) butter
2 old grouse, jointed
100 g (4 oz) gammon, diced
4 onions, peeled and chopped
40 g (1½ oz) plain flour
200 ml (⅓ pint) dry red wine
300 ml (½ pint) game or chicken stock
10 mushrooms, sliced
salt
pepper
1 bay leaf

Melt the butter in a flameproof casserole and fry the grouse, gammon and onions until lightly browned.— Sprinkle over the flour and cook, stirring, for 1 minute. Stir in the wine and stock. Bring to the boil. Add the mushrooms, salt and pepper to taste and the bay leaf. Cover and simmer for about 2 hours or until tender. Remove the bay leaf before serving.

Roast Goose

1 × 4 kg (9 lb) goose, trussed and
    cleaned, with giblets
2 tablespoons clear honey
salt and freshly ground black pepper

The traditional stuffing for Christmas Roast Goose is sage and onion (p. 347), but sausagemeat and apple (p. 349) makes an unusual alternative. Choose one or the other, or stuff the goose with sausagemeat and apple, then form the sage and onion into small balls, coat in flour and shallow fry until crisp. Arrange around the goose when serving. Spoon the chosen stuffing into the cavity of the goose, then sew up both openings with trussing string. Secure with skewers if necessary. Place the goose on a rack in a roasting pan, brush with the honey and sprinkle liberally with salt and pepper. Roast in a fairly hot oven (200°C, 400°F, Gas Mark 6) for

30 minutes to brown the skin, and cover the bird with foil, reduce the heat to moderate (180°C, 350°F, Gas Mark 4) and roast for another 2½ to 3 hours or until the juices run clear when the goose is pierced with a skewer. Baste and turn the bird frequently during cooking, and pour off excess fat. Remove the bird from the oven and discard strings and skewers, if used. Transfer to a warmed serving platter and serve with roast potatoes, seasonal vegetables and a well-flavoured giblet gravy made with the pan juices.
Serves 6

Roast Turkey

1 oven-ready turkey (about 5–6 kg (10–12 lb), with the giblets
50 g (2 oz) butter, softened
salt and freshly ground black pepper

Stuff with sausagemeat and herbs (p. 349) and bacon and corn (p. 349). If only one stuffing is liked, then double the quantity given and use in both neck and body cavities. Any leftover mixture can be formed into small balls, rolled in flour and fried until crisp, then arranged around the bird on the serving platter.

Wash the turkey inside and out and dry thoroughly. Spoon the prepared stuffings into the bird – sausagemeat and herb in the body cavity, bacon and corn in the neck end. Sew both openings with trussing string and secure with skewers if necessary. Brush all over the turkey with softened butter and sprinkle liberally with salt and pepper. Cover with greased greaseproof paper or foil and place on a rack in a roasting pan. Roast in a warm oven (170°C, 325°F, Gas Mark 3) for 3¾ to 4 hours, basting and turning occasionally. Remove the greaseproof or foil 15 minutes before the end of cooking time if a crisp brown skin is liked. To test if done: pierce the thickest part of the thigh with a skewer – the juices should run clear, not pink. Transfer the turkey to a warmed serving platter and remove strings, and skewers if used. Serve with gravy made from the giblets and cooking juices from the bird, jacket baked or roast potatoes, chipolata sausages and a selection of seasonal vegetables.
Serves 10 to 12

Farmhouse Turkey Mould

2 pig's trotters
salt and freshly ground black pepper
4 portions boiling fowl or 2 turkey legs
225 g (8 oz) onions, peeled and chopped
1 teaspoon dried sage

To pickle the pig's trotters, coat them in salt, place in a small basin, sprinkle with more salt and cover the basin. Refrigerate for 2 days.

Wash off all the salt, and place the trotters in a large saucepan with the portions of boiling fowl or the turkey legs, jointed to make 4 portions. Cover with cold water, season with salt and pepper, bring to the boil and skim carefully. Simmer, covered, for 2½ hours or until the meat is tender. Allow to cool.

Remove the trotters and poultry portions on to a clean enamel tray with a slotted draining spoon. Strip the meat from the bones and chop it roughly, discarding the bones and pieces of gristle. Pack the chopped meat into a pudding basin.

Bring the stock to the boil again, add the chopped onion and dried sage, and cook at a fast boil until the onion is tender and the stock reduced by about half. Strain, taste and adjust the seasoning if necessary. Pour just sufficient stock into the basin to cover the meat. Allow to cool and refrigerate overnight.

Turn out on to a serving dish, cut into wedges and surround with salad greens and radish roses.

Turkey Loaf

750 g (1½ lb) cooked turkey meat,
    finely minced
450 g (1 lb) beef sausagemeat
1 onion, peeled and minced
225 g (8 oz) fat bacon, rind removed,
    minced
1 garlic clove, minced
1 tablespoon tomato purée
1 tablespoon dried tarragon
salt
pepper
turkey or chicken stock, to moisten
2 bay leaves

Mix together the turkey meat, sausagemeat, onion, bacon, garlic, tomato
purée and tarragon with salt and pepper
to taste and enough stock to moisten.
Turn into a greased terrine and put the
bay leaves on top. Cover and bake in a
preheated moderate oven (180°C, 350°F,
Gas Mark 4) for 2 hours. Cool under a
weight.

* Turkey Galantine

Follow the recipe for Turkey Loaf
(above) to make the turkey mixture.
Then make the following changes: roll
in a floured cloth and tie the ends.
Poach in simmering water for 2½ hours.
Cool under a weighted plate, and then
chill in the refrigerator for several
hours before slicing to serve.

Turkey Mousse

1 × 70 g (2½ oz) packet aspic jelly
    powder
600 ml (1 pint) turkey or chicken
    stock
225 g (8 oz) cooked boned turkey
    breast, finely diced
1 tablespoon tomato purée
1 teaspoon dried tarragon

2 egg yolks
250 ml (8 fl oz) double cream
100 ml (3 fl oz) brandy
salt
pepper
To garnish:
lettuce leaves
1 chicory, separated into leaves
orange wedges

Make up the aspic with the stock,
according to the directions on the
packet. Cool. Put all the ingredients
into a blender and blend until smooth.
Season with salt and pepper to taste.
Turn into a 1.2 litre (2 pint) capacity
mould and chill until set.

   Line a serving plate with lettuce
leaves and chicory and turn out the
mousse onto it. Garnish with orange
wedges.

Turkey Plait

25 g (1 oz) butter
1 onion, peeled and sliced
75 g (3 oz) button mushrooms, wiped
    and sliced
225 g (8 oz) cooked turkey, boned and
    diced
175 g (6 oz) Gouda cheese, grated
1 small red pepper, deseeded and
    sliced
½ level teaspoon dried mixed herbs
salt and freshly ground black pepper
1 egg, beaten
225 g (8 oz) frozen puff pastry,
    defrosted

Melt the butter in a saucepan and cook
the sliced onion and mushrooms over
moderate heat for 5 minutes, stirring
occasionally. Stir in the diced turkey,
grated cheese, sliced red pepper and
mixed herbs. Season to taste and stir in
most of the beaten egg, reserving a little
for glazing the pastry.

   Roll out the pastry to an oblong
34 × 30 cm (14 × 12 inches). Spoon the
filling down the middle of the pastry,

leaving a wide margin all round. Using a sharp knife cut parallel slits about 1 cm (½ inch) wide, down each side of the oblong. Fold up the top and bottom of the oblong on to the filling. Plait the strips over the filling. Transfer on to a damp baking sheet.

Brush the turkey plait with the remainder of the beaten egg. Cook for 20 minutes in a hot oven (220°C, 425°F, Gas Mark 7) and then reduce heat to fairly hot (190°C, 375°F, Gas Mark 5) for a further 10 minutes.

Serve hot or cold with a green salad.

Rabbit in Mustard Sauce

4 rabbit joints
4 tablespoons French mustard
4 tablespoons seasoned flour for coating
50 g (2 oz) butter
50 g (2 oz) salt pork, rind removed and diced
1 medium-sized onion, peeled and chopped
1 clove of garlic, crushed
300 ml (½ pint) milk
salt and freshly ground black pepper
To garnish:
parsley sprigs
8 large bread croûtons, fried in butter

On the day before you wish to serve the meal soak the rabbit joints for 2 hours in lightly salted water. Remove them and dry them well with absorbent kitchen paper. Coat the joints on all sides with the mustard and leave, covered, in the refrigerator overnight.

Coat the joints with the seasoned flour. Melt the butter in a flameproof casserole. Brown the joints on all sides, then add the diced salt pork, chopped onion and crushed garlic. Cover and cook for another 20 minutes, stirring occasionally. Then add the milk and seasoning and stir. Transfer the casserole to a warm oven (160°C, 325°F, Gas Mark 3) and cook for another 45

minutes. Taste and adjust seasoning.

Place the rabbit joints on a heated serving dish, cover with the sauce from the casserole and garnish with parsley sprigs and the fried bread croûtons.

Roast Partridges

4 streaky bacon rashers
4 young partridges
50 g (2 oz) butter
120 ml (4 fl oz) dry red wine
salt
pepper
4 thick slices of toast
watercress, to garnish

Tie the bacon slices across the breasts of the partridges. Truss the birds, leaving the feet on. Melt the butter in a roasting tin and brown the birds on all sides. Transfer to a preheated moderately hot oven (200°C, 400°F, Gas Mark 6) and roast for 30 to 40 minutes.

After 20 minutes, baste with the wine and season with salt and pepper. Continue to baste at intervals. Serve on the toast with the tin juices poured over, garnished with watercress.

Spatchcocked Partridges

4 young partridges
50 g (2 oz) butter, melted
salt
pepper
watercress, to garnish

With a sharp knife, cut through the partridges from the back, not quite severing them. Open them out and press to flatten them, fixing them open with a skewer through each. Brush with melted butter, season with salt and pepper, and cook under a preheated medium grill until brown and tender. Baste with more butter while cooking. Serve garnished with watercress.

Partridges in Piquant Sauce

4 small partridges, plucked and drawn
50 g (2 oz) lard
3 medium-sized onions, peeled and
  sliced
2 stalks of celery, scrubbed and
  chopped
1 cooking apple, peeled, cored and
  roughly chopped
2 tablespoons flour
300 ml ($\frac{1}{2}$ pint) chicken stock
2 tablespoons Worcestershire sauce
50 g (2 oz) seedless raisins
salt and freshly ground black pepper
150 ml ($\frac{1}{4}$ pint) unsweetened natural
  yogurt
pastry fleurons, to finish

Wash the partridges and dry well with
absorbent kitchen paper. Melt the lard
in a heavy pan and lightly brown the
partridges on all sides. Remove them
from the pan and place in a casserole.
Cook the onion gently in the remaining
fat in the pan for 5 minutes or until limp,
then add the chopped celery and the
apple. Stir in the flour and cook for
another 2 minutes. Gradually add the
stock and the Worcestershire sauce,
bring to the boil and add the raisins.
Add seasoning to taste.

Pour the sauce over the partridges,
cover lightly with foil and cook in a
moderate oven (180°C, 350°F, Gas Mark
4) for 1$\frac{1}{2}$ hours, or until the partridges
are tender. Remove them and place on a
warm serving dish together with the
onions, celery, apples and raisins
strained from the sauce. Taste the
sauce, and adjust the seasoning if
necessary. Stir in the yogurt and reheat
without boiling. Pour a little of the
sauce over the partridges, surround
them with the fleurons and serve the
rest of the sauce separately in a
sauceboat.

To make the fleurons: Defrost and roll
out a small piece of frozen puff pastry
thinly and cut out circles with a small
biscuit cutter. Using the same cutter,
make crescent shapes and ovals from
the circles. Bake on a dampened baking
sheet in a hot oven (220°C, 425°F, Gas
Mark 7) for 10 to 12 minutes or until
golden-brown, raising the oven temperature immediately after removing the
partridges.

Roast Pigeon

4 young pigeons
4 streaky bacon rashers
100 g (4 oz) butter
salt
pepper
4 tablespoons port wine or sherry

Truss the birds, and tie a rasher of
bacon over each breast. Melt the butter
in a roasting tin. Add the birds and
brown lightly on all sides. Season with
salt and pepper and roast in a preheated
hot oven (220°C, 425°F, Gas Mark 7) for
30 minutes, basting from time to time.
At the last basting pour over the port or
sherry. Serve the birds with the juices
from the tin poured over.

Casserole of Pigeon

40 g (1$\frac{1}{2}$ oz) butter
2 large pigeons, halved
100 g (4 oz) streaky bacon rashers,
  rinds removed, finely diced
2 onions, peeled and chopped
1 garlic clove, crushed
40 g (1$\frac{1}{2}$ oz) plain flour
300 ml ($\frac{1}{2}$ pint) game or chicken stock
150 ml ($\frac{1}{4}$ pint) dry red wine
100 g (4 oz) mushrooms, sliced
1 bay leaf
salt
pepper
4 thick slices of toast

Melt the butter in a flameproof
casserole. Add the pigeon halves,
bacon, onions and garlic and fry until

well coloured. Sprinkle over the flour. Mix in well, then stir in the stock and wine. Add mushrooms, bay leaf, salt and the pepper to taste. Bring to the boil, cover and simmer for about $1\frac{1}{2}$ hours or until tender.

Remove the bay leaf and adjust the seasoning. Serve on thick slices of toast, with the sauce poured over.

Pigeons Braised with Cabbage

2 tablespoons chicken fat, or butter
2 large pigeons, split
2 thick slices streaky bacon, rinds
   removed and chopped
2 large carrots, peeled and diced
1 large onion, peeled and chopped
salt and freshly ground black pepper
1 medium-sized cabbage, about $\frac{3}{4}$–1 kg
   ($1\frac{1}{2}$–2 lb), trimmed and quartered
$\frac{1}{2}$ teaspoon ground bay leaves
1 chicken stock cube, crumbled
To garnish:
$\frac{1}{2}$ teaspoon grated lemon rind
1 tablespoon cornflour
2 tablespoons lemon juice

Heat the chicken fat or butter in a large, deep, flameproof casserole and sauté the pigeon halves in it, until lightly coloured on both sides. Remove and keep warm.

Fry the chopped bacon in the casserole until the fat begins to run, then add the diced carrot and chopped onion. Fry until just coloured, then return the pigeon halves to the casserole, breast side down, and season well. Surround with the cabbage quarters, add the ground bay leaves and the stock cube dissolved in 450 ml ($\frac{3}{4}$ pint) boiling water. Bring to the boil. Cover closely, and simmer for 2 to $2\frac{1}{2}$ hours or until the pigeons are tender. (Test with a fine skewer in the leg meat.)

Remove the vegetables and pigeon halves, breast side uppermost on to a warm serving dish with a slotted drain-

ing spoon. Add the grated lemon rind to the sauce. Boil for 1 to 2 minutes to reduce slightly.

Mix the cornflour with the lemon juice and stir into the sauce. Cook, stirring, over moderate heat for 3 minutes. Taste the sauce and adjust the seasoning if necessary. Spoon the sauce over the pigeon breasts. Serve with fluffy boiled rice or buttered noodles.

Pigeon Casserole with Grapes

25 g (1 oz) butter
1 tablespoon vegetable oil
2 pigeons, split
1 medium-sized onion, peeled and
   chopped
100 g (4 oz) button mushrooms, wiped
   and sliced
1 tablespoon flour
150 ml ($\frac{1}{4}$ pint) dry cider
150 ml ($\frac{1}{4}$ pint) strong chicken stock
salt and freshly ground black pepper
100 g (4 oz) seedless grapes
2 teaspoons cornflour
1 tablespoon water

Melt the butter and oil together in a large heavy saucepan or flameproof casserole. Brown the pigeons quickly in the fat on both sides. Remove from the pan. Add the chopped onion to the fat and cook gently, covered, for a few minutes until soft. Add the sliced mushrooms, and fry for 2 minutes. Stir in the flour, cook for 1 minute, then add the cider, stock, seasoning to taste, and bring to the boil.

Return the pigeon halves to the pan, skin side down, and sprinkle the grapes round them. Cover and simmer for $1\frac{1}{2}$ to 2 hours. Remove the pigeon halves and then place, skin side up, on a warm serving dish.

Moisten the cornflour with the water, stir into the sauce and bring back to the boil. Cook gently for 3 minutes then pour over the pigeons.

Casserole of Pigeon Ma Façon

50 g (2 oz) butter
2 large pigeons, halved
1 large onion, peeled and finely
  chopped
100 g (4 oz) bacon rashers, rinds
  removed, diced
1 garlic clove, crushed
40 g (1½ oz) plain flour
300 ml (½ pint) game or chicken stock
150 ml (¼ pint) unsweetened orange
  juice
1 tablespoon black treacle
1 tablespoon tomato purée
1 teaspoon angostura bitters
1 fresh thyme sprig
8 mushrooms, sliced
salt
pepper

Melt the butter in a flameproof
casserole. Add the pigeon halves, onion,
bacon and garlic and fry until lightly
coloured. Sprinkle with the flour and
cook, stirring, for 1 minute. Stir in the
stock, orange juice, treacle, tomato
purée, bitters, thyme, mushrooms and
salt and pepper to taste. Cover and
simmer for about 1 hour or until tender.

Pigeon and Steak Pie

50 g (2 oz) butter
2 large pigeons, jointed
225 g (8 oz) beef skirt, trimmed and
  finely diced
40 g (1½ oz) plain flour
450 ml (¾ pint) brown ale
1 tablespoon tomato purée
1 teaspoon dried tarragon
1 bay leaf
salt
pepper
1 teaspoon Worcestershire sauce
1 small onion, peeled and finely
  chopped
6 mushrooms, sliced

4 streaky bacon rashers, rinds
  removed, diced
225 g (8 oz) frozen puff pastry, thawed
1 egg, beaten

Melt the butter in a saucepan and add
the pigeon joints and beef. Fry until
lightly coloured. Sprinkle over the flour
and cook, stirring, for 1 minute. Stir in
the brown ale. Bring to the boil. Stir in
the tomato purée, tarragon, bay leaf,
salt and pepper to taste and the Worcestershire sauce. Cover and simmer for 2
hours or until tender. Remove the bay
leaf and allow to cool.
  When cold, turn the pigeon mixture
into a pie dish. Stir in the onion, mushrooms and bacon. Cover the dish with
puff pastry, make an air hole and use the
trimmings to decorate the top. Brush
with egg. Bake in a preheated moderately hot oven (200°C, 400°F, Gas
Mark 6) for about 40 minutes.

Pigeon Breasts à la Crème

4 young pigeons
2 onions, peeled and chopped
6 mushrooms, sliced
1 fresh thyme sprig
1 fresh tarragon sprig or ¼ teaspoon
  dried tarragon
150 ml (¼ pint) dry red wine
600 ml (1 pint) game or chicken stock
salt
pepper
250 ml (8 fl oz) double cream
8 slices of toast
parsley sprigs, to garnish

Cut the breasts from the pigeons and
put the carcasses into a saucepan. Add
the onions, mushrooms, herbs, wine and
stock and bring to the boil. Cover and
simmer for about 1 hour.
  Put the pigeon breasts into another
saucepan and strain over the stock
mixture. Poach for about 30 minutes or
until tender. Remove the breasts from
the pan and keep hot.

Reduce the cooking stock by brisk boiling to a scant 300 ml (½ pint). Add salt and pepper to taste and whisk in the cream. Arrange the birds on the toast and pour over the sauce. Garnish with parsley.

Roast Pheasant

2 streaky bacon rashers
1 × 1½ kg (3 lb) pheasant
50 g (2 oz) butter
salt
pepper
150 ml (¼ pint) dry red wine
watercress, to garnish

Tie the bacon across the breast of the pheasant. Truss the bird, leaving the feet on. Melt the butter in a roasting tin and fry the pheasant on all sides until a nice colour. Season with salt and pepper and roast in a preheated hot oven (220°C, 425°F, Gas Mark 7) for 1 hour 20 minutes. After 1 hour, baste with the wine.

To serve, take the legs off for two portions and carve two more from the breasts. Serve the pan juices as gravy. Garnish with watercress.

Faisan Normande

50 g (2 oz) butter
3 Bramley apples, peeled, cored and finely chopped
juice of ½ lemon
4 pheasant breasts
salt
pepper
3 tablespoons double cream
watercress, to garnish

Melt 25 g (1 oz) of the butter in a frying pan. Add the apples and lemon juice and fry gently until softened. Turn two-thirds of the apple into a casserole that will just accommodate the apples and

pheasant breasts.

Fry the breasts in the rest of the butter and put them on top of the apple. Add salt and pepper to taste and the remaining apple. By now the casserole should be well-filled. Sprinkle over the cream. Cover and cook in a preheated moderately hot oven (200°C, 400°F, Gas Mark 6) for 20 to 40 minutes or until tender. The apples and cream should form a delicious sauce. Serve garnished with watercress.

Use the pheasant legs to make a steak and pheasant pie (see below).

Steak and Pheasant Pie

50 g (2 oz) butter
3 onions, peeled and chopped
2 garlic cloves, crushed
4 pheasant legs, jointed into two pieces each
350 g (12 oz) beef skirt, trimmed and finely diced
40 g (1½ oz) plain flour
200 ml (⅓ pint) dry red wine
300 ml (½ pint) game or chicken stock
8 mushrooms, sliced
1 bay leaf
salt
pepper
225 g (8 oz) frozen puff pastry, thawed
1 egg, beaten

Melt the butter in a saucepan and fry the onions, garlic, pheasant and beef until lightly browned. Sprinkle over the flour and cook, stirring, for 1 minute. Stir in the wine and stock. Bring to the boil and add the mushrooms, bay leaf and salt and pepper to taste. Cover and simmer for 1½ hours or until the pheasant is tender. Remove the bay leaf.

Allow to cool, then turn into a pie dish. Cover with puff pastry, make an air hole and decorate the top with the pastry trimmings. Brush with beaten egg and bake in a preheated moderately hot oven (200°C, 400°F, Gas Mark 6) for 45 minutes.

BEEF

Traditional Roast Beef

prime joint of beef on bone, i.e.
   sirloin, ribs, aitchbone, 1¼–2¾ kg
   (2½–6 lb), or a prime joint of beef,
   boned and rolled, i.e. sirloin, ribs,
   topside
25–50 g (1–2 oz) dripping
salt and freshly ground black pepper
   (optional)
For the Yorkshire puddings:
50 g (2 oz) plain flour
pinch of salt
1 egg
150 ml (¼ pint) milk
a little dripping

Wipe the meat and trim if necessary.
Weigh and calculate the cooking time
required. For joints on the bone allow
20 minutes per 450 g (1 lb), plus 20
minutes over; for a boned and rolled
joint allow 25 minutes per 450 g (1 lb),
plus 25 minutes over; to give a medium
cooked joint. For rare-cooked meat cut
the cooking time by 5 minutes per 450 g
(1 lb), and for a very well cooked joint
add 5 minutes per 450 g (1 lb).

Place the joint in a roasting tin with
the thickest layer of fat upwards. Cover
with dripping and season lightly. Cook
in a hot oven (220°C, 425°F, Gas Mark
7), basting several times, and roast
potatoes alongside the joint. Serve with
Yorkshire puddings, horseradish sauce
and a thin gravy made using the pan
juices.

Beef can also be roasted in a moderately hot oven (190°C, 375°F, Gas
Mark 5), allowing 25 minutes per 450 g
(1 lb), plus 25 minutes over, for meat on
the bone; 30 minutes per 450 g (1 lb), plus
30 minutes over, for boned and rolled
joints; to give medium cooked meat.
Increase or decrease the times slightly
for well cooked or rare meat.

To make Yorkshire puddings, sieve
the flour with a pinch of salt into a bowl,
add the egg and gradually beat in the
milk to give a smooth batter. Add a little
dripping to four individual Yorkshire
pudding tins, or 10–12 patty tins, and
put into an oven (220°C, 425°F, Gas
Mark 7), until the fat is really hot. Pour
in the batter and cook for 15 to 20
minutes until well puffed up and browned. To make one large pudding, use
double the quantity and a 20 cm (8 inch)
square tin, increase the cooking time to
35 to 40 minutes.

† Pot Roast of Brisket

1 kg (2 lb) piece of rolled brisket
25 g (1 oz) flour
salt
freshly ground black pepper
50 g (2 oz) lard or margarine
1 large onion, peeled and sliced
2 large carrots, scraped and sliced
600 ml (1 pint) hot brown stock or
   water and ½ beef stock cube
2 tablespoons tomato purée

bouquet garni
450 g (1 lb) potatoes, peeled and
quartered if large
450 g (1 lb) packet frozen green beans
or fresh beans

Coat the meat in the flour seasoned
with salt and pepper. Heat the lard or
margarine in the cooker and brown the
meat on all sides. Add the onion and
carrots and fry lightly. Lift out the meat
and vegetables and drain the excess
lard or margarine from the cooker. Add
the stock or water and stock cube,
tomato purée and bouquet garni to the
cooker. Stir well to remove any residues
from the base of the cooker. Put the
trivet into the cooker, stand the joint on
the trivet and surround the joint with
the vegetables. Close the cooker, bring
to H pressure and cook for 35 minutes.
Reduce the pressure quickly. Move the
meat over to one side of the cooker and
add the lightly salted potatoes. If liked
wrap the potatoes in a piece of greaseproof paper if you do not want them to
absorb any sauce. Bring the liquid back
to the boil and add a separator containing the lightly salted beans. Close the
cooker, bring to H pressure and cook for
a further 5 minutes. Reduce the pressure quickly.

Lift out the beans and potatoes and
keep hot. Lift out the meat, remove the
string, slice and keep hot. Remove the
trivet and bouquet garni from the
cooker. Mash the onion and carrots
into the sauce and serve over the sliced
meat with the potatoes and beans. Hand
any extra sauce separately.

Fondue Bourguignonne

1½ kg (3 lb) fillet steak, cut into 2.5
cm (1 inch) cubes
salt
freshly ground black pepper
vegetable oil for cooking
1 garlic clove, peeled and cut in half
(optional)

Sprinkle the steak with plenty of salt
and pepper and divide into six equal
amounts. Arrange on individual plates.
Heat the oil slowly in a saucepan on the
stove, with the garlic clove (if using).
When very hot, pour into a fondue pot
and keep hot over a spirit flame on the
table. Hand sauces such as Mushroom
and Tomato Sauce (p. 351), Mustard
Sauce (p. 356) and Anchovy Sauce
(p. 355) separately; stir before serving.
Serves 6

Potted Hough
or Shin of Beef

450 g (1 lb) hough or shin of beef
2 rashers streaky bacon
1 carrot, peeled
1 onion, peeled and stuck with a few
cloves
450 ml (¾ pint) water
½ teaspoon salt
freshly ground black pepper

Cut the beef into very small pieces. Put
into a flameproof casserole with the
bacon, carrot and onion. Add the water
and bring to the boil. Remove any scum
with a slotted draining spoon, season to
taste and cover with a close-fitting lid.
Cook in a cool oven (150°C, 300°F, Gas
Mark 2) for 3 hours.

Remove the vegetables and the rind
from the bacon, and discard. Chop the
beef and bacon finely. Put the meat into
a 1 litre (1¾ pint) basin or mould. Strain
over sufficient stock to cover and put in
a cool place. When cold cover with foil
and chill in a refrigerator overnight
until set.

This jellied meat mould is delicious
served sliced in sandwiches or with
potatoes and a green salad.

Boiled Brisket of Beef and Dumplings

1½ kg (3 lb) salted brisket of beef or
  silverside
bouquet garni (see p. 364)
3–4 medium onions, peeled
225 g (8 oz) carrots, scraped and
  sliced
1 medium turnip, peeled and
  quartered
2 small leeks
1 stalk celery, washed and chopped
8 Dumplings (see p. 364)

Ask the butcher how long the brisket
has been in brine: if longer than 3 days,
it may need soaking in cold water for 3
to 4 hours before cooking.

Put the joint in a large pan, cover
with cold water and add the bouquet
garni. Bring slowly to the boil, then
lower the heat to simmer, skim off any
scum and simmer gently for 2 hours.
Add the onions, carrots, which can be
left whole if small, and turnip to the
pan. Clean the leeks and thickly slice
the white part. Add the leeks and celery
to the pan and continue cooking for 30
minutes.

Make the dumplings and arrange
them round the meat. Cover tightly and
continue cooking for 15 minutes or
until well risen. Place the meat on a
warm serving platter and leave it to set
before removing the skewers and string.
Remove the dumplings and vegetables
with a slotted spoon and arrange them
round the joint. Garnish with parsley.
Discard the bouquet garni and pour
300 ml (½ pint) of the stock into a cold
saucepan. Remove the fat with kitchen
paper. Reheat, taste and adjust the
seasoning and serve separately in a
warm sauce boat.

Continental Pot Roast of Beef

1½ kg (3 lb) piece topside, silverside or
  brisket or flank of beef
2 onions
225 g (8 oz) carrots
50 g (2 oz) beef dripping or butter
120 ml (4 fl oz) red wine
bouquet garni with celery (see p. 364)
1 teaspoon salt
6–8 peppercorns
beef stock
750 g (1½ lb) potatoes (optional)

As topside and silverside are very lean,
ask the butcher to wrap a piece of
larding fat round the joint when trussing it. This is not necessary if using
brisket or flank which contain fat and
are cheaper cuts.

Peel and quarter the onions, wash
and scrape the carrots. Heat the fat in a
flameproof casserole and brown the
meat quickly all over in the hot fat. Add
the onion and the carrots and brown
lightly.

Add the wine, bouquet garni, salt
and peppercorns. Cover tightly and
cook over a very low heat until tender,
about 2 hours. Check the meat occasionally, and if the liquid has evaporated add a little stock as required.

Scraped new potatoes or peeled and
quartered old potatoes may be added to
the casserole about 1 hour before the
end of the cooking time. When cooked,
place the meat and vegetables on a
warm serving dish. Discard the
bouquet garni. Remove the fat from the
gravy by drawing kitchen paper across
it. Taste and adjust seasoning and
strain the gravy into a gravy boat.

Spiced Silverside

1½–1¾ kg (3–3½ lb) piece of salted
  silverside
2 onions, peeled and sliced, or 8
  button onions, peeled
1 leek, trimmed, sliced and washed
4 large carrots, peeled and halved
2 sticks celery, scrubbed and sliced
2 bay leaves
8–12 whole cloves
50 g (2 oz) soft brown sugar
½ teaspoon ground cinnamon
½ teaspoon dry mustard
2 tablespoons orange juice

Place the joint in a saucepan with the
vegetables and bay leaves and cover
with water. Bring to the boil, remove
the scum, then cover and simmer gently
for about 2½ hours. Allow to cool
slightly in the liquor then drain and
place in a roasting tin.

Stud the fat with the cloves. Mix
together the sugar, cinnamon, mustard,
and orange juice and spread over the
meat. Cook in a moderate oven (180°C,
350°F, Gas Mark 4) for 30 minutes or
until tender, basting occasionally.
Remove and keep warm, place the vege
tables around the joint.

Stir 450 ml (¾ pint) of the cooking
liquor into the pan drippings and bring
to the boil for 3 minutes. Season to taste
and serve with the joint.

Gaelic Steaks

50 g (2 oz) butter
1 tablespoon oil
1 large onion, peeled and finely
  chopped
1 clove garlic, crushed (optional)
salt
freshly ground black pepper
4 fresh home-produced sirloin steaks
3–4 tablespoons whisky
2 tablespoons finely chopped parsley
1 teaspoon lemon juice

Melt the butter and oil together in a
large heavy frying pan. Add the onion
and garlic (if using) and sauté gently for
about 5 minutes without colouring.
Season the steaks lightly with salt and
generously with pepper. Add to the pan
and fry quickly for 2 to 4 minutes on
each side (depending on how rare they
are required to be). Warm the whisky,
add to the pan and flambé. Stir in the
parsley and lemon juice. Turn the
steaks over and cook gently for ½ to 1
minute. Taste and adjust the seasonings, if necessary. Serve immediately.

Steak Sophia

8 thin slices fillet steak
2 cloves garlic, crushed
salt and freshly ground black pepper
50 g (2 oz) butter
2 tablespoons finely chopped onion
2 teaspoons Worcestershire sauce
1 tablespoon lemon juice
2 tablespoons finely chopped parsley
2–4 tablespoons brandy
3–4 tablespoons double cream
  (optional)
fried button mushrooms (optional), to
  garnish

Beat the steaks lightly, rub all over
with crushed garlic and season lightly.
Melt the butter in a large frying pan and
fry the onion until soft. Add the steaks
and fry quickly for 1 to 2 minutes on
each side. Add the Worcestershire
sauce, lemon juice, parsley and seasonings. Ignite the brandy, add to the pan
and simmer for 1 to 2 minutes. Stir in the
cream (if using) and reheat without
boiling. Taste and adjust the seasonings
and serve garnished with fried button
mushrooms, if liked.

Steak Parcels

40 g (1½ oz) butter
100 g (4 oz) mushrooms, cleaned,
    trimmed and chopped
1 clove garlic, crushed
1 teaspoon French mustard
1 tablespoon finely chopped parsley
salt and freshly ground black pepper
4 minute steaks about 150–175 g (5–6
    oz) each
450 g (1 lb) puff pastry
beaten egg to glaze
deep fat for frying
To garnish:
watercress
chicory
carrot slices

Melt half the butter in a pan and fry the
mushrooms and garlic until soft. Stir in
the mustard and parsley, season well
and leave to cool. Season the steaks
lightly, then fry quickly in the remaining butter for 1–1½ minutes each side.
Remove from pan, spread with mushroom mixture. Cool. Roll out the
pastry thinly and cut out circles large
enough to enclose each steak. Position
steaks on the pastry, brush the edges
with beaten egg and press together to
enclose the steaks completely. Make
sure the pastry is securely pinched
together. Turn the parcels over and
brush with egg. Decorate with the
pastry trimmings and brush again with
egg. Heat the fat to about 180°C/350°F,
or until a cube of bread browns in it in
20 seconds, and carefully lower the
parcels into the fat, two at a time. Fry
for about 5 minutes, turning over once,
until golden brown. Drain on absorbent
kitchen paper. Garnish with watercress, chicory, carrot sticks, if liked.

Fruited Beef Olives

350 g (12 oz) topside of beef
40 g (1½ oz) beef dripping
1 medium-sized onion, peeled and
    roughly chopped
25 g (1 oz) flour
450 ml (¾ pint) beef stock
2 teaspoons salt
freshly ground black pepper
For the stuffing:
5 tablespoons fresh white
    breadcrumbs
1 tablespoon shredded beef suet
4 dried apricots, soaked and chopped
1 rasher lean bacon, diced
1 teaspoon dried or 1 tablespoon fresh
    chopped mixed herbs
salt
freshly ground black pepper
1 egg, lightly beaten
8 stuffed green olives, to garnish

Cut the meat into slices across the
grain, about 7.5 × 10 cm (3 × 4 inches).
Flatten the slices by laying them between sheets of greaseproof paper and
batting out with a rolling pin.
    Prepare the stuffing by mixing all the
ingredients together well. Spread over
the slices of meat. Roll up the meat
tightly and secure the rolls with
wooden cocktail sticks or with cotton
thread.
    Melt the dripping in a small casserole
and brown the beef olives quickly on all
sides. Remove them and fry the chopped
onion until limp. Sprinkle in the flour
and cook gently for another 2 minutes,
stirring constantly, until the flour is
golden-brown. Gradually stir in the
stock and seasoning to taste. Bring to
the boil, add the beef olives, cover with
the lid and simmer gently for 2 hours.
    Transfer the beef olives to a heated
serving dish. Remove the cocktail
sticks or cotton thread. Garnish each
roll with an olive. Pour over a little of
the sauce and serve the remainder separately. If liked, garnish each roll with
a parsley sprig instead of an olive.

Beef Olives with Walnuts

1 onion, peeled and finely chopped
4 rashers streaky bacon, derinded and
  chopped
1 clove garlic, crushed
25 g (1 oz) butter
75 g (3 oz) fresh breadcrumbs
50 g (2 oz) shelled walnuts, roughly
  chopped
1 tablespoon finely chopped parsley
salt and freshly ground black pepper
1 large egg, beaten
4 slices topside of beef, beaten flat
2 tablespoons oil
25 g (1 oz) flour
450 ml (¾ pint) beef stock
2–3 tablespoons dry sherry or white
  wine
To garnish:
few walnut halves
parsley sprigs

Fry the onion, bacon and garlic in
melted butter until lightly browned.
Stir in the breadcrumbs, walnuts, parsley and seasonings and bind together
with the egg. Divide into four and put
one portion on each beef slice. Roll up
beef slices to enclose the fillings and
then secure with wooden cocktail
sticks.

Fry in the heated oil until browned
all over then transfer the olives to an
ovenproof casserole. Stir the flour into
the pan drippings and cook for 1 minute
then gradually add the stock and sherry
and bring to the boil. Season well and
pour over the olives. Cover and cook in
a warm oven (160°C, 325°F, Gas Mark 3)
for about 1¼ hours, or until tender.

Skim off any fat from the surface,
taste and adjust the seasonings. Garnish with the walnut halves and parsley
sprigs before serving.

† Beef, Bacon and Bean Hotpot

2 tablespoons vegetable oil
1 large onion, peeled and finely
  chopped
1 garlic clove, peeled and crushed
750 g (1½ lb) chuck steak, cut into 2.5
  cm (1 inch) chunks
225 g (8 oz) streaky bacon, de-rinded
  and chopped
1 × 400 g (14 oz) can tomatoes
2 tablespoons tomato purée
2 teaspoons prepared French mustard
1 tablespoon black treacle, brown
  sugar or golden syrup
150 ml (¼ pint) water
6 handfuls, scant 300 ml (½ pint) red
  kidney beans, soaked overnight and
  drained
salt
freshly ground black pepper

Heat the oil in the pressure cooker, add
the onion and fry over gentle heat until
soft. Add the garlic, beef and bacon,
then fry over brisk heat until the meat is
browned on all sides. Stir in the water,
tomatoes, tomato purée, mustard,
treacle and beans, then add salt and
pepper to taste. Bring to the boil.

Cover with the lid and bring up to
pressure according to manufacturer's
instructions. Cook at H pressure for 20
minutes, reduce the pressure quickly
and remove the cover. Taste and adjust
the seasoning. Serve hot accompanied
with freshly boiled rice.
Serves 4 to 6

Variation:
Substitute dried haricot beans for the
kidney beans.

† Beef and Bean Casserole

75 g (3 oz) haricot beans
boiling water
50 g (2 oz) lard or margarine
1 large onion, peeled and sliced
2 carrots, peeled and sliced
450 g (1 lb) shin of beef, trimmed and
    cubed
600 ml (1 pint) hot brown stock or
    water and ½ beef stock cube
2 tablespoons tomato purée
salt
freshly ground black pepper
1 bay leaf
2 teaspoons cornflour
a little cold water
finely chopped parsley, to garnish

Put the haricot beans into a basin, cover with boiling water and leave to stand for 1 hour. Melt the lard or margarine in the cooker. Add the onion and carrots and fry until lightly coloured. Add the meat and sauté until evenly browned. Remove the cooker from the heat, stir in the stock or water and stock cube, tomato purée, salt, pepper, bay leaf and the drained haricot beans. Return to the heat and bring to the boil. Close the cooker, bring to H pressure and cook for 20 minutes. Reduce the pressure slowly. Remove the bay leaf and add the cornflour, blended with a little cold water. Bring to the boil, stirring constantly and simmer for 1 minute. Taste and adjust the seasoning as necessary and sprinkle with a little chopped parsley to serve.

Boeuf Bourguignonne

675 g (1½ lb) topside of beef
200 ml (7 fl oz) red wine
1 clove garlic, crushed
1 bay leaf
25 g (1 oz) dripping or lard
100 g (4 oz) streaky bacon, derinded
    and diced
12 button onions, peeled
1 tablespoon flour
200 ml (7 fl oz) beef stock
salt and freshly ground black pepper
2–3 tablespoons brandy (optional)
100 g (4 oz) button mushrooms,
    cleaned and trimmed

Trim the meat and cut into 2.5 cm (1 inch) cubes. Place in a bowl with the wine, garlic and bay leaf; cover and leave for several hours, or overnight, in a cold place.

Drain the meat thoroughly. Melt the fat in a pan and fry the meat quickly until well browned all over. Transfer to an ovenproof casserole. Fry the bacon and onions until lightly browned and transfer to the casserole. Stir the flour into the fat in the pan and cook for 1 minute then gradually add the wine marinade and stock and bring to the boil. Season to taste and pour into the casserole. Cover and cook in a warm oven (160°C, 325°F, Gas Mark 3) for 1½ hours. Warm the brandy (if using), ignite and add to the casserole with the mushrooms. Return to the oven for 15 to 30 minutes until tender. Discard the bay leaf, taste and adjust the seasonings before serving. A little extra stock may be required.

Flemish Carbonnade of Beef

¾ kg (1½ lb) top rump or chuck steak, cut into thin slices
50 g (2 oz) lard
225 g (8 oz) onions, peeled and sliced
100 g (4 oz) mushrooms, washed and sliced
2–3 tablespoons flour
2 teaspoons brown sugar
300 ml (½ pint) brown ale
beef stock as required
salt
freshly ground pepper
bouquet garni (p. 364)
40–50 g (1½–2 oz) butter
6 thick slices French bread
continental mustard
parsley sprigs, to garnish

Cut the beef into strips about 3½–5 cm (1½–2 inches) wide. Heat the lard and quickly fry the slices of beef until brown on both sides, then remove them from the casserole. Add the onions and mushrooms and fry until the onions are transparent. Remove the casserole from the heat and stir in sufficient flour to absorb the lard and add the sugar.

Return the casserole to the heat and fry the flour, stirring, until the roux is caramel coloured. Reduce the heat and gradually stir in the ale. Bring to the boil, add the steak and sufficient stock to cover. Season to taste with salt and freshly ground pepper and add the bouquet garni. Cover and cook in the centre of preheated oven (160°C, 325°F, Gas Mark 3) for 1½ hours. Remove the bouquet garni.

Spread butter on one side of the bread slices and mustard on the other. Arrange the slices, butter side uppermost, on top of the meat. Continue cooking for 20 to 30 minutes on the top shelf of the oven until the meat is tender and the bread has soaked up the gravy underneath and become crisp and crusty on top. Garnish with parsley.

Chunky Beef with Herb Dumplings

1 × 225 g (8 oz) packet suet dumpling mix
1 teaspoon dried mixed herbs
2 tablespoons vegetable oil
1 large onion, peeled and finely chopped
1 × 400 g (14 oz) can tomatoes
1 tablespoon tomato purée
1 tablespoon Worcestershire sauce
pinch of sugar
salt
freshly ground black pepper
2 × 425 g (15 oz) cans chunky steak in rich gravy
1 × 275 g (10 oz) can carrots, drained and chopped

Make 12 small dumplings according to the packet directions, adding half the dried mixed herbs to the mix before adding the water. Set aside. Heat the oil in a pan, add the onion and fry over gentle heat until soft, stirring occasionally. Add the tomatoes and break up with a spoon, then stir in the tomato purée, Worcestershire sauce, sugar, remaining herbs and salt and pepper to taste. Bring to the boil, lower the heat and add the dumplings. Cover and cook over the lowest possible heat for 15 minutes, shaking the pan occasionally. Do not stir or this will break up the dumplings.

Add the chunky steak and carrots, shaking the pan to mix the ingredients together. Cover and cook for 5 to 10 minutes until heated through and bubbling. Taste and adjust seasoning and serve immediately.

Variations:
Canned peas or broad beans can be used instead of the carrots.

Beef in Guinness

1 kg (2 lb) chuck steak, cut into cubes
300 ml ($\frac{1}{2}$ pint) Guinness
40 g (1$\frac{1}{2}$ oz) flour
salt
freshly ground black pepper
40 g (1$\frac{1}{2}$ oz) dripping or lard
1 large onion, peeled and sliced
1 beef stock cube dissolved in 300 ml
  ($\frac{1}{2}$ pint) hot water
1 tablespoon Worcestershire sauce
1 tablespoon soft brown sugar
1 tablespoon tomato purée
4 carrots, peeled and sliced
4 medium potatoes, peeled and cut
  into cubes

Put the meat in a bowl, pour over the Guinness and stir well. Leave to marinate overnight. The next day, strain the marinade and reserve. Coat the meat in the flour seasoned with salt and pepper. Melt the fat in a flameproof casserole, add the meat and fry briskly until browned on all sides. Remove from the casserole with a slotted spoon and set aside. Add the onion to the casserole and fry gently until golden. Return the meat to the casserole with the reserved marinade and stir well.

Add the remaining ingredients, except the potatoes, cover and cook in a preheated cool oven (150°C, 300°F, Gas Mark 2) for 1$\frac{1}{2}$ hours. Taste and adjust the seasoning, add the potatoes and cook for a further 45 minutes or until the meat and potatoes are tender.

Paprika Beef Goulash

2 tablespoons vegetable oil
1 large onion, peeled and finely
  chopped
1 tablespoon paprika
1 green pepper, cored, seeded and
  finely chopped
1 red pepper, cored, seeded and finely
  chopped

2 × 425 g (15 oz) cans chunky steak in
  rich gravy
2 tablespoons tomato purée
salt
freshly ground black pepper
225 g (8 oz) button mushrooms, finely
  sliced
soured cream or plain unsweetened
  yogurt, to serve

Heat the oil in a pan, add the onion and paprika and fry over gentle heat for 5 minutes, stirring occasionally.

Add the peppers and fry for 5 minutes until soft, then add the chunky steak, tomato purée and salt and pepper to taste. Stir well to mix, then cook gently for 10 minutes until hot and bubbling. Stir the mushrooms into the pan and cook for a further 5 minutes. Serve immediately with boiled rice and soured cream or yogurt handed separately.

Variation:
Canned mushrooms can be used instead of fresh ones.

Cidered Beef with Dumplings

550 g (1$\frac{1}{4}$ lb) braising steak
a little seasoned flour
2 tablespoons dripping or lard
1 large onion, peeled and chopped
3 sticks celery, scrubbed and sliced
300 ml ($\frac{1}{2}$ pint) dry cider
300 ml ($\frac{1}{2}$ pint) beef stock
salt and freshly ground black pepper
For the dumplings:
100 g (4 oz) self-raising flour
pinch of salt
50 g (2 oz) shredded suet
1 teaspoon mixed herbs
water to mix

Trim the beef and cut into 2.5 cm (1 inch) cubes. Toss in seasoned flour. Melt the fat and fry the meat until well browned then transfer to an ovenproof casserole.

Fry the onion and celery gently for a few minutes in the same fat then stir in 1 tablespoon seasoned flour and cook for 1 minute. Add the cider and stock and bring to the boil. Season to taste and pour over the beef. Cover and cook in a warm oven (160°C, 325°F, Gas Mark 3) for 1½ hours, or until the meat is almost tender.

Meanwhile, to make the dumplings, mix together the flour, a pinch of salt, suet and herbs and mix to a soft dough with water. Form into 8 balls. Add to the casserole and continue cooking for a further 20 to 30 minutes or until the dumplings are cooked. Taste and adjust the seasonings before serving.

Spanish Beef

2 tablespoons vegetable oil
1 onion, peeled and finely chopped
1 garlic clove, peeled and crushed
2 green or red peppers, cored, seeded and finely chopped
2 × 425 g (15 oz) cans chunky steak in rich gravy
2 tablespoons tomato purée
½ teaspoon dried tarragon
pinch of sugar
salt
freshly ground black pepper
50 g (2 oz) stuffed olives

Heat the oil in a pan, add the onion, garlic and peppers and fry over gentle heat for 10 minutes, stirring occasionally. Add the remaining ingredients, except the olives, and cook over gentle heat for 10 minutes until bubbling. Add the olives and heat through for 5 minutes. Taste and adjust seasoning.

Serve with instant mashed potato, pre-cooked rice or crusty French bread and butter.

† Mexican Beef Casserole

50 g (2 oz) lard or margarine
1 large onion, peeled and sliced
1 large green pepper, cored, seeded and sliced
750 g (1½ lb) stewing beef, trimmed and cubed
25 g (1 oz) flour
salt
freshly ground black pepper
1 teaspoon chilli powder
300 ml (½ pint) hot brown stock or water and ½ beef stock cube
1 × 400 g (14 oz) can tomatoes
1 × 100 g (4 oz) packet frozen sweetcorn kernels

Heat the lard or margarine in the cooker, add the onion and pepper and fry until both are beginning to colour. Lift out and drain well. Coat the meat in flour seasoned with salt and pepper. Brown the meat in the hot lard or margarine, lift out and drain well. Stir the chilli powder into the cooking juices, add the hot stock or water and stock cube and stir well to remove any residues from the base of the cooker. Return the meat and vegetables to the cooker together with the tomatoes and sweetcorn. Stir and bring to the boil. If the liquid is too thick add a little more water to the cooker. Close the cooker, bring to H pressure and cook for 20 minutes. Reduce the pressure quickly. Stir well, taste and adjust the seasoning as necessary. Serve with pasta or rice.

† Braised Beef with Peppers

50 g (2 oz) lard or margarine
1 onion, peeled and sliced
2 red peppers, cored, seeded and
  sliced
750 g (1½ lb) chuck steak, cut into
  four 2.5 cm (1 inch) thick slices
450 ml (¾ pint) hot brown stock or
  water and ½ beef stock cube
100 g (4 oz) sweetcorn kernels
salt
freshly ground black pepper

Heat the lard or margarine in the
cooker and sauté the onion and peppers
until both are beginning to soften. Lift
out and drain well. Brown the meat on
both sides in the hot lard or margarine.
Lift out and drain off the excess lard or
margarine from the cooker. Add the
stock or water and stock cube to the
cooker and stir well to remove any
residues from the base of the cooker.
Put the vegetables and sweetcorn into
the cooker, place the meat slices on top
and season with salt and pepper. Close
the cooker, bring to H pressure and
cook for 20 minutes. Reduce the pressure quickly. Taste and adjust the
seasoning as necessary before serving.

Beef Stroganoff

550–675 g (1¼–1½ lb) rump or fillet
  steak
50 g (2 oz) butter
1 teaspoon oil
2 large onions, peeled and thinly
  sliced
225 g (8 oz) button mushrooms,
  cleaned, trimmed and sliced
salt and freshly ground black pepper
200–300 ml (7 fl oz–½ pint) soured
  cream
chopped chives or parsley, to garnish

Trim the steak and cut into narrow
strips about 5 cm × 6 mm (2 inches × ¼

inch). Melt 25 g (1 oz) butter in a pan,
add the oil and fry the onion until soft
and just beginning to colour. Add the
mushrooms and continue for 3 to 4
minutes. Remove from the pan and keep
warm. Add the remaining butter to the
pan and, when hot, fry the steak quickly
for 4 to 5 minutes, stirring frequently.
Return the onions and mushrooms to
the pan and season. Stir in the soured
cream and heat through quickly for 2
minutes. Taste and adjust the seasonings and serve immediately, sprinkled
with chives or parsley.

† Rogan Gosht

2 tablespoons vegetable oil
1 large onion, peeled and finely
  chopped
1 garlic clove, peeled and crushed
2 tablespoons curry paste
½ teaspoon chilli powder, or to taste
750 g (1½ lb) chuck steak, cut into
  2.5 cm (1 inch) chunks
2 tablespoons flour
salt
freshly ground black pepper
300 ml (½ pint) water
1 tablespoon vinegar
1 beef stock cube
2 green or red peppers, cored, seeded
  and chopped
4 tomatoes, quartered
cornflour, to thicken (optional)

Heat the oil in the pressure cooker, add
the onion and fry over gentle heat until
soft. Add the garlic, curry paste and
chilli powder and fry for 5 minutes,
stirring constantly.
  Meanwhile, coat the beef in the flour
seasoned with salt and pepper. Add to
the cooker and fry over brisk heat until
browned on all sides. Stir in the water
and vinegar and scrape up the sediment
from the bottom of the cooker, then
bring to the boil. Add the stock cube and
stir to dissolve.
  Cover with the lid, then bring up to

pressure according to manufacturer's instructions. Cook at H pressure for 15 minutes. Reduce the pressure quickly, remove the cover and add the peppers and tomatoes. Cover the cooker again, bring back to pressure and cook for a further 5 minutes. Reduce the pressure quickly and remove the cover. Taste and adjust the seasoning of the sauce. Thicken, if liked, by mixing cornflour to a paste with a little water, stir into the sauce and return to the heat. Bring to the boil, stirring constantly, and cook until the sauce thickens. Serve hot with freshly boiled rice, mango chutney and plain yogurt.

Beef and Chestnut Pie

550 g (1¼ lb) braising steak
25 g (1 oz) butter
1 tablespoon oil
12 button onions, peeled
2 tablespoons flour
450 ml (¼ pint) beef stock
4 tablespoons wine
salt and freshly ground black pepper
225 g (8 oz) chestnuts, lightly roasted
    and peeled
For the pastry:
160 g (6 oz) plain flour
pinch of salt
40 g (1½ oz) margarine
40 g (1½ oz) lard or white fat
water to mix
beaten egg or milk

Trim the meat and cut into 2.5 cm (1 inch) cubes. Fry in butter and oil until well browned. Transfer to an ovenproof casserole. Fry the onions until lightly browned and add to the casserole. Stir the flour into the pan, cook for 1 minute, gradually add stock and wine, bring to the boil. Season well, add the chestnuts and pour over the beef. Cover and cook in a moderate oven for about 1¼ hours, until tender. Pour into a pie dish and leave to cool.

To make the pastry, sieve the flour with a pinch of salt, add the fats and rub in until the mixture resembles fine crumbs. Add enough water to mix. Roll out slightly larger than the top of the dish and cut a 2.5 cm (1 inch) wide strip all round. Place the strip on the wetted rim of the dish, brush with water. Position the lid. Trim edges, crimp and decorate with pastry trimmings. Brush with egg or milk and cook in a hot oven (220°C, 425°F, Gas Mark 7) for 15 minutes. Continue in a moderate oven (180°C, 350°F, Gas Mark 4) for 25 to 30 minutes, until pastry is cooked.

Stewed Steak and Kidney

750 g (1¾ lb) chuck steak
175–225 g (6–8 oz) ox kidney
2–3 tablespoons flour
50 g (2 oz) lard or beef dripping
1 tablespoon chopped onion
stock or water to cover
salt
freshly ground pepper

Cut the steak into 3½ cm (1½ inch) cubes, removing any fat and gristle. Cut the kidney into smaller chunks than the meat, discarding the fatty core. Toss steak and kidney in flour in a paper bag. Shake off any surplus flour. Fry the onion in hot lard or beef dripping in a sauté pan until transparent. Add the steak and kidney and fry, stirring, until nicely browned. Cover with stock or water and season with salt and freshly ground pepper to taste.

Bring to the simmer and cook very gently on top of the stove or in a slow oven until the meat is tender, about 1½ to 2 hours.

For pie filling (see p. 128), allow the meat to cool and skim off the fat.

Steak and Kidney Pudding

500 g (1¼ lb) stewing steak
225 g (8 oz) ox kidney
flour for coating
225 g (8 oz) Suet crust pastry (p. 361)
salt
freshly ground pepper
approx. 125 ml (¼ pint) beef stock or
   water

Grease a 1.2 litre (2 pint) pudding basin.
Cut the steak into 3 cm (1¼ inch) chunks,
discarding any fat and gristle. Cut the
kidney into smaller pieces, discarding
the fatty core. Put the flour in a clean
paper bag and toss the meat in it. This
will ensure it is evenly coated.

Roll out the suet crust into a circle 5
mm (¼ inch) thick and 10 cm (4 inches)
all round larger than the top of the
basin. Cut a quarter out of the circle
and reserve for the lid. It will also make
the lining pastry fit better.

Lift the pastry into the basin, centre
it carefully and ease it into the basin so
the cut edges overlap slightly. Damp
and seal these edges. Press the pastry
evenly against side of basin so there are
no pleats.

Trim excess pastry off around the top
edge of the basin. Put in the steak and
kidney a layer at a time, seasoning each
layer with salt and pepper. Add sufficient stock or water to come a quarter
of the way up the filling. Fold pastry
edge over on top of filling, and brush
with water.

Gather the remaining triangle of
pastry into a ball, and roll it out into a
circle to fit the top of the basin. Lay it on
top of the filling and press the pastry
edges together. Cover and steam for 3½
to 4 hours.

Remove the pudding from the steamer
and allow it to shrink slightly before
turning it out. Alternatively, wrap the
basin in a clean napkin and serve the
pudding in the basin. Serve hot with
Onion gravy (p. 355) handed separately
if wished.

Steak, Kidney and Mushroom Pie

Steak and kidney pie filling (p. 127)
100 g (4 oz) mushrooms, sliced
225 g (8 oz) Rough puff pastry (p. 362)
1 beaten egg, for glazing
parsley sprig, to garnish

Put a pie funnel in the centre of a 1.2
litre (2 pint) pie dish. This is to make a
vent for steam to escape during baking,
so the pastry will not be soggy underneath. Pack the cold filling round the
funnel and then cover with the sliced
mushrooms.

Roll out the pastry 5 mm (¼ inch) thick
and cut a strip of pastry, the same width
as the lip of the pie dish, off the outside
edge of the pastry. Damp the lip with a
brush and press the pastry strip firmly
on. Damp and press the joins together.

Damp the pastry strip. Roll the rest of
the pastry on to the rolling pin and
unroll it over the dish.

Press the pastry edges together on the
lip of the dish. Trim edges around rim
with a sharp knife.

With the back of the forefinger of the
left hand, press the pastry lid down and
slightly off the edge of the pie dish, and
with the back of the knife, held horizontally in the other hand, knock the
pastry back, flaking the edge.

Flute the edge by pressing down with
the left thumb, and pulling the pastry
back towards the pie dish with the back
of the knife held vertically in the other
hand. Pull the pastry with the knife do
not cut it.

Insert a skewer into the pie funnel,
through the pastry, to make a hole so
that the steam can escape. Cut a slit on
top of the pie on each side of the funnel.
Brush the top of the pie with beaten egg,
but not the flaked edge.

Roll out the pastry trimmings and cut
a strip 2.5 cm (1 inch) wide and cut
diagonally across to make 6 diamond
shapes for leaves. With the back of the
knife, mark 'veins' down the centre of

each leaf and short lines on either side.

Brush the top surface of each leaf with beaten egg. Hold the points of the leaf at each end and twist. Place the leaf in position on top of the pie – take care not to block the slits for steam.

Roll out another strip of pastry $3\frac{1}{2}$ cm ($1\frac{1}{2}$ inches) wide. Cut evenly spaced slits three quarters of the way across to form a fringe. Brush with beaten egg. Roll the pastry strip round a skewer with the point protruding 2.5 cm (1 inch) beyond the uncut edge.

Insert the point of the skewer into the pie funnel. Press the base of the roll of pastry firmly onto the pie. Remove the skewer and with the point open out the petals of the pastry flower. Preheat the oven to 220°C, 425°F, Gas Mark 7. Place the pie on a baking sheet and bake on the upper shelf for at least 20 minutes or until the pastry is well risen and turning brown. Then reduce the heat to 200°C, 400°F, Gas Mark 6 for a further 30 minutes for the pie to cook through. If the pastry is turning too brown, cover the top with a paper bag to protect it. Serve the pie hot, garnished with a sprig of parsley.

† Beef and Vegetable Pie

50 g (2 oz) lard or margarine
450 g (1 lb) stewing beef, trimmed and cubed
1 onion, peeled and sliced
2 carrots, scraped and sliced
300 ml ($\frac{1}{2}$ pint) brown stock or water and $\frac{1}{2}$ beef stock cube
salt
freshly ground black pepper
2 tablespoons tomato purée
1 × 100 g (4 oz) packet frozen peas
For the pastry:
175 g (6 oz) flour
pinch of salt
40 g ($1\frac{1}{2}$ oz) margarine
40 g ($1\frac{1}{2}$ oz) lard
2 tablespoons cold water
a little milk

Heat the lard or margarine in the cooker. Sauté the beef and vegetables until the beef is browned and the vegetables are beginning to colour. Remove the cooker from the heat. Stir in the stock or water and stock cube, salt, pepper and tomato purée. Stir well to remove any residues from the base of the cooker. Close the cooker, bring to H pressure and cook for 15 minutes. Reduce the pressure quickly. Taste and adjust the seasoning as necessary.

While the meat is cooking make the pastry. Sift the flour and salt into a mixing bowl. Add the fats, cut into small pieces and rub into the flour until the mixture resembles fine breadcrumbs. Stir in sufficient water to form a firm dough that leaves the sides of the bowl cleanly. Turn on to a floured board and knead lightly. If possible wrap in foil or greaseproof paper and chill in the refrigerator for 15 to 30 minutes.

Transfer the meat mixture to a 900 ml ($1\frac{1}{2}$ pint) pie dish and stir in the frozen peas. Roll out the pastry to fit the top of the pie dish. Cut a strip of pastry to go round the lip of the pie dish. Wet the lip and press on the strip of pastry. Wet the strip and cover with the pastry lid, sealing the edges well and making a steam hole in the centre of the pie crust. Decorate the top with leaves made from pastry trimmings. Brush with a little milk. Bake in a fairly hot oven (200°C, 400°F, Gas Mark 6) for 25 minutes or until the pastry is golden brown.

Minced Beef and Kidney Pie

225 g (8 oz) flour
pinch of salt
100 g (4 oz) lard, cut into pieces
2–3 tablespoons cold water
For the filling:
25 g (1 oz) dripping
1 small onion, peeled and chopped
450 g (1 lb) minced beef
100 g (4 oz) ox kidney, trimmed and
    finely chopped
300 ml (½ pint) water
1 teaspoon gravy powder
salt and freshly ground black pepper
1 tablespoon cornflour
a little milk to glaze
parsley sprigs, to garnish

Sift the flour and salt into a bowl. Rub in the lard until the mixture resembles fine breadcrumbs. Stir in just sufficient water to hold the mixture together, then form into a smooth ball. Wrap in foil or greaseproof paper and chill in the refrigerator for 30 minutes.

Meanwhile, melt the dripping in a saucepan. Add the chopped onion and fry, stirring constantly, for 3 to 4 mintes. Add the minced beef and kidney and continue to fry, stirring until all the meat is brown and no lumps remain. Add the water, gravy powder and seasoning. Bring to the boil stirring constantly. Cover and simmer for 1 hour. Alternatively, cook in a pressure cooker for 20 minutes.

Blend the cornflour with a little cold water. Add to the meat mixture and stir constantly until thickened. Simmer for a further 3 minutes. Cool.

Divide the pastry into two and roll out one half on a floured surface to form a circle to fit the base of a 20 cm (8 inch) pie dish. Spoon in the meat mixture. Roll out the remaining pastry for the lid. Lay this over the filling, dampen the edges and press well together to seal. Flute the edge with finger and thumb or with a fork. Decorate the top with 'leaves' using any pastry trimmings.

Brush the pie with milk and make a slit in the centre for the steam to escape.

Place the pie dish on a baking sheet and bake in a fairly hot oven (200°C, 400°F, Gas Mark 6) for 20 minutes, or until golden-brown on top. Serve garnished with sprigs of parsley.

Meat Pie with Potato Crust

50 g (2 oz) dripping
1 large onion, peeled and chopped
salt and freshly ground black pepper
1 tablespoon flour
500 g (1¼ lb) stewing beef, diced
225 g (8 oz) lean pork, diced
1 small swede, peeled and diced
2 tablespoons orange juice
250 ml (8 fl oz) beef stock
For the potato crust:
100 g (4 oz) self-raising flour
175 g (6 oz) potatoes, peeled, cooked
    and mashed
40 g (1½ oz) shredded beef suet
grated rind of 1 orange

Melt the dripping in a large frying pan and brown the chopped onion in it. Season the flour and use to coat the meat. Brown on all sides in the same fat. Transfer the onion and meat mixture to a casserole, add the swede, orange juice and stock which should just come to the level of the contents. Cover the casserole and cook in a moderate oven (180°C, 350°F, Gas Mark 4) for about 1 hour.

Meanwhile, prepare the potato crust by mixing together the flour, mashed potatoes, suet, orange rind and seasoning to taste. Knead lightly. Remove the lid from the casserole and using it as a pattern, pat out the pastry with clean floured hands to the shape of the casserole.

Stir the meat mixture, place the crust on top, making a hole in the centre to allow the steam to escape. Replace the lid and cook for a further 20 minutes.

Minced Beef and Aubergine Fiesta

450 g (1 lb) lean minced beef
1 large onion, peeled and chopped
salt and freshly ground black pepper
450 g (1 lb) aubergines
boiling water
1 × 400 g (14 oz) can tomatoes, drained
225 g (8 oz) mushrooms, sliced
1 clove of garlic, crushed
¼ teaspoon salt
100 g (4 oz) Edam cheese, grated
chopped parsley, to garnish

Fry the minced beef in a pan in its own fat until it is browned. Remove from the pan with a slotted draining spoon, leaving the fat behind. Fry the chopped onion in the fat until soft but not browned. Add to the minced beef with seasoning to taste. Place the beef mixture in a lightly greased ovenproof dish.

Peel the aubergines, cut into 2.5 cm (1 inch) slices and cut each slice into 4 triangular pieces. Put in a saucepan, cover with boiling water and cook for 10 minutes. Drain well. Roughly chop the tomatoes and mix with the aubergines, sliced mushrooms, crushed garlic and ¼ teaspoon salt. Spread over the minced beef. Bake uncovered in a fairly hot oven (200°C, 400°F, Gas Mark 6) for about 20 minutes. Sprinkle over the grated cheese and bake for a further 10 minutes, until the cheese has melted. Garnish with chopped parsley.

Beefeater Pie

50 g (2 oz) dripping
1 large onion, peeled and finely chopped
1 clove of garlic, crushed
225 g (8 oz) minced beef
2 tablespoons tomato purée
300 ml (½ pint) beef stock
3 tablespoons quick cook oats
salt and freshly ground black pepper
4 slices white bread
1 × 75 g (3 oz) jar chicken and bacon spread
2 tomatoes, sliced
chopped parsley, to garnish

Melt the dripping in a saucepan, add the chopped onion and crushed garlic and fry gently until limp. Add the minced beef and fry until crumbly, stirring occasionally. Stir in the tomato purée and the stock, and sprinkle in the oats. Continue stirring until the mixture comes to the boil, then season to taste. Reduce the heat, cover and simmer for 30 minutes, stirring frequently.

Five minutes before the beef mixture is cooked, remove the crusts from the bread and spread each slice with the chicken and bacon spread. Sandwich 2 slices, spread side inside, together. Toast both sides of the sandwiches lightly and then cut each one into 4 triangles. Spoon the beef mixture into a flameproof dish and arrange the tomato slices on top. Place under a hot grill for a minute or two to heat the tomato slices, then arrange the sandwich triangles around the edge of the dish and sprinkle with chopped parsley.

† Minced Beef and Pasta Casserole

25 g (1 oz) lard or margarine
1 onion, peeled and chopped
1 garlic clove, crushed
450 g (1 lb) minced beef
300 ml ($\frac{1}{2}$ pint) hot brown stock or
    water and $\frac{1}{2}$ beef stock cube
1 × 225 g (8 oz) can tomatoes
1 × 219 g (7$\frac{3}{4}$ oz) can baked beans
$\frac{1}{2}$ teaspoon dried mixed herbs
2 teaspoons paprika pepper
2 teaspoons Worcestershire sauce
75 g (3 oz) pasta whirls or shells
salt
freshly ground black pepper
freshly chopped parsley

Heat the lard or margarine in the cooker, add the onion and garlic and fry until the onion is beginning to soften. Add the minced beef and brown quickly. Carefully drain off any excess lard or margarine from the cooker. Stir in the remaining ingredients except the salt, pepper and parsley. Season with a little salt and pepper. Close the cooker, bring to H pressure and cook for 7 minutes. Reduce the pressure quickly. Taste and adjust the seasoning as necessary. Serve garnished with a little chopped parsley.

Beef with Cheese Cobbler

25 g (1 oz) dripping
450 g (1 lb) lean minced beef
2 tablespoons flour
450 g (1 lb) onions, peeled and
    quartered
8 small pickled onions
2 tablespoons tomato purée
$\frac{1}{2}$ teaspoon sugar
$\frac{1}{2}$ teaspoon dried thyme
1 bay leaf, crushed
salt and freshly ground black pepper
300 ml ($\frac{1}{2}$ pint) water
For the cheese cobbler:
225 g (8 oz) self-raising flour
$\frac{1}{2}$ teaspoon dry mustard
salt and freshly ground black pepper
40 g (1$\frac{1}{2}$ oz) butter
75 g (3 oz) Cheddar cheese, finely
    grated
few drops Tabasco sauce
150 ml ($\frac{1}{4}$ pint) water
1 tablespoon milk

Melt the dripping in a frying pan and lightly fry the minced beef until brown, stirring occasionally. Transfer the meat to a casserole, sprinkle with the flour and stir well. Add the quartered onions, pickled onions, tomato purée, sugar, herbs and seasoning to taste. Add the water or just sufficient water to cover the surface. Put the lid on the casserole and cook in a moderate oven (180°C, 350°F, Gas Mark 4) for 1 hour.

To make the cheese cobbler sift the flour. Add the dry mustard and salt and pepper to taste to the sifted flour. Rub in the butter until the mixture resembles fine breadcrumbs, mix in the grated cheese and Tabasco, and blend to a soft dough with the water. Roll out on a floured surface until 1 cm ($\frac{1}{2}$ inch) thick. Cut into rounds with a 7 cm (2$\frac{1}{2}$ inch) fancy cutter, and arrange on top of the meat mixture overlapping the circles. Brush the tops of the cobblers with the milk and return the uncovered casserole to the oven. Bake for a further 30 to 40 minutes or until golden.

Courgette Moussaka

8 tablespoons vegetable oil
1 onion, peeled and finely chopped
1 garlic clove, peeled and crushed
750 g (1½ lb) minced beef
3 tablespoons tomato purée
1 teaspoon ground allspice
pinch of mixed dried herbs
5 tablespoons water
salt
freshly ground black pepper
450 g (1 lb) courgettes, sliced
1 × 450 g (1 lb) can new potatoes, drained and sliced
1 × 300 ml (½ pint) packet cheese sauce mix
300 ml (½ pint) milk
1 egg

Heat 2 tablespoons of the oil in a large shallow pan, add the onion and garlic and fry over gentle heat until soft. Add the meat and fry until browned, breaking it up constantly with a spoon. Stir in the tomato purée, allspice, herbs, water and salt and pepper to taste, then bring to the boil, stirring constantly. Lower the heat and simmer for 25 minutes.

Meanwhile, heat half the remaining oil in a frying pan, add some of the courgettes and fry gently until golden brown on both sides, drain. Fry the remaining courgettes in the same way, adding more oil when necessary.

Put the courgettes in a thick layer on top of the meat mixture, then cover with a layer of potatoes. Make the cheese sauce with the milk according to packet directions, leave to cool for a few minutes, then beat in the egg and salt and pepper to taste. Pour over the potatoes, put under a very low grill for 10 minutes, turning the pan occasionally to ensure even browning. Serve hot with a salad.

Variations:
Substitute sliced fried aubergines for the courgettes. The potatoes can be omitted for a less substantial dish.

Cornish Pie

450 g (1 lb) minced beef
175 g (6 oz) potato, peeled and finely chopped
2 carrots, peeled and finely chopped
1 large onion, peeled and finely chopped
1 teaspoon mixed herbs
salt and freshly ground black pepper
pinch of ground nutmeg
For the pastry:
300 g (12 oz) plain flour
pinch of salt
75 g (3 oz) margarine
75 g (3 oz) lard or white fat
water to mix
beaten egg or milk to glaze

Mix together the mince, potato, carrots, onion and herbs and season the mixture very well with salt, pepper and nutmeg.

To make the pastry, sieve the flour into a bowl with a pinch of salt, add the fats and rub in until the mixture resembles fine breadcrumbs. Add sufficient water to mix to a pliable dough. Knead lightly then roll out two-thirds of the pastry on a floured surface to fit an oblong tin approx 28 × 18 × 4 cm (11 × 7 × 1½ inches) deep.

Add the filling, pressing it down evenly. Roll out the remaining pastry to make a lid, damp the edges, place on pie and press the edges well together. Trim off the surplus pastry and crimp the edges. Use the pastry trimmings to decorate the top.

Brush with egg or milk and cook in a hot oven (220°, 425°F, Gas Mark 7) for 20 to 25 minutes, until beginning to brown; then reduce oven temperature to moderate (180°C, 350°F, Gas Mark 4) and continue for a further 35 to 40 minutes. Serve hot or cold.

Beef and Parsnip Pie

1 large onion, peeled and chopped
1 clove garlic, crushed
2 sticks celery, scrubbed and chopped
1 tablespoon dripping
450 g (1 lb) minced beef
1 tablespoon flour
1 tablespoon tomato purée
150 ml ($\frac{1}{4}$ pint) stock
salt and freshly ground black pepper
1 teaspoon basil
350 g (12 oz) potatoes, peeled and
  boiled
450 g (1 lb) parsnips, peeled and
  boiled
40–50 g (1$\frac{1}{2}$–2 oz) butter

Fry the onion, garlic and celery in the melted dripping until soft. Add the mince and cook gently for 10 minutes, stirring occasionally. Stir in the flour and tomato purée and then the stock, seasonings and herbs. Bring to the boil, cover and simmer gently for 15 to 20 minutes. Taste and adjust seasonings. Turn into an ovenproof dish.

Meanwhile mash the potatoes and parsnips together, add butter and then seasonings to taste and beat until smooth. Either spread or pipe over the meat. Use a large plain vegetable nozzle for piping. Cook in a moderately hot oven (200°C, 400°F, Gas Mark 6) for 30 to 40 minutes until the top is browning.

Instant potato mash may be used in place of boiled potatoes.

Ham and Beef Fricassée

1 ham bone with a little meat
1 bouquet garni (p. 364)
1 small onion, peeled
1 slice of white bread, crust removed
1 tablespoon corn oil
450 g (1 lb) lean minced beef
2 tablespoons seedless raisins
1 tablespoon flour
salt and freshly ground black pepper

On a clean chopping board remove all the lean meat from the ham bone. Put the bone on to boil with enough water just to cover it. Add the bouquet garni and simmer for 30 minutes.

Mince the ham with the onion, then put the bread through the mincer. Heat the corn oil in a flameproof casserole and fry the minced beef gently until brown, turning constantly. Add the ham mixture and the raisins, sprinkle with the flour, and season to taste. Cook, still stirring, for a further 2 minutes. Measure 150 ml ($\frac{1}{4}$ pint) of the ham stock and add to the casserole. Cover and simmer for 30 minutes. Add a little more ham stock if the mixture becomes too dry. Taste and adjust the seasoning if necessary. Serve with piped mashed potatoes.

Stuffed Peppers

4 green peppers, cored and seeded,
  tops reserved
2 tablespoons vegetable oil
1 onion, peeled and finely chopped
225 g (8 oz) minced beef
1 × 225 g (8 oz) can tomatoes
2 tablespoons tomato purée
1 teaspoon dried oregano
salt
freshly gound black pepper
100 g (4 oz) ($\frac{1}{2}$ cup) long-grain rice,
  cooked

Put the peppers in a bowl, cover with boiling water, then leave for at least 10 minutes. Meanwhile, heat the oil in a pan, add the onion and fry over gentle heat until soft. Add the meat and fry until browned, breaking it up constantly with a spoon. Stir in the remaining ingredients except the rice and bring to the boil. Simmer for 15 minutes until the liquid has reduced, then remove from the heat and stir in the ready-cooked rice.

Preheat the oven at medium temperature for 5 minutes. Drain the peppers then stand them in an ovenproof dish. Divide the meat and rice mixture equally between the peppers, spooning any surplus mixture around them. Put the tops on the peppers, then bake in the centre of the oven for 20 minutes. Transfer to the floor of the oven and bake for a further 20 minutes. Serve hot with a tomato sauce, mixed salad and garlic bread, if liked.

Variation:
Add 100 g (4 oz) mushrooms, finely chopped, to the stuffing mixture and halve the quantity of rice.

Paprika Mince

1 large onion, peeled and sliced
1 clove garlic, crushed
1 tablespoon dripping or oil
450 g (1 lb) minced beef
1 tablespoon flour
1 tablespoon paprika
1 tablespoon tomato purée
4 tomatoes, peeled and quartered
salt and freshly ground black pepper
150 ml ($\frac{1}{4}$ pint) stock
1 tablespoon wine vinegar
$\frac{1}{2}$ teaspoon caraway seeds (optional)
To garnish:
150 ml ($\frac{1}{4}$ pint) soured cream
finely chopped parsley

Fry the onion and garlic in the dripping or oil until lightly browned. Stir in the mince and cook gently for about 5 minutes, stirring frequently. Add the flour, paprika, tomato paste, tomatoes, seasonings, stock, vinegar and caraway seeds (if using). Bring to the boil, transfer to an ovenproof casserole, cover and cook in a warm oven (160°C, 325°F, Gas Mark 3) for 1 hour.

Spoon the soured cream over the meat and sprinkle with parsley. Serve with boiled noodles.

† Beef Risotto

25 g (1 oz) butter or margarine
1 small onion, peeled and coarsely chopped
1 small green pepper, cored, seeded and coarsely chopped
350 g (12 oz) minced beef
100 g (4 oz) mushrooms, washed and coarsely chopped
225 g (8 oz) long-grain rice
600 ml (1 pint) brown stock or water and $\frac{1}{2}$ beef stock cube
1 teaspoon Worcestershire sauce
salt
freshly ground black pepper
2 tablespoons chopped parsley
25 g (1 oz) Parmesan cheese

Heat the butter or margarine in the cooker and fry the onion and green pepper until both are beginning to soften. Add the beef and fry until lightly browned. Carefully drain off any excess butter or margarine from the cooker. Return the cooker to the heat and add the mushrooms, rice, stock or water and stock cube, Worcestershire sauce and salt and pepper. Stir well to remove any residues from the base of the cooker. Close the cooker, bring to H pressure and cook for 6 minutes. Reduce the pressure quickly. Return the open cooker to a low heat and stir with a fork to separate the rice grains. Stir in the parsley and taste and adjust the seasoning as necessary. Serve sprinkled with finely grated Parmesan cheese.

Thatched Meat Loaf

3 slices of bread, crusts removed,
   broken into pieces
450 g (1 lb) minced beef
1 onion, peeled and finely chopped
2 tablespoons Worcestershire sauce
1 egg, beaten
1 teaspoon dried mixed herbs
salt
freshly ground black pepper
1 × 100 g (4 oz) packet instant mashed
   potato mix
600 ml (1 pint) of boiling water
1 knob of butter

Put the bread in a small bowl, then
cover with water. Leave to stand for 10
minutes, then squeeze dry. Mix the
bread with the beef, onion, Worcestershire sauce, egg, herbs and salt and
pepper to taste.
   Preheat the oven at medium temperature for 5 minutes. Press the mixture
into a greased 450 g (1 lb) loaf tin or
ovenproof dish and cover with foil.
Bake in the centre of the oven for 1
hour, or until the juices run clear when
the centre of the loaf is pierced with a
skewer or knife.
   Remove the loaf from the oven and
leave to stand in the tin or dish for 10
minutes. Meanwhile, make the potato
mix with the water according to packet
directions, then beat in the butter and
salt and pepper to taste. Drain off the
excess fat and juices from the loaf, then
turn the loaf out on to a baking sheet.
Spread the potato over the loaf to cover
it completely, then rough up the surface
with a fork.
   Return to the oven and bake at high
temperature for 20 minutes, turning the
baking sheet round half way through
cooking. Serve hot with seasonal vegetables or baked beans.

Variation:
Omit the potato topping and serve the
meat loaf cold with a salad tossed in a
vinaigrette.

Savoury Meat Loaf

225 g (8 oz) minced beef
225 g (8 oz) minced pork
1 × 75 g (3 oz) packet sage and onion
   stuffing mix
2 eating apples, peeled
1 egg, beaten
4 tablespoons hot water
salt
freshly ground black pepper

Preheat the oven at medium temperature for 5 minutes. Put the beef, pork
and stuffing mix in a bowl. Grate the
apple flesh into the bowl. Add the egg,
water and salt and pepper, then stir well
to mix.
   Press the mixture into a greased 450 g
(1 lb) loaf tin or ovenproof dish and
cover with foil. Bake in the centre of the
oven for 1 hour, or until the juices run
clear when the centre of the loaf is
pierced with a skewer or knife. Remove
the loaf from the oven, then leave to
stand for 5 minutes. Drain off the excess
fat and juices from the loaf, then turn
the loaf out on to a serving dish and
leave until cold. Cut into slices and
serve with salads. This is ideal for
picnics.

Variations:
Use all minced beef or pork, or a different stuffing mix. Sausage meat can
also be used instead of the pork. Alternatively, serve hot with a tomato and
mushroom sauce, (p. 351) boiled new
potatoes and a seasonal vegetable.

Curried Beef Loaf

350 g (12 oz) minced beef
salt and freshly ground black pepper
2 teaspoons curry powder
2 tablespoons mango chutney
1 onion, peeled and finely chopped
50 g (2 oz) fresh breadcrumbs
1 large egg, beaten

For the sauce:
1 medium-sized onion, peeled and
  chopped
50 g (2 oz) butter or margarine
1–2 teaspoons curry powder
40 g (1½ oz) flour
450 ml (¾ pint) stock
2 tablespoons chopped gherkins, to
  garnish

Mix the mince with plenty of seasonings, the curry powder, chutney, onion
and breadcrumbs and bind together
with the egg. Turn into a well greased
450 g (1 lb) loaf tin and press well down.
Stand in a baking tin containing 4 cm
(1½ inches) water and cook in a warm
oven (160°C, 325°F, Gas Mark 3) for
1½–1¾ hours until firm to the touch and
cooked through.

Meanwhile, to make the sauce, fry
the onion in butter until soft then stir in
the curry powder and flour. Cook for 1
minute then gradually add the stock
and bring to the boil for 2 minutes.
Season to taste and stir in the gherkins.

Turn the loaf out on to a serving dish
and serve with the hot sauce. Garnish
with gherkins, if liked.

Cabbage Dolmades

25 g (1 oz) butter
1 onion, peeled and chopped
4 rashers streaky bacon, derinded and
  chopped
225 g (8 oz) minced beef
50 g (2 oz) long grain rice, cooked
25 g (1 oz) olives, chopped
4 teaspoons soy sauce
salt and freshly ground black pepper
12 large cabbage leaves
300 ml (½ pint) seasoned boiling stock
1 tablespoon cornflour
2 teaspoons tomato purée

Melt the butter in a pan and fry the
onion and bacon until lightly coloured.
Stir in the mince and cook for 5 minutes,
stirring frequently. Stir in the cooked

rice, olives, 3 teaspoons of the soy sauce
and the seasonings. Blanch the cabbage
leaves in boiling salted water for 3
minutes, then drain. Divide the mixture
between the cabbage leaves and roll up
to enclose the filling. Place in a lightly
greased ovenproof casserole and pour
over the boiling stock. Cover the casserole and cook in a warm oven (160°C,
325°F, Gas Mark 3) for 40 minutes.

Strain off the cooking liquor into a
small pan. Add the cornflour blended in
a little cold water, the tomato purée and
the remaining soy sauce and bring to
the boil for 2 minutes. Taste and adjust
the seasonings. Pour back over the
dolmades.

Rice Rissoles

350 g (12 oz) lean minced beef
225 g (8 oz) cooked long-grain rice
1 large onion, peeled and finely
  chopped
50 g (2 oz) Cheddar cheese, grated
1 tablespoon chopped dill pickles
salt and freshly ground black pepper
3 eggs
2 tablespoons cold water
flour for coating
vegetable oil for frying

Stir together in a large bowl the minced
beef, rice, chopped onion, grated
cheese, chopped pickles and seasoning.
Break in 2 eggs, mix thoroughly, and
form with floured hands into 12 balls.
Beat the remaining egg with the water
and use to coat the balls. Roll them in
flour and refrigerate on a plate, slipped
inside a polythene bag for at least 1
hour to become firm.

Fry in deep hot fat (190°C/375°F) until
a rich golden-brown.

Mexican Meatballs

2 tablespoons vegetable oil
1 small onion, peeled and finely
   chopped
$\frac{1}{2}$ red pepper, cored, seeded and finely
   chopped
$\frac{1}{2}$ green pepper, cored, seeded and
   finely chopped
$\frac{1}{2}$ teaspoon chilli powder, or to taste
2 × 425 g (15 oz) cans beef meatballs in
   tomato sauce
1 tablespoon wine vinegar
1 tablespoon soy sauce
2 teaspoons brown sugar
salt
freshly ground black pepper
plain unsweetened yogurt, to finish

Chilli powders vary in strength, depending on the brand used. Since chilli is a strong spice it is wise to use it cautiously until you have found the degree of strength you prefer.

Heat the oil in a pan, add the vegetables and chilli powder and fry over moderate heat for 5 minutes until lightly coloured, stirring occasionally.

Add remaining ingredients, except the yogurt, and stir gently to mix. Cook over moderate heat for a further 5 minutes until bubbling. Taste and adjust seasoning and then serve immediately with yogurt swirled on top. Serve with boiled rice and a green salad.

Chilli Con Carne

450 g (1 lb) minced beef
2 large onions, peeled and thinly
   sliced
1–2 teaspoons chilli powder
salt
freshly ground black pepper
paprika
1 × 822 g (1 lb 13 oz) can peeled
   tomatoes
1 × 454 g (16 oz) can red kidney beans,
   drained

Fry the mince slowly in a non-stick pan for approximately 10 minutes, stirring frequently. Add the onion and chilli powder and cook gently for a further 5 minutes. Season well with salt, lightly with pepper and paprika, add the canned tomatoes and bring to the boil. Cover and simmer very gently for 1–1$\frac{1}{4}$ hours, adding a little boiling water during cooking, if necessary, and stirring occasionally.

Add the beans, taste and adjust the seasonings and continue for a further 15 to 20 minutes.

Serve in earthenware bowls and eat with a spoon and accompany with lots of hot crusty bread.

Curried Meatballs

450 g (1 lb) minced beef
1 onion, peeled and finely chopped
1 tablespoon curry powder
salt
freshly ground black pepper
1 teaspoon Worcestershire sauce
75 g (3 oz) sultanas
25 g (1 oz) fresh breadcrumbs
1 egg, beaten
flour for coating
fat for frying
1 onion, peeled and finely sliced
2 carrots, peeled and diced
15 g ($\frac{1}{2}$ oz) flour
2 teaspoons tomato purée
450 ml ($\frac{3}{4}$ pint) beef stock

Mix together the mince, onion, 1 teaspoon of the curry powder, the seasonings, Worcestershire sauce, 25 g (1 oz) of the sultanas and the breadcrumbs and bind together with the egg. Divide into 16 and shape into balls then coat in flour. Fry in a little fat until browned all over then transfer to an ovenproof casserole.

Retain 1 tablespoon fat in the pan and fry the onion and carrots until lightly coloured. Stir in the remaining curry powder, flour and tomato purée and cook for 1 to 2 minutes. Gradually add the stock and bring to the boil. Season, add the remaining sultanas and pour over the meatballs. Cover and cook in a moderate oven (180°C, 350°F, Gas Mark 4) for about 45 minutes, or until tender.

Taste, adjust the seasonings and serve the meatballs with boiled rice.

Pan Pizza

1 × 150 g (5 oz) packet pizza base mix
2 tablespoons vegetable oil
1 onion, peeled and finely chopped
1 garlic clove, peeled and crushed
    with ½ teaspoon salt
1 × 425 g (15 oz) can minced beef in
    rich gravy
2 tablespoons tomato purée
½ teaspoon ground allspice
freshly ground black pepper
3 tomatoes, finely sliced
freshly chopped parsley

Make the pizza base according to packet directions. Roll out the dough to a circle large enough to fit inside a non-stick skillet or frypan. Brush the inside of the pan with oil, place the dough in the bottom and leave in a warm place for 10 to 15 minutes until it starts to rise. Put the pan over the lowest possible flame, cover tightly and cook for 10 minutes.

Meanwhile, heat the oil in a separate pan, add the onion and garlic and fry gently until golden. Stir in the remaining ingredients, except the tomatoes and parsley, cook for about 5 minutes until bubbling. Taste and adjust seasoning. Spoon the minced beef mixture over the pizza base, and cover with the tomato slices. Cover and continue cooking over gentle heat for a further 20 minutes. Sprinkle with parsley, cut into wedges and serve hot with a selection of fresh salads.

Serves 3 to 4

Tagliatelle alla Bolognese

25 g (1 oz) butter
50 g (2 oz) bacon or ham, chopped
1 small onion, peeled and chopped
1 stalk celery, chopped
50 g (2 oz) mushrooms, sliced
100 g (4 oz) minced beef
50 g (2 oz) chicken livers, chopped
1 tablespoon tomato purée
120 ml (4 fl oz) red wine
120 ml (4 fl oz) stock
pinch of dried basil or marjoram
1 teaspoon sugar
pinch of nutmeg
salt
freshly ground pepper
225 g (8 oz) tagliatelle

Melt the butter in a saucepan and fry the bacon, onion, celery and mushrooms gently until softened. Add the minced beef and chicken livers and fry, stirring well, until nicely browned.

Add the tomato purée and fry for a minute or two. Stir in the wine and stock. Add the herbs, sugar, nutmeg and salt and pepper to taste. Bring to the simmer, cover and cook gently for 30 to 40 minutes.

When the sauce is ready, cook the tagliatelle in plenty of boiling lightly salted water and drain it well. Lift it into a warm serving bowl with wooden pasta forks.

Spoon the bolognese sauce into the centre of the tagliatelle. Hand the grated Parmesan cheese separately and serve with a tossed green salad.

Italian Pasta Pot

2 tablespoons vegetable oil
1 onion, peeled and finely chopped
750 g (1½ lb) minced beef
2 tablespoons tomato purée
1 × 400 g (14 oz) can tomatoes
150 ml (¼ pint) water
½ teaspoon dried oregano or basil
salt
freshly ground black pepper
5 handfuls, 300 ml (½ pint) cut
   macaroni
100 g (4 oz) Cheddar cheese

Heat the oil in a large shallow pan, add
the onion and fry over gentle heat until
soft. Add the meat and fry until browned, breaking it up constantly with a
spoon. Stir in the remaining ingredients
except the cheese, then bring to the boil,
stirring constantly. Lower the heat and
simmer for 25 minutes, then taste and
adjust seasoning. Remove from the heat
and grate the cheese over the top of the
mixture. Put under a hot grill for 10
minutes until golden brown. Serve hot
with a tossed green salad.

Variations:
Any kind of pasta can be used – broken
spaghetti, tagliatelle or pasta shells.

Barbecued Spaghetti

2 tablespoons vegetable oil
1 medium-sized onion, peeled and
   finely chopped
1–2 tablespoons curry powder
3 tablespoons peanut butter
2 teaspoons tomato purée
small strip of lemon rind
300 ml (½ pint) chicken stock
salt and freshly ground black pepper
225–350 g (8–12 oz) spaghetti

Heat the oil in a saucepan. Add the
chopped onion and fry until just beginning to turn golden. Stir in the curry
powder and fry for a few seconds. Add
the peanut butter, tomato purée, lemon
rind, stock and seasoning to taste.
Bring to the boil, stirring constantly,
cover and simmer for about 15 minutes,
stirring occasionally. Remove the piece
of lemon rind. Taste and add more
seasoning if necessary.

Meanwhile, cook the spaghetti in
plenty of boiling lightly salted water.
Drain well. Add the spaghetti to the
sauce and mix until well coated. Serve
hot with fried or grilled sausages or
beefburgers.

Beef and Macaroni Bake

225 g (8 oz) short-cut macaroni
salt and freshly ground black pepper
1 large onion, peeled and sliced
1–2 cloves garlic, crushed
2 carrots, peeled and chopped
1–2 tablespoons oil
450 g (1 lb) minced beef
150 ml (¼ pint) stock
100 g (4 oz) mushrooms, cleaned,
   trimmed and chopped
1 bay leaf
½ teaspoon Worcestershire sauce
1 teaspoon oregano
25 g (1 oz) butter or margarine
25 g (1 oz) flour
300 ml (½ pint) milk

75 g (3 oz) English Mature Cheddar
  cheese, grated
tomato wedges, to garnish

Cook the macaroni in plenty of boiling
salted water, as directed on the packet,
or until just tender. Drain.

Fry the onion, garlic and carrots in
the oil until soft and lightly coloured.
Add the mince and continue for 5 minutes, stirring frequently. Add the stock,
mushrooms, bay leaf, Worcestershire
sauce and seasonings, cover and simmer for 15 to 20 minutes. Discard the
bay leaf. Taste and adjust the seasonings and stir in the oregano.

To make the sauce, melt the butter or
margarine in a pan and stir in the flour.
Cook for 1 minute then gradually add
the milk and bring to the boil, stirring
continuously. Simmer for 3 minutes,
season to taste and stir in 50 g (2 oz)
cheese until melted.

In a lightly greased ovenproof dish
layer up one-third of the cooked macaroni followed by half the meat and
half the sauce. Continue with half the
macaroni, remaining meat, remaining
macaroni and finally the sauce.
Sprinkle with grated cheese and cook in
a moderately hot oven (200°C, 400°F,
Gas Mark 6) for about 40 minutes until
well browned.

Serve hot, garnished with wedges of
tomato and with a green salad.

Lasagne Verdi

8–12 sheets lasagne verdi
salt and freshly ground black pepper
2 tablespoons oil
1 onion, peeled and finely chopped
2 sticks celery, scrubbed and finely
  chopped
1 carrot, peeled and finely chopped
1 clove garlic, crushed
350 g (12 oz) minced beef
1 × 225 g (8 oz) can peeled tomatoes
2 tablespoons tomato purée
4 tablespoons red wine

1 teaspoon oregano
1 bay leaf
For the Béchamel sauce:
600 ml (1 pint) milk
few slices raw onion
1 bay leaf
40 g (1½ oz) butter
40 g (1½ oz) flour
25–50 g (1–2 oz) cheese, grated
1 tablespoon Parmesan cheese, grated

Cook the lasagne in boiling salted
water with 1 tablespoon oil added, following the directions on the packet.
Drain on absorbent kitchen paper.

Fry the onion, celery, carrot and
garlic in the remaining oil for 5 minutes. Stir in the mince and cook for a
further 5 minutes, stirring frequently.
Add the tomatoes, tomato purée, wine,
seasonings, oregano and bay leaf, cover
and simmer for about 40 minutes, stirring occasionally and adding a little
more liquid if necessary.

Meanwhile, to make the Béchamel
sauce, place the milk in a pan with the
onion and bay leaf, bring slowly to the
boil and leave to cool. Melt the butter in
a pan, stir in the flour and cook for 1
minute. Strain the infused milk and
gradually add to the roux, stirring continuously until boiling. Simmer for 2
minutes then taste and adjust the
seasonings. Use the lasagne to line a
lightly greased ovenproof dish about 5
cm (2 inches) deep. Spread with a layer
of meat sauce and then a layer of
Béchamel sauce. Continue to layer the
lasagne and sauces until used up, finishing with a layer of Béchamel sauce.

Sprinkle with a mixture of Cheddar
and Parmesan cheese and cook in a
moderately hot oven (200°C, 400°F, Gas
Mark 6) for about 25 minutes until
golden brown and bubbling.

Spicy Beef Cakes in Tomato Sauce

2 slices of bread, crusts removed,
  broken into pieces
450 g (1 lb) minced beef
1 onion, peeled and very finely
  chopped
1 tablespoon tomato purée
1 tablespoon Worcestershire sauce
salt
freshly ground black pepper
flour for coating
2 tablespoons vegetable oil
1 × 225 g (8 oz) can tomato sauce
½ teaspoon dried oregano or basil
soured cream or plain unsweetened
  yogurt, to finish

Put the bread in a small bowl and cover
with water. Leave to stand for 10 minutes, then squeeze dry. Mix the bread
with the beef, onion, tomato purée,
Worcestershire sauce and salt and
pepper to taste. Form the mixture into 8
flat cakes, then coat in flour. Heat the
oil in a frying pan, add the beef cakes
and fry over brisk heat for 5 minutes on
each side. Lower the heat and pour over
the sauce. Sprinkle with oregano or
basil. Cover and cook gently for 25
minutes, then spoon over soured cream
or yogurt. Served with boiled rice.

Savoury Pancakes

2 tablespoons cooking oil
1 large onion, peeled and finely
  chopped
350 g (12 oz) minced beef
1 × 50 g (2 oz) can anchovies, drained
  and soaked in milk for 30 minutes
1 teaspoon dill powder
2 tablespoons tomato purée
300 ml (½ pint) soured cream
about 8 tablespoons beef stock to
  moisten
freshly ground black pepper
600 ml (1 pint) pancake batter (p. 363)

Heat the oil in a pan, add the onion and
cook gently for approximately 5 minutes until soft and lightly coloured. Add
the minced beef and cook until
browned, stirring occasionally.

Drain the anchovies and pound to a
paste with a pestle and mortar. Add to
the pan with the dill, tomato purée and 2
tablespoons soured cream. Stir well to
combine and add enough stock to moisten. Season with plenty of pepper, then
cook very gently for 20 minutes, stirring
occasionally. Taste and adjust seasoning. Meanwhile, make the pancakes,
using twice as much batter for each
pancake as stated in the recipe for Basic
Batter Mixture (p. 363). Keep each pancake warm while making the remainder. When all the pancakes are made,
lay each one flat on a board, put a few
spoonfuls of filling on each, then roll up
and place on a warmed serving platter.
Keep warm while filling and rolling the
remainder.

Heat the remaining soured cream
until bubbling, pour over the pancakes
and serve immediately.

Chunky Burgers with Piquant Dressing

450 g (1 lb) minced beef
40 g (1½ oz) fresh breadcrumbs
salt
freshly ground black pepper
¼ teaspoon ground mace
1 tablespoon finely chopped parsley
4 tablespoons tomato pickle (or other
  chunky pickle)
1 egg, beaten
flour for coating
oil or dripping for frying
For the dressing:
4 tablespoons thick mayonnaise
2 tablespoons tomato pickle
2 teaspoons lemon juice
¼ teaspoon finely grated lemon rind
To garnish:
chicory spears
coarsely grated carrot

Mix the beef with the breadcrumbs, seasonings, mace, parsley and pickle and bind together with the egg. Divide into four and shape into round flat cakes. (For smaller burgers divide the mixture into eight.) Coat evenly with flour. Fry in hot shallow fat for about 10 minutes each side until well browned and cooked through. Drain on absorbent kitchen paper and keep warm.

To make the dressing, mix together all the ingredients and season to taste.

Serve garnished with chicory and coarsely grated carrot.

Corned Beef Cheeseburgers

350 g (12 oz) lean cut corned beef
1 medium-sized onion, peeled
1 egg
1 tablespoon Worcestershire sauce
50 g (2 oz) quick cook oats
1 tablespoon chopped parsley
salt and freshly ground black pepper
vegetable oil for frying
4 slices processed cheese
1 tomato

Place the corned beef in a medium-sized bowl and mash it with a fork until completely broken down. Grate the onion straight into the corned beef. Beat the egg and add to the meat mixture with the Worcestershire sauce, oats, parsley and seasoning to taste. Mix together thoroughly and allow the mixture to stand for 5 minutes. Divide into 4 equal parts and shape each into a round approx. 2.5 cm (1 inch) thick.

Heat a little oil in a frying pan and cook the burgers for 2 to 3 minutes on each side, until golden-brown. Remove from the pan and drain well on absorbent kitchen paper.

Meanwhile, heat the grill. Place the burgers in the grill pan and top each with a slice of cheese. Place under the grill until the cheese melts. Top with tomato slices. Serve with baps.

Beef Croquettes with Quick Béarnaise Sauce

6 spring onions, cleaned, trimmed, finely chopped
2 rashers lean bacon, derinded and chopped
40 g (1½ oz) butter
25 g (1 oz) flour
150 ml (¼ pint) beef stock
225 g (8 oz) cooked beef, minced
1 tablespoon finely chopped parsley
salt
freshly ground black pepper
2 eggs, beaten
100 g (4 oz) fresh breadcrumbs
oil or fat for deep frying
For the sauce:
6 tablespoons thick mayonnaise
2 teaspoons tarragon vinegar
2 spring onions, cleaned, trimmed, finely chopped
1 teaspoon chopped tarragon, fresh or dried
parsley sprig, to garnish

Fry the onions and bacon gently in the melted butter until soft and lightly coloured. Stir in the flour and cook gently until pale brown. Gradually add the stock and bring to the boil, stirring continuously. Simmer for 2 minutes then remove from the heat and stir in the beef, parsley and seasonings to taste. Cool.

Divide into eight and shape into barrels on a floured surface. Dip into, or brush with, egg then coat in breadcrumbs; repeat this process again pressing well in. Chill until required; even overnight, if wished.

To make the sauce, blend all the ingredients together, season to taste and place in a sauce boat.

Heat deep fat to 190°C/375°F, or until a cube of bread browns in 20 seconds, and fry the croquettes for 4 to 5 minutes until well browned and cooked through. Drain on absorbent kitchen paper, garnish with a parsley sprig and serve hot with the sauce.

Beef and Horseradish Pasties

225 g (8 oz) minced beef
1 onion, peeled and finely chopped
50 g (2 oz) potato, peeled and finely
  chopped
1 carrot, peeled and coarsely grated
salt and freshly ground black pepper
1 tablespoon creamed horseradish
For the pastry:
200 g (8 oz) plain flour
pinch of salt
50 g (2 oz) margarine
50 g (2 oz) lard or white fat
water to mix
beaten egg or milk to glaze

Mix the mince with the onion, potato,
carrot, plenty of seasonings and the
horseradish.

To make the pastry, sieve the flour
with a pinch of salt into a bowl. Add the
fats and rub in until the mixture resembles fine breadcrumbs. Add sufficient water to mix to a pliable dough.
Roll out two-thirds of the pastry on a
floured surface and use to line four
individual Yorkshire pudding tins. Fill
with the meat mixture and cover with
pastry lids, dampened around the edges.
Press the edges well together and crimp.
Decorate the tops with the pastry
trimmings.

Brush with egg or milk and cook in a
hot oven (220°C, 425°F, Gas Mark 7) for
15 minutes. Reduce oven temperature to
moderate (180°C, 350°F, Gas Mark 4)
and continue for 25 to 30 minutes until
golden brown. Serve hot.

Corned Beef Hash

1 × 100 g (4 oz) packet instant mashed
  potato mix
450 ml (¾ pint) boiling water
2 large knobs of butter
¼ teaspoon mustard powder
freshly ground black pepper
1 × 350 g (12 oz) can corned beef,
  shredded
1 onion, peeled and finely chopped

Put the potato mix in a bowl, then
gradually stir in the boiling water. Add
half the butter, the mustard and plenty
of pepper and beat well to mix. Fold in
the corned beef.

Melt the remaining butter in a non-
stick frying pan, add the onion and fry
over gentle heat until soft. Add the
potato mixture and fry over brisk heat
for 10 minutes. Stir the mixture and
turn it over occasionally, flatten it into
a cake shape with a spatula and smooth
the top. Fry over moderate heat for 5
minutes or until golden brown underneath. Invert a plate over the pan and
turn the hash out onto the plate. Slide
back into the pan and fry for a further 5
minutes or until golden brown on the
underside. Cut into wedges and serve
hot with baked beans.

Oxtail Provençale

1 large oxtail, cut up
seasoned flour
2 tablespoons oil
2 onions, peeled and sliced
1–2 cloves garlic, crushed
2 large carrots, peeled and sliced
2 sticks celery, scrubbed and sliced
1 × 400 g (14 oz) can peeled tomatoes
1 tablespoon tomato purée
600 ml (1 pint) stock
2 teaspoons oregano
salt and freshly ground black pepper
12 black olives

Trim the oxtail of excess fat and coat
the pieces in seasoned flour. Fry in the
oil until evenly browned all over. Transfer to a large ovenproof casserole.

Fry the onions and garlic in the same
oil until lightly coloured then add to the
casserole with the carrots, celery, tomatoes, tomato purée, stock, oregano
and plenty of seasonings. Cover tightly

and cook in a warm oven (160°C, 325°F, Gas Mark 3) for 3 hours.

If possible, cool and chill overnight in order to remove the layer of fat easily. If not, spoon off all the fat from the surface before continuing. Add the olives, taste and adjust the seasonings and return the casserole to the oven for another hour before serving.

† Cheesy Beef Roll

175 g (6 oz) self-raising flour
½ teaspoon salt
50 g (2 oz) finely grated Cheddar
  cheese
75 g (3 oz) shredded beef suet
approx. 150 ml (¼ pint) cold water
900 ml (1½ pints) boiling water
little lemon juice
For the filling:
225 g (8 oz) minced beef
1 small onion, peeled and finely
  chopped
1 tablespoon Worcestershire sauce
salt
freshly ground black pepper

Sift the flour and salt into a mixing bowl. Add the cheese and suet and stir thoroughly. Gradually add sufficient water until a smooth, elastic dough is formed which leaves the sides of the bowl cleanly. Turn out on to a floured board and knead lightly. Roll into an oblong a little narrower than the base of the cooker and approximately 5 mm (¼ inch) thick.

For the filling, mix together the beef, onion and Worcestershire sauce and add a little salt and pepper. Spread the filling evenly over the pastry, almost to the edges. Wet the edges with a little water and roll up swiss-roll style, sealing the edges well. Place the roll, seamside down, on a double thickness of greased greaseproof paper or a greased piece of aluminium foil. Wrap loosely, making a pleat in the centre to allow for expansion and tie at the ends. Have the water and lemon juice boiling in the cooker and add the trivet, rim side down. Place the roll on to the trivet. Close the cooker and steam, without the weights, for 10 minutes. Raise the heat, bring to L or H pressure and cook for 30 or 20 minutes accordingly. Reduce the pressure slowly. Serve with fresh green vegetables.

Fried Silverside Sandwiches

25 g (1 oz) butter
8 large slices white bread
4 tablespoons sweet brown pickle
4 slices beef silverside, cooked
2 eggs, beaten
75 ml (3 fl oz) milk
freshly ground black pepper
vegetable oil for frying
mustard and cress, to garnish

Thinly butter the slices of bread and spread with the pickle. Lay the slices of beef silverside on 4 of the bread slices and cover with the remaining slices, so that the pickle helps the bread to adhere to the meat. Place the sandwiches on a board, press firmly together and cut each one across diagonally to make 2 triangles.

Beat up the eggs with the milk, season with a little black pepper and pour into a shallow dish. Dip the sandwiches in the egg mixture, using food tongs to turn them. Make sure they are completely coated.

Heat a little oil in a frying pan and quickly fry the triangles on both sides until golden-brown. Serve hot garnished with mustard and cress.

PORK

Eskdale Pork

50 g (2 oz) fresh breadcrumbs
75 g (3 oz) salami, diced
finely grated rind and juice of 1 small
    orange
1 tablespoon finely chopped parsley
1 teaspoon dried thyme
salt and freshly ground black pepper
1 egg, beaten
1¼ kg (2½ lb) piece lean belly pork,
    boned and scored
a little oil
1 tablespoon flour
300 ml (½ pint) stock
1 teaspoon tomato purée
To garnish:
orange slices
fresh parsley
salami cones

Combine the breadcrumbs, salami,
orange rind, parsley, thyme and seasonings and bind together with the egg.
Trim the pork, removing any gristle or
bone. Spread the stuffing over the inside
of the pork and roll up to enclose the
stuffing. Secure with skewers and fine
string. Place in a roasting tin and rub
the skin lightly with oil, then rub with
salt. Cook in a moderately hot oven
(190°C, 375°F, Gas Mark 5) for about 2
hours until well browned, crispy and
cooked through. Baste once or twice
during cooking and roast potatoes
alongside the joint. Remove meat and
keep warm. Use the pan drippings and
the flour, stock, orange juice, tomato
purée and seasonings to make a gravy.

Garnish pork with orange slices,
parsley and salami cones, and serve
with roast potatoes.
Serves 6

Roast Stuffed Blade of Pork

1 blade of pork weighing approx.
    1¾ kg (3½ lb)
apple and nut stuffing (p. 349)
oil for coating
salt
freshly ground pepper

Ask the butcher to bone the joint and to
score the skin deeply to make crackling.
Pack the stuffing into the cavity where
the bone was removed. Secure with
skewers and string. Preheat the oven to
220°C, 425°F, Gas Mark 7. Weigh the
stuffed joint and allow 25 minutes per
450 g (1 lb), plus 25 minutes. Put bones
on to make stock for the gravy (p. 6).

Grease a roasting pan, put in the
joint, brush all over with oil and
sprinkle the skin generously with salt
to help crisping. Place in the oven, just
above the centre, and cook for 30 minutes or until the skin is golden brown
and crispy. Reduce heat to 190°C, 375°F,
Gas Mark 5 and cook for 70 minutes, or
until the juice is amber coloured and
the crackling is crisp. Pork must
NEVER be underdone.

Place the joint on a warm serving dish. Allow the residue to settle in the pan and carefully pour off the fat into a pork dripping pot. Strain in bone stock or use liquor from accompanying vegetables. Scrape up the pan juices and stir over a brisk heat until reduced and a good colour. Season to taste with salt and freshly ground pepper and strain into a warm gravy boat. Serve the pork with Apple sauce (p. 350). Roast potatoes and a fresh green vegetable.

Pork Stuffed Peppers

65 g (2½ oz) butter
1 onion, peeled and finely chopped
4 rashers streaky bacon, derinded and chopped
450 g (1 lb) lean minced pork
25 g (1 oz) fresh breadcrumbs
1–2 teaspoons dried tarragon
2 tomatoes, peeled and chopped
salt and freshly ground black pepper
4 green peppers
450 ml (¾ pint) hot chicken stock
40 g (1½ oz) flour

Melt 25 g (1 oz) butter in a pan and fry the onion and bacon until soft. Add the mince and cook gently for 5 to 10 minutes, stirring frequently. Stir in the breadcrumbs, tarragon, tomatoes and seasonings. Wash and dry the peppers, cut the tops off and remove the seeds. Stand in a greased ovenproof casserole and fill with the pork mixture. Pour the hot stock around the peppers, cover and cook in a moderate oven (180°C, 350°F, Gas Mark 4) for ¾–1 hour until tender.

Drain off the cooking liquor and make up to 450 ml (¾ pint) with more stock, if necessary. Keep the peppers warm. Melt the remaining butter in a pan, stir in the flour and cook for 1 minute. Gradually add the cooking liquor and bring to the boil for 3 minutes. Taste and adjust the seasonings. Serve the peppers with the sauce in a sauce boat.

Indonesian Pork

225 g (8 oz) long-grain rice
salt and freshly ground black pepper
65 g (2½ oz) butter
1 large onion, peeled and chopped
2 carrots, peeled and diced
1 clove garlic, crushed
1½ teaspoons curry powder
½ teaspoon ground coriander
½ teaspoon chilli powder
½ teaspoon caraway seeds (optional)
1 tablespoon soy sauce
350–450 g (¾–1 lb) cold lean roast pork, diced
225 g (8 oz) frozen peas, freshly cooked
1 large egg

Cook the rice in plenty of boiling salted water until just tender – about 12 minutes. Drain very thoroughly.

Melt 50 g (2 oz) butter in a heavy-based saucepan and fry the onion, carrots and garlic very gently until soft but only lightly coloured, stirring frequently. Add the curry powder, coriander, chilli powder, caraway seeds, soy sauce and seasonings and cook gently for 1 minute. Add the diced pork and continue gently, stirring continuously for 5 minutes, until well heated. Add the cooked rice and continue for a further 8 to 10 minutes until piping hot. Add the peas. Taste and adjust the seasonings.

Whisk the egg with 1 tablespoon water and a pinch of salt. Melt the remaining butter in a frying pan, pour in the egg mixture and cook, without stirring, until set. Turn out and cut into narrow strips. Turn the pork mixture into a hot serving dish and garnish with the strips of omelette.

† Pork with Prune Stuffing

100 g (4 oz) prunes
cold water
75 g (3 oz) fresh white breadcrumbs
finely grated rind of 1 lemon
salt
freshly ground black pepper
1 egg, beaten
1½ kg (3 lb) blade bone joint of pork,
    boned and rinded
50 g (2 oz) lard or margarine
600 ml (1 pint) hot brown stock or
    water and ½ beef stock cube
2 teaspoons cornflour
little water
small bunch watercress, to garnish

Soak the prunes in cold water for several hours or overnight. Drain and dry well. Cut in half, remove the stones and chop. Mix the prunes with the breadcrumbs, lemon rind and a little salt and pepper. Bind with sufficient egg to make a firm stuffing.

Make a deep slit in the flesh side of the pork and pack the stuffing into the slit. Make the joint into a roll and secure at intervals with string. Sprinkle well with salt and pepper.

Heat the lard or margarine in the cooker and brown the joint quickly and evenly all over.

Lift out and drain off any excess lard or margarine from the cooker. Add the stock or water and stock cube and the trivet, rim side down. Stand the joint on the trivet. Close the cooker, bring to H pressure and cook for 15 minutes per 450 g (1 lb) stuffed weight.

Reduce the pressure quickly. Lift out the joint, remove the string and place on a warmed serving platter and keep hot while making the sauce.

Mix the cornflour with a little water and add to the cooker. Cook over a gentle heat, stirring constantly, until the sauce thickens. Taste and adjust the seasoning as necessary and serve separately in a gravy boat with the pork. Garnish with watercress.

Pork Fillet with Mushrooms and Soured Cream

500 g (1¼ lb) pork fillet
2–3 tablespoons flour
100–175 g (4–6 oz) button mushrooms
50 g (2 oz) lard or unsalted butter
2 tablespoons sherry or vermouth
150 ml (¼ pint) soured cream
¼ teaspoon dried savory or mixed
    herbs
salt
freshly ground pepper
250 ml (8 fl oz) stock or bouillon
cooked rice or Duchess potatoes
    (p. 56) to serve
To garnish:
fried mushroom caps
paprika pepper or chopped parsley

Trim any fat or skin from the fillet and cut the meat across into slices about 2.5 cm (1 inch) thick. Flatten the slices slightly with a rolling pin. Coat with flour, shaking off any surplus. Trim off the mushroom stalks, rinse the caps under cold running water and dry on absorbent kitchen paper.

Heat the lard or butter in a sauté pan; when a slight haze rises from the fat, add the pork slices in a single layer. Fry briskly until crisp underneath, turn and fry the other side. Add the mushrooms and cook for 5 minutes, shaking the pan frequently.

Pour in the sherry or vermouth and bubble up, scraping up the juices from the bottom of the pan: this is called deglazing. Cook gently for a minute or two so that the liquids combine.

Lower the heat and stir in the soured cream. Add the herbs, salt and pepper to taste and mix well. Stir in sufficient stock to just cover the pork. Cook gently for 5–10 minutes or until the pork is tender. Taste and adjust the seasoning as necessary.

Make a border of cooked rice or Duchess potatoes and spoon in the pork and sauce. Garnish with fried mushroom caps arranged in a pattern and paprika or chopped parsley.

As an alternative to soured cream, stir 2 tablespoons of lemon juice into 150 ml ($\frac{1}{4}$ pint) double cream. If using a bouillon cube instead of stock, remember it is salty, so taste and adjust the seasoning as necessary.

Military Pork Jalousie

40 g ($1\frac{1}{2}$ oz) butter
1 small onion, peeled and chopped
40 g ($1\frac{1}{2}$ oz) flour
300 ml ($\frac{1}{2}$ pint) stock or milk
salt and freshly ground black pepper
2 tablespoons Military or other chunky pickle
350 g (12 oz) lean cooked pork, finely chopped
1 × 368 g (13 oz) packet frozen puff pastry, thawed
beaten egg, to glaze
mustard and cress, to garnish

Melt the butter in a pan and fry the onion until soft. Stir in the flour and cook for 1 minute. Gradually add the stock or milk and bring to the boil, stirring continuously. Season, add the pickle and pork and simmer gently for 4-5 minutes. Taste and adjust the seasonings and leave to cool.

Roll out the pastry and cut into two pieces 28 × 15 cm (11 × 6 inches). Place one on a dampened baking sheet and spread the filling over the pastry leaving a 2.5 cm (1 inch) margin all round. Brush the border with water. Roll the other piece out to 30 × 18 cm (12 × 7 inches) then fold in half lengthwise and cut into the fold at 1 cm ($\frac{1}{2}$ inch) intervals to within 2.5 cm (1 inch) of the edge, leaving 5 cm (2 inches) at each end. Unfold the pastry, placing it carefully over the filling. Press the edges well together and 'knock up' with a knife. Brush the pastry with beaten egg.

Cook in a hot oven (220°C, 425°F, Gas Mark 7) for about 15 minutes then reduce oven temperature to moderately hot (190°C, 375°F, Gas Mark 5) and continue for a further 20 to 25 minutes until well risen and golden brown. Serve hot or cold, garnished with mustard and cress.

Variation:
Other cold meats can be used in place of the cooked pork.

Roast Pork with Bacon and Sage

$1\frac{1}{4}$ kg ($2\frac{1}{2}$ lb) loin of pork, boned and rolled
salt and freshly ground black pepper
6 rashers lean back bacon, derinded
2 teaspoons freshly chopped sage, or 1 teaspoon dried sage
40 g ($1\frac{1}{2}$ oz) fresh breadcrumbs
1 egg yolk
a little oil
2 teaspoons flour
300 ml ($\frac{1}{2}$ pint) stock
1 teaspoon tomato purée

Unroll the pork and cut the flesh a little to open it out. Season the inside lightly and lay the bacon evenly over the surface. Combine the sage and breadcrumbs and bind together with the egg yolk. Spread over the bacon. Re-roll the pork to enclose the filling. Secure with string and skewers and weigh the joint. Place in a roasting tin, rub the rind with oil and then with salt. Cook in a moderately hot oven (190°C, 375°F, Gas Mark 5), allowing 30-35 minutes per 450 g (1 lb) weight, plus 30 minutes over (depending on the thickness of the joint). Baste occasionally. Remove the joint to a serving dish and keep warm.

Drain off the fat from the pan but reserve 1 tablespoon. Stir the flour into this fat and cook for a few minutes until beginning to brown. Stir in the stock and tomato purée, season and bring to the boil for 3 minutes. Serve the gravy with the sliced joint.
Serves 6

† Apricot Stuffed Tenderloins

2 medium pork tenderloins, approx.
    450 g (1 lb) each
50 g (2 oz) fresh white breadcrumbs
1 tablespoon chopped fresh sage
1 small onion, peeled and grated
1 × 422 g (15 oz) can apricots, drained
salt
freshly ground black pepper
4 tablespoons cooking oil
300 ml (½ pint) hot white stock or
    water and ½ chicken stock cube
300 ml (½ pint) dry white wine
beurre manié made with 25 g (1 oz)
    butter, mixed with 1 tablespoon
    flour
small bunch of watercress, washed
    and trimmed, to garnish

Carefully slice each tenderloin almost
through lengthways, open out and flatten slightly by beating with a rolling
pin. Mix together the breadcrumbs,
sage and onion. Chop all but 8 of the
apricots and reserve these for garnish.
Add the chopped apricots to the stuffing
and season lightly with salt and pepper.
Spread the stuffing along the centre of
each tenderloin, fold over and secure
with string at close intervals. Heat the
oil in the cooker and brown the meat
carefully on all sides. Lift the meat out
and drain off the excess oil from the
cooker. Add the stock or water and
stock cube and wine to the cooker.
Return to the heat and stir well to
remove any residues from the base of
the cooker. Replace the meat and
season lightly with salt and pepper.
Close the cooker, bring to H pressure
and cook for 20 minutes. Reduce the
pressure quickly. Lift out the meat,
remove the string and place on a warm
dish, keep hot. Return the open cooker
to the heat, add the beurre manié in
small pieces, stirring constantly. Cook
until the sauce is thickened. Taste and
adjust the seasoning before serving the
sauce around the meat. Garnish with
reserved apricot halves and watercress.

† Pork Chops with Herbs

25 g (1 oz) lard or margarine
4 pork chops
450 ml (¾ pint) hot brown stock or
    water and ½ beef stock cube
1 onion, peeled and chopped
½ teaspoon chopped fresh sage
½ teaspoon chopped fresh thyme
1 teaspoon chopped fresh parsley
salt and freshly ground black pepper
2 teaspoons flour
little water

Heat the lard or margarine in the
cooker and brown the chops on both
sides. Lift the chops out and drain off
the excess lard or margarine from the
cooker. Add the stock or water and
stock cube to the cooker and stir well to
remove any residues from the base of
the cooker. Place the trivet, rim side
down, in the cooker. Place the chops on
the trivet and carefully sprinkle each
with a mixture of the onion, herbs salt
and pepper. Close the cooker, bring to H
pressure and cook for 10 minutes.
Reduce the pressure quickly. Carefully
lift out the chops with herb topping to a
warm dish and keep hot. Return the
open cooker to the heat and add the
flour blended with a little water. Cook,
stirring continuously, until boiling and
thickened. Taste and adjust the seasoning. Serve sauce around the chops.

Sweet-sour Pork and Pasta

450 g (1 lb) pork shoulder steaks
salt and freshly ground black pepper
4 tablespoons vinegar
2 tablespoons brown sugar
2 tablespoons soy sauce
50 g (2 oz) butter
1 × 400 g (14 oz) can tomatoes
1 tablespoon tomato purée
juice and grated rind of 1 large
    orange
350 g (12 oz) pasta shells

Cut the pork into thin strips. Put into a shallow dish with seasoning, vinegar, brown sugar and soy sauce. Cover and chill in the refrigerator overnight. Remove the meat from the marinade and drain well. Heat the butter in a pan and fry the pork strips gently until browned on all sides. Add the marinade, canned tomatoes and their liquid, tomato purée and orange juice and rind. Cover and simmer for 30 to 35 minutes.

Meanwhile, cook the pasta in rapidly boiling salted water, for about 6 to 8 minutes, until just tender. Drain well. Pile up the cooked pasta on to a warm serving dish and spoon over the sweet-sour pork sauce.

† Pork and Cheese Escalopes

75 g (3 oz) fresh white breadcrumbs
50 g (2 oz) Cheddar cheese, finely grated
25 g (1 oz) shredded beef suet
1 teaspoon dried sage
salt
freshly ground black pepper
1 egg, beaten
4 pork escalopes (approx. 100 g (4 oz) each), beaten
25 g (1 oz) butter or oil
450 ml (¾ pint) white stock or water and ½ chicken stock cube
For the sauce:
25 g (1 oz) butter or margarine
25 g (1 oz) flour
a little milk
75 g (3 oz) Cheddar cheese, finely grated

For the stuffing, mix together the breadcrumbs, cheese, suet, sage and salt and pepper. Bind with the beaten egg. Divide the stuffing between the escalopes and spread to the edges. Roll up the escalopes and secure with string. Heat the butter or oil in the cooker, add the escalopes and brown quickly on all sides. Lift out and drain well. Drain off excess butter or oil from the cooker.

Pour in the stock or water and stock cube and return to the heat. Stir well to remove any residues from the base of the cooker. Return the escalopes to the cooker with a little salt and pepper. Close the cooker, bring to H pressure and cook for 12 minutes. Reduce the pressure quickly. Lift out the escalopes to a warmed serving dish and keep hot, remove the string. Strain the cooking liquid and make up to 450 ml (¾ pint) with the milk from the sauce.

Melt the butter or margarine in the rinsed and dried cooker, add the flour and cook for 1 to 2 minutes. Remove from the heat and stir in the liquid gradually. Return to the heat and bring to the boil. Stir constantly and simmer for 1 minute. Remove from the heat, stir in the cheese, taste and adjust the seasoning as necessary before pouring the sauce over the pork escalopes.

Quick Paella

2 × 150 g (5 oz) packets Spanish or mixed vegetable rice
1 large knob of butter
1 × 450 g (1 lb) can pork shoulder, cut into thin strips
100 g (4 oz) fresh or frozen peeled prawns, defrosted
½ green pepper, cored, seeded and finely chopped
½ red pepper, cored, seeded and finely chopped
freshly ground black pepper
1 lemon, quartered

Cook the rice for 20 minutes according to packet directions. Stir in the remaining ingredients except the lemon quarters. Heat through for 5 minutes, stirring occasionally, then serve immediately with lemon quarters.

Serendipity Chops

4 pork chops
salt and freshly ground black pepper
25 g (1 oz) butter
40 g (1½ oz) fresh breadcrumbs
½ teaspoon ground mace
½ teaspoon dried thyme
1 tablespoon finely chopped parsley
25 g (1 oz) shelled walnuts, chopped
    (optional)
4 tablespoons stock
To garnish:
lemon wedges
parsley sprigs

Trim the chops and season with salt and pepper. Melt the butter in a frying pan and fry the chops quickly on both sides until browned. Transfer to a shallow ovenproof casserole large enough to take the chops in one layer. Mix together the breadcrumbs, mace, thyme, parsley, walnuts (if using) and seasonings to taste. Spoon evenly over the chops and pour the remaining fat in the frying pan over the topping. Add stock to the casserole and cover with foil or a lid. Cook towards the top of a moderately hot oven (200°C, 400°F, Gas Mark 6) for 20 minutes, remove the foil and continue for a further 10 to 20 minutes, until the chops are tender and the topping is crispy. Garnish with lemon wedges and parsley.

Cheesy Topped Pork

4 lean pork chops
salt and freshly ground black pepper
25 g (1 oz) butter
1 green pepper, washed, deseeded and
    thinly sliced
4 tomatoes, peeled and sliced
1½ teaspoons dried rosemary
50 g (2 oz) Cheddar cheese, grated

Trim the pork and season lightly on both sides. Cook in the grill pan under a

moderate heat for about 10 minutes. Meanwhile melt the butter in a small pan and fry the pepper until soft. Turn the chops over and cook for a further 8 to 10 minutes until cooked through. Spoon the peppers on top of the chops, cover with sliced tomatoes and sprinkle with the herbs. Place under the grill for 3 to 4 minutes to heat through the topping. Sprinkle with cheese, then return to a hot grill until brown and bubbling. Serve at once.

† Chinese Pork with Mushrooms

750 g (1½ lb) boned shoulder or
    sparerib of pork, cut into 2.5 cm (1
    inch) chunks
3 tablespoons soy sauce
2 tablespoons cornflour
2 garlic cloves, peeled and crushed
1 teaspoon ground ginger
freshly ground black pepper
2 tablespoons vegetable oil
1 bunch of spring onions, trimmed
    and chopped
450 ml (¾ pint) water
1 chicken stock cube
100 g (4 oz) button mushrooms, sliced
    if large
50 g (2 oz) salted cashew nuts

Put the pork in a bowl with the soy sauce, cornflour, garlic, ginger and pepper to taste. Stir well to mix. Heat the oil in the pressure cooker, add the onions and fry over gentle heat for 5 minutes. Add the pork and fry over brisk heat until browned on all sides, stirring constantly. Stir in the water and scrape up the sediment from the bottom of the cooker, then bring to the boil. Add the stock cube and stir to dissolve.

Cover with the lid, then bring up to pressure according to manufacturer's instructions. Cook at H pressure for 10 minutes, reduce the pressure quickly, remove the cover and add the mushrooms and cashew nuts. Cover the cooker again, bring back to pressure and cook for a further 5 minutes.

Reduce the pressure quickly and remove the cover. Taste and adjust the seasoning, adding more soy sauce and ginger if a stronger flavour is liked. Serve hot with freshly boiled rice or noodles and fresh or canned bean sprouts.

Variations:
Use 2 green peppers, cored, seeded and finely chopped, instead of the sliced mushrooms.

Substitute 4 boned chicken breasts, skinned and sliced, for the pork. Cook for 5 minutes at H pressure.

† Pork Chops with Apple and Cheese Sauce

4 pork chops
2 teaspoons prepared French mustard, or to taste
salt
freshly ground black pepper
2 tablespoons vegetable oil
2 large cooking apples, cored, seeded and thickly sliced
100 g (4 oz) Cheddar cheese
150 ml (¼ pint) chicken stock

Remove the rind and cut off all the fat from the chops. Spread the chops with the mustard and sprinkle liberally with salt and pepper. Heat the oil in the pressure cooker, add the chops and fry over brisk heat until browned on both sides. Cover the chops with a layer of sliced apples and grate the cheese over the top. Pour in the stock and bring to the boil.

Cover with the lid, then bring up to pressure according to manufacturer's instructions. Cook at H pressure for 10 minutes, then reduce the pressure quickly and remove the cover. Taste and adjust the seasoning. Serve hot with seasonal vegetables.

Sweet'n'sour Pork Balls

450 g (1 lb) lean pork, minced
1 clove garlic, crushed
50 g (2 oz) fresh breadcrumbs
salt and freshly ground black pepper
1 egg, beaten
flour for coating
25 g (1 oz) lard or white fat
For the sauce:
1 green pepper, washed, deseeded and thinly sliced
1 red pepper, washed, deseeded and thinly sliced
small can crushed pineapple, or 4 canned pineapple rings, chopped
75 g (3 oz) sugar
4 tablespoons cider vinegar
2–3 tablespoons soy sauce
300 ml (½ pint) stock or water
4 teaspoons cornflour

Combine the pork with the garlic, breadcrumbs and plenty of seasonings and bind together with the egg. Divide into 20 pieces and shape into small balls. Dip each in the flour. Heat the lard in a pan and fry the balls gently for approximately 15 to 20 minutes, turning frequently, until golden brown and cooked through, keep warm.

Meanwhile, blanch the peppers for 5 minutes and drain. Mix with the pineapple. Place the sugar in a pan with the vinegar, soy sauce and stock and bring to the boil. Add the peppers and pineapple and simmer for 5 minutes. Blend the cornflour with a little cold water and add to the sauce. Bring back to the boil and simmer for a further 3 to 4 minutes. Taste and then adjust the seasonings.

Drain the pork balls on absorbent kitchen paper and serve hot with boiled rice and the sauce spooned over.

† Pork Spareribs in Cider

2 tablespoons cooking oil
4 pork sparerib chops, trimmed
1 onion, peeled and chopped
2 stalks celery, scrubbed and chopped
450 ml (¾ pint) dry cider
salt and freshly ground black pepper
½ teaspoon dried sage
2 teaspoons cornflour
little water

Heat the oil in the cooker and brown the chops well on both sides. Add the onion and celery and cook until both are beginning to colour. Remove the chops and vegetables from the cooker and drain off any excess oil from the cooker. Away from the heat add the cider to the cooker. Stir to remove any residues from the base of the cooker. Return the chops and vegetables to the cooker with a little salt, pepper and the sage. Close the cooker, bring to H pressure and cook for 10 minutes. Reduce the pressure quickly. Lift out the chops to a warm dish and keep hot. Return the open cooker to the heat. Add the cornflour blended with a little cold water and stir constantly. Bring to the boil and simmer for 1 minute. Taste and adjust the seasoning as necessary before serving the sauce with the chops.

Pork and Apple Casserole

25 g (1 oz) dripping or lard
4 thick slices belly pork
1 clove of garlic, crushed
4 juniper berries
2 medium-sized onions, peeled and chopped
2 medium-sized cooking apples, peeled, cored and chopped
salt and freshly ground black pepper
150 ml (¼ pint) apple juice
1 kg (2 lb potatoes,) peeled and thickly sliced
15 g (½ oz) butter

Melt the dripping or lard in a frying pan. Add the pork slices and fry until golden-brown on both sides.

Arrange the meat in a shallow casserole. Add the crushed garlic and juniper berries and cover with a layer of chopped onion and apple. Season to taste. Pour on the apple juice and cover with overlapping potato slices. Dot with butter, cover and bake in a cool oven (160°C, 325°F, Gas Mark 3) for 1½ hours. Remove the lid and cook for a further 30 minutes to brown the top.

† Barbecued Pork Chops with Orange Rice

25 g (1 oz) lard or margarine
4 pork chops
1 small onion, peeled and chopped
450 ml (¾ pint) hot brown stock or water and ½ beef stock cube
1 tablespoon tomato purée
3 tablespoons vinegar
2 tablespoons demerara sugar
1 teaspoon mustard powder
1 teaspoon Worcestershire sauce
salt
freshly ground black pepper
225 g (8 oz) easy-cook, long-grain rice
300 ml (½ pint) canned unsweetened orange juice
150 ml (¼ pint) water
1 tablespoon cornflour
little water
1 fresh orange, to garnish

Heat the lard or margarine in the cooker, brown the chops on both sides, remove from the cooker and fry the onion lightly. Lift out and then drain excess lard or margarine from the cooker. Put onion back into cooker with the brown stock or water and stock cube, tomato purée, vinegar, sugar, mustard powder and Worcestershire sauce. Stir well to remove any residues from the base of the cooker. Put the trivet into the cooker, place the chops on top and season lightly with salt and pepper. Close the cooker, bring to H pressure and cook for 4 minutes. Reduce the pressure quickly. Stand an ovenproof dish or solid separator containing the rice, orange juice, water and a little salt on top of the chops. Cover with a piece of greaseproof paper. Close the cooker, bring to H pressure and cook for 6 minutes. Reduce the pressure slowly. Lift out the rice, stir with a fork to separate the grains and transfer to a warmed serving dish. Keep hot. Place the chops on the rice. Remove the trivet, return the open cooker to the heat and add the cornflour blended with a little water. Bring to the boil and stir continuously until thickened. Taste and adjust seasoning. Pour the sauce over chops and garnish with orange slices.

Pork and Pepper Casserole

2 tablespoons vegetable oil
1 onion, peeled and finely chopped
750 g (1½ lb) pork fillet, cut into small cubes
1½ tablespoons flour
2 tablespoons soy sauce
few drops of Tabasco sauce
6 tablespoons undiluted orange squash
300 ml (½ pint) water
1 chicken stock cube
freshly ground black pepper
2 red or green peppers, cored, seeded and cut into rings
100 g (4 oz) Chinese egg noodles, broken into pieces

Heat the oil in a pan, add the onion and fry over gentle heat until soft. Coat the pork in the flour, then fry until browned on all sides. Stir in the soy and Tabasco sauces, orange squash and water. Bring to the boil, add the stock cube and stir to dissolve. Add pepper to taste, cover and simmer for 1 hour or until the pork is tender. Add the peppers and noodles 10 minutes before end of cooking, stirring to separate noodles. Adjust seasoning.

Barbecued Pork

25 g (1 oz) butter
1 teaspoon oil
900 g (2 lb) pork spare ribs (American-style)
2 large onions, peeled and sliced
4 tablespoons demerara sugar
1½ teaspoons salt
1 teaspoon paprika
1 tablespoon tomato purée
1 tablespoon Worcestershire sauce
2 tablespoons malt vinegar
4 tablespoons lemon juice
200 ml (7 fl oz) water
175 g (6 oz) dried apricots, soaked overnight, or a 1 × 425 g (15 oz) can apricots, halved and drained
black olives, to garnish

Melt the butter in a pan, add the oil and then fry the spare ribs quickly until browned. Transfer to an ovenproof casserole.

Fry the onions in the same fat until lightly browned, then drain off any excess fat from the pan. Blend together all the other ingredients, except the apricots, and add to the onion. Bring to the boil and simmer for 3 to 4 minutes. Pour over the pork, cover and cook in a moderately hot oven (200°C, 400°F, Gas Mark 6) for 45 minutes, basting several times.

Drain the apricots and add to the sauce. Return to the oven for a further 15 to 30 minutes, until really tender. Spoon off any excess fat from the surface and serve garnished with olives.

Somerset Pork

4 boneless pork slices
2 tablespoons seasoned flour
40 g (1½ oz) butter
175 g (6 oz) button mushrooms,
   cleaned and trimmed
300 ml (½ pint) dry cider
good dash of Worcestershire sauce
salt and freshly ground black pepper
100 ml (4 fl oz) double cream
finely chopped parsley, or sprigs, to
   garnish

Trim the pork and coat in seasoned flour. Fry in the melted butter until browned on both sides and almost cooked through. Remove from the pan and keep warm.

Add the mushrooms to the pan and cook gently for 2 to 3 minutes. Stir in the remaining flour and cook for 1 minute, then gradually add the cider and bring to the boil. Add the Worcestershire sauce, salt and freshly ground black pepper and replace the pork. Cover and simmer for about 10 minutes. Stir in the cream, taste and adjust the seasonings and reheat without boiling. Serve sprinkled with parsley, or garnished with sprigs.

Stroganoff-style Pork

550 g (1¼ lb) pork fillet
25 g (1 oz) butter
2 tablespoons oil
1 onion, peeled and finely sliced
100 g (4 oz) mushrooms, cleaned,
   trimmed and finely sliced
4 tomatoes, peeled and sliced
200 ml (7 fl oz) chicken stock
salt and freshly ground black pepper
150 ml (¼ pint) soured cream
finely chopped parsley, to garnish

Cut the pork into thin strips and fry in a mixture of butter and oil for 5 minutes, stirring occasionally, then remove from the pan. Fry the onion in the same fat until lightly browned, then add the mushrooms and continue for 5 minutes. Add the tomatoes, stock and seasonings and bring to the boil. Return the pork to the pan, cover and simmer for about 20 minutes or until the meat is tender and the liquid is reduced by about half. Stir in the cream and bring back just to the boil. Taste and adjust the seasonings. Serve liberally sprinkled with parsley.

Pork Goulash

675 g (1½ lb) pork fillet
50 g (2 oz) butter
1 tablespoon oil
2 onions, peeled and sliced
1 tablespoon paprika
2 tablespoons flour
2 teaspoons tomato purée
1 × 225 g (8 oz) can peeled tomatoes
450 ml (¾) pint stock
salt and freshly ground black pepper
1 green pepper, washed, deseeded and
   thinly sliced
4 tablespoons double cream
½ teaspoon finely grated lemon rind

Cut the pork into thin strips. Melt 25 g (1 oz) butter and the oil in a pan and fry the pork for 5 minutes. Remove the pork, add the remaining butter to the pan and, when melted, fry the onions until soft. Stir in the paprika, flour and tomato purée and cook for 1 minute. Add the tomatoes and stock, season well and bring to the boil. Add the pepper and return the pork to the pan. Cover and simmer for about 45 minutes until tender.

Taste and adjust the seasonings, mix the cream with the lemon rind, and serve spooned on top of the goulash.

† Paprika Pork

750 g (1½ lb) boned pork shoulder,
   trimmed and cubed
seasoned flour
50 g (2 oz) butter or oil
2 garlic cloves, crushed
3 teaspoons paprika pepper
300 ml (½ pint) white stock or water
   and ½ chicken stock cube
150 ml (¼ pint) dry sherry
100 g (4 oz) mushrooms, cleaned and
   thickly sliced
1 bay leaf
salt
150 ml (¼ pint) fresh single cream

Coat the pork pieces in seasoned flour and shake off any excess flour. Heat the butter or oil in the cooker and sauté the pork pieces until evenly browned. Lift the pork out and drain well. Stir the garlic and paprika pepper into the cooking juices. Away from the heat add the stock or water and stock cube and sherry and stir well to remove any residues from the base of the cooker. Return the pork to the cooker with the mushrooms, bay leaf and a little salt. Close the cooker, bring to H pressure and cook for 15 minutes. Reduce the pressure quickly and remove the bay leaf. Taste and adjust the seasoning as necessary and stir the cream into the sauce just before serving. Do not reheat after the cream has been added. Serve with plain rice or buttered noodles.

BACON, HAM & SAUSAGE

Bacon Collar with Apricots

1–1½ kg (2–3 lb joint) collar bacon
1 bouquet garni (p. 364)
100 g (4 oz) dried apricots
450 g (1 lb) parsnips, peeled and
    quartered
25 g (1 oz) sultanas
salt
freshly ground black pepper
1 teaspoon cornflour (optional)
1 tablespoon water (optional)

Put the joint in a basin, cover with cold water and soak overnight. Drain and place in a casserole with the bouquet garni and almost cover with fresh water. Put the lid on the casserole and cook in a moderate oven (180°C, 350°F, Gas Mark 4) for 1 hour.

Add the apricots, parsnips, sultanas, a little pepper, and salt if needed. Cook covered, for a further 1 hour. Discard the bouquet garni.

Take out the bacon, remove the rind, slice the meat and place on a heated serving dish garnished with the apricots and parsnips. Serve the sauce separately.

If a slightly thicker sauce is required, moisten the cornflour with the water and stir into the casserole 15 minutes before the joint is done.

Serve with boiled or mashed potatoes, and do not add salt to the water when cooking them in case the bacon sauce is slightly salty.

† Bacon Collar – Danish Style

Unsmoked collar joint of bacon up to
    1½ kg (3 lb) in weight
cold water
900 ml (1½ pints) lager
1 small onion stuck with 6 cloves
1 bay leaf
a few black peppercorns
a little chopped parsley, to garnish
For the sauce:
25 g (1 oz) butter or margarine
25 g (1 oz) flour
150 ml (¼ pint) milk
salt
freshly ground black pepper

Put the bacon into the cooker and cover with cold water. Bring to the boil, remove from the heat and drain well. Place the trivet, rim side down, in the cooker and stand the bacon on the trivet. Add the lager, onion, bay leaf and peppercorns, which have been crushed in a paper bag with a rolling pin. Close the cooker, bring to H pressure and cook for 12 minutes per 450 g (1 lb). Reduce the pressure quickly. Lift out the joint and allow to cool slightly before removing the skin. Keep hot. Drain off the cooking liquid, reserving 300 ml (½ pint) for the sauce. Rinse and dry the cooker.

Melt the butter or margarine in the cooker, add the flour and cook for a few moments. Remove from the heat and add the milk and reserved cooking liquid, stirring well. Return to the heat and bring to the boil, stirring constantly. Simmer for 1 minute. Taste and adjust the seasoning as necessary. Slice the bacon thickly and arrange on a serving dish. Pour the sauce along the centre of the meat slices and garnish with a little chopped parsley. Serve with buttered new potatoes and a green vegetable.

To serve cold: allow the joint to cool in the cooking liquid. Strip off the skin and coat the fat with browned breadcrumbs.

Serve with a crisp, fresh salad in a vinaigrette dressing. When chicory is in season, this is delicious with watercress, cucumber and fresh mint.

Tomato Baked Bacon

1½ kg (3 lb) prime collar joint bacon
16–20 cloves
350 g (12 oz) button onions, peeled
15 g (½ oz) butter
450 g (1 lb) tomatoes, peeled and quartered
1 teaspoon basil
150 ml (¼ pint) dry white wine
2 tablespoons breadcrumbs
salt and freshly ground black pepper

Place the joint in a saucepan and cover with cold water. Bring to the boil and simmer for an hour. Drain and remove the skin and place the bacon in an ovenproof casserole. Stud the fat with cloves.

Fry the onions in melted butter until browned and arrange around the joint. Add the tomatoes to the casserole, sprinkle with basil and add the wine. Cover and cook in a moderately hot oven (190°C, 375°F, Gas Mark 5) for 35 to 40 minutes, until tender.

Remove the lid, sprinkle the breadcrumbs over the fat and return to the oven for 10 minutes. Taste the juices and adjust seasonings before serving. Serves 6.

Bacon Toad

450 g (1 lb) collar bacon
1 onion, peeled
1–2 teaspoons mixed herbs
salt
freshly ground black pepper
3 eggs
fat for cooking
100 g (4 oz) plain flour
250 ml (½ pint) milk
For the sauce:
25 g (1 oz) butter
25 g (1 oz) flour
pinch of salt
300 ml (½ pint) milk
2 tablespoons finely chopped parsley (optional)

Remove the rind and any bone or gristle from the bacon and mince with the onion. Add the herbs and seasonings and bind together with 1 beaten egg. Divide into 16 and shape into small balls. Fry these balls quickly in a little fat until lightly browned all over.

To make the batter, sieve the flour with a pinch of salt into a bowl, make a well in the centre, add the 2 eggs and gradually beat in the milk to give a smooth batter.

Heat 1 tablespoon fat in a baking tin approx 28 × 35 cm (11 × 9 inches) making sure the whole tin is coated. Add the bacon balls and cook in a preheated hot oven (220°C, 425°F, Gas Mark 7) for 5 minutes. Pour the batter into the tin and continue cooking for a further 30 to 40 minutes or until well risen and golden brown.

Meanwhile, to make the sauce, melt the butter in a pan. Stir in the flour and cook for 1 minute, then gradually add the milk and bring to the boil, stirring continuously. Season to taste, add the parsley and simmer for 3 minutes. Serve the sauce with the bacon toad.

Bacon Hotpot

1 kg (2 lb) forehock of bacon joint,
  boned and rolled
4–6 leeks, cleaned and sliced
25 g (1 oz) butter
4 carrots, peeled and sliced
450 g (1 lb) potatoes, peeled and
  thinly sliced
salt and freshly ground black pepper
300 ml ($\frac{1}{2}$ pint) ham stock

Soak the bacon in cold water for several hours then drain and place in a saucepan and cover with fresh cold water. Bring to the boil, remove the scum, cover and simmer gently for 1 hour. Remove from the saucepan, strip off the skin and cut into 2.5 cm (1 inch) cubes.

Fry the leeks gently in butter for 5 minutes then layer with the carrots, potatoes and bacon in an ovenproof casserole, finishing with a layer of potato. Season the stock and pour into the casserole. Cover and cook in a moderately hot oven (190°C, 375°F, Gas Mark 5) for 45 minutes, then remove the lid and continue for a further 20 to 30 minutes, until tender.

Variation:
Half the stock can be replaced with sweet cider if preferred.

† Bacon Casserole with Cider

100 g (4 oz) lentils
600 ml (1 pint) boiling water
750 g (1$\frac{1}{2}$ lb) unsmoked collar bacon
  or forehock, boned, trimmed and
  cut into 2.5 cm (1 inch) cubes
25 g (1 oz) butter or margarine
1 large onion, peeled and sliced
3 stalks celery, scrubbed and coarsely
  chopped
2 small leeks, washed and cut into
  2.5 cm (1 inch) pieces (reserve a
  little top leaf for garnish)

300 ml ($\frac{1}{2}$ pint) dry cider
300 ml ($\frac{1}{2}$ pint) white stock or water
  and $\frac{1}{2}$ chicken stock cube
freshly ground black pepper
pinch of dried sage
1 tablespoon cornflour
little water

Put the lentils in a basin, cover with water and soak for 1 hour. Place the bacon in the cooker with sufficient cold water to cover and bring to the boil. Discard water and put the bacon to one side. Rinse and dry the cooker. Heat the butter or margarine in the cooker and sauté the vegetables until they are beginning to colour. Add the bacon, drained lentils, cider, white stock or water and stock cube, pepper and sage and stir well. Close the cooker, bring to H pressure and cook for 15 minutes. Reduce the pressure slowly. Blend the cornflour with a little cold water and add to the cooker. Return the open cooker to the heat. Cook, stirring constantly, until the sauce is boiling and thickened. Taste and adjust the seasoning. Garnish with chopped leek tops.

Fidget Pie

225 g (8 oz) flour
pinch of salt
100 g (4 oz) lard cut into small pieces
2–3 tablespoons cold water
For the filling:
1 large potato, peeled and chopped
1 large onion, peeled and chopped
225 g (8 oz) smoked streaky or collar
  bacon, diced
1 large cooking apple, peeled, cored
  and chopped
salt and freshly ground black pepper
150 ml ($\frac{1}{4}$ pint) water
a little milk to glaze

Sift the flour and salt into a bowl, add the lard and rub in with the fingertips until the mixture resembles fine breadcrumbs. Add enough cold water to mix to a stiff dough with a palette knife. Knead lightly on a floured surface for 1 minute until smooth. Wrap in foil or greaseproof paper and chill in the refrigerator for 30 minutes.

Grease a 1 litre (1¾ pint) pie dish and into it put layers of the potato, onion and lastly the diced bacon and apple mixture, seasoning each layer well. Add the water.

Roll out the pastry fairly thickly, to fit the top of the pie dish, cutting a strip to go round the lip of the dish from the trimmings. Dampen the strip with cold water and put the pastry lid on top of this, pressing down well to seal. Cut two small steam vents in the lid. Decorate the top of the pie with the rest of the pastry trimmings. Brush with milk.

Bake in a fairly hot oven (200°C, 400°F, Gas Mark 6) for about 30 minutes or until the pastry is golden-brown. Reduce the temperature to 160°C, 325°F, Gas Mark 3 and cook for a further 1 hour, covering the pastry with foil, if necessary, to prevent it from becoming too brown. Serve hot.

Cheese and Bacon Frizzles

1 large potato, peeled and grated
½ onion, peeled and very finely chopped
50 g (2 oz) Cheddar or Edam cheese, grated
4 rashers back bacon, de-rinded and finely chopped
4 tablespoons self-raising flour
1 egg, beaten
freshly ground black pepper
4 tablespoons vegetable oil

Put all the ingredients in a bowl, except the oil, and beat well. Heat the oil in a large non-stick frying pan. Add the mixture to the pan in spoonfuls and fry for 7 minutes on each side until golden brown and crisp. Serve immediately with a mixed salad or baked beans.
Makes 8

Bacon and Onion Pudding

200 g (8 oz) self-raising flour
½ teaspoon salt
75 g (3 oz) shredded suet
1 teaspoon mixed herbs
water to mix
For the filling:
550 g (1¼ lb) piece of lean bacon, derinded and diced
freshly ground black pepper
2 onions, peeled and sliced
4 tablespoons stock or water

Put a large saucepan of water to boil and thoroughly grease a 1 litre (2 pint) pudding basin.

Sieve the flour and salt into a bowl. Mix in the suet and herbs and mix to a soft dough with water. Cut off a quarter of the pastry for the lid and roll the remainder into a circle about twice the diameter of the top of the basin. Carefully lower the circle into the basin and press to the sides without tearing or creasing.

Season the bacon with pepper only and mix with the onions. Place in the pastry lined basin and add the stock. Roll out the remaining pastry for the lid, dampen the edges and place on top of the meat. Press the edges well together and trim. Cover securely with greased paper and then foil or a pudding cloth. Lower the basin into the pan so that the water comes half to two-thirds of the way up the side of the basin. Simmer gently for 4 hours, filling up the pan with more boiling water as necessary.

Remove the coverings and serve straight from the basin.

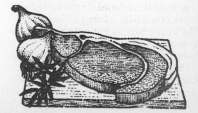

† Bacon, Leek and Sage Pudding

200 g (8 oz) self-raising flour
½ teaspoon salt
100 g (4 oz) shredded beef suet
¼ pint cold water
For the filling:
175 g (6 oz) unsmoked streaky bacon rashers, rinded
1 leek, cleaned and thinly sliced
1 teaspoon fresh sage or ½ teaspoon dried sage
salt
freshly ground black pepper
900 ml (1½ pints) boiling water
a little lemon juice

Sift the flour and salt into a mixing bowl. Stir in the suet and gradually add the water until a smooth elastic dough is formed, which leaves the sides of the bowl cleanly. Turn on to a floured board and knead lightly. Roll the pastry into an oblong a little narrower than the base of the cooker and approximately 5 mm (¼ inch) thick. Put a layer of streaky bacon rashers over the pastry, slightly overlapping each rasher, to within 2.5 cm (1 inch) of the edges. Cover evenly with the sliced leek, sage and a little salt and pepper. Brush the edges of the pastry with a little water and roll up, swiss-roll style, sealing all the edges well. Place the roll, seam-side down, on a greased double thickness of grease-proof paper or on a well-greased piece of aluminium foil. Wrap loosely, making a pleat in the centre to allow for expansion. Secure the greaseproof paper with string at the ends. Have the boiling water and a little lemon juice ready in the cooker. Add the trivet rim side down. Carefully stand the pudding on the trivet, close the cooker and steam gently, without the weights, for 10 minutes. Bring to H pressure and cook for 20 minutes or L pressure and cook for 30 minutes. Reduce the pressure slowly. Serve sliced with a brown gravy and vegetables.

Boiled Gammon with Pease Pudding

450 g (1 lb) yellow split peas, washed, covered with hot water and soaked overnight
1 corner gammon joint, about 1½ kg (3 lb), soaked in cold water overnight
1 bouquet garni (p. 364)
salt and freshly ground black pepper
50 g (2 oz) butter
Vegetables for the soup:
4 medium-sized carrots, peeled and chopped
4 medium-sized onions, peeled and chopped
4 leeks, white and pale green part washed, trimmed and chopped
6 large celery stalks, scrubbed and chopped
Vegetables for the first meal:
4 medium-sized carrots, peeled and quartered
4 medium-sized onions, peeled and quartered
4 leeks, white and pale green part washed and halved
1 small swede, peeled and cut into large chunks

This recipe provides a nourishing and substantial meal for one day and a filling soup for the next.

Drain the split peas, rinse under cold running water and tie all but a handful in a scalded muslin cloth. Drain the gammon and place in a large saucepan with the bouquet garni, loose and tied peas, seasoning and soup vegetables. Cover with about 2 litres (3½ pints) cold water and bring to the boil, skimming with a slotted draining spoon. Lower the heat and simmer gently for about 1½ hours (allowing 25 to 30 minutes per 450 g (1 lb) or until the gammon is tender. Taste the soup and adjust the seasoning if necessary.

Remove the gammon from the pan, strip off the rind and keep the joint hot. Turn the peas from the muslin into a serving dish. Add the butter and beat with a fork until smooth. Taste and adjust the seasoning, if necessary, and keep hot. Meanwhile add the vegetables for the first meal to the saucepan. Bring back to the boil and simmer for 15 minutes or until tender.

Remove the vegetables for the first meal carefully with a slotted draining spoon. Serve with the gammon, pease pudding, English mustard and, if desired, plain boiled potatoes or wholemeal bread. Any remaining pease pudding may be blended into the soup to be served the following day or fried gently in a little butter and served with bacon.

In the interest of economy, this dish may be prepared with a gammon shank or forehock.

Bacon Chops with Prunes

4 thick bacon chops
50–100 g (2–4 oz) large prunes, soaked
1 large cooking apple, peeled, cored and thinly sliced
To garnish:
25 g (1 oz) butter
2 cooking apples, cored and cut into rings
parsley sprigs

Trim off the rind and cut a deep 'pocket' through the fat into the 'eye' of each bacon chop. Remove the stones from the prunes and chop roughly. Mix with the apple and use to fill the pockets. Secure with wooden cocktail sticks. Place on a grill rack and cook under a moderate heat for 5 to 7 minutes each side until cooked through. Keep warm.

Melt the butter and fry the apple rings until golden brown. Arrange apple rings on top of the chops and garnish with parsley sprigs.

Savoury Bacon Pie

25 g (1 oz) butter
1 large onion, peeled and chopped
250 g (9 oz) plain flour
300 ml ($\frac{1}{2}$ pint) milk
salt
freshly ground black pepper
$\frac{1}{2}$ teaspoon Worcestershire sauce
$\frac{1}{2}$–1 teaspoon mixed herbs
175 g (6 oz) cooked ham or bacon, chopped
50 g (2 oz) margarine
50 g (2 oz) lard or white fat
water to mix
2 hard-boiled eggs, sliced
2 large tomatoes, peeled and sliced
beaten egg or milk, to glaze

Melt the butter in a pan and fry the onion until soft. Stir in 25 g (1 oz) flour and cook for 1 minute then gradually add the milk and bring to the boil. Season well, add the Worcestershire sauce and herbs and simmer for 3 minutes. Stir in the ham, taste and adjust the seasoning and cool.

Sieve the remaining flour with a pinch of salt into a bowl, add the fats and rub in until the mixture resembles fine breadcrumbs. Add sufficient water to mix to a pliable dough. On a floured surface roll out two-thirds of the pastry and use to line a 20 cm (8 inch) pie plate or tin. Spoon half the filling into the pastry, cover with the eggs and then the remaining filling. Lay the tomatoes on top. Roll out the remaining pastry for a lid, damp the edges, put in position and trim off the excess pastry. Press the edges well together and crimp. Make a hole in the centre of the lid and decorate around it with pastry trimmings.

Brush with egg or milk and cook in a hot oven (220°C, 425°F, Gas Mark 7) for 20 minutes, then reduce oven temperature to moderate (180°C, 350°F, Gas Mark 4) and continue for 20 to 25 minutes until the pastry is a light golden brown.
Serve hot or cold.

Pigs in Blankets

4 rashers streaky bacon, derinded
prepared French mustard
4 frankfurters
2 tablespoons vegetable oil
4 long soft rolls
butter for spreading
75–100 g (3–4 oz) coleslaw

Spread one side of the bacon rashers
with a little mustard. Wrap a bacon
rasher around each frankfurter, with
the mustard on the inside. Heat the oil
in a frying pan. Add the frankfurters
and fry for 10 minutes over brisk heat,
shaking the pan occasionally until the
bacon is browned on all sides.

Meanwhile, split the rolls in half
lengthways and spread the cut surfaces
with butter and a little mustard, if liked.
Place one frankfurter in each roll, then
top with coleslaw.

Variations:
Skinless sausages can be substituted for
the frankfurters, although they will
need to be cooked an extra 5 minutes.

Any kind of salad can be used instead
of coleslaw, or the rolls can be filled
with tomato and cucumber slices and
lettuce, then dressed with mayonnaise.

Bacon and Cheese Slice

25 g (1 oz) butter
25 g (1 oz) flour
250 ml (8 fl oz) milk
1 teaspoon made mustard
75 g (3 oz) English Mature Cheddar
   cheese, grated
salt and freshly ground black pepper
225 g (8 oz) cooked ham or bacon,
   finely chopped
4 stuffed olives, sliced
For the pastry:
200 g (8 oz) plain flour
pinch of salt
50 g (2 oz) margarine

50 g (2 oz) lard or white fat
water to mix
2 hard-boiled eggs, thickly sliced
beaten egg or milk, to glaze
cucumber slices, to garnish

Melt the butter in a pan, stir in the flour
and cook for 1 minute. Gradually add
the milk and bring to the boil, stirring
continuously. Simmer for 3 minutes
then stir in the mustard and cheese and
season to taste; add the ham or bacon
and the stuffed olives and leave the
filling to cool.

Sieve the flour with a pinch of salt
into a bowl. Add the fats and rub in until
the mixture resembles fine breadcrumbs. Add sufficient water to bind to
a pliable dough. Turn out on to a floured
surface and roll out thinly to a 30 cm (12
inch) square. Place half the filling down
the centre of the pastry, lay the eggs on
top and cover with the remaining filling. Cut the sides of the pastry into
diagonal strips 2 cm (¾ inch) wide and
plait these pieces evenly to enclose the
filling completely. Transfer to a dampened baking sheet and brush the top
with egg or milk. Cook in a hot oven
(220°C, 425°F, Gas Mark 7) for 20 minutes then reduce oven temperature to
moderate (180°C, 350°F, Gas Mark 4)
and continue for a further 15 to 20
minutes until the pastry is golden
brown. Serve hot or cold. Garnish with
slices of cucumber.

Bacon with Sage
and Onion Sauce

2 bacon knuckles
2 teaspoons sugar
1 bay leaf
50 g (2 oz) butter
2 onions, peeled and thinly sliced
50 g (2 oz) flour
450 ml (¾ pint) milk
150 ml (¼ pint) cooking liquor
salt and freshly ground black pepper
2–3 teaspoons dried sage

Put the bacon knuckles into a saucepan and just cover with water. Add the sugar and bay leaf and bring to the boil. Remove the scum, cover and simmer for 1½ hours or until the bacon is tender.

To make the sauce, melt the butter in a pan and fry the onions very gently until soft but not coloured, stir in the flour and cook for 1 minute then gradually add the milk and bring to the boil. Add sufficient cooking liquor to give the required consistency. Season to taste, add the sage and simmer for 3 to 4 minutes.

Remove the skin from the knuckles, strip the meat off the bone and arrange on a hot serving dish. Either pour the sauce over the bacon or serve separately in a sauce boat.

Pickled Bacon Puffs

40 g (1½ oz) butter
1 small onion, peeled and finely chopped
50 g (2 oz) mushrooms, cleaned, trimmed and chopped
25 g (1 oz) flour
150 ml (¼ pint) chicken stock
4 tablespoons milk
salt
freshly ground black pepper
175 g (6 oz) cooked ham, finely chopped
3 pickled walnuts, chopped
225 g (8 oz) frozen puff pastry, thawed
beaten egg, to glaze
watercress sprigs, to garnish

Melt the butter in a pan and fry the onion and mushrooms gently until soft. Stir in the flour and cook for 1 minute then gradually add the stock and milk and bring to the boil, stirring frequently. Simmer for 3 minutes then season to taste and stir in the ham and the pickled walnuts and leave the filling to cool.

Roll out one-third of the pastry thinly and cut into four 13 cm (5 inch) circles.

Place on a dampened baking sheet and spoon the filling on to the pastry leaving a 1.5 cm (½ inch) margin all round. Roll out the remaining pastry and cut into four 15 cm (6 inch) rounds. Brush the pastry margins with water and position the lids. Press the edges very well together, then 'knock up' the edges and crimp. Make 2 slits in the top of each puff and decorate with the pastry trimmings.

Brush with beaten egg and cook in a hot oven (220°C, 425°F, Gas Mark 7) for about 25 minutes until the pastry is well risen and golden brown. Serve the pickled bacon puffs hot or cold, garnished with watercress.

Glazed Gammon

1¾–2 kg (4 lb) gammon or prime collar joint
4 cloves
1 bay leaf
100 g (4 oz) demerara sugar
2 tablespoons wine vinegar
1 tablespoon honey

Weigh the joint and calculate the cooking time, allowing 20–25 minutes per 450 g (1 lb), plus 25 minutes over (depending on thickness of joint). Place in a saucepan and cover with water (The joint can be soaked for 2–6 hours before cooking.) Add the cloves, bay leaf and 25 g (1 oz) sugar and bring to the boil. Remove scum, cover and simmer gently for half the total cooking time.

Drain the joint, wrap in aluminium foil and cook in a preheated moderate oven (180°C, 350°F, Gas Mark 4) until 30 minutes before the end of the total cooking time.

Unwrap foil, strip off the skin and score the fat into diamonds. Heat the vinegar and honey together and brush over the fat. Sprinkle with the remaining sugar, pressing it well in, and return to the oven for the remaining cooking time. Serve hot or cold.

Quick Bacon Pizza

200 g (8 oz) self-raising flour
salt and freshly ground black pepper
50 g (2 oz) butter or margarine
1 tablespoon finely chopped parsley or
   oregano
1 egg, beaten
a little milk to mix
1 × 225 g (8 oz) can peeled tomatoes,
   partly drained
225 g (8 oz) streaky bacon rashers,
   derinded and lightly fried
100 g (4 oz) English Mature Cheddar
   cheese, grated
$\frac{1}{2}$ × 65 g (2$\frac{1}{2}$ oz) can anchovies, drained
8 stuffed olives, halved

Sieve the flour into a bowl with the
seasonings. Add the fat and rub in until
the mixture resembles fine breadcrumbs. Add the herbs and egg and
sufficient milk to mix to a fairly soft
dough. Knead lightly and shape into a
20 cm (8 inch) round. Slide on to a very
lightly greased baking sheet. Spoon the
tomatoes on top, breaking them up a
little, and cover with the halved bacon
rashers. Cook for 15 minutes in a very
hot oven (230°C, 450°F, Gas Mark 8).

Remove from the oven, cover with
cheese and arrange the anchovies and
olives on top in a lattice pattern. Return
to the oven for 5 to 10 minutes until the
cheese is bubbling. Serve hot.

Ham and Egg Supper

1 kg (2 lb) new potatoes, scrubbed and
   halved
salt and freshly ground black pepper
2 large knobs of butter
1 onion, peeled and finely sliced
2 green or red peppers, cored, seeded
   and finely sliced
1 × 450 g (1 lb) can cooked ham, cut
   into thin strips
2 tablespoons vegetable oil
4 eggs

Put the potatoes in a pan of boiling
salted water, bring back to the boil,
cover and simmer for 10 minutes. Drain,
leave to cool slightly and slice thickly.
Melt the butter in a large frying pan,
add the onion and peppers and fry over
gentle heat until soft. Add the potatoes
and fry for about 15 minutes until
golden brown, turning often during
cooking.

Add the ham and fold into the potato
mixture until evenly mixed. Add salt
and pepper to taste, heat through for 5
minutes. Meanwhile, fry the eggs in the
oil in a separate pan. Arrange the eggs
on top of the potato mixture and serve
immediately.

Lasagne Ham Rolls

1 tablespoon vegetable oil
175 g (6 oz lasagne) (about 8 sheets)
8 thin slices ham
2 tablespoons French mustard
100 g (4 oz) Cheddar cheese, grated
salt
freshly ground black pepper
1 × 425 g (15 oz) can mushroom soup
2 large tomatoes, sliced
parsley sprigs, to garnish

Bring a large pan of lightly salted water
to the boil and add the oil. Lower the
sheets of lasagne, one at a time, into the
pan and cook for 5 minutes. Drain well
and lay the sheets of lasagne on a large
piece of greased greaseproof paper or
foil. Lay a slice of ham on top of each
sheet of lasagne and spread with French
mustard. Sprinkle with grated cheese
and season to taste. Roll up each sheet
of lasagne, enclosing the ham and
cheese filling.

Place the rolls in a greased, shallow
ovenproof dish. Pour over the mushroom soup and arrange the slices of
tomato on top. Bake in a preheated
fairly hot oven (190°C, 375°F, Gas Mark
5) for 30 minutes. Serve hot garnished
with parsley sprigs.

Ham and Vegetables au Gratin

2 large knobs of butter
1 large onion, peeled and sliced into rings
225 g (8 oz) mushrooms, finely sliced
1 kg (2 lb) potatoes, peeled and very thinly sliced
salt
freshly ground black pepper
4 thick slices of boiled ham, cut into chunks
1 × 300 ml (2 pint) packet country herb sauce mix
300 ml ($\frac{1}{2}$ pint) milk
3–4 tablespoons golden breadcrumbs

Melt half the butter in a large frying pan, add the onion and fry over gentle heat until soft. Add the mushrooms and fry for 5 minutes, stirring constantly. Remove from the pan and set aside. Melt the remaining butter in the pan, then remove from the heat.

Put a layer of potatoes in the bottom of the pan and sprinkle with salt and pepper. Cover with a layer of onion and mushrooms, then with some of the ham. Repeat these layers until all the ingredients are used up, finishing with a layer of potatoes. Return the pan to a very low heat.

Make the sauce with the milk according to packet directions, then pour over the potatoes. Cover loosely with foil and cook over very low heat for about 35 minutes or until the potatoes are tender. Remove the foil and sprinkle the breadcrumbs over the top.

Put under a preheated hot grill for 10 minutes, until golden brown all over, turning the pan occasionally to ensure even browning. Serve hot.

Variations:
Any kind of cooked or canned meat can be used instead of the boiled ham.

If liked, the ham can be omitted and the vegetable dish served with chops, steaks, gammon or cold meat.

Parmesan Ham

1 × 3 kg (6 lb) joint of gammon on the bone
$\frac{1}{2}$ teaspoon ground mixed spice
6 cloves
2 bay leaves
2 tablespoons wine vinegar
2–3 tablespoons redcurrant jelly
50–75 g (2–3 oz) dried breadcrumbs
50–75 g (2–3 oz) Parmesan cheese, grated
freshly ground black pepper
100 g (4 oz) butter
few rings of fresh or canned pineapple, to garnish

Soak the gammon in several changes of cold water for a minimum of 12 hours, preferably overnight, then rinse under cold running water.

Tie the joint securely with string. Put in a saucepan, cover with cold water and add the mixed spice, cloves, bay leaves and wine vinegar. Bring to the boil, skim the scum with a slotted spoon, then lower the heat, half cover with a lid and simmer gently for 2 to 2$\frac{1}{2}$ hours until the ham is tender when pierced in the centre with a skewer.

Remove from the pan, leave until cold, then remove the string and cut off the rind, leaving a thin layer of fat. Brush this surface of the ham with redcurrant jelly. Mix the breadcrumbs and Parmesan cheese together, add black pepper to taste, then sprinkle and press this mixture on to the redcurrant jelly to cover it completely.

Place the ham in a roasting pan with the butter and bake in a preheated fairly hot oven (190°C, 375°F, Gas Mark 5) for 30 to 40 minutes until the coating is golden brown, basting the ham occasionally with the butter. Remove from the pan and leave until completely cold. Cut a few slices from the ham and arrange with the whole ham on a carving board. Garnish with pineapple.
Serves 12–15

Gammon with Peaches

1 × 425 g (15 oz) can peach halves
1 tablespoon grated onion
1 tablespoon finely chopped parsley
salt and freshly ground black pepper
a little ground cinnamon
40 g (1½ oz) fresh breadcrumbs
4 thin gammon slices
1 tablespoon lemon juice
½ teaspoon dry mustard
20 whole cloves
2 tablespoons demerara sugar
watercress sprigs, to garnish

Reserve four peach halves for garnish and finely chop the remainder. Mix with the onion, parsley, seasonings, cinnamon and breadcrumbs and bind together with a little peach juice.

Divide the stuffing mixture between the gammon placing it in the centre of each slice. Fold over to enclose completely and secure with wooden cocktail sticks, if necessary. Place in a shallow ovenproof dish. Combine 150 ml (¼ pint) peach juice with the lemon juice, mustard and a little black pepper. Pour over the gammon and cook, uncovered, in a moderate oven (180°C, 350°F, Gas Mark 4) for 40 minutes.

Baste the gammon and place a peach half studded with cloves on each roll or arranged at either end of the serving dish. Sprinkle with sugar and return to the oven for 10 minutes before serving garnished with watercress sprigs.

Ham Mousse

40 g (1½ oz) caster sugar
1 tablespoon dry mustard
½ teaspoon salt
freshly ground black pepper
3 large eggs, beaten
6 tablespoons wine vinegar
1 tablespoon powdered gelatine
  (15 g/½ oz packet)
2 tablespoons water

150 ml (¼ pint) double cream
1 tablespoon creamed horseradish
350 g (12 oz) cooked ham, finely
  chopped or minced
cooked asparagus, to garnish

Mix together the sugar, dry mustard, salt, pepper and eggs. Bring the vinegar to the boil and whisk into the egg mixture. Return to the pan and cook over a very gentle heat until thickened, stirring continuously. Do not boil or the sauce will curdle.

Dissolve the gelatine in the water in a small basin over a pan of hot water, cool slightly then add to the sauce. Cool, then stir in the cream, horseradish and ham. Pour into a well greased 900 ml (1½ pint) fluted mould and chill until set. Turn out on to a serving dish and garnish with the asparagus before serving.

Sausage and Bacon Piperade

350 g (12 oz) pork, or pork and beef,
  chipolatas
12 long rashers streaky bacon,
  derinded
1 large onion, peeled and thinly sliced
2–3 cloves garlic, crushed
50 g (2 oz) butter
2 × 184 g (6½ oz) cans pimientos,
  drained
450 g (1 lb) tomatoes, peeled and
  quartered
salt and freshly ground black pepper
To garnish:
parsley sprigs (optional)
wedges of hard-boiled egg (optional)

Prick the chipolatas and wind a rasher of bacon around each one; secure with wooden cocktail sticks if necessary. Either grill or fry, until well browned and cooked through, and keep warm.

Meanwhile, fry the onion and garlic gently in butter until soft, but not brown. Cut the pimientos into thin strips, add to the pan with the tomatoes and cook gently for 7 to 8 minutes, until soft. Season well to taste and turn out on to a warm dish.

Drain the chipolatas on absorbent paper then place on the piperade. Garnish with parsley sprigs, and wedges of hard-boiled egg, if liked.

Spicy Ham Fritters

1 × 100 g (4 oz) packet pancake and batter mix
about 200 ml ($\frac{1}{3}$ pint) milk
1 × 350 g (12 oz) can chopped ham loaf
curry paste
vegetable oil for shallow frying

Make up a coating batter with the mix and the milk according to packet directions. Cut the ham loaf into 8 equal slices, spread one side of each slice with a little curry paste. Heat the oil in a non-stick frying pan. Dip the ham slices into the batter one at a time until evenly coated. Fry in the hot oil for 5 minutes on each side until golden brown and crisp, then drain on paper towels. Serve immediately with a tomato salad and crisp French bread and butter.

Toad in the Hole

8 large beef or pork sausages
batter mixture (p. 363)

Grease a shallow baking dish or roasting pan. Put the beef or pork sausages in the pan and bake in a preheated oven at 220°C, 425°F, Gas Mark 7, turning occasionally, until they are evenly browned. Arrange the sausages evenly in the dish, whisk the batter well and pour it round the sausages. Return the dish to the oven and bake for 20 to 30 minutes or until the batter is well risen, crisp and golden. Serve immediately.

Sausage, Egg and Bacon Pie

350 g (12 oz) puff pastry
225 g (8 oz) beef sausages, cooked and chopped
4 hard-boiled eggs, shelled and chopped
175 g (6 oz) lean bacon, chopped
1 onion, peeled and grated
salt and freshly ground black pepper
1 egg, beaten, to glaze
150 ml ($\frac{1}{4}$ pint) soured cream

Divide the pastry into 2 equal portions, and roll each one to a circle about 22.5 cm (9 inches) in diameter. Line a shallow pie plate with one circle of pastry. Mix the chopped, cooked sausages with the chopped hard-boiled egg, chopped bacon, grated onion and seasoning. Spoon evenly on to the pastry-lined plate, leaving a 2.5 cm (1 inch) rim around the edge. Brush pastry rim with beaten egg. Cover the filling with the remaining circle of pastry, and trim off any excess. Pinch the pastry edges together to seal. Brush the top of the pastry with beaten egg. Make a small steam vent in the centre of the pie, and decorate with shapes cut from the pastry trimmings. Brush these with more beaten egg.

Bake in a fairly hot oven (200°C, 400°F, Gas Mark 6) for 40 minutes. Remove from the oven and carefully make the hole in the top of the pie crust slightly larger. Stir the soured cream to thin it and carefully pour it through a small funnel into the pie. Leave for a few minutes before serving.
Serves 6

Savoury Shortcake

100 g (4 oz) bacon pieces or streaky bacon, derinded
225 g (8 oz) skinless pork sausages, thinly sliced
100 g (4 oz) button mushrooms, wiped and sliced
100 g (4 oz) quick cook oats
100 g (4 oz) self-raising flour
50 g (2 oz) grated Parmesan cheese
pinch of salt
1 teaspoon mixed dried herbs
100 g (4 oz) margarine
approx. 150 ml ($\frac{1}{4}$ pint) milk to bind and glaze

Cut the bacon into very small pieces. Place in a frying pan and fry gently until the fat begins to run. Stir in the sliced sausages and mushrooms. Allow the mixture to become quite cold.

Mix together the oats, self-raising flour, half the Parmesan cheese, the salt and the mixed herbs in a bowl. Rub in the margarine until the mixture resembles coarse breadcrumbs. Add sufficient milk to make a fairly stiff dough.

Divide the mixture into 2 equal portions and roll each out on a floured board to a circle approx. 20 cm (8 inches) in diameter. Place one half in the bottom of a well-greased 20 cm (8 inch) ovenproof dish. Pile the cold sausage mixture on top and cover with the remaining round of dough, pressing the edges together well down into the dish. Brush the top with milk and sprinkle the remaining Parmesan cheese on top. Bake in a fairly hot oven (190°C, 375°F, Gas Mark 5) for 30 to 35 minutes.

Sausagemeat Flan

450 g (1 lb) fresh sausagemeat
1 small onion, peeled and finely chopped
50 g (2oz) fresh breadcrumbs
salt and freshly ground black pepper

1 egg, beaten
3 leeks, trimmed, thickly sliced and washed
25 g (1 oz) butter
25 g (1 oz) flour
scant 250 ml ($\frac{1}{2}$ pint) milk
$\frac{1}{2}$ teaspoon mustard
75 g (3 oz) English Mature Cheddar cheese, grated

Mix the sausagemeat with the onion, breadcrumbs, seasonings and beaten egg. Use to line a lightly greased 18 cm (7 inch) flan dish. Cook in a moderately hot oven (200°C, 400°F, Gas Mark 6) for 25 to 30 minutes until well browned and cooked through. Meanwhile, cook the leeks in salted water until tender and then drain very thoroughly. Melt the butter in a pan, stir in the flour and cook for 1 minute, then gradually add the milk and bring to the boil for 2 minutes. Season to taste, then stir in the mustard and most of the cheese until melted. Add the leeks and pour into the flan. Sprinkle with the remaining cheese and return to the oven or place under a moderate grill until the cheese is lightly browned, about 10 minutes. Serve hot.

Chipolata Cheese Pie

225 g (8 oz) plain flour
salt and freshly ground black pepper
50 g (2 oz) margarine
50 g (2 oz) lard or white fat
water to mix
225 g (8 oz) chipolata sausages
2 teaspoons dripping
225 g (8 oz) tomatoes, peeled and sliced
1 large egg
150 ml ($\frac{1}{4}$ pint) milk
pinch of garlic powder
50 g (2 oz) Cheddar cheese, grated

Sieve the flour with a pinch of salt into a bowl, add fats and rub in until the mixture resembles fine breadcrumbs. Add sufficient cold water to mix to a pliable dough. Brown the chipolatas lightly in melted dripping, then drain well. Roll out two-thirds of the pastry and use to line a 20 cm (8 inch) flan tin or ring. Lay half the tomatoes in the base, cover with the chipolatas and fill in the gaps with the remaining tomatoes. Beat the egg with the milk, seasonings and garlic and pour into the pastry case. Sprinkle with the cheese.

Roll out the remaining pastry, cut into narrow strips and arrange in a lattice pattern over the filling. Cook in a hot oven (220°C, 425°F, Gas Mark 7) for 15 minutes, then reduce oven temperature to moderate (180°C, 350°F, Gas Mark 4) and continue for 30 to 40 minutes until the filling is golden brown and firm to the touch. Serve hot or cold.

Shooter's Roll

450 g (1 lb) pork sausagemeat,
   without herbs
100 g (4 oz) lean bacon rashers,
   derinded and chopped
1 small onion, peeled and finely
   chopped
1 teaspoon dried sage
100 g (4 oz) mushrooms, cleaned,
   trimmed and finely chopped
salt and freshly ground black pepper
350 g (12 oz) frozen puff pastry,
   thawed
beaten egg to glaze
salads, to garnish

Combine the sausagemeat, bacon, onion, sage, mushrooms and seasonings to taste. Roll out the pastry thinly on a lightly floured surface and trim to a rectangle approx. 30 × 25 cm (12 × 10 inches). Form the sausagemeat mixture into a brick shape down the centre of the pastry. Fold over the sides and ends of pastry, damping with water, to enclose the filling completely. Place on a lightly greased or non-stick baking sheet with the pastry joins underneath. Decorate the roll with the pastry

trimmings and brush all over with beaten egg. Make two cuts in the top and bake in a very hot oven (230°C, 450°F, Gas Mark 8) for 15 minutes. Reduce oven temperature to moderately hot (190°C, 375°F, Gas Mark 5) and continue for a further 35 to 40 minutes. Cover the top with foil if over browning.

Remove carefully from the baking sheet and cool. Chill thoroughly before serving, sliced, with salads.

Sausage Nuggets

3 hard-boiled eggs, chopped
75 g (3 oz) English Mature Cheddar
   cheese, grated
2 tablespoons tomato ketchup
salt
freshly ground black pepper
450 g (1 lb) fresh sausagemeat
2 tablespoons very finely chopped
   onion
flour for coating
1 egg, beaten
golden crumbs for coating
deep fat for frying
To garnish:
lettuce leaves
carrot sticks

Mix together the chopped eggs, grated cheese, ketchup, and seasonings to taste. Divide into four equal portions and form into balls. Combine the sausagemeat with the onion and divide into four. Mould each piece of sausagemeat around a cheese and egg ball to give an egg shape. Roll first in flour, then dip in beaten egg and finally coat in breadcrumbs; chill until required.

Heat the deep fat until it is hot enough to brown a cube of bread in 20 to 30 seconds – 180–190°C, 350–375°F. Fry the nuggets for about 15 minutes, or until crisp, golden brown and cooked through. Drain an absorbent kitchen paper and serve hot or cold with a garnish of lettuce and carrot sticks.

Sausages with Horseradish Mayonnaise

450 g (1 lb) pork sausages
4 tablespoons French dressing
For the horseradish mayonnaise:
2 egg yolks
1 tablespoon wine vinegar
2 teaspoons French mustard
300 ml (½ pint) olive oil
salt and freshly ground black pepper
4 tablespoons whipped cream
1 tablespoon creamed horseradish
2 stalks of celery, scrubbed and
   chopped
2 eating apples, diced
2 tablespoons diced gherkin

Grill the pork sausages for about 10 minutes, until golden-brown all over and cooked through. While they are still warm put them into a shallow dish and spoon over the French dressing. Cover the dish and chill in the refrigerator for 2 hours.

To make the horseradish mayonnaise, beat the egg yolks with the wine vinegar and then add the French mustard. Gradually add the oil, in a fine trickle, whisking continuously until it is all absorbed. Season to taste and stir in the whipped cream and creamed horseradish. Fold in the celery, apple and gherkin.

Arrange the marinated sausages on a serving platter and spoon over the horseradish mayonnaise. Serve with rye bread.

Oatmeal Sausages with Hollandaise Sauce

450 g (1 lb) pork sausages with herbs
1 egg, beaten
50 g (2 oz) rolled oats
450 g (1 lb) cooked, chopped spinach
25 g (1 oz) butter
salt and freshly ground black pepper
a little ground nutmeg

For the sauce:
4 tablespoons wine vinegar
2 tablespoons water
6 peppercorns, crushed
4 egg yolks
100–175 g (4–6 oz) softened butter
a little lemon juice
tomato, to garnish

Prick the sausages then dip in beaten egg. Coat thoroughly in the oats and place in a greased ovenproof dish. Cook, uncovered, in a hot oven (220°C, 425°F, Gas Mark 7) for 35 to 40 minutes, until they are well browned, crisp and cooked through.

Meanwhile, heat the spinach in melted butter and season to taste with salt, pepper and nutmeg. Turn into a serving dish and keep warm.

To make the sauce, put the vinegar, water and peppercorns in a small pan and bring to the boil. Boil until reduced by half then strain into a basin. Place over a saucepan of gently simmering water. Beat in the egg yolks and cook very gently until the sauce thickens, stirring continuously. Beat in the butter, a little at a time until the sauce has a thin coating consistency. Season to taste with salt and pepper, sharpen with a little lemon juice.

Drain the sausages and arrange on the spinach. Garnish with tomato. Serve with the warm sauce.

Six Layer Dinner

2 large knobs of butter
1 large Spanish onion, peeled and
   finely sliced
450 g (1 lb) pork sausages
1 × 300 g (10 oz) can condensed tomato
   soup
1 × 75 g (3 oz) packet country stuffing
   mix
1 × 100 g (4 oz) packet frozen
   sweetcorn
1 × 100 g (4 oz) packet instant mashed
   potato mix

600 ml (1 pint) boiling water
salt
freshly ground black pepper

Melt half the butter in a frying pan, add the onion and fry over gentle heat until soft and lightly coloured. Remove the onion with a slotted spoon and set aside. Add the sausages to the pan, fry until brown on all sides, then transfer to the bottom of an ovenproof dish. Cover with the onion, then the tomato soup. Sprinkle over half the stuffing mix, then the sweetcorn. Preheat the oven at medium temperature for 5 minutes. Make the potato mix with the water according to packet directions, then beat in the remaining butter and salt and pepper to taste. Spread over the ingredients in the dish, then sprinkle with the remaining stuffing mix. Bake in the centre of the oven for 30 minutes, then serve hot.

Variations:
Any vegetables can be used instead of the ones given here – try fresh tomatoes, frozen or canned peas, sliced canned carrots or baked beans.

Quick Cassoulet

2 tablespoons vegetable oil
1 large onion, peeled and sliced
450 g (1 lb) chipolata sausages
100 g (4 oz) streaky bacon, chopped
1 × 436 g (15 oz) can red kidney beans, drained
150 ml ($\frac{1}{4}$ pint) beef stock
salt and freshly ground black pepper
8 thin slices French bread
50 g (2 oz) Cheddar cheese, grated

Heat the oil in a frying pan. Add the onion and fry gently for 5 minutes. Add the chipolata sausages and the chopped bacon and fry gently for a further 5 minutes, turning the sausages occasionally.
    Put the sausages, onion and bacon

into a casserole. Add the drained red kidney beans, stock and seasoning to taste. Cover and cook in a moderate oven (180°C, 350°F, Gas Mark 4) for 40 minutes. Remove the lid and cover the sausage and bean mixture with slices of French bread. Sprinkle with the grated cheese and return the cassoulet to the oven for a further 10 to 15 minutes, until the cheese bubbles.

Sausage and Bacon Casserole

450 g (1 lb) pork or beef sausages
1 tablespoon dripping
12 rashers streaky bacon, derinded and rolled
1 large onion, peeled and sliced
2 large carrots, peeled and sliced
100 g (4 oz) button mushrooms, cleaned, trimmed and halved
300 ml ($\frac{1}{2}$ pint) stock
4–6 tablespoons red wine
1 teaspoon dried thyme
salt and freshly ground black pepper
$\frac{1}{2}$ teaspoon Worcestershire sauce
4 tomatoes, peeled and halved
cornflour (optional)

Brown the sausages in the melted dripping then transfer to an ovenproof casserole. Fry the bacon in the same fat until lightly browned and add to the casserole. Add the onion, carrots and mushrooms to the pan and cook gently for 5 minutes. Stir in the stock, wine, thyme, seasonings and Worcestershire sauce and bring to the boil. Pour into the casserole, cover and cook in a moderate oven (180°C, 350°F, Gas Mark 4) for 40 minutes. Remove any fat from the surface, taste and adjust the seasonings and add the tomatoes. Return the casserole to the oven and continue cooking for 20 minutes.
    This dish can be thickened with a little cornflour if preferred. Moisten the cornflour with water and stir into the casserole gradually.

Sausage and Salami Tattie Ash

450 g (1 lb) fresh sausages
1 tablespoon dripping
1 large onion, peeled and sliced
450 g (1 lb) small new potatoes, scraped or scrubbed
2 carrots, peeled and cut into sticks
1 large leek, trimmed, sliced and washed
100 g (4 oz) salami, diced
salt and freshly ground black pepper
1 teaspoon Worcestershire sauce
scant 400 ml ($\frac{3}{4}$ pint) stock
To garnish:
salami slices (optional)
chopped parsley (optional)

Fry the sausages quickly in melted dripping until well browned all over; drain and cut each one in half. Fry the onion in the same fat until lightly browned, then drain well. Place the sausages, onion, potatoes (which can be left in their skins, if preferred), carrots, leeks, salami and seasonings in an oven-proof casserole. Add the Worcester-shire sauce to the stock and pour into the casserole. Cover and cook in a moderate oven (180°C, 350°F, Gas Mark 4) for about 1 hour or until tender.

Taste and adjust the seasonings, garnish with salami and parsley, if liked.

Risotto

1 large knob of butter
1 large onion, peeled and chopped
2 × 150 g (5 oz) packets savoury tomato rice
900 ml (1½ pints) hot water
1 × 50 g (2 oz) packet quick dried mixed vegetables
freshly ground black pepper
100 g (4 oz) piece of garlic sausage, diced
6 small frankfurters, sliced
grated Parmesan cheese, to serve

Melt the butter in a large saucepan, add the onion and fry over gentle heat until soft. Stir in the rice and fry for a further 5 minutes, stirring occasionally. Pour in the water, stir once, then bring to the boil. Add the mixed vegetables and pepper to taste, cover tightly and cook over gentle heat for 20 minutes until most of the liquid has been absorbed. Stir in the garlic sausage and frankfur-ters and cook for a further 5 minutes until heated through. Taste and adjust seasoning, then serve immediately with a tossed mixed salad and the Parmesan handed separately.

Sausage Kedgeree

450 g (1 lb) chipolata sausages
2 eggs
175 g (6 oz) long-grain rice
50 g (2 oz) butter
salt
freshly ground black pepper
4 tablespoons chopped parsley
lemon twists, to garnish

Grill the chipolata sausages until golden-brown on all sides and cooked through. Cut into bite-sized pieces. Put the eggs into cold water, bring to the boil and simmer for 10 minutes. Remove the eggs, lightly crack the shells and plunge them into a bowl of cold water. Cook the long-grain rice in rapidly boiling salted water for about 10 minutes until just tender. Drain thoroughly and toss with a fork to separate the grains. Shell the hard-boiled eggs and chop roughly. Melt the butter in a pan, add the sausage pieces and the cooked rice and season to taste. Add the chopped hard-boiled egg and stir with a fork over a gentle heat for a few minutes, until the kedgeree is heated through. Add nalf the chopped parsley and pile up on a hot serving dish. Sprinkle with the remaining chopped parsley. Serve hot, garnished with lemon twists.

LAMB

Spring Lamb Cobbler

900 g (2 lb) middle neck of lamb
25 g (1 oz) dripping or lard
2 tablespoons flour
2 tablespoons tomato purée
600 ml (1 pint) stock or water
4 onions, peeled and sliced
2 leeks, cleaned and sliced
4 carrots, peeled and sliced
1 bay leaf
salt and freshly ground black pepper
For the scone topping:
200 g (8 oz) self-raising flour
50 g (2 oz) butter or margarine
1 egg, beaten
4 tablespoons milk

Trim the meat and cut into serving pieces. Melt the fat in a flameproof casserole and fry the meat until evenly browned. Dredge with the seasoned flour and continue to cook until flour is browned. Gradually stir in the tomato purée and stock and bring to the boil. Add the onions, leeks, carrots, bay leaf and seasonings and simmer for about 1¼ hours until tender. Discard the bay leaf, taste and adjust seasonings.

Sieve the flour with a pinch of salt into a bowl, add the fat and rub in until the mixture resembles fine bread-crumbs. Add the beaten egg and sufficient milk to mix to a fairly soft dough. Roll out the dough to 1½ cm (½ inch) thickness, cut into 5 cm (2 inch) rounds and place in an overlapping circle around the edge of the casserole to make a border on top of the lamb. Brush with milk and cook in a hot oven (220°C, 425°F, Gas Mark 7) for 10 to 15 minutes until well risen, golden brown and firm to the touch. Serve at once.

Grapefruit Stuffed Shoulder of Lamb

1½ kg (3 lb) shoulder of lamb, boned
For the stuffing:
75 g (3 oz) fresh white breadcrumbs
2 teaspoons chopped parsley
grated rind of 1 grapefruit
50 g (2 oz) sultanas
salt and freshly ground black pepper
1 egg, beaten
To garnish:
grapefruit segments
parsley sprigs

Spread out the boned shoulder, skin side down, on a board. Mix all the ingredients for the stuffing together. Cover the shoulder with the stuffing mixture and roll up neatly. Tie tightly with string in two places. Place in a roasting tin and put in the centre of a moderate oven (180°C, 350°F, Gas Mark 4) for 25 minutes per 450 g (1 lb) of the stuffed weight. Remove the strings and serve on a warm platter surrounded by grapefruit segments placed alternately with parsley sprigs.
Serves 6

Lamb and Leek Pudding

225 g (8 oz) self-raising flour
1 teaspoon salt
100 g (4 oz) shredded beef suet
150 ml ($\frac{1}{4}$ pint) water
For the filling:
3 thin leeks, washed and sliced in
    rings
450 g (1 lb) boned lamb shoulder or
    best end of neck, trimmed of fat and
    cut into small cubes
2 tablespoons seasoned flour for
    coating
1 beef stock cube, crumbled
salt and freshly ground black pepper
1 teaspoon dried thyme

To make the pastry, sift the flour and
salt into a bowl. Stir in the shredded
suet. Mix in just sufficient of the water
to make a smooth dough that leaves the
sides of the bowl clean. Turn out on to a
lightly floured board and knead for 1
minute.

Form into 2 balls, 1 twice as large as
the other. Roll the larger ball into a
round big enough to line a 1 litre ($1\frac{3}{4}$
pint) pudding basin. Grease the pudding
basin. Ease the pastry into position,
making cuts down the sides of the
pastry with clean kitchen scissors, if
necessary, and sealing these together
after brushing the cut edges with water.

Wash the sliced leeks thoroughly in a
colander and drain well. Coat the cubed
lamb with seasoned flour. Put both into
the basin in alternate layers. Mix the
crumbled stock cube, seasoning to taste
and the dried thyme, with sufficient cold
water to come halfway up the contents.
Form the reserved pastry into a lid and
place on top, sealing the edges of the
pastry with cold water.

Cover the pudding with greased foil,
making a pleat in the centre to allow for
expansion. Tie a piece of string tightly
round the bowl under the lip and across
the top to form a handle. Place in a
steamer or large saucepan of simmering
water, making sure the water does not
come more than halfway up the sides of
the basin. Cover and steam for 3 hours,
topping up the water level when
necessary.

Remove the basin by the string
handle, using the handle of a wooden
spoon slipped under the string. Take off
the foil and serve in wedges, taking care
to spoon out a reasonable proportion of
the filling with each serving. Diced
carrots and peas make a good
accompaniment.

Colonial Goose

2 kg ($4\frac{1}{2}$ lb) leg of lamb, boned
25 g (1 oz) butter
1 small onion, peeled and chopped
100 g (4 oz) prunes, soaked
1 eating apple, peeled, cored and
    chopped
75 g (3 oz) fresh breadcrumbs
salt and freshly ground black pepper
1 teaspoon fresh or dried rosemary,
    finely chopped
1 egg, beaten
150 ml ($\frac{1}{4}$ pint) dry white wine
a little melted butter
2 tablespoons flour
300 ml ($\frac{1}{2}$ pint) stock
To garnish:
cooked courgettes, sliced
cooked whole prunes
fresh rosemary (optional)

Ask the butcher to bone out the leg of
lamb – this may have to be ordered in
advance. Melt the butter and fry the
onion until soft. Chop and stone the
prunes and add to the chopped onion
with the apple, breadcrumbs, seasonings and rosemary. Bind together with
the egg and use to stuff the bone cavity.
Sew the joint back into shape with a
trussing needle and fine string – but not
too tightly or the skin will split during
cooking. Place in a polythene bag,
lining a bowl, add the wine and leave
to marinate for 4–6 hours, turning
occasionally.

Remove the joint, weigh and place in a roasting tin. Brush with melted butter and cook in a moderate oven (180°C, 350°F, Gas Mark 4), allowing 25 minutes per 450 g (1 lb), plus 30 minutes over. Baste occasionally and cover with foil when sufficiently browned. Remove the string from the joint, place joint on a serving dish and keep warm. Pour off the fat from the roasting tin and stir the flour into the pan juices. Cook for a few minutes then stir in the wine marinade and stock. Bring to the boil and simmer for 2 minutes. Taste and adjust the seasonings and strain into a sauce boat. Garnish the joint with slices of courgette, whole prunes, and sprigs of rosemary if available.

Pot Roast Lamb with Fennel

1½ kg (3 lb) loin of lamb joint
1 tablespoon dripping
salt and freshly ground black pepper
1 large bulb of fennel, cleaned and
  roughly chopped
1 onion, peeled and chopped
½ teaspoon finely grated lemon rind
1 tablespoon lemon juice
about 300 ml (½ pint) boiling stock
1 tablespoon cornflour

Trim the lamb and brown the joint all over in melted dripping. Place in an ovenproof casserole and season well. Arrange the fennel and onion around the joint, add the lemon rind and juice and stock. Cover tightly and cook in a moderately hot oven (190°C, 375°F, Gas Mark 5) for about 1½ hours or until tender.

Strain off the cooking liquor, make up to 300 ml (½ pint) with more stock if necessary and thicken with cornflour blended in a little cold water. Boil for 2 minutes, then taste and adjust the seasonings.

Slice the lamb, surround it with the fennel and serve with the sauce.
Serves 6

† Orange Lamb Shoulder

1½ kg (3 lb) boned shoulder of lamb
salt
freshly ground black pepper
75 g (3 oz) fresh white breadcrumbs
75 g (3 oz) mushrooms, cleaned and
  chopped
50 g (2 oz) sultanas
1 small onion, peeled and grated
½ teaspoon dried marjoram
finely grated rind of 2 oranges
1 egg, beaten
25 g (1 oz) lard or margarine
750 ml (1¼ pints) hot brown stock or
  water and ½ beef stock cube
To finish:
2 tablespoons redcurrant jelly
2 teaspoons cornflour
little water

Trim the lamb of any excess fat. Lay the lamb, skin side down, and season the upper surface with salt and pepper. Mix together the breadcrumbs, mushrooms, sultanas, onion, marjoram, orange rind and a little salt and pepper. Bind together with the egg. Spread the stuffing over the surface of the meat to within 2.5 cm (1 inch) of the edges. Roll up as tightly as possible and secure at intervals with string. Heat the lard or margarine in the cooker and brown the lamb evenly all over. Lift out and drain off the excess lard or margarine from the cooker. Add the hot stock or water and stock cube to the cooker, stir well to remove any residues from the base of the cooker. Put the trivet into the cooker, rim side down and place the lamb on the trivet. Close the cooker, bring to H pressure and cook for 55 minutes. Reduce the pressure quickly. Lift out the joint to a warm serving dish, remove the string and keep hot. Remove the trivet from the cooker. Return the open cooker to the heat, stir in the redcurrant jelly and the cornflour blended with a little water. Simmer and stir constantly until thickened. Adjust seasoning and serve with the lamb.

Spiced Leg of Lamb

1 × 2 kg (4 lb) leg of lamb
1 garlic clove, peeled and cut into
    slivers
1 tablespoon ground coriander
1 tablespoon ground cumin
1 tablespoon flour
6 black peppercorns, crushed
1 teaspoon salt
2 tablespoons tomato purée
2 teaspoons lemon juice
50 g (2 oz) lard or dripping
450 ml ($\frac{3}{4}$ pint) hot beef stock

Score the skin of the lamb and insert the garlic slivers. Mix together the spices, flour, peppercorns, salt, tomato purée and lemon juice in a bowl and brush all over the lamb. Chill in the refrigerator overnight. Put the lamb in a roasting pan with the lard or dripping. Roast on the top shelf of a very hot oven (230°C, 450°F, Gas Mark 8) for 15 to 20 minutes until the meat is browned, basting occasionally. Pour the hot stock into the pan, lower the heat to moderate (180°C, 350°F, Gas Mark 4) and roast for approximately 1$\frac{1}{2}$ hours or until the juices run pink when the meat is pierced with a skewer. Spoon the stock over the lamb from time to time during cooking.

Remove the meat from the pan and leave in a warm place before carving. Transfer the pan to the top of the stove and boil the stock to reduce to a thick gravy. Taste and adjust seasoning before serving.
Serves 4–6

Roast Apricot Lamb

100 g (4 oz) dried apricots, soaked
    overnight
25 g (1 oz) butter
1 medium-sized onion, peeled and
    finely chopped
finely grated rind of $\frac{1}{2}$ lemon
2 tablespoons finely chopped parsley

salt and freshly ground black pepper
good pinch of ground mixed spice
50 g (2 oz) long-grain rice, cooked
1 small egg, beaten
small shoulder of lamb, boned, about
    1$\frac{1}{2}$ kg (3 lb)
a little dripping or oil
300 ml ($\frac{1}{2}$ pint) stock
2–3 teaspoons cornflour

To make the stuffing, cook the apricots in the soaking water for 10 minutes then drain, reserving the liquor; chop the fruit. Melt the butter and fry the onion gently until soft. Remove from the heat and stir in the lemon rind, parsley, seasonings, spice, cooked rice and apricots; bind together with the egg.

Put the lamb on to a board and spread the stuffing over the inside. Roll the joint carefully making sure all the stuffing is enclosed. Secure with skewers and string and weight the joint. Place in a roasting tin, spread with a little dripping and season lightly. Cook in a hot oven (220°C, 425°F, Gas Mark 7), allowing 25 minutes per 450 g (1 lb) weight and 25 minutes over, basting occasionally. Remove the joint and keep warm. Use the pan drippings, 150 ml ($\frac{1}{4}$ pint) reserved apricot juice, stock and seasonings to taste to make a gravy, and thicken with the cornflour.
Serves 6

† Lamb Bourguignonne

2 tablespoons cooking oil
225 g (8 oz) small pickling onions,
    peeled
1 garlic clove, crushed
750 g (1$\frac{1}{2}$ lb) lamb from shoulder or
    leg, cubed
100 g (4 oz) unsmoked streaky bacon,
    rinded and chopped
100 g (4 oz) button mushrooms,
    cleaned
2 tablespoons tomato purée
450 ml ($\frac{3}{4}$ pint) red wine (Burgundy-
    type)

salt and freshly ground black pepper
To finish:
1 tablespoon flour
little water
a little freshly chopped parsley

Heat the oil in the cooker. Sauté the onions and garlic until they are beginning to colour. Add the meat and bacon and fry until the meat is evenly browned. Add the mushrooms, tomato purée, wine and a little salt and pepper. Stir well to remove any residues from the base of the cooker and bring to the boil. Close the cooker, bring to H pressure and cook for 12 minutes. Reduce the pressure quickly. Blend the flour with a little water. Return open cooker to heat. Stir in the blended flour gradually and cook until thickened, stirring constantly. Taste and adjust the seasoning as necessary. Garnish with a little chopped parsley.

† Navarin of Lamb

25 g (1 oz) lard or margarine
1 large onion, peeled and sliced
1 garlic clove, crushed
2 breasts of lamb, chopped into single rib pieces
25 g (1 oz) flour
salt
freshly ground black pepper
1 × 400 g (14 oz) can tomatoes
300 ml (½ pint) white stock or water and ½ chicken stock cube
225 g (8 oz) carrots, scraped and sliced
1 teaspoon mixed herbs
To finish:
1 tablespoon flour
little water
a little freshly chopped parsley

Heat the lard or margarine in the cooker. Sauté the onion and garlic until both are beginning to colour. Lift out and drain well. Coat the meat pieces in the flour, seasoned with salt and pepper

and fry until evenly browned all over. Lift out and drain well. Drain off any excess lard or margarine from the cooker. Return the cooker to the heat and stir in the tomatoes, stock or water and stock cube, carrots and herbs. Stir well to remove any residues from the base of the cooker. Return the meat, onion and garlic to the cooker. Close the cooker, bring to H pressure and cook for 12 minutes. Reduce the pressure quickly. Skim off any excess fat. Blend the flour with a little water. Return the open cooker to the heat and stir in the blended flour. Cook until thickened, stirring constantly. Taste and adjust the seasoning as necessary. Garnish with a little chopped parsley.

Crispy Lamb

1 large or 2 small breasts of lamb, boned
salt and freshly ground black pepper
1 egg, beaten
golden crumbs for coating
deep fat for frying
6 tablespoons thick mayonnaise
2 tablespoons capers
1 tablespoon finely chopped parsley
lemon wedges, to garnish

Trim the lamb of skin, gristle and excess fat. Place in a saucepan of well seasoned water and bring to the boil. Cover and simmer for 15 minutes then drain the lamb and cool. Cut into narrow strips; dip into the beaten egg and then coat thoroughly in breadcrumbs. Chill until required. Heat the fat to 180°C/350°F, or until a cube of bread browns in it in 30 seconds, and fry the lamb, a few pieces at a time, for 4 to 5 minutes until golden brown. Drain on absorbent paper and keep warm.

Mix together the mayonnaise, capers and parsley, add seasonings to taste and place in a bowl. Serve with the hot crispy lamb garnished with lemon wedges.

Fillet of Lamb en Croûte

2 large fillets of lamb
25 g (1 oz) butter
1 small onion, peeled and finely
   chopped
1 clove garlic, crushed
100 g (4 oz) mushrooms, cleaned,
   trimmed and chopped
salt
freshly ground black pepper
1 teaspoon dried rosemary
1 tablespoon finely chopped parsley
350 g (12 oz) frozen puff pastry,
   thawed
beaten egg to glaze
To garnish:
rosemary sprigs (if available)
potato croquettes

Trim the lamb fillets and lay one on top
of the other. Secure with thin string.
Fry quickly in hot melted butter until
sealed all over. Remove and set aside
until cool.

Fry the onion and garlic in the same
fat until soft, then stir in the
mushrooms and cook gently for 3 to 4
minutes. Remove from the heat, season
well and stir in the rosemary and
parsley and leave to cool.

Roll out the pastry to a rectangle.
Spread the mushroom mixture in a strip
down the centre of the pastry. Remove
the string from the lamb and lay lamb
on top of the mushrooms. Fold over the
pastry to enclose the lamb, dampening
the edges to seal. Place on a dampened
baking sheet with the joins underneath
and decorate the top with pastry
trimmings. Brush with beaten egg and
cook in a very hot oven (230°C, 450°F,
Gas Mark 8) for 10 minutes, then reduce
oven temperature to moderately hot
(190°C, 375°F, Gas Mark 5) and continue
for 50 to 60 minutes until the pastry is
golden brown. Cover the pastry with
foil when sufficiently browned.

Serve in slices, garnished with sprigs
of fresh rosemary, and potato
croquettes, with a thin gravy.

Spanish Lamb Chops

25 g (1 oz) butter
4 loin of lamb chops
1 large onion, peeled and sliced
1 clove garlic, crushed
1 pepper (red or green), deseeded and
   chopped
175 g (6 oz) long-grain rice
about 750 ml (1¼ pints) stock
pinch of saffron or ½ teaspoon
   turmeric
salt and freshly ground black pepper
100 g (4 oz) frozen peas

Melt the butter in a large heavy frying
pan and brown the chops on both sides.
Remove from the pan. Fry the onion,
garlic and pepper in the same fat until
soft. Stir in the rice and continue for 2
minutes. Add the stock, saffron or turmeric and seasonings and bring to the
boil. Replace the chops and cover the
pan. Simmer gently for 20 minutes.
Turn the chops over, stir in the peas and
add a little more boiling stock if necessary. Re-cover and continue to simmer
gently for about 20 minutes or until the
lamb and rice are tender and the liquid
has been absorbed. Taste and adjust the
seasonings as necessary and serve
straight from the pan.

A few mussels and/or peeled prawns
can be added to the rice, if liked, with
the peas.

Roast Crown of Lamb

2 best ends of neck of lamb (12
   cutlets) or a crown of lamb
little oil
For the stuffing:
25 g (1 oz) butter
1 large onion, peeled and finely
   chopped
2 sticks celery, scrubbed and finely
   chopped
100 g (4 oz) brown breadcrumbs
pinch of garlic powder

salt and freshly ground black pepper
50 g (2 oz) salted peanuts, chopped
75 g (3 oz) long-grain rice, cooked
1 level teaspoon curry powder
1 large egg, beaten
To garnish:
freshly cooked peas
cooked whole baby carrots

To make a crown of lamb, remove the chine bones from the best ends. Cut across the bone ends of the meat about 2.5 cm (1 inch) from the bone tips and scrape away all the fat and flesh to leave the bones bare. Place the joints back to back and sew together with the bones curving outwards to give a crown shape, using a trussing needle and fine string. Brush lightly all over with oil.

To make the stuffing, melt the butter in a pan and fry the onion and celery until soft, then stir in all the other ingredients, binding together with the egg. Use to fill the centre of the crown giving a domed top.

Weigh the stuffed crown and place in a roasting tin. Cover the bone tips with foil to prevent burning, and cover the stuffing with foil to keep it moist during cooking. Cook in a moderate oven (180°C, 350°F, Gas Mark 4), allowing 30 minutes per 450 g (1 lb) weight and 30 minutes over. Baste outside of the crown once or twice during cooking and remove the foil from the stuffing for the last half hour.

To serve, place the crown on a serving dish and remove the foil. Decorate bone tips with cutlet frills and surround the crown with whole carrots and peas. Use the pan drippings to make a thin gravy.

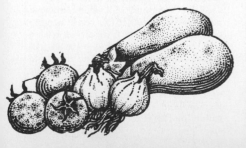

Mixed Grill

2 lamb cutlets or loin chops
2 pork sausages
oil for brushing
2 lamb's kidneys
2 large tomatoes
salt
freshly ground black pepper
sugar
butter
4 large mushrooms
2 rashers streaky bacon
mint butter (p. 353)
watercress, to garnish

Trim the cutlets or chops, removing any skin and surplus fat. Place on an oiled grid with the sausages. Brush the cutlets and sausages with oil. Put under a preheated grill and cook until brown (about 5 minutes), turning the sausages as necessary, but not the cutlets.

Meanwhile, slit the kidneys down the back, peel off the skin and remove the fatty core with scissors. Skewer them open so they will not curl when cooking. Brush with oil. Halve the tomatoes crossways, not downwards. Season with salt, pepper and sugar to taste and dot with butter. Remove the mushroom stalks, season the black side with salt and pepper and dot with butter, ready to be grilled.

Stretch the bacon rashers with the back of a knife and remove the rind and gristle. Roll up the rashers and skewer them. When the cutlets are brown on the first side, turn with tongs and then add the kidneys, bacon rolls, tomatoes and mushrooms. Turn the kidneys, sausages and bacon rolls as necessary but not the cutlets or vegetables.

When the cutlets are brown on the second side, place them on a dish or two individual plates and arrange the rest of the mixed grill round them. Top the cutlets with the mint butter, garnish with fresh watercress and serve with Chips (p. 54) or Sauté potatoes (p. 55). Serves 2

Chilli Lamb Chops

4 loin of lamb chops
salt and freshly ground black pepper
4 thin slices of lemon
2 large onions, peeled and thinly
    sliced
2 teaspoons chilli powder
1 × 298 g (10½ oz) can condensed
    tomato soup
To garnish:
lemon slices
parsley sprigs

Trim the chops, season lightly and place
in a shallow ovenproof dish with a slice
of lemon on each one. Blanch the onions
in boiling water for 3 minutes then
drain thoroughly and lay them over the
chops. Mix the chilli powder into the
soup with seasonings and heat gently.
Pour over the chops, cover and cook in a
moderately hot oven (200°C, 400°F, Gas
Mark 6) for approximately 45 minutes or
until tender.

Remove any excess fat from the
surface, taste and adjust seasonings
and garnish with lemon slices and
parsley sprigs.

† Lemon and Mushroom Breast of Lamb

50 g (2 oz) fresh white breadcrumbs
1 teaspoon finely grated lemon rind
2 tablespoons lemon juice
50 g (2 oz) mushrooms, cleaned and
    chopped
1 small onion, peeled and finely
    chopped
½ teaspoon dried rosemary
salt
freshly ground black pepper
1 egg, beaten
1 kg (2 lb) breast of lamb, trimmed
    and boned
25 g (1 oz) lard or margarine
450 ml (¾ pint) hot brown stock or
    water and ½ beef stock cube

Mix together the breadcrumbs, lemon
rind and juice, mushrooms, onion, rosemary and salt and pepper. Bind with the
egg. Lay the lamb, skin side down, and
spread the stuffing over the lamb to
within 2.5 cm (1 inch) of the edges. Roll
up and tie securely at intervals with
string. Heat the lard or margarine in
the cooker and brown the lamb well on
all sides. Lift out and drain off any
excess lard or margarine from the
cooker. Add the hot stock or water and
stock cube and stir well to remove any
residues from the base of the cooker.
Put the trivet in the cooker, rim side
down. Stand the joint on the trivet and
season well with salt and pepper. Close
the cooker, bring to H pressure and
cook for 30 minutes, then reduce the
pressure quickly. Remove the string
from the meat before serving.

Dressed Lamb Cutlets

8 neck cutlets of lamb
beaten egg and breadcrumbs for
    coating
lard or clarified butter for frying
1 kg (2 lb) creamy mashed potatoes
fresh mint or parsley sprigs, to
    garnish

Remove the chine bone from the chops
and trim off the surplus fat. Cut 2.5 cm (1
inch) of meat off the ends of the rib
bones and scrape the bones clean.

Coat the chops with egg and crumbs
and leave the coating to harden. Fry in
hot fat for 5 minutes on each side,
turning once. Drain on kitchen paper.

Make a mound of creamy mashed
potatoes in the centre of a warm serving
platter and mark in it a pattern with a
fork or spoon handle. Put a cutlet frill
on the end of each cutlet bone and stand
the cutlets round the potatoes with the
frills in the centre. Garnish with sprigs
of fresh mint or parsley. Serve with
Cumberland sauce (p. 350) or Tartare
sauce (p. 352) if liked.

Honeyed Lamb Chops

4 loin of lamb chops
salt and freshly ground black pepper
15 g ($\frac{1}{2}$ oz) butter
1 tablespoon finely chopped mint
2–3 tablespoons honey
$\frac{1}{2}$ teaspoon finely grated lemon rind
lemon slices, to garnish

Trim the lamb and season lightly. Place in a grill pan and dot with butter. Cook under a moderate grill for 8 to 10 minutes until well browned. Turn the chops over and continue for 2 to 3 minutes.

Mix together the mint, honey and lemon rind and spread over the chops. Continue to cook for 5 to 8 minutes until well browned and cooked through. Serve with the pan juices spooned over, and garnish with lemon slices, and sprigs of fresh mint, when available.

Stuffed Breasts of Lamb in Cider

2 large breasts of lamb, boned
salt and freshly ground black pepper
65 g (2$\frac{1}{2}$ oz) butter
2 medium-sized onions, peeled and
  chopped
75 g (3 oz) cooked rice
50 g (2 oz) raisins
2 teaspoons dried thyme
40 g (1$\frac{1}{2}$ oz) flour
300 ml ($\frac{1}{2}$ pint) stock
150 ml ($\frac{1}{4}$ pint) dry cider or white wine
fresh thyme or parsley, to garnish

Trim the breasts of lamb of any gristle, membrane and excess fat. Cut each one in half and season lightly. Melt 25 g (1 oz) butter and fry one onion until lightly browned. Stir in the rice, raisins, half the thyme and plenty of seasonings. Divide stuffing between the four pieces of lamb, spreading it evenly over the inside of the meat. Roll each piece up and secure with wooden cocktail sticks. Place in a roasting tin and cook in a hot oven (220°C, 425°F, Gas Mark 7) for $\frac{3}{4}$ to 1 hour, or until well browned and cooked through. Baste several times during cooking. Remove to a serving dish and keep warm. To make the sauce, melt the remaining butter and fry the second onion until soft. Stir in the flour and cook for 1 minute, then gradually add the stock and cider or wine and bring to the boil for 2 minutes. Add the remaining thyme and seasonings to taste. Garnish the lamb with fresh herbs, and serve with the sauce.

Barbecued Lamb Chops

1 kg (2 lb) lamb chops, trimmed of fat
salt
freshly ground black pepper
2 tablespoons honey
2 tablespoons soy sauce
2 tablespoons tomato ketchup
2 garlic cloves, peeled and crushed
300 ml ($\frac{1}{2}$ pint) boiling water
1 chicken stock cube
1 tablespoon cornflour

Preheat the oven at high temperature for 5 minutes. Put the chops in a roasting tin, sprinkle with salt and pepper, then roast in the centre of the oven for 15 minutes on each side. Meanwhile, put the honey, soy sauce, ketchup and garlic in a heatproof bowl. Add the water and stock cube and stir until dissolved. Pour over the chops, then turn the oven down to medium temperature and continue roasting for a further 30 minutes or until the chops are tender. Baste occasionally with the sauce and turn the chops over during cooking. Mix the cornflour to a paste with a little water. Transfer the roasting tin to the top of the stove, stir in the cornflour paste, then cook until the sauce thickens, stirring constantly. Taste and adjust the seasoning, then serve hot with seasonal vegetables.

Stuffed Breast of Lamb

1 kg (2 lb) breast of lamb, boned and
    trimmed
salt and freshly ground black pepper
4 large potatoes, scrubbed
parsley sprigs to garnish
For the stuffing:
100 g (4 oz) fresh white breadcrumbs
1 small onion, peeled and finely
    chopped
1 medium-sized carrot, peeled and
    grated
1 medium-sized turnip, peeled and
    grated
1 tablespoon chopped parsley
½ teaspoon dried sage
salt and freshly ground black pepper
1 egg, lightly beaten

Sew the breast of lamb together to make
one piece, if necessary, and sprinkle
with a little seasoning. Prick the potatoes well.

To make the stuffing, mix together
the white breadcrumbs, chopped onion,
grated carrot, grated turnip, chopped
parsley and sage. Season with salt and
pepper. Bind together with the lightly
beaten egg. Spread the stuffing over the
inside of the breast of lamb. Roll up
tightly and secure with string. Place
into a roasting tin. Put the potatoes
round the joint. Bake in a moderate
oven (180°C, 350°F, Gas Mark 4) for 1
hour. Turn the potatoes over to coat
evenly with the pan juices. Bake for
another 45 minutes. Serve garnished
with parsley sprigs.

Barbecued Lamb Spare Ribs

1 large breast of lamb, cut into ribs
600 ml (1 pint) water
1 tablespoon malt vinegar
For the sauce:
1 tablespoon soy sauce
1 tablespoon clear honey
1 tablespoon plum or other red jam
1 teaspoon malt vinegar
½ teaspoon Worcestershire sauce
½ teaspoon dry mustard
½ teaspoon tomato ketchup
½ teaspoon lemon juice
salt and freshly ground black pepper

Remove any excess skin and fat from
the ribs. Put the water and vinegar into
a saucepan and bring to the boil. Place
the ribs in the boiling water and
simmer, covered, for about 15 minutes.
Remove the ribs and drain well. Place
them in a roasting tin.

Mix together all the ingredients for
the sauce in a small saucepan and
simmer for 4 minutes. Taste and adjust
the seasoning if necessary.

Pour the sauce over the meat and
cook, covered, in a moderate oven
(180°C, 350°F, Gas Mark 4) for 30
minutes. Increase the temperature to
(200°C, 400°F, Gas Mark 6) and cook for
a further 20 minutes. Transfer to a hot
serving dish. Serve with boiled rice.

Lamb Cutlets Arlene

8 lamb cutlets
salt and black pepper
40 g (1½ oz) butter
175 g (6 oz) mushrooms, cleaned,
    trimmed and chopped
3 tablespoons capers
6 tablespoons chopped gherkins
1 tablespoon wine vinegar
To garnish:
chopped parsley
tomato wedges

Trim cutlets and season well. Place on a grill rack and dot with 15 g ($\frac{1}{2}$ oz) butter. Cook under a moderate grill for 8 to 10 minutes each side until just cooked through.

Meanwhile, melt the remaining butter in a pan and fry the mushrooms until soft. Add the capers, gherkins, vinegar and seasonings and cook gently for 5 minutes.

Serve the lamb cutlets on a hot dish, decorated with cutlet frills, if liked, and the mushroom mixture spooned over the eyes of the cutlets. Garnish with parsley, tomato wedges, if liked.

Armoured Cutlets

225 g (8 oz) frozen puff pastry, thawed
4 lamb cutlets
25 g (1 oz) butter
1 teaspoon curry powder
salt
freshly ground black pepper
1 egg, beaten
To garnish:
lettuce leaves
mustard and cress

On a floured surface roll out the pastry into a narrow strip. Leave to rest.

Trim any excess fat and gristle from the cutlets. Soften the butter and beat in the curry powder and seasonings to taste, then spread evenly over one side of each cutlet. Cut the pastry lengthwise into strips about 2.5 cm (1 inch) wide and brush with beaten egg. Use the pastry to wind evenly round the cutlets in overlapping circles until completely enclosed, keeping the egg-glazed side on the outside. Place on a greased baking sheet and cook in a very hot oven (230°C, 450°F, Gas Mark 8) for 10 minutes. Reduce oven temperature to moderate (180°C, 350°F, Gas Mark 4) and continue for a further 20 minutes or until well browned and puffy.

Serve hot garnished with lettuce and mustard and cress.

Chinese Cutlets

4 lamb cutlets
salt and freshly ground black pepper
300 ml ($\frac{1}{2}$ pint) chicken stock
2 tablespoons tomato ketchup
1 tablespoon soy sauce
2 teaspoons cornflour
1 onion, peeled and chopped
1 green pepper, washed, deseeded and sliced
1 tablespoon oil
175 g (6 oz) mushrooms, cleaned, trimmed and sliced
1 × 454 g (16 oz) can bean sprouts, drained
1 tablespoon sherry
2 eggs
25 g (1 oz) butter

Trim the cutlets, season well and cook on the grill rack under a moderate heat for 8 to 10 minutes each side.

Meanwhile, to make the sauce, place the stock, ketchup and soy sauce in a pan, add seasonings, blend in the cornflour and bring to the boil, stirring continuously, for 3 minutes.

Fry the onion and pepper in oil until soft, add the mushrooms and continue for 5 minutes. Stir in the bean sprouts, sherry and one-third of the sauce and simmer for 5 minutes. Beat the eggs with seasonings and 2 tablespoons water and use, with the butter, to make two large flat omelettes in a frying pan. Cut each in half.

To serve, place the bean sprout mixture in a hot serving dish. Place the cutlets on top. Roll up each piece of omelette and lay on the cutlets. Serve the remaining sauce in a sauce boat.

† Lamb Italian

8 lamb cutlets
25 g (1 oz) lard or margarine
8 small onions, peeled
1 × 225 g (8 oz) can tomatoes
1 garlic clove, crushed
50 g (2 oz) mushrooms, washed and
  thickly sliced
150 ml (¼ pint) water
1 teaspoon dried oregano
salt
freshly ground black pepper
2 teaspoons cornflour
little water

Trim all but a thin layer of fat from the cutlets. Heat the lard or margarine in the cooker. Fry the cutlets and onions until the cutlets are brown on both sides. Remove both from the cooker and drain well. Pour off the remaining lard or margarine from the cooker. Return the cooker to the heat and add the tomatoes, garlic, mushrooms, water and oregano. Stir well to remove any residues from the base of the cooker. Return the cutlets and onions to the cooker with a little salt and pepper. Close the cooker, bring to H pressure and cook for 8 minutes. Reduce the pressure quickly. Lift out the cutlets and vegetables to a warm dish and keep hot. Return the cooker to the heat and stir in the cornflour blended with a little water. Bring to the boil stirring constantly. Taste and adjust the seasoning as necessary before pouring the sauce over the cutlets.

Aubergine Moussaka

675 g (1½ lb) aubergines (about 3)
salt and freshly ground black pepper
3–4 tablespoons oil
2 large onions, peeled and thinly
  sliced
450 g (1 lb) lean raw lamb, minced
1 × 226 g (8 oz) can peeled tomatoes
2 tablespoons tomato purée
4 tablespoons stock
For the topping:
2 large eggs
100 g (4 oz) plain cottage cheese,
  sieved
6 tablespoons single cream

Wash and dry the aubergines, slice them and sprinkle lightly with salt; leave to stand for 30 minutes. Rinse off the salt, drain thoroughly and dry on absorbent kitchen paper. Fry the aubergines in 2–3 tablespoons oil until lightly browned. Drain and use to line a large shallow ovenproof casserole.

Fry the onions in the remaining oil until soft then add the meat and cook gently for about 10 minutes, stirring occasionally. Add the tomatoes, tomato purée, stock and plenty of seasonings and cook for a further 5 minutes. Spoon over the aubergines and cook, uncovered, in a moderate oven (180°C, 350°F, Gas Mark 4) for about 45 minutes, until cooked through.

Beat together the eggs, cottage cheese and cream, season well and spoon over the meat. Return to the oven for a further 25 to 30 minutes until the topping is set and lightly browned.

Variation:
Raw minced beef may be used in place of lamb for an equally tasty dish.

Haggis Pudding

225 g (8 oz) self-raising flour
1 teaspoon salt
100 g (4 oz) shredded beef suet
scant 150 ml (¼ pint) water
For the filling:
2 tablespoons cooking oil
2 medium-sized onions, peeled and
  finely chopped
225 g (8 oz) lamb's liver, sliced
225 g (8 oz) boned shoulder of mutton
  or lamb, minced
50 g (2 oz) can anchovies

100 g (4 oz) medium oatmeal
100 g (4 oz) shredded beef suet
2 tablespoons finely chopped parsley
finely grated rind and juice of 1
  lemon
salt
freshly ground black pepper
about 4 tablespoons red wine or beef
  stock

To make a traditional haggis it is necessary to have a sheep's pluck (lights, liver and heart) and stomach bag, both of which are difficult to obtain. This is an adaption of the traditional haggis, and is steamed in a pudding basin. It should be served with plenty of rich brown gravy, mashed 'nips' and jacket baked potatoes.

To make the pastry: sieve the flour and salt into a mixing bowl. Stir in the shredded suet. Mix in the water gradually to form a smooth elastic dough that leaves the sides of the bowl. Turn out on to a floured board, knead lightly, then roll into a circle large enough to line the inside of a 1 litre (2 pint) pudding basin. Cut out one quarter of the circle for the lid and reserve. Grease the inside of the basin and fit in the pastry lining, joining the edges in the basin with water. Set aside.

To make the filling: heat the oil in a pan, add the onions and fry gently until soft and lightly coloured. Transfer to a mixing bowl and add the liver to the pan, with more oil if necessary. Fry the liver briskly until browned on all sides, then remove from the pan and set aside to cool. Add the lamb to the pan and fry until browned, stirring constantly. Put in the mixing bowl with the onion.

Soak the anchovies in milk for 30 minutes. Drain them and mince with the liver until fine, then mix into the lamb and onion mixture with the oatmeal and beef suet. Stir in the parsley, lemon rind and juice, and plenty of salt and pepper. Add the red wine or stock gradually until the mixture is soft but not wet.

Spoon the haggis into the pastry-lined pudding basin. Roll out the reserved pastry for the lid and place on top of the haggis. Tuck in the edges and seal with a little water. Cover with a circle of foil with a pleat in the centre. Tie securely with string. Place in the top of a steamer or double boiler, or in a large pan of gently bubbling water, and steam for 2½ hours. Remove from the pan, leave to rest 5 minutes, then remove coverings and turn haggis out on to a warmed serving platter; or serve straight from the pudding basin. Serve immediately.

Serves 6–8

Casseroled Lamb with Pears

1 kg (2 lb) middle and best end neck
  of lamb
2 teaspoons ground ginger
6 medium-sized cooking pears, peeled
  and cored
4 medium-sized potatoes, peeled and
  diced
4 tablespoons dry cider
salt
freshly ground black pepper
450 g (1 lb) frozen whole French
  beans
2 teaspoons snipped chives, to garnish
  (optional)

Trim the excess fat from the lamb. In a non-stick, or slightly greased frying pan brown the pieces in their own fat on both sides, then transfer them to a casserole. Sprinkle with the ground ginger. Quarter the cooking pears and place in a layer over the meat. Arrange the diced potatoes over the pears. Add the dry cider and season well.

Cover and cook in a warm oven (160°C, 325°F, Gas Mark 3) for 1¼ hours, adding the French beans for the last 30 minutes of cooking time. Taste and adjust the seasoning as necessary. If liked, serve garnished with snipped fresh chives.

Curried Neck of Lamb

1¼ kg (2½ lb) middle neck of lamb
1 tablespoon ground coriander
1 teaspoon turmeric
½ teaspoon powdered cumin
¼ teaspoon chilli powder
¼ teaspoon ground cinnamon
pinch of ground cloves
1–2 teaspoons curry paste
25 g (1 oz) dripping or lard
2 onions, peeled and sliced
1 clove garlic, crushed
450 ml (¾ pint) stock or water
salt
freshly ground black pepper

Trim the lamb and cut into small pieces.
Combine the spices with the curry paste
and a little water to mix. Melt the fat in
a pan and fry the onions and garlic until
soft. Add the spice paste and fry for 5
minutes, stirring frequently. Add the
meat, mixing well, and cook gently for
about 15 minutes, turning occasionally.
Add the stock and bring to the boil.
Cover and simmer gently for about 1½
hours or until tender. Add a little more
boiling liquid if necessary during
cooking, but there should not be too
much liquid at the end, as this is a
dryish type of curry.

Taste and adjust seasonings and
serve with freshly boiled rice and a
selection of curry accompaniments: ie,
poppadums, mango chutney, salted
peanuts, sliced tomatoes with onion,
sliced banana, etc.

Variation:
Whole coriander can be used if you
crush the seeds thoroughly first.

Stuffed Onion Dumplings

4 medium-sized onions, 175–225 g (6–8
    oz) each, peeled
salt
freshly ground black pepper

For the filling:
25 g (1 oz) butter
50 g (2 oz) mushrooms, cleaned,
    trimmed and chopped
1 clove garlic, crushed
4 rashers streaky bacon, derinded and
    chopped
225 g (8 oz) cooked lamb, finely
    chopped or minced
8 stuffed olives, chopped
50 g (2 oz) cooked rice
For the pastry:
300 g (12 oz) plain flour
pinch of salt
75 g (3 oz) margarine
75 g (3 oz) lard or white fat
water to mix
beaten egg or milk to glaze

Cook the onions in boiling salted water
for 10 minutes then drain and cool.

Melt the butter and fry the mushrooms, garlic and bacon gently for 5
minutes. Stir in the lamb, olives, rice
and season well, cool.

Sieve the flour with a pinch of salt
into a bowl, rub in fats until the mixture
resembles fine breadcrumbs. Add
enough water to mix to a pliable dough.

Using a small spoon, scoop out the
centres of the onions leaving an outer
shell and base about 1 cm (½ inch) thick.
Fill the centre with the lamb mixture
pressing it well in. Roll out the pastry
and cut into 4 rounds about 20 cm (8
inch) in diameter. Place the onions,
filling end downwards, on the pastry,
dampen pastry edges and wrap round to
completely enclose the onions in pastry.

Stand the dumplings in a lightly
greased baking tin with the seams
underneath. Decorate the tops with
pastry leaves made from the trimmings
and brush with egg or milk. Cook in
moderately hot oven (200°C, 400°F, Gas
Mark 6) for 20 minutes then reduce oven
temperature to warm (160°C, 325°F, Gas
Mark 3) and continue for a further 1–1¼
hours, until the onions feel tender when
pierced with a skewer. Serve hot.

Use the scooped-out insides of the
onions in some other dish or soup.

Boiled Lamb with Dill Sauce

1¼ kg (2½ lb) best end of neck of lamb
salt and freshly ground black pepper
1 bay leaf
fresh dill sprigs (see recipe)
For the sauce:
50 g (2 oz) butter
50 g (2 oz) flour
2 tablespoons wine vinegar
1 tablespoon lemon juice
2 teaspoons sugar
1 egg yolk
2 tablespoons double cream
2 tablespoons finely chopped dill or
  drained capers

Trim the lamb and put in a saucepan with the seasonings, bay leaf and sprigs of dill. Add about 1¼ litres (2 pints) water and bring to the boil. Remove any scum from the surface, cover and simmer gently for 1¼–1½ hours or until tender. Drain the joint and keep warm.

Strain and reserve 600 ml (1 pint) cooking liquor. Melt the butter in a pan, stir in the flour and cook for 1 minute. Gradually add the liquor and bring to the boil for 2 minutes more, stirring continuously. Remove from the heat. Add the vinegar, lemon juice, sugar, egg yolk, cream and half the dill and reheat gently but without boiling. Taste and adjust the seasonings.

Serve the lamb with some sauce poured over and with the remaining dill sprinkled on top. Garnish with parsley sprigs, if liked.

Variation:
Dried dill can be used when fresh dill is not available; or drained capers can be used instead.

Lamb Noisettes with Spicy Tomato Sauce

50 g (2 oz) butter or margarine
4 noisettes of lamb or loin or chump
  chops
salt and freshly ground black pepper
1–2 cloves garlic, crushed
100 g (4 oz) button mushrooms,
  cleaned, trimmed and sliced
150 ml (¼ pint) red wine
  (Burgundy type)
150 ml (¼ pint) tomato ketchup
150 ml (¼ pint) beef stock
2 teaspoons cornflour (optional)
To garnish:
watercress sprigs
fried bread triangles

Melt 25 g (1 oz) of the butter in a frying pan. Season the noisettes generously and put into the melted fat. Cover the pan and cook gently for 8 to 10 minutes. Turn the noisettes over and continue for a further 8 to 10 minutes until cooked right through.

Meanwhile melt the remaining butter in a small pan and fry the garlic for 1 to 2 minutes. Add the mushrooms and continue gently for 2 to 3 minutes. Stir in the wine, ketchup and stock, add seasonings and bring to the boil. Simmer gently, uncovered, for 10 to 15 minutes, stirring occasionally, until slightly reduced. Thicken with cornflour blended in a little cold water (if using) and bring back to the boil for 2 minutes. Taste and adjust seasonings.

Drain noisettes on absorbent kitchen paper, then serve with the sauce spooned over, garnished with watercress and fried bread.

Variation:
Chops can be cooked in the same way as noisettes.

Lamb Beanpot

2 breasts of lamb
1 tablespoon dripping
2 onions, peeled and sliced
1–2 cloves garlic, crushed
2 large carrots, peeled and sliced
1 tablespoon flour
300 ml ($\frac{1}{2}$ pint) stock
4 tablespoons white wine or cider
1 × 225 g (8 oz) can peeled tomatoes
salt and freshly ground black pepper
1 × 425 g (15 oz) can red kidney beans,
    drained
25 g (1 oz) Edam cheese, grated
25 g (1 oz) browned breadcrumbs

Trim the lamb of skin, gristle and fat and cut into thin strips. Fry in the melted dripping until golden brown, then remove from the pan.

Drain off all but 1 tablespoon fat from the pan then fry the onions, garlic and carrots for 4 to 5 minutes, stirring frequently. Sprinkle in the flour and cook for 1 minute. Gradually add the stock and wine or cider and bring to the boil. Add the tomatoes and seasonings, return the lamb to the pan and cover. Simmer gently for 30 minutes, adding a little more stock, if necessary.

Add the drained beans and continue for about 40 minutes or until tender. Taste and adjust the seasonings and skim off any fat from the surface.

Sprinkle the top with a mixture of the cheese and crumbs and brown under a hot grill.

Minted Lamb Pasties

200 g (8 oz) plain flour
pinch of salt
50 g (2 oz) margarine
50 g (2 oz) lard or white fat
water to mix
175 g (6 oz) cooked lamb, finely diced
1 small onion, peeled and finely
    chopped
3 tablespoons cooked peas
100 g (4 oz) boiled potatoes, chopped
salt and freshly ground black pepper
2 teaspoons freshly chopped mint or 1
    teaspoon dried mint
beaten egg, to glaze

Sieve the flour with a pinch of salt into a bowl. Add the fats and rub in until the mixture resembles fine breadcrumbs. Add sufficient cold water to mix to a pliable dough and knead lightly until smooth. Wrap in foil and chill for 30 minutes if possible.

If using raw diced lamb, it should be fried gently in 25 g (1 oz) butter for 5 to 10 minutes before mixing with the other ingredients.

Mix together the chopped lamb, onion, peas, potato, salt and pepper to taste and the mint.

Roll out the pastry on a floured surface and cut into four circles 18 cm (7 inches) in diameter. Divide the meat mixture between these, placing it in the centre of each. Damp the pastry edges and bring together at the top to form a pasty. Press well together and crimp the edge. Place on a dampened baking sheet and brush with beaten egg. Cook in a hot oven (220°C, 425°F, Gas Mark 7) for 15 minutes, then reduce oven temperature to moderate (180°C, 350°F, Gas Mark 4) and continue for 15 to 20 minutes, until well browned.

Serve hot or cold with tomato wedges.

† Lamb Hot-pot

100 g (4 oz) small haricot beans
boiling water
50 g (2 oz) lard or margarine
1 kg (2 lb) middle or scrag neck of
    lamb, chopped and trimmed
1 large onion, peeled and sliced
1 turnip or parsnip, peeled and cubed
2 large carrots, peeled and sliced
750 ml (1$\frac{1}{4}$ pints) hot brown stock or
    water and $\frac{1}{2}$ beef stock cube
salt

freshly ground black pepper
1 bay leaf
1 tablespoon cornflour
a little cold water
finely chopped parsley, to garnish

Place the beans in a basin. Cover with boiling water and leave to soak for 1 hour. Heat the lard or margarine in the cooker and brown the meat evenly on both sides. Lift out and drain well. Fry the vegetables until they are beginning to colour. Remove the cooker from the heat and carefully drain off any excess lard or margarine. Add the stock or water and stock cube, salt, pepper and bay leaf to the cooker. Stir well to remove any residues from the base of the cooker. Return the meat and drained beans to the cooker. Close the cooker, bring to H pressure and cook for 15 minutes. Reduce the pressure slowly and remove the bay leaf. Blend the cornflour with a little water. Return the open cooker to the heat and add the blended cornflour. Cook, stirring constantly, until thickened. Taste and adjust the seasoning as necessary and serve garnished with chopped parsley.

Lancashire-style Hot-pot

8 middle neck lamb chops
2 lambs' kidneys, skinned, cored and roughly chopped
2 onions, peeled and sliced
2 carrots, peeled and diced
1 small turnip, peeled and diced
salt and freshly ground black pepper
300 ml ($\frac{1}{2}$ pint) stock
450 g (1 lb) potatoes, peeled and thinly sliced

Trim the chops, removing any excess fat, and place in an ovenproof casserole. Add the kidneys, onions, carrots, turnip and plenty of seasonings. Pour in the stock and arrange the potatoes in overlapping circles over the contents of the casserole. Cover and cook in warm oven (160°C, 325°F, Gas Mark 3) for about 2 hours or until the meat and potatoes are tender. Remove the lid, raise oven temperature to moderately hot (200°C, 400°F, Gas Mark 6) and continue for about 20 minutes to brown the potatoes.

Two or three sprigs of fresh mint can be added when available.

VEAL

Veal and Vegetable Casserole

1 kg (2 lb) pie veal, cubed
salt and freshly ground black pepper
2 tablespoons vegetable oil
1 clove of garlic, crushed
6 spring onions, trimmed and chopped
2 small turnips, peeled and diced
225 g (8 oz) baby carrots, scrubbed
½ teaspoon dried thyme
½ teaspoon dried marjoram
4 medium-sized potatoes, peeled and
    thinly sliced
300 ml (½ pint) water
1 chicken stock cube, crumbled
150 ml (¼ pint) dry cider
To finish:
100 g (4 oz) cottage cheese
1 teaspoon snipped chives
1 tablespoon chopped parsley
salt and freshly ground black pepper

Sprinkle the meat with salt and pepper. Heat the oil in a large frying pan, add the meat, crushed garlic and chopped spring onions and cook for 5 minutes. turning several times to brown the meat on all sides. Remove with a slotted draining spoon to a casserole.

Cook the diced turnips and carrots in the oil left in the pan for 5 minutes. Add the vegetables to the meat in the casserole, sprinkle in the herbs and cover with a layer of potato slices.

Mix together the water, chicken stock cube and the cider in a saucepan,
bring to the boil and pour into the casserole. Cover and cook in a cool oven (150°C, 300°F, Gas Mark 2) for 2 hours. Taste and adjust seasoning if necessary.

Mix the cottage cheese with the snipped chives and chopped parsley and a little seasoning, if liked, and spread over the potatoes. Raise the heat to fairly hot (200°C, 400°F, Gas Mark 6) for a further 10 minutes to form a cheesy crust. Serve at once.

Pot Roast Veal Provençale

1¼ kg (2½ lb) shoulder of veal, boned
    and rolled
1 tablespoon dripping
salt
freshly ground black pepper
1 large onion, peeled and sliced
1 tablespoon tomato purée
1 × 400 g (14 oz) can peeled tomatoes
150 ml (¼ pint) dry white wine
good pinch of sugar
a little garlic powder or crushed
    garlic
a little chopped parsley, to garnish

Brown the joint all over in melted dripping; season lightly and place in an ovenproof casserole.

Fry the onion in the same fat until soft, add the tomato purée, canned tomatoes and wine and bring to the boil. Season well, add the sugar and pour over the veal. Sprinkle the outside of the veal with garlic and cover the casserole tightly. Cook in a moderately hot oven (190°C, 375°F, Gas Mark 5) for 1 hour.

Baste well then continue for a further hour or until tender. Taste and adjust the seasonings. To serve slice the veal, surround with the sauce and garnish with parsley, if liked.
Serves 5–6.

Veal Stew with Piped Potato

450 g (1 lb) pie veal
1 tablespoon seasoned flour for coating
25 g (1 oz) lard
1 medium-sized onion, peeled and chopped
1 small parsnip, peeled and diced
1 small turnip, peeled and diced
1 teaspoon caraway seed
300 ml (½ pint) beef stock
salt
freshly ground black pepper
1 tablespoon chopped parsley, to garnish
For the mashed potato:
450 g (1 lb) potatoes
50 g (2 oz) butter
2 tablespoons milk
salt and freshly ground black pepper

Turn the veal in the seasoned flour. Melt the lard in a saucepan and quickly brown the meat in it. Add the chopped onion, diced parsnip and turnip and the caraway seed. Cook for a further 3 minutes, stirring all the time. Add the stock, season to taste and simmer, covered, for 1 hour.

While the stew is cooking, boil the potatoes and mash with the butter and milk until smooth and creamy, adding seasoning to taste. When the stew is ready to serve, put the mashed potato in a forcing bag and pipe around the edge of the dish and sprinkle with chopped parsley.

Vitello Tonnato

675 g (1½ lb) boned leg of veal, rolled
1 bay leaf
6 peppercorns
1 carrot, peeled and sliced
1 onion, peeled and sliced
2 sticks celery, scrubbed and chopped
stock or water
1 × 65 g (2½ oz) can tuna fish
1 can anchovy fillets, drained
150 ml (¼ pint) olive oil
2 egg yolks
1 tablespoon lemon juice
salt and freshly ground black pepper
To garnish:
capers
lemon slices
parsley sprigs

Place the veal in a saucepan with the bay leaf, peppercorns, vegetables and sufficient stock to cover barely. Bring to the boil, remove the scum, cover and simmer gently for about 1 hour or until tender. Drain and cool.

Meanwhile thoroughly mash the tuna fish with 4 anchovy fillets and 1 tablespoon oil, then add the egg yolks and either press through a sieve or liquidise until very smooth. Stir in the lemon juice and gradually beat in the remaining oil, a little at a time, until the sauce is smooth and has the consistency of thin cream. Season to taste.

Slice the veal thinly and arrange in a shallow dish. Spoon the sauce over to coat completely, cover the dish and chill overnight.

Before serving, garnish with the remaining anchovies, capers, lemon slices and parsley.
Serves 6.

Cranberry Glazed Veal

1½ kg (3 lb) shoulder of veal, boned
    and rolled, or loin of veal
salt and freshly ground black pepper
1 onion, peeled and finely chopped
25 g (1 oz) butter
6 tablespoons cranberry sauce
6 tablespoons red wine
300 ml (½ pint) stock
1 tablespoon cornflour
To garnish:
lattice potatoes
bacon rolls
French beans (optional)

Lightly season the joint and place in a
deep casserole. Fry the onion in the
butter until soft. Add half the cranberry
sauce and the wine and bring to the boil.
Pour over the veal. Cook in a hot oven
(220°C, 425°F, Gas Mark 7), allowing 30
minutes per 450 g (1 lb), plus 30 minutes
over. Baste joint every 15 minutes for
the first 1½ hours. Spoon the remaining cranberry sauce over the joint,
cover the casserole and continue to
cook for the remaining time. Remove
the joint to a serving dish and keep
warm.
    Spoon the fat from the juices in the
casserole, add the stock and thicken
with cornflour blended in a little cold
water. Bring back to the boil for 2
minutes, taste and adjust the seasonings and serve with the veal. Garnish
with potatoes, bacon rolls, and French
beans, if liked.
Serves 6.

Orange Stuffed Veal Roast

1¼–1½ kg (2½–3 lb) boned and rolled
    shoulder of veal
salt and freshly ground black pepper
1 cooking apple, peeled, cored and
    chopped
1 small onion, peeled and finely
    chopped

grated rind of 1 orange
flesh of 2 oranges, diced
50 g (2 oz) fresh breadcrumbs
1 tablespoon finely chopped parsley
1 egg, beaten
6 rashers streaky bacon
dripping
glazed orange slices, to garnish

Open out the joint and season the inside
lightly. Combine the apple, onion,
orange rind and flesh, breadcrumbs,
parsley and seasonings, and bind together with the egg. Spread over the
veal, roll up and secure with skewers
and string. Weigh the joint and place in
a roasting tin. Lay the bacon over the
joint and spread liberally with dripping.
Cook in a hot oven (220°C, 425°F, Gas
Mark 7), allowing 30 minutes per 450 g
(1 lb), plus 30 minutes over, and basting
the joint every 15 minutes for the first 1½
hours. Cover the meat tightly with foil
and continue for the remaining cooking
time. Serve the joint garnished with
glazed orange slices and with a thin
gravy made from the pan juices and if
liked parsley for colour.
    To glaze orange slices, place them in
a roasting tin alongside the joint for the
last 15 minutes.
Serves 6.

Veal Croquettes
with Mushroom Sauce

350 g (12 oz) lean pie veal
1 onion, peeled
225 g (8 oz) fresh sausagemeat
salt and freshly ground black pepper
Tabasco sauce
¼ teaspoon ground mace
1 egg, beaten
fresh breadcrumbs for coating
fat for frying
25 g (1 oz) butter
1 onion, peeled and finely chopped
For the sauce:
100 g (4 oz) mushrooms, cleaned,
    trimmed and sliced

300 ml (½ pint) stock
2 teaspoons cornflour
3 tablespoons soured cream (optional)

Finely mince the veal and onion and mix with the sausagemeat, seasonings, a dash of Tabasco, mace and half the beaten egg. Divide into four and form into flat triangle shapes. Dip in the beaten egg and coat in breadcrumbs; then fry gently in shallow fat for 10 to 12 minutes each side, until cooked through and well browned. Drain the croquettes on absorbent kitchen paper and keep warm.

Meanwhile, to make the sauce, fry the onion in butter until soft then add the mushrooms and continue for 2 to 3 minutes. Add the stock, seasonings and a good dash of Tabasco sauce and bring to the boil. Simmer the sauce for 10 minutes then thicken with the corn-flour, blended in a little cold water, and return to the boil for 2 minutes.

Taste and adjust the seasonings and stir in the soured cream (if using). Reheat gently and serve with the croquettes.

Minted Veal Pie

450 g (1 lb) lean pie veal
1 onion, peeled
25 g (1 oz) butter
50–100 g (2–4 oz) mushrooms, cleaned, trimmed and chopped
1 tablespoon flour
150 ml (¼ pint) stock
2 teaspoons dried mint
salt
freshly ground black pepper
200 g (8 oz) plain flour
50 g (2 oz) margarine
50 g (2 oz) lard or white fat
water to mix
milk to glaze

Mince the veal and onion coarsely. Cook gently in a pan with the butter for 10 minutes, stirring occasionally. Add

the mushrooms and continue cooking for 2 minutes. Stir in the flour, followed by the stock, mint and seasonings, and bring to the boil for 2 minutes. Taste and adjust the seasonings and cool.

Sieve the 200 g (8 oz) flour and a pinch of salt into a bowl, add the fats and rub in until the mixture resembles fine breadcrumbs. Add sufficient water to mix to a pliable dough. Roll out half the pastry, use to line a 20 cm (8 inch) pie plate or shallow tin, and spoon in the filling. Roll out the remaining pastry and cut into about 28 4 cm (1½ inch) rounds. Brush with milk and place in overlapping circles all over the filling to make a lid. Glaze again with milk and cook in a hot oven (220°C, 425°F, Gas Mark 7) for 20 minutes. Reduce oven temperature to moderate (180°C, 350°F, Gas Mark 4) and cook for a further 20 to 30 minutes, until browned.

Veal Jessica

4 veal cutlets
salt and freshly ground black pepper
1 clove garlic, crushed
40 g (1½ oz) butter
1 onion, peeled and thinly sliced
1 × 400 g (14 oz) can peeled tomatoes
2 tablespoons red wine
100 g (4 oz) mozarella cheese, sliced
fresh herbs, to garnish

Trim the cutlets, season with salt and pepper and rub with the garlic. Fry in the melted butter until well browned on both sides. Transfer to a shallow oven-proof casserole. Fry the onion in the same fat until soft and arrange over veal. Cover with the partly drained tomatoes and wine, season lightly. Cover and cook in a moderate oven (180°C, 350°F, Gas Mark 4) for about 45 minutes, or until tender. Remove the lid, cover the veal with cheese and place under a moderate grill until cheese has melted and lightly browned. Serve at once garnished with herbs.

Veal and Spinach Cannelloni

8 cannelloni
salt and freshly ground black pepper
65 g (2½ oz) butter
1 onion, peeled and chopped
350 g (12 oz) pie veal, minced
225 g (8 oz) frozen chopped spinach, thawed
pinch of nutmeg
40 g (1½ oz) flour
450 ml (¾ pint) milk
75 g (3 oz) mature Cheddar cheese, grated

Cook the cannelloni in boiling salted water according to the instructions on the packet. Drain well.

Melt 25 g (1 oz) butter in a pan and fry the onion until soft, stir in the veal and cook gently for 15 minutes, stirring frequently. Add the drained spinach, seasonings and nutmeg, cook for 10 minutes. Melt the remaining butter in a pan, stir in the flour, cook for 1 minute. Gradually add the milk and bring to the boil, stirring continuously. Season to taste and simmer for 3 minutes. Stir 150 ml (¼ pint) sauce into the veal mixture; taste and adjust seasonings.

Stuff the cannelloni with the veal and place in a greased shallow ovenproof dish. Now add 50 g (2 oz) cheese to remaining sauce and pour over the cannelloni. Sprinkle with the remaining cheese and cook in a moderately hot oven (200°C, 400°F, Gas Mark 6) for about 30 minutes until golden brown and bubbling.

Veal Bigarade

4 escalopes of veal, beaten flat
salt and freshly ground black pepper
40 g (1½ oz) butter
2 tablespoons wine vinegar
2 tablespoons caster sugar
finely grated rind of 1 orange
juice of 3 large oranges
2 tablespoons lemon juice
300 ml (½ pint) white stock
1 tablespoon cornflour (optional)
2 tablespoons brandy
To garnish:
1 orange, thinly sliced
watercress sprigs

Trim the veal and season lightly with salt and pepper. Melt the butter in a large frying pan and cook the escalopes gently for 3 to 4 minutes on each side. Keep warm.

Meanwhile heat the vinegar and sugar together in a small pan, without stirring, until caramel coloured. Add the orange rind, fruit juices and stock and bring to the boil. Simmer gently, uncovered, for 5 minutes, stirring occasionally. Blend the cornflour (if using) in a little cold water and add to the sauce; bring to the boil for 2 minutes. Add to the escalopes in the pan and cook gently for 5 minutes, spooning the sauce over the meat continuously. Warm the brandy, set alight and add to the pan. Stir until evenly mixed, taste and adjust seasonings.

Serve immediately, garnished with twists of orange and watercress.

Veal and Lemon Cobbler

1 large onion, peeled and sliced
25 g (1 oz) butter
1 tablespoon oil
675 g (1½ lb) pie veal
25 g (1 oz) flour
450 ml (¾ pint) white stock
salt and freshly ground black pepper
finely grated rind of 1 small lemon
1 tablespoon lemon juice
100 g (4 oz) mushrooms, cleaned, trimmed and sliced
For the scone topping:
200 g (8 oz) self-raising flour
a little salt and pepper
50 g (2 oz) butter or margarine
finely grated rind of ½ small lemon

1 egg, beaten
approx. 4 tablespoons milk to mix and
   glaze
parsley, to garnish (optional)

Fry the onion in the butter and oil until
soft, but not coloured, in a flameproof
casserole. Trim the veal and cut into 2.5
cm (1 inch) cubes, then add to the pan
and fry for about 5 minutes until well
sealed. Stir in the flour and cook for 1
minute then gradually add the stock
and bring to the boil. Season well, add
the lemon rind and juice and cover the
casserole. Cook in a warm oven (160°C,
325°F, Gas Mark 3) for 1¼ hours, or until
tender. Stir the mushrooms into the
casserole.
   To make the topping, sift the flour
and a little salt and pepper into a bowl.
Rub in the fat until the mixture resembles fine breadcrumbs, then stir in
the lemon rind. Add the egg and sufficient milk to mix to a fairly soft dough.
Roll out to 1.5 cm (½ inch) thickness on a
floured surface and cut into 5 cm (2
inch) rounds. Arrange these scones in
an overlapping circle round edge of the
casserole to make a border on top of
the veal. Brush with milk and cook in a
hot oven (220°C, 425°F, Gas Mark 7) for
10 to 15 minutes until well risen, golden
brown and firm to the touch. Serve at
once. Garnish with parsley, if liked.

Creamy Veal Olives

4 small escalopes of veal, beaten flat
salt and freshly ground black pepper
2 slices cooked ham, halved
2 large eggs, hard-boiled and halved
50 g (2 oz) butter
300 ml (½ pint) seasoned white stock
2 tablespoons dry white wine
   (optional)
100 g (4 oz) button mushrooms,
   cleaned, trimmed and quartered
20 g (¾ oz) flour
4 tablespoons double cream
parsley, to garnish

Trim the escalopes and season lightly.
Place half a slice of ham and half an egg
on each one; roll up and secure with
wooden cocktail sticks. Heat 25 g (1 oz)
butter in a pan and fry the veal olives
until browned all over. Transfer to a
shallow ovenproof casserole. Pour on
the stock and wine, cover and cook in a
moderate oven (180°C, 350°F, Gas Mark
4) for 1 hour. Drain off the liquor and
reserve. Keep the olives warm. Melt the
remaining butter in a pan and fry the
mushrooms gently for 2 minutes. Stir in
the flour and cook for 1 minute.
Gradually add the liquor and bring to
the boil. Season to taste and simmer for
2 minutes. Stir in the cream and reheat
gently without boiling. Pour over the
olives and garnish with parsley.

Cumberland Veal

4 veal escalopes, beaten
salt and freshly ground black pepper
50 g (2 oz) butter
1 medium-sized onion, peeled and
   chopped
150 ml (¼ pint) port
4 tablespoons white stock
1 tablespoon redcurrant jelly
100 g (4 oz) mushrooms, cleaned,
   trimmed and sliced
2 teaspoons lemon juice
100 ml (4 fl oz) double cream
parsley sprigs, to garnish (optional)

Trim the veal and season lightly with
salt and pepper. Melt the butter in a
large frying pan and fry the onion until
soft. Add the veal and cook for 2 to 3
minutes each side. Add the port, stock,
redcurrant jelly and seasonings and
bring to the boil. Add the mushrooms
and cover the pan. Simmer gently for 10
to 15 minutes until the veal is tender.
Taste and adjust the seasonings and
sharpen with lemon juice. Stir in the
cream and heat gently to just below
boiling point. Serve garnished with
parsley sprigs, if liked.

Raised Picnic Pie

350 g (12 oz) pie veal
450 g (1 lb) cooked ham
1 small onion, peeled
salt and freshly ground black pepper
good pinch of ground mace
For the hot water pastry:
110 g (4½ oz) blended white vegetable
   fat
150 ml (¼ pint) water
300 g (12 oz) plain flour
1 egg, beaten
2 teaspoons powdered gelatine
300 ml (½ pint) stock
mixed salads, to garnish

Finely mince the veal with 100 g (4 oz)
ham and the onion. Season well, add the
mace and mix thoroughly. Cut remaining ham into thin strips.

To make the hot water pastry, melt
the fat in the water and bring to the boil.
Sieve the flour with ½ teaspoon salt into
a bowl. Add the boiling liquid and mix
to a soft dough. Knead lightly then roll
out three-quarters of the pastry and use
to line an 18–20 cm (7–8 inch) round,
loose-bottomed cake tin, or a game pie
mould. (Keep the remaining pastry
covered in the bowl.) Place half the
minced meat in the bottom, cover with
strips of ham and then the remaining
mince. Press down evenly. Roll out
the remaining pastry for a lid, brush the
edges with water and position. Press
edges well together, trim and crimp.
Decorate the top with pastry trimmings
and make a hole in the centre. Brush
with beaten egg and cook in a fairly hot
oven (200°C, 400°F, Gas Mark 6) for 30
minutes. Reduce oven temperature to
warm (160°C, 325°F, Gas Mark 3) and
continue for 1¼–1½ hours, covering with
foil when sufficiently browned.

Dissolve the gelatine in the stock and
season well. As the pie cools, fill up with
the stock through the central hole.
Chill until firm then turn out and serve
with mixed salads.
Serves 6–8.

Stuffed Courgettes

1 small onion, peeled and chopped
25 g (1 oz) butter
225 g (8 oz) minced veal
25 g (1 oz) fresh breadcrumbs
salt and freshly ground black pepper
1 teaspoon finely chopped mint
1 egg yolk
8 medium-sized courgettes
150 ml (¼ pint) white stock
225 g (8 oz) freshly boiled spaghetti
50 g (2 oz) mild Emmenthal cheese,
   finely grated

Fry the onion in the butter until soft
then stir in the minced veal and cook
very gently for 10 minutes, stirring
frequently. Remove from the heat and
stir in the breadcrumbs, seasonings,
mint and egg yolk.

Wash and trim the courgettes and cut
in half lengthwise. Discard some of the
seeds and fill each courgette with the
veal mixture. Put the two halves back
together and secure with cotton, or
wooden cocktail sticks. Place in a
lightly greased shallow ovenproof dish
and pour the stock around. Cover and
cook in a moderate oven (180°C, 350°F,
Gas Mark 4) for about 45 minutes until
tender.

Remove the cotton or sticks and serve
on a bed of boiled spaghetti, tossed in a
little butter and seasoned, with the
grated cheese handed separately in a
bowl.

Veal Montmorency

4 veal escalopes, beaten flat, or 4 veal
   cutlets
salt and freshly ground black pepper
25 g (1 oz) butter
1 tablespoon oil
1 × 400 g (14 oz) can black cherries
4 tablespoons Madeira
2 teaspoons lemon juice
150 ml (¼ pint) white stock

2 teaspoons cornflour
To garnish:
watercress sprigs
lattice potatoes (optional)

Trim the veal and season lightly on both sides. Heat the butter with the oil in a large frying pan and fry the escalopes for 2 to 3 minutes on each side, or fry the cutlets until browned on both sides. Drain the cherries and add the juice to the pan with the Madeira, lemon juice and stock. Bring to the boil, cover and simmer gently, about 10 minutes for the escalopes and 20 to 25 minutes for the cutlets, or until tender. Skim any fat from the surface of the juices, taste and adjust seasonings. Blend the cornflour with a little cold water and stir into the sauce. Bring to the boil, add the cherries and simmer for a further 5 minutes. Serve garnished with water cress, and lattice potatoes if liked.

Saltimbocca

8 small, very thin slices of veal
1 tablespoon lemon juice
salt and freshly ground black pepper
8 fresh sage leaves or a little dried
    sage
8 small, thin slices prosciutto or
    cooked ham
40 g (1½ oz) butter
3–4 tablespoons Marsala
To garnish:
croûtons
sage leaves

Ask the butcher to flatten the veal, or place the pieces between two sheets of waxed paper and beat flat with a mallet or chopper. Rub each piece with lemon juice and season lightly. Lay a sage leaf on each piece or sprinkle it with a little dried sage. Cover with prosciutto or cooked ham. Roll up and secure with wooden cocktail sticks.
   Melt the butter in a pan and fry the rolls gently until golden brown all over.

Add the Marsala and bring to the boil. Cover and simmer gently for about 20 minutes, or until tender. Taste and adjust the seasonings and serve with the juices poured over and garnished with croûtons and sage leaves.

Osso Bucco

1 kg (2 lb) shin of veal
salt and freshly ground black pepper
25 g (1 oz) butter
1 tablespoon oil
1 large onion, peeled and chopped
4 sticks celery, scrubbed and sliced
2 large carrots, peeled and sliced
150 ml (¼ pint) dry white wine
1 teaspoon lemon juice
300 ml (½ pint) white stock
½ teaspoon dried rosemary
1 × 400 g (14 oz) can peeled tomatoes
2 teaspoons cornflour (optional)
To garnish:
lemon rind
chopped parsley

Ask the butcher to saw the veal into 4 pieces. Trim and season. Melt the butter in a pan, add the oil and fry the veal until browned all over. Remove from the pan.
   Fry the onion, celery and carrots until just beginning to colour then pour off any excess fat from the pan. Add the wine and lemon juice and replace the veal. Bring to the boil, cover and simmer very gently for 45 minutes.
   Add the stock, rosemary, tomatoes and seasonings. Bring back to the boil, cover and simmer for a further hour or until the meat is tender. If liked, thicken with the cornflour blended in a little cold water and boil for 2 minutes.
   Taste and adjust seasonings, if necessary. Sprinkle with a mixture of lemon rind and chopped parsley before serving, if liked.

OFFAL

Spiced Liver

cooking oil for frying
1 large onion, peeled and sliced into
    rings
450 g (1 lb) lamb's liver, sliced into
    thin bite-sized pieces
flour for coating
$\frac{1}{2}$ teaspoon crushed cardamom seeds
1 teaspoon ground coriander
$\frac{1}{2}$ teaspoon crushed black peppercorns
2 cloves, finely crushed
about 300 ml ($\frac{1}{2}$ pint) water
To garnish:
4 back bacon rashers, rinds removed,
    crisply fried and chopped
4 tomatoes, quartered and fried

Heat 2 tablespoons of oil in a frying pan.
Add the onion and fry gently for 5
minutes or until golden. Coat the liver
in flour seasoned with the cardamom
seeds and coriander, pepper and cloves.
Add to the pan and fry gently until
golden-brown on both sides.

Cover the liver with the water, stir
well and continue to cook for about 10
minutes, stirring occasionally. To test if
the liver is cooked, prick with a fork;
if juices are faintly pink the liver is
ready to serve. Transfer the liver and
sauce to a hot serving platter and arrange on a bed of plain boiled rice and
sweetcorn. Top with the bacon pieces
and garnish the edge of the platter with
the fried tomato quarters.

Serve immediately.

Chicken Liver Risotto

65 g (2$\frac{1}{2}$ oz) butter
1 tablespoon vegetable oil
225 g (8 oz) long-grain rice
175 g (6 oz) chicken livers
175 g (6 oz) button mushrooms, wiped
    and thinly sliced
2 tablespoons tomato purée
450 ml ($\frac{3}{4}$ pint) chicken stock
sprigs of parsley, to garnish
Parmesan cheese

Heat 50 g (2 oz) of the butter and the oil
in a non-stick saucepan or one with a
heavy base. Add the rice and cook,
stirring from time to time, until just
transparent.

Meanwhile, toss the chicken livers
and sliced mushrooms in the remaining
butter until the livers are just firm.
Using kitchen scissors, snip up the
livers into bite-sized pieces. Add the
livers and mushrooms to the rice.

Dissolve the tomato purée in the hot
stock, pour over the rice and bring to
the boil. Stir gently, reduce the heat,
cover and simmer for about 20 minutes,
or until the rice is tender and all the
liquid has been absorbed. Fluff up and
serve hot, garnished with sprigs of
parsley. Hand grated Parmesan cheese
separately.

Liver Stroganoff

1 large knob of butter
1 onion, peeled and finely chopped
450 g (1 lb) lamb's liver, sliced into
  very thin strips
1 tablespoon tomato purée
1 tablespoon Worcestershire sauce
juice of 1 lemon
225 g (8 oz) button mushrooms, finely
  sliced
salt and freshly ground black pepper
150 ml (¼ pint) soured cream

Melt the butter in a pan, add the onion
and fry over gentle heat until soft. Add
the liver and fry for 5 minutes, stirring
constantly. Stir in the remaining ingredients except the cream, then cook
for a further 5 minutes, stirring occasionally. Remove from the heat and stir
in the cream, return the pan to a low
heat and warm through. Taste and
adjust seasoning and serve with a
tossed green salad and boiled rice.

Fried Liver and Bacon

450 g (1 lb) sliced calves' or lamb's
  liver
8 bacon rashers, back or streaky
4 tomatoes
salt and freshly ground pepper
50 g (2 oz) lard or cooking fat
1 tablespoon chopped onion
120 ml (4 fl oz) red or white wine or
  stock
parsley sprigs, to garnish

Cut out any gristle from the liver and
coat with flour, shaking off any surplus.
Stretch the bacon rashers with back of a
knife and cut off the rind and gristle.
Halve the tomatoes crosswise, not
down, and season with salt and pepper.
  Arrange the bacon rashers in a frying
pan and heat slowly until nicely crisp-
ed. Remove to a warm serving dish. Add
the lard or fat to the pan, heat it and fry

the tomatoes quickly, first outside and
then cut side, until they begin to go
golden. Place them on the serving dish
and keep it warm.
  Put in the liver slices carefully to
avoid splashing. Fry briskly until crisp
underneath, turn and fry the other side.
Do not overcook or the liver will be
hard. Remove to the serving dish. Add
the chopped onion to the fat and fry,
stirring, until it is just beginning to
change colour.
  Pour in the wine or stock and bring to
the boil, scraping up the juices from the
bottom of the pan. Add a little extra
stock or water if needed. Season to taste
with salt and pepper. Arrange the liver
slices overlapping on serving dish with
bacon rashers. Pour the hot gravy over
the liver and garnish with the tomatoes
and parsley.

Liver and Bacon Marsala

450 g (1 lb) lambs' liver, sliced
seasoned flour for coating
40 g (1½ oz) butter
8 rashers streaky bacon, derinded and
  halved
4 tablespoons Marsala
150 ml (¼ pint) beef stock
1 teaspoon lemon juice
salt and freshly ground black pepper
To garnish:
chopped parsley
potato crisps

Trim the liver and coat in seasoned
flour. Melt the butter in a frying pan
and fry the bacon until lightly coloured.
Remove from the pan. Fry the liver until
browned on both sides. Add the Marsala, stock and lemon juice and season
well. Return the bacon to the pan and
simmer gently until the liver is tender
and the sauce syrupy, about 15 minutes.
Taste and adjust the seasonings, if
necessary. Arrange on a serving dish
and garnish with parsley and potato
crisps. Serve immediately.

Liver with Lemon Glaze

8–12 slices lambs' liver
a little seasoned flour
25 g (1 oz) butter
1 tablespoon oil
For the glaze:
2 tablespoons oil
3 tablespoons stock
finely grated rind of ½ lemon
3 tablespoons lemon juice
2 tablespoons finely chopped onion
good pinch of dried thyme
salt and freshly ground black pepper
To garnish:
lemon slices
parsley sprigs

Trim the liver and coat in seasoned flour. Fry in the melted butter and oil for 5 to 8 minutes each side, until well browned and cooked through – but do not overcook or the liver will become hard. Drain on absorbent kitchen paper and keep warm.

Meanwhile, place all the ingredients for the glaze in a small pan and bring to the boil. Simmer gently for 5 to 6 minutes, taste and adjust the seasonings, add to the pan the liver was cooked in and blend with the pan juices. Simmer for 2 to 3 minutes.

Arrange the liver on a flat dish and spoon the glaze over. Garnish with lemon and parsley.

Orchard Liver

450 g (1 lb) lambs' liver, sliced
2 tablespoons seasoned flour
25 g (1 oz) butter
1 tablespoon oil
3 medium-sized cooking apples, approx. 350 g (12 oz) peeled, cored and sliced
1 tablespoon finely chopped parsley
1 teaspoon finely chopped thyme
1–2 teaspoons finely chopped dill or fennel

300 ml (½ pint) stock
salt and freshly ground black pepper
sprigs of fresh herbs, to garnish

Coat the liver evenly in the seasoned flour. Melt the butter in a frying pan and add the oil. Fry the liver for 2 to 3 minutes each side until well sealed. Remove from the pan. Add the apples and fry gently for 4 to 5 minutes, taking care not to break up the slices. Sprinkle in the herbs and add the stock. Bring to the boil, season to taste and replace the liver. Cover the pan and simmer gently for 10 to 15 minutes until tender. Taste and adjust the seasonings.

Serve very hot, garnished with sprigs of fresh thyme, fennel and/or dill.

Stuffed Lambs' Hearts

4 lambs' hearts
1 small onion, peeled and finely chopped
2 rashers streaky bacon, derinded and chopped
2 small sticks celery, scrubbed and finely chopped
25 g (1 oz) butter
75 g (3 oz) cooked rice
salt and freshly ground black pepper
good pinch of ground mace
40 g (1½ oz) raisins
300 ml (½ pint) stock
1 tablespoon vinegar
1 tablespoon cornflour
freshly cooked carrots and peas, to garnish

Wash the hearts very thoroughly, slit open a little and remove any tubes or gristle. Wash again and dry well. Fry the onion, bacon and celery in the melted butter until lightly browned. Add the rice, seasonings, mace and raisins and mix well. Use to stuff the cavities in the hearts then tie into shape with fine string if necessary. Place the hearts in an ovenproof casserole just large enough to take them. Bring the stock to the boil, add the vinegar, season well and add to the casserole. Cover and cook in a warm oven (160°C, 325°F, Gas Mark 3) for 2–2½ hours, until tender.

Strain off the liquor and thicken with cornflour blended in a little cold water. Bring to the boil for 2 minutes, taste and adjust the seasonings.

Arrange the hearts on a serving dish, spoon the sauce over and garnish with carrots and peas.

Liver Risotto

50 g (2 oz) butter
2 large onions, peeled and chopped
2 rashers streaky bacon, derinded and chopped
350 g (12 oz) lamb's or pig's liver, trimmed and cut into cubes
225 g (8 oz) long-grain rice
100 g (4 oz) button mushrooms, cleaned, trimmed and quartered
1 × 225 g (8 oz) can peeled tomatoes
½–1 teaspoon marjoram (optional)
600 ml (1 pint) beef stock
salt
freshly ground black pepper
100 g (4 oz) freshly cooked peas
Parmesan cheese (optional)

Melt the butter in a heavy based pan. Fry the onions, bacon and liver for about 5 minutes until they are beginning to colour and the liver is well sealed.

Stir in the rice and cook for a few minutes more. Add the mushrooms, tomatoes, marjoram (if using), stock and seasonings and bring slowly up to the boil. Mix well, then cover and simmer over a very gentle heat, without stirring, for about 25 minutes, or until the rice is tender and the liquid almost completely absorbed.

Taste and adjust the seasonings, stir in the peas and serve piled on a hot dish. Sprinkle well with Parmesan cheese, if liked.

Lambs' Tongues with Herb Dumplings

4 small lambs' tongues
1 tablespoon salt
2 large onions, peeled and sliced
1 bouquet garni (p. 364)
25 g (1 oz) butter
1 tablespoon flour
2 tablespoons capers
2 tablespoons lemon juice
For the dumplings:
225 g (8 oz) self-raising flour
100 g (4 oz) shredded beef suet
½ teaspoon dried thyme
salt
freshly ground black pepper

Wash the tongues thoroughly. Put into a large saucepan, cover with water and add the salt. Bring to the boil, and drain. Cover the tongues with fresh water, add the sliced onion and bouquet garni, and bring to the boil. Reduce the heat, cover and simmer for 1¼ hours, or until the tongues are tender. Remove the tongues and leave to cool, then skin and take out any little bones. Cool the stock so that it is easier to skim off the fat from the surface. Remove the bouquet garni.

Melt the butter in a small saucepan and gradually stir in the flour. Cook for 2 minutes, stirring all the time. Add the stock (if necessary, make up to 450 ml (¾ pint) with boiling water), the capers and lemon juice. Stir continuously until all the liquid has been added and the sauce has thickened.

Prepare the dumpling mixture by mixing together the flour, suet, thyme, seasoning and enough water to form a fairly stiff dough. Form the dough into about 12 round dumplings keeping hands well floured.

Dice the tongues, put into a casserole and cover with the sauce. Place the dumplings on top so that the surface is completely covered. Bake in a fairly hot oven (190°C, 375°F, Gas Mark 5) for 30 minutes.

Layered Liver and Bacon

15 g (½ oz) lard
450 g (1 lb) pig's liver, thinly sliced
4 rashers streaky bacon, rind removed
2 medium-sized onions, peeled and
    chopped
2 medium-sized cooking apples,
    peeled, cored and chopped
1 teaspoon dried thyme
1 tablespoon chopped parsley
salt and freshly ground black pepper
8 tablespoons fresh white
    breadcrumbs
300 ml (½ pint) hot water

Grease the inside of a casserole with the lard. Place half the sliced liver in a layer at the bottom and cover with 2 rashers of bacon. Mix together the chopped onion, apple, herbs and seasoning and place half the mixture over the bacon slices. Sprinkle half the breadcrumbs over it. Continue to fill the casserole with another layer each of liver, bacon and onion and apple mixture, finishing with the breadcrumbs. Pour in the hot water or just sufficient to cover the surface. Put the lid on the casserole and cook in a moderate oven (180°C, 350°F, Gas Mark 4) for 1½ hours. Remove the lid, add a little more hot water if the contents appear too dry, and cook for another 30 minutes to allow the surface to brown.

Braised Lambs' Tongues

4 lambs' tongues
2 onions, peeled and sliced
1 tablespoon oil
2 carrots, peeled and diced
1 × 225 g (8 oz) can peeled tomatoes
salt and freshly ground black pepper
about 450 ml (¾ pint) stock
1 tablespoon freshly chopped parsley
1 tablespoon capers or chopped
    gherkins
bacon rolls, to garnish

Wash the tongues thoroughly and trim if necessary. Fry the onions in oil until golden brown then transfer to an oven-proof casserole. Lay the tongues on the onion and surround with the carrots and tomatoes. Season well, pour in sufficient stock just to cover and sprinkle with the parsley, and capers or gherkins. Cover and cook in a moderate oven (180°C, 350°F, Gas Mark 4) for about 1½ hours, until tender. Taste and adjust the seasonings. The tongues can be removed and skinned, and then reheated again in the sauce before serving, if preferred. Serve garnished with bacon rolls.

Hearts Victoriana

3 large or 4 small lambs' hearts
25 g (1 oz) butter or margarine
2 onions, peeled and sliced
2 tablespoons flour
600 ml (1 pint) stock
2 teaspoons basil or oregano
salt and freshly ground black pepper
50 g (2 oz) sultanas or raisins
1 large cooking apple, peeled, cored
    and sliced
apple slices, to garnish (optional)

Wash the hearts thoroughly and cut into 1 cm (½ inch) slices, discarding any gristle and tubes. Fry the hearts in melted butter or margarine until well browned and then transfer to an oven-proof casserole. Fry the onions in the same fat until soft then stir in the flour and cook for 1 minute. Gradually add the stock and bring to the boil. Add the herbs, seasonings, and the sultanas or raisins, and pour over the hearts. Cover tightly and cook in a warm oven (160°C, 325°F, Gas Mark 3) for 1½ hours.

Skim off any fat, taste and adjust the seasonings and add the apple. Continue to cook for a further 30 minutes or until tender.

Garnish with apple slices dipped in lemon juice, if liked.

Glazed Lambs' Tongues

4 lambs' tongues
4 cloves
1 small onion, peeled
1 teaspoon salt
1 bay leaf
1 × 2.5 cm (1 inch) piece of cinnamon
    stick
3 tablespoons malt vinegar
4 small tomatoes
1 tablespoon lemon juice
1 teaspoon gelatine

Wash the tongues well in cold running water and place in a saucepan. Stick the cloves in the onion and add onion to tongues together with the salt, bay leaf and cinnamon stick. Cover with cold water and bring to the boil. Put on the lid and simmer for 45 minutes. Add the vinegar and continue to simmer for a further 30 minutes. Take out the tongues, allow to cool, skin and remove any small bones from the cut ends.

Stand the tongues on their sides with their bases towards the centre, on a serving plate, and place the tomatoes between the tongues.

Strain 7 tablespoons of the cooking liquid into a small saucepan and add the lemon juice. Mix the gelatine with 2 tablespoons of the remaining cold stock and leave until it has softened and become spongy. Stir the softened gelatine into the liquid in the saucepan and heat until it has completely dissolved. Allow to cool and become syrupy.

Slowly spoon the setting glaze over the tongues and repeat several times to achieve a really good coating.

Serve with green salad and either rice or potato salad.

Seville Heart Pie

1–1¼ kg (2–2½ lb) ox heart
3 tablespoons oil
2 large onions, peeled and sliced
3 tablespoons flour
450 ml (¾ pint) stock
finely grated rind and juice of 1 large
    orange
salt and freshly ground black pepper
2 tablespoons port (optional)
1 orange, peeled and cut into
    segments
675 g (1½ lb) creamed potato
julienne strips of orange (see recipe),
    to garnish

Cut the heart into narrow strips, removing any tubes and gristle, then wash very thoroughly and dry. Fry in the oil until lightly browned and transfer to an ovenproof casserole. Fry the onion in the same fat until soft, then stir in the flour and cook for 1 minute. Gradually add the stock and bring to the boil for 2 minutes. Stir in the orange rind, juice, seasonings and port (if using). Pour into the casserole, cover and cook in a cool oven (150°C, 300°F, Gas Mark 2) for about 3 hours, or until tender, adding a little more stock, if necessary, during the cooking.

Remove the lid, taste and adjust the seasonings and stir in the orange segments. Pipe the potato over the casserole, leaving a gap in the centre. Return to a moderately hot oven (200°C, 400°F, Gas Mark 6) for about 30 minutes, until the potato is lightly browned. Serve sprinkled with julienne strips of orange.

To make julienne strips, finely pare the rind from a firm orange, free the white pith, using a potato peeler. Cut into very thin long strips and then simmer gently in boiling water for 10 minutes, or until tender. Drain well.

Pressed Ox Tongue

1 ox tongue, fresh or pickled, about
    1¾–2¾ kg (4–6 lb)
bouquet garni (p. 364)
1 onion, peeled and sliced
2 carrots, peeled and sliced
few black peppercorns
mixed salads, to garnish

If pickled, soak the tongue in cold water
for several hours. Place the tongue in a
saucepan with the bouquet garni,
onion, carrot and peppercorns and
cover with cold water. Bring to the boil,
remove the scum, cover and simmer
gently for 2½–3 hours if pickled and 4½–6
hours if fresh, until tender. Plunge into
cold water when ready and strip off the
skin, removing any pieces of bone and
gristle.

Put the tongue into a conveniently
sized cake tin or basin. (A 2¾ kg (6 lb)
tongue fits into an 18 cm (7 inch) round
cake tin.) Add a little stock, put a plate
on top and weight down heavily until
cold and set. Turn out and serve with
salads.

To serve hot, sprinkle the skinned
tongue with toasted breadcrumbs, garnish with wedges of lemon and serve
with a parsley sauce.

Kidney Pancakes

100 g (4 oz) plain flour
pinch of salt
2 eggs
300 ml (½ pint) milk
lard or oil for frying
For the filling:
50 g (2 oz) butter
8–10 lambs' kidneys, skinned, cored
    and chopped
100 g (4 oz) mushrooms, cleaned,
    trimmed and chopped
40 g (1½ oz) flour
300 ml (½ pint) beef stock
salt and freshly ground black pepper

good dash of Worcestershire sauce
150 ml (¼ pint) single cream
40 g (1½ oz) flaked almonds, toasted
a little melted butter
parsley sprigs, to garnish

To make the batter, sift the flour with a
pinch of salt into a bowl and make a well
in the centre, add the eggs and a little
milk and mix to a smooth thick batter.
Continue adding the milk and beat until
smooth. Use to make 8 thin pancakes in
a small greased frying pan. Stack up on
a plate with foil between each and keep
the pancakes warm.

For the filling, melt the butter in a
pan and fry the kidneys for about 5
minutes until well sealed, add the mushrooms and continue for 2 to 3 minutes.
Stir in the flour followed by the stock,
seasonings and Worcestershire sauce.
Bring to the boil, cover and simmer for
about 10 minutes or until tender. Stir in
the cream and half the almonds and
reheat without boiling. Taste and
adjust the seasonings. Divide the filling
between the pancakes and roll up.

Place the pancakes in a lightly
greased shallow ovenproof dish and
brush with melted butter. Sprinkle with
the remaining almonds, cover with foil
and cook in a moderate oven (180°C,
350°F, Gas Mark 4) for about 20 minutes, until piping hot. Garnish with
parsley sprigs.

Kidney in Oriental Sauce

450 g (1 lb) ox kidney
1 tablespoon vegetable oil
300 ml (½ pint) dry ginger ale
2 teaspoons malt vinegar
salt and freshly ground black pepper
25 g (1 oz) butter
100 g (4 oz) mushrooms, wiped and
    sliced
25 g (1 oz) flaked almonds
25 g (1 oz) sultanas
1 tablespoon gravy powder
3 tablespoons cold water

Cut the ox kidney in slices about 2 cm ($\frac{3}{4}$ inch) thick. Remove the core and chop the slices. Heat the vegetable oil in a saucepan and fry the pieces of kidney, turning several times, until lightly coloured all over, about 3 minutes. Add the ginger ale, vinegar and seasoning and bring to the boil. Simmer, covered, for 30 minutes. Meanwhile melt the butter in a frying pan and cook the sliced mushrooms for 3 minutes, turning frequently. Add the fried mushrooms, flaked almonds and sultanas to the kidney mixture, stir well and simmer for a further 10 minutes. Dissolve the gravy powder in the cold water and stir into the saucepan. Bring to the boil, stirring constantly. Simmer for a further 5 minutes. Taste and adjust the seasoning if necessary. Serve with boiled rice.

Kidney and Sausage Casserole

225 g (8 oz) chipolata sausages, halved
25 g (1 oz) butter or margarine
6–8 lambs' kidneys, skinned, halved and cored
1 large onion, peeled and chopped, or 8 button onions, peeled
15 g ($\frac{1}{2}$ oz) flour
300 ml ($\frac{1}{2}$ pint) stock
4 tablespoons red wine or sherry (optional)
salt and freshly ground black pepper
$\frac{1}{2}$ teaspoon dried dill
675 g (1$\frac{1}{2}$lb) creamed potato
beaten egg or melted butter, to glaze
chopped parsley, to garnish

Fry the chipolatas in the melted fat, until lightly browned, in a fireproof casserole. Remove from the pan. Fry the kidneys until well sealed, then remove. Fry the onion until soft then stir in the flour and cook for 1 minute. Gradually add the stock and wine or sherry and bring to the boil. Replace the sausages and kidneys, season well and add the herbs. Cover the casserole and cook in a moderate oven (180°C, 350°F, Gas Mark 4) for 30 to 40 minutes, until tender.

Meanwhile, pipe the potato around a shallow heatproof dish, brush it with egg or melted butter and brown under a hot grill.

To serve, spoon the sausage and kidney mixture into the potato-lined dish and sprinkle with chopped parsley.

Kidneys Portugaise

3 tablespoons oil
2 onions, peeled and finely chopped
2 cloves garlic, crushed
1 large red pepper, washed, deseeded and chopped
2 tablespoons tomato purée
1 × 400 g (14 oz) can peeled tomatoes, chopped
4 tablespoons beef stock or water
$\frac{1}{2}$ teaspoon Worcestershire sauce
dash of Tabasco sauce
1 tablespoon lemon juice
salt and freshly ground black pepper
25 g (1 oz) butter
8–10 lambs' kidneys, skinned, halved and cored
black olives, to garnish

Heat 2 tablespoons oil in a pan, add the onions and garlic and fry gently until soft. Add the pepper and continue gently for 4 to 5 minutes. Stir in the tomato purée, tomatoes, stock, Worcestershire sauce, Tabasco, lemon juice and seasonings. Bring to the boil, cover and simmer gently for 15 minutes, stirring occasionally.

Meanwhile, heat the remaining oil and the butter in another pan. Add the kidneys and fry gently for 8 to 10 minutes, stirring frequently, until well sealed and almost cooked through. Add the tomato mixture, cover and simmer gently for a further 5 to 10 minutes. Taste and adjust seasonings. Serve with boiled rice and garnish with black olives.

Cidered Kidneys

4 rashers lean back bacon, derinded
    and chopped
1 large onion, peeled and sliced
1 clove garlic, crushed
25 g (1 oz) butter
10 lambs' kidneys, skinned, halved
    and cored
a little seasoned flour
450 ml (¾ pint) dry cider
salt and freshly ground black pepper

Fry the bacon, onion and garlic in the
butter until soft, about 5 minutes. Coat
the kidneys in seasoned flour and add to
the pan. Fry gently for 7 to 8 minutes,
turning several times, until well sealed
and almost cooked through. Stir in 1
tablespoon seasoned flour then gradually add the cider to the pan. Bring to
the boil, stirring continuously, then
simmer, uncovered, for about 10 minutes, until the kidneys are tender and
the sauce has reduced to a syrupy consistency. Then taste and adjust the
seasonings.

Kidneys à l'Orange

4 rashers streaky bacon, derinded and
    chopped
2 onions, peeled and thinly sliced
40 g (1½ oz) butter
8–10 lambs' kidneys, skinned, halved
    and cored
2 tablespoons seasoned flour
½ teaspoon paprika
300 ml (½ pint) stock
finely grated rind and juice of 1 large
    orange
salt and freshly ground black pepper
2 teaspoons tomato purée
orange wedges, to garnish

Fry the bacon and onions in the butter
until soft. Coat the kidneys in seasoned
flour and add to the pan. Cook gently for
5 minutes, turning frequently until well

sealed. Stir in the remaining flour and
paprika, cook for 1 minute then gradually add the stock, orange rind and
juice. Bring slowly to the boil, season
well and add the tomato paste. Cover
and simmer gently for about 20 minutes
until tender, adding a little more stock
during cooking, if necessary. Taste and
adjust seasonings and serve garnished
with orange wedges.

Kidney Fritters with Mustard Sauce

25 g (1 oz) butter
125 g (5 oz) flour
300 ml (½ pint) stock
salt and freshly ground black pepper
1 tablespoon wine vinegar
1 tablespoon French mustard
25–50 g (1–2 oz) stuffed olives, sliced
10–12 lambs' kidneys, skinned,
    quartered and cored
flour for coating
1 large egg
150 ml (¼ pint) milk
1 teaspoon oil
deep fat for frying
tomato wedges, to garnish

To make the sauce, melt the butter in a
pan, stir in 25 g (1 oz) flour and cook for 1
minute, gradually add the stock and
bring to the boil for 3 minutes, stirring
frequently. Season to taste, stir in the
vinegar and mustard and simmer for 2
minutes. Add the olives and keep warm.
    Prepare the kidneys and coat in flour.
Sieve the remaining flour with a pinch
of salt into a bowl. Add the egg and
sufficient milk to beat to a smooth
batter, then beat in the remaining milk.
Heat the fat to 180–190°C/350–375°F, or
until a cube of bread browns in it in 20
seconds. Dip the pieces of kidney in the
batter, a few at a time, then drop into
the hot fat and cook for 4 to 5 minutes
until golden brown and crispy. Drain
the fritters on absorbent kitchen paper
and keep warm. Garnish with tomato.

BARBECUES & BUFFETS

Shish Kebabs

1¼ kg (2½ lb) piece top of leg of lamb
4 tablespoons oil
2 tablespoons wine vinegar
2 tablespoons lemon juice
1 clove garlic, crushed
salt and freshly ground black pepper
1 small onion, peeled and finely
  chopped
8 bay leaves
8 thick slices of raw onion, blanched
To garnish:
parsley sprigs
lemon wedges

Trim the lamb and cut into 2.5 cm (1 inch) cubes. Place the oil in a bowl with the vinegar, lemon juice, garlic, seasonings and chopped onion. Add the meat and leave in a cool place to marinade for at least 2 hours, turning several times.

Drain the cubes of meat and thread on to 4 long skewers, alternating with the bay leaves and slices of onion. Cook under a moderately hot grill for about 10 minutes each side, until browned and cooked through; or cook over a charcoal barbecue until tender. Garnish with lemon wedges and parsley and serve with a plain or savoury rice.

Sausages and Bacon Skewers

300–350 g (10–12 oz) slices gammon
  2 cm (¾ inch) thick
1 × 425 g (15 oz) can peach halves
225 g (8 oz) chipolatas, halved
8 fresh bay leaves
8 button onions, peeled and blanched
For the coleslaw:
350 g (12 oz) finely shredded white
  cabbage
2 large carrots, peeled and coarsely
  grated
1 tablespoon finely chopped parsley
25 g (1 oz) shelled walnuts, roughly
  chopped
3–4 tablespoons French dressing

Cut the gammon into 2 cm (¾ inch) cubes after discarding the rind. Drain the peaches and cut each piece in half. Arrange the gammon, pieces of peach, chipolatas, bay leaves and onions on 4 long skewers. Cook under a moderate grill for about 15 minutes, turning several times and brushing regularly with peach juice, until the chipolatas and bacon are cooked through. Serve on a bed of coleslaw. To prepare the coleslaw, combine the cabbage, carrots, parsley, walnuts and French dressing. Toss the vegetables and nuts together to ensure they are evenly coated.

If liked, the coleslaw can be topped with finely chopped herbs.

Marinaded Beef Kebabs

150 ml (5 fl oz) natural yogurt
150 ml (¼ pint) tomato juice
2 teaspoons Worcestershire sauce
pinch of cayenne
1 teaspoon dried sage
½ teaspoon marjoram
1 tablespoon finely chopped onion
salt and freshly ground black pepper
450 g (1 lb) rump steak
8 mushrooms, cleaned
4 tomatoes, halved
1 green pepper, washed, deseeded and
    cut into 8
saffron rice

Mix together the yogurt, tomato juice,
Worcestershire sauce, cayenne, herbs,
onion and seasonings. Trim the steak
and cut into 2.5 cm (1 inch) cubes. Place
in the marinade and leave for 4 to 5
hours, turning occasionally. Drain the
meat and thread on to 4 long skewers,
alternating with the mushrooms, tomatoes and pepper. Cook under a hot grill
for about 10 minutes each side, brushing with the marinade frequently and
turning the meat once or twice until
well browned but not overcooked.

Heat the marinade gently, without
boiling, taste and adjust the seasonings
and serve with the kebabs and put on a
bed of saffron rice.

To make saffron rice, add a few grains
of saffron or a little powdered turmeric
to the boiling salted water before
adding the rice.

Sheftalia

1¼ kg (2½ lb) boned lean lamb
1 large onion, peeled and chopped
2 garlic cloves, peeled and crushed
    with 1 teaspoon salt
6 tablespoons finely chopped parsley
1 small egg, beaten
1 teaspoon ground allspice
freshly ground black pepper

flour seasoned with salt and pepper
    for coating
vegetable oil for cooking
few fresh rosemary sprigs

Mince the lamb, onion, garlic and parsley together several times until the
mixture is fine and smooth. Stir in the
egg and allspice and black pepper to
taste and mix until evenly blended.
Form the mixture into thin sausage
shapes, approximately 6 cm (2½ inches)
long, and roll between well-floured
hands until the kebabs are firm and
lightly coated in flour. Chill in the
refrigerator for 24 hours, then thread
carefully on to oiled kebab skewers and
brush gently with oil. When the barbecue charcoals are hot, put a few
rosemary sprigs on the well-oiled barbecue grid. Place the kebabs on top and
cook for 10 to 15 minutes, turning the
kebabs during cooking, and brushing
with more oil from time to time. Remove
from the barbecue and serve hot with
yogurt and a tomato and onion salad
sprinkled with plenty of finely chopped
fresh coriander or parsley.
Makes about 40.

Liver and Bacon Kebabs

450 g (1 lb) lambs' liver in a piece
4 tablespoons oil
2 tablespoons lemon juice
salt and freshly ground black pepper
12 rashers streaky bacon, derinded
    and rolled
8 large button mushrooms, cleaned
    and trimmed
8 fresh bay leaves
4 large tomatoes, halved
saffron rice
150 ml (¼ pint) stock

Cut the liver into 2 cm (¾ inch) cubes and
place in a bowl with the oil, lemon juice
and seasonings and marinade for 1–2
hours.

Drain the liver well and arrange on

four long skewers with the bacon rolls, mushrooms and bay leaves. Place on the grill rack and cook under a moderate grill for about 5 minutes each side, brushing once or twice with the marinade, until browned. Grill the tomatoes alongside the kebabs. Place on a bed of saffron rice (see recipe for Marinaded Beef Kebabs, left) with the tomatoes to garnish. Keep warm. Add the stock to the pan juices and bring to the boil for 1 to 2 minutes. Taste and adjust the seasonings and pour over the kebabs.

Pork and Lemon Brochettes

550–675 g (1¼–1½ lb) pork fillet
2 onions, peeled, thickly sliced and
  blanched
2 tablespoons lemon juice
a little oil
For the sauce:
200 ml (7 fl oz) stock
1 tablespoon soy sauce
good dash of Worcestershire sauce
1 teaspoon lemon juice
salt and freshly ground black pepper
1 teaspoon cornflour
2 tomatoes, peeled, deseeded and
  chopped
To garnish:
lemon wedges
watercress sprigs

Trim the pork and cut into thin strips about 4 cm (1½ inches) long by 1.5 cm (½ inch) thick. Arrange on 4 long skewers, pushing the meat fairly tightly together and interspersing with slices of onion. Brush the pork first with lemon juice and then with oil. Place on a grill rack and cook under a moderate heat until the meat is well browned and cooked through, about 8 to 10 minutes each side. Brush with the oil several times during cooking.

Meanwhile, to make the sauce, place the stock, soy sauce, Worcestershire sauce, lemon juice and seasonings in a pan and bring to the boil. Thicken with

the cornflour blended in a little cold water and add the tomato. Simmer for 5 minutes, then serve with the kebabs. Garnish with lemon wedges and sprigs of watercress.

Sweet and Sour Pork Kebabs

about 1½ kg (3 lb) pork fillet
  (tenderloin) cut into cubes
salt and freshly ground black pepper
For the marinade:
6 tablespoons vegetable oil
finely grated rind and juice of 1½
  grapefruits
3 tablespoons dark soft brown sugar
3 tablespoons soy sauce
2 tablespoons black treacle
3 fresh green chillis, finely chopped
1 × 5 cm (2 inch) piece fresh root
  ginger, peeled, chopped and
  pounded to a paste with a pestle in
  a mortar
1 teaspoon Tabasco sauce

Put the pork in a large bowl and sprinkle liberally with salt and pepper. Mix all the ingredients for the marinade together, beating briskly to combine thoroughly. Pour over the pork and stir well so that each cube of meat is coated in the marinade. Chill in the refrigerator for 24 hours, stirring the meat and marinade together from time to time. Let stand at room temperature for 1 to 2 hours before cooking.

Thread the cubes of pork on to 8–10 oiled kebab skewers while the barbecue charcoals are heating. When they are hot, place the kebabs on the grid and cook for approximately 15 minutes, turning the skewers regularly to ensure even cooking and brushing the pork with the remaining marinade.

Serve immediately with chilled ratatouille and jacket potatoes, or hot French bread and a tossed green salad. Hand yogurt separately.
Serves 8–10

Marinade for Meat

strip of finely pared orange rind
2 tablespoons wine vinegar
150 ml ($\frac{1}{4}$ pint) red wine or sherry
freshly ground black pepper
1 teaspoon coarse salt
2 teaspoons soft brown sugar
few sprigs fresh thyme (or rosemary
    for lamb)
few drops Worcestershire sauce

Put all the ingredients together in a
bowl and mix well. Add the meat and
sufficient cold water barely to cover.
Cover the bowl and put in the refrigerator or cold place for up to 24 hours,
turning the meat occasionally. Before
cooking, drain the meat well and brush
with oil or melted butter. Heat the
marinade gently and bring up to the
boil. Simmer for 5 minutes and serve as
a sauce with the meat.

Salted Nuts

6 tablespoons corn oil
75 g (3 oz) butter
450 g (1 lb) shelled mixed nuts
    (almonds, peanuts, cashews,
    walnuts, etc.)
salt

Heat the oil and butter in a skillet or
frying pan until foaming. Add the nuts
and fry for 5 minutes, shaking the pan,
until browned on all sides. Remove from
pan with a slotted spoon and drain well
on absorbent kitchen paper. Sprinkle
with salt to taste, allow to cool, then
heap into serving dishes or bowls.

* Devilled Nuts

Follow the recipe for Salted Nuts
(above), with this change: add 1 teaspoon of cayenne pepper with the salt.

Lemon Barbecue Sauce

40 g ($1\frac{1}{2}$ oz) butter
1 clove garlic, crushed
1 small onion, peeled and thinly
    sliced
2 teaspoons flour
200 ml (7 fl oz) dry white wine
grated rind of 1 lemon
juice of 2 lemons
1 lemon, thinly sliced
few drops Tabasco sauce
salt and freshly ground black pepper
pinch of chilli powder
sugar to taste
chopped parsley (optional)

Melt the butter and fry the garlic and
onion gently until soft. Stir in the flour
followed by the wine, lemon rind and
juice and bring to the boil, stirring
continuously. Add the sliced lemon,
Tabasco, seasonings, chilli powder and
sugar to taste and simmer for 5 minutes.
Taste and adjust the seasonings and
serve hot with chopped parsley added, if
liked. Serve with any meats.

Variation:
Dry cider or half wine and half stock
may be used in place of all wine.

Tomato Barbecue Sauce

1 tablespoon vinegar
$1\frac{1}{2}$ tablespoons brown sugar
$1\frac{1}{2}$ teaspoons mustard
$\frac{1}{4}$ teaspoon freshly ground black
    pepper
$\frac{3}{4}$ teaspoon salt
good pinch cayenne
good pinch grated lemon rind
1 teaspoon lemon juice
1 small onion, peeled and finely
    chopped
25 g (1 oz) butter
4 tablespoons tomato ketchup
1 tablespoon Worcestershire sauce
8 stuffed olives, chopped

Place all the ingredients, except the olives, with 4 tablespoons water, in a small saucepan and bring slowly to the boil. Cover and simmer gently for about 15 minutes, stirring from time to time, then stir in the olives. Serve hot or cold in a bowl to eat with any barbecued meats. This sauce will keep for several days in a covered container in the refrigerator and the quantities can be doubled up to serve larger numbers.

Mackerel Salad Open Sandwiches

6 large slices of rye or wholemeal bread
butter for spreading
2 × 120 g (4¼ oz) cans mackerel fillets in tomato sauce, flaked
2 teaspoons lemon juice
2 tablespoons mayonnaise
freshly ground black pepper
To garnish:
4 hard-boiled eggs, sliced
24 gherkins, drained

Spread the bread with plenty of butter, then cut neatly into quarters with a sharp knife. Mix the flaked mackerel with the lemon juice, mayonnaise and pepper to taste, then spread on the buttered bread, dividing the mixture equally among the quarters. Decorate the top of each quarter with a slice of egg and a gherkin fan.

To make gherkin fans: slice gherkin into four length-wise, keeping gherkin in one piece at the base. Spread the four slices out in a fan shape, holding the base firmly.
Makes 24

Hot Cheese and Herb Loaf

1 long French loaf
50 g (2 oz) butter
225 g (8 oz) cream cheese, softened

2 tablespoons finely chopped parsley
2 tablespoons snipped chives
2 tablespoons finely chopped thyme, marjoram or basil
salt and freshly ground black pepper

Cut the loaf in half lengthwise and spread the inside cut surfaces with butter. Beat the cream cheese with the herbs until thoroughly combined, adding salt and pepper to taste.

Spread the cheese mixture on the butter, dividing it equally between each half. Put the loaf back together again, wrap in foil, then place directly on oven shelf. Bake in a fairly hot oven (200°C, 400°F, Gas Mark 6) for 10 minutes, open the foil wrapping and continue baking for a further 5 minutes or until the loaf is crisp and the cheese is hot.

Remove from the oven, discard foil, cut loaf into thick slices and transfer to a bread basket or board.
Serve immediately
Cuts into 12–14 slices

Garlic Sausage and Cheese Open Sandwiches

1 × 225 g (8 oz) packet (7 slices) pumpernickel bread
100 g (4 oz) cream cheese
salt and freshly ground black pepper
28 thin slices of garlic sausage, rind removed
28 pimiento-stuffed green olives, cut in halves

Cut the pumpernickel slices into quarters and spread each one thickly with the cream cheese. Sprinkle with salt and pepper to taste. Fold each slice of garlic sausage in half, then cut almost in two. Twist each half in opposite directions then place on the cream cheese, pressing down gently to adhere. Arrange an olive half on each side of the sausage. Sprinkle with more salt and pepper.
Makes 28

Herb Bread

1 long French loaf
100 g (4 oz) butter, softened
4 tablespoons finely chopped herbs
(parsley, chives, marjoram)

Cut the bread into 2.5 cm (1 inch) thick slices without cutting right through the base. Cream the butter and herbs together in a bowl until thoroughly combined, then spread on the cut surfaces of the bread.

Wrap the loaf in foil, place directly on oven shelf and bake in a fairly hot oven (200°C, 400°F, Gas Mark 6) for 10 minutes, then open the foil wrapping and continue baking for a further 5 minutes or until the loaf is crisp. Remove from the oven, unwrap and serve hot.

* Garlic Bread

Follow the recipe for Herb Bread (above) with this change: substitute 2 garlic cloves, peeled and crushed, for the herbs.

Danish Pork and Prune Open Sandwiches

5 large slices of white bread, crusts removed
butter for spreading
1 × 198 g (7 oz) can Danish cured pork
1 × 113 g (4 oz) carton cottage cheese with chives
salt and freshly ground black pepper
10 prunes, halved and pitted
10 large orange slices, peel, pith and pips removed
watercress or parsley sprigs, to garnish (optional)

Use day old bread or the toppings will not adhere to their bases, and pierce each 'sandwich' with a cocktail stick, if you like. Garnish the platter with sprigs of watercress or parsley if liked.

Spread the bread with plenty of butter and cut each slice neatly into quarters with a sharp knife. Cut the pork lengthwise into 10 slices, then cut each slice in half. Place one slice of pork on each piece of bread, and cut to the same size if necessary. Put 1 heaped teaspoon cottage cheese on each quarter and sprinkle with salt and pepper. Place a prune half on top of the cottage cheese and press down firmly, then cut the orange slices into quarters and arrange two quarters on either side of the prunes to form a 'butterfly'.
Makes 20

Finger and Fork Platter

Celery boats
Trim the stalks of 1 large head of celery, scrub thoroughly and cut into 5 cm (2 inch) lengths. Beat 225 g (8 oz) cream cheese until soft with a wooden spoon, then stir in 2 tablespoons anchovy essence, 50 g (2 oz) finely chopped walnuts, and freshly ground black pepper to taste. Fill mixture into celery pieces and sprinkle with a little paprika pepper.

Stuffed eggs
Halve 12 hard-boiled eggs lengthwise, scoop out the yolks carefully and mash with a fork. Mix with 150 ml ($\frac{1}{4}$ pint) thick homemade mayonnaise (p. 42), 1 tablespoon curry paste (or to taste), salt and freshly ground black pepper to taste. Pipe into the reserved egg whites and decorate each with a slice of stuffed olive.
Makes 24 halves

Cucumber canoes
Trim 2 cucumbers and score the length of each with the prongs of a fork. Cut in half lengthwise, scoop out the flesh from the inside, place in a sieve, sprinkle with salt and leave to drain for

30 minutes. Pat dry with absorbent kitchen paper, then mix with 175 g (6 oz) roughly chopped peeled prawns, 3 tablespoons thick mayonnaise and 2 tablespoons snipped chives. Season liberally with salt and freshly ground black pepper. Cut each cucumber half into approximately 6 'canoes', spoon in the filling and sprinkle each one with a little cayenne pepper.
Makes 24

Stuffed tomatoes
Cut 8 firm but ripe tomatoes in half. Scoop out the flesh carefully with a teaspoon (this can be used in soups or casseroles, if liked.) Sieve 225 g (8 oz) cottage cheese and mix with 100 g (4 oz) finely chopped boiled ham and 1 teaspoon Tabasco sauce (or to taste). Season well with salt and freshly ground black pepper. Spoon the filling into the tomato cases, mounding it in the centre. Cut 16 stoned olives in quarters and arrange in a flower motif on top of the cottage cheese mixture.
Makes 16 halves

Mushroom caps
You will need 450 g (1 lb) deep cup-shaped mushrooms for these. Wipe them clean and carefully break the stalks from the caps. Fry the caps gently in a little butter for 1 minute on each side. Chop the stalks finely and fry until golden in a little butter with 1 medium-sized onion, peeled and finely chopped, and 50 g (2 oz) fine white breadcrumbs. Transfer to a mixing bowl and stir in 100 g (4 oz) finely chopped garlic sausage. Spoon into the mushroom caps, sprinkle with 50 g (2 oz) grated Parmesan cheese, and cayenne pepper to taste, and put under a hot grill for a few minutes until golden brown. Transfer to a serving platter. When cool sprinkle with finely chopped parsley.

Cheesy Sausage Rolls

225 g (8 oz) flour
pinch of salt
pinch of cayenne pepper
100 g (4 oz) butter or margarine
50 g (2 oz) Cheddar cheese, finely grated
1 egg yolk
pinch of dried mixed herbs
225 g (8 oz) pork sausagemeat
a little milk, to glaze

Sieve the flour, salt and cayenne pepper into a bowl. Add the butter or margarine in pieces and rub together with the fingertips until the mixture resembles fine breadcrumbs. Beat the egg yolk. Stir in the grated cheese and the yolk and draw the mixture together with the fingertips to form a smooth dough. Form into a ball, wrap in foil and chill in the refrigerator for at least 30 minutes. Divide the dough in two and roll each piece out on a lightly floured board to an oblong shape approximately 10 cm (4 inches) wide.

Mix the dried herbs into the sausagemeat, divide in two and roll with floured hands into long sausage shapes. Place the sausagemeat on the dough and fold over to enclose. Brush the edges with a little milk and press firmly to seal. Brush all over the dough with milk, then cut into 2.5 to 5 cm (1 to 2 inch) lengths.

Place the sausage rolls on a baking sheet and bake just above the centre of a fairly hot oven (200°C, 400°F, Gas Mark 6) for 15 minutes. Reduce the heat to moderate (180°C, 350°F, Gas Mark 4) and continue baking for another 10 to 15 minutes until the pastry is golden brown and crisp. Remove from the oven, transfer to a warmed serving platter and serve warm.
Makes about 15–20

Canapés

slices of white, wholemeal or granary
  bread
or
cheese straws (p. 24)
or
crispbreads, crackers or savoury
  biscuits
butter for frying
selection of toppings (see recipe)

Ideally, canapés should be small
enough to eat in one or two bites.
Remove crusts from white, wholemeal
or granary bread, toast lightly on both
sides and cut slices into halves or quarters or stamp into small rounds with a
pastry cutter after toasting. As an alternative to toasting, the bread can be
lightly fried in butter – but be sure to
drain well on absorbent kitchen paper
before using. If preferred, the canapé
base can be made of savoury cheese
pastry – use a recipe for cheese straws,
or see the recipe for Cheesy Sausage
Rolls (p. 215). Roll the pastry out thinly
and stamp into 6 cm (2½ inch) or 7.5 cm (3
inch) rounds and other shapes with a
pastry cutter. Another alternative is to
use crispbreads, crackers and savoury
biscuits as bases. For an eye-catching
spread, combine different shapes, tex-
tures and toppings on large serving
platters and top with a selection of the
following:

Cream cheese toppings
Mix 100 g (4 oz) softened cream cheese
with:
1. 50 g (2 oz) pimiento-stuffed green
olives, finely chopped. Season to taste.
Spread on to buttered canapés and top
with 1 slice of stuffed olive.
2. 25 g (1 oz) finely chopped walnuts and
½ teaspoon cayenne pepper. Season to
taste. Spread on to buttered canapés
and top each with half a walnut.
3. Half a cucumber, peeled, seeded and
finely chopped. Season to taste. Spread
on to buttered canapés and top each

with a generous sprinkling of snipped
fresh chives.
4. 50 g (2 oz) pitted dates, finely chopped. Season to taste. Spread on to buttered canapés.
5. Four rashers of crisply fried streaky
bacon, rinds removed, finely chopped.
Season to taste. Spread on to buttered
canapés and top with two strips of green
pepper.

Salmon topping
Drain a 225 g (8 oz) can red salmon and
flake with a fork. Fold lightly into 4
tablespoons mayonnaise blended with a
few drops of Tabasco sauce. Spread on
to buttered canapés, sprinkle with a
little cayenne pepper and garnish with
watercress sprigs.

Sardine topping
Drain a 124 g (4½ oz) can sardines in
olive oil. Mash well with a fork and
combine with 2 teaspoons lemon juice
and 2 tablespoons mayonnaise or natural yogurt. Season the mixture with
plenty of freshly ground black pepper.
Refrigerate for 30 minutes or until
needed, then spread on to butter-fried
canapés and top each with 2 small onion
rings and 1 small parsley sprig.

Tuna topping
Drain a 198 g (7 oz) can tuna and flake
with a fork. Fold lightly into 4 tablespoons soured cream and season well
with salt and freshly ground black
pepper. Spread on to buttered canapés
and top each with a gherkin fan (see
recipe for Mackerel Salad, p. 213).

Savoury butters
Combine 100 g (4 oz) softened butter
with any one of the following, blending
well with a wooden spoon. Spread or
pipe on to canapés and refrigerate until
serving time.
Anchovy: Drain a 50 g (2 oz) can anchovies in olive oil, cover with milk and
leave to soak for 30 minutes. Drain well,
pound to a paste with a pestle and
mortar and blend into butter, with

freshly ground black pepper to taste.
Blue cheese: Soften 50 g (2 oz) Danish
Blue/Gorgonzola cheese with a wooden
spoon. Blend into butter.
Watercress: Chop 1 bunch watercress
very finely and blend into butter.
Season with plenty of salt. This butter is
an attractive bright green in colour.
Chilli: Blend 3 tablespoons chilli relish
and the finely grated rind of ½ lemon
into the butter, with salt and pepper to
taste.

Smoked Salmon Rolls

For the horseradish cream:
150 ml (¼ pint) double cream
2 tablespoons grated horseradish or
    horseradish sauce
1 teaspoon wine vinegar
salt and freshly ground black pepper
To make the rolls:
450 g (1 lb) smoked salmon thinly
    sliced
1 × 429 g (15 oz) can asparagus spears,
    drained
lemon wedges, to garnish

To make the horseradish cream: whip
the cream until thick, then beat in the
horseradish, wine vinegar, and salt and
pepper to taste.
Cut the salmon into pieces approximately 7.5 cm (3 inches) square and cut
each asparagus spear in half. Lay the
salmon pieces flat on a board, place one
piece of asparagus in the centre of each
piece of salmon, spoon a little of the
horseradish cream over the asparagus
and roll up the salmon neatly. Arrange
on a serving platter and garnish with
lemon wedges.
Makes about 34

Sausages in Foil

24 cocktail sausages
2 tablespoons oil
1 large onion, peeled and thinly sliced
2 dessert apples, cored and chopped
salt and freshly ground black pepper
25 g (1 oz) butter
25 g (1 oz) flour
300 ml (½ pint) cider

Cut 4 large squares of foil, turning up
the edges, and place 6 cocktail sausages
in the centre of each.
Heat the oil in a frying pan. Add the
sliced onion and fry gently until soft.
Add the chopped apple and cook gently
for a further 3 minutes. Season to taste.
Spoon the apple and onion mixture over
the cocktail sausages on the foil
squares. (If liked, fry the sausages for a
few minutes first to brown them.)
Heat the butter in a small saucepan.
Stir in the flour and cook for 1 minute.
Gradually add the cider and bring to the
boil, stirring constantly. Simmer until
the sauce thickens. Spoon the cider
sauce over the sausages, onion and
apple.
Fold up the foil and pinch the edges
well together to seal in the ingredients.
Stand the foil parcels on a baking tray.
Cook in a fairly hot oven (190°C, 375°F,
Gas Mark 5) for 30 minutes.

Variation:
Instead of cocktail sausages, you can
use chipolatas; just twist each chipolata, to make 3 smaller sausages.

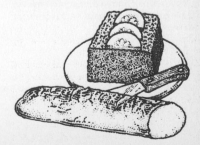

Stuffed Fresh Dates

450 g (1 lb) fresh dates
450 g (1 lb) block of marzipan

Stone the dates, slitting with a sharp
knife and removing the stone carefully.
Divide the block of marzipan into equal
portions, the same number as the dates,
and shape each piece into a long oval.
Insert a roll of marzipan into each date
to replace the stone. Arrange the stuffed
dates on a platter or in paper sweet
cases, in small dishes.

Potato Choux Puffs

1 quantity choux pastry (p. 361)
450 g (1 lb) potatoes, boiled and
    mashed
salt and freshly ground black pepper
pinch of grated nutmeg
oil for deep frying

Beat the choux pastry and mashed
potato together in a bowl, season to
taste and add the grated nutmeg. Put
the potato and choux mixture into a
piping bag fitted with a 1 cm ($\frac{1}{2}$ inch)
plain nozzle.
    Heat the oil in a deep-fat fryer or
saucepan until it is hot enough to turn a
stale bread cube golden in 45 seconds
(185°C/360°F). Pipe out the choux mixture, cutting it into 1 cm ($\frac{1}{2}$ inch)
lengths, and allowing them to drop
gently into the hot oil. Fry for 1 to 2
minutes, until puffed and golden-brown.
Drain on absorbent paper and serve hot.
Serves 6

Cheesy Cocktail Biscuits

175 g (6 oz) flour
pinch of paprika pepper
1 teaspoon dry mustard
100 g (4 oz) butter
75 g (3 oz) Gouda cheese, grated
2 teaspoons anchovy essence
1 egg, beaten
For the filling:
50 g (2 oz) butter
50 g (2 oz) Gouda cheese, grated
4 anchovy fillets, finely chopped
For the topping:
25 g (1 oz) Gouda cheese, grated

Sift the flour, paprika pepper and mustard together in a bowl and rub in the
butter until the mixture resembles
coarse breadcrumbs. Add the grated
cheese and anchovy essence and bind
with half the egg.
    Roll out thinly on a floured board and
cut out circles with a small round
pastry cutter.
    Place the biscuits on baking sheets.
Brush the tops of half the biscuits with
the remaining egg then, sprinkle on
a little grated Gouda cheese before
baking. These will make the top of the
biscuit sandwich.
    Bake in a fairly hot oven (200°C,
400°F, Gas Mark 6) for 10 to 15 minutes
until golden.
To make the filling: beat the butter and
grated cheese together until soft, add
the chopped anchovy fillets and use to
sandwich the plain and cheese-topped
biscuits together.

Surprise Thatched Cottage

1 large white or brown loaf
450 g (1 lb) cocktail sausages, cooked
$\frac{1}{2}$ cucumber, sliced
100 g (4 oz) cream cheese
about 75 g (3 oz) potato sticks
1 stick, celery, trimmed and scrubbed
2 slices of processed cheese

Cut the top off the loaf and reserve to make the roof. Scoop the bread from the inside of the loaf and fill the hollow with cocktail sausages. Place on a board or serving platter. Place the cucumber slices to form a thick layer on top of the loaf. Spread the roof thickly with cream cheese, reserving some for the chimney, windows and doors, then place on top of the cucumber slices.

Press the potato sticks into the cream cheese to form the thatch. Cut the celery stick in two, then cut in half lengthwise. Sandwich two of the halves together with cream cheese, press into the top of the house for the chimney, then add two potato sticks to resemble the smoke.

Cut the cheese slices into squares to make windows for the front, back and sides of the cottage, and cut two oblong shapes to make front and back doors. Stick these shapes on to the loaf with a little cream cheese and use potato sticks to make frames for the windows, a knocker and letterbox for the front door. Use the remaining two pieces of celery to make a porch above the door.

Sausage Rolls

225 g (8 oz) rough puff pastry

1 beaten egg, for glazing

Preheat the oven to 200°C, 425°F, Gas Mark 7. Roll out the pastry into a rectangle 5 mm ($\frac{1}{4}$ inch) thick and about 15 cm (6 inches) wide, divide it lengthwise in half. Divide the sausagemeat in half and, on a floured board, roll it into 2 long thin sausage shapes. Place one on each pastry strip, just right of the centre. Brush the pastry edges with beaten egg and fold the pastry over the sausage meat.

Press the pastry edges firmly together and knock up with the back of the knife like a pie edging. Cut the pastry rolls into equal 5 cm (2 inch) lengths or larger

if preferred. Place on a dampened baking tray and brush with beaten egg. Cut 2 or 3 slits across the top of each roll for the steam to escape.

Bake just above the centre of the oven for 25 to 30 minutes or until well risen and golden brown. Serve hot with mustard.

If serving the rolls cold, use Flaky Pastry (p. 362) instead of the rough puff pastry.

Blue Cheese Dip

50 g (2 oz) unsalted butter, softened
350 g (12 oz) Gorgonzola cheese, rind
    removed and softened
about 6 tablespoons milk
4 sticks of celery, trimmed, scrubbed
    and finely chopped
75 g (3 oz) walnuts, finely chopped
freshly ground black pepper

Whip the butter with an electric or rotary beater until light and soft, then gradually beat in the cheese a little at a time until it is thoroughly combined. Gradually stir in the milk until a creamy consistency is obtained, then fold in three-quarters of the celery and one-third of the walnuts. Add black pepper to taste and transfer to a serving bowl. Combine the remaining celery and walnuts and sprinkle over the top of the dip. Chill in the refrigerator before serving.

Serve chilled dips in shallow bowls with a selection of crisp raw vegetables, savoury biscuits and crisps for 'dipping'. Guests can then help themselves. Serves about 12

Devilled Crab Dip

350 g (12 oz) cream cheese
4–6 tablespoons thick homemade
    mayonnaise (p. 42)
2 teaspoons chilli sauce
2 teaspoons Worcestershire sauce
salt
freshly ground black pepper
1 medium-sized cucumber, peeled,
    seeded and finely diced
pinch of sugar
1 × 150 g (5 oz) packet frozen crabmeat,
    thawed
¼ teaspoon cayenne pepper

Beat the cream cheese with a wooden
spoon until soft, then gradually beat in
the mayonnaise until a soft, creamy
consistency is obtained. Stir in the
sauces, and salt and pepper to taste.

Sprinkle the diced cucumber with the
sugar and stir into the cheese mixture,
then fold in the crabmeat. Taste and
adjust seasoning, then spoon into a
serving bowl, sprinkle with the cayenne
pepper and chill in the refrigerator
before serving.
Serves about 10

Glühwein

1 litre bottle dry red wine
300 ml (½ pint) water
2 tablespoons sugar, or to taste
1 cinnamon stick, broken in two
1 bay leaf
1 lemon struck with a few cloves

Pour the wine and water into a large
saucepan, add the sugar and heat gently
until the sugar dissolves. Float the
remaining ingredients on top of Glüh-
wein and heat gently for 5 to 10 minutes.
Do not allow to boil. Taste for sweetness, adding more sugar as necessary,
then strain and serve hot in heatproof
glasses or stoneware goblets.
Fills 8–10 glasses

Punch

1 litre bottle rosé wine
8 tablespoons rum
2 tablespoons sugar, or to taste
1 large orange, sliced, pips discarded
1 lemon, sliced, pips discarded
1 cinnamon stick, broken in two
pinch of grated nutmeg
4 cloves

Pour the wine and rum into a large
saucepan, add the sugar and heat gently
until the sugar dissolves. Float remaining ingredients on top of punch and
heat gently for 10 to 15 minutes. Do not
allow to boil. Taste for sweetness, then
strain and serve hot with orange and
lemon slices in heatproof glasses or
stoneware goblets.
Fills about 8 glasses

Lemonade

3 lemons, halved
1¾ litres (3 pints) water
450 g (1 lb) sugar, or to taste
2 tablespoons citric acid

This quantity makes 1¾ litres (3 pints).
Squeeze the lemons and set the juice
aside. Cut the lemon skins into thick
slices, then put in a pan with the water.
Bring to the boil, remove from heat and
add lemon juice, sugar and citric acid.
Stir to dissolve the sugar, then leave to
cool. Strain into a jug, cover and chill in
the refrigerator.

Serve diluted with water to taste. Use
within 1 week if kept in the refrigerator,
or 1 to 2 days if kept at cool room
temperature.

PUDDINGS & DESSERTS

Eve's Pudding

450 g (1 lb) cooking apples
75 g (3 oz) demerara sugar
finely grated rind of 1 lemon
100 g (4 oz) caster sugar
100 g (4 oz) butter or margarine
¼ teaspoon vanilla essence
2 eggs, beaten
100 g (4 oz) self-raising flour
sugar for dredging

Peel, core and slice the apples into a buttered ovenproof dish in layers, sprinkling each layer with demerara sugar and grated lemon rind. Cream the caster sugar and butter together until light and fluffy. Add the vanilla essence to the eggs and beat in very gradually, adding a little flour if mixture looks like curdling. Fold in the remaining flour and spread the sponge mixture evenly over the fruit.

Bake in a moderate oven (180°C, 350°F, Gas Mark 4) for 35–40 minutes until well risen and golden brown. Test the sponge topping with a skewer, which should come out clean. Dredge with sugar and serve hot with custard.

Variation:
Vary by adding some blackberries, or substituting sliced pears for the apples. In season use gooseberries, rhubarb with grated orange rind, or halved plums or apricots.

Butterscotch Upside Down Pudding

4 pineapple rings
4 cherries
100 g (4 oz) demerara sugar
50 g (2 oz) butter or margarine
50 g (2 oz) chopped walnuts
For the batter:
2 eggs, separated
¼ teaspoon vanilla essence
1 tablespoon melted butter
100 g (4 oz) caster sugar
100 g (4 oz) plain flour
1 teaspoon baking powder

Grease a 20 cm (8 inch) shallow cake tin and arrange the pineapple slices on the bottom with a cherry in the centre of each. Dissolve the sugar and melt the butter in a saucepan over gentle heat, then stir in the nuts. Mix well and pour over the pineapple slices being careful not to dislodge the cherries.

Beat the egg yolks with the vanilla and melted butter until creamy. Whisk the egg whites until stiff but not brittle and fold in the sugar and the egg yolk mixture. Sieve together the flour and baking powder and fold in carefully. Pour the batter into the tin and spread it evenly.

Bake in a preheated warm oven (160°C, 325°F, Gas Mark 3) for 30 minutes or until firm and golden. Turn out pudding upside down on a platter and serve hot or cold with cream.

Black Cap Castle Puddings

100 g (4 oz) blackcurrant jam
100 g (4 oz) butter or margarine
100 g (4 oz) caster sugar
¼ teaspoon vanilla essence
2 eggs, beaten
100 g (4 oz) self-raising flour
1–2 tablespoons warm water

Grease 4 Castle Pudding tins or dariole moulds and put 1 teaspoon of blackcurrant jam in the bottom. Cream butter and sugar until light and fluffy. Add vanilla essence to eggs and beat in very gradually, adding a little of the flour if the mixture starts to curdle. Fold in remaining flour. Add 1–2 tablespoons warm water to produce a soft dropping consistency. Two-thirds fill the moulds with mixture, leaving room for the puddings to rise.

The puddings are now ready to be either baked or steamed.

To bake:
Place the puddings on a baking tray in a preheated moderate oven (180°C, 350°F, Gas Mark 4) for 25 minutes or until well risen and golden brown. Test the puddings with a skewer and when cooked allow to shrink slightly before unmoulding. If necessary, trim the tops so that when inverted the puddings will stand level on the serving plate. Serve hot with Blackcurrant Jam Sauce (p. 359) or cold with chilled custard.

To steam:
Place the puddings in a roasting tin with just enough water to come halfway up the moulds. Lay a sheet of greased kitchen foil on top, but do not tuck tightly round the roasting tin as the steam must be allowed to escape. Cook in a preheated moderate oven (180°C, 350°F, Gas Mark 4) for 50 minutes and test with a skewer, which should come out clean. Turn out and serve hot as above with Blackcurrant Jam Sauce or hot custard.

Country Jam Pudding

175 g (6 oz) self-raising flour
40 g (1½ oz) caster sugar
50 g (2 oz) butter or margarine
1 egg, beaten
3–4 tablespoons jam, lemon curd or mincemeat

Mix the flour and sugar together. Rub in the fat with the tips of the fingers until the consistency of breadcrumbs. Mix into a stiff dough with the egg and a little water. Knead lightly and divide in half. Roll out thinly into 2 rectangles of the same size. Place one on a greased baking sheet, prick and spread with preserve, leaving a margin round the edge. Brush the margin with water and place the second rectangle on top. Press the edges together and pinch with finger and thumb into flutes. Prick the top in a pattern with a fork. Bake in a preheated moderately hot oven (200°C, 400°F, Gas Mark 6) for 15–20 minutes until risen and golden brown. Remove from oven, sprinkle with caster sugar and cut into squares. Serve hot with custard or cold with cream.

Raspberry Lemon Sauce Pudding

225 g (8 oz) raspberries
25 g (1 oz) butter
100 g (4 oz) caster sugar
finely grated rind and juice of 1 large lemon
150 ml (¼ pint) milk
2 eggs, separated
25 g (1 oz) plain flour

Spread the raspberries over the base of a 600 ml (1 pint) soufflé dish.

Cream together the butter and 2 tablespoons caster sugar with the lemon rind. Beat in the lemon juice. Whisk the milk into the egg yolks and beat very gradually into the creamed mixture, alternating with flour and remaining sugar until well blended. Whisk the egg whites until stiff but not brittle and fold into the lemon mixture.

Pour the pudding mixture over the raspberries and place the dish in a roasting tin with 2.5 cm (1 inch) of water in the bottom. Cook for 40–45 minutes in a moderately hot preheated oven (190°C, 375°F, Gas Mark 5) until the top is golden brown and set. Serve hot with a jug of single cream, or cold decorated with piped whipped cream and some fresh raspberries.

Portuguese Walnut Pudding

225 g (8 oz) broken walnuts
$\frac{1}{4}$ teaspoon mixed spice
4 eggs, separated
225 g (8 oz) caster sugar
50 g (2 oz) walnut halves
25 g (1 oz) butter
1 tablespoon Kirsch

Grind the broken walnuts or chop finely and mix with the spice. Whisk the egg yolks and sugar together until pale and creamy. Whisk the egg whites until stiff but not brittle and fold into the egg yolk mixture alternately with the ground walnuts.

Turn into a buttered 750 ml (1$\frac{1}{4}$ pint) mould, leaving room for the pudding to rise, and cover with greased foil. Steam for 1$\frac{1}{2}$ hours until set and springy to the touch; or test with a skewer. Allow to shrink slightly before unmoulding on to a serving dish. Meanwhile fry the walnut halves in the butter until slightly crisp, then add the Kirsch.

Serve hot, garnished with the fried walnuts and accompanied by a bowl of Sherry Foam Sauce (p. 359); or cold, decorated with whipped cream in generous swirls and walnuts.

Rhubarb Pudding

100 g (4 oz) self-raising flour
pinch of salt
50 g (2 oz) butter or margarine, cut into pieces
100 g (4 oz) sugar
450 g (1 lb) young rhubarb, trimmed, cleaned and cut into 2.5 cm (1 inch) slices
150 ml ($\frac{1}{4}$ pint) milk

Sift the flour and salt into a mixing bowl. Add the fat and rub into the flour with the fingertips until the mixture resembles fine breadcrumbs. Stir in the sugar and rhubarb and beat in the milk to make a thick batter. Turn into a buttered 1 litre (1$\frac{3}{4}$ pint) baking dish and bake in a fairly hot oven (200°C, 400°F, Gas Mark 6) for 30 to 40 minutes. Serve at once with caster sugar.

Brown Betty

450 g (1 lb) rhubarb
100 g (4 oz) caster sugar
100 g (4 oz) fresh white breadcrumbs
finely grated rind and juice of 1 orange
75 g (3 oz) butter, melted

Wipe the rhubarb and chop into 2.5 cm (1 inch) lengths. Mix together the sugar, breadcrumbs and orange rind. Butter a 1.2 litre (2 pint) ovenproof dish and fill with alternate layers of rhubarb and breadcrumbs; sprinkle each layer with melted butter and orange juice. End with breadcrumbs and butter. Bake in a moderately hot oven (190°C, 375°F, Gas Mark 5) for 45 minutes until crisp and golden. Serve hot with cream or custard.

Variation:
The original recipe uses apples, and plums and gooseberries also make excellent Brown Betties.

Rich Chocolate Pudding

75 g (93 oz) plain chocolate
50 g (2 oz) butter or margarine
150 ml (¼ pint) milk
65 g (2½ oz) caster sugar
¼ teaspoon vanilla essence
2 eggs, separated
125 g (5 oz) white breadcrumbs

Put the chocolate and butter in a bowl and melt over a saucepan of hot water. Remove from heat and stir until smooth. Warm the milk and add it gradually. Stir in the sugar. Add vanilla to the beaten egg yolks and stir into the chocolate. Mix in breadcrumbs. Whisk the egg whites until stiff but not brittle and fold into the mixture. Turn into a well-greased 900 ml (1½ pint) pudding mould. Cover closely with greased foil and steam for 1½-2 hours until well risen and springy to the touch. Allow to shrink before unmoulding. Serve hot with Chocolate Sauce (p. 357) or with cream.

Almond and Apricot Pudding

50 g (2 oz) dried apricots
100 g (4 oz) sponge cake crumbs
50 g (2 oz) ground almonds
75 ml (3 fl oz) single cream or top of the milk
75 ml (3 fl oz) milk
50 g (2 oz) butter or margarine
50 g (2 oz) caster sugar
finely grated rind of 1 lemon
¼ teaspoon almond essence
2 eggs, separated

Cover the apricots with 300 ml (½ pint) of water, bring to simmering point and cook gently until required.

Put the sponge cake crumbs and ground almonds into a bowl, pour over the cream and milk and leave to soak, stirring occasionally. Cream the butter

and sugar with the lemon rind until light and fluffy. Add almond essence to the egg yolks; beat in, alternately with the crumb mixture. Drain, chop and add half the apricots. Whisk the egg whites until stiff but not brittle and fold into the mixture. Turn into a well-greased 900 ml (1½ pint) pudding mould and cover with well-greased kitchen foil. Steam for 1¾-2 hours until well risen. Test with a skewer; it should come out clean. Leave to shrink slightly before unmoulding.

Serve hot with Apricot Sauce (p. 360), made with remaining apricots.

Variation:

Canned pineapple instead of apricots can be used for this featherlight pudding, and if you have sponge finger biscuit trimmings left over from another dessert you can use them instead of cake crumbs.

Steamed Cherry Pudding

175 g (6 oz) fresh red or black cherries
75 g (3 oz) brown or white breadcrumbs
3 tablespoons sugar
finely grated rind of ½ lemon
300 ml (½ pint) single cream or evaporated milk
2 eggs, separated
For the cherry sauce:
100 g (4 oz) fresh cherries
150 ml (¼ pint) water
40 g (1½ oz) caster sugar
juice of ½ lemon
2 teaspoons cornflour
1 tablespoon Cherry Brandy or Kirsch (optional)

Remove stalks and stones from the cherries. Mix with the breadcrumbs, sugar and lemon rind. Heat cream or evaporated milk, bring to the boil and pour over the mixture.

Whisk the egg whites until stiff, but not brittle. Beat the yolks with a fork and stir into the pudding mixture. Fold in the whites and turn into a well-buttered 600 ml (1 pint) bowl or pudding mould. Cover with greased foil then, steam for 1½ hours until well risen and firm to the touch. Meanwhile make the Cherry Sauce. Remove stalks and stones from the cherries and put in a small saucepan with the water, sugar and lemon juice. Cover and simmer for 15 minutes. Mix the cornflour to a thin paste with 2 tablespoons water and stir in 2 tablespoons of the cherry liquid. Blend this mixture back into the saucepan and simmer, stirring well, for 2 minutes. Remove from heat and add the Cherry Brandy or Kirsch if using.

When the pudding is cooked, allow to shrink slightly before unmoulding on to a warm serving plate. Pour on the Cherry Sauce.

Delicate Orange Pudding

100 g (4 oz) glacé cherries
50 g (2 oz) angelica
100 g (4 oz) unsalted butter
100 g (4 oz) caster sugar
grated rind and juice of 1 orange
2 eggs, beaten
75 g (3 oz) self-raising flour
50 g (2 oz) fresh white breadcrumbs
3 tablespoons lemon jelly marmalade
1 large orange, peeled and thinly
  sliced

Roughly chop the glacé cherries and angelica. Soften butter slightly then cream with the sugar until light and fluffy. Add the orange rind. Gradually beat in the eggs. Sift the flour, mix with the breadcrumbs and fold into the creamed mixture. Stir in the orange juice, cherries and angelica to distribute the fruit evenly through the mixture.

Coat the base and sides of a 1 kg (2 lb) loaf tin with the jelly marmalade and cover with overlapping orange slices. Pour the pudding mixture into the tin.

Stand it in a roasting tin, half filled with water, and bake in a preheated fairly hot oven (200°C, 400°F, Gas Mark 6) for 45 minutes.

Turn out on a serving dish and serve hot with custard or lightly whipped double cream.

Baked Apple Dumplings

225 g (8 oz) suet crust (p. 361)
4 medium apples
4 heaped teaspoons brown sugar or
  mincemeat
1 egg white, beaten
4 teaspoons caster sugar

Roll out the suet crust thinly into a square and cut into four equal pieces. Peel and core the apples and put one in the centre of each pastry square. Fill the apple centre with brown sugar or mincemeat. Brush the edge of each pastry square with water, draw the corners up to meet over the centre of each apple and press the edges firmly together. Decorate with pastry leaves. Put on a greased baking tin. Brush with egg white and sprinkle with sugar. Bake in a hot oven (200°C, 400°F, Gas Mark 6) for 30 minutes. Serve hot with Rum Butter.

* Steamed Apple Dumplings

Prepare apples and wrap in suet crust as in the recipe for Baked Apple Dumplings (above). Place each dumpling upside down on a square of greased foil large enough to wrap loosely round it, allowing room for the pastry to rise. Place the dumplings in a steamer over a saucepan of boiling water and cook for 45–60 minutes. Serve hot with Apricot Jam Sauce (p. 359).

Guard's Pudding

175 g (6 oz) fresh breadcrumbs, white
  or brown
75 g (3 oz) caster sugar
2 eggs, beaten
75 g (3 oz) butter, melted
4 tablespoons raspberry jam
¼ teaspoon bicarbonate of soda
1 teaspoon water

Mix the breadcrumbs and sugar well
together. Stir in the eggs, the melted
butter and jam. Dissolve the bicarbonate of soda in the water and stir
thoroughly into the mixture. Turn into
a well-greased 900 ml (1½ pint) pudding
mould. Cover with greased foil and
steam for 2 hours until set. Allow to
shrink before unmoulding. Serve hot
with custard or cream.

Prune Tutti Frutti Pudding

75 g (3 oz) prunes
50 g (2 oz) glacé cherries
50 g (2 oz) dried apricots
25 g (1 oz) angelica
100 g (4 oz) butter
100 g (4 oz) caster sugar
finely grated rind and juice of 1
  lemon
2 eggs
75 g (3 oz) self-raising flour
50 g (2 oz) fresh white breadcrumbs
2 tablespoons apricot jam

Select 3 large prunes and put in a
saucepan with water to cover. Simmer
for 10 minutes, then leave to soak.

Snip the flesh off the stones of the
remaining prunes with scissors. Halve
and set aside 3 large glacé cherries and
chop the remainder. Chop the apricots
and angelica. Prepare a steamer saucepan and well grease a 900 ml (1½ pint)
pudding basin.

Cream the butter and sugar with the
lemon rind until light and fluffy. Whisk

the eggs and beat in a little at a time.
Mix together the flour and breadcrumbs
and fold in lightly. Add the lemon juice
and fold in the chopped prunes,
cherries, apricots and angelica.

Coat the bottom of the bowl with the
apricot jam. Slit the plumped prunes in
half, discard stones and arrange on the
jam with the halved cherries. Carefully
spoon in the pudding mixture.

Cover the bowl with greased foil and
steam for 1½–2 hours. Test with a
skewer, remove from heat and allow
pudding to shrink slightly before unmoulding on to a warm platter. Serve
with Apricot Jam Sauce (p. 359).

Viennese Caramel Pudding

300 ml (½ pint) milk
50 g (2 oz) granulated sugar
50 g (2 oz) diced brown bread without
  crust
50 g (2 oz) sultanas
50 g (2 oz) glacé cherries, quartered
2 egg yolks
75 ml (3 fl oz) single cream
1–2 tablespoons sweet sherry
lemon juice to taste
For the meringue:
2 egg whites
50 g (2 oz) caster sugar
To decorate:
3 glacé cherries, halved
12 small diamonds of angelica
caster sugar

Put the milk to heat slowly. Meanwhile
make the caramel. Spread the granulated sugar over the base of a thick
saucepan, place over gentle heat and
stir carefully until dissolved. Increase
heat and boil briskly *without stirring*,
until rich caramel colour. (If too pale it
will not taste of toffee, if too dark it will
be bitter.) Remove from heat and pour
in about a cupful of milk very gradually,
as it will bubble up fiercely. Return to
heat and stir until caramel and milk are
blended. Stir caramel mixture carefully

into remaining milk.

Mix together the diced bread, sultanas and cherries, pour over the caramel milk and leave for 20 minutes to swell. Stir in the beaten egg yolks, cream and sherry. Sharpen to taste with lemon juice. Pour into a greased ovenproof dish and bake in the centre of a preheated moderate oven (180°C, 350°F, Gas Mark 4) for 30 minutes or until set.

Whisk the egg whites to a stiff snow and fold in the caster sugar. Pile on top of pudding, covering carefully. Ruffle or swirl top, decorate with cherries and angelica and sprinkle with sugar. Return to oven for 20 minutes or until crisp and golden. Serve hot or cold.

Variation:
White bread can be used instead of brown, or, for a sweeter pudding, diced sponge fingers.

Queen of Puddings

75 g (3 oz) fresh white breadcrumbs
25 g (1 oz) granulated sugar
2 teaspoons finely grated lemon rind
25 g (1 oz) butter or margarine
450 ml (¾ pint) milk
2 eggs, separated
2 tablespoons raspberry jam
50 g (2 oz) caster sugar
sugar for dredging
To decorate:
glacé cherries
angelica

Mix together the breadcrumbs and granulated sugar. Add the lemon rind and butter to the milk and heat gently until the butter melts, then pour over the breadcrumbs. Stir well and leave to swell for 30 minutes. Beat the egg yolks and blend into the cooled mixture. Pour into a well-greased 900 ml (1½ pint) ovenproof dish. Bake in a preheated warm oven (160°C, 325°F, Gas Mark 3) for 30 minutes or until firm and set. Warm the jam and spread over the

pudding. Whisk the egg whites until stiff and dry. Sieve and fold in the caster sugar and pile on top of the pudding. Swirl or ruffle the top and dredge with sugar. Decorate with glacé cherries and angelica. Return the pudding to the oven and bake for 30 minutes or until crisp and golden. Serve hot or cold.

Variation:
Vary this old favourite by putting raspberries or blackberries in the bottom of the dish.

Four Fruit Layer Pudding

225 g (8 oz) suet crust (p. 361)
175 g (6 oz) blackberries
175 g (6 oz) caster sugar
225 g (8 oz) apricots, halved and stoned
225 g (8 oz) red or purple plums, halved and stoned
225 g (8 oz) pears, sliced

You can use a selection of any fresh or dried fruit for this pudding, but it looks at its best when the layers of different fruits are of contrasting colours as suggested here.

Grease a 1.2 litre (2 pint) pudding basin and prepare a steamer. Roll out suet crust thinly. Cut out a small circle to fit the bottom of the basin and come 1.5 cm (½ inch) up the side to form a cap. Spread with blackberries and sprinkle with sugar. Cut out a larger circle of pastry and cover fruit. Spread with apricots, cut side uppermost, and sprinkle with sugar. Cut out a larger circle of pastry and spread with plums and sugar. Cut out and cover with another circle of pastry. Spread with sliced pears and sugar and cover with remaining pastry to form a lid. Tie greased foil over basin and steam for 2½–3 hours. Remove from heat, allow to shrink and turn out on to a warm platter. Serve hot with cream or Syrup Sauce (p. 359).

Five-cup Pudding

1 × 200 ml (7 fl oz) teacup self-raising
flour
1 × 200 ml (7 fl oz) teacup currants or
chopped seedless raisins
1 × 200 ml (7 fl oz) teacup soft brown
sugar
1 × 200 ml (7 fl oz) teacup shredded
beef suet
1 × 200 ml (7 fl oz) teacup milk
1 teaspoon ground mixed spice
(optional)

Put all the dry ingredients into a mixing
bowl. Add the milk and stir well to mix.
Pour the mixture into a well-greased 1
litre (1¾ pint) pudding basin leaving a
2.5 cm (1 inch) space at the top. Cover
the top with greased greaseproof paper
or foil, make a pleat in the centre and tie
on with string round the rim.
    Place the basin in a large pan of
gently bubbling water and steam for 3
hours. Remove the basin carefully from
the pan, discard the greaseproof paper
or foil and turn the pudding out on a hot
serving dish. Serve hot with custard.

Bramble and Apple Hat

225 g (8 oz) suet crust (p. 361)
450 g (1 lb) cooking apples
225 g (8 oz) blackberries
2–3 tablespoons brown or white sugar
75 ml (3 fl oz) cold water

Grease a 1.2 litre (2 pint) pudding basin.
Roll out the suet crust into a circle
about 6 mm (¼ inch) thick. Cut out a
quarter and line the basin (see p. 361).
Peel, core and slice the apples and fill
the basin, layering the apples with
blackberries and sugar. Gather the remaining suet crust into a ball and roll it
out into a circle to put on top of the
fruit. Damp the edge all round.
    Trim the lining pastry neatly about
1.5 cm (½ inch) above the lid, fold the

edges over and press on to the lid. Cover
the basin and steam the pudding for 3
hours. Lift out and allow to shrink
slightly. Place a hot serving platter on
top, invert the platter and basin together and unmould carefully. Serve
hot with a bowl of brown sugar and
custard.
Variation:
Fill with any fresh fruit in season or
with dried apricots, peaches or prunes
which have been soaked overnight.

* Pear and Walnut Pudding

Follow the recipe for Bramble and
Apple Hat (above), with these changes:
slice pears and chop walnuts, flavour
with finely grated lemon rind or crushed coriander seeds and brown sugar.

* Plum, Apricot or Greengage Pudding

Follow the recipe for Bramble and
Apple Hat (above), with these changes:
halve and stone plums, apricots or
greengages and layer with granulated
sugar.

* Gooseberry Pudding

Follow the recipe for Bramble and
Apple Hat (above), with these changes:
top and tail gooseberries, layer with
demerara sugar and grated nutmeg.

* Rhubarb Pudding

Follow the recipe for Bramble and
Apple Hat (above), with these changes:
cut rhubarb in 2.5 cm (1 inch) lengths,
flavour with grated orange rind and
juice or chopped stem ginger and sugar.

College Pudding

50 g (2 oz) plain flour
1 teaspoon baking powder
½ teaspoon mixed spice
pinch of salt
50 g (2 oz) shredded suet
25 g (1 oz) white or brown sugar
75 g (3 oz) mixed currants, raisins and
   sultanas
25 g (1 oz) chopped candied peel or
   glacé cherries
50 g (2 oz) fresh breadcrumbs
1 egg, beaten
4–5 tablespoons milk

Prepare a steamer and butter a 900 ml
(1½ pint) pudding basin. Sift the flour,
baking powder, spice and salt into a
mixing bowl and mix in the suet, sugar,
fruit and breadcrumbs. Stir in the egg
and sufficient milk to produce a soft
consistency which drops off the spoon
in 5 seconds.

Turn the mixture into the pudding
basin, which should be two-thirds full.
Cover with greased foil or snap-on lid.
Steam for 2 to 2½ hours. When cooked,
allow the pudding to shrink slightly
then cover the basin with a hot serving
plate, hold it firmly and invert. Carefully lift off the basin. Serve the pudding
hot with Custard (p. 358) or Brandy
butter (p. 353) if liked.

* Spotted Dick or
Currant Duff

Follow the recipe for College Pudding
(above), with this change: use 100 g (4
oz) currants instead of mixed fruit.
Serve with Custard (p. 358) if liked.

* Date or Fig Pudding

Follow the recipe for College Pudding
above), with these changes: use 100 g (4
oz) chopped dates or figs instead of dried
fruit and add the grated rind of ½ lemon.
Delicious served with Orange custard
(p. 358).

* Marmalade Pudding

Follow the recipe for College Pudding
(above), with these changes: use ½ teaspoon bicarbonate of soda instead of
baking powder and stir in 2 tablespoons
marmalade instead of fruit. Serve with
marmalade, heated and thinned with a
little water.

Baked Roly-poly Pudding

225 g (8 oz) suet crust (p. 361)
75–100 g (3–4 oz) warm jam
milk and sugar for glazing (optional)

Roll out the suet crust about 6 mm (¼
inch) thick into a rectangle about
25 × 20 cm (10 × 8 inches). Spread evenly
with warm jam leaving a border about
1.5 cm (½ inch) wide all round. Fold this
border over the jam and brush with
water. Roll up, not too tightly, from one
of the shorter sides. Press the top edge
down, seal it and press the ends
together.

Turn roly-poly upside down on a piece
of greased foil or greaseproof paper
large enough to come halfway up the
sides of the roll. Tie loosely about 5 cm
(2 inches) from each end, leaving room
for the pastry to rise. Cut 4 slits across
pastry top to allow the steam to escape.
Brush lightly with milk and sprinkle
with sugar; alternatively dredge with
sugar after baking. Bake in a hot oven
(200°C, 400°F, Gas Mark 6) for 30–40
minutes until well risen and golden.
Remove paper case and transfer to a
serving dish. Serve hot with cream or
custard.

* Steamed Roly-poly

Follow the recipe for Baked Roly-poly Pudding (above), with these changes: prepare a saucepan of boiling water with steamer on top. Make the roly-poly. Turn it upside down on a sheet of greased foil large enough to wrap round it, leaving room for the pastry to rise. Seal the joins on top and at the ends by pleating or rolling them firmly together. Place in the steamer and cook for 1½–2 hours. When cooked, open foil and roll pudding carefully on to a warm serving dish. Serve hot with custard or Jam Sauce (p. 359).

* Mincemeat and Syrup Roly-poly

Follow the recipe for either Baked or Steamed Roly-poly Pudding, with this change: spread suet crust with mincemeat and trickle over 2–3 tablespoons golden syrup.

Plum Pudding

225 g (8 oz) pitted prunes, soaked overnight in cold water, drained and finely chopped
225 g (8 oz) seedless raisins
225 g (8 oz) sultanas
225 g (8 oz) currants
225 g (8 oz) mixed dried fruit
225 g (8 oz) carrots, peeled and grated
225 g (8oz) shredded beef suet
450 g (1 lb) fresh white breadcrumbs
225 g (8 oz) self-raising flour
225 g (8 oz) sugar
¼ teaspoon salt
½ teaspoon baking powder
½ teaspoon mixed spice
½ teaspoon grated nutmeg
finely grated rind and juice of 1 lemon
3 eggs, beaten

300 ml (½ pint) stout
milk to mix
flour for sealing

This is a very old recipe for a traditional, rich Christmas pudding, and it is one that improves in flavour the longer it is kept. If you like, you can continue the old custom of burying a silver threepenny or sixpenny piece in the pudding before steaming – but wrap it in foil first.

Put the dried fruit, carrots, suet, breadcrumbs, self-raising flour and sugar in a large mixing bowl and stir well to mix. Add the remaining dry ingredients and stir to combine. Stir in the lemon rind and juice, eggs and stout and continue stirring until all the ingredients are thoroughly combined, adding enough milk to make a soft dropping consistency.

Spoon the mixture into greased pudding basins to come within 2.5 cm (1 inch) of each rim, packing the mixture down well with the back of a spoon. Cover the top of each with a circle of greased greaseproof paper. Put a thick layer of flour on top of the greaseproof, pressing it down well with the back of a spoon, then cover with another circle of greaseproof paper. Cover the basins with a pudding cloth, muslin or aluminium foil, leaving room for the puddings to rise during cooking. Tie securely just beneath the rim.

Place the puddings in the top of a steamer or double boiler, or in a large pan of gently bubbling water, and steam for at least six hours, checking and topping up the water level from time to time during cooking.

Remove puddings from the pan and leave until cold. Check that the puddings are tightly sealed – the flour will have become a solid paste – and renew the top piece of greaseproof and the cloth if necessary. Store in a cool dry place. Steam again for 2 to 3 hours before serving. Serve with hot custard or brandy butter (see p. 353).

Makes about 5 × 450 g (1 lb) puddings.

Snowdon Pudding

100 g (4 oz) raisins
25 g (1 oz) glacé cherries, halved
100 g (4 oz) shredded suet
100 g (4 oz) breadcrumbs
25 g (1 oz) ground rice
finely grated rind of 1 lemon
75 g (3 oz) lemon marmalade
2 eggs, beaten
3–4 tablespoons milk

Prepare a steamer and well grease a 1.2 litre (2 pint) pudding mould. Decorate the mould with some of the raisins and the glacé cherries, cut side down. Mix together the rest of the raisins with the dry ingredients. Stir in the marmalade and eggs and add enough milk to make a soft dropping consistency. Spoon carefully into the pudding mould so as not to disarrange the fruit. Cover well with greased foil and steam for 1½–2 hours. Remove from heat and allow to shrink slightly before unmoulding.

Danish Apple Crunch

1 kg (2 lb) Bramley apples
sugar to taste
100 g (4 oz) butter
100 g (4 oz) breadcrumbs
100 g (4 oz) brown sugar
150–300 ml (¼–½ pint) whipping cream
1 bar chocolate flake

Make a purée with the apples, sweeten to taste and cool. Heat the butter in a frying pan, stir in the breadcrumbs and fry lightly. Mix in the brown sugar and continue cooking until the breadcrumbs are crisp, but not hard. Remove the pan from the heat and stir the crumbs until cool. Put alternate layers of apple purée and fried crumbs in a glass bowl, finishing with crumbs. When cold, whip the cream, swirl over and decorate with spikes of chocolate flake. Chill until needed.

Camper's Crumble

2 × 400 g (14 oz) cans apple and
    raspberry pie filling
1 × 225 g (8 oz) packet crumble mix

Put the pie filling in a shallow cake tin and heat until bubbling. Sprinkle over the crumble mix, cover and cook over gentle heat for 10 minutes. Transfer to a very low grill and grill for about 5 minutes until an even golden brown, turning the tin as necessary.

Christmas Crumble

100 g (4 oz) mincemeat
150 ml (¼ pint) cold water
finely grated rind of 1 orange
2 teaspoons cornflour
1 tablespoon rum or brandy
2 teaspoons sugar
For the topping:
100 g (4 oz) butter
50 g (2 oz) demerara sugar
100 g (4 oz) quick cook oats
To decorate:
150 ml (¼ pint) double cream
25 g (1 oz) chopped walnuts

Place the mincemeat with the cold water and orange in a saucepan. Bring to the boil, reduce the heat and simmer for 5 minutes. Moisten the cornflour with 1 tablespoon of water and stir it into the mincemeat, then add the rum or brandy and the sugar. Bring to the boil, stirring constantly. Cook for 1 minute then allow to become quite cold.

To make the topping, melt the butter in a saucepan and stir in the demerara sugar and oats until well coated. Place half the oat mixture in the bottom of a trifle dish, cover with the mincemeat sauce and top with the remaining oat mixture. Whip the cream until just holding its shape then spread lightly over the centre of the crumble and sprinkle with the chopped walnuts.

Apple Charlotte with Brown Breadcrumbs

450 g (1 lb) cooking apples, peeled
　cored and sliced
2 tablespoons water
100 g (4 oz) soft brown sugar
100 g (4 oz) fresh brown breadcrumbs
2 tablespoons demerara sugar
½ teaspoon ground cinnamon
2 tablespoons shredded beef suet

Put the sliced apples into a saucepan with the water and simmer for 10 to 15 minutes until tender. Sweeten.

Mix breadcrumbs, demerara sugar and cinnamon.

Place half the sweetened apple in a greased pie dish. Cover with half the crumb mixture, then the remaining apple and finally top with the remaining crumb mixture. Sprinkle the surface with the shredded suet.

Cover the dish with greased grease-proof paper or foil and bake in a moderate oven (180°C, 350°F, Gas Mark 4) for 30 to 40 minutes. Serve very hot with custard or cream.

Mandarin Charlotte Russe

1 × 312 g (11 oz) can mandarin oranges
1 × 135 g (4¾ oz) packet lemon jelly
15 g (½ oz) angelica
18 Boudoir biscuits
300 ml (½ pint) whipping cream
1–2 tablespoons Orange Curaçao or
　Cointreau (optional)

Rinse a 600 ml (1 pint) Charlotte mould with cold water. Drain the fruit. Dissolve the jelly thoroughly in 300 ml (½ pint) boiling water and add the fruit syrup making the liquid up to 450 ml (17 fl oz) with water if necessary.

Pour a thin layer of liquid jelly into the bottom of the mould and put in refrigerator to set.

Cut off one rounded end of the Boudoir biscuits so they are 1.5 cm (½ inch) shorter than the mould.

When the first layer of jelly is set, arrange some of the mandarin sections on it in an attractive pattern with angelica diamonds, dipping each piece in liquid jelly before you put it in place. Refrigerate until set. When the pattern is firm cover with another layer of jelly and refrigerate. Meanwhile whip the cream until fairly stiff and fold in the liqueur if using.

When the jelly in the mould is firm dip the sugared side of the biscuits one at a time in liquid jelly and stand them closely together all round the sides of the mould, sugar side out. Fill the centre with alternate layers of cream and mandarin sections, ending with cream.

Slowly spoon remaining jelly down sides of mould between the biscuits, which will gradually absorb it. When jelly shows at the rim of the mould, chill Charlotte until required. Unmould and decorate with the remaining cream and extra fruit if desired.

Crispy Pear Charlotte

450 g (1 lb) pears
5 tablespoons brown sugar
4 tablespoons apricot jam
6 slices white bread
100 g (4 oz) butter, melted

Peel, core and slice the pears. Put half in a well-buttered 1.2 litre (2 pint) oven-proof dish. Sprinkle with 2 tablespoons sugar and spread with 2 tablespoons jam. Cover with remaining pears, 2 tablespoons sugar and jam.

Remove crusts from the bread and cut each slice into 4 triangles. Dip into melted butter and arrange on top of the pears, covering them completely. Sprinkle with remaining sugar. Bake in moderately hot oven (190°C, 375°F, Gas Mark 5) for 30–40 minutes until crisp and golden. Serve hot with cream.

Caramel Plum Charlotte

2 × 450 g (1 lb) cans plums in syrup
1 teaspoon ground cinnamon
finely grated rind of 1 orange
finely grated rind of 1 lemon
5–6 thick slices of brown bread, crusts
    removed
butter for spreading
6 tablespoons soft brown sugar

Put 1 can of plums in a large shallow pan. Drain off the juice from the remaining can, then add to the plums in the pan. Sprinkle with the cinnamon and orange and lemon rinds.

Meanwhile, spread the bread thickly with butter and cut each slice in half. Arrange on top of the plums butter side up, to cover them completely, then sprinkle over the sugar. Put under a low to moderate grill for about 10 minutes until the sugar has caramelized, turning the pan occasionally to ensure even browning. Remove from the grill and leave to cool for 5 minutes. Serve lukewarm with fresh cream or ice cream.

Variations:
Use canned gooseberries or rhubarb instead of the plums. Or use 1 kg (2 lb) fresh fruit and poach it with sugar first.

Summer Pudding

900 g (2 lb) mixed soft fruit as
    available: raspberries, blackberries,
    red or blackcurrants and cherries
100–175 g (4–6 oz) caster sugar
about ½ a sandwich loaf

Pick over the fruit, removing stalks and stones. This should leave 700 g (1½ lb) of prepared fruit. Put the fruit and sugar in a thick pan over very gentle heat and stir gently occasionally until fruit is tender and juice has run, about 15–20 minutes. Cool and sweeten to taste.

Slice the bread fairly thinly – about 6 mm (¼ inch) – and remove crusts. Line the bottom of a soufflé dish or 900 ml (1½ pint) pudding basin, cutting the bread to fit neatly together. Cut more slices in fingers to fit closely round the dish or basin, leaving no gaps. Half fill the dish with fruit, cover with sliced bread, add remaining fruit and cover closely with more bread. Spoon over remaining juice to soak the bread and just fill the dish. Reserve any surplus juice. Fit a small plate into the top of the dish, put on a 900 g (2 lb) weight and chill overnight.

To unmould, place serving dish on top of basin and invert both together quickly. Carefully lift off the basin. (Use a serving dish which will hold the juice when it runs out.) If there are any little white patches of bread, spoon over the reserved juice. Serve with cream.

Bread and Butter Pudding

6 slices white bread
50–75 g (2–3 oz) butter
50 g (2 oz) sultanas, currants or mixed
    dried fruit
40–50 g (1½–2 oz) caster sugar
2 large or 3 small eggs
600 ml (1 pint) milk

Remove crusts from bread and spread thickly with butter. Cut each slice into four, either squares or triangles. Butter a 1.2 litre (2 pint) ovenproof dish, preferably rectangular. Arrange buttered bread over the bottom of the dish and sprinkle with fruit and sugar. Put in another layer of bread, the rest of the fruit and half the remaining sugar. Cover with remaining bread, butter side uppermost and sprinkle on the rest of the sugar. Beat the eggs well into the milk and pour over the pudding. Leave to stand for 30 minutes or so to allow the bread to absorb the milk. Bake in a warm oven (170°C, 325°F, Gas Mark 3) for 45–60 minutes until set and the top is crisp and golden. Serve hot.

Raspberry Charlotte

1 × 135 g (4¾ oz) packet raspberry jelly
450 g (1 lb) fresh or frozen
    raspberries, thawed
24 sponge fingers
100 g (4 oz) caster sugar
4 teaspoons powdered gelatine
2 tablespoons lemon juice
2 tablespoons water
450 ml (¾ pint) fresh double cream
3 egg whites

Make up the jelly with 300 ml (½ pint)
water. Leave until beginning to set,
then spoon half into a 20 cm (8 inch)
charlotte mould. Arrange some raspberries on top of the jelly and sprinkle
with a little sugar. Brush sides of
sponge fingers with some jelly, then line
the mould with the fingers by standing
them upright in the jelly closely together. Spoon any remaining jelly into
the mould. Chill until set. Meanwhile,
put the remaining raspberries and
sugar in a saucepan and heat gently for
5 minutes or until soft.

Leave to cool, purée in a blender, then
sieve.

Sprinkle the gelatine over lemon
juice and water in a bowl and leave to
stand until spongy. Put the bowl over a
pan of hot water and stir over low heat
until dissolved. Leave to cool slightly,
then stir into the raspberry purée.
Leave until just beginning to thicken.
Whip cream until thick, then fold into
the purée, reserving some for decoration. Beat egg whites until stiff and
fold these in. When jelly has set in
mould spoon in the raspberry cream.
Trim ends of sponge fingers, cover with
foil or a plate and chill in refrigerator
for several hours or overnight until
ready to serve.

If the charlotte is difficult to unmould, dip the base of the mould very
quickly in a bowl of hot water. Serve
with cream.

Three Raspberry charlottes will serve
10–12

Swiss Raspberry Charlotte

1 × 425 g (15 oz) can raspberries
1 tablespoon cornflour
1 egg yolk, beaten
75 ml (3 fl oz) single cream
1–2 tablespoons lemon juice
sugar to taste
18 Boudoir biscuits
For the Swiss meringue:
1–2 egg whites
2 tablespoons fruit syrup
125 g (4 oz) icing sugar, sieved

Strain the juice off the fruit, measure
and add water to make up to 225 ml (8 fl
oz). Put cornflour in a small saucepan,
blend with a little juice into a smooth
paste and then stir in remaining juice.
Heat, stirring steadily with a wooden
spoon, and simmer for 3–5 minutes until
thickened and clear. Remove from heat.
Mix the egg yolk and cream together
and stir gradually into the sauce. Add
lemon juice and sugar to taste.

Cut one rounded end from each
Boudoir biscuit. Pour a thin layer of
raspberry cream in the bottom of a 15
cm (6 inch) soufflé dish and stand the
biscuits round the dish. Fill with layers
of fruit and cream. Cover the cream
with a layer of drained fruit, then another layer of cream, a layer of fruit and
cover with the remaining cream.

To make the Swiss Meringue put one
egg white, fruit syrup and icing sugar
(or 2 egg whites and icing sugar) in a
bowl over a saucepan of simmering
water. Whisk together with a rotary
whisk until thick and making soft
peaks. Remove from heat and whisk
until cool. Flavour to taste with lemon,
vanilla or fruit juice.

Put the meringue mixture into a forcing bag and pipe on to the Charlotte,
covering the filling and rising pyramid
style in the centre. Bake in a moderate
oven (150°C, 300°F, Gas Mark 2) for 20
minutes or until the meringue is delicately coloured. Serve cold with
whipped cream.

Cherry Clafoutis

450 g (1 lb) ripe cherries
50 g (2 oz) plain flour
pinch of salt
50 g (2 oz) caster sugar
2 eggs, beaten
300 ml ($\frac{1}{2}$ pint) milk
40 g ($1\frac{1}{2}$ oz) butter
1 tablespoon cherry brandy or rum
    (optional)

Remove the stalks and stones from the cherries – a cherry stoner is best for this. Sift the flour and salt into a mixing bowl. Whisk in 2 tablespoons of the caster sugar, then gradually blend in beaten eggs. Heat the milk until luke-warm and pour it slowly into the batter whisking all the time.

Melt the butter and brush some of it over a shallow baking dish. Whisk the remaining butter into the batter. Add the cherry brandy or rum, if used. Spread the cherries over the base of the dish and pour the batter over them. Bake in the centre of a preheated oven (220°C, 425°F, Gas Mark 7) for 30 to 35 minutes or until golden brown and set. Sprinkle with the remaining sugar and serve hot.

Fruity Griddle Cakes

2 eggs, separated
125 g (4 oz) plain flour
2 teaspoons baking powder
2 tablespoons caster sugar
150 ml ($\frac{1}{4}$ pint) milk
1 tablespoon melted butter
2 apples or 2 bananas
warmed honey, golden syrup or lemon
    juice, to serve

You can use a thick frying pan if you have no griddle. Whisk the egg whites until stiff. Sieve the flour, baking powder and 1 tablespoon sugar into a bowl. Beat the egg yolks lightly and mix in with the milk and melted butter. Beat this mixture into the dry ingredients. Peel and coarsely grate the apples, discarding the core; or peel and chop bananas. Fold the fruit into the batter and then the whisked egg whites. Heat the griddle or frying pan and grease lightly. It is hot enough when a drop of water spits and splutters. Drop the batter on the hot griddle in tablespoons, allowing room for spreading. In a minute or two, when puffed and bubbly, flip over and brown the other side. Sprinkle with remaining sugar and serve with warmed honey, golden syrup or fresh lemon juice.

Friar's Omelette

3 large Bramley apples, about 700 g
    ($1\frac{1}{2}$ lb)
finely grated rind of 1 lemon
pinch of ground cloves or cinnamon
50–75 g (2–3 oz) granulated sugar
3 egg yolks, beaten
100 g (4 oz) white or brown
    breadcrumbs
75 g (3 oz) butter or margarine

Wipe and core the apples. Pour sufficient water into a roasting tin to cover the base thinly and put in the apples. Lay a sheet of well-buttered foil on top and bake in a moderately hot oven 190°C, 375°F, Gas Mark 5) for 30 minutes or until tender; test with a skewer. Remove from oven and scrape out the pulp into a basin. Add the lemon rind, spice and sugar to taste. Beat in the egg yolks.

Well butter a 900 ml ($1\frac{1}{2}$ pint) pie dish or shallow casserole and spread a thick layer of breadcrumbs in the bottom. Pour over the apple mixture and cover with remaining crumbs. Dot all over with little knobs of butter or melt the butter and pour it over. Return to oven and bake for 30 minutes or until crisp and golden on top. Serve hot with cream or custard.

Poor Knights of Windsor

8 slices French bread, cut about 6 mm
   ($\frac{1}{4}$ inch) thick
2 whole eggs or 4 yolks
50 ml (2 fl oz) sweet sherry
100 ml (4 fl oz) milk
2 teaspoons caster sugar
butter or vegetable oil for frying
For the cinnamon sugar:
2 tablespoons caster sugar
2 teaspoons ground cinnamon

Remove the crusts from the bread and
lay in a shallow dish. Beat together the
eggs, sherry, milk and sugar. Clarify the
butter by heating it in a saucepan until
it stops bubbling. Remove from heat,
allow to settle and strain it slowly
through a fine sieve into the frying pan,
leaving behind the sediment. This will
stop the butter from browning too
quickly. Alternatively, use vegetable
oil, which does not need clarifying.

Reheat the fat until a piece of dry
bread crisps quickly. Pour egg mixture
over the bread, leave a moment and
turn over. Lift each slice out on a fish
slice, allow surplus liquid to drip back
into the dish, and slide bread into hot
fat. Fry until golden underneath, turn
and fry other side. Drain on soft paper.

Mix together the sugar and cinnamon, sprinkle thickly on each fritter
and serve at once. Children may like
warm jam or honey instead.

* Fried Jam Sandwiches

Convert left over jam sandwiches into a
treat for the next day by cutting off the
crusts, dipping them in egg and milk
and frying them like Poor Knights of
Windsor (above).

Prune and Apricot Snowballs

8 large prunes (soaked overnight)
8 dried apricots (soaked overnight)
40 g ($1\frac{1}{2}$ oz) butter or margarine
150 ml ($\frac{1}{4}$ pint) water
75 g (3 oz) plain flour, sieved
2 eggs, beaten
deep fat for frying
crystallised ginger; or glacé cherries;
   or blanched almonds
50–75 g (2–3 oz) icing sugar, sieved

A wineglass of sherry added to the
soaking water for the fruit will improve
the flavour.

Remove the prunes and apricots from
the soaking liquid, slit down one side,
remove prune stones and leave fruit to
drain.

Dissolve the butter in the water over
a gentle heat, then bring to the boil
and tip in the flour. Beat well with a
wooden spoon over moderate heat until
the dough forms a smooth ball. Add the
beaten egg *very* gradually, beating well
between each addition.

Stuff the drained fruit with a knob of
ginger, a glacé cherry or a blanched
almond and press firmly together. Heat
fat to 190°C/375°F. You can test it by
dropping in a teaspoon of dough, which
should rise at once to the surface and
start to crisp. Take up tablespoons of
dough and drop them carefully into
the hot fat. Use a teaspoon to push the
dough off the tablespoon. Fry until
puffed up, golden and crisp.

As each one is ready, remove from the
fat with a slotted spoon, slit and stuff
hollow centre with the stuffed fruit.
Roll in the icing sugar and keep warm.
Serve at once.

Jersey Jumbles

125 g (4 oz) plain flour
pinch of salt
1 teaspoon baking powder
pinch of ground ginger
pinch of ground nutmeg
25 g (1 oz) butter or margarine
25 g (1 oz) caster sugar
1 egg, beaten
deep fat for frying
caster sugar for dredging
honey or syrup

Sieve the flour, salt, baking powder and spices into a basin. Rub in the fat with the finger tips. Mix in the sugar. Stir in the egg, adding a little water if necessary; the dough should be fairly stiff. Roll out on a floured board until about 1.5 cm ($\frac{1}{2}$ inch) thick. Cut into 7 cm (3 inch) rounds. With a smaller cutter, remove the centres to leave rings. Work up remaining dough, roll out and cut into strips 7 × 2.5 cm (3 × 1 inch). Shape each one into twists.

Heat the fat to 190°C/375°F; test by dropping in a piece of dough which should rise at once and start to swell. Drain the jumbles on soft paper and dredge with sugar. Serve with warmed honey or syrup.

Greek Almond Fritters

50 g (2 oz) ground almonds
25 g (1 oz) caster sugar
$\frac{1}{4}$ teaspoon ground cinnamon
2–3 teaspoons lemon juice
100 g (4 oz) plain shortcrust pastry
    (p. 363)
deep fat for frying
4 tablespoons honey
2 tablespoons orange juice

Mix the almonds, sugar and cinnamon. Add the lemon juice and knead well together. Roll out the pastry very thinly and cut into 8 cm (3 inch) squares. Put a small piece of filling in the centre of each square, damp the edges and fold over into triangles; press edges firmly together.

Heat the fat to 190°C, 375°F (a piece of dough dropped in should rise and crisp quickly). Fry the fritters a few at a time until golden all over. Drain on soft paper and keep warm while frying the next batch.

Heat the honey and orange juice together and dip in each fritter, coating it well. Serve hot as soon as possible. For parties you can make and fry the fritters in advance. Reheat them in a moderately hot oven (190°C, 375°F, Gas Mark 5) and dip them into the orange honey syrup just before serving.

Variation:
Vary the filling by using ground walnuts instead of almonds, or slit and seeded grapes.

Peach Condé

$\frac{1}{2}$ teaspoon ground cinnamon
1 × 425 g (15 oz) can creamed rice
1 × 400 g (14 oz) can peach halves,
    drained
4 glacé cherries, halved, to finish

Stir the cinnamon into the rice. Chop the peaches finely, reserving 4 halves for decoration. Layer the rice and peaches in 4 individual glasses, starting and ending with a layer of rice. Top with the reserved peach halves and decorate with halved glacé cherries. Chill before serving.

Variation:
You can vary the fruit, according to taste and availability.

Fruit Fritters

300 ml ($\frac{1}{2}$ pint) basic coating batter,
    without egg (p. 364)
2 bananas
2 apples, cooking or dessert
juice of 1 lemon
4 pineapple slices, fresh or canned
4 apricots or plums
1 egg white
1–2 teaspoons cinnamon
caster sugar
deep fat for frying

Peel the bananas and cut into quarters.
Peel the apples, cut into thick rings and
core with a corer. Sprinkle the bananas
and apples with lemon juice to prevent
them browning. Cut a fresh, peeled
pineapple into slices and remove the
core. Drain the canned pineapple slices
and dry on absorbent kitchen paper.
Halve and stone the apricots or plums.
    Prepare the deep fat. Put in the frying
basket and heat the fat to 190°C/375°F.
Just before frying, whisk the egg white
until stiff but not brittle and, with
concave spatula or large cook's spoon,
fold it into the batter quickly and evenly.
    Dip the prepared fruit into the batter,
using a 2-pronged cook's fork. The
prongs can be inserted into the hole in
the centre of the apple and pineapple
rings. Draw the cooked fruit across the
edge of the bowl so excess batter drops
back into it. Lower the fruit into the fat
and fry until the batter is crisp and
golden. Do not overcrowd the pan.
    Use a large slotted spoon to turn the
fritters.
    Lift the frying basket out of the pan
and allow the fat to drain back into the
pan. Place the fritters on absorbent
kitchen paper to drain. Mix the cinnamon with 2 to 3 tablespoons caster
sugar and sprinkle it over the fritters.
Keep the fritters warm while reheating
the oil and frying the next batch. Serve
immediately, arranged on a paper doily
in a warm serving dish and hand extra
caster sugar separately.

Cold Rice Crème

75 g (3 oz) round-grain rice
600 ml (1 pint) milk
25 g (1 oz) sugar
1 egg, separated
15 g ($\frac{1}{2}$ oz) butter
1 packet orange jelly
few glacé cherries, halved, to
    decorate

Put the rice, milk and sugar in a
saucepan. Bring to the boil, stir well,
reduce the heat, cover and simmer for 30
minutes, stirring occasionally. Lightly
beat the egg yolk, stir into the rice
mixture with the butter, then remove
from the heat. Dissolve the jelly in 150
ml ($\frac{1}{4}$ pint) boiling water and allow to
cool. Stir into the rice mixture. Whisk
the egg white until stiff and fold into the
rice and jelly mixture, then pour into an
oiled ring mould. Chill well until set.
Turn out on a serving dish and decorate
with halved glacé cherries.

Lockshen Pudding

225 g (8 oz) egg vermicelli
2 teaspoons salt
50 g (2 oz) butter
50 g (2 oz) sultanas
50 g (2 oz) candied peel, chopped
50 g (2 oz) blanched almonds, cut into
    slivers
$\frac{1}{4}$ teaspoon ground cinnamon
50 g (2 oz) caster sugar
2 eggs, beaten

Drop vermicelli into 2 litres ($3\frac{1}{2}$ pints)
boiling water with 2 teaspoons salt and
cook uncovered for about 5 minutes or
until just tender, stirring occasionally.
Pour the vermicelli into a colander and
drain well. Cut the butter into small
pieces. Return the drained vermicelli to
the pan. Add the butter and stir gently
until melted. Mix in the sultanas, candied peel, half the almonds and the

cinnamon blended with the sugar. Add the beaten eggs and mix well.

Pour into a buttered ovenproof dish and scatter over the remaining almonds. Bake in a preheated moderate oven (180°C, 350°F, Gas Mark 4) for 30 minutes or until set and crisp on top. Serve hot with cream.

Sago Cream

600 ml (1 pint) milk
40 g (1½ oz) small sago
¼ teaspoon vanilla essence
50 g (2 oz) granulated sugar
75 ml (3 fl oz) whipping cream
1 egg white
½ teaspoon grated nutmeg

Heat the milk in a saucepan, sprinkle on the sago and cook over gentle heat, stirring frequently, for about 20 minutes until sago is soft. Add vanilla, sweeten to taste with sugar and pour into a bowl to cool.

Whip the cream until thickened, then the egg white until stiff but not brittle. Fold them together lightly and then into the sago. Turn out into a pudding dish or 4 individual bowls or glasses. Sprinkle with nutmeg. Serve cold with Raspberry Jam Sauce (p. 359).

Variations:
This pudding can also be made with semolina, seed or flaked tapioca. If using whole rice, cook 10 minutes longer, about 30 minutes in all.

Spiced Semolina

600 ml (1 pint) milk
40 g (1½ oz) semolina
90 g (3½ oz) caster sugar
2 teaspoons mixed spice
finely grated rind of ½ lemon
50 g (2 oz) sultanas
2 eggs, separated

Heat the milk in a saucepan and sprinkle on the semolina. Bring to the boil, stirring constantly, and cook for a few minutes until it resembles the consistency of porridge.

Remove the pan from the heat, stir in 2 tablespoons of sugar, the spice, lemon rind and sultanas. Beat the egg yolks with a fork and stir into them 2 tablespoons of the cooked semolina. Blend this mixture into the pudding and pour into a greased ovenproof dish.

Whisk the egg whites to a stiff snow and fold in the remaining sugar, reserving a tablespoonful for sprinkling on top. Pile the meringue on the pudding, covering it completely. Swirl or ruffle the top and sprinkle with sugar. Bake on the second shelf of a preheated moderately hot oven (190°C, 375°F, Gas Mark 5) for 20 minutes until crisp and golden. Serve hot.

Sweet Indian Rice

3 tablespoons pudding rice
2 tablespoons seedless raisins
2 tablespoons flaked blanched almonds
2 tablespoons honey
2 tablespoons sugar, or to taste
600 ml (1 pint) milk
½ teaspoon ground mixed spice or cinnamon
1 knob of butter

Preheat the oven at high temperature for 5 minutes. Put all the ingredients in an ovenproof dish, then bake in the centre of the oven for 30 minutes. Lower the temperature to medium, transfer the dish to the floor of the oven and continue cooking for a further 30 minutes or until the rice is tender.

Hot Chocolate Soufflé

100 g (4 oz) plain chocolate
4 tablespoons black coffee
40 g (1½ oz) butter
40 g (1½ oz) plain flour
225 ml (8 fl oz) milk
50 g (2 oz) caster sugar
¼ teaspoon vanilla essence
3 egg yolks
4 egg whites
icing sugar to glaze
To serve:
150 ml (¼ pint) single cream
2–3 tablespoons rum or Tia Maria

Chocolate is a rich, rather heavy ingredient and it is essential to use an extra egg white in this soufflé to get a really light, fluffy texture.

Prepare a 15 cm (6 inch) soufflé dish and preheat the oven (190°C, 375°F, Gas Mark 5). Break up chocolate and put in a bowl with the black coffee over a saucepan of hot water to melt.

Melt butter in a small saucepan, remove from heat and blend in flour. Gradually add milk, bring to the boil and simmer, stirring, for 3 minutes. Stir melted chocolate until smooth and blend into the sauce. Stir in sugar until dissolved and the vanilla. Remove from heat, cool slightly and gradually beat in egg yolks.

Whisk the egg whites until stiff but not brittle, in a large bowl. Pour over the chocolate mixture, about a third at a time, and fold it in quickly and lightly.

Pour into prepared soufflé dish. With a teaspoon dig a little trench, about 1.5 cm (½ inch) deep, about 2.5 cm (1 inch) from the rim of the dish all round. This will give an impressive 'crown' to the soufflé when it rises.

When the soufflé has baked for 25 minutes, draw the oven shelf forward, dredge with icing sugar and return to the oven for 5 minutes to caramelise. Serve immediately with single cream flavoured with rum or Tia Maria. The liqueur can be added to the soufflé mixture, but as it is very volatile and therefore evaporates in hot mixtures it will have more effect in the cream.

To prepare a soufflé dish
Choose the right size so the soufflé can rise well above the dish. For a 2-egg soufflé, use a 13 cm (5 inch) dish; for a 3-egg soufflé a 15 cm (6 inch) dish and for a 4-egg soufflé an 18 cm (7 inch) dish. Cut a band of double greaseproof paper long enough to overlap by 5 cm (2 inches) round the dish and wide enough to stand 8 cm (3 inches) above it. Grease the inside of the dish and the top half of paper band. Wrap it round the outside of the dish with the fold at the base and secure with string.

To prepare the oven for a soufflé
Move top shelf to centre of oven and preheat to required temperature (190°C, 375°F, Gas Mark 5). If the temperature is too low the soufflé texture will be dry like sponge cake. It should be well risen, the top golden and firm to the touch but the centre still soft and creamy.

Points to watch
1. The basis of a hot soufflé is a butter and flour roux made into a thick sauce with milk, coffee, fruit juice or purée, into which the egg yolks are beaten. Cool slightly before adding yolks or they will curdle.
2. Do not try to fold the whisked egg whites into the sauce in a small saucepan. Pour the sauce over the whisked egg whites in a large bowl, about a third at a time; fold and cut it in lightly and quickly.
3. Do not remove paper collar until serving as a cold draught can collapse the soufflé in minutes.

Steamed Apricot Soufflé

300 ml (½ pint) apricot purée
40 g (1½ oz) butter
40 g (1½ oz) plain flour
sugar to taste
3 egg yolks, beaten
1 tablespoon lemon juice
3–4 egg whites
2 tablespoons flaked almonds
Apricot sauce (p 360)

Stewed fresh, dried or canned fruit can be used for this recipe. Strain and purée the fruit, measure and make up to 300 ml (½ pint) with the liquid. Use the surplus liquid for the sauce. The amount of sugar to use in the soufflé mixture will depend on the original sweetness of the purée. Greengages, plums, raspberries, loganberries or blackberries can replace the apricots.

Prepare a 15 cm (6 inch) soufflé dish and the oven (190°C, 375°F, Gas Mark 5). Melt butter in a small saucepan, remove from heat and blend in flour. Stir in the apricot purée, bring to the simmer and cook, stirring for 3–5 minutes. Sweeten to taste. Cool slightly and gradually beat in egg yolks. Add lemon juice. Whisk egg whites into a stiff but not dry snow and fold into mixture. Pour into prepared soufflé dish and stand it in a roasting tin with sufficient cold water to come halfway up. Bake for 1 hour or until soufflé is set and springy to the touch.

Meanwhile toast flaked almonds under the grill and make the sauce. When the soufflé is ready, brush the top with a little of the sauce and sprinkle on the almonds. Serve immediately, with the sauce separately.

Coffee Praline Soufflé

50 g (2 oz) caster sugar
50 g (2 oz) unblanched almonds
For the soufflé:
3 eggs, separated
75 g (3 oz) caster sugar
2 tablespoons instant coffee granules
175 ml (6 fl oz) boiling water
12 g (½ oz) (1 envelope) powdered gelatine
3 tablespoons cold water
300 ml (½ pint) double cream
2 tablespoons Tia Maria (optional)

Prepare a 15 cm (6 inch) soufflé dish (see p. 240). First make the praline so that it has time to cool. Put the sugar and almonds into a small thick saucepan over gentle heat. When the sugar is dissolved, stir carefully to coat the almonds and continue cooking until rich golden brown and smelling of toffee. Pour on to an oiled baking tin, spreading it out. When cold and brittle, remove and chop small.

Mix the egg yolks and sugar in a large bowl. Dissolve the coffee in the boiling water and add gradually. Whisk over a saucepan of boiling water until thick and foamy. Remove from heat and continue whisking until cold. Soak the gelatine in the cold water, dissolve over gentle heat and stir into the soufflé mixture. Place in a basin of cold water with ice and stir gently from time to time until beginning to set.

Meanwhile whisk egg whites until stiff but not dry. Whip cream into soft peaks and fold about two-thirds into the coffee mixture. Fold in egg whites and half the praline. Mix in the Tia Maria if using. Turn into the soufflé dish, smooth top and chill. When set, peel off paper collar with the help of a knife dipped in hot water. Coat the sides of the soufflé with some of the remaining praline. Whip remaining cream stiff enough to pipe and decorate the top of the soufflé. Finally garnish with the rest of the praline.

Fresh Orange and Lemon Soufflé

3 eggs separated
175 g (6 oz) caster sugar
100 ml (4 fl oz) orange juice
50 ml (2 fl oz) lemon juice
12 g ($\frac{1}{2}$ oz) (1 envelope) powdered gelatine
300 ml ($\frac{1}{2}$ pint) whipping cream; or 150 ml ($\frac{1}{4}$ pint) evaporated milk, with 1 tablespoon lemon juice
2 tablespoons Orange Curaçao, Cointreau or Grand Marnier (optional)
To decorate:
crystallised orange and lemon slices
pistachio nuts or angelica
double cream (optional)

Prepare a 15 cm (6 inch) soufflé dish (see p. 240). Whisk the egg yolks, sugar and fruit juice in a large bowl over a saucepan of boiling water (take care the water does not touch the bowl), until the mixture is thick and foamy and falls from the whisk in ribbons which hold their shape for a few seconds before sinking back into the mixture. Remove from heat. Dissolve the gelatine in a cup with 3–4 tablespoons of the boiling water from the pan. When thoroughly dissolved, whisk into the fruit mixture. Set aside to chill and thicken. Whisk the egg whites until stiff but not brittle. Whip the cream to a soft peak. (If using evaporated milk, whisk it with a tablespoon of lemon juice until it doubles in bulk.) When the fruit mixture has thickened and is beginning to set, fold in the cream and then the egg whites. Fold in the liqueur last. Turn the mixture into the soufflé dish, smooth the top and refrigerate until set. Peel off the paper collar with the help of a knife dipped in hot water. Cut the orange and lemon slices into small wedges, halve or chop the pistachio nuts (or angelica) and decorate to taste, with whipped cream if using. Stand the soufflé dish on a dessert plate to serve.

* Raspberry, Loganberry or Apricot Soufflé

Follow the recipe for Orange and Lemon Soufflé (above), with these changes: use a purée of fresh, frozen or canned fruit instead of the juice. If using canned fruit, strain off the juice, then purée the fruit, measure and make up to 175 ml (6 fl oz) with juice. This gives you a good thick purée.

Sharpen the soufflé mixture with lemon juice to taste just before folding in the egg whites. If adding liqueurs Kirsch is a good choice with Raspberry and Loganberry Soufflé; apricot brandy with Apricot.

* Fresh Tangerine Soufflé

Follow the recipe for Orange and Lemon Soufflé (above), with these changes: use tangerine instead of orange juice. Kirsch or the orange based liqueurs are suitable for flavouring. Decorate with tangerine segments, or the rind first blanched in boiling water and then cut into an attractive design.

* Fresh Grapefruit Soufflé

Follow the recipe for Orange and Lemon Soufflé (above), with these changes: use 100 ml (4 fl oz) grapefruit juice and 50 ml (2 fl oz) orange juice instead of lemon.

Sweet Soufflé Omelette

2 eggs, separated
2 teaspoons water
15 g ($\frac{1}{2}$ oz) butter
2 tablespoons whole fruit jam, heated
caster sugar

Light the grill or preheat the oven to 220°C, 425°F, Gas Mark 7. Whisk the egg whites until soft peaks are formed. Whisk the egg yolks with the water and fold into the whites.

Heat the butter, pour in the eggs and level the top. Allow the bottom to set and turn golden without stirring. Lift the edge with a palette knife to check the colour.

Put the pan under the grill or in the top of the oven for 1–2 minutes until well risen and setting. Spoon the hot jam down the centre.

Fold the omelette in half over the filling and slide it onto a warm plate. Dust with caster sugar and serve immediately.

Variations:
Use fresh or canned fruit instead of jam, well sugared or flavoured with liqueur. Alternatively, the finished omelette can be flamed in rum. Use 1 tablespoon rum, warm it, set light to it with a match and pour flaming over the omelette. Serve at once.

Lemon Pancakes (Crêpes)

300 ml (½ pint) basic batter mixture (p. 363)
caster sugar for dredging
cooking oil or melted lard
juice of 1 lemon

300 ml (½ pint) of batter mixture will make approx 10–12 pancakes. Use a thick pan reserved for omelettes and pancakes as it should not be washed but wiped clean with kitchen paper or a damp cloth.

Whisk the pancake batter with a rotary beater and pour it into a jug. Place a sheet of greaseproof paper on a working surface beside the stove and dredge the paper with caster sugar. Heat a small thick frying pan about 18–20 cm (7–8 inches) in diameter and brush it lightly with cooking oil or fat;

too much fat will mix with the batter and make it heavy. When the fat is hot, lift the pan off the burner and pour in just enough batter to cover thinly the base. Twist and tilt the pan so the batter runs evenly over the base. If you have any 'holes', fill them with a little extra batter. If you have too much batter in the pan, pour it off quickly or your pancake will be too thick. Put the pan back on the heat and cook until the batter bubbles all over. Loosen the edges with a palette knife and when the batter is set and bubbly, slip the knife under the pancake and flip it over. If it lands slightly off centre, shake it back into place. Do not poke the pancake or it will tear.

When the pancake is golden underneath, flick it out of the pan, upside down, onto the sugared paper. The first side cooked should now be underneath. Sprinkle the top with sugar and then with lemon juice. Pick up the front edge of the paper and tilt it so the pancake rolls up neatly away from you. Lift it with the palette knife on to a warm serving dish. Regrease and reheat the pan for the next pancake.

* Caribbean Pineapple Pancakes

Follow the recipe for Lemon Pancakes (above), with these changes: make 2 thin pancakes for each person. Fill each one with 2 tablespoons heated chopped pineapple, fresh or canned, and sprinkle with demerara sugar. Place 2 filled pancakes on each serving plate and dredge generously with caster sugar. Heat a metal skewer and press it in criss-cross pattern on to the sugar which will caramelise in a lattice design. Pour over a spoonful of flaming rum and serve at once.

'Pennywise' Pancakes

100 g (4 oz) plain flour
1 egg
150 ml (¼ pint) milk
150 ml (¼ pint) water
1 tablespoon vegetable oil
vegetable oil for frying

To make up the batter, place the flour, egg, milk, water and oil in a bowl and whisk vigorously until smooth.

Heat a little oil in a pancake pan, add about 2 tablespoons of the batter and swirl it round the pan to coat the base evenly. Cook until the top surface just becomes set and dry then toss or flip the pancake over using a palette knife and cook the other side until golden.

Slip the cooked pancake on to a warm serving plate and keep hot. Add a little more oil to the pan before cooking each pancake and continue until all the batter has been used. If cooking in a non-stick pan you may not require to add any more oil. Serve sprinkled with caster sugar and lemon juice.
Makes 8

Crêpes Suzette

100 g (4 oz) unsalted butter
finely grated rind and juice of 1
  orange
100 g (4 oz) caster sugar
8 thin pancakes (p. 243)
2 tablespoons Orange Curaçao,
  Cointreau or Grand Marnier
2 tablespoons brandy

Cream the butter with the orange rind. Add the sugar, a tablespoonful at a time, pouring a little orange juice on the butter, and beat both together to prevent the liquid separating from the fat. Stop adding juice when it starts to curdle.

The Suzette Butter can be prepared in advance and refrigerated or frozen until required.

When you are ready to serve, heat the Suzette Butter gently in a chafing dish or frying pan (this can be done on a side table in the dining room) and then put pancakes in one at a time, spooning the sauce over them. Fold each pancake in half and then in half again, push to the side of the pan and to leave room for the next one.

When all the pancakes are folded and the sauce slightly reduced and thickened, pour over the orange liqueur. Warm the brandy in a ladle or small pan, tilt into the flame so that it ignites and pour over the pancakes. Shake the pan to liven the flames. Serve two pancakes for each helping and spoon on more sauce.

Apple Batter Pudding

450 g (1 lb) cooking apples
brown sugar
300 ml (½ pint) basic batter mixture
  (p. 363)
caster sugar for dredging

Peel, core and thickly slice the cooking apples. Generously butter a shallow ovenproof dish and heat it in a preheated oven at 220°C, 425°F, Gas Mark 7. Put in the apples and sprinkle generously with brown sugar. Return the dish to the oven for 10 minutes. Whisk the basic batter mixture and pour it over the apples. Replace dish in oven and then bake for 30 minutes or until the batter is well risen and golden brown. Dredge with caster sugar and serve immediately.

Apricot Pancake Layer

8 thin pancakes (p. 243)
For the filling:
1 × 425 g (15 oz) can apricot halves
2 teaspoons arrowroot
3 tablespoons orange jelly marmalade
1 tablespoon flaked almonds

Fry the pancakes and keep them warm
while you prepare the filling.

Drain the apricot halves and cut each
one into 4 neat slices. Moisten the
arrowroot with 1 tablespoon of the
apricot syrup and put the remaining
syrup in a saucepan with the marmalade. Stir over gentle heat until the
marmalade has melted. Add the moist-
ened arrowroot and bring to the boil,
stirring constantly. Cook gently until
the mixture thickens and clears, stirring all the time. Fold in the apricot
slices.

Place one pancake on an ovenproof
plate and cover with a little of the
apricot filling. Continue in layers arranging a few good slices on top of the
last pancake. Scatter with the flaked
almonds and place in a moderate oven
(180°C, 350°F, Gas Mark 4) for about 15
minutes. Serve warm, cut into wedges.
For special occasions, decorate with
extra apricot slices.

Normandy Pancakes

4 medium Bramley apples
50 g (2 oz) unsalted butter
50 g (2 oz) soft brown or caster sugar
8 thin pancakes (p. 243)
For the sauce:
50 g (2 oz) unsalted butter
50 g (2 oz) caster sugar
150 ml (¼ pint) cider
2 tablespoons Calvados or brandy, to
serve

Peel, core and cut apples into short
slices. Fry in melted butter until just
coloured. Spoon fried apples down the
centre of each pancake and sprinkle
with sugar. Fold over the sides of each
pancake. Arrange in buttered oven dish.

Melt butter and sugar over a moderate heat, add cider and boil briskly for
3–4 minutes. Pour over stuffed pancakes. Bake in moderately hot oven
(190°C, 375°F, Gas Mark 5) for 20 minutes or until heated through.

Warm Calvados or brandy in a ladle,
tilt sideways into a gas flame or use a
taper to ignite and pour over pancakes.
Serve while flaming. Allow 2 pancakes
per helping and hand cream separately.

Meringue Shells
or Flan Case

For meringue topping:
25 g (1 oz) sugar for each egg white
For shells or cases:
50 g (2 oz) sugar for each egg white

Meringue is made with stiffly whisked
egg white blended with sugar and it is
essential that the egg is carefully separated and that the bowl and whisk are
perfectly clean and dry. Even a drop of
egg yolk, grease or water will prevent
the white from whisking stiffly. For a
small amount, a balloon whisk can be
used, but a rotary whisk is quicker for
larger quantities. When using an electric mixer, special care is needed to
obtain the right consistency for piping.

To make a meringue topping for a
pudding or tart, 25 g (1 oz) sugar to each
egg white will be sufficient. This will
give a crisp, golden surface when
cooked for 30 minutes in a moderate
oven, but it will be soft underneath. To
make meringue shells or flan cases,
which must be crisp all through, you
need 50 g (2 oz) sugar to each egg white
and the meringue must be baked very
slowly for 1 to 2 hours according to size.
Unfilled shells can be stored for several
days in an airtight tin, or frozen. Once
filled, the meringue will soon soften.

Ten-Minute Pancakes

100 g (4 oz) plain flour
2 teaspoons baking powder
1 tablespoon caster sugar
1 egg, separated
150 ml ($\frac{1}{4}$ pint) milk
1 tablespoon melted butter
50 g (2 oz) sultanas or currants or
  seedless raisins

Sift the flour, baking powder and caster sugar into a mixing bowl. Make a well in the centre and quickly stir in the egg yolk, milk and melted butter; do not beat it. Whisk the egg white until stiff, and fold it in quickly and lightly. Sprinkle on the dried fruit and fold it in. Heat and lightly grease the griddle. It is the right temperature when a drop of water splutters on the surface. Drop the batter off the point of a large metal spoon, allowing room for spreading. Cook for 2–3 minutes until the bubbles burst through the batter, turn with a palette knife and cook until golden. When cooked, wrap the pancakes in a clean cloth to keep them warm and soft. Serve with butter, honey or jam.

Peach Meringue Flan

2 egg whites
100 g (4 oz) caster sugar
150 ml ($\frac{1}{4}$ pint) double cream
450 g (1 lb) fresh or canned peaches,
  sliced
chopped pistachio nuts, to decorate

Line a baking tray with non-stick parchment or greaseproof paper. Draw on it in pencil 2 circles 18 cm (7 inches) in diameter. Lightly oil the greaseproof paper. Preheat the oven to 140°C, 275°F, Gas Mark 1. Meanwhile make meringue mixture with the egg whites and caster sugar (see p. 245).

Fit a large nozzle into a forcing bag and fill it with meringue mixture. Pipe a ring of meringue round one circle just inside the pencil line. Pipe onto the parchment 8 to 12 baby rosettes with a base the same width as the meringue ring. Pipe the remaining mixture into the other circle and spread it out evenly into a flat disc.

Bake the meringues in the preheated oven on a low shelf for 1 hour or until crisp when tapped. Remove the meringues from the oven. Lift off the rosettes with a knife. Turn the parchment upside down on the table and carefully peel it off the meringue ring and disc. If you try to prise the meringues off the parchment they are liable to splinter.

Shortly before serving, whip the cream and pipe a ring round the edge of the flat base. Place the meringue ring on top and press it down gently. Arrange the peach slices on the base in concentric circles. Pipe a little cream on the base of the rosettes and press them onto the ring. Decorate the flan with the remaining whipped cream and chopped pistachio nuts.

Strawberry Meringue Flan

2 egg whites
100 g (4 oz) caster sugar
150 ml ($\frac{1}{4}$ pint) double cream
450 g (1 lb) strawberries

Line a baking sheet with non-stick parchment or greaseproof paper. Draw two 18 cm (7 inch) circles in pencil. Lightly oil the greaseproof paper.

Whisk the egg whites until very stiff and dry. Sieve in 2 tablespoons of sugar and whisk again until very stiff and shiny. Sieve and fold in the remaining sugar quickly and lightly. Do not overfold or the meringue will fall. Fill the meringue mixture into a large forcing bag with a large rose nozzle.

Pipe a ring of meringue round one circle just inside the pencil mark. Pipe 8 small rosettes round about with a base the same width as the piped ring. Pipe remaining meringue mixture into the other circle and spread it out evenly into a flat disc.

Bake in preheated slow oven (140°C, 275°F, Gas Mark 1) for about 1 hour until crisp. Remove from oven, lift off rosettes. Turn paper upside down on the table and peel paper off the meringue ring and disc. If you lift meringues off the paper they may break.

Shortly before serving whip the cream and pipe a ring round the edge of the flat disc. Place meringue ring on top and press down gently. Pipe cream on base of rosettes and press them on top of the ring. Halve the strawberries, if large, and arrange them neatly in meringue case. Decorate with remaining cream.

Pavlova Cake

3 egg whites
175 g (6 oz) caster sugar
1 teaspoon cornflour
$\frac{1}{4}$ teaspoon vanilla essence
1 teaspoon lemon juice
For the filling:
300 ml ($\frac{1}{2}$ pint) whipping cream
100 g (4 oz) strawberries, hulled, or raspberries
100 g (4 oz) stoned cherries
4 ripe apricots or greengages, halved
2 ripe peaches, sliced
To decorate:
100 g (4 oz) redcurrants
1 egg white
2 tablespoons caster sugar

Draw an 18 cm (7 inch) circle on non-stick parchment or lightly-oiled grease-proof paper and place on a baking sheet. Whisk the egg whites until very stiff and dry. Sieve and whisk in half the sugar and continue whisking until the mixture is stiff and shiny. Sieve the remaining sugar with the cornflour and fold into the mixture with the vanilla essence and lemon juice.

Spread the meringue on the circle and build up into a bowl-shaped shell, swirling the meringue round the outside of the shell. Bake in the centre of a slow oven (150°C, 300°F, Gas Mark 2) for $1\frac{1}{4}$–$1\frac{1}{2}$ hours until firm and delicately coloured. Allow to cool before removing the parchment or paper. The shell can be prepared in advance and stored in an airtight container until required.

Wash and dry the redcurrants. Beat the egg white until liquid. Dip little bunches of the redcurrants into this and then into the sugar. Chill in the refrigerator to crystallise.

Whip the cream and set 2 tablespoons aside for the topping with some of the prepared fruit. Fold the rest of the fruit carefully into the cream and pile in the centre of the meringue. Top with the remaining fruit, swirl the rest of the cream in the centre and decorate with the crystallised redcurrants.

Ginger Meringue Nests

6 tablespoons ginger marmalade
1 tablespoon undiluted orange squash
6 meringue nests
6 scoops of vanilla ice cream
fresh pouring cream, to serve

Put the marmalade and orange squash in a pan and heat gently until melted, stirring occasionally. Leave to cool. Put the meringues in individual serving bowls, then put one scoop of ice cream in each. Pour the sauce over the ice cream, then serve immediately with fresh pouring cream handed separately.
Serves 6

Meringues Chantilly

2 egg whites
100 g (4 oz) caster sugar
150 ml ($\frac{1}{4}$ pint) double cream
extra caster sugar
vanilla essence to taste
chopped walnuts, to decorate

Preheat the oven to 120–140°C, 250–275°F, Gas Mark $\frac{1}{2}$–1. Line a baking tray with non-stick parchment or grease and flour a baking sheet – bang it to spread the flour evenly. Using a rotary whisk and a large bowl, beat the egg whites until they are stiff and dry and hang on the whisk when shaken. Sift 2 tablespoons of the caster sugar over the whisked whites and beat again until stiff and shiny.

Sift half the remaining sugar over the whites and, using a concave spatula or large cook's spoon, fold it in, scooping the mixture up from the bottom of the bowl and folding it over the top. Sift the rest of the sugar and fold it in, cutting down through the centre of the mixture. Work very quickly and lightly as too much folding will, most likely, collapse the meringue.

Take 2 large spoons and with one, scoop up a heaped spoonful of meringue. Then with the other, scoop it out of the spoon onto the baking sheet to form a shell shape. Neaten with a knife dipped in cold water. Dredge the shells with caster sugar. The shells can be piped with a large plain or rose nozzle if preferred. Bake the meringue in the oven on a low shelf for about 1 hour or until set and a delicate beige colour. Peel the parchment off meringues, or carefully lift them off the baking sheet with a sharp knife.

Gently press the base of each shell in the centre to make a hollow and return the meringues upside down to the oven for another 30 minutes to dry out. Cool on a wire rack. Whip the cream until stiff. Sweeten with 1 teaspoon caster sugar and flavour with a few drops of vanilla essence. Sandwich the shells together in pairs with cream, which can be piped or spread with a teaspoon. Sprinkle with chopped walnuts. For a buffet, serve in paper cases.

Summer Rose Meringue

225 g (8 oz) icing sugar, sieved
4 egg whites
$\frac{1}{4}$ teaspoon vanilla essence
For the filling:
150 ml ($\frac{1}{4}$ pint) double cream
1–2 tablespoons Kirsch or sherry
2 teaspoons caster sugar
225 g (8 oz) loganberries, raspberries or wild strawberries
15 g ($\frac{1}{2}$ oz) crystallised rose petals

Put the egg whites and icing sugar in a bowl over a saucepan of simmering water and follow the recipe for Swiss Meringue (See Swiss Raspberry Charlotte p. 234). Flavour with vanilla essence. Line 2 baking sheets with non-stick parchment or greaseproof paper and draw 18 circles 7 cm (3 inch). If using greaseproof paper, oil lightly. Put the meringue mixture in a forcing bag with a large rose nozzle. Pipe rings just inside the circles. Fill in 6 rings with more meringue to make flat discs. Bake in preheated slow oven (140°C, 275°F, Gas Mark 1) for 45 minutes or until crisp and delicately coloured. Remove from oven, cool and loosen meringue but keep oven at the above temperature.

Mount 2 meringue rings on each disc, sticking them together with remaining meringue mixture. Return to oven for 20 minutes until firm.

Remove and cool. Whip cream until stiff, fold in Kirsch or sherry and sugar to taste. Fold in prepared berries, pile into baskets and decorate with crystallised rose petals. For buffets serve baskets in paper meringue cases.
Serves 6

Hazelnut Galette

125 g (4 oz) hazelnuts
140 g (4½ oz) plain flour
pinch of salt
50 g (2 oz) caster sugar
75 g (3 oz) butter
For the topping:
75 g (3 oz) caster sugar
For the filling:
300 ml (½ pint) whipping cream
1 tablespoon caster sugar
450 g (1 lb) raspberries

Spread hazelnuts on a baking sheet. Toast under grill, shaking frequently. Rub in a dry cloth to remove skins. Chop 25 g (1 oz) roughly and grind the rest in a mill.

Sieve the flour and salt into bowl and mix in the ground nuts and sugar. Rub in butter with finger tips until of breadcrumb consistency. Knead lightly and chill for 30 minutes or until dough is firm. Shape into a thick roll, divide into 4 and roll out into 4 thin circles.

Place the circles on a greased baking sheet and bake in a preheated moderate oven (180°C, 350°F, Gas Mark 4) for 15–20 minutes until brown and set. Remove from oven and cool.

Put the sugar in a small thick saucepan over gentle heat and stir gently until dissolved. Increase heat and boil briskly without stirring until a rich caramel colour.

Pour some over one biscuit, spreading it evenly with a well oiled knife. Sprinkle the roughly chopped nuts round the edge before the caramel sets.

Prepare the filling shortly before Galette is to be served. Whip cream and fold in sugar. Arrange some raspberries in the centre of the caramelised biscuit. Warm up remaining caramel and trickle it over them, pulling the caramel into strands like spun sugar. Spread the cream over the other biscuits, cover with raspberries and pile the layers on top of each other with the decorated biscuit on top.

Camper's Trifle

6 trifle sponges, cut in half
4 tablespoons jam, for spreading
2 × 300 g (11 oz) cans mandarin
  oranges
1 × 100 g (4 oz) packet orange jelly
1 × 75 g (3 oz) packet instant custard
  mix
1 × 150 ml (5 fl oz) carton double or
  whipping cream, stiffly whipped

Spread the sponges with the jam, sandwich them together and place in the bottom of a deep serving bowl. Drain the mandarins and reserve the juice. Dissolve the jelly in 300 ml (½ pint) boiling water according to packet directions, then stir in enough mandarin juice to make up to 600 ml (1 pint). Pour over the sponge cakes, add half the mandarins and chill until set.

Put the custard mix in a measuring jug, then add boiling water to come up to the 300 ml (½ pint) mark. Stir briskly to make a thick custard. Leave to cool slightly, then spread over the set jelly. Leave until cold, then spread the cream on top. Decorate with the remaining mandarins.
Serves 6 to 8

Variations:
Substitute canned apricot halves or sliced peaches for the mandarins and use a different flavour jelly if liked. If you have any sherry or sweet white wine, pour a few spoonfuls over the sponge cakes before adding the jelly.

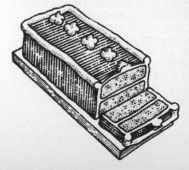

Berries with Cointreau Chantilly

350 g (12 oz) strawberries
175 ml (6 fl oz) whipping cream
175 ml (6 fl oz) single cream
2 tablespoons caster sugar
1-2 tablespoons Cointreau
To decorate:
crushed meringues or ratafias
crystallised mint leaves

Hull the strawberries. Whip the two creams together until stiff and fold in the sugar. Flavour to taste with Cointreau. Fold in the prepared berries and spoon into individual glasses. Chill until required.

Serve topped with crushed meringues or ratafias and garnished with crystallised mint leaves.

Strawberries, raspberries, loganberries or cultivated blackberries can all be used in this quickly-prepared and delicious sweet. Flavour with Cointreau, Grand Marnier, Orange Curaçao or Kirsch according to availability and taste.

Creamy Chocolate Mould

40 g (1½ oz) cornflour
8 tablespoons water
1 large tin evaporated milk
75 g (3 oz) plain chocolate, grated
1-2 tablespoons caster sugar

Mix the cornflour to a smooth paste with 8 tablespoons of cold water. Heat the evaporated milk, add the chocolate and gradually blend in the cornflour mixture. Bring to simmering point and cook, stirring, for 3 minutes until thickened. Remove from heat and sweeten to taste.

Rinse a 600 ml (1 pint) mould with cold water, pour in the mixture and chill. Unmould on to a serving plate. Surround with canned or stewed pears.

Variation:
The chocolate can be replaced by 2 tablespoons cocoa plus ¼ teaspoon vanilla essence and the evaporated milk by 300 ml (½ pint) fresh milk plus an equal quantity of single cream.

Banana and Ginger Dessert

1 × 33 g (1⅓ oz) packet vanilla
    blancmange powder
2 tablespoons sugar
600 ml (1 pint) milk
100 g (4 oz) apricot jam
4 bananas
75 g (3 oz) preserved stem ginger,
    finely chopped
150 ml (¼ pint) double cream
1 teaspoon caster sugar
½ teaspoon vanilla essence

Make up the vanilla blancmange using the sugar and milk, according to the directions on the packet. Pour into a shallow serving dish and allow to set.

Heat the jam and rub through a sieve. Peel the bananas, and cut into halves lengthwise, then scoop out a little 'trough' down the centre of each half. Fill this with pieces of the very finely chopped ginger, reserving larger pieces for the decoration, and brush the sides of the bananas thickly with the jam. Arrange on the set blancmange.

Whip the cream, add the sugar and vanilla essence and pipe down the bananas over the ginger. Decorate with the remaining pieces of ginger.

Atholl Brose

4 tablespoons medium oatmeal or
    ground almonds
3-4 tablespoons whisky
1 tablespoon lemon juice
2 tablespoons heather honey
150 ml (¼ pint) double cream
twists of fresh lemon, to decorate

The Highland version of Syllabub, this is much better made with toasted oatmeal rather than with ground almonds. The amount of honey can be adjusted to taste. Spread the oatmeal on a tin and toast for a few minutes under the grill, shaking frequently so that it browns evenly. Leave to cool.

Mix together the whisky, lemon juice and honey. Gradually whisk in the cream until the mixture stands in soft peaks. Fold in the toasted oatmeal and turn into goblets. Chill until required. Decorate each goblet with a lemon twist and serve with thin shortbread biscuits.

Syllabub

1 lemon
100 ml (4 fl oz) medium white wine
3–4 tablespoons caster sugar
300 ml ($\frac{1}{2}$ pint) double cream
To decorate:
chopped pistachio nuts or crushed
  praline

Grate the rind delicately off the lemon so there is no trace of pith. Put it in a bowl with the strained lemon juice, wine and 3 tablespoons sugar. (You can leave this mixture to infuse if there is time.) Strain out the lemon rind just before using.

Gradually add the cream, whisking steadily until the mixture stands in peaks. Taste and add some more sugar if desired; this will depend on the wine you have used.

Pour the Syllabub into the goblets or custard cups, swirling it up the centre, and chill thoroughly.

Decorate with chopped pistachio nuts or crushed praline and serve with French Tuile Biscuits.

Old Fashioned English Trifle

8 trifle sponge cakes, cut in half
  lengthwise
8 tablespoons red jam
8 tablespoons sherry
1 × 135 g (4$\frac{3}{4}$ oz) packet jelly
4 fresh peaches, skinned, halved and
  stoned
25 g (1 oz) demerara sugar, or to taste
$\frac{1}{2}$ teaspoon ground cinnamon
600 ml (1 pint) cold thick custard
300 ml ($\frac{1}{2}$ pint) whipping cream
To finish:
25 g (1 oz) glacé cherries, halved
few strips of angelica
25 g (1 oz) blanched almonds, split or
  flaked

This trifle is best made with fresh peaches when in season, but if unavailable, use canned peach halves.

Spread the insides of the sponge cakes with jam, then sandwich them together again. Put in the bottom of a large, deep trifle dish or glass fruit bowl, pour over the sherry and leave to soak into the sponge.

Make the jelly according to packet directions, leave until quite cold, then pour over the sponge cakes. Chill in the refrigerator until set, and arrange the peach halves, cut side down, on top of the jelly. Mix the sugar and cinnamon together and sprinkle over the peaches. Spoon the custard over to make an even layer, then chill in the refrigerator for an hour or until set.

Whip the cream until thick and spread over the custard, swirling it with a knife. Decorate the top of trifle, making flowers with cherry 'blooms' and angelica 'leaves'. Arrange almonds decoratively between the flowers. Chill in the refrigerator until serving time.
Serves 12–15

Ginger Syllabub

2 pieces of whole stem ginger, finely
  chopped
2 tablespoons stem ginger syrup
2 tablespoons medium or dry sherry
25 g (1 oz) caster sugar
150 ml ($\frac{1}{4}$ pint) double cream
25 g (1 oz) crystallised ginger,
  chopped, to decorate

Put the stem ginger and syrup, the
sherry and sugar in a bowl and stir to
combine. Set aside.

Whip the cream until thick, then fold
in the ginger mixture, making sure that
it is evenly distributed throughout the
cream. Chill in the refrigerator for several hours. Whip again before serving.
Spoon into two individual glasses and
decorate with the chopped crystallised
ginger.

Serves 2

Zabaglione

3 egg yolks
75 g (3 oz) caster sugar
1 teaspoon finely grated lemon rind
150 ml ($\frac{1}{4}$ pint) medium white wine or
  Marsala

Whisk the egg yolks with the sugar and
lemon rind until white, then whisk in
the wine. Place the bowl over a saucepan of simmering water and continue
whisking until the mixture thickens
and falls in ribbons from the whisk.
Pour into large wineglasses and serve
at once as the mixture is likely to fall.
Serve with sweet biscuits.

Cold Zabaglione

6 egg yolks
75 g (3 oz) caster sugar
finely grated rind of 1 orange
150 ml ($\frac{1}{4}$ pint) Marsala or white wine
50 ml (2 fl oz) double cream
chopped pistachio nuts or orange
  peel, to decorate

Follow the method for making hot Zab-
aglione (above) and when the mixture
has thickened to ribbon consistency,
remove from heat, place in a bowl of
iced water and continue whisking until
cold. Very lightly whisk the cream with
a fork and fold into the mixture. Pour
into goblets and chill in refrigerator
until required.

Before serving decorate with chopped pistachio nuts or fine twists of
orange peel and accompany with sweet
finger biscuits. Alternatively pour over
sliced fresh peaches, strawberries or
fresh fruit salad.

Lemon Flummery

300 ml ($\frac{1}{2}$ pint) water
25 g (1 oz) butter
finely grated rind and juice of 1
  lemon
25 g (1 oz) plain flour
100 g (4 oz) caster sugar
1 egg, separated

Heat the water with the butter and
lemon rind. Mix the flour and sugar in a
bowl. Gradually stir in the hot liquid,
beating smooth. Blend a little of this
mixture into the beaten egg yolk. Mix
this back into the mixture and pour all
back into the saucepan. Cook gently for
5 minutes.

Add the lemon juice and pour into a
cold bowl. Whisk the egg white until
stiff but not dry and fold into the flum-
mery. Serve hot or cold with baked
fruit, fruit compôtes etc.

Lemon Snow

1 × 50 g (2 oz) packet lemon pie filling
300 ml (½ pint) water
2 eggs, separated
4 tablespoons sugar
1 × 25 g (1 oz) packet Dream Topping
multi-coloured sugar strands, to
    decorate

Make the lemon pie filling according to
packet directions with the water and 2
egg yolks. Leave to cool.

Beat the egg whites until stiff, add the
sugar and beat again until shiny. Make
the Dream Topping according to packet
directions, then fold half into the lemon
mixture with the egg whites. Transfer
to individual glasses and spread the
remaining Dream Topping over the top.
Decorate with sprinkled sugar strands
and chill in the refrigerator until firm.

Marrons Mont Blanc

50 g (2 oz) unsalted butter
25 g (1 oz) caster sugar
225 g (8 oz) can purée of *marrons
    glacés*
1–2 tablespoons sherry
lemon juice to taste
150 ml (¼ pint) double cream
ratafia biscuits or miniature
    meringues, to decorate

Cream together the butter and sugar.
Stir the chestnut purée in the tin and
add it gradually to the creamed mixture. Flavour to taste with sherry and
lemon juice, stirring it in gradually to
avoid curdling.

Pile prepared chestnut purée into
centre of individual dessert dishes.
Whip the cream and swirl on to the top
of each little mound. Arrange ratafia
biscuits or miniature meringues round
the base. Chill until required.

Orange Caramel Cream

For the caramel:
100 g (4 oz) caster sugar
3 tablespoons water
For the orange custard:
finely grated rind of 1 orange
300 ml (½ pint) fresh or frozen orange
    juice
3 eggs
40 g (1½ oz) caster sugar

Infuse the orange rind in the juice over
very gentle heat. Warm 4 × 100 ml (4 oz)
dariole moulds in the oven so that the
caramel does not set too quickly.

Put the sugar and water into a thick
saucepan and stir over gentle heat until
dissolved into clear syrup. Boil briskly,
without stirring until rich caramel
colour. Divide between moulds, and
using thick oven gloves as the tins get
burning hot, revolve moulds so that
each is evenly coated. Work quickly
before caramel hardens.

Beat eggs and sugar together until
light and fluffy. Strain in hot orange
juice, mixing well. Pour into prepared
moulds and put them in a baking tin
with 2.5 cm (1 inch) of water. Cover with
greased paper and cook in a preheated
moderate oven (180°C, 350°F, Gas Mark
4) for 1 hour until set and firm. Chill
thoroughly. Unmould into individual
dishes; the melted caramel will run
down as a delicious sauce.

Pineapple Cheese Cream

1 tablespoon gelatine
2 tablespoons hot water
1 × 425 g (15 oz) can pineapple chunks
2 eggs, separated
100 g (4 oz) caster sugar
1 tablespoon lemon juice and grated
  rind of ½ lemon
350 g (12 oz) cottage cheese, sieved
150 ml (¼ pint) double cream
angelica leaves to decorate

Soften the gelatine in the water. Drain the syrup from the pineapple chunks. Whisk the egg yolks and sugar together until thick and creamy. Slowly whisk in 150 ml (¼ pint) pineapple syrup.

Put the mixture into a saucepan, add the softened gelatine and stir over low heat until dissolved. Add the grated lemon rind and leave to cool. Stir in the sieved cottage cheese and lemon juice. Leave until beginning to set. Beat until smooth.

Lightly whip the cream and fold into the mixture. Beat the egg whites until stiff, and finely chop half the pineapple chunks. Now fold the chopped pineapple and beaten egg whites into the mixture. Put into a serving dish or individual glasses, and decorate with the remaining pineapple chunks and angelica leaves. Chill before serving.

Crème Caramel

For the caramel:
100 g (4 oz) caster sugar
4 tablespoons water
For the crème:
450 ml (¾ pint) milk
2 eggs
2 tablespoons sugar
vanilla essence to flavour

Warm, but do not grease four 125 ml (¼ pint) dariole moulds. Put the sugar and water for the caramel in a small thick pan and stir carefully over gentle heat until the sugar is completely dissolved. Do not swirl it up the sides of the pan – use a wet pastry brush to remove any splashes on sides of the pan.

Remove the spoon from the pan, raise heat and boil *without stirring* until a golden caramel colour. To stop the caramel overbrowning, quickly dip base of the pan in cold water. When the caramel is the right colour hold a mould in one hand, wearing oven gloves and pour in the caramel to about 2 cm (¾ inch) deep.

With the other gloved hand, rotate the mould so the caramel coats it evenly. Pour in a little more if needed.

Preheat oven to 190°C, 375°F, Gas Mark 5. Heat the milk in a pan until a rim of bubbles appears round the edge. Beat eggs and sugar together, stir in milk. Add a few drops of vanilla essence.

Pour custard into moulds. Put in a bain marie. Cover with greased paper or foil, cook in centre of oven for 45 minutes or until set. Test by gently shaking moulds; the centre should be as firm as jelly.

Chill the crèmes thoroughly. To unmould, place individual serving bowls over the top of the crèmes, hold the mould and bowl firmly and invert. Give a slight shake and carefully lift off mould. The caramel will run down the crèmes as a golden sauce.

Crème caramel may be cooked in a 600 ml (1 pint) mould. It will require 1 hour or longer to cook.

Strawberries Romanoff

700 g–1 kg (1½–2 lb) strawberries,
  hulled and washed
100 g (4 oz) caster sugar, or to taste
6 tablespoons vodka
3 tablespoons black cherry jam
1½ tablespoons powdered gelatine
3 tablespoons water
600 ml (1 pint) double or whipping
  cream

Purée 225 g (8 oz) strawberries and 50 g (2 oz) sugar in an electric blender until smooth. Transfer to a mixing bowl. Mix the vodka and cherry jam until evenly blended, then stir into the strawberry purée. Slice the remaining strawberries, reserving a few whole ones for decoration, put in a shallow bowl and sprinkle with some more caster sugar (the amount needed will depend on the sweetness of the strawberries). Set aside.

Sprinkle the gelatine over the water in a small heatproof bowl and leave to stand until spongy. Put the bowl in a pan of hot water and stir over low heat until the gelatine has been dissolved. Remove from the heat, leave to cool slightly then stir into the strawberry purée. Leave to stand until the purée begins to thicken. Whip the cream until thick, reserving a few spoonfuls for decoration, then fold into the purée until evenly distributed. Gently stir in the sliced strawberries, pour into a glass serving bowl and chill in the refrigerator until serving time. Decorate with the whole strawberries and piped rosettes of whipped cream.
Serves 10–12

Whipped Pears

1 × 400 g (14 oz) can pear halves
1 × 25 g (1 oz) packet yellow jelly glaze
200 ml (⅓ pint) water
1 × 150 ml (5 fl oz) carton double cream, stiffly whipped
2 egg whites, stiffly whipped
2 tablespoons flaked almonds, to decorate (optional)

Mash the pears and juice to a purée with a fork, set aside. Put the jelly glaze powder and water in a pan and stir to dissolve. Bring to the boil, stirring constantly, then remove from the heat and beat until thick and glossy. Beat into the pear purée until evenly blended,

then beat in the cream. Fold in the egg whites until evenly blended, then leave in a cool place or chill in the refrigerator until set. Sprinkle with the almonds (if using) just before serving.
Serves 6

Variations:
Any kind of canned fruit can be substituted for the pears.

If liked, use a larger can of fruit and reserve a few pieces of fruit to decorate the top of the dessert before mashing remainder.

Raspberry Fool

150 ml (¼ pint) ready-prepared custard or 1 tablespoon custard powder and 150 ml (¼ pint) milk
300 ml (½ pint) raspberry purée
caster sugar
150 ml (¼ pint) whipping cream
chopped pistachio nuts or flaked almonds, to decorate

If using custard powder, mix to a thin paste with a little of the cold milk. Boil up the remaining milk and pour it onto the custard, stirring well. Return the custard to the pan and cook for 1 minute, stirring until it thickens. Cool the custard and mix in the fruit purée. Sweeten to taste with caster sugar. Whip the cream stiffly and fold it into the cold fruit mixture. Pour the fool into individual glasses and top with chopped pistachio nuts or flaked almonds. Serve with lady fingers or crisp petits fours biscuits.

Variations:
Gooseberries or any seasonal soft fruit can be used.

Fluffy Fruit Fool

150 ml (¼ pint) milk
2 eggs, separated
300 ml (½ pint) sweetened rhubarb
  purée (p. 261)
150 ml (¼ pint) double cream
sugar to taste

Warm the milk and add gradually to the
beaten egg yolks. Pour back into the
rinsed saucepan. Stir over gentle heat
until the mixture thickens and clings to
the back of the wooden spoon. Chill
thoroughly and mix into the rhubarb
purée. Whip the cream fairly stiff and
fold in. Sweeten to taste. Whisk the egg
whites until stiff but not brittle and fold
into the fool. Pour into goblets and chill
until required. Serve topped with baby
meringues or ratafias; accompany with
biscuits or sponge fingers.

Quick Gooseberry Fool

1 × 425 g (14 oz) can gooseberries
  drained
1 × 425 g (15 oz) can custard
1–2 drops almond essence
1 × 175 g (6 oz) can dairy cream,
  chilled
2–3 tablespoons flaked blanched
  almonds, to decorate

Mash the gooseberries with a potato
masher. Put in a bowl with the custard
and almond essence and stir well to mix.
Fold in the cream, then spoon into
individual glasses and decorate each
one with a sprinkling of flaked almonds.

Variation:
Any canned fruit can be substituted for
the gooseberries.

Blackberry Mousse

1 × 100 g (4 oz) packet blackcurrant
  jelly
300 ml (½ pint) boiling water
450 g (1 lb) fresh blackberries
4 tablespoons sugar
2 egg whites, stiffly whipped
To decorate:
fresh blackberries
sugar

Dissolve the jelly in the boiling water,
then set aside. Put the blackberries and
sugar in a pan and heat gently for 10
minutes until soft, stirring occasionally. Stir into the jelly, then leave in a
cool place until just beginning to set.
  Fold the egg whites into the blackberry mixture until evenly blended.
Leave in a cool place or chill in the
refrigerator until set. Decorate with
fresh blackberries and then sprinkle
with sugar before serving.
Serves 6

Chestnut Mousse

1 × 100 g (4 oz) packet melt-in-the-bag
  plain chocolate cake covering
1 × 225 g (8 oz) can sweetened
  chestnut purée
2 tablespoons milk
150 ml (¼ pint) double or whipping
  cream, stiffly whipped
1 chocolate flake, crumbled, to finish

If you happen to have some brandy or
sherry, the flavour of this mousse will
benefit from a spoonful or two.
  Melt the chocolate in the bag according to packet directions.
  Meanwhile beat the chestnut purée
in a bowl. Whisk the cream until stiff.
Stir in the melted chocolate and milk
and fold in the whipped cream. Spoon
into a serving dish and sprinkle over the
crumbled chocolate flake to finish the
mousse.

Chocolate Mousse

1 × 100 g (4 oz) bar plain chocolate,
  broken up
1 × 150 g (5 oz) packet marshmallows
4 tablespoons milk
2 eggs, separated
1 × 150 ml (5 fl oz) carton double
  cream
grated chocolate, to decorate

Put the chocolate, marshmallows and
milk in a pan and melt over a gentle
heat, stirring occasionally. Leave to
cool for 5 minutes, then stir in the egg
yolks. Leave until completely cold, then
stir in the cream reserving some for
decoration. Beat the egg whites until
stiff, then fold into the mousse until
evenly blended. Whisk the cream until
stiff. Spoon into individual dishes, then
top with a blob of cream and sprinkle
over the grated chocolate. Chill in the
refrigerator until set.
Serves 6

Mocha Mousse

1 tablespoon gelatine
2 tablespoons cold water
2 tablespoons instant coffee
1 tablespoon cocoa powder
2 tablespoons sugar
300 ml (½ pint) boiling water
200 ml (7 fl oz) evaporated milk,
  chilled
To decorate:
4 tablespoons double cream,
  whipped (optional)
chocolate curls (optional)

Sprinkle the gelatine over the cold
water in a cup and allow to soften for 5
minutes.
Place the instant coffee, cocoa and
sugar in a measuring jug and gradually
add the boiling water, stirring all the
time until dissolved. Add the softened
gelatine and stir well until completely

melted. Allow to cool until mixture is on
the point of setting.
Place the evaporated milk in a bowl
and whisk steadily until it is thick and
fluffy. Gradually whisk in the coffee
mixture and pour into a rinsed 1 litre (1¾
pint) fluted mould. Chill until set then
turn out on a serving dish. If liked,
decorate with rosettes of whipped
cream and chocolate curls.
Chocolate curls can be made quickly
by scraping a clean potato peeler across
the bottom of a block of plain chocolate.

Strawberry Mousse

1 × 400 g (15 oz) can strawberries
1 × 150 g (5 oz) packet strawberry jelly
300 ml (½ pint) evaporated milk,
  chilled

Drain the strawberries, measure the
juice and make up to 450 ml (¾ pint) with
water. Heat 150 ml (¼ pint) of the liquid
to boiling point, pour it over the jelly
and stir to dissolve. Stir in the remaining liquid, then chill until just beginning to set. Fold in the strawberries.
Whip the evaporated milk until thick,
fold it into the jelly and fruit, leaving a
marbled effect if liked. Transfer to individual glasses and chill until firm.

Crème Brûlée with Sugared Raspberries

100 g (4 oz) caster sugar
2 teaspoons vanilla essence
6 egg yolks
900 ml (1½ pints) double cream
50 g (2 oz) demerara sugar
350 g (12 oz) fresh or frozen
   raspberries, thawed

Put two-thirds of the caster sugar, the vanilla essence and egg yolks in a bowl and beat to combine without allowing to become frothy. Set aside.

Put the cream in the top of a double boiler or in a heatproof bowl placed on top of a pan of gently simmering water. Heat until just below boiling point, then immediately pour into the egg yolk mixture, stirring to combine. Strain into a baking dish and put in a bain marie or roasting pan half filled with hot water.

Bake in a cool oven (150°C, 300°F, Gas Mark 2) for 1¼ hours or until just set. Remove dish from bain marie, leave until cold, then chill in the refrigerator overnight if possible. When chilled, sprinkle with the demerara sugar and put under a preheated hot grill until the sugar caramelises.

Remove from grill and leave to cool again. Meanwhile, toss the raspberries in the remaining caster sugar. Cover the top of the crème brûlée with the sugared raspberries and serve chilled straight from the baking dish.

Variation:
Any soft summer fruit can be substituted for the raspberries that top this dessert.

Fresh Fruit Brûlée

For the sugar syrup:
100 g (4 oz) sugar
300 ml (½ pint) water
2 tablespoons Cointreau or brandy
For the fruit salad:
4 crisp eating apples
2 large bananas
225 g (8 oz) black grapes, halved and
   depipped
4 peaches, peeled, halved, stoned and
   sliced
4 pears, peeled, cored and sliced
50 g (2 oz) blanched almonds, split
   and toasted
For the topping:
300 ml (½ pint) double or whipping
   cream
25 g (1 oz) vanilla sugar
100–175 g (4–6 oz) soft brown sugar

The best season for the fruit salad is in the summer, although good ones can be made in the winter with the help of dried fruits and nuts.

To prepare sugar syrup: put the sugar and water in a saucepan and heat gently, without stirring, until the sugar has dissolved. Increase the heat and boil rapidly for approximately 5 minutes until the mixture is syrupy. Remove pan from the heat and leave sugar syrup to cool. Stir in the Cointreau or brandy.

Peel, core and slice the apples and put in a shallow heatproof serving dish. Peel the bananas and slice thinly, add to the apples with the grapes, peaches and pears. Pour over the sugar syrup, folding it into the fruit with the almonds. Be careful not to break or bruise the fruit. Whip the cream with the vanilla sugar until thick, then spoon over the fruit in the dish to cover it. Sprinkle the brown sugar evenly over the cream and put under a preheated hot grill for approximately 5 minutes until the sugar has caramelised. Remove from the grill, leave to cool, then refrigerate until serving time.
Serves 8–10

Fresh Apricot Jelly

225 g (8 oz) granulated sugar
600 ml (1 pint) water
1 thin piece lemon peel
450 g (1 lb) fresh apricots
12 g ($\frac{1}{2}$ oz) (1 envelope) powdered
  gelatine
3 tablespoons hot water
To decorate:
crumbled meringues or ratafias
whipping cream or single cream

Dissolve the sugar in the water. Add the lemon rind and boil for 5 minutes. Add the apricots and cook gently for 10–15 minutes; do not overcook. Lift the fruit out with a draining spoon on to a plate. Remove skins, put these back in the simmering syrup and continue cooking to reduce slightly.

Meanwhile halve and stone the apricots and put them in a glass serving bowl, or divide between individual dishes. Strain and measure off 600 ml (1 pint) of apricot syrup. Dissolve the gelatine in the hot water and stir into the syrup. Pour over the fruit and leave in a cool place to set. Serve decorated with whipped cream and crumbled meringues or accompany with a jug of pouring cream.

Fruit Chartreuse

1 × 135 g (4$\frac{3}{4}$ oz) packet lemon jelly
1 × 312 g (11 oz) can mandarins
225 g (8 oz) cherries or grapes
4 ripe bananas
juice of 1 lemon
whipping cream, to decorate

Break up the jelly and dissolve in 300 ml ($\frac{1}{2}$ pint) boiling water. Add the drained mandarin juice and sufficient cold water to make liquid up to 600 ml (1 pint). Stone cherries or seed grapes. Peel bananas and cut each across into 3 equal pieces. Brush with lemon juice to prevent them from discolouring.

Rinse out a shallow 900 ml (1$\frac{1}{2}$ pint) jelly mould with cold water. Pour a thin layer of jelly over the base and refrigerate until set. When firm arrange mandarin sections and cherries or grapes in an attractive pattern on it, dipping each piece in liquid jelly first. Chill until firm, then cover with a layer of jelly and chill. When set, stand banana sticks around sides of mould, dipping each piece in liquid jelly. Fill centre with mixed fruit, cover with more jelly to fill mould and refrigerate. To serve, unmould and decorate with piped whipped cream and any remaining fruit.

Honey and Lemon Milk Jelly

2 large eggs, separated
2 tablespoons honey, warmed
finely grated rind and juice of 1
  lemon
600 ml (1 pint) creamy milk
12 g ($\frac{1}{2}$ oz) (1 envelope) powdered
  gelatine
2 tablespoons hot water

Beat the egg yolks and honey together until creamy. Add lemon rind to the milk and heat slowly in a thick saucepan without boiling. Whisk a little hot milk into the egg yolk mixture and blend this into the hot milk. Stir over gentle heat until the custard clings to the back of the wooden spoon. Strain into a cold bowl and cool. Dissolve gelatine thoroughly in the hot water and stir into the custard with the lemon juice. Whisk the egg whites until stiff but not brittle and fold into the custard. Reheat until nearly boiling. Rinse a 900 ml (1$\frac{1}{2}$ pint) jelly mould with cold water, pour in mixture slowly, cool and then refrigerate until set. It will separate as it sets into a fluffy top and lemon jelly base which will be reversed when it is unmoulded. Serve with fruit compôte.

Jelly Roll

2 × 227 g (8 oz) cans pineapple rings
1 × 135 g (4¾ oz) packet strawberry or
  raspberry jelly
few grapes, stalks removed and
  washed

You will need a large empty can to use
as a mould – 538 g (1 lb 3 oz) is the most
suitable size and it can be kept for
future use.
  Drain the pineapple rings and
measure the juice. Make the jelly according to packet directions, using the
pineapple juice with the cold water.
  Pour a little of the jelly into the
rinsed-out can to just cover the bottom.
Chill in the refrigerator until set. Place
one pineapple ring carefully on top of
the set jelly, put a grape in the centre,
then pour over more jelly to cover and
chill in the refrigerator until set. Continue making layers of jelly, pineapple
and grapes until the can is full, chilling
each layer of jelly until set before pro-
ceeding with the next layer. Chill in the
refrigerator for 1 hour, then unmould
on to a serving platter.
Cuts into 8 slices

Variations:
You can use a different-flavoured jelly if
preferred, and substitute strawberries,
raspberries, mandarin oranges or nuts
for the grapes used here.

Pear Church Mice

1 × 822 g (1 lb 13 oz) can pear halves
2 × 135 g (4¾ oz) packets lime jelly
21 sultanas, raisins or currants
25 g (1 oz) angelica

Drain the pears and measure the juice.
Make the jelly according to packet
directions, using the pear juice with the
water. Pour into a shallow tin or tray
and chill in the refrigerator until set.

Chop the jelly roughly with a knife
and arrange on a serving board or plate.
Arrange the pear halves on the jelly, cut
side down, then press in the dried fruit
to make two eyes and one nose for each
mouse. Cut the angelica into very fine
strips and stick a few strips on either
side of each nose to form whiskers. Chill
in the refrigerator until serving time.
Makes 7

Yogurt Jelly

1 × 100 g (4 oz) packet blackcurrant
  flavour jelly
1 small carton black cherry yogurt
2 tablespoons honey (optional)

Dissolve the jelly in 300 ml (½ pint)
boiling water according to packet directions. Stir in 150 ml (¼ pint) cold water,
then leave to cool.
  Add the yogurt and honey (if using)
and beat for a few minutes until well
mixed. Chill for several hours or overnight until set. Serve with whipped
cream, or chop the jelly roughly and
serve in individual bowls with ice cream
for the children.
Serves 4–6

Variations:
Any combination of flavours can be
used according to taste – try raspberry
or strawberry jelly with the same
flavour yogurt.
  For a richer, creamier dessert, add
150 ml (¼ pint) whipped cream to the
jelly with the yogurt.
  For a lighter version, use a large 500 g
(1 lb) carton of yogurt instead of the
small one.

Fruit Purée

Fruit purée is an important ingredient in many desserts. If it is thin and watery it will spoil the dish; it must be thick and full of flavour. The fruit can be cooked in a saucepan on top of the stove, or in a casserole in a moderate oven (180°C, 350°F, Gas Mark 4). Do not add sugar until the fruit is cooked as it will toughen the skins. 450 g (1 lb) of fresh fruit will yield about 300 ml (½ pint) of purée.

Apricots, Plums
Wash under running cold water. Cut round the fruit in the natural crease down to the stone. Twist the two halves in opposite directions so that the fruit splits and the stones can be removed. Cover the base of a thick saucepan with water. Add the fruit and cook gently until juice runs. Remove lid and continue cooking until liquid has evaporated. Sieve fruit or mash in a blender. Sweeten to taste.

Raspberries, Loganberries, Strawberries
These do not need to be cooked to make a purée, but must be sieved if you want to get rid of the pips.

Apples
Quarter, peel thinly, remove cores and slice into a bowl of cold water with 2 tablespoons of lemon juice to prevent discoloration. Butter the bottom of a thick saucepan. Put in the drained apples and 2 tablespoons water. Cover and cook gently until juice begins to flow. Remove lid and continue cooking until apples are soft and liquid has evaporated, stirring gently from time to time. Beat into a smooth thick purée with a wooden spoon. Add sugar to taste.

Gooseberries, Blackberries, Redcurrants
Top and tail the fruit with scissors. Wash under running cold water and cook as apricots.

Rhubarb
Cut off the leaves (which contain unwholesome oxalic acid), and the thick white ends of the stalks. Wash or wipe the stalks clean and chop into 2.5 cm (1 inch) lengths. Put into a buttered pan with a sliver of orange rind or two tablespoons orange juice and cook as apples.

Apricot Amber

300 ml (½ pint) sweetened apricot
  purée, still warm
lemon juice to taste
25 g (1 oz) butter
2 eggs, separated
50 g (2 oz) caster sugar

Sharpen the purée to taste with lemon juice. Stir in the butter and beaten egg yolks. Pour the mixture into a greased shallow pie dish. Whisk the egg whites to a stiff snow and fold in the caster sugar. Cover the fruit mixture completely with the meringue and ruffle the top. Dredge with caster sugar. Bake in the centre of a warm oven (160°C, 325°F, Gas Mark 3) for 30 minutes or until meringue is crisp and golden. Serve hot or cold.

Variation:
You can make this pudding equally well with any fruit purée. For a more hearty dish bake in a shortcrust pastry case.

Syrup for Fruit Salad or Compôte

225–350 g (8–12 oz) granulated sugar
600 ml (1 pint) water
thin sliver of lemon or orange rind
1 vanilla pod (optional)

Put the sugar in a pan, add the water
and lemon or orange rind and the vanilla pod, if used. Bring slowly to the
simmer, stirring until sugar is dissolved. When the sugar has completely
dissolved, boil briskly without a lid for 5
minutes, or until syrupy. Pour the syrup
into a bowl to cool and remove the rind
and vanilla pod.

Fruit Compôte

This is made with fruit which has been
gently poached in syrup until it is just
tender but still holding its shape – not
stewed in water into an unappetizing
mush. The fruit can be mixed, or all of
one kind. The syrup may be flavoured
with a stick of cinnamon, or a sliver of
lemon or orange rind, or a vanilla pod. If
you are using dried fruit – apple rings,
pear halves, apricots and prunes – soak
the fruit overnight in cold water and
use the liquor for the syrup.

Apples and Pears:
Peel, quarter and core the apples and
slice them immediately into syrup. Rosy
apples can be left unpeeled to give
colour to the salad.

Plums, Greengages, Apricots:
Wash the fruit and remove the stalks.
Cut the fruit round its natural crease,
twist the two halves in opposite directions and the fruit will split, exposing
the stone which is easily removed. Drop
fruit immediately into syrup.

Peaches:
Plunge the peaches into boiling water
for 2 to 3 minutes and peel. Remove the
stone as for plums. Quarter or slice
each peach and drop into syrup
immediately.

Cherries:
Remove the stalks and wash the
cherries in cold water. Remove stones
with a cherry stoner.

Grapes:
Split grapes down one side and remove
the pips, or leave whole and push a
paper clip into the stem end to extract
the pips.

**Strawberries, Raspberries,
Loganberries, Blackberries:**
Remove the stalks and hulls. Rinse
carefully in cold water.

Bananas:
Peel, slice and drop immediately into
syrup.

Oranges, Tangerines, Grapefruit:
Put the fruit on a plate to catch the
juice. Remove the peel and pith together, sawing downwards with a sharp
knife. Hold the fruit firmly and cut
down to the centre on either side of the
membrane of each segment and remove
the flesh. Put segments and juice in the
salad bowl.

Pineapple:
Cut the pineapple across in thick slices;
cut off the rind and remove centre core
with an apple corer. Cut pineapple into
wedges.

Melon:
Cut the melon in half and discard the
seeds. Scoop the flesh out into balls with
a French scoop, or cut it out in small
chunks. Drop the pieces into syrup. The
empty shell can be used as a basket in
which to serve fruit salad. Van dyke
(that is, cut 'V' shapes) the edges with a
sharp knife.

Dried Fruit Compôte

2 × 225 g (3 oz) packets mixed dried
   fruit (apples, apricots, prunes, figs,
   etc), soaked overnight in cold water
6 tablespoons undiluted orange
   squash
½ teaspoon ground cinnamon
4 tablespoons brown sugar
flaked almonds or chopped mixed
   nuts, to finish

Serve this as a dessert with fresh cream
or ice cream. It is also good at breakfast
time with homemade muesli or other
cereals, and yogurt.

Drain the dried fruits, then put in a pan
with the orange squash, cinnamon and
sugar. Add enough water to just cover
and stir well to mix. Bring to the boil
and simmer for 15 to 20 minutes or until
soft. Leave to cool, then chill. Sprinkle
with nuts before serving.
   Keeps for up to one week.

Baked Apples

4 Bramley apples
4 tablespoons mincemeat or other
   stuffing (see recipe)
50 g (2 oz) butter
2–3 tablespoons brown sugar
75 ml (3 fl oz) cider or water

Preheat the oven to 180°C, 350°F, Gas
Mark 4. Push a corer through the centre
of the apples. Open the hole to 3 cm (1½
inches). With a sharp knife, slit the skin
round the middle or downwards in 6
segments. This prevents the apples bur-
sting during cooking.
   Place the apples in a well-buttered
ovenproof dish. Fill the centres with
mincemeat or other stuffing such as
chopped walnuts and cherries, ground
almonds and honey, or just demerara or
soft brown sugar.
   Top each apple with a knob of butter

and sprinkle with brown sugar. Pour in
sufficient cider or water to cover the
base of the dish and place a piece of
buttered paper on top of the apples.
   Bake in the oven for 30 minutes or
longer according to size. Insert a
skewer to test if they are tender; do not
overcook. Serve hot or cold with pouring cream, custard or vanilla ice cream.

Chocolate Crunch Flan

1 × 200 g (7 oz) packet ginger nuts
approx. 75 g (3 oz) butter or
   margarine, melted
1 × 65 g (2½ oz) packet chocolate
   flavoured Angel Delight
150 ml (¼ pint) milk
2 bananas
150 ml (¼ pint) double cream, stiffly
   whipped
1 chocolate milk flake

Put the biscuits in a bowl, crushed with
the end of a rolling pin, and stir in the
melted butter. Press into the base and
sides of a 20 cm (8 inch) flan dish or
shallow cake tin, then chill until firm.
Beat the Angel Delight with the milk
according to packet directions, spread
in the bottom of the flan. Peel the
bananas and slice finely, arrange them
on top. Spread the cream over the bananas, then crumble over the chocolate.
Serves 6–8

Belgian Fruit Flan

20 cm (8 inch) flan case of sweet
  shortcrust pastry (p. 00)
300 ml ($\frac{1}{2}$ pint) Pâtisserie Cream,
  vanilla flavour (p. 365)
125 g (4 oz) green or black grapes
2 large bananas
juice of $\frac{1}{2}$ lemon
125 g (4 oz) apricot glaze
For the apricot glaze:
125 g (4 oz) apricot jam
1 tablespoon lemon juice

First make the vanilla-flavoured Pâtisserie Cream and leave it to cool,
stirring continuously to prevent a skin
forming. Meanwhile slit the grapes
down one side and remove the pips. Peel
and slice the bananas and pour over the
lemon juice to prevent discoloration.

When the Pâtisserie Cream is cold
spread it in the flan case. Arrange the
fruit on top in an attractive pattern.
Make the Apricot Glaze by dissolving
apricot jam with a little lemon juice
over a low heat. Spoon carefully over
the fruit. To give the flan a professional
finish brush the glaze over the top edges
of the pastry.

Serve the flan the day it is filled or the
pastry will lose its crispness, but the
flan case can be baked in advance and
stored in a tin.

* Raspberry, Strawberry or Cherry Flan

Follow the recipe for Belgian Fruit flan
(above), with this change: prepare 450 g
(1 lb) of fresh raspberries, hulled strawberries or stoned cherries. Flavour the
Pâtisserie Cream with lemon juice and
coat with Redcurrant Glaze.

Devonshire Sponge Flan

100 g (4 oz) butter
100 g (4 oz) caster sugar
2 eggs
100 g (4 oz) self-raising flour, sieved
100 g (4 oz) apricot jam
25 g (1 oz) flaked almonds
juice of 1 orange
450 g (1 lb) ripe plums
150 ml ($\frac{1}{4}$ pint) double or clotted
  cream, to decorate

Cream butter and sugar together until
the mixture is light and fluffy. Whisk
the eggs lightly and add gradually to
creamed mixture, beating well between
each addition. Fold in the flour quickly
and lightly. Turn the mixture into a
well-greased 20 cm (8 inch) sponge flan
ring. Bake in a preheated moderate
oven (180°C, 350°F, Gas Mark 4) for 20
minutes or until well risen and golden.
Allow to shrink and turn out on to a
wire rack. Heat the apricot jam and
brush over the border and sides of flan
case. Toast the almonds under the grill,
spread on greasproof paper and roll the
flan in them until evenly coated. Spoon
orange juice over the inside of the case.

Halve and stone the plums and arrange them overlapping in the flan.
Reheat the apricot jam, thin slightly
with water if necessary and spoon over
fruit. Decorate with whipped cream or
serve with a bowl of clotted cream.

Italian Frangipane Flan

20 cm (8 inch) flan case of sweet
  shortcrust pastry (p. 360)
70 g (2$\frac{1}{2}$ oz) unsalted butter
40 g (1$\frac{1}{2}$ oz) plain flour
1 whole egg plus one yolk
25 g (1 oz) caster sugar
150 ml ($\frac{1}{4}$ pint) milk
2 teaspoons finely grated lemon rind
25 g (1 oz) ratafias or macaroons
1 tablespoon rum

$\frac{1}{4}$ teaspoon vanilla essence
raspberry jam
To decorate:
whipped cream
pistachio kernels, halved or chopped

Melt 40 g (1$\frac{1}{2}$ oz) of the butter in a small saucepan. Remove from heat and blend in the flour. Beat the eggs and stir in gradually. Add the sugar and blend in the milk. Replace the pan on the burner and heat gently, stirring continuously until the mixture thickens and begins to leave the sides of the pan. Remove from fire and stir in the grated lemon rind, crushed ratafias, rum and vanilla essence. Heat the remaining butter in a small pan until it turns nut brown, then stir it into the cream mixture to give it the characteristic frangipane flavour.

Spread the bottom of the flan case with jam. Pour in the frangipane cream and smooth the top.

When cold decorate with rosettes of piped whipped cream and halved or chopped pistachio kernels.

Mincemeat

450 ml ($\frac{3}{4}$ pint) medium or dry cider
450 g (1 lb) dark soft brown sugar
2 kg (4 lb) cooking apples
1 teaspoon mixed spice
1 teaspoon ground cinnamon
450 g (1 lb) currants
450 g (1 lb) seedless raisins
100 g (4 oz) glacé cherries, finely chopped
100 g (4 oz) blanched almonds, finely chopped
finely grated rind and juice of 1 lemon
1 miniature bottle brandy or rum

Put the cider and sugar in a large saucepan and heat gently until the sugar has dissolved.

Meanwhile, peel, core and chop the apples and add to the pan. Stir in the remaining ingredients, except brandy or rum, and bring slowly to the boil, stirring constantly. Then lower the heat, half cover with a lid and simmer for approximately 30 minutes or until the mincemeat has become a soft pulp, stirring occasionally. Turn off the heat and leave mincemeat until quite cold. Stir in the brandy or rum, making sure that it is evenly distributed. Spoon the mincemeat into clean, dry jars with screw-topped lids, covering the top of mincemeat with a circle of greaseproof paper before putting on lids.
Makes about 4 kg (8 lb)

Mincemeat Jalousie

1 × 400 g (14 oz) packet frozen puff pastry, thawed
6 tablespoons mincemeat
1 small egg, beaten
2 tablespoons sugar
1 teaspoon ground cinnamon

Cut the pastry in two, then roll out each piece to an oblong about 25 × 15 cm (10 × 6 inches). Place one piece of pastry on a baking sheet and spread the mincemeat over it, leaving a 2.5 cm (1 inch) margin around the edges.

Preheat the oven at high temperature for 5 minutes. Place the remaining piece of pastry over the mincemeat, brush the edges with water, then press together and flute them to seal. Brush all over the pastry with the egg, then cut diagonal slits in the top piece of pastry. Sprinkle with the sugar and cinnamon, then bake in the centre of the oven for about 25 minutes. Turn the baking sheet round half way through cooking, and cover the pastry with foil if it is becoming too brown. Leave to stand for 5 minutes before serving.

Variations:
Substitute jam or lemon curd for the mincemeat, or 2 peeled, cored and sliced cooking apples, sprinkled with sugar to taste.

Mincemeat Flan

For the pastry:
250 g (8 oz) flour
pinch of salt
125 g (4 oz) butter or margarine
2 tablespoons caster sugar
1 egg yolk
2 tablespoons cold water
For the filling:
6 dessert apples
50 g (2 oz) butter
75 g (3 oz) demerara sugar
finely grated rind and juice of 1
 lemon
300 g (10 oz) mincemeat
For the topping:
3 egg whites
175 g (6 oz) caster sugar

Sieve the flour and salt into a bowl. Add the butter or margarine in pieces and rub into the flour until the mixture resembles fine breadcrumbs. Stir in the caster sugar and egg yolk, then stir in the water and draw the dough together to form a smooth ball. Wrap in foil and chill in the refrigerator for 30 minutes. Roll out the dough on a lightly floured board to a circle large enough to line a 23 cm (9 inch) flan tin or flan ring placed on a baking sheet. Prick the base of the dough with a fork and chill in the refrigerator for another 30 minutes. Line the dough with foil and baking beans and bake blind in a fairly hot oven (190°C, 375°F, Gas Mark 5) for 15 minutes. Remove foil and beans, return to the oven and bake for another 5 minutes until the pastry is golden. Remove the flan ring if used.

Peel apples, core with an apple corer and slice into thin rings. Melt the butter in a pan, add the apple rings, demerara sugar, lemon rind and juice and cook gently for a few minutes until the apples are coated in the mixture. Cool. Arrange half the apple rings in the bottom of the pastry case. Spoon in mincemeat and top with the remaining apples.

Beat the egg whites until stiff, then beat in 1 tablespoon of the caster sugar. Fold in the remaining sugar, reserving 1 tablespoon for dredging. Pipe the meringue on top of the flan to cover the filling completely. Dredge with the reserved sugar and bake in a very cool oven (140°C, 275°F, Gas Mark 1) for 30 minutes until the meringue is golden. Remove from the oven and leave to rest for approximately 15 minutes before serving as a dessert with fresh cream. Or leave until cold, then slice thinly and serve as a tea time treat.

Orange Honey Gingernut Flan

175 g (6 oz) ginger nuts
50 g (2 oz) caster sugar
50 g (2 oz) butter, melted
For the filling:
225 g (8 oz) cottage cheese
150 ml (¼ pint) natural yogurt
1 tablespoon orange blossom honey
finely grated rind and juice of 1 large
 orange
2 teaspoons powdered gelatine
3 tablespoons hot water
To decorate:
75 ml (3 fl oz) double cream
5 crystallised orange slices

Crush the ginger nuts between 2 sheets of greaseproof paper with a rolling pin, or use a liquidiser. Combine with caster sugar and melted butter. Press into a 20 cm (8 inch) pottery flan dish or shallow pie dish. Chill until really firm in the refrigerator.

Sieve the cottage cheese into a bowl and mix in yogurt and honey. Add the orange rind and juice. Dissolve the gelatine thoroughly in the hot water and stir into the mixture. Pour into the flan case and chill in refrigerator for an hour or two until set.

Decorate with piped whipped cream and crystallised orange slices and cut into wedges.

Sweet Summer Flan

225 g (8 oz) fresh raspberries
50 g (2 oz) sugar, or to taste
1 × 150 ml (5 fl oz) carton double or
   whipping cream
1 × 150 ml (5 fl oz) carton single cream
1 small sponge flan case

Chop the raspberries, reserving a few whole ones for decoration. Put the chopped raspberries and sugar in a bowl, stir gently to mix, then leave for 5 to 10 minutes. Meanwhile, put the creams together in a separate bowl and beat until thick. Fold in the chopped raspberries, then spread in the flan case. Use the whole raspberries to decorate the top of the flan. Keep in a cool place until serving time.

Variations:
Any fresh fruit can be used instead of the raspberries – try hulled strawberries, stoned cherries or peaches.

Treacle Tart

175 g (6 oz) plain shortcrust pastry
   (p. 363)
3 rounded tablespoons golden syrup
1 teaspoon finely grated lemon rind
2 rounded tablespoons fresh white
   breadcrumbs

Grease the base, but not the lip, of a 20 cm (8 inch) ovenproof plate or shallow pie dish. Roll the pastry out thinly into a circle. Cut strips off the outside edge the same width as the lip of the plate. Damp the lip and press on the pastry strip; damp the strip. Roll remaining pastry over the pin and unroll over the plate, ease it into the base of the plate and press outer edges firmly together. Trim off surplus pastry, knock-up outside edge with the back of a knife and flute it. Prick bottom of tart all over with a fork.

Warm the syrup with the lemon rind, mix in the breadcrumbs and pour into the tart. Cut pastry trimmings into narrow strips and criss-cross lattice fashion over the filling. Damp the ends of the strips and fix firmly on to pastry edge. Cover with little circles cut out of trimmings. Bake in the centre of preheated moderately hot oven (190°C, 375°F, Gas Mark 5) for 30 minutes or until the pastry is crisp and golden. Serve hot or cold.

Orange Treacle Tart

225 g (8 oz) flour
pinch of salt
50 g (2 oz) margarine, cut into pieces
50 g (2 oz) lard, cut into pieces
2 tablespoons cold water
For the filling:
225 g (8 oz) golden syrup
100 g (4 oz) chunky marmalade
2 tablespoons lemon juice
225 g (8 oz) fresh white breadcrumbs

To make the pastry, sift the flour and salt into a bowl. Rub in the margarine and lard and add just sufficient cold water to make a firm dough. Wrap in foil or greaseproof paper and chill in the refrigerator for 30 minutes.

Roll out the pastry on a floured surface and use to line a 20 cm (8 inch) sandwich tin or a flan dish or flan ring placed on a baking sheet.

To make the filling, mix together the syrup, marmalade and lemon juice until well blended. Add the breadcrumbs and stir until coated with the syrup mixture. Spoon the filling into the pastry case and smooth the top. Bake in a moderate oven (180°C, 350°F, Gas Mark 4) for 25 to 30 minutes, or until golden-brown.

Tarte Française

300 g (10 oz) sweet shortcrust pastry
(p. 360)
For the filling:
225 g (8 oz) sugar
600 ml (1 pint) water
1 kg (2 lb) fresh apricots, halved and
stoned
175 g (6 oz) lemon curd
300 ml ($\frac{1}{2}$ pint) double cream
2 tablespoons arrowroot
2 tablespoons rum, lemon juice or
water
4 tablespoons sieved apricot jam

Make the pastry and chill in the refrigerator for at least 1 hour.

For filling: heat sugar and water gently until the sugar has dissolved, then boil rapidly for 5 minutes. Lower the heat, add half the apricots, simmer gently for 5 minutes until tender but still whole. Remove with a slotted spoon and drain. Repeat with remaining apricots. Strain syrup and reserve. Press the chilled dough into a 30 cm (12 inch) fluted flan tin with removable base. Chill for 30 minutes, then prick the base with a fork, cover with foil and fill with baking beans. Place on a baking sheet and bake blind in a preheated fairly hot oven (190°C, 375°F, Gas Mark 5) for 15 minutes, then remove foil and beans and bake a further 15 minutes until set and golden, remove from the oven and leave to cool.

Spread the lemon curd over the base. Whip the cream until just becoming stiff, then spread over the lemon curd. Arrange the drained apricot halves on top of the cream.

Mix the arrowroot with the rum, lemon juice or water. Return the sugar syrup to the heat, stir in arrowroot mixture and jam, then bring to the boil and simmer until thick. Remove from the heat, leave to cool slightly, then pour over the apricots.

Leave until set before serving.

Cuts into about 12 portions

Harlequin Jam Tart

225 g (8 oz) plain shortcrust pastry
(p. 363)
1 tablespoon raspberry jam
1 tablespoon apricot jam
1 tablespoon gooseberry jam
1 tablespoon blackberry jam

Roll the pastry out thinly and line a 20 cm (8 inch) pie plate as for Treacle Tart (p. 267). With a knife mark the bottom pastry across into 8 equal triangles. Spread each triangle with jam, alternating the colours.

Cut the pastry trimmings into narrow strips and arrange them across the tart, dividing the jams. Damp the end of each strip, press one end on the pastry edge, twist it across the tart and secure on the other side. Cover the ends with cut out pastry shapes. Bake in the centre of preheated moderately hot oven (190°C, 375°F, Gas Mark 5) for 30 minutes.

Norfolk Treacle Custard Tart

125 g (4 oz) plain shortcrust pastry
(p. 363)
4 tablespoons golden syrup
1 teaspoon finely grated lemon rind
15 g ($\frac{1}{2}$ oz) butter
2 tablespoons single cream
1 egg, beaten

Roll pastry out thinly and line a 20 cm (8 inch) flan ring. Prick the bottom. Warm the syrup with the lemon rind. Cut the butter into small pieces and stir it into syrup. Leave until nearly cold. Beat the cream and egg together and blend into the syrup. Pour into the flan case. Bake in the centre of a moderate oven (180°C, 350°F, Gas Mark 4) for 40 minutes or until pastry is crisp and filling is set. Allow to shrink before removing flan ring and slide on to a serving plate. Serve hot or cold.

Tarte au Citron

175 g (6 oz) sweet shortcrust pastry
(p. 360)
For the filling:
50 g (2 oz) butter
finely grated rind and juice of 2
lemons
2 eggs, beaten
225 g (8 oz) caster sugar
75 g (3 oz) ground almonds
For the topping:
2 lemons
For the glaze:
water
225 g (8 oz) sugar

Roll out the shortcrust pastry and line a 20 cm (8 inch) flan dish or flan ring placed on a baking sheet. Flute the edges and prick the base, then chill dough in the refrigerator for another 30 minutes. Line the dough with foil and baking beans and bake blind in a fairly hot oven (190°C, 375°F, Gas Mark 5) for 10 minutes. Remove foil and beans, return to the oven and bake for another 10 to 15 minutes until the pastry is golden and set. Remove from oven and leave to cool.

Put the ingredients for the filling (except the ground almonds) in the top of a double boiler or in a heatproof bowl standing over a pan of gently simmering water. Cook the mixture for 30 to 40 minutes until thick, stirring constantly with a wooden spoon. Remove from the heat and stir in the ground almonds until evenly mixed. Pour into the flan case and leave to set in a cool place overnight.

Meanwhile, prepare the lemon slices for the top of the tart. Slice the lemons thinly and remove the pips. Put the slices in a heatproof bowl, pour over boiling water to cover and leave overnight. The next day, drain the slices, put in a pan and cover with fresh water.

Bring to the boil and simmer gently for 20 to 30 minutes until they are soft. Remove lemon slices with a slotted spoon, reserving the cooking liquid. Dry on absorbent kitchen paper, then arrange on top of the set filling.

To prepare the glaze: make the reserved cooking liquid from the lemon slices up to 300 ml (½ pint) with water. Put in a heavy-based pan with the sugar and heat gently until the sugar has dissolved. Increase the heat and boil rapidly for 7 to 10 minutes until syrupy. Remove from the heat, leave to cool slightly, then spoon over the lemon slices to cover. Leave to set, then remove flan ring, if used. Place flan on a serving platter before serving.
Serves 4–6

Bavarian Prune and Apricot Torte

250 g (9 oz) plain flour
125 g (4½ oz) unsalted butter
125 g (4½ oz) caster sugar
3 egg yolks, beaten
¼ teaspoon vanilla essence
75 ml (3 fl oz) water
For the topping:
100 g (4 oz) prunes, soaked
50 g (2 oz) apricots, soaked
2–3 tablespoons lemon juice
caster sugar for dredging

Sieve the flour and rub in the butter with finger tips until the mixture resembles fine breadcrumbs. Mix in the sugar. Beat egg yolks with vanilla essence and water and stir into dry ingredients. Add a little water if necessary to give a soft dough. Knead lightly on a floured board; pat out into a circle 6 mm (¼ inch) thick and place in a greased 20 cm (8 inch) sandwich tin. Chill for 30 minutes. Stone prunes and arrange on top of the torte with the apricots. Sprinkle with lemon juice and caster sugar. Bake in a preheated hot oven (200°C, 400°F, Gas Mark 6) for 15 minutes, reduce heat (180°C, 350°F, Gas Mark 4) and cook for 10 minutes or until set. Serve hot or cold with cream.

Raspberry Linzer Torte

125 g (5 oz) plain flour
½ teaspoon ground cinnamon
1 teaspoon instant coffee powder
50 g (2 oz) ground hazelnuts
75 g (3 oz) butter
65 g (2½ oz) caster sugar
finely grated rind of ½ lemon
2 egg yolks or 1 whole egg, beaten
For the filling:
approx. 5 heaped tablespoons 275 g
    (10 oz) raspberry jam or fresh
    raspberries with 2 tablespoons
    sugar
To glaze:
1 egg white, beaten
caster sugar

Sift the flour, cinnamon and coffee into
a mixing bowl and mix in the ground
nuts. Cut the fat into the flour and rub
in to a breadcrumb consistency. Mix in
the sugar and lemon rind.

Stir in the beaten egg and knead into
a soft dough. Chill for at least 30 minutes. Grease an 18–20 cm (7–8 inch) pie
plate. Roll out the dough into a round,
put into the plate and with floured
fingers work it out until it lines the
plate, about ½ cm (¼ inch) thick. Trim
edges neatly. Work up the trimmings
and roll out to ½ cm (¼ inch) thick and
cut into narrow strips.

Prick the bottom of the pie and spread
with raspberry jam or crushed fresh
raspberries sweetened with caster
sugar. Lay the strips of pastry across
the filling in a lattice pattern. Trim the
ends and press them into the edge of the
pie. Brush the pastry with beaten egg
white and dust with caster sugar. Bake
in a preheated moderate oven (180°C,
350°F, Gas Mark 4) for 40 minutes or
until set.

Serve cold in the pie plate or lift out
when cold.

Nut Torte

50 g (2 oz) unblanched almonds
50 g (2 oz) walnuts
4 eggs, separated
125 g (5 oz) caster sugar
Mocha Butter Cream (½ quantity)
    (p. 320)
For the caramel topping:
75 g (3 oz) sugar
3 tablespoons water
25 g (1 oz) walnut halves

Line the base and grease two 18 cm (7
inch) sandwich tins.

Mince the nuts in a mouli grater or
electric grinder. Whisk together the egg
yolks and caster sugar in a mixing bowl
until a pale lemon colour. Whisk the
whites until stiff but not too dry. Using
a concave spatula or large cooking
spoon, fold the whites and nuts into the
egg yolks and sugar until well blended,
but do not overfold. Pour into the sandwich tins and level off. Bake on the
same shelf in the centre of a preheated
moderate oven (180°C, 350°F, Gas Mark
4) for 30 minutes or until set. The top
should spring back when gently pressed. Remove from the oven and allow
to shrink slightly before turning out on
a wire tray to cool. When cold, place
one half of the torte on a large serving
plate, spread with Mocha Butter Cream
and put the other one on top.

Caramel topping: oil the edge of the
plate so any drips of caramel can be
easily removed. Dissolve the sugar in
the water in a small saucepan over a low
heat. Stir until the syrup is clear, but do
not allow to boil. When clear, raise the
heat and boil rapidly without stirring
until a rich caramel colour. Use immediately or the caramel will burn and
turn too dark and make the torte bitter.
Pour the caramel on top of the torte,
spreading it with an oiled palette knife
neatly to the edge. Arrange the walnuts
on top quickly before the caramel gets
hard. Press the back of a knife into the
caramel marking it into 8 portions to

make it easier to cut when serving. When the remaining caramel in the pan has cooled slightly, dip the end of the knife in it and draw it up in threads and trickle them over the nuts, or pull into spun sugar.

If you are not planning to serve the torte until the following day, it is advisable to delay making the caramel until then as it absorbs moisture in the air and loses its crispiness.

Baked Stuffed Peaches

4 large peaches
2 tablespoons rum or brandy
For the stuffing:
25 g (1 oz) caster sugar
50 g (2 oz) unsalted butter
50 g (2 oz) ratafia biscuits
1 egg yolk, beaten

To make the stuffing, cream the sugar and 25 g (1 oz) of the butter together in a bowl. Crush the ratafia biscuits between two sheets of greaseproof paper, using a rolling pin, and work them into the creamed mixture. Bind with the beaten egg yolk.

Plunge the peaches into boiling water for 2 to 3 minutes, then peel off the skin. Slit the peaches round the natural crease, and remove the stones. Grease a shallow ovenproof dish with the rest of the butter and put in the peach halves cut side up. Divide the stuffing into eight and fill the peach halves, doming the stuffing neatly. Cover the peaches with buttered greaseproof paper or foil and bake in a preheated oven (180°C, 350°F, Gas Mark 4) for 20 minutes or until just cooked. Heat the brandy or rum in a small pan, set light to it and pour it flaming over the peaches. Serve immediately with whipped double or clotted cream.

Fruit Slices

225 g (8 oz) flour
pinch of salt
150 g (5 oz) butter or margarine
2 teaspoons caster sugar
2–3 tablespoons cold water
For the filling:
1 tablespoon cornflour
150 ml ($\frac{1}{4}$ pint) water
75 g (3 oz) sugar
350 g (12 oz) mixed dried fruit
(sultanas, raisins, currants)
1 teaspoon ground cinnamon
To glaze:
cold water
caster sugar

Sift the flour and salt into a bowl. Rub in the fat with the fingertips until the mixture resembles fine breadcrumbs. Stir in the sugar and add just sufficient water to hold the mixture together, then form into a smooth ball. Wrap in foil or greaseproof paper and chill in the refrigerator for 30 minutes.

To make the filling, blend the cornflour to a smooth paste with a little of the water. Stir in the remaining water and place in a saucepan. Add the sugar, fruit and cinnamon and bring to the boil, stirring constantly, until the mixture thickens. Cook for 1 minute then allow to cool.

Divide the pastry into 2 equal portions. Roll out one half to line a greased 30 × 22.5 cm (12 × 9 inch) Swiss roll tin. Cover the base with the fruit mixture and spread evenly. Roll the remaining pastry to cover. Lay this over the filling, dampen the edges and press together to seal. Flute with your finger and thumb or press with the back of a fork. Brush with a little water and dredge with the caster sugar. Bake in a fairly hot oven (190°C, 375°F, Gas Mark 5) for about 25 minutes, or until pale golden.

Cut into 5 × 11 cm (2 × 4$\frac{1}{2}$ inch) slices and allow to cool before removing carefully from the tin.
Makes 12

Paskha

50 g (2 oz) maraschino cherries,
  drained and chopped
50 g (2 oz) chopped mixed peel
50 g (2 oz) blanched almonds, finely
  chopped
50 g (2 oz) seedless raisins
finely grated rind of 1 lemon
1 tablespoon dry sherry
350 g (12 oz) carton cottage cheese
100 g (4 oz) cream cheese
100 g (4 oz) caster sugar
120 ml (4 fl oz) carton double cream
2 teaspoons powdered gelatine
3 tablespoons lemon juice
To decorate:
a little oil
about 12 glacé cherries, halved

Put the maraschino cherries, mixed
peel, almonds, raisins and lemon rind in
a small bowl, stir in the sherry and mix
well until the sherry is absorbed. Set
aside.

Mix the cottage and cream cheeses
together, then beat in the sugar. Beat
the cream until thick and fold into the
cheese with the fruit and nut mixture.

Sprinkle the gelatine over the lemon
juice in a small heatproof bowl, leave
until spongy, then place the bowl in a
pan of hot water and stir over low heat
until the gelatine has dissolved.
Remove from the heat, leave to cool
slightly, then fold into the cheese mixture. Line a 12.5 cm (5 inch) clay flower
pot with a large piece of muslin or a
clean tea-towel, spoon in the cheese and
fold the cloth over the top. Cover with a
saucer, place heavy weights on top,
stand in a bowl and chill in the refrigerator overnight.

The next day, remove the weights and
saucer and unfold the cloth. Invert a
serving platter over the pot and turn
out the paskha. Brush lightly with oil,
then press halved glacé cherries around
the top and bottom edges. Chill in the
refrigerator until serving time.
Serves 6–8

Peppermint Chocolate Pears

10–12 mint chocolate creams
4 ripe Comice pears
50 g (2 oz) crystallised ginger or glacé
  cherries, chopped
150 ml (¼ pint) single cream
25 g (1 oz) walnuts, chopped

Cut up the chocolate mints and put
them in a bowl over a saucepan of
simmering water to melt.

Core pears from the bottom, leaving
top with stalk intact. Peel and slice a
sliver off the base so that pears will
stand upright. Stuff with chopped
ginger or cherries and place each pear
in a small dessert dish.

Heat the cream, without boiling and
add to the peppermint cream. Stir until
smooth and pour over the pears.
Sprinkle with chopped walnuts and
serve at once.

Pears in Red Wine

4 even-sized pears
150 ml (¼ pint) red wine
100 g (4 oz) caster sugar
approx. 300 ml (½ pint) water
1 long sliver lemon rind

Choose a deep flameproof casserole just
large enough to take the pears standing
up. Put in the wine, sugar, 150 ml (¼ pint)
of the water and the lemon rind. Bring
to the boil on top of the stove and
simmer until syrupy. Peel the pears,
leave on the stalks and level off the
base. Stand the pears in the casserole
and pour over the wine syrup. Add
sufficient water just to cover the pears.
Put on the lid and cook in a preheated
oven at 160°C, 325°F, Gas Mark 3 for 1½
hours or until just tender; test with a
skewer to see if they are ready.

Chill thoroughly and serve with
whipped or thin cream.

Brown Bread Ice-cream

175 ml (3 oz) wholemeal breadcrumbs
100 g (4 oz) caster sugar
175 ml (6 fl oz) double cream
100 ml (4 fl oz) single cream
100 g (4 oz) icing sugar, sieved
1 egg, separated
2 tablespoons rum or Marsala
To decorate:
50 g (2 oz) crushed peanut brittle or
   praline
whipping cream (optional)

Spread the crumbs on a baking tray and
sprinkle with the caster sugar. Bake in
a moderately hot oven (190°C, 375°F,
Gas Mark 5) until crisp and golden,
shaking the tray from time to time.
Spread on a cold plate to cool.

Whisk the double and single cream
together, gradually adding the icing
sugar. Beat the egg yolk with the rum or
Marsala and whisk into the cream.

Whisk the egg white until stiff but not
brittle and fold into the mixture with
the breadcrumbs. Turn into a 600 ml (1
pint) mould, cover tightly with foil and
freeze. To unmould dip briskly into hot
water and turn out.

Decorate with crushed peanut brittle
or praline and serve with butterscotch or
chocolate sauce. Alternatively serve in
individual glasses or goblets, pour over
the sauce, top with whipped cream and
nut brittle.

Chocolate Cream Ice

50 g (2 oz) plain chocolate
600 ml (1 pint) single cream
75 g (3 oz) caster sugar
3 egg yolks, beaten
2–3 tablespoons Marsala or sweet
   sherry
To decorate:
whipping cream
crystallised violets
pistachio nuts or walnuts

An ice-cream made with a chocolate
custard base which can be varied by
flavouring it with instant coffee or rum,
or given a crunchy texture by folding in
2–3 tablespoons of praline with the egg
whites.

Break up chocolate and melt in a
bowl over hot water. Put the cream over
the gentle heat. Add a little hot cream to
the melted chocolate, stir until smooth
and blend back into cream with the
sugar. Add 2–3 tablespoons of plain
chocolate mixture to the egg yolks and
stir this mixture back into the pan.
Continue to stir over gentle heat (in a
double boiler if preferred) until cream
thickens into a thin custard and coats
the back of the wooden spoon. Do not
boil or it will separate.

Cool, stirring occasionally to prevent
a skin forming, then add Marsala or
sherry. Pour into moulds or freezing
tray and freeze until stiff. Serve decorated with whipped cream, crystallised violets and chopped nuts.

Banana Boats

1 × 50 g (2 oz) bar plain chocolate,
   broken into pieces
2 tablespoons water
1 × 150 ml (5 fl oz) carton double
   cream
1 × 300 ml (10 fl oz) carton vanilla ice
   cream
4 bananas
2 tablespoons chopped nuts

Put the chocolate and water in a non-
stick pan and heat gently until melted,
stirring occasionally. Remove from the
heat, leave to cool slightly, then stir in
half the cream. Beat the remaining
cream until stiff. Slice the bananas in
two lengthways, then place in individual shallow bowls. Top with scoops
of ice cream, then drizzle over the
melted chocolate. Top each boat with
whipped cream, sprinkle with nuts and
serve immediately.

Iced Raspberry Parfait

450 g (1 lb) fresh raspberries
2 egg whites
100 g (4 oz) caster sugar
4 tablespoons water
2 tablespoons lemon juice
300 ml ($\frac{1}{2}$ pint) double cream
To decorate:
whipping cream
whole raspberries or crystallised rose
  petals

Sieve the raspberries. If using canned fruit strain off the juice, sieve the fruit, measure the purée and make up to 300 ml ($\frac{1}{2}$ pint) with some of the juice. Whisk the egg whites to stiff snow.

Put the sugar and water in a small saucepan and place over gentle heat. Stir until sugar has dissolved, then bring to the boil and cook rapidly without stirring until the syrup will form a thread (120°C, 250°F). Allow the syrup to stop bubbling, then pour slowly on to the beaten egg whites in a thin steady stream, holding the saucepan well above the basin and stirring continuously with a wooden spoon. When all the sugar is in, continue to beat until the mixture is thick and shiny and forms soft peaks. Stir in the fruit purée and lemon juice. Whip the cream into soft peaks but not stiff and gradually fold in the fruit mixture. Sharpen to taste with lemon juice.

Pour into a mould or individual dariole tins and freeze. Remove Parfait from freezer into the refrigerator 1 hour before serving. Dip the mould briefly in hot water to unmould. Decorate with whipped cream and whole raspberries or crystallised rose petals. Serve with wafer biscuits or plain petits fours.

Variation:
Fresh loganberries, strawberries or apricots can be substituted for the raspberries, or if fresh fruit is not available any tinned fruit except strawberries can be used.

Slimline Orange Sorbet

175 ml (6 fl oz) frozen or fresh orange
  juice
1 large orange
300 ml ($\frac{1}{2}$ pint) natural yogurt
12 g ($\frac{1}{2}$ oz) (1 envelope) powdered
  gelatine
4 tablespoons hot water
2 egg whites
fresh mint or borage sprigs, to
  decorate

Defrost the frozen orange juice. Grate the rind finely off the orange and add to the juice. Mix into the yogurt. Dissolve gelatine in hot water, blend with the mixture and leave to thicken.

Whisk the egg whites to a stiff snow and when the yogurt begins to set, fold in carefully. Pour the sorbet mixture into a freezer container and freeze.

Peel the pith off the orange. Take a sharp knife and cut down to the centre of the orange on either side of each section and lift it out from between the dividing membranes.

To serve fill individual glasses with spoonfuls of frozen sorbet interspersed with orange sections. Garnish with sprigs of fresh mint or borage.

Iced Melon Sorbet

1 small honeydew melon
100 g (4 oz) caster sugar
1 lemon
1 egg white
To decorate:
150 ml ($\frac{1}{4}$ pint) whipping cream
4 Maraschino or glacé cherries
8 fresh mint leaves or angelica
  diamonds

Cut the melon in half lengthwise, discard the pips and scoop out the flesh. Put this in a blender with the sugar and 2 tablespoons of juice squeezed from the lemon. Whisk until the sugar is dissolved. Pour into a freezer container and freeze until mushy.

Meanwhile cut the two pieces of melon shell in half lengthwise. Reform each into original shape, using two bowls of matching size lined with kitchen foil. Chill in refrigerator.

When the melon mixture is mushy turn into a bowl and whisk. Whisk egg white until stiff and fold into melon mixture; sharpen to taste with lemon juice. Pour into two melon shells, cover with foil and freeze. About 1 hour before required separate into four sections using a knife dipped into hot water. Place wedges on four dessert plates. Using a rose nozzle, pipe a zig-zag of whipped cream along the top of each wedge. Place a cherry in the centre with a frosted mint or angelica leaf on either side. Return to the refrigerator until serving.

If you cannot get a small melon for 4 servings, use half a large one and cut it into 4 wedges.

Pineapple Sorbet

1 ripe fresh pineapple, about 1½ kg (3 lb), cut in half lengthwise
2 egg whites
For the sugar syrup:
100 g (4 oz) sugar
300 ml (½ pint) water

Scoop out the pineapple flesh and juice, reserving the pineapple shells, and purée in an electric blender. Transfer to a mixing bowl.

To make the sugar syrup: put sugar and water in a heavy-based saucepan, then heat gently until the sugar has dissolved. Increase the heat and boil rapidly for 7 to 10 minutes until syrupy, then remove from the heat and leave until cold. Mix the pineapple purée and sugar syrup together, pour into a freezer tray and freeze in the ice box of the refrigerator or in the freezer. Leave until the mixture becomes mushy.

Turn the mixture into a bowl and beat with an electric or rotary beater. Beat the egg whites until stiff, then fold into the pineapple mixture. Spoon the mixture into the pineapple shells and return to the ice box or freezer.

Freeze for at least 2 hours or overnight. Transfer to main part of refrigerator 15 minutes before serving.

Fire and Ice

4 medium Bramley apples
25 g (1 oz) butter or margarine
4 tablespoons demerara sugar
about 75 ml (3 fl oz) cider or water
1 family block vanilla ice-cream
4 shelled walnuts or crushed gingernuts

Wipe and core the apples. With a sharp knife, slit the skin round the 'equator'. Place the apples in a well-buttered fireproof dish and fill their centres with demerara sugar. Add sufficient cider or water to cover base of baking dish. Cover with a buttered sheet of greaseproof paper or foil. Bake in a preheated moderately hot oven (190°C, 375°F, Gas Mark 5) for 30 minutes until tender – test with a skewer and do not overcook. Remove from oven, lift skin carefully off the apples and place in individual dishes or bowls.

Keep the apples warm while you boil the liquid in the base of the dish briskly until reduced to a syrupy consistency. Pour over the apples. Top each apple with a generous helping of ice-cream and a shelled walnut or crushed gingernut. Serve immediately.

Chocolate Ripple Pears

100 g (4 oz) plain chocolate
3 tablespoons golden syrup
75 ml (3 fl oz) single cream
4 ripe dessert pears
1 family block vanilla and chocolate
   ice-cream
25 g (1 oz) ratafia biscuits, to decorate

First make the Chocolate Cream Sauce.
Break up the chocolate and melt in a
bowl over hot water. Blend in golden
syrup. Heat the cream, without boiling,
and gradually stir into the chocolate
mixture. Keep warm over the hot water.
(If serving cold, remove from heat and
stir occasionally until chilled.)

Core, halve and peel the pears. Put
two scoops of vanilla and chocolate ice-
cream in each dessert dish and arrange
a half pear on either side. Pour over the
hot Chocolate Cream Sauce and decorate with ratafia biscuits, either
whole or crushed.

Peach Melba

1 × 200 g (7 oz) can raspberries
2 tablespoons icing sugar
1 teaspoon arrowroot or cornflour
1 tablespoon water
1 × 300 ml (10 fl oz) carton vanilla ice
   cream
4 fresh peaches, skinned, halved and
   stoned

Work the raspberries through a sieve
into a small pan. Stir in the icing sugar.
Mix the arrowroot or cornflour to a
paste with the water, then stir into the
pan. Bring to the boil, stirring constantly, then simmer for 1 to 2 minutes
until thick and glossy. Leave to cool.

Divide the ice cream equally between
4 individual bowls, then arrange two
peach halves on either side of the ice
cream. Pour over the sauce and serve
immediately.

Pineapple Igloos

3 egg whites
175 g (6 oz) caster sugar
4 pineapple slices
600 ml (1 pint) strawberry ice-cream
To decorate:
glacé cherries
angelica leaves
caster sugar

Preheat the oven to 230°C, 450°F, Gas
Mark 8 and place a shelf near the top.
Whisk the egg whites until very stiff
and dry. Sieve in 4 tablespoons sugar
and continue whisking until stiff and
shiny. Fold in the remaining sugar.

Place the pineapple slices on 4 ovenproof glass dishes. Pile the ice-cream
evenly on top so that it does not project
over the edge. Swirl the meringue over
each one, covering the ice-cream and
pineapple completely. Be careful to seal
the edges right on to the plates or the
ice-cream will melt and leak.

Decorate with glacé cherries and angelica and dredge with caster sugar. Put
the dishes on a baking sheet and bake
for 4–5 minutes, until they are delicately coloured and crisp. Serve at once.

Spiced Apple Pie

225 g (8 oz) shortcrust pastry, plain or
   rich (p. 363 or 361)
75 g (3 oz) white or brown sugar
1 tablespoon flour
$\frac{1}{4}$ teaspoon grated nutmeg
$\frac{1}{4}$ teaspoon ground cinnamon
finely grated rind and juice of 1
   orange
finely grated rind of 1 lemon
750 g (1½ lb) cooking apples, sliced
50 g (2 oz) sultanas
1 tablespoon lemon juice
40 g (1½ oz) butter, melted
To glaze:
milk or beaten egg white
granulated sugar

Preheat the oven to 200°C, 400°F, Gas Mark 6. Grease the base of a 20 cm (8 inch) round shallow pie dish. Divide the pastry in half and roll out one half thinly into a round. Damp the lip of the pie dish, line it with the pastry and prick all over the base with a fork. Mix together the sugar, flour and spices and rub a little over the pastry base. Add grated orange and lemon rind to remainder. Arrange the sliced apples in the dish, sprinkle each layer with sultanas, sugar mixture, fruit juice and melted butter.

Roll out the other piece of pastry into a round about 5 cm (2 inches) larger all round than the top of the pie dish. Damp the edge of the bottom pastry. Lift the other piece on the rolling pin and unroll it across the top of the pie. Press the two edges firmly together and with a sharp knife trim off the surplus pastry and knock it back.

To flute the edge: with the left forefinger, press the pastry edge down and slightly off the rim of the dish and with the thumb and forefinger of the other hand press the pastry into a peak. Repeat evenly round the edge of the pie. Make a few slits in the top of the pie to allow the steam to escape while it is cooking.

Bake in the oven for 20 minutes or until the pastry is well risen and turning golden. Lower the heat to 190°C, 375°F, Gas Mark 5 and cook for another 25 minutes, or until the filling is cooked. Serve hot with cream or custard.

Iced Plum Pudding

300 ml ($\frac{1}{2}$ pint) double cream
1 × 225 g (8 oz) can condensed milk
1 teaspoon mixed spice
$\frac{1}{2}$ teaspoon grated nutmeg
4 teaspoons instant coffee powder
25 g (1 oz) chopped citron peel
50 g (2 oz) chopped walnuts
75 g (3 oz) seedless raisins
75 g (3 oz) sultanas

75 g (3 oz) glacé cherries, chopped
finely grated rind of 1 orange
$\frac{1}{2}$ teaspoon vanilla essence
2–3 tablespoons rum or brown sherry
To decorate:
1 tangerine
1–2 tablespoons rum or brandy

Whisk half of the cream together with the condensed milk, spices and coffee. Pour into a refrigerator tray and freeze until stiffened. Turn into a bowl and whisk again until light and creamy. Whip remaining cream to soft peak and fold into the mixture with the fruit, nuts and orange rind. Flavour to taste with vanilla and rum or sherry. Pour into a pudding mould and freeze hard.

Move mould from freezer to refrigerator about 1 hour before required. Cut tangerine in half; then carefully scoop out pulp from one half.

To serve, dip mould quickly into hot water and unmould onto a serving platter. Decorate with rosettes of whipped cream and quartered glacé cherries. Alternatively make a hollow in the top and place a half tangerine shell inside. Warm 1 or 2 tablespoons rum, fill the shell, set alight and serve immediately.

Blackberry and Pear Pie

225 g (8 oz) blackberries
450 g (1 lb) cooking pears
4–5 tablespoons sugar
225 g (8 oz) plain shortcrust pastry
   (p. 00)
caster sugar for dredging

Pick over the blackberries, removing any hulls, and wash if necessary. Quarter the pears, then peel, core and slice them. Fill a deep 900 ml (1½ pint) pie dish with the fruit, piling the layers of sliced pears and blackberries into a dome. Sprinkle each layer with sugar. Add 2 tablespoons water.

On a floured board, roll out the pastry 5 mm (¼ inch) thick to the same shape as the top of the pie dish but a little larger. Damp the lip of the dish. Cut off and press on strips of pastry, damp the strips and cover with the remaining pastry. Flute the edge if you wish, but to distinguish a fruit from a meat pie, the edge should really be crimped with the tines of a fork. With the left thumb, press the knocked back pastry edge down firmly and holding the fork vertically, press tines of fork against outer edge of pastry, marking it in grooves.

It is not correct to decorate the top of the pie with pastry leaves as for steak pie; instead, prick through the pastry with the fork in a simple design.

Bake in a preheated oven (200°C, 400°F, Gas Mark 6) for 30–40 minutes, until the fruit is cooked and the pastry is crisp and golden. Remove the pie from oven, place it on serving dish and dredge with caster sugar. Serve with clotted or pouring cream or custard.

Variations:
Use ¾ kg (1½ lb) sliced apples and 1 teaspoon ground cinnamon or cloves mixed with brown sugar.

Use 1 kg (2 lb) rhubarb, cleaned and sliced, with 1 teaspoon ground ginger mixed with sugar.

Use 1 kg (2 lb) plums, apricots or greengages, halved and stoned or same amount of gooseberries, topped and tailed, with white or brown sugar.

Cherry Brandy Pie

900 g (2 lb) cherries, stoned
75 g (3 oz) granulated sugar
225 g (8 oz) plain or sweet shortcrust pastry (p. 363 or 360)
50 ml (2 fl oz) Cherry Brandy
75 ml (3 fl oz) double cream, warmed
caster sugar for dredging

Light the oven. Fill a 900 ml (1½ pint) oval pie dish with the stoned cherries, sugaring each layer.

Roll out the pastry thinly in an oval, 5 cm (2 inches) wider than the top of the pie dish all round. Cut a strip of pastry, the same width as the lip of the dish, off outside edge of the pastry. Damp the lip and press pastry strip firmly down on it. Damp the strip, lift the rest of the pastry on the rolling pin and unroll it over the dish. Press the pastry edges together and trim off the surplus with a sharp knife. Holding the knife horizontally and using the back of it, knock up the pastry edge. Keep the thumb or crooked forefinger of the other hand on the pie, so the pastry is kept firmly pressed to the lip of the dish. Mark the outer edge neatly with the tines of a fork or flute it. Prick the top to allow the steam to escape.

Bake in the preheated moderately hot oven (200°C, 400°F, Gas Mark 6) for 20 minutes, then reduce heat (190°C, 375°F, Gas Mark 5) and continue cooking for 25 minutes until the fruit is cooked.

Remove from oven and cut neatly round the lid of the pie just inside the lip; lift off carefully. Pour the cherry brandy over the fruit and then the cream. Replace the lid, dredge with sugar and return to the oven for 5 minutes. Serve hot.

Coffee and Walnut Pie

175 g (6 oz) sweet shortcrust pastry (p. 360)
2 tablespoons apricot jam
75 g (3 oz) butter
75 g (3 oz) caster sugar
1 egg, beaten
40 g (1½ oz) walnuts, finely chopped
100 g (4 oz) self-raising flour
4 teaspoons liquid coffee essence
1 tablespoon milk
150 ml (¼ pint) soured cream
walnuts, coarsely chopped, to decorate

Roll out pastry and line a 20 cm (8 inch) flan ring. Prick base and spread with apricot jam. Cream butter and sugar together until light and fluffy; gradually beat in egg. Fold in walnuts and flour. Mix coffee essence with milk then blend into mixture. Turn into pastry case and smooth top.

Bake in the centre of preheated hot oven (220°C, 425°F, Gas Mark 7) for 15 minutes. Reduce heat to moderate (160°C, 325°F, Gas Mark 3) and bake for a further 25 minutes or until cooked; test with a skewer which should come out clean. Warm soured cream, but do not overheat. Pour over pie and return to oven for 5 minutes. Remove from the oven, scatter chopped walnuts on top and serve immediately.

This pie is also very good served cold: spread lemon-flavoured glacé icing over the filling instead of the soured cream and decorate with walnut halves.

Grapefruit Meringue Pie

1 plain shortcrust flan case (p. 363) 18–20 cm (7–8 inch) baked blind
2 tablespoons cornflour
225 ml (8 fl oz) unsweetened grapefruit juice, canned or frozen
about 75 g (3 oz) caster sugar
2 egg yolks, beaten
For the meringue:
2 egg whites
50 g (2 oz) caster sugar, sieved
caster sugar for dredging

Blend the cornflour with a little of the grapefruit juice to a smooth paste in a small saucepan. Gradually stir in remaining juice. Heat gradually, stirring continuously with a wooden spoon, then simmer gently for 3 minutes or until the mixture thickens and clears. Remove from heat and sweeten to taste. Cool slightly and gradually beat in the egg yolks. Pour into the flan case and smooth the top.

To make the meringue, whisk the egg whites until very stiff and dry. Fold in the sugar quickly and lightly. Spoon the meringue mixture round the outside edge of the pie and work towards the centre. Make sure the filling is completely covered and there are no little gaps round the pastry edge or the meringue will 'weep'. Dredge with caster sugar. Bake in the centre of a preheated moderate oven (160°C, 325°F, Gas Mark 3) for 25–30 minutes or until set and golden coloured. Serve hot or cold, decorated with sugared grapefruit peel if available.

Crispy Chocolate Pie

25 g (1 oz) butter
2 tablespoons golden syrup
75 g (3 oz) plain chocolate, melted
100 g (4 oz) corn flakes
300 ml ($\frac{1}{2}$ pint) Basic sweet white
  sauce (p. 357)
150 ml ($\frac{1}{4}$ pint) black cherry yogurt
150 ml ($\frac{1}{4}$ pint) whipping cream
few small sweets, to decorate

Melt the butter and golden syrup together in a saucepan over gentle heat. Add the melted chocolate and the corn flakes and mix well until the flakes are well coated with the chocolate mixture. Spoon on to a 20 cm (8 inch) pie plate, and press to the base and sides with a metal spoon, building up the edges slightly to make a lip around the outside. Chill well until firm.

Meanwhile, make up the white sauce and allow it to get cold. Stir in the yogurt.

Whip the cream until thick, reserve half for the decoration and fold the remainder into the yogurt mixture. Pour the filling into the pie case and chill until set. Serve decorated with rosettes of whipped cream and a few small sweets.

* Instant Strawberry and Chocolate Pie

Follow the recipe for Crispy Chocolate Pie (above), with these changes: if time is short, a packet of strawberry instant dessert made up with milk can be used as a filling. Alternatively, substitute strawberry yogurt for the black cherry yogurt.

Spiced Pear Pie

225 g (8 oz) plain shortcrust pastry
  (p. 363)
40 g (1$\frac{1}{2}$ oz) granulated sugar
40 g (1$\frac{1}{2}$ oz) soft brown sugar
1 tablespoon plain flour
$\frac{1}{4}$ teaspoon grated nutmeg
$\frac{1}{4}$ teaspoon ground cinnamon
finely grated rind and juice of 1
  orange
finely grated rind of $\frac{1}{2}$ lemon
1 tablespoon lemon juice
900 g (2 lb) cooking pears
50 g (2 oz) sultanas
40 g (1$\frac{1}{2}$ oz) butter, melted
To glaze:
milk
granulated sugar

Light the oven and grease the base of a 20 cm (8 inch) round shallow pie dish. Damp the lip of the dish.

Divide the pastry in half. Roll out one half thinly, line the pie dish and prick all over the base. Mix together the granulated sugar, brown sugar, flour and spices. Rub a little of the mixture over the pastry lining. Add the grated orange and lemon rind to the remainder of the pastry.

Peel, core and slice the pears. Arrange them in layers in the dish, sprinkling each layer with sultanas, sugar mixture, fruit juices and melted butter.

Roll out the other piece of dough into a circle about 5 cm (2 inches) larger all round than the top of the pie. Damp the edge of the lining pastry, lift the other piece on the rolling pin and unroll it across the top of the pie.

Press the two edges firmly together and with a sharp knife trim off the surplus dough. Knock the two edges together with the back of the knife and flute the edge. Make a few slits in the top of the pie to allow the steam from the fruit to escape. Brush lightly with milk and sprinkle with granulated sugar to give a glazed finish.

Bake in a moderately hot oven (200°C, 400°F, Gas Mark 6) for 20 minutes until the pastry is well risen and turning colour; lower the heat (190°C, 375°F, Gas Mark 5) and continue baking for 25 minutes or until the pie is cooked through. Serve hot with cream.

Variation:
Apples can be used instead of pears as an excellent alternative.

Kentucky Raisin Pie

175 g (6 oz) sweet shortcrust pastry (p. 360)
150 g (5 oz) seedless raisins
¼ teaspoon bicarbonate of soda
4 tablespoons hot water
50 g (2 oz) soft brown sugar
For the topping:
100 g (4 oz) plain flour
½ teaspoon ground cinnamon
¼ teaspoon ground nutmeg
¼ teaspoon ground ginger
50 g (2 oz) butter
50 g (2 oz) soft brown sugar

Roll out the pastry thinly and line a 20 cm (8 inch) greased pie plate. Pinch the edge of the pastry with finger and thumb into a decorative border. Prick the pastry base all over through to the plate and cover with raisins. Mix the bicarbonate of soda with the water and the brown sugar and pour it over the raisins.

Sieve the flour and spices together. Cut in the butter and rub it in with the tips of the fingers until the consistency of breadcrumbs. Mix in the sugar and spread over the raisin filling.

Bake in a preheated hot oven (220°C, 425°F, Gas Mark 7) for 10 minutes until the pie begins to brown. Reduce the heat (160°C, 325°F, Gas Mark 3) and continue cooking for 20 minutes until the filling is set.

Serve hot or cold, with whipped cream if wished.

Lemon Meringue Pie

1 × 18–20 cm (7–8 inch) plain or sweet shortcrust flan case, baked blind (p. 363 or p. 360)
1 large or 2 small lemons
2 tablespoons cornflour
2 egg yolks, beaten
sugar to taste
For the meringue topping:
2 egg whites
50 g (2 oz) caster sugar
glacé cherries and angelica leaves to decorate
extra caster sugar for dredging

Grate the rind finely off the lemons. Squeeze out the juice, measure it and make it up to 225 ml (8 fl oz) with water. In a small saucepan blend the cornflour to a thin paste with a little of the lemon liquid. Gradually stir in the rest of the lemon liquid and rind, bring to simmer and cook for 3 to 4 minutes, stirring steadily. Blend 2 tablespoons of the mixture into the egg yolks and stir this back into the saucepan. Sweeten to taste.

Cool the filling, pour it into the flan case and smooth over. Preheat the oven to 160°C, 325°F, Gas Mark 3. Whisk the egg whites until very stiff and dry. Sift and fold in the sugar quickly and lightly. Spoon the meringue round the edge of the filling and then fill in the centre.

Be sure that the meringue is well sealed to the pastry edge or the steam from any uncovered filling will make the meringue 'weep'.

Swirl the top of the meringue with a spatula or palette knife. Decorate with glacé cherries and angelica leaves. Dredge lightly with caster sugar and bake in the centre of the oven for 30 minutes or until crisp and golden.

Pumpkin Pie

225 g (8 oz) flour
pinch of salt
65 g (2 oz) butter or margarine
50 g (2 oz) lard
2 tablespoons caster sugar
finely grated rind of 1 lemon
1–2 tablespoons cold water
For the filling:
454 g (16 oz) can unseasoned pumpkin
   purée
1 small can evaporated milk
   (equivalent to 450 ml, $\frac{3}{4}$ pint)
2 tablespoons honey
100 g (4 oz) soft brown sugar
juice of 1 lemon
1 teaspoon ground ginger
1 teaspoon ground cinnamon
$\frac{1}{2}$ teaspoon grated nutmeg
pinch of salt
2 eggs, beaten

Sieve the flour and salt into a bowl. Add
the butter or margarine and lard in
pieces and rub into the flour with the
fingertips until the mixture resembles
fine breadcrumbs. Stir in the sugar and
lemon rind and enough cold water to
bind the mixture together. Form into a
ball, wrap in foil and chill in the refrigerator for at least 30 minutes.
   Roll out the dough on a lightly
floured board and use to line a 24 cm (9$\frac{1}{2}$
inch) fluted flan tin with removable
base. Reserve the leftover pieces of
dough for the lattice. Place on a baking
sheet, prick the base, then chill in the
refrigerator for another 30 minutes.
Meanwhile, make the filling: put all the
filling ingredients in a bowl and stir
well to combine. Pour into the flan case.
Roll out the reserved pieces of dough
and cut into strips to form a lattice on
top of the filling. Seal with a little
water. Bake in a fairly hot oven (190°C,
375°F, Gas Mark 5) for 45 minutes or
until the filling is set and the pastry
golden.
   Remove from the oven and leave to
cool. Before serving, remove from the
flan tin, and place on a serving platter.
Serve with plenty of whipped double
cream.
Serves 6–8

Flamed Jamaican Bananas

4 large under-ripe bananas
40 g (1$\frac{1}{2}$ oz) butter
juice of $\frac{1}{2}$ large lemon
2 tablespoons rum
To decorate:
brown sugar
single cream

Peel the bananas and halve lengthwise.
Heat the butter in a flameproof dish and
fry the bananas, cut side down. When
golden, turn over, sprinkle with lemon
juice, and fry until the underneath is
colouring. Warm the rum in a ladle,
ignite and pour over bananas. Serve
while still flaming accompanied with a
bowl of brown sugar and a jug of single
cream. If no flameproof dish is available
use a frying pan.

Glazed Bananas

1 large knob of butter
3 tablespoons soft brown sugar
3 tablespoons undiluted orange
   squash
1 tablespoon golden syrup
$\frac{1}{4}$ teaspoon ground cinnamon
2 bananas, peeled and split in half
   lengthways

Melt the butter in a non-stick frying
pan. Add the sugar, orange squash,
syrup and cinnamon and heat gently
until melted, stirring constantly. Add
the bananas and cook over gentle heat
for 10 minutes until soft and glazed,
spooning the sauce over them during
the cooking. Serve hot with chilled
cream or ice cream.
Serves 2

Floating Islands with Bananas

2 egg whites
50 g (2 oz) caster sugar
For the custard:
600 ml (1 pint) milk
2 egg yolks
50 g (2 oz) granulated sugar
1 tablespoon cornflour
$\frac{1}{4}$ teaspoon vanilla essence
2 bananas
2 tablespoons lemon juice
25 g (1 oz) flaked chocolate

Heat the milk for the custard in a wide pan. Whisk egg whites until stiff and dry. Sieve in half the caster sugar and whisk again until stiff and glossy. Fold in remaining sugar. Scoop up meringue mixture in tablespoons and poach in the hot milk; simmer about 5 minutes until set. Lift out with a draining spoon on to oiled greaseproof paper to drain.

Beat egg yolks and sugar together until pale lemon colour and blend in cornflour. Gradually mix in the hot milk left from cooking meringues. Pour mixture back into the milk pan and stir over very gentle heat until thickened; do not boil. Add vanilla essence. Slice bananas over the base of a serving bowl, sprinkle with lemon juice and cover with custard. Sprinkle with sugar to prevent a skin forming. Arrange meringues on top and sprinkle them with flaked chocolate. Serve cold.

Fresh Pineapple Pyramid

1 medium pineapple
3–4 tablespoons caster sugar
175 ml (6 fl oz) double cream
2 tablespoons Kirsch (optional)
225 g (8 oz) strawberries; or
   raspberries; or cherries

Cut the top off the pineapple complete with leaves and set aside. Level off the bottom and discard the fibrous base. Stand the pineapple on a chopping board and with a large sharp knife, working downwards from the top, cut off the skin all round. Cut the pineapple across in thick slices – 1.5 cm ($\frac{1}{2}$ inch). Remove the core from each slice with an apple corer and sprinkle with sugar. Whip the cream stiffly, sweeten to taste and add Kirsch if using. Hull and halve the strawberries, pick over the raspberries or stone the cherries.

Reform the pineapple in an upright position on a serving platter, spreading a layer of cream covered with prepared fruit between each slice. Replace the top, with leaves, wrap in clingfilm and refrigerate until required. When serving use a pastry slice to remove top and serve one slice complete with whipped cream and strawberries to each guest.

Variation:
In winter, orange or mandarin sections can replace the summer fruit.

Honeydew and Pineapple Basket

1 ripe honeydew melon
4 slices pineapple, fresh or canned
3–4 tablespoons condensed milk
  (sweet)
50 g (2 oz) ground almonds
1 tablespoon lemon juice

Cut top third off melon and discard pips. Scoop flesh out of both parts with a sharp spoon and cut in pieces. Vandyke the edges of melon shells by cutting small triangles all around to give a zig-zag effect.

Chop the pineapple and mix with melon flesh, condensed milk, ground almonds and lemon juice. Pack this mixture into larger melon shell and pile it up in the centre. Put melon lid on at an angle and secure at back with cock-tail sticks. Wrap melon completely in clingfilm or foil and chill thoroughly. Serve garnished with fresh leaves and/or flowers and crushed ice.

Oranges Che Yang

1 × 311 g (11 oz) can mandarin oranges
300 ml ($\frac{1}{2}$ pint) sweetened apple purée
  (p. 00)
25 g (1 oz) preserved stem ginger,
  chopped
1 teaspoon grated nutmeg
1 tablespoon clear honey
2 teaspoons lemon juice
2 tablespoons ginger syrup

Drain the mandarin segments from the syrup. Mix the fruit with the apple purée, chopped ginger, grated nutmeg, honey, lemon juice and ginger syrup.

Serve in small glasses with Chantilly Cream (p. 365).

French Apple and Ginger Cake

225 g (8 oz) caster sugar
150 ml ($\frac{1}{4}$ pint) cider
150 ml ($\frac{1}{4}$ pint) water
2 tablespoons ginger syrup
piece of thin lemon rind
900 g (2 lb) dessert apples
50 g (2 oz) sultanas
50 g (2 oz) chopped preserved ginger
To decorate:
150 ml ($\frac{1}{4}$ pint) double cream
preserved ginger

Use ginger preserved in syrup, not the sugary crystallised ginger.

Line the base of an 18–20 cm (7–8 inch) cake tin with kitchen foil and brush all over lightly with oil.

Dissolve the sugar in the cider and water, add the ginger syrup and lemon rind and bring to the boil. Wash and core the apples, slice thinly and add to the syrup. Simmer very gently, without a lid, until the apple slices are transparent. Stir occasionally, taking care not to break the slices.

When the apple slices are cooked, lift them out of the syrup with a draining spoon and arrange in layers in the tin, sprinkling each layer with sultanas and chopped ginger. When all the apple is in cover with a heavy oiled plate which fits in the top of the tin. Chill in the refrigerator, preferably overnight.

To serve remove plate and place a large platter over the tin. Invert both together quickly, and carefully remove the tin and foil. Decorate the cake with piped whipped cream and preserved ginger.

Variation:
Pears can be used instead of apples.

CAKES, BISCUITS & SWEETS

French Easter Cake

For the Genoese sponge:
75 g (3 oz) flour, sieved
25 g (1 oz) cornflour, sieved
4 eggs, beaten
100 g (4 oz) caster sugar
100 g (4 oz) unsalted butter, melted
  and cooled
For the butter icing:
175 g (6 oz) butter
450 g (1 lb) icing sugar, sieved
2 tablespoons hot water
100 g (4 oz) plain cooking chocolate,
  broken into pieces
2 tablespoons liquid coffee
few miniature Easter eggs, to
  decorate

To make the sponge: grease three 18 cm (7 inch) round shallow cake tins and line the bases.

Sieve the flour and cornflour together and set aside. Put the eggs and sugar in a heatproof bowl and stand over a pan of simmering water. Beat with a balloon whisk, electric or rotary beater until the mixture becomes thick. Remove from the heat and continue beating until the mixture is cool.

Slowly stir the melted butter into the mixture dribbling it in gradually from the side of the bowl, then sieve half the flour and cornflour over the bowl and fold in gently. Repeat with the remaining flour and cornflour.

Pour the mixture into the prepared tins and bake in the centre of a fairly hot oven (190°C, 375°F, Gas Mark 5) for 20 to 25 minutes, until well risen and firm to the touch.

Meanwhile, make the butter cream: beat the butter in a bowl until light, then gradually beat in the icing sugar a little at a time, adding hot water as the mixture becomes too stiff to beat. Put one quarter of the butter cream in a separate bowl. Set aside. Put the chocolate pieces and liquid coffee in a heatproof bowl and stand over a pan of gently simmering water.

Heat gently until the chocolate has melted, stirring occasionally to help break up the pieces, then remove from the heat and stir into the separate quarter of butter cream.

Spread some of this chocolate butter cream on top of two of the cakes and sandwich the three cakes together. Put the cake on a stand and spread the top and sides with most of the unflavoured butter cream. Stir the leftover unflavoured butter cream into the remaining chocolate butter cream and put into a forcing bag fitted with a small star tube. For an attractive decoration, work as follows. Pipe small stars around the top edge of the cake and join the stars together by piping a line between each one. Pipe vertical lines around the sides of the cake beneath the stars, working from the bottom upwards. Repeat the top edge decoration around base. Decorate with Easter eggs. Cuts into 8–10 slices.

Basic Whisked Sponge

3 eggs
¼ teaspoon vanilla essence
75 g (3 oz) caster sugar
75 g (3 oz) plain flour
For the filling and topping:
250 g (9 oz) Chocolate butter cream
 (p. 320)
2 tablespoons finely chopped walnuts
9 walnut halves
chopped pistachio nuts or angelica
 leaves to decorate

Grease two 18 cm (7 inch) sandwich tins
and dust with a mixture of 1 teaspoon
each of sugar and flour. Preheat the
oven to 190°C, 375°F, Gas Mark 5.

Whisk the eggs, vanilla and sugar
together until really pale; the mixture
should fall off the whisk in ribbons
which hold their shape on top of the
mixture on the bowl for several seconds
before sinking.

Sift half the flour and fold it into the
egg mixture quickly and lightly. Sift
and fold in remaining flour. Pour the
mixture into the sandwich tins, tilt
them to spread it out evenly. Bang the
tin on the table to settle mixture. Bake
cakes on the same oven shelf for 20
minutes until well risen and golden and
tops are springy to touch. Remove the
cakes from the oven allow to shrink
slightly before turning out on to a wire
tray to cool.

Take one-third of the chocolate
butter cream and mix in the chopped
walnuts. Sandwich the two sponges together with this filling. Spread the rest
of the butter cream neatly over the top
of the cake. Make a swirling pattern
with a knife, or mark it into squares
with the tines of a fork. Arrange the
walnut halves on top and finish with
lines or groups of chopped pistachio
nuts or small angelica leaves.

Family Sponge

175 g (6 oz) butter or margarine
175 g (6 oz) sugar
3 eggs
225 g (8 oz) self-raising flour
pinch of salt
2 tablespoons milk
4 tablespoons jam
caster sugar to sprinkle

Cream the butter and sugar together
until pale and fluffy. Add the eggs one at
a time beating well after each addition.
Fold in the flour and salt with the milk.

Turn the mixture into a greased 20 cm
(8 inch) square cake tin lined with
greased greaseproof paper. Bake in a
moderate oven (180°C, 350°F, Gas Mark
4) for 30 to 35 minutes, or until well
risen and golden-brown. The cake will
have shrunk slightly from the sides of
the tin.

Turn the cake out on a wire rack to
cool. When cold split into 2 layers and
sandwich together with the jam and
sprinkle with caster sugar. Serve cut
into squares.

* Coconut Cake

Follow the recipe for Family sponge
(above), with the following changes:
add 75 g (3 oz) desiccated coconut with
the flour, spread a little more jam over
the top of the finished cake and sprinkle
coconut round the edge.

* Fruit Cake

Follow the recipe for Family sponge
(above), with the following changes:
add the grated rind of 1 orange to the
creamed mixture and 75 g (3 oz) mixed
dried fruit, (sultanas, raisins, currants)
with the flour. Bake a little longer, for
40 to 45 minutes.

* Cup Cakes

Follow the recipe for Family sponge (above), with the following changes: bake the mixture in paper cases in well-greased bun tins for about 15 minutes. Top with glacé icing or brush with melted red currant jelly and sprinkle with coconut. With either finish, top with half a glacé cherry.

Basic Genoese Sponge

40 g (1½ oz) unsalted butter
3 large eggs
75 g (3 oz) caster sugar
75 g (3 oz) plain flour

This quantity makes one 18 cm (7 inch) cake. Prepare two 18 cm (7 inch) sandwich tins or a Swiss roll tin 30 × 20 cm (12 × 8 inches). Heat the butter gently until liquid, then leave for any sediment to settle.

Put the eggs and sugar in a mixing bowl. Whisk with an electric beater, or by hand with a rotary whisk over a bowl of simmering water until the mixture is thick enough to show the trail of the whisk. Take care the water does not touch the bottom of the bowl. If over-heated the sponge will be tough.

Sift the flour and fold in half of it carefully. Pour half the melted butter round the edge of the mixture and fold it in. Fold in the remaining flour alternately with the rest of the butter, taking care not to use any sediment. Work quickly and lightly or the butter will sink to the bottom.

Pour into the two sandwich tins or Swiss roll tin and bake in the preheated oven (190°C, 375°F, Gas Mark 5) for 20 to 25 minutes, until golden and springy to the touch. Allow the cake(s) to shrink slightly, then turn out on to a wire tray until cool.

When cold, fill and ice the cake as for Victoria Sandwich Cake (p. 289).

Fresh Orange Sponge

1 orange
2 tablespoons golden syrup
100 g (4 oz) butter or margarine
100 g (4 oz) caster sugar
2 eggs
100 g (4 oz) plain flour
2 teaspoons baking powder
1–2 tablespoons warm water

Prepare a steamer saucepan and a greased 900 ml (1½ pint) pudding basin.

With a fine grater remove rind from the orange, avoiding the pith, then peel off all pith. Cut the orange into slices, on a plate so as to catch the juice. Spread the syrup over the bottom of the basin and arrange orange slices on it. Cream the butter and sugar until light and fluffy together with the grated rind. Whisk the eggs with a fork and add, a tablespoonful at a time, beating well between each addition. Should the mixture start to curdle, add a spoonful or two of the flour each time egg is added. Sieve the flour and baking powder together and fold quickly and lightly into the mixture. Add the orange juice and mix in a tablespoonful or so of warm water to produce a soft dropping consistency (it should fall off the wooden spoon by the time you count five).

Spoon the mixture into the basin on top of the orange slices. Cover with greased foil and put into a steamer. Cover and cook for 1½ hours or so until the pudding is set. To test, remove foil and insert a skewer; it should come out clean.

Remove pudding from pan and allow to shrink slightly before turning out on a warm serving platter. Serve with Orange Foam Sauce (p. 359) or orange-flavoured custard.

Sponge in the Pan

1 × 400 g (14 oz) can peach halves
4 tablespoons soft brown sugar
1 large knob of butter
½ teaspoon ground cinnamon
1 × 150 g (5 oz) packet sponge mix
1 egg
2 tablespoons sugar
2 tablespoons milk

Drain the peaches and pour the juice into a 18–20 cm (7–8 inch) non-stick saucepan. Add the brown sugar, butter and cinnamon and bring to the boil, stirring constantly. Lower the heat and simmer until dark and thick. Meanwhile, make the sponge mix according to packet directions with the egg, sugar and milk.

Arrange the peaches cut sides uppermost in the saucepan. Spoon over the sponge batter evenly and smooth the top. Cover and cook over low heat for 30 minutes or until the sponge is set. Leave to stand for 10 minutes, then invert a plate over the pan, and turn the sponge out on to the plate, peach side uppermost. Serve with fresh cream or vanilla ice cream.
Serves 5–6

Variations:
Any kind of canned fruit can be used instead of the peaches.

Butterfly Cakes

100 g (4 oz) butter or margarine, softened
100 g (4 oz) caster sugar
2 eggs, beaten
75 g (3 oz) self-raising flour
pinch of salt
25 g (1 oz) cocoa powder
1 tablespoon warm water
For the butter icing:
50 g (2 oz) butter
100 g (4 oz) icing sugar, sieved

2 tablespoons water
1 small packet chocolate buttons
chocolate vermicelli, to decorate

Cream the butter or margarine and sugar together until light and fluffy, then gradually beat in the eggs a little at a time. Sieve the flour, salt and cocoa powder together and gradually fold into the butter and sugar mixture. Beat in the warm water. Divide the mixture between 20 small paper cake cases and bake in a fairly hot oven (190°C, 375°F, Gas Mark 5) for 15 minutes until risen and golden brown. Remove from the oven and leave to cool. Meanwhile, make the butter icing: beat the butter until soft, then gradually beat in the icing sugar a little at a time, adding 1 tablespoon water when the mixture becomes too stiff to beat. Put the chocolate buttons and the water in to a small heavy-based saucepan and heat gently until melted, stirring from time to time. Beat the melted chocolate into the butter icing until evenly distributed.

Cut the tops off the cakes and cut in half. Put a blob of butter cream icing on top of each cake and press in the tops to form wings. Sprinkle each butterfly with chocolate vermicelli.
Makes 20

Apple Cake

225 g (8 oz) self-raising flour
1 teaspoon salt
100 g (4 oz) butter
450 g (1 lb) cooking or dessert apples, peeled, cored and chopped
100 g (4 oz) caster sugar
2 eggs, beaten
25 g (1 oz) soft brown sugar

Sift the flour and salt into a mixing bowl. Cut the fat into the flour and rub in to a breadcrumb consistency. Mix in the apples, caster sugar and eggs. Turn into a greased 20–23 cm (8–9 inch) cake tin. Level off the top and sprinkle with the brown sugar. Bake in a preheated moderately hot oven (200°C, 400°F, Gas Mark 6) for 30 to 40 minutes.

Allow to shrink slightly before turning out on to serving platter.

Serve hot with clotted cream, or split and buttered. If eating cold, cool on a wire tray and serve with butter.

Angel Cake

100 g (4 oz) plain flour
175 g (6 oz) caster sugar
5–6, about 175 ml (6 fl oz) egg whites
½ teaspoon cream of tartar
½ teaspoon vanilla or almond essence
lemon curd
To decorate:
Lemon Glacé Icing (p. 318)
crystallised lemon slices

This quantity makes one 18 cm (7 inch) cake. Sift the flour and sugar together 3 to 4 times. Beat the egg whites until foaming; add the cream of tartar and whisk until stiff but not dry. Sift the flour and sugar on to the whisked egg whites carefully, about 2 tablespoonfuls at a time, then fold in the flavouring essence. Turn the mixture into an ungreased 18 cm (7 inch) angel cake tin. Bake in a preheated moderate oven (160°C, 325°F, Gas Mark 3) for 1 hour or until a skewer inserted comes out clean. Remove from the oven and invert on to a wire tray. Leave until quite cold before turning out of the tin. This is a sweet cake and it is best to choose a sharp filling for contrast. Slice the cake across in three, or down into 8. Spread the slices with lemon curd and reassemble the cake.

Spread the top with Lemon Glacé Icing (p. 318) and decorate with crystallised lemon slices.

Victoria Sandwich

150 g (6 oz) butter or margarine
150 g (6 oz) caster sugar
3 eggs, beaten
150 g (6 oz) plain flour
2 teaspoons baking powder
1 2 tablespoons water
extra caster sugar for dredging

Grease two 18 cm (7 inch) sandwich tins. If the tins do not have a lever to release the sponge, line the base of each with a round of buttered greaseproof paper. Preheat the oven to 190°C, 375°F, Gas Mark 5.

Cream the butter and sugar together until light and fluffy, then gradually beat in the eggs a spoonful at a time. Sift the flour and baking powder together and fold it into the mixture. Add a little water to give a soft dropping consistency – it should drop off the spoon in 5 seconds.

Divide the mixture between the two tins, and smooth the top. Bake both cakes side by side in the oven for 20 minutes or until they are well risen and golden. When cooked, they will be springy to the touch and beginning to shrink away from the side of the tin. Allow the cakes to shrink slightly, then turn them out upside down on a wire tray to cool.

When cool, remove the cakes from the tray, spread one with jam, place the other on top and dredge with caster sugar.

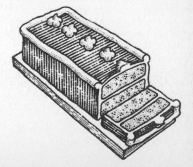

Numeral Cakes

225 g (8 oz) butter or margarine,
  softened
225 g (8 oz) caster sugar
4 eggs, beaten
225 g.(8 oz) self-raising flour
pinch of salt
2–3 tablespoons warm water
3 tablespoons jam
For the icing:
150 g (5 oz) butter
350 g (12 oz) icing sugar, sieved
2 tablespoons hot water
food colouring
Smarties or sugared roses
candles

The quantities given above are sufficient to make two cakes to form the
number ten. If you are making one of
the smaller numbers you will obviously
have to trim to waste, but any trimmings can be used for making trifles, or
simply eaten by the children!

Grease an 18 cm (7 inch) ring mould
and an 18 cm (7 inch) square shallow
cake tin. Prepare the cake mixture as in
the recipe for Butterfly Cakes (see p. 00)
and divide the mixture between the two
tins. Bake in a fairly hot oven (190°C,
375°F, Gas Mark 5) for 30 minutes or
until risen and golden brown. Remove
from the oven, turn out on to a wire rack
and leave to cool.

Cut the ring cake in half horizontally,
spread one of the cut surfaces with some
of the jam, then sandwich the two
halves together again. Cut the square
cake in half vertically, spread the top of
one half with the remaining jam and
sandwich the two halves together, one
on top of the other.

To make the icing: beat butter until
soft, then gradually beat in the icing
sugar a little at a time, adding the water
gradually as the mixture becomes too
stiff to beat. Add a few drops of food
colouring according to taste.

Spread the icing smoothly over the
two cakes, then press Smarties or roses

around the edges. Place candles on top
of the cake and make the child's name
with more Smarties or roses, if wished.

Instructions for making other numbers:
2 Half of one circular cake, plus one
square cake cut and sandwiched together as above, then cut into two
pieces, one slightly longer than the
other. Trim to shape.
3 Half of one circular cake, plus one
square cake cut and sandwiched together as above, then cut into two equal
pieces. Trim at the joins and shape.
4 Two square cakes, each one cut and
sandwiched together as above. Cut 5 cm
(2 inch) off each cake and use the four
pieces to make the number.
5 Half of one circular cake, plus one
square cake cut and sandwiched together as above, then cut into two
pieces, one slightly longer than the
other. Trim to shape.
6 One circular cake, plus one square
cake cut and sandwiched together as
above. Trim to shape at the join with the
circle.
7 Two square cakes, each one cut and
sandwiched together as above. Trim at
the join.
8 Two circular cakes. Trim at the join.
9 One circular cake, plus one square
cake cut and sandwiched together as
above. Trim to shape at the join with the
circle.

Lemon Curd
and Caraway Cakes

150 g (6 oz) soft margarine
100 g (4 oz) caster sugar
150 g (6 oz) lemon curd
225 g (8 oz) self-raising flour
pinch of salt
1 teaspoon caraway seeds
3 eggs, beaten

Cream the margarine and sugar together until light and fluffy. Beat in the
lemon curd. Sift the flour and salt and

mix in the caraway seeds. Beat the eggs into the creamed mixture, one at a time, with 2 tablespoons flour each time. Fold in the remaining flour. Spoon the mixture into greased patty pans until three quarters full. Bake in a preheated moderate oven (180°C, 350°F, Gas Mark 4) for 20 minutes until golden and firm to the touch. Allow the cakes to shrink slightly, then remove from tins and cool on a wire tray.
Makes about 30

Variation:

For parties, top with Lemon Curd Glacé Icing. Mix 75 g (3 oz) sifted icing sugar with 3 teaspoons lemon curd into a spreading consistency. Swirl over the tops of the cakes and decorate each one with 3 mimosa balls or a tiny crystallised lemon slice.

Teisen Tel (Honey Cake)

225 g (8 oz) plain flour
½ teaspoon bicarbonate of soda
1 teaspoon ground cinnamon
100 g (4 oz) butter
100 g (4 oz) soft brown sugar
3 eggs, separated
100 g (4 oz) honey, warmed
approx. 2 tablespoons warm water
For the topping:
50 g (2 oz) caster sugar
1 tablespoon warm honey

Sift the flour with the bicarbonate of soda and cinnamon. Cream the butter and sugar together until light and fluffy. Beat in the egg yolks gradually and then the warmed honey. Fold in the flour adding a little warm water if the mixture gets too stiff. Beat one egg white until stiff but not too dry and fold it in lightly.

Turn the mixture into a greased 20 cm (8 inch) round cake tin with a loose bottom. Bake in a preheated moderately hot oven (200°C, 400°F, Gas Mark 6) for 15 minutes. Lower the heat to 185°C,

375°F, Gas Mark 5 for a further 15 to 20 minutes. Remove from the oven and allow it to shrink slightly before turning it out. Beat the remaining 2 egg whites until stiff. Fold in the sifted sugar quickly and lightly.

Put the cake on a baking sheet and brush it all over with warmed honey. Swirl the meringue over with a palette knife, drawing it up in points. Return to a preheated moderate oven (160°C, 325°F, Gas Mark 3) for 15 minutes or until the meringue is set and delicately coloured. Serve cold.

Yorkshire Jam Cake

350 g (12 oz) plain flour
pinch of salt
3 teaspoons baking powder
175 g (6 oz) butter or margarine
175 g (6 oz) caster sugar
1 large or 2 small eggs, lightly beaten
a little water
50 g (2 oz) jam, warmed
To glaze:
milk
caster sugar

Sift the flour, salt and baking powder into a mixing bowl. Cut the fat into the flour and rub in to a breadcrumb consistency. Mix in the sugar thoroughly. Stir in the eggs with a palette knife. Mix to a soft but not sticky dough, adding a little water if necessary. Shape into a ball and cut in half. On a floured board, roll each half out into a circle 1.5 cm (½ inch) thick. Place one on a greased baking sheet, prick it all over and spread with the warm jam, leaving a narrow margin round the edge. Cover with the remaining half of the dough, and pinch the edges firmly together. Brush the top with milk and sprinkle with sugar. Bake in the centre of a preheated moderately hot oven (190°C, 375°F, Gas Mark 5) for 30 to 35 minutes, until well risen and golden brown. Cool on a wire tray.

Almond and Cherry Cake

225 g (8 oz) butter
225 g (8 oz) caster sugar
5 eggs, beaten
225 g (8 oz) self-raising flour, sifted
100 g (4 oz) ground almonds
1 teaspoon almond essence
100 g (4 oz) glacé cherries, washed,
    dried and quartered

Put the butter and sugar in a bowl and beat together until light and fluffy. Beat in the eggs a little at a time, adding a little flour with each addition. Coat the cherries in the flour, then fold in any remaining flour with the almonds until evenly blended. Beat in the essence and cherries. Line a greased deep 20 cm (8 inch) square cake tin with greased greaseproof paper, then spoon in the mixture.

Bake just below the centre of a pre-heated moderate oven (180°C, 350°F, Gas Mark 4) for 1¼ hours or until a skewer inserted in the centre comes out clean. Leave to cool in the tin, then remove the greaseproof paper. Wrap in cling film, overwrap in a polythene bag and store in an airtight container until ready to serve.
Makes 24 slices

White Walnut Cake

225 g (8 oz) butter or soft (tub)
    margarine
275–350 g (10–12 oz) caster sugar
225 g (8 oz) plain flour
3 teaspoons baking powder
pinch of salt
250 ml (8 fl oz) milk
4 egg whites
75–100 g (3–4 oz) walnuts, chopped
¼ teaspoon vanilla essence (optional)
To finish:
Chocolate Sour Cream Frosting or
    American Frosting (see p. 319)
9 walnut halves

This quantity makes one 18–20 cm (7–8 inch) cake. Line and grease three 18 cm (7 inch) sandwich tins or one 20 cm (8 inch) round cake tin. Cream the fat and sugar together until light and fluffy. Sift together the flour, baking powder and salt and mix them in alternately with the milk, a third at a time. Whisk the egg whites until stiff but still moist, and fold into the mixture, alternating with the chopped nuts. Flavour with the vanilla if liked. Pour the mixture into the tin(s) and bake in a pre-heated moderate oven (180°C, 350°F, Gas Mark 4) for about 30 minutes for 3 tins or 1 hour for 1, or until springy to the touch. Split the large cake into 3 when cold.

Spread the layers with Chocolate Sour Cream Frosting, sandwich together and swirl the remainder over the top and sides of the cake. Alternatively fill and frost with American Frosting. Decorate with walnut halves.

Orange, Carrot and Nut Cake

100 g (4 oz) butter
175 g (6 oz) caster sugar
1 teaspoon ground cinnamon
1 teaspoon grated orange rind
2 eggs, lightly beaten
75 g (3 oz) raw carrot, finely grated
50 g (2 oz) walnuts, finely chopped
1 tablespoon orange juice
225 g (8 oz) self-raising flour
pinch of salt

Cream the butter and sugar together in a bowl until pale and fluffy. Beat in the ground cinnamon and orange rind. Gradually add the eggs, beating well after each addition. Stir in the grated carrot, chopped nuts and orange juice. Sift the flour and salt together and fold into the creamed mixture.

Turn into a greased 20 cm (8 inch) cake tin lined with greased greaseproof paper and smooth the top. Bake in a warm oven (160°C, 325°F, Gas Mark 3) for 45 to 55 minutes, or until the centre of the cake springs back when lightly pressed with a fingertip. Turn out on a wire rack to cool. If liked, the cake can be decorated with orange glacé, butter icing, or sifted icing sugar.

Picnic Cake
(Quick Fruit Cake)

225 g (8 oz) plain flour
1 teaspoon baking powder
1 teaspoon mixed spice
grated rind of ½ lemon or grated rind of 1 orange
100 g (4 oz) butter or margarine
100 g (4 oz) caster sugar
50 g (2 oz) sultanas
50 g (2 oz) currants, cleaned
50 g (2 oz) seedless raisins
2 eggs, beaten
4 glacé cherries
4 walnut halves
extra sugar for sprinkling

Sift the flour, baking powder and spice into a mixing bowl and add the grated lemon or orange rind. Chop up the fat and rub it in lightly to give breadcrumb consistency. Add the sugar, sultanas, currants and raisins and mix well. Stir in the beaten eggs and, if necessary, add a little water to give a soft dropping consistency – the mixture should drop off the spoon in 5 seconds.

Put the mixture into a greased 15 cm (6 inch) round cake tin. Arrange the glacé cherries and walnut halves on top. Sprinkle with a little sugar.

Bake in a preheated moderately hot oven (190°C, 375°F, Gas Mark 5) for 15 minutes then reduce the heat to 180°C, 350°F, Gas Mark 4 and bake for a further 1¼ hours or until the cake is done. Test with a skewer, which when inserted in the centre should come out clean. Allow the cake to shrink a little in the tin, then turn it out onto a wire tray to cool.

* Rock Buns

Follow the recipe for Picnic Cake (above) with these changes: make up the Picnic cake mixture into a fairly stiff dough – if too soft the buns will spread instead of being rocky. Using a fork, put the mixture into small heaps on a greased baking tin. Bake in a preheated oven at 220°C, 425°F, Gas Mark 7 for about 15 minutes or until set and golden brown.

Ginger Snaps

75 g (3 oz) butter
75 g (3 oz) dark soft brown sugar
2 tablespoons golden syrup
2 tablespoons black treacle
175 g (6 oz) self-raising flour
2 teaspoons ground ginger

Put the butter, sugar, syrup and treacle in a pan and heat gently until melted, stirring occasionally.

Sift the flour and ginger into a bowl, then stir in the melted mixture until the dough draws together. Put teaspoonfuls of the mixture on lightly greased baking sheets, spacing them well apart. Press down with the fingertips to form flat round shapes. Bake in a preheated moderate oven (180°C, 350°F, Gas Mark 4) for 7 to 10 minutes.

Leave to set on the baking sheets for a few minutes, then transfer to a wire rack and leave to cool completely. Wrap neatly in foil and store in an airtight container.

Makes about 30

Honey and Ginger Cake

225 g (8 oz) plain flour
1 teaspoon ground ginger
100 g (4 oz) butter or margarine
50 g (2 oz) caster sugar
100 g (4 oz) stem ginger, chopped
1 teaspoon bicarbonate of soda
150 ml ($\frac{1}{4}$ pint) milk
50 g (2 oz) clear honey
1 egg, beaten

Line the base of a 15 cm (6 inch) cake tin with lightly buttered greaseproof paper. Sift the flour and ground ginger into a mixing bowl. Cut the fat into the flour and rub in to a breadcrumb consistency. Mix in the sugar and stem ginger.

Dissolve the bicarbonate of soda in half the milk and stir into the honey. Make a well in the dry ingredients and stir in the milk mixture and beaten egg. Mix to a soft dropping consistency adding more milk as required.

Turn into the prepared tin and level the top. Bake in the centre of a preheated moderate oven (170°C, 325°F, Gas Mark 3) for about 1 hour, until set and golden. Allow to shrink slightly, remove from the tin and cool on a wire tray.

Rich Gingerbread

100 g (4 oz) butter or margarine
175 g (6 oz) black treacle
50 g (2 oz) golden syrup
50 g (2 oz) soft brown sugar
150 ml ($\frac{1}{4}$ pint) milk
2 eggs, beaten
225 g (8 oz) plain flour
2 teaspoons mixed spice
2 teaspoons ground ginger
1 teaspoon bicarbonate of soda
50 g (2 oz) sultanas or seedless raisins
  (optional)
50 g (2 oz) chopped stem ginger
  (optional)

Grease a 1 kg (2 lb) loaf tin. Line the bottom with a strip of non-stick parchment or greaseproof paper. Preheat the oven to 150°C, 300°F, Gas Mark 2. Weigh a mug and measure into it the required weight of treacle.

Put the fat, treacle, golden syrup and sugar in a saucepan and heat it gradually until melted. With a wooden spoon, stir in the milk, cool slightly and stir in the beaten eggs.

Sift together into a bowl the flour, spice, ginger and bicarbonate of soda. Make a well in the centre of the dry ingredients, stir in the egg mixture and beat vigorously until smooth. Sprinkle over the dried fruit and fold it in. Repeat with the chopped ginger, if used.

Pour the mixture into the prepared tin. Bake in the centre of the oven for 1$\frac{1}{2}$ to 2 hours. Test with a skewer, which will come out clean when the gingerbread is cooked. Allow the gingerbread to shrink slightly in the tin before turning it out onto a wire tray.

Variation:

For parties: when cold, spread the top of the gingerbread with 100 g (4 oz) white Lemon flavoured glacé icing (see page 318) and decorate with pieces of crystallized (not stem) ginger.

Sticky Pear Gingerbread

2 firm pears
8 glacé cherries
50 g (2 oz) unsalted butter
2 tablespoons caster sugar
For the gingerbread:
100 g (4 oz) butter or margarine
175 g (6 oz) black treacle
50 g (2 oz) golden syrup
50 g (2 oz) soft brown sugar
150 ml ($\frac{1}{4}$ pint) milk
2 eggs, beaten
225 g (8 oz) plain flour
2 teaspoons mixed spice
2 teaspoons ground ginger
1 teaspoon bicarbonate of soda

Well grease an 18–20 cm (7–8 inch) cake tin. Peel, core and slice the pears evenly. Arrange the pear slices and the cherries on the base of the tin in a circle. Cream together the butter and caster sugar and spread over the pears.

Put the butter or margarine, treacle, syrup and brown sugar in a saucepan and heat gradually until melted. Add the milk, cool slightly and stir in the beaten eggs.

Sieve together the flour, spices and soda and blend in the egg mixture. Beat smooth and carefully pour over the pears. Bake on the middle shelf of a preheated cool oven (150°C, 300°F, Gas Mark 2) for 1½ hours. Test with a skewer; it should come out clean. Allow to shrink before turning out upside down on a serving plate. Serve hot with custard or cold with cream.

Sticky Date Gingerbread

225 g (8 oz) butter
225 g (8 oz) dark soft brown sugar
100 g (4 oz) golden syrup
100 g (4 oz) black treacle
500 g (1 lb) flour
1 tablespoon ground ginger
2 teaspoons ground cinnamon
2 eggs, beaten
150 ml (¼ pint) milk, warmed
1½ teaspoons bicarbonate of soda
100 g (4 oz) sugar rolled chopped
    dates

Put the butter, sugar, syrup and treacle in a pan and heat gently until melted, stirring occasionally. Remove the pan from the heat.

Sift the flour, ginger and cinnamon into a large bowl and make a well in the centre. Pour in the melted mixture and beat well to combine. Beat in the eggs. Mix the milk and bicarbonate of soda together and add to the mixture with the dates.

Line the bottom of a greased roasting tin, approximately 35 × 25 cm (14 × 10

inch) with greased greaseproof paper. Pour in the mixture. Bake just below the centre of a preheated cool oven (150°C, 300°F, Gas Mark 2) for 1¼ hours or until a skewer inserted in the centre comes out clean.

Leave to cool in the tin, then remove the greaseproof paper. Cut the gingerbread into two, wrap each half individually in foil and overwrap in polythene bags. Store in an airtight container. When ready to serve cut into squares and spread with butter.

Makes 30 slices

Quick Chocolate Sandwich Cake

50 g (2 oz) cooking fat
50 g (2 oz) golden syrup
250 ml (8 fl oz) milk
175 g (6 oz) plain flour
25 g (1 oz) cocoa
50 g (2 oz) sugar
1 teaspoon bicarbonate of soda
3 teaspoons baking powder
1 tablespoon wine vinegar
1 tablespoon water
¼ teaspoon vanilla essence
To finish:
raspberry jam
icing sugar

This quantity makes one 18 cm (7 inch) cake. Grease two 18 cm (7 inch) sandwich tins. Melt the fat and syrup in the milk in a saucepan over moderate heat. Mix well and cool.

Sift the dry ingredients into a mixing bowl. Pour in the cooled liquid and beat well. Add the vinegar, water and vanilla, then beat again. Pour the mixture into the sandwich tins. Spread out evenly and cook in the centre of a preheated hot oven (220°C, 425°F, Gas Mark 7) for 15 to 20 minutes. Remove from the oven and cool on a wire tray. Sandwich together with raspberry jam and dredge the top with icing sugar sifted through a paper doyley.

Jam Swiss Roll

3 eggs
75 g (3 oz) caster sugar
½ teaspoon vanilla essence
75 g (3 oz) plain flour
1 tablespoon warm water
100 g (4 oz) warmed jam
extra caster sugar for dredging

Line a 23 × 30 cm (9 × 12 inch) Swiss roll tin with greaseproof paper or non-stick parchment. Cut a rectangle 5 cm (2 inches) larger all round than the tin. Grease bottom of the tin to prevent paper slipping about. Lay paper in tin and, using the handle of a metal spoon, press paper into the angle all round base of the tin, making a firm crease. Using scissors, snip the paper from each corner down to corner of the tin. Brush with oil; this is not necessary with non-stick parchment.

Preheat oven to 220°C, 425°F, Gas Mark 7. Make up sponge mixture. Pour into the tin and spread it evenly into corners with a spatula. Bake near top of oven for 8 to 10 minutes, until golden and springy to touch. Meanwhile wring out a clean teacloth in hot water. Spread it on the table, place a sheet of greaseproof paper on top and dredge lightly with sugar. This will facilitate the rolling up.

When the sponge is ready – do not overcook it or it will be brittle to roll up – turn it upside down on the sugared greaseproof paper. Carefully ease up the edges of the lining paper and peel it off. With a long knife trim off the crisp side edges of the sponge. Cut a shallow slit, parallel with the bottom edge and 1 cm (½ inch) above it.

Spread the warmed jam over the sponge. Turn the bottom edge up and tuck it in so the first roll is fairly tight. Then, using the paper, continue rolling more lightly and evenly into a neat roll with the joint underneath.Place the Swiss roll on a serving plate and dredge with a little more caster sugar.

Raspberry and Cream Swiss Roll

3 eggs
75 g (3 oz) caster sugar
75 g (3 oz) plain flour
1 tablespoon warm water
¼ teaspoon vanilla essence
sugar for dredging
For the filling:
225 g (8 oz) raspberries
300 ml (½ pint) whipping cream
2 tablespoons caster sugar
angelica leaves or pistachio nuts, to
  decorate

Line a 23 × 30 cm (9 × 12 inch) swiss roll tin with greaseproof paper. Brush lightly and evenly with oil or melted unsalted fat.

Whisk the eggs and sugar together until light and fluffy and the mixture falls off the whisk in ribbons. Lightly fold in sieved flour. Mix in water and vanilla essence quickly. Pour mixture into lined tin and spread evenly into corners. Bake near top of preheated hot oven (220°C, 425°F, Gas Mark 7) for 8–10 minutes until golden and the centre springs back lightly when touched.

Meanwhile wring out a clean teatowel in hot water. Spread it on the table, place a sheet of greaseproof paper on top and dredge it lightly with sugar.

Turn sponge out upside down on the sugared paper. Carefully ease off edges of lining paper and strip it off. Quickly trim off crisp edges of sponge with a sharp knife. Cut a shallow slit, parallel with the bottom edge and 1.5 cm (½ inch) above it. Turn bottom edge in neatly for the first roll, then continue to roll with the paper inside. Cool on a wire rack.

Meanwhile crush the raspberries with a fork, reserving a few whole ones for decorating. Whip cream until it forms soft peaks, set some aside for decoration and fold raspberries into the rest. Sweeten to taste.

Unroll sponge, spread with filling and re-roll carefully. Place on a serving plate with join underneath. Whip remaining cream into stiff peak and pipe on to sponge. Garnish with reserved raspberries and angelica or nuts.

Variation:
The filling can be made with strawberries, loganberries or blackberries instead of raspberries.

Almond and Chocolate Layer Cake

50 g (2 oz) unsalted butter
4 large eggs
100 g (4 oz) caster sugar
100 g (4 oz) plain flour
25 g (1 oz) nibbed almonds
¼ teaspoon almond essence
Chocolate Joy Icing (see p. 318)
2–3 tablespoons flaked almonds, toasted

This quantity makes one 18 cm (7 inch) cake. Line the base of a round 18 cm (7 inch) cake tin. Grease and dust with a flour and caster sugar mixture. Follow carefully the method for the basic recipe for Genoese Sponge (p. 287): melt the butter and set aside to cool and for sediment to sink. Now whisk the eggs and sugar until white and thick. Fold in the flour, almond nibs, butter and almond essence.

Pour into the prepared tin and bake in the centre of a preheated moderately hot oven (190°C, 375°F, Gas Mark 5), for about 1 hour until well risen and springy to the touch. Test with a skewer which will come out clean when the cake is cooked. Allow to shrink slightly and turn on to a wire tray to cool.

When quite cold, cut across into 3 layers. Spread the two bottom layers with Chocolate Joy and re-assemble the cake. Swirl the rest of the Chocolate Joy over the top and sides of the cake. Arrange a ring of almonds round the rim on the top of the cake and put the remainder in the centre.

Chocolate Roulade

6 eggs, separated
¼ teaspoon vanilla essence
225 g (8 oz) caster sugar
50 g (2 oz) cocoa
For the filling:
100 g (4 oz) plain chocolate
2 tablespoons water
450 ml (¾ pint) Chantilly Cream (see p. 365); or double cream, whipped
To decorate:
150 ml (¼ pint) double cream
crystallised violets or lilac
mint leaves or angelica diamonds

Line a 33 × 21 cm (13 × 8½ inch) swiss roll tin with greased greaseproof paper.

Whip egg yolks, vanilla essence and sugar until creamy. Sieve and fold in cocoa. Whisk egg whites until stiff but not brittle and fold into mixture. Pour into prepared tin and spread evenly into corners.

Bake in preheated oven (180°C, 350°F, Gas Mark 4) for 20 minutes or until set and springy to the touch, but still soft. Do not overcook or it will crack when rolled up. Remove from oven, allow to shrink slightly and turn out upside down on greased greaseproof paper.

Break up chocolate and melt with the water in a bowl over a saucepan of simmering water. Stir until smooth and spread over cake. Cover with Chantilly Cream (p. 365) or whipped cream. Roll up like Swiss Roll (p. 296).

Remove to a serving platter and decorate with ribbons of piped whipped cream, crystallised flowers and mint leaves, angelica or nuts.
Serves 8

Black Forest Cherry Cake

1 × 425 g (15 oz) can black cherries
1 teaspoon arrowroot
1 chocolate-flavoured sponge
    sandwich
150 ml (¼ pint) double cream, stiffly
    whipped
1 chocolate milk flake

Drain and pit the cherries, reserving
the juice. Mix the arrowroot with a
little of the juice in a pan, then stir in
the remaining juice and bring slowly to
the boil. Simmer for a few minutes until
the sauce thickens, stirring constantly.
Remove from the heat, pour into a jug
and leave to cool.

Separate the two layers of the cake
and cut the top layer into serving portions. Fold the cherries into the cream,
then spread over the bottom layer of the
cake. Fit the portions of cake back
together on top at an angle, then
crumble over the chocolate.

Serve the sauce separately.

Devil's Food
Chocolate Cake

100 g (4 oz) plain chocolate, broken
    up
125 g (5 oz) butter
100 g (4 oz) dark brown sugar
1 tablespoon golden syrup
200 g (7 oz) plain flour
25 g (1 oz) cocoa
1 teaspoon bicarbonate of soda
2 eggs, beaten
100 ml (4 fl oz) milk
To finish:
450 g (1 lb) American Frosting (p. 319)
50 g (2 oz) plain chocolate
2 tablespoons water

This quantity makes one 20 cm (8 inch)
cake. Line the base and grease 2
straight-sided 20 cm (8 inch) layer cake
tins. Heat the chocolate in a saucepan
with the butter, sugar and syrup until
just melted.

Sift the flour, cocoa and bicarbonate
of soda into a mixing bowl. Make a well
in the centre and stir in the cooled
melted ingredients. Stir in the eggs and
beat well, then mix in the milk. Pour the
mixture into the prepared tins and bake
in a preheated moderate oven (180°C,
350°F, Gas Mark 4) for 30 minutes or
until set. Allow to cool in the tins before
turning out on to a wire tray to cool.

When cold sandwich together with
some of the American Frosting and coat
the top and sides with the rest, swirling
it with a palette knife, working quickly
before it sets. When the frosting has set,
melt the chocolate with the water in a
bowl over a pan of hot water. Stir until
smooth and trickle it across the top of
the cake from the tip of a spoon in a
lattice pattern. Serve with whipped
cream or icecream.

Chocolate
Refrigerator Cake

1 × 100 g (4 oz) bar plain chocolate,
    broken up
100 g (4 oz) unsalted butter
5 tablespoons golden syrup
1 × 225 g (8 oz) packet rich tea
    biscuits
2 tablespoons chopped nuts
2 tablespoons chopped glacé cherries

Put the chocolate, butter and golden
syrup in a pan and heat gently until
melted, stirring occasionally. Meanwhile, put the biscuits in a bowl and
crush to fine crumbs with the end of a
rolling pin. Add the melted mixture,
nuts and cherries and stir well to mix.
Line the base of a small non-stick pan
with silver kitchen foil.

Press the mixture into the pan, then
chill in the refrigerator overnight. Turn
out, remove the foil, then cut into thin
slices to serve.
Makes about 12 slices

Cut and Come Again Cake

225 g (8 oz) self-raising flour
1 teaspoon salt
1 teaspoon baking powder
1 teaspoon ground mixed spice
225 g (8 oz) wholemeal flour
225 g (8 oz) dark soft brown sugar
225 g (8 oz) butter
175 g (6 oz) sultanas
175 g (6 oz) currants
175 g (6 oz) seedless raisins
50 g (2 oz) glacé cherries, quartered
50 g (2 oz) cut mixed peel
finely grated rind and juice of 1
  orange
3 tablespoons thick cut marmalade
300 ml ($\frac{1}{2}$ pint) sweet stout

Sift the self-raising flour, salt, baking powder and spice into a large bowl. Stir in the wholemeal flour and sugar, then rub in the butter with the fingertips. Add the dried fruit, cherries and peel, orange rind, juice and marmalade. Stir well to mix, then stir in enough sweet stout to give a soft dropping consistency. Spoon the mixture into a greased deep 20 cm (8 inch) square cake tin lined with greased greaseproof paper, then smooth the top. Bake just below the centre of a preheated moderate oven (170°C, 325°F, Gas Mark 3) for 2¼ hours until a skewer inserted in the centre comes out clean. Cover with foil if the cake becomes too brown during baking.

Leave to cool in the tin then remove the greaseproof paper. Wrap in foil, overwrap in a polythene bag and store in an airtight container.
Makes 24 slices

Mixer Fruit Cake

225 g (8 oz) self-raising flour
2 teaspoons mixed spice
1 teaspoon baking powder
100 g (4 oz) soft brown sugar
175 g (6 oz) mixed dried fruit
100 g (4 oz) soft margarine
2 eggs
2 tablespoons water

This quantity makes one 15 cm (6 inch) cake.

This is a one-stage cake made with soft (tub) margarine which does not need to be rubbed into the flour before adding the other ingredients. It is ideal for the electric mixer, but be careful not to overbeat the mixture. If no mixer is available use a wooden spoon.

Grease a 15 cm (6 inch) round cake tin and line the base. Sift the flour, mixed spice and baking powder into the mixing bowl, mix in the sugar and dried fruit lightly with the fingers. Add the margarine, eggs and water and beat with a wooden spoon or in the electric mixer until well combined. Turn into the prepared tin and smooth the top. Bake in the centre of a preheated moderate oven (170°C, 325°F, Gas Mark 3) for about 1¾ hours or until a skewer inserted comes out clean. Allow the cake to shrink slightly. Turn out on to a wire tray, remove the lining paper and leave to cool.

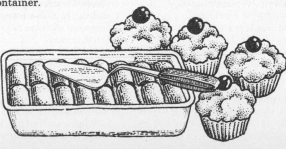

Anniversary Cake

350 g (12 oz) butter or margarine
350 g (12 oz) soft brown sugar
6 eggs, beaten
350 g (12 oz) flour
pinch of salt
1 teaspoon baking powder
1 teaspoon mixed spice
1 teaspoon grated nutmeg
1 teaspoon ground cinnamon
350 g (12 oz) sultanas
350 g (12 oz) currants
225 g (8 oz) seedless raisins
100 g (4 oz) mixed candied peel
175 g (6 oz) glacé cherries, finely
  chopped
75 g (3 oz) blanched almonds, finely
  chopped
finely grated rind and juice of 1
  lemon
4 tablespoons brandy, rum or sherry
700 g (1½ lb) Almond Paste (see p. 320)

Grease a 23 cm (9 inch) square cake tin and line with a double layer of greaseproof paper. Brush with oil.

Beat the butter until soft and light, add the sugar and cream together until light and fluffy. Beat in the eggs a little at a time, adding a little of the measured flour if the mixture shows signs of separating. Sieve the flour with the salt, baking powder and spices into a large mixing bowl. Stir in the dried fruit, candied peel, glacé cherries and almonds and mix thoroughly. Fold into the butter and sugar, adding the lemon rind and juice and half the spirits. Mix well together, then spoon into the prepared tin. Spread level.

Bake in a warm oven (170°C, 325°F, Gas Mark 3) for 3½ hours or until a skewer inserted in the centre of the cake comes out clean. Cover the cake with foil if it becomes too brown during cooking. When cooked, remove from the oven and leave to cool slightly. Prick a few holes in the top of the cake with a skewer and spoon over the remaining spirits.

Leave until cold, then turn out of the tin and remove the greaseproof paper. Wrap in aluminium foil and store in an airtight tin for at least a month to improve the flavour, spooning over more spirits from time to time, if wished. Cover with Almond Paste before icing and decorating.

Scots Seed Cake

100 g (4 oz) butter or margarine
100 g (4 oz) caster sugar
2 large eggs, separated
1 tablespoon whisky or brandy
100 g (4 oz) plain flour
¼ teaspoon baking powder
¼ teaspoon grated nutmeg
50 g (2 oz) blanched almonds,
  shredded
50 g (2 oz) candied orange peel,
  chopped
25 g (1 oz) candied citron peel,
  chopped
To finish:
caraway seeds
granulated sugar

This quantity makes one 15 cm (6 inch) cake.

Line the sides and base of a round 15 cm (6 inch) cake tin. Cream the fat and sugar until light and fluffy. Gradually beat in the egg yolks. Whisk the egg whites until stiff but not brittle, and fold in alternately with the flour, sifted with the baking powder and nutmeg. Fold in the almonds, candied peel and whisky or brandy. Turn into the prepared tin. Sprinkle with caraway seeds and granulated sugar.

Bake in the centre of a preheated moderate oven (160°C, 325°F, Gas Mark 3), for 1½ hours or until set and golden. Test with a skewer which should come out clean when inserted into the centre. Allow the cake to shrink slightly. Turn out on to a wire tray, remove the lining paper and leave to cool.

Dundee Cake

100 g (4 oz) sultanas
100 g (4 oz) seedless raisins
100 g (4 oz) currants
50 g (2 oz) chopped mixed peel
50 g (2 oz) halved glacé cherries
50 g (2 oz) blanched almonds
275 g (10 oz) plain flour
1 teaspoon mixed spice
225 g (8 oz) butter or margarine
225 g (8 oz) soft brown sugar
grated rind of 1 lemon
4 eggs, beaten
little milk to finish

Line a 20 cm (8 inch) round cake tin.

Pick over the fruit, clean the currants, if necessary, by rubbing them in flour in a wire sieve. Set aside some almonds for decoration and cut the remainder into long slivers. Sieve the flour and spice into a mixing bowl and mix in the fruit and nuts.

Cream the fat and sugar together with the grated lemon rind until light and fluffy. Beat in the eggs a spoonful at a time, beating well between additions. Fold in the flour, fruit and nuts. The mixture should drop off the spoon in 5 seconds, add a spoonful of water if needed.

Spoon the cake mixture into the lined tin, spreading it evenly. Now make a large hollow in the centre. This will fill in during the first hour of baking and the cake will rise evenly instead of in a dome. Split the remaining almonds, toss them in a saucer of milk and arrange them on top of the cake.

Bake in the centre of a preheated oven (160°C, 325°F, Gas Mark 3) for 2 to 3 hours. If the top is browning too quickly, cover it with brown paper. Test by inserting a skewer, not a cold knife, into the centre of the cake; it will come out clean when the cake is cooked.

When cooked, remove the cake from the oven and allow it to cool in the tin. If the top has cracked, turn the cake upside down on a cooling tray and the weight will close any cracks. When cool, lift off the tin and peel off the paper. When quite cold, put the cake in an airtight tin or seal it in a plastic bag and store for four weeks before cutting.

Porter Cake

350 g (12 oz) plain flour
$\frac{1}{4}$ teaspoon mixed spice
175 g (6 oz) butter or margarine
275 g (10 oz) soft brown sugar
450 g (1 lb) mixed dried fruit
50 g (2 oz) glacé cherries, chopped
50 g (2 oz) walnuts, chopped
or
50 g (2 oz) blanched almonds, shredded
grated rind of 1 lemon
$\frac{1}{2}$ teaspoon bicarbonate of soda
150 ml ($\frac{1}{4}$ pint) warm stout
3 eggs, beaten

Line and grease a 20 cm (8 inch) round cake tin and tie a band of brown paper round the outside of the tin and 5 cm (2 inches) above it to protect the top of the cake during baking. Sift the flour and mixed spice into a mixing bowl. Cut the fat into the flour and rub in to a breadcrumb consistency. Stir in the sugar, fruit, nuts and grated lemon rind and mix well. Dissolve the bicarbonate of soda in the warm stout and add to the beaten eggs. Stir this into the dry ingredients and mix well.

Pour into the prepared tin and bake in the centre of a preheated cool oven (140°C, 275°F, Gas Mark 1) for 2 hours or until set. Reduce the heat to 120°C, 250°F, Gas Mark $\frac{1}{2}$ for a further hour or until a skewer inserted comes out clean.

Allow to cool in the tin before turning out. Do not cut the same day. It is best if kept to mature in an airtight tin.

Pineapple Gâteau

4 eggs
175 g (6 oz) caster sugar
50 g (2 oz) plain flour
50 g (2 oz) potato flour or cornflour
1 teaspoon baking powder
1 large tin pineapple or 6–8 slices
300 ml (½ pint) whipping cream
2 tablespoons Kirsch
1 tablespoon pistachio nuts, chopped, to garnish

Whisk the eggs and sugar until mixture falls in ribbons off the whisk. Sieve together the plain flour, potato flour and baking powder. Fold a little at a time into the whisked mixture. Turn into a 20 cm (8 inch) greased cake tin. Bake in a preheated moderately hot oven (190°C, 375°F, Gas Mark 5) for 30–40 minutes until well risen and springy to the touch. Allow to shrink slightly then turn out on to a wire cooling rack. Meanwhile drain pineapple slices. Cut half of them into wedges and halve remainder. Whip the cream until stiff. Mix 2 tablespoons of pineapple syrup with the Kirsch. When sponge is cold split in half. Put one half on a serving plate and spoon over pineapple syrup and Kirsch. Arrange pineapple wedges on top and spread with whipped cream. Cover with top half of the sponge. Arrange pineapple half slices on top in a circle, pipe on remaining cream and garnish with chopped pistachio nuts.
Serves 6–8

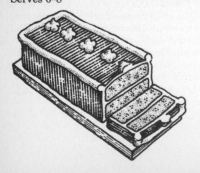

Gâteau St Honoré

40 g (1½ oz) butter or margarine
150 ml (¼ pint) water
75 g (3 oz) plain flour, sieved
2 eggs, beaten
For the gâteau:
100 g (4 oz) sweet shortcrust pastry (see p. 360)
300 ml (½ pint) Pâtisserie Cream (see p. 365); or 300 ml (½ pint) Chantilly Cream (see p. 365)
rum or vanilla essence to taste
75 g (3 oz) caster sugar
crystallised rose and violet petals, to decorate

Melt the butter in the water, bring to the boil and tip in the flour. Beat until smooth over gentle heat until the dough leaves the sides of the pan. Cool and beat in the eggs very gradually, 1 tablespoon at a time. If you do this too quickly dough will be too soft to pipe.

Roll out the sweet shortcrust into a round about 20 cm (8 inches) across. Place on a greased baking sheet and prick well. Damp the outside edge of the round. With a forcing bag and a 1.5 cm (½ inch) plain nozzle pipe a ring of choux pastry on top of the damp edge.

Pipe the rest of the choux pastry in small 'buns' the same width as the ring, on another greased baking sheet. Place shortcrust base on a shelf near the top of preheated oven (220°C, 425°F, Gas Mark 7), with small puffs below it. Bake for 15 minutes and reduce heat (190°C, 375°F, Gas Mark 5), reverse baking trays. Cook for a further 20 minutes. Remove from oven and cool pastry. Slit choux ring and puffs to allow steam to escape. Flavour cream with rum or vanilla. When cold, fill puffs.

Heat the caster sugar in small thick saucepan over gentle heat until it turns golden. Dip base of puffs in caramel and fix on ring. Trickle remaining caramel on top of puffs and quickly decorate with rose and violet petals alternately. Pile remaining cream into centre.

Apricot Rum Baba

125 g (4 oz) plain flour
$\frac{1}{4}$ teaspoon salt
10 g ($\frac{1}{4}$ oz) fresh yeast; or 1$\frac{1}{2}$ teaspoons
dried
2 tablespoons caster sugar
50 ml (2 fl oz) warm milk
2 eggs, beaten
65 g (2$\frac{1}{2}$ oz) butter, creamed
For the rum syrup:
100 g (4 oz) caster sugar
175 ml (6 fl oz) water
100 ml (4 fl oz) rum
For the decoration and filling:
apricot glaze (see p. 264)
225 g (8 oz) apricots, fresh or canned
angelica
150 ml ($\frac{1}{4}$ pint) double cream

Sieve flour and salt into a bowl and put
to warm. Cream the yeast with the
sugar, add the warm milk and beaten
eggs. Gradually stir into the flour and
beat to a smooth batter. Cover the bowl
with a clean cloth and leave in a warm
place to prove for about 45 minutes or
until the dough has doubled in bulk.
Beat in the butter gradually. Half fill a
greased 18 cm (7 inch) Baba ring and
leave in warm place until the dough
rises to the rim. Bake in a preheated
moderately hot oven (200°C, 400°F, Gas
Mark 6) for 10 minutes, then reduce to
moderate (180°C, 350°F, Gas Mark 4)
and cook for 30 minutes or until a skewer
inserted comes out clean. Remove from
oven. Leave for 5–10 minutes. Turn out
on to shallow pie dish, upside down.

Dissolve the sugar in the water, then
boil fast until reduced to a syrup. Cool
slightly and add the rum. Prick the
Baba and spoon over the syrup. Baste
frequently until completely absorbed.

Coat the Baba with Apricot Glaze (see
Belgian Fruit Flan p. 264). Arrange 8
apricot halves on the top and brush with
glaze. Cut the angelica into leaves and
insert between apricots. Cut up remaining apricots, fold into the whipped
cream and pile into the centre.

Saffron Cake

$\frac{1}{2}$ teaspoon saffron threads
150 ml (6 fl oz) milk
15 g ($\frac{1}{2}$ oz) fresh yeast
or
1$\frac{1}{2}$ teaspoons dried yeast with 1
teaspoon sugar
450 g (1 lb) plain flour
pinch of salt
$\frac{1}{4}$ teaspoon ground cinnamon
$\frac{1}{4}$ teaspoon ground nutmeg
$\frac{1}{4}$ teaspoon mixed spice
50 g (2 oz) caster sugar
150 ml (5 fl oz) cream or 100 g (4 oz)
butter, softened
1 tablespoon citron peel, chopped
50 g (2 oz) currants
50 g (2 oz) sultanas
Sweet Milk Glaze (2 tablespoons
sugar dissolved in 2 tablespoons hot
milk)

Crumble the saffron threads into a
cup. Heat half the milk to boiling point
and pour 3 tablespoons on to the saffron, leave for at least 10 minutes to
infuse. Add the cold milk to the hot to
cool it, add the yeast (with the sugar if
using dried yeast) and mix until smooth.

Sift the flour, salt and spices into a
warm mixing bowl and mix in the sugar.
Stir in the cream, add the saffron liquid
and the remainder of the milk and beat
into a soft dough. Add a little warm
water if necessary. Mix in the peel and
dried fruit. Cover and leave in a warm
place until doubled in bulk.

Knock back the dough, put it into a
warmed and greased 18–20 cm (7–8 inch)
cake tin and leave in a warm place until
doubled in bulk. Bake in the centre of a
preheated moderately hot oven (200°C,
400°F, Gas Mark 6) for 15 minutes, then
reduce the heat to 190°C, 375°F, Gas
Mark 5 or put the cake on a lower shelf
for a further 15 to 20 minutes or until
cooked. Test with a skewer. Allow to
shrink slightly before turning out on to
a wire tray to cool. Brush with hot glaze
while still warm.

Cheesecake with Grapes

1 × 200 g (7 oz) packet plain chocolate
  digestive biscuits
50 g (2 oz) roasted hazelnuts, finely
  chopped
75 g (3 oz) butter, melted
For the filling:
350 g (12 oz) black or green grapes,
  halved and depipped
700 g (1½ lb) cream cheese
2 eggs, beaten
100 g (4 oz) caster sugar
2 tablespoons honey
finely grated rind and juice of 1
  lemon

Put the biscuits between two sheets of
greaseproof paper and crush finely with
a rolling pin. Put in a mixing bowl with
the hazelnuts and melted butter and stir
to combine. Using a metal spoon, press
into the base and sides of a lightly oiled
18 cm (7 inch) loose-bottomed spring-
form pan. Chill in the refrigerator for at
least 1 hour until set. Put a layer of
grapes, cut side down, in the bottom of
the pan, arranging them as close together as possible. Reserve the remaining grapes for decorating the top of the
finished cheesecake.

Beat the cream cheese in a bowl until
light and fluffy, then beat in the eggs a
little at a time. Fold in the sugar,
reserving 2 tablespoons, then honey,
lemon rind and juice.

Pour this mixture over the grapes in
the pan, then place on a baking sheet
and bake in a preheated cool oven
(150°C, 300°F, Gas Mark 2) for approximately 1¼ hours or until the filling is set.
Turn off the oven, leave cheesecake in
the oven until completely cold, then
transfer to the refrigerator and chill
overnight.

Remove cheesecake carefully from
pan and transfer to a serving platter.
Arrange the reserved grapes in a circular pattern on the top and sprinkle
with the remaining sugar.
Serves 10–12

Unbaked Apricot Cheesecake

50 g (2 oz) butter or margarine
100 g (4 oz) digestive biscuits, crushed
½ teaspoon ground cinnamon
For the filling:
1 × 425 g (15 oz) can apricot halves
350 g (12 oz) cottage cheese, sieved
75 g (3 oz) caster sugar
grated rind and juice of 1 large lemon
1 tablespoon gelatine
150 ml (¼ pint) whipping cream
flaked almonds (optional)

Place the butter or margarine in a
saucepan. Stir over moderate heat until
just melted, but do not allow it to
colour. Remove from the heat, stir in
the biscuit crumbs and ground cinnamon and mix well. Press the crumb
mixture into the base of a greased loose-
bottomed 17.5 cm (7 inch) cake tin,
smoothing well with the back of a metal
spoon. Chill in the refrigerator while
preparing the filling.

Drain the apricot halves, reserve the
syrup, and liquidize in an electric blender or pass through a sieve. Place the
apricot purée, sieved cottage cheese,
sugar and lemon rind and juice together
in a bowl and beat until smooth.
Measure 2 tablespoons of the reserved
apricot syrup in a small basin, sprinkle
on the gelatine and stir well. Place the
basin in a pan of hot water and stir until
the gelatine has completely dissolved.
Cool and add to the cheese mixture.
Whip the cream until thick and fold into
the cheese mixture. Turn on to the
chilled biscuit base and allow to set.
Remove the cake tin and serve the
cheesecake on its base on a plate. If
liked, sprinkle with flaked almonds.

Cherry Cheesecake

1 × 200 g (7 oz) packet ginger biscuits
100 g (4 oz) butter or margarine,
    melted
1 × 300 ml (10 fl oz) carton double
    cream
4 tablespoons icing sugar
225 g (8 oz) cream cheese
1 × 400 g (14 oz) can cherry pie filling

Put the biscuits in a bowl and crush to
fine crumbs with the end of a rolling pin.
Add the melted butter or margarine and
stir well to mix. Press the mixture into
the bottom and sides of a 20 cm (8 inch)
flan dish, then chill for about 30 minutes
until firm.

Beat the cream until thick, then beat
in the icing sugar and cream cheese
until well blended. Spread the mixture
over the base of the flan. Spread the pie
filling on top to cover the cream mixture
completely.

Chill until serving time.
Serves 6

Variations:

Use any kind of pie filling, or use fresh
fruit such as stoned cherries, seedless
grapes, sliced bananas, halved strawberries or whole raspberries – and
sprinkle with sugar to taste.

Chocolate, Rum and Raisin Cheesecake

150 g (5 oz) digestive biscuits
75 g (3 oz) butter
50 g (2 oz) demerara sugar
For the filling:
40 g (1½ oz) raisins
25 ml (1 fl oz) rum
2 eggs, separated
50 g (2 oz) caster sugar
1 teaspoon instant coffee
5 tablespoons boiling water
12 g (½ oz) (1 envelope) powdered
    gelatine

50 g (2 oz) plain chocolate
225 g (8 oz) cream cheese
150 ml (¼ pint) double cream
2 tablespoons milk
To decorate:
150 ml (¼ pint) double cream
chocolate flakes or crystallised
    flowers and leaves

Soak the raisins in rum, preferably
overnight. Put the biscuits between two
sheets of greaseproof paper and crush
with a rolling pin until fine. Melt the
butter and stir in the crumbs and sugar.
Stir over gentle heat until well blended
and press into a greased 23 cm (9 inch)
flan dish or tin with a loose base. Chill
in the refrigerator for at least an hour to
harden well.

Mix egg yolks, sugar and the coffee
dissolved in 2 tablespoons of the boiling
water in the top of a double saucepan or
in a bowl. Place over boiling water and
stir steadily until the mixture clings to
the back of the wooden spoon.

Dissolve gelatine thoroughly in 3
tablespoons of boiling water, stir into
the egg mixture and remove from heat.
Break up the chocolate into pieces.
Melt the chocolate with a little water in
a bowl over boiling water. Stir until
smooth and blend into mixture. Set
aside until cool.

Beat the cream cheese and when the
chocolate mixture is cold, stir it gradually into the cream cheese. Whisk the
cream with the milk to soft peaks and
fold into the mixture. Whisk the egg
whites until stiff but not brittle and fold
into mixture. Stir in the rum-soaked
raisins. Pour into flan dish or tin and
refrigerate until firmly set.

Decorate with piped whipped cream
and chocolate flakes or crystallised
flowers and leaves.

Variation:

Vary this by using sweet sherry instead
of rum or omitting the raisins alto-
gether and using a double quantity of
chocolate.
Serves 6–8

Éclairs

Choux pastry (see p. 361)
150 ml (¼ pint) double cream, whipped
or flavoured custard

Preheat the oven to 200°C, 400°F, Gas
Mark 6. Place a forcing bag fitted with a
1.5 cm (⅝ inch) plain nozzle in a jug.
Turn back the open end of the bag and
spoon the choux pastry into the bag.
Squeeze the dough well down the bag to
eliminate air bubbles.

Grease and flour a baking sheet.
Mark evenly spaced lines 7.5 cm (3
inches) long with the handle of a
wooden spoon. Hold the forcing bag in
your right hand and, with your left
thumb and one finger on the nozzle to
guide it, force out the dough onto
marked lines, cutting off at end of each
line with a knife.

Bake in the oven for 30 to 35 minutes
until well risen, crisp and golden. When
tapped they should sound hollow,
remove the éclairs from the tray, make a
slit in the side of each to allow steam to
escape; cool on a rack. When cold, fill
with whipped cream or flavoured custard using a forcing bag and plain
nozzle.

* Chocolate Éclairs

Choux pastry (see p. 361)
For the glacé icing:
75 g (3 oz) icing sugar
25 g (1 oz) cocoa
water to mix
¼ teaspoon vanilla essence

Follow the recipe for Éclairs (above) to
bake and fill the éclairs then make the
chocolate glacé icing as follows: sift the
icing sugar with the cocoa into a bowl.
Mix in a spoonful of water at a time
until the icing is of spreading consistency. Flavour with vanilla essence.
Spread the icing over the top of the
éclairs, using a knife dipped in hot
water and put into paper cases. If
making a large quantity, the éclairs can
be dipped top downwards into the icing.

* Strawberry or Raspberry Éclairs

Follow the recipe for Éclairs (above),
with these changes: fill éclairs with
whipped cream and sliced strawberries
or whole raspberries and coat with
Lemon glacé icing (p. 318), tinted with
pink colouring.

Cream Buns

Choux pastry (p. 361)
whipped cream
icing sugar

Put the choux pastry into a piping bag
fitted with a large star nozzle. Pipe
small round, raised shapes on to
greased and floured baking sheets, leaving space for spreading. Each round of
choux should be about 5 cm (2 inches) in
diameter. Bake as for éclairs (see left),
and make a small hole in the base of
each cooked bun, to allow the steam to
escape. Once cold, fill the buns with
whipped cream and dust with sifted
icing sugar.
Makes 10–12

Profiteroles

Choux pastry (p. 361)
whipped cream
icing sugar, sifted, or Chocolate sauce
(p. 357)

Put the choux pastry into a piping bag
fitted with a 1 cm (½ inch) plain nozzle.
Pipe very small raised mounds, no more
than 2.5 cm (1 inch) in diameter, on to

greased and floured baking sheets, leaving space for spreading. Bake as for éclairs (left), but for only 20 minutes, and make a small hole in the base of each cooked profiterole to allow the steam to escape. Once cold, fill with whipped cream. Arrange the profiteroles in a pyramid on a serving dish, and either dust with sifted icing sugar or top with chocolate sauce.

Apple Buns

225 g (8 oz) plain flour
1 teaspoon cream of tartar
$\frac{1}{2}$ teaspoon bicarbonate of soda
pinch of salt
100 g (4 oz) butter or margarine
100 g (4 oz) caster sugar
1 egg
1–2 tablespoons water
approx. 300 ml ($\frac{1}{2}$ pint) thick
    sweetened apple purée from 450 g
    (1 lb) cooking apples (p. 261)
$\frac{1}{2}$ teaspoon ground coriander
caster sugar or whipped cream, to
    finish

Sift the flour, cream of tartar, bicarbonate of soda and salt into a mixing bowl. Cut the fat into the flour and rub in to a breadcrumb consistency. Mix in the sugar, stir in the beaten egg and add a little water to mix to a stiff but not sticky dough, like shortcrust pastry. Roll out to 5 mm ($\frac{1}{4}$ inch) thick, divide in half and cut one half into rounds and line greased bun tins. Put 1 to 2 teaspoons of apple purée in each one. Cut the remaining pastry into smaller rounds, put them on top and press the pastry edges firmly together. Work up the trimmings, roll out and make more buns. Bake near the top of a preheated hot oven (220°C, 425°F, Gas Mark 7) for 15 minutes or until well risen and golden. Serve hot dredged with caster sugar, or cool on a wire tray and serve each bun topped with a swirl of cream.
Makes 12–18

Almond Buns

175 g (6 oz) plain flour
$\frac{1}{2}$ teaspoon baking powder
pinch of salt
75 g (3 oz) butter or margarine
50 g (2 oz) caster sugar
1 egg, beaten
For the almond paste:
50 g (2 oz) ground almonds
25 g (1 oz) caster sugar
25 g (1 oz) icing sugar
1 egg yolk
squeeze of lemon juice
For the topping:
1 egg white, beaten
flaked almonds

Sift the flour, baking powder and salt into a mixing bowl. Cut the fat into the flour and rub in to a breadcrumb consistency. Stir in the sugar and bind into a stiff dough with the beaten egg, adding a spoonful of water if necessary.

To make the almond paste, mix together the ground almonds and sugars. Bind with the egg yolk into a stiff paste, and flavour to taste with the lemon juice. Roll into 16 marbles using sugared fingers.

Roll the dough into a sausage shape and divide into 16 equal portions. Shape into balls on a floured board and flatten slightly. Place a marble of almond paste in the centre of each bun and gather the edges together over it. Turn upside down and place on a greased baking sheet. Brush the buns with the beaten egg white and sprinkle with flaked almonds. Bake in a preheated hot oven (220°C, 425°F, Gas Mark 7) for 15 minutes or until well risen and golden brown. Cool on a wire tray.
Makes 16

Coffee Walnut Buns

100 g (4 oz) plain flour
100 g (4 oz) wholemeal flour
pinch of salt
2 teaspoons baking powder
100 g (4 oz) butter or margarine
75 g (3 oz) soft brown sugar
50 g (2 oz) walnuts, chopped
1 egg
2 tablespoons coffee essence
milk to mix
For the topping:
Coffee Glacé Icing (see p. 318)
halved walnuts

Sift the flour, salt and baking powder
into a mixing bowl. Cut the fat into the
flour and rub in to a breadcrumb consistency. Mix in the sugar and chopped
nuts. Beat the egg and coffee essence
together, then stir into the mixture
adding milk to give a stiff dough.

Using 2 forks heap the mixture in
rocky mounds on a greased baking
sheet. Bake near the top of a preheated
moderately hot oven (200°C, 400°F, Gas
Mark 6) for 15 to 20 minutes. Remove
from the tins and cool on a wire tray.
Ice and top with half a walnut.
Makes 12–16.

Danish Pastries

225 g (8 oz) plain flour
pinch of salt
25 g (1 oz) butter or lard
15 g ($\frac{1}{2}$ oz) fresh yeast
or
1$\frac{1}{2}$ teaspoons dried yeast
15 g ($\frac{1}{2}$ oz) caster sugar
5 tablespoons warm water
1 egg, beaten
125 g (5 oz) butter
225 g (8 oz) Almond paste (see p. 320)
  finished weight
thin Glacé Icing (see p. 318) for
  glazing

This quantity makes 14 pastries.

Sift the flour and salt into a warm
mixing bowl and rub in the lard. Blend
the yeast with the sugar and water.
Leave for 10 minutes to froth if using
dried yeast. Stir into the flour with the
beaten egg and mix to a soft dough.
Turn on to a floured board and knead
lightly for about 5 minutes until
smooth. Put in an oiled polythene bag
and refrigerate for 10 minutes.

Cream the butter with a palette knife
and shape into a 'brick'. Roll out the
dough into a rectangle 1 cm ($\frac{1}{2}$ inch)
thick. Spread the butter evenly over
half the dough leaving a border 2.5 cm (1
inch) round the edge. Fold over the
other half of the dough, seal the edges
with a rolling pin and give the pastry a
quarter turn. Repeat three times, chilling for 10 minutes between each rolling.
Put in the polythene bag and chill for at
least 30 minutes before shaping.

Roll out the dough slightly and divide
in half. Roll one half into a rectangle
30 × 20 cm (12 × 8 inches). Cut into 6 10
cm (4 inch) squares.

Divide the marzipan into 14 pieces,
roll 6 into little balls and flatten
slightly. Place one in the centre of each
square and brush with beaten egg.
Draw up the corners together in the
centre and seal with the beaten egg.
Place the pastries on a baking sheet,
cover and leave in a warm place for
about 20 minutes until puffy. Brush
with beaten egg and bake in a hot oven
(220°C, 425°F, Gas Mark 7) for 15 to 20
minutes or until crisp and golden.
Brush with Icing and cool on a wire
tray.

Roll the second half of the pastry into
a 25 cm (10 inch) square and divide into
4 quarters. Cut each square diagonally
making 8 triangles. Roll the remaining
pieces of Marzipan into tiny sausage
shapes. Place in the centre of the long
side of each triangle. Brush the pastry
edges with beaten egg and roll up with
the point underneath. Curve into a
crescent shape. Place on a baking sheet.
Prove, glaze and bake as before.

Chocolate Chews

50 g (2 oz) caster sugar
2 tablespoons golden syrup
75 g (3 oz) butter
225 g (8 oz) quick cook oats
3 tablespoons cocoa powder
1 teaspoon vanilla or rum essence
25 g (1 oz) walnuts, chopped
50 g (2 oz) seedless raisins, chopped

Place the sugar, syrup and butter in a saucepan. Stir over a gentle heat until the sugar has dissolved. Bring the mixture to the boil, remove from the heat and stir in the oats, cocoa powder, vanilla or rum essence, chopped walnuts and chopped raisins.

Mix very thoroughly and spread in a buttered 20 cm (8 inch) square cake tin. Chill in the refrigerator until firm then cut into 5 cm (2 inch) squares. Remove from the tin with a palette knife and store in an airtight container.
Makes 16

Oven Scones

25–50 g (1–2 oz) butter or margarine
225 g (8 oz) plain flour
½ teaspoon salt
4 teaspoons baking powder
approx. 150 ml (¼ pint) milk
milk or flour to finish

Preheat the oven to 230°C, 450°F, Gas Mark 8 and heat a baking sheet. Sift the flour, salt and baking powder into a mixing bowl. Chop up the fat and rub it into the flour until the mixture resembles coarse breadcrumbs.

Make a well in the centre and pour in most of the liquid. Mix to a soft spongy dough, adding more liquid as needed. Turn on to a well floured board and quickly knead out any cracks to make a smooth dough.

Pat out dough, or roll lightly, until 1.5 cm (¾ inch) thick. Cut into rounds with floured scone cutter 6 cm (2½ inches) wide put onto warmed baking sheet. Reshape remaining dough into a ball, flatten slightly, cut into quarters. Put triangles on baking sheet.

Brush the scones with milk for a glossy top, or dust with flour for a soft crust. Bake near the top of the oven for 7 to 10 minutes until the scones are well risen and golden brown. Remove from the oven and wrap in a tea cloth if to be served hot, or cool on a wire tray.

* Cheese Scones

Follow the recipe for Oven scones (above) with the following changes: add 75–100 g (3–4 oz) grated mature cheese to the dry ingredients with 1 teaspoon dry mustard. Mix the dough with 150 ml (¼ pint) milk.

* Girdle Scones

Follow the recipe for Oven scones (above), with these changes: replace the baking powder with 1 teaspoon bicarbonate of soda and 2 teaspoons cream of tartar and adding 2 tablespoons caster sugar. Divide the dough in half and roll it into 2 rounds 1 cm (½ inch) thick. Cut each round into 6 triangles. Cook on the greased girdle for 5 minutes until well risen and golden underneath, then turn and cook for a further 10 minutes or until nicely browned and cooked through.

* Sultana Scones

Follow the recipe for Oven scones (above) with the following changes: add 50 g (2 oz) sultanas and 1–2 tablespoons caster sugar to the dry ingredients and mix with 1 beaten egg and 75 ml (3 fl oz) water. Glaze with milk.

Eccles Cakes

100 g (4 oz) currants
50 g (2 oz) butter, melted
50 g (2 oz) soft brown sugar
pinch of grated nutmeg
225 g (8 oz) Flaky Pastry (see p. 362)
To glaze:
1 egg white, beaten
caster sugar

This quantity makes 8 to 10 cakes.

Mix together the currants, butter, brown sugar and nutmeg. Roll out the pastry to 5 mm ($\frac{1}{4}$ inch) thick and cut into 10 cm (4 inch) rounds. Put a teaspoonful of filling in the centre of each round and damp the border. Pull the pastry together over the filling and squeeze together. Turn the pastries over and roll out until the fruit begins to show through. Score the top with a sharp knife into a diamond pattern. Brush with egg white and sprinkle with caster sugar. Bake in a preheated hot oven (230°C, 450°F, Gas Mark 8) for 15 minutes or until well risen and golden brown. Serve hot or cold.

Irish Potato Cakes

500 g (1 lb) floury potatoes
50 g (2 oz) butter
salt and pepper to taste
approx. 100 g (4 oz) plain flour
butter for filling

Boil, dry and mash the potatoes in a mouli. While still hot, beat in the butter. Season well with salt and freshly ground pepper. Work in sufficient flour to bind into a dough.

On a floured board, knead the dough lightly and divide it in half. Shape each piece into a round 1 cm ($\frac{1}{2}$ inch) thick. Then cut each round into 6 or 8 farls (triangles).

Well grease the heated girdle. Lift the farls onto the girdle with a palette knife or a fish slice and cook for about 5 minutes until nicely browned underneath. Turn and cook until golden brown. Split the potato cakes, fill with a slice of butter and serve very hot with grilled sausage or bacon.

* Sweet Potato Cakes

Follow the recipe for Irish potato cakes (above) with the following changes: sprinkle the butter with caster sugar before closing the cakes.

* Apple Potato Cakes

Follow the recipe for Irish potato cakes (above) with the following changes: fill with chopped apple, sugar and butter before closing the cakes.

Carleton Cakes

100 g (4 oz) plain flour
25 g (1 oz) ground rice
1 teaspoon baking powder
75 g (3 oz) butter or margarine
50 g (2 oz) caster sugar
2 eggs, separated
25 g (1 oz) candied citron peel, chopped
25 g (1 oz) blanched flaked almonds, shredded
3 tablespoons water
1 thin slice candied citron peel, to decorate

This quantity makes 12 cakes.

Sift the flour, rice and baking powder together. Cream the fat with the sugar until light and fluffy. Stir in the egg yolks and beat well. Mix in the flour, then the citron peel and almonds. Stir in the water and beat until smooth. Beat the egg whites until stiff but not brittle. Fold them into the mixture. Spoon into well greased patty pans. Cut the citron peel slice into small wedges and place one in the centre of each cake. Bake in a preheated moderately hot oven (200°C, 400°F, Gas Mark 6) for about 15 minutes. Remove from the tins and cool on a wire tray. Best when freshly baked.

Fruity Parkin

75 g (3 oz) butter or margarine
100 g (4 oz) dark soft brown sugar
150 g (5 oz) golden syrup
75 g (3 oz) black treacle
finely grated rind and juice of 1
  lemon
175 g (6 oz) self-raising flour
pinch of salt
2 teaspoons ground ginger
175 g (6 oz) medium oatmeal
4 dried apricots, soaked overnight
  drained and finely chopped
50 g (2 oz) sultanas
50 g (2 oz) pitted dates, chopped
about 6 tablespoons milk

Put the butter or margarine, sugar, syrup and treacle in a saucepan and heat gently until dissolved, stirring occasionally. Remove from the heat and stir in the lemon rind and juice.

Sieve the flour, salt and ginger into a bowl, then stir in the oatmeal and dried fruit. Stir in the melted mixture, then enough milk to make a soft dropping consistency. Beat well to combine. Grease a 22.5 × 14 × 5 cm (9 × 5½ × 2 inch) baking tin and line the base with greased greaseproof paper. Pour in the parkin and bake in a moderate oven (180°C, 350°F, Gas Mark 4) for approximately 45 minutes until firm to the touch. Remove from the oven, leave to cool in the tin for a few minutes, then turn out on to a wire rack. Leave until completely cold, then peel off the greaseproof paper and store in an airtight tin for at least three days before cutting and eating.
Cuts into about 12 pieces

Munchy Muesli Squares

225 g (8 oz) muesli (p. 364)
3 tablespoons thick honey
3 tablespoons golden syrup
50 g (2 oz) butter, softened

Put all the ingredients in a bowl and beat together until well mixed. Spread the mixture in a buttered 20 cm (8 inch) square tin, then bake in a preheated moderate oven (180°C, 350°F, Gas Mark 4) for 35 minutes until golden brown. Leave to cool in the tin for 5 minutes, then cut into squares and leave in the tin to cool completely. Remove the squares from the tin, wrap neatly in foil and store in an airtight container.
Makes 16

Oat Crisps

150 g (5 oz) butter
50 g (2 oz) golden syrup
100 g (4 oz) demerara sugar
75 g (3 oz) quick cook oats
50 g (2 oz) desiccated coconut
100 g (4 oz) plain flour
1 teaspoon bicarbonate of soda
1 teaspoon hot water

Place the butter, syrup and sugar in a large saucepan. Heat gently until the butter has melted and the sugar dissolved. Mix together the oats, coconut and flour, then stir into the melted mixture. Dissolve the bicarbonate of soda in the hot water and stir into the oat mixture. Allow to cool for a few minutes then form into 18 balls.

Place the balls well apart on greased baking sheets. Leave plenty of space for spreading. Bake in a warm oven (160°C, 325°F, Gas Mark 3) for 15 to 20 minutes, or until evenly browned. Leave to cool slightly and set before removing them with a palette knife. Transfer to a wire rack to cool completely. Store in an airtight container.

Hot Cross Squares

25 g (1 oz) fresh yeast, or 4 teaspoons
  dried yeast and 1 teaspoon sugar
300 ml ($\frac{1}{2}$ pint) warm milk and water
  mixed
450 g (1 lb) strong plain flour
1 teaspoon salt
$\frac{1}{2}$ teaspoon mixed spice
$\frac{1}{2}$ teaspoon ground cinnamon
$\frac{1}{2}$ teaspoon grated nutmeg
50 g (2 oz) caster sugar
50 g (2 oz) butter
1 egg, beaten
50 g (2 oz) currants
50 g (2 oz) chopped mixed peel
To finish:
100 g (4 oz) shortcrust pastry dough,
  made with 100 g (4 oz) flour, 50 g
  (2 oz) butter, 1 tablespoon water
50 g (2 oz) sugar
2 tablespoons water

Cream the fresh yeast with a little of the
milk and water. (If using dried yeast,
stir the sugar into the milk and water
and sprinkle the dried yeast over.)
Leave in a warm place for 10 minutes or
until frothy.

Meanwhile sieve the flour, salt and
spices into a warm mixing bowl. Stir in
the caster sugar. Rub in the butter with
the fingertips. Make a well in the centre
of the flour, pour in the frothy yeast
mixture and liquid, the egg, currants
and mixed peel. Mix together with the
hands until a soft dough is formed. Turn
out on to a lightly floured board and
knead for 10 minutes until smooth. Roll
out the dough to a rectangle to fit a
roasting pan about 30 × 23 cm (12 × 9
inches), brush the inside of the pan with
butter and put in the dough. Mark into
twelve squares with a sharp knife.
Leave in a warm place for about 1 hour
until almost doubled in bulk.

Roll out the shortcrust pastry dough
on a floured board and cut into three 30
cm (12 inch) strips and four 23 cm (9
inch) strips. Place the strips on top of
the risen dough, forming a criss-cross
pattern to make crosses on the twelve
squares. Use a little water to stick the
strips on. Bake in the centre of a fairly
hot oven (190°C, 375°F, Gas Mark 5) for
20 minutes or until browned on top.
Remove from the oven, leave to cool for
a few minutes, then cut into twelve
squares. Transfer to a wire rack.

Put the sugar and water into a heavy-
based pan and heat gently until the
sugar has dissolved. Increase the heat
and boil rapidly for a few minutes until
a syrup is formed. Remove from the heat
and brush over the squares until all the
syrup is used. Leave until cool before
splitting in two and spreading with
butter.
Makes 12

Tea Brack

500 g (1 lb) mixed dried fruit
4 tablespoons thick honey
300 ml ($\frac{1}{2}$ pint) strained cold tea
2 eggs, beaten
50 g (2 oz) butter, melted
2 tablespoons milk
500 g (1 lb) self-raising flour

Put the fruit, honey and tea in a large
bowl and stir well to mix. Cover with a
cloth and leave to soak overnight. Beat
in the remaining ingredients until
evenly mixed, then spoon into a greased
deep 18 cm (7 inch) square cake tin lined
with greased greaseproof paper.

Bake just below the centre of a preheated moderate oven (170°C, 325°F,
Gas Mark 3) for $1\frac{1}{4}$ to $1\frac{1}{2}$ hours or until a
skewer inserted in the centre comes out
clean. Cover the top of the cake with
foil if it becomes too brown during
baking.

Remove it from the oven and leave to
cool in the tin, then remove the greaseproof paper. Wrap in foil, overwrap in a
polythene bag and store in an airtight
container. Serve cut into thin slices and
spread with butter.
Makes 24 slices

Chocolate Crispies

100 g (4 oz) milk chocolate, broken
  into squares
2 tablespoons milk
2 tablespoons golden syrup
100 g (4 oz) cornflakes, lightly crushed
50 g (2 oz) desiccated coconut

Put the chocolate, milk and golden
syrup into a heavy-based saucepan and
heat gently until melted, stirring occasionally to mix the ingredients together. Put the cornflakes in a mixing bowl
and stir in the chocolate mixture and
the coconut. Stir to combine, then
divide mixture equally between 12 to 14
paper bun cases. Chill in the refrigerator for an hour or so until set, then
store in an airtight tin.
Makes 12–14

Easter Biscuits

75 g (3 oz) butter or margarine
75 g (3 oz) caster sugar
1 egg, beaten
175 g (6 oz) self-raising flour
pinch of salt
$\frac{1}{2}$ teaspoon mixed spice
50 g (2 oz) currants
1–2 tablespoons milk
To finish:
1 egg white, lightly beaten
caster sugar for sprinkling

Cream together the butter or margarine
and sugar in a mixing bowl until light
and fluffy, then beat in the egg. Sieve
the flour, salt and mixed spice and fold
into the creamed mixture with the currants. Beat well to mix, adding enough
milk to make a soft pliable dough.
Knead lightly until dough is smooth,
and then roll out on a floured board to
6 mm ($\frac{1}{4}$ inch) thick. Stamp into rounds
with a pastry cutter.
  Put biscuits on greased baking
sheets, allowing room for expansion.

Bake in the centre of a moderate oven
(180°C, 350°F, Gas Mark 4) for 10 minutes. Remove from the oven, brush
with the egg white and sprinkle with
caster sugar. Return to the oven and
continue cooking for a further 10 minutes or until the biscuits are golden
and crisp. When cooked, leave biscuits
to cool for a few minutes. Transfer to a
wire rack to cool completely. Store in
an airtight tin.
Makes 16–18

Peanut Biscuits

275 g (10 oz) self-raising flour
$\frac{1}{2}$ teaspoon ground cinnamon
275 g (10 oz) margarine
225 g (8 oz) soft brown sugar
100 g (4 oz) salted peanuts, finely
  chopped
100 g (4 oz) seedless raisins
1–2 tablespoons milk

Sift the flour and cinnamon together.
Cream the margarine and sugar together until light and fluffy. Fold in the
flour with the chopped peanuts and
raisins and sufficient milk to make a
soft dough.
  Using half the mixture, drop teaspoonfuls on to two baking sheets,
allowing room to spread. Bake in a
moderate oven (180°C, 350°F, Gas Mark
4) for 10 minutes. Remove with a palette
knife and cool on a wire rack while
baking the second batch.
Makes approx. 48

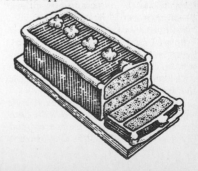

Spiced Sultana Cookies

225 g (8 oz) self-raising flour
1 teaspoon ground mixed spice
pinch of salt
100 g (4 oz) wholemeal flour
100 g (4 oz) demerara sugar
150 g (5 oz) butter
1 large egg, beaten
50 g (2 oz) sultanas
a little extra demerara sugar, for
   sprinkling

Sift the self-raising flour, spice and salt into a bowl. Stir in the wholemeal flour and the sugar. Rub in the butter with the fingertips, then stir in the egg to give a stiff dough.

Turn the dough out onto a floured surface and work in the sultanas with the fingertips, until evenly distributed throughout the dough. Sprinkle with plenty of flour if the dough becomes too sticky. Form into a ball, wrap in foil, then chill in the refrigerator for at least 30 minutes until firm.

Roll out small pieces of the dough on a floured surface and cut into rounds using a 5 cm (2 inch) fluted biscuit cutter. Dredge the dough and surface with flour while rolling and cutting as the dough is rich and sticky.

Place on baking sheets, prick all over with a fork, then sprinkle with demerara sugar. Bake in a preheated moderate oven (180°C, 350°F, Gas Mark 4) for 10–12 minutes until golden brown and set.

Transfer immediately to a wire rack and leave to cool. Wrap neatly in foil and store in an airtight container.
Makes 30–35

Fresh Strawberry Shortcake

225 g (8 oz) plain flour
pinch of salt
3 teaspoons baking powder
75 g (3 oz) butter
75 g (3 oz) caster sugar
approx. 75 ml (3 fl oz) milk
40 g (1½ oz) butter, melted
350 g (12 oz) fresh strawberries, hulled
1–2 tablespoons caster sugar
150 ml (6 fl oz) whipping or double
   cream, whipped

Sift the flour, salt and baking powder into a mixing bowl. Cut the fat into the flour and rub in to a breadcrumb consistency. Add the caster sugar and mix to a soft dough with the milk. Turn on to a floured board and knead for about 1 minute. Divide in half and roll each half into a round on a greased baking sheet, brush one round with melted butter and place the other round on top. Bake in the centre of a preheated hot oven (220°C, 425°F, Gas Mark 7) for 20 to 30 minutes or until firm and golden brown. Separate the two rounds and cool on a wire tray. Put aside 9 even-sized strawberries for decoration. Slice the remaining strawberries in half.

When the shortcake is cold, spread the sliced berries on the bottom layer, sprinkle with sugar and replace the top. Spread the cream over the top of the shortcake and ruffle it up. Decorate with the selected strawberries.

Variation:
To make small shortcakes, cut the rolled dough into 7.5 cm (3 inch) rounds and bake for about 20 minutes.

Iced Cookies

225 g (8 oz) flour
pinch of salt
100 g (4 oz) sugar
125 g (4 oz) butter or margarine
1 egg yolk
1-2 tablespoons cold water
For the glacé icing:
100 g (4 oz) icing sugar, sieved
1-2 tablespoons hot water
few drops each of bright red, yellow,
  green and blue food colourings

Sift the flour and salt into a mixing bowl and stir in the sugar. Cut the butter or margarine into pieces and work into the flour and sugar with the fingertips. Stir in the egg and enough cold water to draw the mixture together. Form the dough into a ball, wrap in foil and chill in the refrigerator for at least 30 minutes. Roll out the chilled dough on a well-floured board and stamp into approximately 50 shapes with small fancy cookie cutters. Place on greased baking sheets and bake in a moderate oven (180°C, 350°F, Gas Mark 4) for approximately 10 minutes until the cookies are set and golden. Remove from the oven and cool on a wire rack. Meanwhile, make the glacé icing: put the icing sugar in a bowl and gradually beat in the hot water, adding enough to let the icing coat the back of a spoon. Divide the icing into three or four and add different food colourings to each. Spread immediately on top of the biscuits, then leave to set unless decorations are to be added.

If liked, the round cookies can be made into faces with currants for eyes, halved glacé cherries for noses and a curved strip of orange or lemon rind for the mouth. Dogs and cats can also have faces made in this way. Star-shaped cookies can be decorated with silver dragees at each point. Add decorations immediately after icing, then leave to set. Store in an airtight tin.
Makes about 50

Strawberry and Hazelnut Shortcake

100 g (4 oz) butter
75 g (3 oz) caster sugar
100 g (4 oz) roasted hazelnuts, finely
  ground
175 g (6 oz) flour
450 ml (¾ pint) double or whipping
  cream
50 g (2 oz) icing sugar
450 g (1 lb) strawberries, hulled and
  washed

Assemble this cake just before serving time. Cream the butter and caster sugar together until light and fluffy, then beat in the hazelnuts and flour a little at a time. Form the mixture into three equal balls and chill in the refrigerator for at least 30 minutes until firm. With floured fingers, press each ball into a 20 cm (8 inch) circle on parchment paper placed on a baking sheet. Mark one of the circles into eight triangles with a sharp knife. Bake in the centre of a fairly hot oven (190°C, 375°F, Gas Mark 5) for 15 to 20 minutes or until golden brown (if necessary, bake each circle separately as the pastry will cook too quickly if not baked in the centre of the oven). Remove from the oven and cut through the eight triangles of the one circle to separate them. Leave the pastry for 5 to 10 minutes to cool slightly and become firm, then carefully ease off the parchment paper. Leave to cool. Whip the cream until thick with most of the icing sugar, reserving a little. Slice the strawberries, reserving four for decoration, and fold into the whipped cream.

Place one whole round of hazelnut pastry on a serving platter and spread with half the strawberry and cream mixture. Place the second round of pastry on top and spread with the remaining strawberries and cream. Arrange the eight 'triangles' on top of the cake, dust with icing sugar and decorate each with a strawberry.
Serves 8

Rich Scots Shortbread

225 g (8 oz) plain flour
100 g (4 oz) rice flour or ground rice
100 g (4 oz) caster sugar
pinch of salt
225 g (8 oz) unsalted butter

Sift the two flours (or flour and rice), sugar and salt, into a mixing bowl. Soften the butter slightly, cut it up and rub it into the dry ingredients with your fingers. When it starts to bind, gather it together with one hand into a ball. Knead it on a lightly floured board until it is a soft, smooth and pliable dough.

Place a 20 cm (8 inch) flan ring on a greased baking tray and put in the dough. Press it out evenly with your knuckles to fit the ring. With the back of a knife, mark it into 6 or 8 triangles. Prick right through to the baking sheet with a fork in a neat pattern. Chill for at least 1 hour before baking to firm it up.

Bake in the centre of a preheated cool oven (150°C, 300°F, Gas Mark 2) for 45 minutes to 1 hour or until it is a pale biscuit colour but still soft. Remove from the oven and leave to cool and shrink before removing the ring, then dust lightly with caster sugar. When cold store in an airtight tin.

Rum Truffles

100 g (4 oz) plain chocolate, broken
   into pieces
3 tablespoons rum
100 g (4 oz) stale fruit cake
100 g (4 oz) ground almonds
50 g (2 oz) icing sugar, sifted
2 tablespoons apricot jam, sieved
15 g ($\frac{1}{2}$ oz) cocoa powder
50 g (2 oz) chocolate vermicelli

Put the chocolate and rum in a heatproof bowl and stand over a pan of gently simmering water. Heat until the chocolate melts, stirring occasionally to make a smooth mixture.

Meanwhile, crumble the cake and ground almonds together in a bowl with the fingertips. Pour in the melted chocolate and the icing sugar and stir well to combine. Turn out on to a board sprinkled with icing sugar and knead lightly until smooth.

Shape the mixture into approximately 25 balls and brush with the jam. Put the cocoa and vermicelli together in a bowl and shake to combine. Add the truffles one at a time and shake the bowl until each truffle is evenly coated. Chill in the refrigerator until firm, and then pack in sweet cases.

Makes about 25

Bonfire Toffee

100 g (4 oz) butter
225 g (8 oz) soft brown sugar
225 g (8 oz) golden syrup
walnut halves

Use the largest saucepan available for making toffee as this will help prevent the toffee boiling over and sticking to top of the cooker.

Brush a large shallow tin with a little of the butter and set aside.

Put the remaining butter in a saucepan and heat gently until melted. Add the sugar and syrup and heat gently until the sugar has dissolved, stirring occasionally. Increase the heat and boil the mixture rapidly for approximately 10 minutes until the temperature reaches 155°C (310°F) on a sugar thermometer. Watch to make sure it does not boil over. Remove from the heat and pour into the prepared tin. Leave to cool for 10 to 15 minutes, then mark into squares and put a walnut half in the middle of each. Leave until completely cold, then remove the toffee from the tin, break it up into separate squares and store in an airtight container.

Makes about 450 g (1 lb)

Toffee Treats

500 g (1 lb) demerara sugar
225 g (8 oz) butter, cut into pieces
2 tablespoons golden syrup
175 g (6 oz) cut mixed nuts

Put all the ingredients in a heavy pan and heat gently until the sugar has dissolved, stirring occasionally. Increase the heat and boil rapidly for 4 to 5 minutes until thick, stirring constantly with a wooden spoon. Spread immediately in a buttered Swiss roll tin 28 × 20 cm (11 × 8 inch), using a palette knife. Leave for 5 minutes until just beginning to set, then cut into squares and leave in the tin until cold. Store in an airtight container, interleaving the layers with greaseproof paper.
Makes about 750 g (1¾ lb)

Toffee Apples

10 dessert apples, washed and dried
10 wooden sticks
For the toffee:
350 g (12 oz) soft brown sugar
50 g (2 oz) butter
100 g (4 oz) golden syrup
1 teaspoon lemon juice
150 ml (¼ pint) water

Remove the stalks from the apples and push a wooden stick into each one.
Put all the ingredients for the toffee into a heavy-based saucepan and heat gently until dissolved, stirring occasionally. Increase the heat and boil rapidly, without stirring, until the toffee mixture reaches a temperature of 145°C (290°F) on a sugar thermometer. Remove from the heat.
Carefully dip the apples in the toffee one at a time. Make sure that they are completely covered in the toffee, then plunge into cold water. Stand on well-oiled greaseproof paper until set.
Makes 10

Vanilla Fudge

1 large can sweetened condensed milk
500 g (1 lb) light soft brown sugar
50 g (2 oz) butter
½ teaspoon vanilla essence

Put all the ingredients in a heavy-based pan and heat gently until the sugar has dissolved, stirring occasionally. Then increase the heat and boil rapidly for 5 minutes, stirring constantly with a wooden spoon until the mixture becomes thick and dark.
Remove from the heat and continue stirring vigorously for 2 minutes until the mixture begins to look grainy. Pour immediately into a buttered 20 cm (8 inch) square shallow tin. Leave for 5 minutes until just beginning to set, then cut into squares and leave in the tin until cold. Remove the fudge from the tin, break into squares and pack in an airtight container.
Makes about 750 g (1¾ lb)

Variations:
Chopped nuts, raisins or grated chocolate can be added to the fudge if liked. Stir into the mixture after removing from the heat.

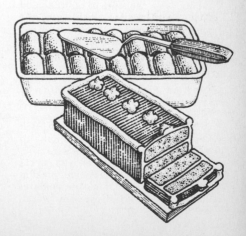

Royal Icing

3 egg whites
450–700 g (1–1½ lb) icing sugar, sieved
1 tablespoon glycerine
yellow or blue food colouring

Put the egg whites in a clean bowl and break up with a fork. Add the icing sugar a little at a time, beating well with a wooden spoon after each addition. Keep adding the icing sugar until the icing is smooth and coats the back of the spoon, then stir in the glycerine. Stir gently for a few minutes to reduce air bubbles.

Pour the icing into an airtight container and cover with a lid, or cover the bowl with a damp cloth and place in a polythene bag. Leave to stand for several hours, preferably overnight. Next day, stir the icing gently to reduce air bubbles.

Put 4 tablespoons icing in a separate bowl, cover with a lid or damp cloth and set aside in a cool place. Colour the remaining icing blue if it is for a silver wedding cake, yellow for a golden wedding cake.

To ice the cake: stand it on a wire rack over a tray and pour all the icing on to the top of the cake. Gently lift and tip the tray to make the icing flow evenly down the sides of the cake and use a palette knife to help make the icing cover the entire surface of the cake. Gently prick any air bubbles that form on the surface of the icing, working quickly before the icing begins to dry. Immediately scoop up the surplus icing, put in a bowl and cover with a lid or damp cloth. Leave both cake and icing in a cool place overnight.

The next day, run a sharp pointed knife around the base of the cake to make sure that it is free of the wire rack. Put a few blobs of icing on a 28 cm (11 inch) square silver cake board, pick up the cake using the flat of your hands on the sides and place it carefully on the board.

Chocolate Joy Icing

225 g (8 oz) icing sugar
50 g (2 oz) cocoa
50 g (2 oz) unsalted butter
1 egg yolk
¼ teaspoon vanilla essence
3–4 tablespoons warm water

Sift the icing sugar and cocoa together. Cream the butter until light and fluffy and beat in the icing sugar and cocoa. Flavour the egg yolk with the vanilla, add 2 to 3 tablespoons warm water and beat into the butter cream. Add a little more water if necessary to make a spreading consistency.

Glacé Icing

100 g (4 oz) icing sugar
water to mix
vanilla essence

Sift the icing sugar into a small bowl. Gradually stir in the water, a spoonful at a time, to give a spreading consistency. Add a few drops of vanilla essence. Use at once as it sets quickly. Sufficient for an 18 cm (7 inch) cake.

* Lemon or Orange Glacé Icing

Follow the recipe for Glacé Icing (above), with these changes: use strained lemon or orange juice instead of water to mix.

* Coffee Glacé Icing

Follow the recipe for Glacé Icing (above), with this change: sift 2 teaspoons instant coffee powder with the icing sugar.

Sugar Roses

1½ teaspoons powdered gelatine
30 ml (2 fl oz) boiling water
about 500 g (1 lb 2 oz) icing sugar,
   sieved
few drops of food colouring (optional)

Sugar roses are an elaborate and delicate decoration to be added on top of an iced cake for a special occasion.

Dissolve the gelatine in the boiling water. Stir in enough icing sugar to make a firm putty-like paste and add food colouring if wished. If storing, keep in polythene.

Pinch out small pieces of paste to form petals, dipping your fingers in a little cornflour as you work. Wrap these petals around a pyramid of paste, using a little water to make them stick. Make a large rose with eight or ten large petals for the centre of the design, then make smaller roses with fewer petals, grading them down to rosebuds with only three or four petals. Cut off the bases of the pyramids at an angle and press on to the cake with small blobs of icing.

Chocolate Sour Cream Frosting

75 g (3 oz) plain chocolate, broken
   into pieces
2 tablespoons water
225 g (8 oz) icing sugar
approx. 75 ml (3 fl oz) soured cream

Put the chocolate in a bowl with the water over a saucepan of simmering water. The hot water must not touch the bottom of the bowl. When soft, stir until smooth and creamy. Sift the icing sugar into a bowl and gradually stir in 2 tablespoons soured cream. Mix in the melted chocolate and add a little more soured cream to give a thick coating consistency.

American Frosting

450 g (1 lb) granulated sugar
250 ml (8 fl oz) water
2 egg whites
¼ teaspoon vanilla essence
or
2 teaspoons coffee essence
or
2 teaspoons lemon juice

Dissolve the sugar in the water over gentle heat, stirring. Do not allow to boil until the syrup is clear. When dissolved, raise the heat and boil rapidly, without stirring, to 120°C/240°F, until it forms a 'thread' when trickled off a spoon. If not hot enough, the frosting will not set, if overboiled it will set hard too soon.

Meanwhile whisk the egg whites in a large bowl until stiff and dry. When the syrup is ready, remove from the heat and allow the bubbles to subside. Holding the saucepan well above the bowl, pour the syrup in a thin stream over the egg whites, beating continuously with a wooden spoon. Add the flavouring and continue beating until the frosting loses its shiny appearance and *begins* to look like cotton wool. Use immediately before it sets.

Vanilla Butter Cream

75 g (3 oz) butter
175 g (6 oz) icing sugar, sifted
¼ teaspoon vanilla essence or other
   flavouring
1-2 teaspoons warm water

Cream the butter until soft and gradually beat in the icing sugar. Add the flavouring essence and a little warm water if necessary to give a smooth pliable texture. This amount will cover the top and sides of an 18 cm (7 inch) sponge sandwich or be sufficient for a filling and topping.

* Orange and Lemon Butter Cream

Follow the recipe or Vanilla Butter Cream (above), with these changes: cream the butter and sugar with the finely grated rind of $\frac{1}{2}$ lemon or 1 small orange, use the strained juice instead of water. Add a little at a time or the butter cream will curdle.

* Coffee Butter Cream

Follow the recipe for Vanilla Butter Cream (above), with these changes: add 2 teaspoons instant coffee powder to the icing sugar. Cream with the butter, add a little water if necessary.

* Mocha Butter Cream

Follow the recipe for Vanilla Butter Cream (above), with these changes: add 1 teaspoon instant coffee powder and 1 tablespoon cocoa or chocolate powder to the icing sugar. Cream with the butter, add a little water.

Chocolate Butter Cream

Follow the recipe for Vanilla Butter Cream (above), with these changes: replace 25 g (1 oz) icing sugar with 25 g (1 oz) cocoa or chocolate powder. Flavour to taste with vanilla essence.

* Walnut Butter Cream

Follow the recipe for Vanilla Butter Cream (above), with these changes: add 2 tablespoons finely chopped walnuts to the finished vanilla, chocolate, coffee or mocha butter cream.

Almond Paste

350 g (12 oz) ground almonds
175 g (6 oz) caster sugar
175 g (6 oz) icing sugar, sieved
1 egg
3 egg yolks
1–2 tablespoons lemon juice
few drops of almond or vanilla essence (optional)
about 3 tablespoons sieved apricot jam, warmed

Put the almonds and sugars in a bowl and mix well. Beat the egg and egg yolks together with half the lemon juice, and the essence if using. Add to the almond mixture and mix carefully until the paste comes together, adding more lemon juice if necessary, but do not overwork. To add to cake work as follows: brush the top of the cake with apricot jam. Halve almond paste and roll out one piece on a board sprinkled with icing sugar, to a round slightly larger than the cake. Lift on to the rolling pin and lay over the cake. Trim.

Brush the sides of the cake with the remaining jam. Roll out the remaining paste into a rectangle, long enough to go half round cake and twice as deep; cut into two. Press one piece at a time on to the cake, cutting away any excess along the top. Smooth the joins with a palette knife, smooth the top of the cake with a rolling pin and roll a straight-sided jar round the sides. Leave to dry for at least one week before icing.

BREADS & TEABREADS

Apple and Walnut Loaf

175 g (6 oz) granary or wholemeal
   flour
175 g (6 oz) plain flour
½ teaspoon salt
2 teaspoons bicarbonate of soda
¼ teaspoon cream of tartar
75 g (3 oz) butter or margarine
50 g (2 oz) caster sugar
225 g (8 oz) cooking or dessert apples,
   peeled, cored and finely chopped
50 g (2 oz) walnuts, chopped
100 g (4 oz) honey
75 ml (2½ fl oz) buttermilk or soured
   milk
1 egg

This quantity makes 1 loaf.

Sift the flours, salt, soda and cream of tartar into a mixing bowl. Cut the fat into the flour and rub in to a breadcrumb consistency. Mix in the sugar with the apples and walnuts, reserving 2 tablespoons of nuts. Mix thoroughly. Dissolve the honey in the buttermilk or soured milk and beat in the egg.

Stir the liquid into the dry ingredients and mix well. Turn the mixture into a prepared 23 × 13 cm (9 × 5 inch) loaf tin. Scatter the remaining nuts over the top. Bake in the centre of a preheated moderate oven (180°C, 350°F, Gas Mark 4) for 1¼ hours or until a skewer inserted comes out clean. Leave to shrink slightly before lifting out on to a wire tray to cool.

Banana Nut Bread

225 g (8 oz) butter
225 g (8 oz) caster sugar
2 tablespoons thick honey
4 eggs, beaten
500 g (1 lb) self-raising flour
½ teaspoon salt
½ teaspoon bicarbonate of soda
4 medium ripe bananas, peeled and
   mashed
100 g (4 oz) walnuts, roughly chopped

Put the butter, sugar and honey in a bowl and beat together until light and fluffy. Beat in the eggs a little at a time, adding a little flour with each addition. Sift remaining flour, salt and soda together, then fold into the creamed mixture. Beat in the bananas and nuts.

Spoon the mixture into two greased 1 kg (2 lb) loaf tins lined with greased greaseproof paper. Bake just below the centre of a preheated moderate oven (180°C, 350°F, Gas Mark 4) for 1¼ hours or until well risen and a skewer inserted in the centre comes out clean.

Leave to cool in the tin, then remove the greaseproof paper. Wrap each cake in foil, overwrap in polythene bags and store in airtight containers. Serve cut into thick slices and spread with butter, if liked.

Makes 24 slices

Cheese and Bacon Loaf

100 g (4 oz) streaky bacon or pieces
100 g (4 oz) plain flour
100 g (4 oz) wholemeal flour
1 teaspoon bicarbonate of soda
½ teaspoon cream of tartar
½-1 teaspoon dry mustard
50 g (2 oz) butter or margarine
75-100 g (3-4 oz) grated mature
  cheese
1 egg, beaten
150 ml (¼ pint) milk
To finish:
milk
grated cheese

This quantity makes 1 loaf. Remove
rind and gristle from the bacon. Put the
bacon in a cold frying pan and cook
slowly until very crisp, then chop

Sift the flours, bicarbonate of soda,
cream of tartar and mustard into a
mixing bowl. Cut the fat into the flour
and rub into a breadcrumb consistency.
Mix in the grated cheese and chopped
bacon thoroughly. Stir in the egg and
milk and mix to a very soft dough.

Turn on to a floured board and knead
lightly and quickly into a smooth
dough. Shape into a large round bun
and place on a greased baking sheet.
Brush with milk and cover with grated
cheese. With a sharp knife slash the top
across into four and then into eight
equal triangles.

Bake in the centre of a moderately
hot oven (200°C, 400°F, Gas Mark 6) for
35 to 40 minutes until well risen and
golden brown. Test with a skewer which
will come out clean when cooked.

* Cheese and Bacon Buns

Follow the recipe for Cheese and Bacon
Loaf (above), with these changes: divide
and shape the dough into buns and bake
as for Herb Rolls (p. 330).
Makes 8 to 12 buns

Apricot and Walnut Loaf

225 g (8 oz) wholemeal flour
225 g (8 oz) strong white flour
25 g (1 oz) sugar
100 g (4 oz) dried apricots, snipped
50 g (2 oz) walnuts, chopped
15 g (½ oz) fresh yeast
or
1½ teaspoons dried yeast with 1
  teaspoon sugar
300 ml (½ pint) warm milk and water
50 g (2 oz) butter, cut up
1 egg, beaten
warm honey or Sugar Syrup (2
  tablespoons sugar dissolved in 2
  tablespoons hot water or milk), to
  glaze

This quantity makes 2 small loaves.

Sift the wholemeal and strong white
flours into a warm mixing bowl. Mix in
the sugar, dried apricots and chopped
walnuts.

Dissolve the yeast in half the warm
milk and water, adding the sugar if
using dried yeast. Leave for 10 minutes
or until frothy.

Dissolve the butter in the remaining
warm milk and water. Stir in the beaten
egg. Add all the liquids to the dry
ingredients and mix to a smooth dough.
Knead well, cover and put into a bowl in
a warm place to prove until doubled in
bulk.

Turn on to a floured board, knock
back the dough and divide in half. Put
into 2 small warmed and greased loaf
tins. Cover and prove in a warm place
until the dough fills the tins.

Bake in a preheated hot oven (230°C,
450°F, Gas Mark 8) for 20 minutes.
Reduce the heat to 200°C, 400°F, Gas
Mark 6 and cook for a further 15 to 20
minutes. Brush with warm honey or
sugar glaze and return to the oven for 4
to 5 minutes for the glaze to set. Allow
to shrink slightly for a few minutes
before unmoulding and leaving to cool
on a wire tray. Store in an airtight
container.

Currant Loaf

15 g (¼ oz) fresh yeast
or
1½ teaspoons dried yeast
1 teaspoon sugar
approx. 450 ml (¾ pint) warm milk
750 g (1½ lb) strong white flour
1 teaspoon salt
50 g (2 oz) butter or margarine, cut up
225 g (8 oz) currants
Sugar Syrup (2 tablespoons sugar
    dissolved in 2 tablespoons hot water
    or milk), to glaze

This quantity makes 2 small loaves, or 1 loaf and eight buns. Add the yeast with the sugar to 150 ml (¼ pint) of the warm milk and leave to froth. Sift the flour and salt into a warm bowl and rub in the fat to a breadcrumb consistency. Mix in the currants, make a well in the centre and add the yeast liquid. Stir into a fairly soft dough with as much remaining milk as necessary. Turn out on to a floured board and knead until smooth and elastic.

Cover and leave to rise in a warm place until doubled in bulk. Knock back and shape into 2 small loaves or into 1 medium loaf and use the other half for Currant Buns (below). Prove for about 20 minutes or until the dough rises to the top of the tin.

Bake in the centre of a preheated hot oven (230°C, 450°F, Gas Mark 8) for 15 to 20 minutes. Reduce the heat to 190°C, 375°F, Gas Mark 5, and continue cooking for 30 minutes or until the loaves sound hollow when tapped on the bottom. Brush the top with sweetened milk or sugar syrup and return to the oven for two minutes for the glaze to set. Turn out on a wire tray and leave to cool. Serve freshly baked or toasted and buttered.

* Currant Buns

Follow the recipe for Currant Loaf (above), with these changes: pinch off pieces of the Currant Loaf dough after it has risen and been knocked back. They should weigh about 50 g (2 oz) each. Shape, prove, bake and glaze as for Penny Buns (below). Serve freshly baked or split, toasted and buttered.

Ginger and Peanut Loaf

350 g (12 oz) self-raising flour
pinch of salt
1 teaspoon ground ginger
50 g (2 oz) soft brown sugar
75 g (3 oz) sultanas
50 g (2 oz) preserved stem ginger,
    chopped
75 g (3 oz) unsalted peanuts
75 g (3 oz) butter
4 tablespoons black treacle
2 eggs
150 ml (¼ pint) milk

Grease a 1 kg (2 lb) loaf tin and line the base with a piece of greased greaseproof paper. Sift the flour, salt and ground ginger together into a bowl. Add the sugar, sultanas, stem ginger and peanuts.

Put the butter and treacle into a saucepan and heat gently until melted. Add the treacle mixture to the dry ingredients, and gradually beat in the eggs and the milk until well blended. Pour the mixture into the prepared loaf tin and bake in a warm oven (160°C, 325°F, Gas Mark 3) for 1¼ hours.

Allow the loaf to cool slightly and then turn out on a wire rack and strip off the lining paper.

Grant Stone Ground Loaf

750 g (1½ lb) stone ground flour
15 g (½ oz) sea salt
25 g (1 oz) margarine or butter
15 g (½ oz) Barbados sugar
approx. 450 ml (¾ pint) warm water
15 g (½ oz) fresh yeast

This quantity makes 1 large and 1 small loaf, or 3 small loaves. Sift the flour and salt into a mixing bowl and warm for 5 minutes. Rub in the fat. Crumble the yeast into 150 ml (¼ pint) of the warm water and add the sugar. Stir until dissolved and leave for 10 minutes to froth up. Pour the yeast liquid into the flour and stir in the rest of the water. Mix well and if necessary add more warm water.

Pour or spoon the dough into the warmed and greased tins – 3 small tins or 1 large and 1 small. They should be only half-filled. Put the tins in a polythene bag, and leave in a warm place to rise until doubled in bulk. This should take about 30 minutes. If under-proved, the loaf will have too close a texture; if over-proved, the bread will be spongy. Remove the polythene and bake in a preheated moderately hot oven (200°C, 400°F, Gas Mark 6) for 45 minutes to 1 hour according to size. Test by tapping the top crust with the knuckles to see if it sounds hollow. Allow to cool and shrink slightly before turning out to cool on a wire tray.

Spiced Fruit Loaf

225 g (8 oz) wholemeal flour
225 g (8 oz) strong white flour
2 teaspoons salt
1 teaspoon mixed spice
50 g (2 oz) caster sugar
10 g (¼ oz) lard
100 g (4 oz) dried apricots
50 g (2 oz) chopped walnuts (optional)
100 g (4 oz) sultanas
50 g (2 oz) seedless raisins
15 g (½ oz) fresh yeast
or
2 teaspoons dried yeast
300 ml (½ pint) warm water
For the toping:
25 g (1 oz) butter or margarine
25 g (1 oz) caster sugar
40 g (1½ oz) plain flour

Sift flour, salt, mixed spice and sugar into a large bowl. Tip any bran left in the sieve into the bowl. Rub in the fat. Snip up the apricots with scissors and mix into the flour with the walnuts, sultanas and raisins. Dissolve the yeast in the warm water and make up the dough as for Quick Brown Bread (see p. 329), and knead well. Line the base of 2 greased 450 g (1 lb) loaf tins with a strip of non-stick parchment or buttered greaseproof paper. Divide dough in half, shape each piece into a roll and place in the tins. Put into polythene bags, leave in a warm place for about 1 hour or until doubled in bulk. Make the topping by rubbing together the butter, sugar and flour to a rough breadcrumb consistency. Cover the dough evenly. Bake in the centre of an oven (200°C, 400°F, Gas Mark 6) for 40–45 minutes. Allow to shrink for 10 minutes then turn out onto a wire tray to cool.

Malt Loaf

25 g (1 oz) fresh yeast
or
15 g (½ oz) dried yeast with 1 teaspoon sugar
150 ml (¼ pint) warm water
450 g (1 lb) soft white flour
1 teaspoon salt
50–75 g (2–3 oz) sultanas (optional)
100 g (4 oz) malt extract
1 tablespoon black treacle
25 g (1 oz) butter or margarine
Sugar Syrup (2 tablespoons sugar dissolved in 2 tablespoons hot water or milk), to glaze

Dissolve the yeast in the warm water, adding the sugar if using dried yeast. Leave for 10 minutes or until frothy. Sift the flour and salt into a warm bowl and mix in the sultanas, if using. Heat the malt, treacle and fat gently in a small pan until liquid, then cool slightly. Stir the yeast liquid and malt mixture into the dry ingredients and mix to a soft, sticky dough, adding more warm water if necessary. Turn the dough on to a floured board and knead until firm and elastic.

Divide the dough in half, shape and put into 2 greased 450 g (1 lb) loaf tins. Cover and leave to prove until the dough rises to the top of the tins. Malt dough rises slowly so this may take up to 2 hours. Bake in the centre of a preheated moderately hot oven (200°C, 400°F, Gas Mark 6) for 30 to 40 minutes. When cooked, remove the loaves, brush the tops with sugar syrup and return to the oven for two minutes. Turn out on a wire tray and allow to cool.

Bran Loaf

100 g (4 oz) wholemeal or plain flour
1 teaspoon cream of tartar
$\frac{1}{2}$ teaspoon baking powder
1 tablespoon caster sugar
$\frac{1}{2}$ teaspoon salt
100 g (4 oz) bran
50 g (2 oz) butter or margarine
150 ml ($\frac{1}{4}$ pint) buttermilk or 150 ml ($\frac{1}{4}$ pint) milk soured with 2 teaspoons lemon juice

This quantity makes 1 large or 2 small loaves. Sift the flour, cream of tartar, baking powder, sugar and salt into a mixing bowl. Mix in the bran. Cut the fat into the flour and rub in to a breadcrumb consistency. Stir in the buttermilk and mix thoroughly. Turn into a prepared 23 × 13 cm (9 × 5 inch) loaf tin and smooth the top.

Alternatively, divide between 2 small tins. Bake in the centre of a preheated

moderately hot oven (190°C, 375°F, Gas Mark 5) for about 1 hour (less for small loaves) or until a skewer inserted comes out clean. Allow to shrink slightly, remove from the tin and allow to cool on a wire tray.

Rich Bran Fruit Loaf

225 g (8 oz) soft brown sugar
100 g (4 oz) All Bran
225 g (8 oz) mixed dried fruit (currants, raisins, sultanas)
1 tablespoon shredded dried orange peel
1 tablespoon golden syrup
250 ml (8 fl oz) milk
1 egg, beaten
1 large banana, peeled and mashed
100 g (4 oz) self-raising flour

Place the sugar, All Bran, dried fruit, orange peel, syrup and milk in a bowl and stir well. Allow to soak overnight.

The next day, add the beaten egg, mashed banana and flour and mix thoroughly.

Turn the mixture into a greased 1 kg (2 lb) loaf tin and bake in a moderate oven (180°C, 350°F, Gas Mark 4) for about 1 hour, until the cake is cooked, or until a skewer inserted in the centre comes out clean.

Turn out on a wire rack to cool slightly.

Chelsea Buns

225 g (8 oz) strong white flour
15 g (½ oz) fresh yeast
or
1½ teaspoons dried yeast with 1
    teaspoon sugar
½ teaspoon salt
100 ml (4 fl oz) warm milk
25 g (1 oz) butter or lard
1 egg, beaten
40 g (1½ oz) butter, melted
75 g (3 oz) mixed dried fruit (sultanas,
    currants, raisins)
2 tablespoons chopped mixed peel
50 g (2 oz) soft brown sugar
¼ teaspoon ground cinnamon or
    nutmeg
caster sugar for sprinkling
2 tablespoons clear honey, warmed or
    Sweet Milk Glaze (2 tablespoons
    sugar dissolved in 2 tablespoons hot
    milk), to glaze

This quantity makes 9 buns. Grease and
warm an 18 cm (7 inch) square cake tin.
Put 50 g (2 oz) of the flour into a warm
mixing bowl, add the yeast (with the
sugar if using dried yeast) and blend in
the milk smoothly. Leave in a warm
place for 10 to 20 minutes or until
frothy. Sift the rest of the flour with the
salt into another bowl and rub in the
hard fat. Mix into the yeast batter with
the beaten egg. Beat until the dough
leaves the sides of the bowl. Turn on to a
floured board and knead into a smooth
dough. Cover and leave to rise until
doubled in bulk.

Knock back the dough and roll out
into a 30 × 23 cm (12 × 9 inch) rectangle.
Brush with melted butter and cover with
dried fruit, chopped peel and brown
sugar, mixed with the spice. Trickle
over the remaining butter. Roll up the
dough like a Swiss roll and cut into nine
2.5 cm (1 inch) slices. Place, cut side
down, in the greased tin. Prove for
about 30 minutes until the dough is
puffy and the buns are just touching.
Sprinkle with caster sugar and bake

in a preheated hot oven (220°C, 425°F,
Gas Mark 7) for 15 to 20 minutes.
Remove from the oven and brush with
warm honey or Sweet Milk Glaze while
still hot. Allow to cool slightly before
separating the buns.

Penny Buns

500 g (1¼ lb) strong white flour
15 g (½ oz) fresh yeast
1 teaspoon sugar
approx. 600 ml (1 pint) warm milk
50 g (2 oz) butter, cut up
1 egg, beaten
75 g (3 oz) currants
50 g (2 oz) sugar
Sugar Syrup (2 tablespoons sugar
    dissolved in 2 tablespoons hot water
    or milk), to glaze

This quantity makes about 16 buns. Sift
half the flour into a warm bowl. Blend
the yeast with the sugar, and add 150 ml
(¼ pint) of the warm milk. Mix into a firm
dough, adding a little more milk if
necessary. Beat well with your hand or
a wooden spoon. Cover and leave to rise
for 30 to 40 minutes. Dissolve the butter
in the remaining milk. Pour this into
the beaten egg and stir well.

Mix the liquid into the risen dough
with the remaining flour, the currants
and the sugar. Beat well and leave to
rise in a warm place until doubled in
bulk. Knock back the dough and scoop
off pieces of dough weighing about 50 g
(2 oz) each.

Shape each piece into a smooth ball,
place on a greased baking sheet and
flatten slightly; alternatively, half-fill
well greased bun tins. Cover and prove
until springy to the touch. Bake in a
preheated hot oven (220°C, 425°F, Gas
Mark 7) for about 15 minutes or until
cooked. Remove and brush with
sweetened milk or sugar syrup, then
replace in the oven for a few moments
for the glaze to dry. Lift onto a wire tray
and allow to cool.

Sugared Bun Cluster

450 g (1 lb) risen bread dough (p. 332)
demerara sugar
milk
4 tablespoons honey, melted
25 g (1 oz) chopped or flaked nuts

This quantity makes 8 bun clusters. Divide the bread dough into 8 even-sized portions. Work a little demerara sugar into each portion of dough, kneading it gently on a very lightly floured surface, to form a smooth ball. Arrange the shaped pieces of dough in a greased 20 cm (8 inch) sandwich tin, so that they just touch.

Cover the tin with a large polythene bag and leave in a warm place for about 20 minutes until risen.

Brush the top of the bun cluster with milk. Spoon over the melted honey and sprinkle the surface with extra demerara sugar and the nuts. Bake in a very hot oven (230°C, 450°F, Gas Mark 8) for 15 minutes, then reduce the heat to fairly hot (200°C, 400°F, Gas Mark 6) for a further 10 minutes. Carefully turn out the bun cluster on a wire rack and allow to cool.

Honey Twist

15 g (½ oz) fresh yeast
or
10 g (¼ oz) dried yeast with 1 teaspoon sugar
50 ml (2 fl oz) warm water
150 ml (¼ pint) warm milk
50 g (2 oz) butter or margarine
40 g (1½ oz) sugar
1 egg yolk, beaten
350 g (12 oz) strong white flour
1 teaspoon salt
50 g (2 oz) chopped mixed peel
50 g (2 oz) sultanas
For the topping:
50 g (2 oz) butter or margarine
25 g (1 oz) sugar
3 tablespoons honey
1 egg white

Dissolve the yeast in the warm water, adding the sugar if using dried yeast. Leave for 10 minutes or until frothy. Put the butter or margarine and sugar in a bowl. Pour in the milk and stir until dissolved. Cool slightly and add the yeast liquid. Stir in the beaten egg yolk. Sift and stir in the flour and salt. Add the peel and sultanas. Beat until smooth. Turn on to a floured board and knead lightly, adding more flour if necessary. Put into a warm bowl, cover and prove until doubled in bulk.

Meanwhile cream the fat and sugar together for the topping. Mix in the honey and finally the unbeaten egg white. Turn the risen dough on to a floured board and knead for 4 to 5 minutes. Roll out onto a long sausage shape not more than 4 cm (1½ inches) thick. Take care not to twist or break it. Coil this loosely into a warmed and greased 25 cm (10 inch) sandwich tin, working from the outside into the centre. Cover and prove in a warm place until springy to the touch. Pour over the topping and spread it evenly.

Bake in a preheated moderately hot oven (200°C, 400°F, Gas Mark 6) for 15 minutes. Reduce the heat to 180°C, 350°F, Gas Mark 4 for a further 30 minutes or until cooked. Test with a skewer which will come out clean when the bread is ready. Cool on a wire tray.

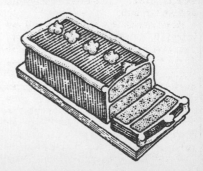

Welsh Cakes

225 g (8 oz) self-raising flour
pinch of salt
100 g (4 oz) butter
50 g (2 oz) sugar
50 g (2 oz) currants
25 g (1 oz) chopped nuts
1 egg
2 tablespoons milk
vegetable oil or fat for greasing the
    griddle

This quantity makes 8 to 10 cakes. Sift
the flour and salt together into a bowl.
Rub in the butter until the mixture
resembles fine breadcrumbs. Add the
sugar, currants and chopped nuts and
mix to a fairly stiff dough with the egg
and the milk. Knead the dough lightly
on a floured surface and roll out until
about 5 mm (¼ inch thick). Cut into 5 cm
(2 inch) rounds with a biscuit cutter.

Grease and warm a griddle or heavy-
based frying pan. The griddle is hot
enough when a piece of the mixture
placed on it turns golden-brown underneath in 30 seconds.

Cook the Welsh cakes for 2 to 3
minutes on each side. Serve warm with
plenty of butter.

Lardy Cake

350 g (12 oz) strong white flour
1 teaspoon salt
10 g (¼ oz) lard
10 g (¼ oz) fresh yeast
250 ml (8 fl oz) water
For the filling:
100 g (4 oz) lard
75 g (3 oz) sultanas
25 g (1 oz) chopped mixed peel
100 g (4 oz) sugar
To glaze:
milk
caster sugar

Make the dough according to the recipe
for basic White Bread dough (p. 332).
Knead well, cover and leave in a warm
place to rise until doubled in bulk. Turn
on to a well floured board and knock
back the dough. Roll it out thinly to
about 1.5 cm (½ inch) then cut an 18 × 46
cm (7 × 18 inch) rectangle. Mark across
into 3 equal sections. Dot the top two
thirds with half the lard and sprinkle
with half the sultanas, mixed peel and
sugar.

Fold up the bottom third of the dough,
then fold over the top third. Seal the
edges with the rolling pin, give a quarter turn and roll out again into a rec-

tangle as for Flaky Pastry (p. 362). Repeat with the rest of the lard, fruit and sugar; fold and turn. Roll and fold once again.

Line a roasting tin, approximately 25 × 20 cm (18 × 8 inches) with foil and grease it. Put in the dough and leave in a warm place for 30 minutes or until risen and doubled in bulk. Brush with milk and sprinkle with sugar. Mark into squares with the back of a knife and bake in a preheated moderately hot oven (200°C, 400°F, Gas Mark 6) for 35 to 40 minutes.

Leave in the tin for the cake to soak up any fat which has leaked out. For a crisper under crust, cool on a wire tray.

Quick Brown Bread

225 g (8 oz) wholemeal flour and 225 g (8 oz) strong white flour
or
450 g (1 lb) wholemeal flour
2 teaspoons salt
2 teaspoons caster sugar
10 g ($\frac{1}{4}$ oz) lard
10 g ($\frac{1}{2}$ oz) fresh yeast
or
2 teaspoons dried yeast
300 ml ($\frac{1}{2}$ pint) warm water
2 tablespoons cracked wheat or sesame seeds

This quantity makes two 450 g (1 lb) loaves. Sift the flour, salt and sugar into a bowl. Tip any bran left in the sieve into the bowl. Cut up the lard and rub it in with the fingertips. If using fresh yeast, dissolve it in the warm water. If using dried, dissolve 1 teaspoon sugar in 150 ml ($\frac{1}{4}$ pint) water, sprinkle the yeast on top, leave until frothing and add to the flour with the remaining water by making a well in the flour and pouring in the yeast liquid. Mix to a soft dough and beat with a wooden spoon until it leaves the sides of the bowl clean. Add a little extra water if dough is too stiff.

Turn onto a floured board and knead well. Divide the dough in half and shape each piece into a roll to half-fill two greased 450 g (1 lb) loaf tins. Brush the top of the dough with slightly salted water and sprinkle with cracked wheat or sesame seeds. Place the tins in lightly oiled plastic bags, close loosely and leave in a warm place until the dough is doubled in bulk, about 1 hour. Remove the dough from the bags and place on a baking sheet. Bake in the centre of a preheated oven (230°C, 450°F, Gas Mark 8) for 40 to 45 minutes until well risen and the loaf sounds hollow when the bottom is tapped. Turn out and cool on a wire tray.

* Round Cob Loaves

Follow the recipe for Quick Brown Bread (above), with these changes: divide the dough in half, shape each piece into a round and place on a greased baking sheet. Finish tops as for tin loaves, prove until doubled in bulk and bake as for Quick brown bread.

* Soft Brown Rolls

Follow the recipe for Quick Brown Bread (above), with these changes: divide the dough and shape as for Dinner rolls (p. 332). Place the rolls 2 cm ($\frac{3}{4}$ inch) apart on a baking tray and dust generously with flour. Cover with polythene and leave to prove until doubled in bulk. Bake just above the centre of a preheated oven (230°C, 450°F, Gas Mark 8) for 20 to 30 minutes. The rolls will spread against each other but are easily separated and will have a soft surface instead of a crust.

Granary Bread

750 g (1½ lb) granary meal
2 teaspoons salt
15 g (½ oz) fresh yeast
or
2 teaspoons dried yeast with 1
   teaspoon sugar
approx. 500 ml (18 fl oz) warm water
1 tablespoon vegetable oil or melted
   lard

This quantity makes 2 loaves and rolls,
or 3 loaves.

Put the granary meal and salt into a
warm bowl – it is too coarse to put
through a flour sieve, so just aerate it
with the fingers. Blend the yeast with
300 ml (½ pint) warm water, adding the
sugar if using dried yeast. Leave to
froth. Add the oil or fat to the remaining
water, and mix with the yeast liquid.
Stir into the flour and mix into a soft
dough, adding a little more warm water
if necessary. Do not skimp the liquid
when using coarse meals or the bread
will be hard. Beat well with a wooden
spoon, turn on to a floured board and
knead for about 10 minutes until firm
and elastic. Round up the dough into a
ball and put in an oiled bag or a container and leave to prove until doubled
in bulk. Knock back the dough. Divide
dough into two pieces weighing 400 g
(14 oz) each. Shape each piece into a
round and place on a floured baking
sheet. Bake in a preheated hot oven
(230°C, 450°F, Gas Mark 8) for 30 minutes or until cooked. You will have
sufficient dough over to make Brown
Rolls (p. 329).

Herb Soda Bread

225 g (8 oz) wholemeal flour
225 g (8 oz) plain flour
2 teaspoons salt
1 teaspoon bicarbonate of soda
50 g (2 oz) butter or margarine
100 g (4 oz) grated onion
100 g (4 oz) grated celery
2 tablespoons chopped fresh parsley
1 tablespoon chopped fresh mint or
   chervil
275 ml (9 fl oz) milk
3 teaspoons lemon juice
milk and sesame or poppy seeds, to
   finish

This quantity makes 1 loaf.

Sift the flours, salt and bicarbonate of
soda into a mixing bowl. Cut the fat into
the flour and rub in to a breadcrumb
consistency. Add the grated onion,
celery and herbs, rubbing in with the
finger tips until thoroughly mixed. Stir
the lemon juice into the milk and mix
into a soft dough with the dry ingredients. Turn on to a well floured
board and knead lightly into a smooth
round ball. Place on a floured baking
sheet and flatten into a circle of about
20 cm (8 inches). Brush with milk and
cover with the seeds. With a sharp knife
slash the top into 4 equal portions. Bake
near the top of a preheated moderately
hot oven (200°C, 400°F, Gas Mark 6) for
35 to 40 minutes until well risen and
golden brown. Test with a skewer which
will come out clean when cooked. Cool
on a wire tray.

* Herb Rolls

Follow the recipe for Herb Soda Bread
(above), with these changes: mix and
knead the dough as above. Pinch off
pieces weighing 75 g (3 oz) each and roll
into balls. Place on a warmed, floured
baking sheet leaving room between for
expansion. Flatten the tops, brush with
milk and cover with poppy or sesame
seeds. Bake near the top of a preheated
moderately hot oven (200°C, 400°F, Gas
Mark 6) for 20 minutes, or until well
risen and golden brown. Cool on a wire
tray. Serve fresh with ham or cheese, or
toasted with crispy bacon.
Makes 8 rolls.

Irish Buttermilk Soda Bread

450 g (1 lb) plain or wheatmeal flour
1–2 teaspoons salt
1 teaspoon bicarbonate of soda
300 ml (½ pint) buttermilk
3–4 tablespoons water

This quantity makes 1 loaf.

Sift the flour, salt and bicarbonate of soda into a mixing bowl. Stir in the buttermilk and add a little water if necessary to make a soft dough. Turn out on to a floured board, knead lightly and quickly and shape into a smooth round bun.

Cut a deep cross right across the top of the loaf so that when baked it can be divided into 4 'farls', as they are called. Place on a warmed and floured baking sheet. Bake just above the centre of a preheated moderately hot oven (200°C, 400°F, Gas Mark 6) for 30 to 35 minutes or until well risen and nicely browned. For a soft crust, remove from baking sheet and wrap in a teacloth, for a crisp crust, cool on a wire tray.

Oatmeal Bread

225 g (8 oz) medium oatmeal
450 ml (¾ pint) milk
15 g (½ oz) fresh yeast
or
1½ teaspoons dried yeast with 1
    teaspoon sugar
4 tablespoons warm water
2–3 teaspoons salt
50 g (2 oz) butter or lard, melted
225 g (8 oz) strong white or
    unbleached flour
To finish:
milk
coarse oatmeal

This quantity makes 1 small loaf and 8 rolls or 2 small loaves.

Put the oatmeal in a mixing bowl and add the milk. Leave to soak overnight for the oatmeal to absorb the milk. Dissolve the yeast in the warm water, adding the sugar if using dried yeast, and leave to froth. Mix the yeast liquid into the oatmeal which will be of porridge consistency, with the salt and melted fat.

Sift and beat in sufficient white flour to make a smooth, very soft dough. Knead thoroughly on a thickly floured board, adding more flour if necessary. (Dough hooks on a mixer at lowest speed will cut the kneading time to about 5 minutes.) Replace in a warm bowl, cover with a damp cloth and leave in a warm place to prove for 1½ to 2 hours or until the dough has doubled in bulk. Knock back the dough on a board sprinkled with medium oatmeal. Divide in two and put one half into a small warmed and greased tin. It should half-fill the tin. Cover and prove for about 45 minutes or until the dough rises to the top of the tin.

Brush with milk and sprinkle with coarse oatmeal. Bake in a preheated hot oven (220°C, 425°F, Gas Mark 7) for 20 to 30 minutes. Lower the heat to 160°C, 325°F, Gas Mark 3 and bake for a further 15 to 20 minutes. Remove from tin and tap the bottom to see if it sounds hollow. Cool on a wire tray. Serve sliced and buttered with cream cheese or preserves.

* Soft Oatmeal Rolls

Follow the recipe for Oatmeal Bread (above), with these changes; round up the remaining dough after knocking back, and divide into 8 equal portions. Roll into smooth balls and put into warmed and greased bun or muffin tins. They should be only half-filled. Cover and prove until doubled in bulk. Brush with milk and sprinkle with coarse oatmeal. Bake in a preheated hot oven (220°C, 425F, Gas Mark 7) for 20 to 30 minutes with the Oatmeal Bread. Cool on a wire tray.

White Bread

750 g (1½ lb) strong white flour
2 teaspoons salt
15 g (½ oz) lard
15 g (½ oz) fresh yeast
or
1½ teaspoons dried yeast, with 1
    teaspoon caster sugar
450 ml (¾ pint) tepid water

This quantity makes two 450 kg (1 lb)
loaves.

Sift the flour and salt into a warmed
bowl and rub in the lard. Blend the fresh
yeast with the water. If using dried
yeast, dissolve the sugar in the water,
sprinkle in the yeast and leave until
frothing. Make a well in the flour and
pour in the yeast liquid all at once. Stir
and beat with a wooden spoon until the
dough leaves the sides of the bowl.

Gather the dough into a ball, turn it
onto a floured board and then flatten
slightly. Hold the front of the dough
with one hand, and with the other pull
up the further edge, stretch it and fold it
over towards you.

Press the folded dough down firmly
and, with a punching movement, push it
away from you, using the heel of your
hand. Give the dough a quarter turn
and repeat the stretching, folding and
punching – developing a rocking movement – for at least 10 minutes, until the
dough is firm and elastic and does not
stick to the fingers.

Shape the dough into a round and put
it into a lightly oiled polythene bag and
set it aside to rise until it has doubled in
bulk – 45 to 60 minutes in a warm place
for a quick rise, 1½ to 2 hours at room
temperature, 8 to 12 hours in a cold
larder, 12 to 14 hours in a refrigerator.
Refrigerated dough must be left for
about 1 hour at room temperature
before being shaped.

Grease two 450 g (1 lb) loaf tins or one
1 kg (2 lb) tin. For 2 small loaves divide
the risen dough in half. Flatten each
piece firmly with the knuckles to knock

out any air bubbles, then knead again
for 2 to 3 minutes. Stretch each piece of
dough into a rectangle with a width
equal to the length of the tin. Fold the
dough in three or roll it up like a Swiss
roll and place it in the tins, with the join
underneath and pat into shape to fit
neatly into the corners.

Brush the top of the dough with
lightly salted water. Place the tins in
the oiled polythene bags and leave in a
warm place to 'prove', until the dough
rises to the top of the tins and is springy
to the touch. Remove the tins from the
bags, set them on a baking sheet and
brush the dough again with the salted
water. Bake in the centre of a preheated
oven (230°C, 450°F, Gas Mark 8), for 30
to 40 minutes, until well risen and
golden brown.

When cooked, the loaf shrinks
slightly from the sides of the tin and
sounds hollow when tapped on the
bottom. Turn out and allow to cool on a
wire tray.

For an extra crusty finish, return the
unmoulded loaves to the oven for a
further 5 to 10 minutes.

* Dinner Rolls

Follow the recipe for White Bread
(above), with these changes: after the
risen dough has been divided in half and
'knocked back', shape each half into a
round and divide into 6 or 8 equal
portions. Roll each portion into a ball
on the floured palm of your hands, then
press it down on the board and flatten it
slightly. Arrange the rounds on a baking tray, allowing room to swell, cover
with polythene and leave to prove until
doubled in size. Bake in a preheated
oven (230°C, 450°F, Gas Mark 8) for 15
to 20 minutes, until crisp and golden.

Rye Bread

25 g (1 oz) dried yeast
2 tablespoons black treacle
900 ml (1½ pints) water
1 tablespoon salt
1 kg (2 lb) wholewheat flour
450 g (1 lb) rye flour
25 g (1 oz) butter
1 egg, beaten with a pinch of salt
cracked wheat or bran

Make the rye bread dough as for the basic White Bread dough (p. 332), using the mixed wholewheat and rye flours, and the black treacle in place of the sugar. Allow the dough to rise for 45 minutes and then knead lightly.

Divide the risen dough into 2 equal portions. Shape each one into a long, oval loaf. Put the shaped loaves on greased baking sheets, brush the surface with the beaten egg mixture and sprinkle with cracked wheat or bran.

Make several diagonal cuts in the surface of the loaves with a sharp knife. These cuts allow the loaves to rise or 'bloom' well, hence the name 'bloomer'. Bake in a very hot oven (230°C, 450°F, Gas Mark 8) for 20 minutes, then reduce the heat to fairly hot (200°C, 400°F, Gas Mark 6) for a further 20 minutes.

Cottage Loaf

1½ kg (3 lb) risen bread dough (p. 332)
flour for dredging

Cut off about one quarter of the dough for the 'knob' of the cottage loaf. Knead the larger piece of dough into a smooth, even round and put it on a greased baking sheet. Form the smaller piece of dough into a smooth even ball. Brush the top of the larger piece of dough with water and put the 'knob' centrally on top. Fix the top position by pressing the floured handle of a wooden spoon right through centre of base of bottom piece of dough, pulling the spoon handle out carefully.

Cover the shaped loaf with a large polythene bag and leave in a warm place for about 30 minutes until it has risen. The dough should seem light and spongy.

Dredge the top very lightly with flour. Bake in a very hot oven (230°C, 450°F, Gas Mark 8) for 15 minutes, then reduce the heat to moderate (180°C, 350°F, Gas Mark 4) for a further 20 minutes. Cool on a wire rack.

* Individual Cottage Loaves

Follow the recipe for Cottage Loaf (above), with these changes: use 75 g (3 oz) risen dough for each loaf, breaking off a portion for the knob. Mould as above, but only bake for the first 15 minutes.

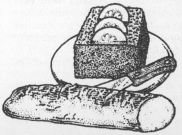

Baps

ingredients as for basic White Bread
  dough
1 teaspoon dried yeast

This quantity makes approx. 30 baps.

Make up the basic bread dough as on
page 332, using the extra dried yeast,
and leave to rise.

Divide the risen dough into 75 g (3 oz)
portions. Form each piece into a smooth
ball and roll it into a flat round on a
lightly floured surface. Arrange the
shaped baps on floured baking sheets,
leaving space between each one to
allow for spreading.

Cover with a large polythene bag and
leave in a warm place for about 20
minutes until risen. The baps should be
light and fluffy. Press the floured handle
of a wooden spoon into the centre of
each bap, and then dredge the tops
lightly with flour. Bake in a hot oven
(220°C, 425°F, Gas Mark 7) for 10 minutes. Cool the cooked baps between
folded clean tea towels so that they
keep a soft, spongy texture.

Wholewheat Popover Rolls

450 g (1 lb) risen wholewheat bread
  dough (p 329)
1 egg, beaten with a pinch of salt
cracked wheat or bran

This quantity makes 12 rolls.

Brush the insides of 12 small dariole
moulds or castle pudding tins with
melted butter. Divide the risen wholewheat bread dough into 12 even-sized
portions and drop into the prepared
moulds or tins.

Cover with a large polythene bag and
leave in a warm place for about 20
minutes until risen. Brush the tops of
the popovers with the beaten egg mixture and sprinkle with a little cracked
wheat or bran. Bake in a hot oven

(220°C, 425°F, Gas Mark 7) for 15 to 20
minutes until well risen and golden-
brown. Turn the popover rolls out of
their tins and tap the bottoms to see
that they are cooked. Place on a wire
rack and allow to cool.

Parker House Rolls

350 g (12 oz) strong white flour
1 teaspoon salt
15 g ($\frac{1}{2}$ oz) fresh yeast
or
2 teaspoons dried yeast
2 teaspoons sugar
120 ml (4 fl oz) warm water
250 ml (8 fl oz) milk
25 g (1 oz) butter, cut up
melted butter for coating
Egg and Water Wash (1 egg beaten
  with 1–2 tablespoons water), to
  glaze

This quantity makes 8 rolls.

Sift the flour and salt into a bowl and
leave in a warm place. Blend the yeast
and sugar into the warm water then
leave to froth. Heat the milk gently.
Add the butter to the milk and when
dissolved pour into the yeast mixture.
Stir this liquid into half the flour and
beat vigorously with a wooden spoon
into a smooth batter. Cover with a damp
cloth and leave in a warm place for 1
hour or until doubled in bulk. Break it
down with a wooden spoon, then gradually add the rest of the flour and beat
into a soft dough.

Turn out on to a floured board and
knead until smooth and elastic. Shape
the dough into a ball and put it into a
warm bowl. Brush with melted butter
and leave to rise again until doubled in
bulk. Knock back the dough on a light
floured board and roll out to about 1 cm
($\frac{1}{2}$ inch) thick. Cut into 8 rounds with 6
cm ($2\frac{1}{2}$ inch) floured cutter or a tumbler.
Brush the rounds with melted butter.
Press a knife handle or pencil firmly
across the centre of each round to make
a deep crease, fold the dough over at the

crease, and press firmly down to seal.

Place the folded rolls on a greased baking sheet leaving room for expansion. Cover and leave to prove. When springy, brush with Egg and Water Wash and bake in a preheated hot oven (220°C, 425°F, Gas Mark 7) for 20 minutes or until puffed and golden. Serve hot straight from the oven, or reheat.

Croissants

225 g (8 oz) strong white flour
1 teaspoon salt
15 g ($\frac{1}{2}$ oz) lard
15 g ($\frac{1}{2}$ oz) fresh yeast
or
1$\frac{1}{2}$ teaspoons dried yeast
100 ml (4 fl oz) warm water
1 teaspoon sugar
1 egg, beaten
75 g (3 oz) butter
1 egg, beaten with 1 teaspoon caster sugar, to glaze

This quantity makes 6 croissants.

Sift the flour and salt into a warm mixing bowl. Rub in the lard. Dissolve the yeast in the warm water with the sugar. Leave to froth, then mix in the beaten egg. Make a well in the centre of the flour, add the yeast mixture and gradually work into a dough. Beat vigorously until it leaves the sides of the bowl clean. Turn on to a floured board and knead for 10 minutes until smooth. Cream the butter with a round-

ed knife and divide into 3 equal portions.

*Roll out the dough into a strip about 18 cm (7 inches) wide and 5 mm ($\frac{1}{4}$ inch) thick. Keep the sides straight and the corners neat. Mark the dough across into 3 equal sections. With a palette knife flake one-third of the butter on to the top of the dough leaving a border of 1 cm ($\frac{1}{2}$ inch). Fold the bottom third up and the top third down, incorporating as much air as possible and seal the edges with the rolling pin as for Flaky Pastry (p. 362). Now give the dough a quarter turn.

Repeat from * twice more, flaking on a third of the butter each time. Work quickly or the butter may melt and make the dough sticky. Put the folded dough in a polythene bag and refrigerate for 30 minutes. Repeat the rolling, folding and turning 3 more times without adding any butter. Replace in the bag, refrigerate for 30 minutes.

To shape the croissants, roll out the dough into a neat strip 56 × 15 cm (22 × 6 inches) and trim the edges. Turn the long side towards you and working from the left, notch the nearest edge at 15 cm (6 inch) intervals, leaving 7.5 cm (3 inches) over at the right hand end. Notch the further edge at 15 cm (6 inch) intervals working from the right. Cut diagonally across the pastry from notch to notch into triangles measuring 15 cm (6 inches) at the base. Set aside the half triangles at each end to cut into fancy shapes, for use as a garnish for fish, chicken or beef dishes. Brush the triangles with the egg and sugar glaze. Roll up loosely from the base, finish with the tip underneath, then curve into a crescent shape. Place the croissants on a clean baking tray, well apart. Cover with a clean cloth and leave in a warm place for 30 minutes or until puffy. Brush lightly with the egg and sugar glaze and bake in a preheated hot oven (220°C, 425°F, Gas Mark 7) for 20 minutes or until well risen and golden. Serve warm with butter and preserves or reheat before serving.

Cheese and Poppy Seed Pinwheels

450 g (1 lb) risen bread dough (p. 332)
1 egg, beaten with a pinch of salt
25 g (1 oz) grated Parmesan cheese
poppy seeds

This quantity makes 12 pinwheels.

Divide the risen bread dough into 12 even-sized portions. Roll each piece into a long thin sausage shape, and flatten lightly with the palm of the hand. Brush each strip of dough with the beaten egg mixture and sprinkle with a little grated Parmesan cheese. Roll up each strip of dough tightly, pressing the ends of the dough to seal.

Stand the pinwheels on greased baking sheets, leaving space for spreading. Brush each pinwheel with the beaten egg mixture and sprinkle the tops with poppy seeds.

Cover with a large polythene bag and leave in a warm place for about 20 minutes until risen. Bake in a hot oven (220°C, 425°F, Gas Mark 7) for 15 minutes.

Edam Tea Ring

225 g (8 oz) plain flour
4½ teaspoons baking powder
1 teaspoon salt
1 teaspoon paprika
225 g (8 oz) Edam cheese, grated
4 tablespoons piccalilli pickle, chopped
1 large egg
150 ml (¼ pint) milk

Sift the flour, baking powder, salt and paprika pepper into a large mixing bowl. Rub in 200 g (7 oz) of the grated cheese and add piccalilli pickle.

Beat the egg and milk together. Pour most of the milk mixture into the cheese mixture, reserving a little for glazing.

Divide the dough into 6 pieces, and form each into a roll. Place these on a baking tray to form a circle, leaving a space between each roll. Brush the rolls with the milk and egg mixture and sprinkle with the remaining cheese.

Bake in a hot oven (220°C, 425°F, Gas Mark 7) for 25 minutes.

Cool on a wire rack. Serve as a circle, or broken up, either hot or cold.

Bridge Rolls

225 g (8 oz) strong white flour
1 teaspoon salt
50 g (2 oz) butter or margarine
15 g (½ oz) fresh yeast
or
1½ teaspoons dried yeast with 1 teaspoon sugar
1 egg, beaten
approx. 100 ml (4 fl oz) warm milk
cream or Egg and Milk Wash (1 egg beaten with 1–2 tablespoons milk), to glaze

This quantity makes 12 to 16 rolls.

Sift the flour and salt into a mixing bowl and leave in a warm place. Cut the fat into the flour and rub in to a breadcrumb consistency. Blend the fresh yeast with the warm milk.

For dried yeast, make the milk slightly warmer, dissolve the sugar in it and sprinkle on the yeast.

When the yeast liquid is frothy, add the beaten egg and mix into the flour to a fairly soft dough, adding extra milk if necessary. Turn on to a floured board and knead until smooth. Put into an oiled polythene bag and leave in a warm place until doubled in bulk.

Knock back the dough on a floured board. Shape into a sausage and divide into 12 or 16 equal-sized pieces. With floured fingers, roll each piece into a torpedo shape and place fairly close together in rows on a lightly greased baking sheet. Cover with polythene and leave to rise for 15 to 20 minutes until the dough springs back when pressed. Brush with cream or egg wash. Bake in the centre of a preheated hot oven (220°C, 425°F, Gas Mark 7) for 15 to 20 minutes according to size. Remove from the oven and if they have baked together, separate carefully. Cool on a wire tray.

Wholemeal Treacle Scones

100 g (4 oz) flour
100 g (4 oz) wholemeal flour
25 g (1 oz) sugar
$\frac{1}{2}$ teaspoon cream of tartar
$\frac{1}{2}$ teaspoon bicarbonate of soda
1 teaspoon ground mixed spice
50 g (2 oz) butter
2 tablespoons black treacle, warmed
7 tablespoons milk

This quantity makes 10 to 12 scones.

Put the dry ingredients into a bowl and stir until thoroughly mixed. Rub in the butter then stir in the warmed treacle and the 6 tablespoons milk.

Turn the dough out on a floured surface and knead lightly. Roll out gently until about 1 cm ($\frac{1}{2}$ inch) thick and stamp out about 10 rounds with a 5 cm (2 inch) cutter.

Place the scones on a greased and floured baking sheet and brush with remaining milk. Bake in a fairly hot oven (190°C, 375°F, Gas Mark 5) for 20 minutes.

English Muffins

450 g (1 lb) strong white flour
1 tablespoon salt
15 g ($\frac{1}{2}$ oz) fresh yeast
or
1$\frac{1}{2}$ teaspoons dried yeast
1 teaspoon sugar
250 ml (8 fl oz) warm milk and water
50 g (2 oz) butter, melted

This quantity makes 8 to 10 muffins.

Sift the flour and salt into a bowl and leave in a warm place. Dissolve the yeast and sugar in 150 ml ($\frac{1}{4}$ pint) of the warm milk and water. Leave to froth, then mix in the fat. Stir all the liquid into the warm flour and beat well until smooth and elastic. Cover and prove in a warm place for 50 minutes or until doubled in bulk. Turn on to a well floured board and knead, working in a little more flour if necessary to make the dough easy to shape. Round up the dough, roll into a thick sausage shape and divide into 8 to 10 portions, about 1-2 cm ($\frac{1}{2}$-$\frac{3}{4}$ inch) thick. Shape each one into a round with straight sides. Put on to a greased baking sheet. Cover and put in a warm place to prove for 30 to 40 minutes or until springy to the touch. Leave room for expansion and be careful not to over-prove as the muffins will lose their shape. Warm the griddle gently and grease lightly with a small piece of lard on a fork. Lift the muffins carefully on to the griddle and cook over very moderate heat for 8 to 10 minutes until pale gold underneath. Turn and cook the other side. Wrap in a cloth and keep warm in a low oven if cooking in batches.

Pikelets

225 g (8 oz) plain or unbleached flour
1 teaspoon salt
15 g ($\frac{1}{2}$ oz) fresh yeast
or
1$\frac{1}{2}$ teaspoons dried yeast
1 teaspoon sugar
150 ml ($\frac{1}{4}$ pint) warm water
1 teaspoon butter
150 ml ($\frac{1}{4}$ pint) warm milk
1 egg, beaten

This quantity makes 20–24 Pikelets.

Sift the flour and salt into a warm bowl. Dissolve the yeast and the sugar in the warm water. Melt the butter in the warm milk and beat in the egg. Stir the yeast liquid and then the milk mixture into the flour. Mix into a smooth batter and beat well. Cover and leave in a warm place for 1 to 1$\frac{1}{2}$ hours until the batter is thick and bubbling.

Warm the griddle and grease with a piece of lard on a fork. When a drop of water splutters on the griddle, it is hot enough. Stir the batter, then use a ladle or jug to pour it on the griddle in round 'puddles', leaving space in between so they are easy to turn. However, the yeast batter does not spread as much as pancake batter.

Cook over moderate heat until bubbles break the top surface and the underneath is pale gold. Using a palette knife, flip over the pikelets and cook the other side until honey coloured. Keep each batch warm in a folded cloth in a low oven.

Sally Lunns

450 g (1 lb) strong white flour
1 teaspoon salt
15 g ($\frac{1}{2}$ oz) fresh yeast
or
1$\frac{1}{2}$ teaspoons dried yeast
1 teaspoon sugar
50 ml (2 fl oz) warm water
125 ml (5 fl oz) single cream or milk
50 g (2 oz) butter
2 eggs, beaten
Sweet Milk Glaze (2 tablespoons sugar
  dissolved in 2 tablespoons hot milk)

This quantity makes 2 Sally Lunns.

Grease and warm two 15 cm (6 inch) round cake tins. Sift the flour and salt into a warm bowl. Dissolve the yeast with the sugar in the water and leave to froth. Warm the cream or milk, dissolve the butter in it and allow to cool slightly. Mix in the beaten eggs and add to the yeast. Make a well in the flour and stir in the liquid. Mix to a smooth soft dough. Cover and leave in a warm place until doubled in bulk. Turn on to a floured board and knead carefully. Divide the dough in half and round up each half into a ball. Put a ball into each tin, cover and leave until it has risen again and fills the tins.

Bake in the centre of a preheated hot oven (220°C, 425°F, Gas Mark 7) for 20 minutes or until golden and a skewer inserted will come out clean. Bring the hot glaze to the boil and brush over the cakes while still in the tin. Allow to shrink before turning out.

Drop Scones

100 g (4 oz) self-raising flour
pinch of salt
25 g (1 oz) sugar
1 egg
150 ml ($\frac{1}{4}$ pint) milk
25 g (1 oz) butter, melted
vegetable oil or fat for greasing the
griddle

This quantity makes approx. 14 scones.

Sift the flour and salt together into a bowl. Stir in the sugar. Add the egg and milk and beat to a smooth batter. Stir in the melted butter which will help to keep the scones moist.

Grease and warm a griddle or heavy-based frying pan. The griddle is hot enough when a little of the mixture dropped on it turns golden underneath in 30 seconds.

Drop the mixture in tablespoonfuls on to the hot griddle, allowing space for spreading, and cook for about 2 minutes. When the scones are slightly puffed and covered with bubbles, turn them over to brown the other side.

Keep the first batch of scones wrapped in a clean tea towel, to prevent them drying out, while you cook the rest.

* Savoury Drop Scones

Follow the recipe for Drop Scones (above), with these changes: omit the sugar, and add 1 small grated onion, 1 teaspoon dry mustard and 50 g (2 oz) grated Parmesan cheese to the batter. Cook as above.

Savoury drop scones make an unusual accompaniment to soups.

English Crumpets

100 g (4 oz) strong white flour
100 g (4 oz) plain flour
2 teaspoons salt
12 g ($\frac{1}{4}$ oz) fresh yeast
1 teaspoon sugar
300 ml ($\frac{1}{2}$ pint) warm milk and water
1 tablespoon vegetable oil
$\frac{1}{2}$ teaspoon bicarbonate of soda
150 ml ($\frac{1}{4}$ pint) warm water

This quantity makes 12 to 14 crumpets.

Sift the flours and salt into a warm bowl. Cream the yeast with the sugar. Add the warmed milk and water, then the oil. Stir into the flour to make a batter and beat vigorously until smooth and elastic. Cover the bowl, put in a warm place and leave until the mixture rises and the surface is full of bubbles (about 1$\frac{1}{2}$ hours). Break it down by beating with a wooden spoon.

Dissolve the bicarbonate of soda in the warm water and stir into the batter. Cover and leave in a warm place to prove for about 30 minutes.

To cook the crumpets, heat and grease the griddle lightly. Grease 5 to 6 crumpet rings 8–9 cm (3–3$\frac{1}{2}$) inches or scone cutters and put them on the griddle to heat. Cook as many crumpets as possible at a time as the batter will not remain bubbly for long.

Put 1 cm ($\frac{1}{2}$ inch) of batter into each ring. Cook gently for 7 to 10 minutes or until the surface sets and is full of tiny bubbles. Using an oven glove for protection, lift off the ring and if the base of the crumpet is pale gold, flip it over and cook for another 3 minutes until the other side is just coloured. If the crumpet batter is set but sticks slightly in the ring, push it out gently with the back of a wooden spoon. Wipe, grease and heat the rings for each batch of crumpets.

PRESERVES & PICKLES

Crab Apple Jelly

crab apples
water
sugar
lemons

Wash the apples, remove any blemished parts and cut them in half. Place in a preserving pan or large saucepan and just cover with water. Bring to the boil and simmer until reduced to a soft pulp. Strain through a jelly bag overnight but do not squeeze the bag or the jelly will be cloudy.

Measure the crab apple juice and place in a preserving pan. Add 500 g (1 lb) sugar and the thinly pared rind of half a lemon to each 600 ml (1 pint) of crab apple juice. Bring slowly to the boil, stirring until the sugar has dissolved. Boil rapidly, skimming if necessary, until the jelly will set firmly when tested.

To test for setting, first remove the pan from the heat. Place a small quantity of jelly on a small plate, cool, then push gently with a fingertip. If the surface wrinkles the jelly is ready.

Have ready sufficient warm dry sterilized jars on a board, and ladle in the jam. Cover at once with waxed paper discs and cling wrap covers. Label the jars with date and recipe title.

The lemon rind may be removed before potting or one piece added to each jar of jelly as preferred.

† Grapefruit Marmalade

1 kg (2 lb) grapefruit, approx. 3
  pips and juice of 2 lemons
1.2 litres (2 pints) water
2 kg (4 lb) preserving or granulated
  sugar, warmed

Wash the grapefruit well. Using a potato peeler or sharp knife, remove the rind from the grapefruit and cut into thin strips. Remove all the pith and pips from the grapefruit. Tie the pith and pips in a piece of clean muslin cloth with the lemon pips. Coarsely chop the grapefruit and place in the cooker with the rind, lemon juice, 600 ml (1 pint) water and the muslin bag, the cooker should not be more than half full. Close the cooker, bring to M or H pressure for 10 or 8 minutes accordingly. Reduce the pressure quickly. Remove the muslin bag from the cooker and allow to cool slightly. Squeeze the bag over the cooked fruit to remove as much juice and pectin as possible, then discard.

Return the open cooker to the heat, add the remaining water and the warmed sugar. Stir over a low heat until the sugar is completely dissolved. Raise the heat and boil rapidly until setting point is reached, approximately 15 minutes. Skim and allow to stand until a thin skin forms. Ladle into warmed, dry jars. Cover with waxed discs, when cold add cellophane covers and label.

Yield approximately 3 kg (6 lb).

† Orange and Ginger Marmalade

1 kg (2 lb) Seville oranges
juice and pips of 2 lemons
25 g (1 oz) root ginger, bruised
1.2 litres (2 pints) water
2 kg (4 lb) preserving or granulated
  sugar, warmed
175 g (6 oz) crystallized ginger, finely
  chopped

Wash the fruit well. Using a potato peeler or sharp knife, remove the rind from the oranges and cut into thin strips or thicker strips if you prefer a coarse-cut marmalade. Halve the oranges, squeeze the juice and remove the pips. Cut the fruit into quarters and remove the pulp. Tie the orange pulp into a piece of clean muslin cloth with the pips from the oranges and lemons and the root ginger. Put 600 ml (1 pint) water, the orange and lemon juice, orange peel and muslin bag into the cooker, the cooker should not be more than half full. Close the cooker and bring to M pressure for 10 minutes OR H pressure for 8 minutes. Reduce the pressure quickly. Remove the muslin bag from the cooker and allow to cool slightly. Squeeze the bag over the cooked peel to remove as much juice and pectin as possible, then discard.

Return the open cooker to the heat, add the remaining water, the warmed sugar and crystallized ginger. Stir over a low heat until the sugar is completely dissolved. Raise the heat and boil rapidly until setting point is reached, approximately 15 minutes. Skim and allow to stand until a thin skin forms. Stir the marmalade before ladling into warmed, dry jars. Cover with waxed discs, when cold add cellophane covers and label.

Yield approximately 3 kg (6 lb).

† Lemon and Lime Marmalade

500 g (1 lb) lemons
500 g (1 lb) limes
900 ml (1½ pints) water
2 kg (4 lb) preserving or granulated
  sugar, warmed

Wash the fruits well. Using a potato peeler or sharp knife remove the rinds from the fruits and cut into thin strips. Remove all the pith and pips from the fruits and tie them into a piece of clean muslin cloth. Cut the fruits coarsely, saving any juice, and put into the cooker with any fruit juice, 450 ml (¾ pint) water and the muslin bag. The cooker should not be more than half full. Close the cooker, bring to M or H pressure for 10 or 8 minutes accordingly. Reduce the pressure quickly. Remove the muslin bag from the cooker and allow to cool slightly. Squeeze the bag over the softened fruit to remove as much juice and pectin as possible and then discard.

Return the open cooker to the heat, add the remaining water and the warmed sugar. Stir over a low heat until the sugar is completely dissolved. Raise the heat and boil rapidly until setting point is reached, approximately 15 to 20 minutes. Skim and allow to stand until a thin skin forms. Ladle into warmed, dry jars. Cover with waxed discs, when cold add cellophane covers and label.

Yield approximately 3 kg (6 lb).

† Apple and Raspberry Jam

1 kg (2 lb) cooking apples, peeled,
  cored and roughly chopped
300 ml ($\frac{1}{2}$ pint) water
500 g (1 lb) raspberries, hulled and
  cleaned
1$\frac{1}{2}$ g (3 lb) preserving, loaf or
  granulated sugar, warmed

Put the prepared apples into the cooker
with the water. Tie the apple peel and
cores into a piece of clean muslin cloth
and add to the fruit. Close the cooker
and bring to M pressure for 4 minutes.
Reduce the pressure slowly. Lift out the
muslin bag and cool slightly. Squeeze
the bag well to obtain as much juice and
pectin as possible, then discard. Add the
raspberries to the cooker.

Return the open cooker to a low heat
and stir in the warmed sugar. Stir over a
low heat until the sugar is completely
dissolved. Boil rapidly until setting
point is reached, approximately 15 to 20
minutes. Transfer to warmed, dry jars.
Cover with waxed discs, when cold add
cellophane covers and label. Store in a
cool dry place.

Yield approximately 2$\frac{1}{2}$ kg (5 lb).

† Bramble Jelly

1$\frac{1}{2}$ kg (3 lb) blackberries, hulled and
  washed
juice of 2 lemons
300 ml ($\frac{1}{2}$ pint) water
granulated or preserving sugar,
  warmed

Put the blackberries into the cooker
together with the strained lemon juice
and water. Close the cooker and bring
to M pressure for 3 minutes. Reduce the
pressure slowly. Press the fruit well
with a wooden spoon to extract the
maximum amount of juice and pectin
then strain through a jelly bag or several thicknesses of muslin. Measure

the juice, and add 500 g (1 lb) sugar for
each 600 ml (1 pint) of juice.

Return the juice to the open cooker
with the warmed sugar. Stir over a low
heat until the sugar is completely dissolved. Boil rapidly until setting point
is reached, approximately 15 to 20 minutes. Transfer to warmed, dry jars.
Cover with waxed discs, when cold add
cellophane covers. Label the jars including the date.

Crab Apple Jam

crab apple pulp
water
sugar
cloves
pared lemon rind tied in a piece of
  muslin

Measure the pulp and place in a preserving pan or large saucepan. Add 2
tablespoons water to each 600 ml (1
pint) of pulp and bring to the boil. Sieve.
Measure the sieved pulp and return to
the pan.

To every 600 ml (1 pint) of pulp add
450 g (1 lb) sugar, 2 cloves and the rind
of half a lemon. Bring to the boil stirring occasionally to dissolve the sugar.
Boil rapidly until setting point is reached. Test as for Crab apple jelly
(p. 340). Remove the muslin bag of
flavouring.

Ladle the jam into the prepared sterilized jars as for Crab apple jelly. Cover
at once with waxed paper discs and
cling wrap covers. Label the jars.

† Damson and Port Wine Jam

1$\frac{1}{2}$ kg (3 lb) damsons
300 ml ($\frac{1}{2}$ pint) water
4 tablespoons port
1$\frac{1}{2}$ kg (3 lb) preserving or granulated
  sugar, warmed
knob of butter

Wash and dry the fruit and prick each damson with a fork. Put the fruit and water into the cooker. Close the cooker and bring to M pressure for 5 minutes. Reduce the pressure slowly. Add the port and warmed sugar. Stir over a low heat until the sugar is completely dissolved. Boil rapidly until setting point is reached, approximately 15 to 20 minutes. Add a small knob of butter to the jam and stir (this will bring the stones to the surface and they can then be removed with a slotted spoon). Transfer to warmed, dry jars. Cover with waxed discs, when cold add cellophane covers and label.

Yield approximately 2½ kg (5 lb).

† Rhubarb and Ginger Jam

1½ kg (3 lb) rhubarb, washed and cut
    into 2.5 cm (1 inch) pieces
juice of 2 lemons
25 g (1 oz) root ginger, bruised
300 ml (½ pint) water
1½ kg (3 lb) preserving or granulated
    sugar, warmed
100 g (4 oz) crystallized ginger, finely
    chopped

Put the rhubarb into the cooker with the strained lemon juice. Put the squeezed lemons and pips into a piece of clean muslin cloth with the ginger, tie securely and add to the fruit with the water. Close the cooker and bring to M pressure only. Reduce the pressure slowly. Remove the muslin bag and discard.

Return the open cooker to the heat, add the warmed sugar and crystallized ginger. Stir over a low heat until the sugar is completely dissolved. Boil rapidly until setting point is reached, approximately 10 minutes. Transfer to warmed, dry jars. Cover with waxed discs, when cold add cellophane covers and label.

Yield approximately 2½ kg (5 lb).

Strawberry and Rhubarb Jam

1 kg (2 lb) rhubarb, leaves and base
    trimmed from the stalks
150 ml (¼ pint) water
3 tablespoons lemon juice
1 kg (2 lb) strawberries, hulled
2 kg (4 lb) preserving sugar
15 g (½ oz) butter
1 bottle liquid pectin

This quantity yields 3 kg (6–7 lb) jam.

Cut the rhubarb stalks into 2.5 cm (1 inch) lengths. Place in a preserving pan with the water and lemon juice. Bring slowly to the boil, simmer for 5 minutes, allow to cool. Add the strawberries, cutting the larger fruit in half. Add the sugar. Allow to stand for 1 hour, stirring occasionally. Place over a low heat and stir continuously until the sugar has dissolved. Add the butter to reduce foaming, bring to a full rolling boil, and boil rapidly for 5 minutes. Remove from the heat, add the pectin and stir well.

Allow to cool for 20 minutes before potting to prevent the fruit from rising to the top of the jars. Have ready sufficient warm, dry, sterilized jars on a board, and pour in the jam. Allow to get completely cold, cover with waxed paper discs and cling wrap covers. Label the jars.

* Raspberry Jam

Follow the recipe for Strawberry and Rhubarb Jam (p. 343), with these changes: as raspberries have a better setting power than strawberries, reduce both the lemon juice and liquid pectin in proportion. You can also use diced marrow flesh or pumpkin flesh to make mixed fruit jams, but make sure the diced flesh is sufficiently tender before adding the berry fruit and sugar.

† Plum and Orange Jam

1 kg (2 lb) plums
finely grated rind and juice of 2 oranges
300 ml ($\frac{1}{2}$ pint) water
1 kg (2 lb) preserving or granulated sugar, warmed

Wash and dry the plums carefully. Cut into halves and remove the stones. Tie the stones into a piece of clean muslin cloth. Put the plums into the cooker with the orange rind and strained juice, muslin bag and water. Close the cooker, and bring to M pressure for 3 minutes. Reduce the pressure slowly. Lift out the muslin bag and discard. Add the warmed sugar and stir over a low heat until the sugar is completely dissolved. Boil rapidly until setting point is reached, approximately 15 to 20 minutes. Transfer to warmed, dry jars. Cover with waxed discs, when cold add cellophane covers and label.

Yield approximately 2 kg (4 lb).

† Lemon Curd

4 large eggs, beaten
350 g (12 oz) caster sugar
finely grated rind of 3 lemons
3 tablespoons lemon juice
75 g (3 oz) unsalted butter, cut into small pieces
300 ml ($\frac{1}{2}$ pint) water

Strain the eggs into an ovenproof container that will fit easily into the cooker. Stir in the sugar, lemon rind, strained juice and butter. Cover with a double thickness of greased greaseproof paper or a piece of greased aluminium foil. Put the water and the trivet into the cooker. Cut up one of the leftover lemons and add to the water to prevent discoloring. Stand the container on the trivet. Close the cooker, bring to H pressure and cook for 15 minutes. Reduce the pressure slowly. Stir the lemon curd well, leave to stand for at least 5 minutes, then stir again before pouring into warmed, dry jars. Cover with waxed discs, when cold add cellophane covers or a lid and label.

Yield approximately 750 g (1$\frac{1}{2}$ lb).

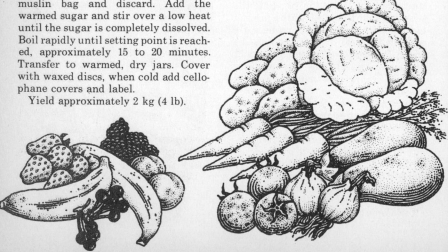

Uncooked Green Tomato Chutney

1 kg (2 lb) green or small tomatoes, halved or quartered
750 g (1½ lb) mild onions, peeled and finely chopped
100 g (4 oz) sultanas
150 g (5 oz) seedless raisins
100 g (4 oz) soft brown sugar
1 tablespoon salt
1 tablespoon dry mustard
½ teaspoon ground ginger
½ teaspoon cayenne pepper
malt vinegar

Mince the tomatoes and chopped onion, and place in a bowl. Add the dried fruit, sugar, salt, mustard, ground ginger and cayenne pepper and mix together thoroughly. Leave to stand for 2 hours to allow the flavours to develop and blend well.

Pack into sterilized jars, leaving a 2.5 cm (1 inch) headspace. Just cover the contents of each jar with cold vinegar. Seal with cling wrap covers and either place in the freezer or refrigerate. Unopened, the chutney will keep in the refrigerator for 3 months, once opened it should be used up, however, within one week.

Yield approximately 2 kg (4 lb).

† Tomato and Red Pepper Chutney

1 kg (2 lb) ripe tomatoes, skinned and chopped
2 red peppers, cored, seeded and chopped
1 large onion, peeled and coarsely chopped
1 garlic clove, crushed
1 teaspoon cayenne pepper
a little salt
225 g (8 oz) demerara sugar
300 ml (½ pint) malt or pickling vinegar

Put all the ingredients into the cooker and stir thoroughly. Close the cooker, bring to H pressure and cook for 5 minutes. Reduce the pressure quickly. Return the open cooker to the heat and boil rapidly until the consistency is thick (this can take from 15 to 30 minutes). Stir occasionally. Transfer to warmed, dry jars. Cover with waxed discs, when cold add cellophane covers and label.

Yield approximately 1½ kg (3 lb).

† Sweetcorn and Pepper Relish

225 g (8 oz) sweetcorn kernels, (frozen or canned)
2 large green peppers, cored, seeded and chopped
1 onion, peeled and finely chopped
½ cucumber, peeled and coarsely chopped
3 stalks celery, scrubbed and finely chopped
4 tomatoes, skinned and chopped
salt
freshly ground black pepper
1 teaspoon ground turmeric
100 g (4 oz) demerara sugar
300 ml (½ pint) pickling or malt vinegar

Put all the ingredients into the cooker and stir well. Close the cooker, bring to H pressure and cook for 5 minutes. Reduce the pressure quickly. Return the open cooker to the heat and boil rapidly until the consistency is thick, approximately 15 to 20 minutes. Transfer to warmed dry jars. Cover with waxed discs, when cold add cellophane covers and label. Store in a very cool place or the refrigerator and use within 3 to 4 weeks.

Yield approximately 750 g (1½ lb).

† Sweet Tomato Chutney

1½ kg (3 lb) ripe tomatoes, skinned
   and chopped
2 large onions, peeled and chopped
2 teaspoons paprika pepper
1 teaspoon mixed spice
1 teaspoon salt
300 ml (½ pint) spiced vinegar
225 g (8 oz) granulated sugar

Put all the ingredients, except the sugar, into the cooker and stir thoroughly. Close the cooker, bring to H pressure and cook for 5 minutes. Reduce the pressure quickly. Add the sugar and stir over a low heat until it is completely dissolved. Raise the heat and cook until the consistency is thick, stirring occasionally (this can take from 15 to 30 minutes). Transfer to warmed, dry jars. Cover with waxed discs, when cold add cellophane covers and label.
   Yield approximately 1½ kg (3 lb).

† Mango Chutney

4 mangoes, a little under-ripe
25 g (1 oz) salt
450 ml (¾ pint) malt vinegar
1 teaspoon cayenne pepper
15 g (½ oz) root ginger, bruised
15 g (½ oz) whole black peppercorns
225 g (8 oz) demerara sugar

Peel mangoes and slice the flesh away from the core. Discard the core, put the flesh into a bowl and sprinkle with the salt. Cover and leave to stand for several hours or overnight.
   Drain and rinse well. Put the mangoes, 300 ml (½ pint) of the vinegar and the cayenne pepper into the cooker. Tie the ginger and peppercorns into a piece of clean muslin cloth and add to the cooker.
   Close the cooker, bring to H pressure and cook for 5 minutes. Reduce pressure quickly. Remove the muslin bag and add the sugar and remaining vinegar to the cooker.
   Heat over a low heat until the sugar is completely dissolved then cook rapidly until the mixture is thick and syrupy (this can take from 15 to 30 minutes). Transfer to warmed, dry jars. Cover with waxed discs, when cold add cellophane covers and label.
   Yield approximately 1 kg (2 lb).

† Mixed Fruit Chutney

225 g (8 oz) prunes
225 g (8 oz) dried apricots
boiling water
500 g (1 lb) cooking apples, peeled,
   cored and chopped
225 g (8 oz) stoned raisins, chopped
1 large onion, peeled and coarsely
   chopped
1 teaspoon pickling spice, tied in
   muslin cloth
1 teaspoon ground ginger
½ teaspoon ground cloves
grated rind of 1 lemon
225 g (8 oz) soft brown or demerara
   sugar
300 ml (½ pint) malt or pickling
   vinegar
a little salt

Put the prunes and apricots into a large basin, cover with boiling water and leave to soak for 10 minutes. Drain, chop the fruits and discard the prune stones. Put the fruits into the cooker with the remaining ingredients. Stir well. Close the cooker, bring to H pressure and cook for 10 minutes. Reduce the pressure quickly. Remove the pickling spice.
   Return the open cooker to the heat and boil rapidly until the consistency is thick (this can take from 15 to 30 minutes). Transfer to warmed, dry jars. Cover with waxed discs, when cold add cellophane covers and label.
   Yield approximately 1½ kg (3 lb).

BASIC RECIPES

Rice and Watercress Stuffing

1 bunch watercress
50 g (2 oz) rice, cooked
1 tablespoon finely chopped celery
1 tablespoon finely chopped onion
chicken or duck liver (if using for
    poultry)
1 teaspoon salt
freshly ground pepper
50 g (2 oz) butter, melted
1 small egg, beaten

This will stuff 1 large chicken.

Wash the watercress, discarding any yellow leaves and long stalks, and chop finely. Add it to the rice with the celery and onion. If using liver, clean it, cutting out any discoloured parts, chop and add to the rice. Season to taste. Mix in the melted butter and beaten egg and use immediately.

Serve with chicken, duck or lamb.

Sage and Onion Stuffing

50 g (2 oz) butter
450 g (1 lb) onions, peeled and finely
    chopped
350 g (12 oz) fresh white breadcrumbs
1 egg, beaten
3 tablespoons dried sage
3–4 tablespoons single cream
salt and freshly ground pepper

Melt the butter in a pan, add the onions and cook gently until golden. Transfer to a bowl and stir in the breadcrumbs, egg and sage. Mix well, adding enough cream or milk to hold the stuffing together. Season to taste with salt and pepper.
Serve with roast goose.

Mushroom Stuffing

50 g (2 oz) streaky bacon or ham,
    chopped
25 g (1 oz) butter or margarine
1 tablespoon finely chopped onion
50 g (2 oz) mushrooms, chopped
50 g (2 oz) rice, cooked
1 tablespoon chopped parsley
or
1 teaspoon dried mixed herbs
salt
pepper
lemon juice to taste

This quantity is sufficient for four cod steaks.

Cook the bacon over a moderate heat until the fat runs. Clean and finely chop the mushrooms. Add the butter or margarine and fry the onion and mushrooms until softened. Stir in the rice and parsley or dried herbs and season to taste with salt, freshly ground pepper and lemon juice.

Serve with fish, tomatoes, peppers or marrow rings.

Prune or Apricot Stuffing

50 g (2 oz) butter
1 onion, peeled and finely chopped
100 g (4 oz) celery, washed and finely
  chopped
100 g (4 oz) carrots, scraped and finely
  chopped
50 g (2 oz) rice, cooked
1 tablespoon chopped parsley
1 teaspoon paprika pepper
salt
freshly ground pepper
lemon juice to taste
50 g (2 oz) prunes or dried apricots,
  soaked overnight, drained and
  chopped

This quantity is sufficient for a crown
roast of lamb or pork or a guard of
honour.

Heat the butter and gently fry the
onion and celery until turning golden.
Add the carrots, rice and parsley. Mix
well and season to taste with paprika
pepper, salt and pepper and sharpen
with lemon juice. Stir in the prunes or
apricots.

Serve with pork, lamb, chicken, duck,
turkey or goose.

Herb Stuffing

100 g (4 oz) fresh breadcrumbs
1 teaspoon dried herbs (see recipe)
1 tablespoon chopped parsley
1 teaspoon grated lemon rind
$\frac{1}{2}$ teaspoon salt
freshly ground pepper
1 small onion, peeled and finely
  chopped
25 g (1 oz) butter, melted
1 egg, beaten
stock or water to bind

Mix together the breadcrumbs, dried
herbs, parsley, lemon rind, salt and
pepper to taste. Mix the onion into the
breadcrumbs, then stir in the melted
butter and beaten egg. Add enough
stock or water to bind the mixture and
mix thoroughly. Leave the breadcrumbs to swell before using or the
stuffing will burst out during cooking.
Use sage or savory for duck or goose;
lemon thyme for fish, chicken, lamb and
veal; mint for lamb. Sufficient for $1\frac{1}{2}$ kg
(3–$3\frac{1}{2}$ lb) shoulder of lamb.

For fish, meat or poultry.

Chestnut Stuffing

50 g (2 oz) streaky bacon
25 g (1 oz) butter or margarine
turkey or goose liver
1 tablespoon chopped onion
1 tablespoon chopped celery
225 g (8 oz) cooked fresh or canned
  chestnuts, chopped
or
225 g (8 oz) unsweetened chestnut
  purée
50 g (2 oz) fresh breadcrumbs
2 teaspoons grated lemon rind
salt
pepper
lemon juice to taste
1 egg, beaten

De-rind and chop the bacon. Cook it
gently until the fat runs. Add the butter
or margarine and fry the chopped liver,
onion and celery until slightly coloured. Stir in the chopped chestnuts or
purée. Add the breadcrumbs and lemon
rind and mix well. Season to taste with
salt and freshly ground pepper and
sharpen with lemon juice. Bind with
beaten egg. Use to stuff the breast of the
bird and put any surplus into the body
cavity.

Serve with turkey and goose.

Sausagemeat and Herb Stuffing

15 g (½ oz) butter
1 large onion, peeled and finely
  chopped
225 g (8 oz) pork sausagemeat
100 g (4 oz) fresh white breadcrumbs
2 teaspoons dried mixed herbs
1 tablespoon finely chopped parsley
1 egg, beaten
salt and freshly ground black pepper

Melt butter in a pan, add the onion and cook gently until soft and lightly coloured. Transfer to a bowl, stir in the remaining stuffing ingredients with plenty of salt and pepper and mix thoroughly. Serve with roast turkey.
Serves 10–12

Bacon and Corn Stuffing

15 g (½ oz) butter
1 large onion, peeled and finely
  chopped
225 g (8 oz) streaky bacon, rinds
  removed and chopped
1 × 225 g (8 oz) packet frozen
  sweetcorn
salt
50 g (2 oz) shredded beef suet
100 g (4 oz) fresh white breadcrumbs
1 egg, beaten
freshly ground black pepper

Melt butter in a pan, add the onion and cook gently until soft and lightly coloured. Remove the onion from the pan with a slotted spoon and put in a bowl. Add the bacon to the pan, cook until crisp and golden, then transfer to the bowl. Cook the sweetcorn in boiling salted water for 5 minutes, then drain and add to the bowl with the remaining stuffing ingredients. Season to taste with salt and pepper and mix well.
  Serve with roast turkey.
Serves 10–12

Sausagemeat and Apple Stuffing

50 g (2 oz) butter
2 medium-sized onions, peeled and
  finely chopped
liver from goose, finely chopped
225 g (8 oz) pork sausagemeat
2 large cooking apples
175 g (6 oz) brown breadcrumbs

Melt the butter in a pan, add the onions and cook gently until golden. Add the liver and sausagemeat and cook until browned, breaking up and stirring constantly. Peel, core and chop the apples and add to the pan. Continue cooking for 5 minutes, stirring constantly, then transfer to a bowl and stir in the breadcrumbs. Season and mix well.
  Serve with roast goose.

Apple and Nut Stuffing

50 g (2 oz) salted peanuts
1 Bramley cooking apple
50 g (2 oz) butter
1 small onion, finely chopped
2 tablespoons finely chopped celery
50 g (2 oz) fresh breadcrumbs
1 tablespoon chopped parsley
1 teaspoon dried savory
salt
freshly ground pepper
lemon juice

This quantity is sufficient for 1½ kg (3–3½ lb) blade of pork. Chop the peanuts thoroughly. Peel, core and chop the apple. Heat the butter and then fry peanuts until golden. Add the apple, onion and celery and cook until softened. Stir in the breadcrumbs, parsley and savory. Season well with salt and pepper and lemon juice, to taste. Mix and leave for 20 minutes before using, so that the breadcrumbs can absorb the moisture and swell. Serve with roast pork, duck or goose.

Horseradish Cream

2 tablespoons grated horseradish
150 ml (¼ pint) soured cream
1 teaspoon French mustard
1 teaspoon caster sugar
salt
freshly ground pepper

Mix the horseradish into the soured cream. Add the mustard and sugar and salt and pepper to taste. The same quantity of double cream sharpened with 2 teaspoons lemon juice may be used instead of the soured cream.

Serve with roast beef, smoked mackerel or eel.

Gooseberry Sauce

225 g (8 oz) gooseberries
3–4 tablespoons water
25 g (1 oz) butter
sugar to taste

Top and tail the gooseberries. Put them in a pan with the water, cover and cook until soft. Whisk the gooseberries until smooth and continue cooking until they form a thick purée. Stir in the butter and add sugar to taste.

Serve with mackerel or pork chops.

Apple Sauce

450 g (1 lb) apples
2–3 tablespoons water
25 g (1 oz) butter
sugar to taste

Peel, core and slice the apples. Put the water in a pan, add the apples, cover and cook gently until soft. Remove the lid, beat until smooth and continue cooking gently until thickened. Stir in the butter and add sugar to taste.

Serve with roast pork or sausages.

Cumberland Sauce

1 orange
1 lemon
4 tablespoons redcurrant jelly
4 tablespoons port
2 teaspoons cornflour
1 tablespoon water

Grate the rind of the orange and lemon very finely with a grater. Squeeze out the juices and put them in a pan with the grated rind and redcurrant jelly. Heat gently and stir until the jelly is dissolved. Add the port. Mix the cornflour with the water and stir in 2 tablespoons of the sauce. Return the mixture to the pan and cook, stirring, until the sauce thickens and clears.

Serve with baked ham, grilled gammon steaks, cold duck, roast venison or ham.

Bread Sauce

1 medium onion
4 cloves
400 ml (¾ pint) milk
1 bay leaf
salt
freshly ground pepper
75 g (3 oz) diced white bread (without crust)
knob of butter
3–4 tablespoons cream

Peel the onion and stud it with cloves, then put it in a small pan with the milk, bay leaf and salt and pepper. Bring the milk slowly to the boil, remove the pan from the heat, cover and leave in a warm place for 20 minutes to allow the flavours to infuse. Add the bread and, after 20 minutes, remove the onion and bay leaf. Add the butter, whisk until smooth. Stir in the cream, taste and adjust seasoning.

Serve with roast chicken, turkey, guinea fowl or pheasant.

Tomato Sauce

50 g (2 oz) butter or 1 tablespoon
  olive oil
1 medium onion
1 stalk celery
1 × 65 g (2½ oz) can tomato purée
1–2 tablespoons flour
120 ml (4 fl oz) red wine
300 ml (½ pint) stock
pinch each of dried basil and
  marjoram
2 teaspoons sugar
lemon juice
salt
freshly ground black pepper

Peel and dice the onion and chop the
celery.

Heat the butter or oil and fry the
chopped vegetables until they begin to
change colour. Add the tomato purée
and fry for 2 to 3 minutes, stirring well.
Remove from the heat and blend in
enough flour to absorb the fat. Gradually stir in the wine and stock and add
the herbs. Bring to the boil, stirring,
add the sugar and season with salt,
pepper and lemon juice. Reduce the
heat and simmer for 20 minutes, until
sauce has reduced. Serve with pasta.

Mushroom
and Tomato Sauce

vegetable oil for frying
1 small onion, peeled and finely
  chopped
1 garlic clove, peeled and crushed
  with ½ teaspoon salt
100 g (4 oz) button mushrooms,
  cleaned and chopped
6 tomatoes, skinned, seeded and
  chopped
pinch of sugar
few drops of Tabasco sauce
2 tablespoons tomato chutney
150 ml (¼ pint) thick mayonnaise
freshly ground black pepper

Heat a little oil in a pan, add the onion
and garlic and cook gently for approximately 5 minutes until soft and lightly
coloured. Add the mushrooms and tomatoes, increase the heat and cook a
further few minutes until the mixture
thickens and reduces. Remove from the
heat, leave to cool, then stir in the
remaining ingredients with pepper to
taste. Taste and adjust seasoning. Chill
in the refrigerator until serving time.

Hollandaise Sauce

2 egg yolks
lemon juice to taste
100 g (4 oz) unsalted butter
salt to taste
cold water

Cut the butter up into small even-sized
pieces. Put the egg yolks and 1 tablespoon lemon juice in a bowl over a
saucepan of simmering water. Take
care the water does not touch the
bottom of the bowl. Put a cup of cold
water and a teaspoon on the side.

Stir the egg yolk and lemon juice
together over low heat until the mixture begins to thicken. Stir in the
butter, one piece at a time. Allow each
piece to melt before adding the next.

At the first sign of 'scrambling'
remove the bowl from the saucepan and
add a teaspoon of cold water. Continue
adding butter and replace the bowl
over saucepan, adding cold water as
required. When all the butter is incorporated, remove sauce from the heat
and season to taste with salt and lemon
juice. Serve at once as it will separate if
allowed to become cold.

Serve warm with fish, chicken, asparagus, artichokes or broccoli.

Tartare Sauce

2 teaspoons finely chopped capers
2 teaspoons finely chopped gherkins
1 teaspoon finely chopped shallots
2 tablespoons finely chopped fresh
  parsley
150 ml ($\frac{1}{4}$ pint) Mayonnaise
mustard and lemon juice to taste

Mix the finely chopped ingredients into
the mayonnaise and season to taste
with mustard and lemon juice. Serve
with fish.

Mint Sauce

1 teacup fresh mint leaves
1 tablespoon caster sugar
2 tablespoons boiling water
approx. 2 tablespoons cider vinegar

Chop the mint leaves finely with the
caster sugar and put them in a
sauceboat. Add the boiling water and
stir until the sugar is dissolved. Add
sufficient vinegar to cover the mint.
Leave to infuse. Serve with roast lamb
or grilled lamb chops.

Beurre Manié

2 tablespoons butter
2 tablespoons flour

Kneaded butter and flour used to thick-
en soups, sauces and casseroles. Mash
the butter together with the flour, using
a fork; add a teaspoonful at a time to a
gently simmering soup, casserole or
sauce until it has thickened to desired
consistency.

Do not boil hard or the sauce will
separate, but cook long enough to
remove the starchy taste of raw flour.
Surplus beurre manié can be closely
wrapped and stored in the refrigerator.

Clarified Butter

Sediment-free butter used for shallow
frying.

Heat unsalted butter gently until
foaming, but do not allow it to brown.

Remove the pan from the heat and
allow the sediment to settle. Strain the
butter through a fine nylon sieve or
muslin.

Leave it until cold, then lift the solid
fat off the liquid.

Garlic Butter

hot French bread
2–4 cloves garlic
4 tablespoons creamed butter

Press or chop finely 2 to 4 cloves of
garlic and beat into 4 tablespoons
creamed butter. Season to taste with
salt and freshly ground pepper. Serve
with grilled meat or for flavouring
vegetables.

Parsley Butter

1 tablespoon finely chopped parsley
2 tablespoons creamed butter
salt
lemon juice to taste

Beat 1 tablespoon finely chopped parsley into every 2 tablespoons creamed
butter. Season with salt and sharpen to
taste with lemon juice. Roll into a
sausage shape, wrap and chill. Slice and
use as a garnish or for grilled fish or
meat or for flavouring cooked
vegetables.

Croûtons

slices of bread
oil for deep frying
or
butter for shallow frying

Slice bread 1 cm ($\frac{1}{2}$ inch) thick. Remove the crusts and cut the bread into dice. Deep fry in hot oil or shallow fry in butter until golden. Drain on soft paper. Serve at once with soup or as a filling for Savoury Omelettes (p. 64), or store in an airtight container or freezer.

Mint Butter

2 tablespoons fresh mint
50 g (2 oz) softened butter
lemon juice to sharpen

Beat the mint into the butter and sharpen to taste with lemon juice. Shape into a roll and chill between sheets of plastic. When hard, cut into slices and use for garnish.

Cumberland Rum Butter

100 g (4 oz) unsalted butter
2 teaspoons grated lemon rind
100 g (4 oz) soft brown sugar
3 tablespoons rum

Cream the butter with the lemon rind and beat in the sugar and rum as for Brandy butter. Chill until hard and serve with baked apples, steamed puddings, etc.

Brandy Butter

100 g (4 oz) unsalted butter
100 g (4 oz) caster sugar
3 tablespoons brandy

Cream the butter until soft. Beat in the sugar a tablespoon at a time, with a teaspoon of brandy, adding it very gradually so the sauce will not curdle. Chill until hard and serve with Christmas pudding, mince pies, etc.

Espagnole Sauce

1 medium onion
100 g (4 oz) carrots
50 g (2 oz) mushrooms
1 stalk celery
2 rashers streaky bacon
50 g (2 oz) butter or lard
2–3 tablespoons flour
50 ml (2 fl oz) dry sherry
100 ml (4 fl oz) tomato juice
300 ml ($\frac{1}{2}$ pint) brown stock
pinch of mixed dried herbs
salt
freshly ground black pepper
lemon juice to taste

Peel and chop the onion. Scrape and chop the carrots. Wash and chop the mushrooms and celery. De-rind and chop the bacon. Melt the butter or lard and fry the vegetables and bacon (*mirepoix*) until just golden.

Remove the pan from the heat and stir in the flour. Return the pan to the heat and fry, stirring continuously, until the roux is caramel brown. Remove the pan from the heat.

Gradually blend in the sherry, tomato juice and then the stock. Use a long-handled spoon to avoid scalding from the steam. Add the herbs, salt, pepper, lemon juice and bring to the simmer, still stirring. Cover and cook gently for 45 minutes or until the vegetables are tender. Stir occasionally to prevent the sauce sticking to the pan.

Pass the sauce through a mouli-légumes or sieve. Reheat and taste and adjust the seasoning. If preferred, the sauce can be left unsieved.

* Burgundy Sauce

Follow the recipe for Espagnole Sauce (above), with these changes: add 100 ml (4 fl oz) red wine instead of sherry before stirring in the tomato juice. Serve with steak or gammon.

* Madeira or Marsala Sauce

Follow the recipe for Burgundy Sauce (left) but use 50 ml (2 fl oz) Madeira or Marsala wine instead of red wine. Sweet sherry or Vermouth is an acceptable substitute. Serve with ham, kidney and liver.

* Bigarade Sauce

Follow the recipe for Burgundy Sauce (left), with these changes: add the grated rind and juice of 2 oranges and 1 small lemon, 2 tablespoons redcurrant jelly and 50 ml (2 fl oz) port. Cook until the jelly is melted and the sauce has slightly reduced. Serve with duck, goose, hare and venison.

* Sauce Robert

Follow the recipe for Espagnole Sauce (left), with these changes: fry 2 tablespoons finely chopped onion in some melted butter until well softened. Add 150 ml ($\frac{1}{4}$ pint) dry white wine and 2 teaspoons wine vinegar and boil briskly until reduced by half. Add the mixture to 300 ml ($\frac{1}{2}$ pint) Espagnole sauce with 1 tablespoon mild French mustard. Add 1 teaspoon sugar or to taste. Serve with pork or lamb.

Thick Gravy

approx. 2 tablespoons fat and meat juices
1–2 tablespoons flour
300 ml ($\frac{1}{2}$ pint) brown stock or vegetable liquid

Carefully pour off the fat from the roasting pan until only 2 tablespoons are left with the juices from the joint.

Stir in enough flour to absorb the fat
and fry, stirring steadily, until well-
browned.

Gradually blend in the brown stock
or vegetable liquid and cook briskly for
about 5 minutes until the sauce has
thickened. Season to taste with salt and
pepper. Serve with roast joints.

* Onion Gravy

Follow the recipe for Thick Gravy
(left), with these changes: peel and
chop a large onion. Cook until softened
in 2 tablespoons fat, add 2 tablespoons
of flour and continue as for Thick gravy.

Coating Sauce

25 g (1 oz) butter or margarine
25 g (1 oz) flour
300 ml ($\frac{1}{2}$ pint) liquid

Melt the butter or margarine in a small
thick saucepan over moderate heat. Do
not allow it to brown.

Remove the pan from the heat, add
the flour and stir with a wooden spoon
until the butter and flour are smoothly
blended.

Gradually stir in the milk; keep the
pan off the heat or sauce will thicken
unevenly and be lumpy. Season to taste
with salt and freshly ground pepper or
ground nutmeg.

Return the pan to the heat and stir
steadily until sauce thickens. Simmer
gently for 4–5 minutes until the flour is
cooked. If there are any lumps, whisk
until smooth. Coat the back of the
wooden spoon with sauce to check the
consistency.

* Binding Sauce (Panada)

50 g (2 oz) butter
50 g (2 oz) flour
300 ml ($\frac{1}{2}$ pint) liquid

Follow the recipe for Coating Sauce
(above).

* Pouring Sauce

15 g ($\frac{1}{2}$ oz) butter
15 g ($\frac{1}{2}$ oz) flour
300 ml ($\frac{1}{2}$ pint) liquid

Follow the recipe for Coating Sauce
(left).

* Anchovy Sauce

15 g ($\frac{1}{2}$ oz) butter
15 g ($\frac{1}{2}$ oz) flour
150 ml ($\frac{1}{4}$ pint) milk
150 ml ($\frac{1}{4}$ pint) court bouillon (p. 7)
1–2 tablespoons anchovy essence

Make a Pouring Sauce with the butter,
flour, milk and court bouillon. Add
essence to taste. Serve with fish.

* Lemon Sauce

Follow the recipe for Pouring Sauce
(above), with this change: add 2 tablespoons lemon juice to the sauce. Serve
with vegetables, fish and chicken.

* Sour Cream Sauce

Follow the recipe for Coating Sauce
(left), with this change: add 4 tablespoons soured cream to the sauce. Serve
with vegetables, fish, chicken and veal.

* Caper Sauce

Follow the recipe for Coating Sauce (p. 355), with this change: add 1 table-spoon finely chopped capers and 1 tea-spoon caper liquid to the sauce. Serve with lamb and pork.

* Cheese Sauce

Follow the recipe for Coating Sauce (p. 355), with these changes: add 50–75 g (2–3 oz) grated cheese to the sauce. Season with 1 teaspoon French mustard and paprika to taste. Serve with vege-tables, fish, chicken and pasta.

* Egg Sauce

Follow the recipe for Pouring Sauce (p. 355), with these changes: add 2 chop-ped, hard-boiled eggs and 1 tablespoon chopped fresh parsley or chives to the sauce. Season well with salt and freshly ground pepper. Serve with grilled fish and chicken or turkey.

* Mustard Sauce

Follow the recipe for Pouring Sauce (p. 355), with this change: add 1 to 2 tablespoons continental mustard to the sauce. Serve with fish.

* Onion Sauce

Follow the recipe for Coating Sauce (p. 355), with these changes: boil 1 large, peeled and chopped onion in just sufficient water to cover until tender. Drain well and stir into the sauce. If liked, add 2 tablespoons single cream or evaporated milk.

* Parsley Sauce

Follow the recipe for Pouring Sauce (p. 355), with this change: add 2 table-spoons finely chopped parsley to the sauce. Serve with vegetables, grilled fish and chicken or turkey.

* Mushroom Sauce

175 g (6 oz) sliced button mushrooms
1 tablespoon lemon juice
50 g (2 oz) butter
1 tablespoon dry sherry (optional)
300 ml ($\frac{1}{2}$ pint) coating sauce

Follow the recipe for Coating Sauce (p. 355), with these changes: sprinkle the sliced button mushrooms with 1 tablespoon lemon juice and sauté in the butter until golden and stir into the sauce. If liked, add 1 tablespoon dry sherry to the finished sauce.

* Béchamel Sauce

1 small onion, peeled
1 bay leaf
8 peppercorns
300 ml ($\frac{1}{2}$ pint) milk
15 g ($\frac{1}{2}$ oz) butter
15 g ($\frac{1}{2}$ oz) flour
3–4 tablespoons cream (optional)

Heat the onion, bay leaf and pepper-corns in the milk for 20 minutes, strain, and use to make a Pouring Sauce with the butter and flour, following the recipe for Coating Sauce (p. 355). Serve in place of Coating Sauce.

Variations:
Use 150 ml ($\frac{1}{4}$ pint) each of milk and well-flavoured Coating Sauce (p. 355).

For rich Béchamel, reduce sauce by simmering for 8–10 minutes and finish with the cream.

Rich Lemon Sauce

300 ml ($\frac{1}{2}$ pint) water
1 chicken stock cube, crumbled
thinly pared rind of $\frac{1}{2}$ lemon
25 g (1 oz) butter
20 g ($\frac{3}{4}$ oz) flour
3 tablespoons lemon juice
1 egg yolk
2 tablespoons single cream or
  evaporated milk
salt and freshly ground white pepper

This quantity makes 450 ml ($\frac{3}{4}$ pint).

Place the water, crumbled stock cube, lemon rind, butter and flour into a saucepan. Place over a moderate heat and whisk constantly until the sauce comes to the boil. Cook gently for 2 minutes until thickened and smooth, stirring frequently.

Beat together the lemon juice and egg yolk in a bowl, beat in a little of the hot sauce then return this mixture to the pan and reheat without boiling. Stir in the cream or evaporated milk and season to taste. Serve with chicken, fried fish or grilled fish.

Cranberry Sauce

225 g (8 oz) fresh or frozen cranberries
100–150 g (4–6 oz) sugar
finely grated rind and juice of 1
  orange

Put the cranberries in a pan, stir in 100 g (4 oz) of sugar and the orange rind and juice. Pour in enough water to just cover the fruit and bring to the boil. Lower heat and simmer the sauce gently for about 30 minutes until the cranberries are tender and split open.

Remove sauce from the heat, leave to cool slightly, then rub through a sieve. Taste and add more sugar if necessary. Pour into a serving bowl and chill in the refrigerator. Serve with roast turkey. Serves 6

Simple Sweet White Sauce

600 ml (1 pint) milk
2 tablespoons caster sugar
25 g (1 oz) cornflour

Place the milk, sugar and cornflour in a saucepan. Whisk over moderate heat until the sauce comes to the boil. Simmer for 2 minutes until smooth and thickened, stirring all the time. To make a basic vanilla sauce, add $\frac{1}{2}$ teaspoon vanilla essence and stir well.

⋆ Chocolate Sauce

Follow the recipe for Simple Sweet White Sauce (above), with these changes: add 1 tablespoon cocoa with the cornflour when making up the sauce. To make a nutty-flavoured chocolate sauce add half a 75 g (3 oz) bar of hazelnut or peanut chocolate, broken into squares. Stir into the hot sauce until melted.

⋆ Coffee Sauce

Follow the recipe for Simple Sweet White Sauce (above), with these changes: dissolve 2 teaspoons instant coffee powder in 1 tablespoon boiling water and stir into the sauce with 15 g ($\frac{1}{2}$ oz) unsalted butter. Stir until smooth.

Custard

3 egg yolks
1 tablespoon caster sugar
300 ml ($\frac{1}{2}$ pint) milk
$\frac{1}{4}$ teaspoon vanilla essence

Whisk the egg yolks and sugar together in a bowl until they are well blended. In a small saucepan heat the milk until it is nearly boiling.

Whisk the heated milk gradually into the egg yolk mixture. Place the bowl over a saucepan of simmering water or pour the mixture into the top of a double saucepan with hot water in the lower container.

Stir over the heat until the custard thickens and coats the back of the wooden spoon in a creamy film. If the custard is cooked over direct heat it is very liable to curdle.

Add the vanilla essence and more sugar if desired. Strain and serve warm or pour into a cold bowl and allow to cool, stirring occasionally to prevent a skin forming.

* Sherry Custard

Follow the recipe for Custard (above), with these changes: reduce the quantity of milk by 3 tablespoons and replace this with 3 tablespoons sweet sherry which should be stirred into the custard when cooked.

* Orange Custard

Follow the recipe for Custard (above), with these changes: finely grate the rind of 1 large orange. Then squeeze out the juice, discarding the pips. Reduce the quantity of milk by 3 tablespoons and infuse the rind in the milk as it heats. Add the strained orange juice to the custard when cooked.

* Coffee Custard

Follow the recipe for Custard (left), with this change: mix 2 teaspoons instant coffee with the sugar and egg yolks before adding the hot milk. Heat in a double saucepan as before. Serve either hot or cold.

Sherried Custard Sauce

300 ml ($\frac{1}{2}$ pint) milk
2 egg yolks, beaten
2 tablespoons caster sugar
2 tablespoons sweet sherry

Place the milk in a saucepan and bring just to boiling point. Beat together the egg yolks and sugar, then add a little of the scalded milk and beat well. Add this mixture to the rest of the milk and cook over a pan of simmering water or pour the mixture into the top of a double saucepan with hot water in the lower container, until the sauce will coat the back of a wooden spoon, stirring all the time. Do not boil. Remove from the heat, cover the surface with a circle of greaseproof paper and allow to cool.

When sauce is cold, stir in sherry.

Strawberry Sauce

1 × 200 g (7 oz) can strawberries
150 ml ($\frac{1}{4}$ pint) water
juice of $\frac{1}{2}$ lemon
2 teaspoons arrowroot

Work the strawberries and juice through a sieve into a pan. Stir in the water and lemon juice, then heat through to boiling point. Mix the arrowroot to a paste with a little water, then add to the pan and simmer until the sauce thickens, stirring constantly. Leave to cool before pouring over the ice cream.

Orange Foam Sauce

25 g (1 oz) unsalted butter
finely grated rind and juice of 1
 orange
1 tablespoon plain flour
50 g (2 oz) caster sugar
1 egg, separated
lemon juice to taste

Cream the butter with the orange rind.
Mix the flour and sugar and beat into
butter. Add water to the orange juice to
make up to 150 ml ($\frac{1}{4}$ pint). Add to beaten
egg yolk and beat into mixture. Do not
worry if it curdles; it will become
smooth as it cooks.

Stir the sauce over gentle heat until it
thickens and the flour is cooked. Just
before serving, whisk egg white stiff but
not dry and fold into sauce. Sharpen
with lemon juice if liked.

* Sherry Foam Sauce

Follow the recipe for Orange Foam
Sauce (above), with this change: substitute 50 ml (2 fl oz) sherry for the
lemon juice but do not omit the grated
rind of the lemon.

* Lemon Foam Sauce

Follow the recipe for Orange Foam
Sauce (left), with this change: use lemon
rind and juice for the orange.

Marmalade Sauce

4 tablespoons marmalade
150 ml ($\frac{1}{4}$ pint) hot water
1 teaspoon cornflour
2 tablespoons cold water
lemon juice to taste

Heat marmalade and hot water in a
small pan. Mix cornflour to a smooth
paste with the cold water. Draw pan
from heat and blend in the cornflour
mixture. Boil for 3 minutes and sharpen
to taste with lemon juice.

* Jam or Syrup Sauce

Follow the recipe for Marmalade Sauce
(above), with these changes: substitute
either jam or 3 tablespoons syrup for the
marmalade.

Chocolate Nut Sauce

1 × 50 g (2 oz) bar plain chocolate,
 broken into pieces
1 knob of butter
1 tablespoon golden syrup
2 tablespoons icing sugar
2 tablespoons cold water
2 tablespoons chopped mixed nuts

Put the chocolate, butter and syrup in a
pan and heat gently until melted, stirring occasionally. Sprinkle in the icing
sugar and beat until smooth, then
remove from the heat and stir in the
water and nuts. Leave to stand for 10
minutes before pouring over ice cream.

Fruit Sauce

1 × 425 g (15 oz) can fruit
2 teaspoons cornflour
3 tablespoons reserved fruit juice
sugar and lemon juice to taste

Strain the juice from the fruit. Sieve the fruit, measure it and make it up to 300 ml (½ pint) with fruit juice and bring to the boil. Blend the cornflour to a smooth paste with the reserved fruit juice and stir it into the sauce. Cook gently, stirring steadily until the sauce thickens and clears. Flavour to taste with sugar and lemon juice. A tablespoon of a fruit liqueur can be added.

Apricot Sauce

25 g (1 oz) dried apricots, cooked
1 tablespoon cornflour
300 ml (½ pint) apricot liquor
1–2 tablespoons caster sugar
75 ml (3 fl oz) single cream
1–2 teaspoons lemon juice

Drain and sieve the apricots. Put the cornflour in a small saucepan and gradually blend in the measured apricot liquor and sugar. Bring to the simmer and cook, stirring, for 3 minutes. Cool slightly and gradually add cream. Sweeten to taste and flavour with 1–2 teaspoons lemon juice.

Serve with Almond and Apricot pudding (p. 224).

Sweet Shortcrust Pastry

175 g (6 oz) plain flour
pinch of salt
50 g (2 oz) butter or margarine
50 g (2 oz) lard or shortening
2 teaspoons caster sugar
1 egg yolk, beaten
cold water to mix

This quantity is sufficient to line a flan case measuring 20–22 cm (8–9 inches) across.

Sieve the flour and salt into a mixing bowl. Cut in the fat and toss until covered with flour. Rub in the fat with the tips of the fingers, lifting your hands well above the bowl to incorporate as much air as possible. Add the sugar and mix thoroughly.

Stir a tablespoon of water into the egg yolk and mix into the pastry. Stir in sufficient cold water, using a palette knife, to make a fairly stiff dough. Turn on to a floured board and knead lightly to remove cracks. Cover and put into a cool larder or refrigerator to relax for at least 30 minutes before rolling out.

Cheese Shortcrust

175 g (6 oz) plain flour
¼ teaspoon salt
pinch of dried mustard
75 g (3 oz) butter and lard, or
   margarine and lard
75 g (3 oz) mature dry Cheddar
   cheese, grated
1 egg yolk
cold water to mix

Makes one 18–20 cm (7–8 inch) flan case or 18 tartlet cases or barquettes (boat shapes), i.e. 175 g (6 oz) pastry.

Sift the flour, salt and mustard into a mixing bowl. Cut up the fat and rub in as for Plain shortcrust (p. 363). Mix in the grated cheese thoroughly. Mix the egg yolk with 2 tablespoons cold water and stir it in, adding extra water as needed. Bind the ingredients into a soft but not sticky dough. Knead the dough on a floured board. Leave the pastry to relax in a cool place before rolling it out. Bake in a preheated oven (200°C, 400°F, Gas Mark 6).

Rich Shortcrust

100 g (4 oz) plain flour
pinch of salt
75 g (3 oz) butter and lard, or
    margarine and lard
1 egg yolk
1-2 tablespoons water

This quantity makes one 15–18 cm (6–7 inch) flan case, or 100 g (4 oz) pastry.

Sift the flour and salt into a mixing bowl. Cut up the fat and rub it in as for Plain shortcrust (p. 363). Beat the egg yolk and water together and stir it into the flour, adding more water if required. Work to a soft, but not sticky dough. Knead the dough lightly on a floured board and leave it to relax in a cool place for at least 30 minutes before rolling it out. Bake in a preheated oven at 200°C, 400°F, Gas Mark 6.

Suet Crust Pastry

225 g (8 oz) self-raising flour or 225 g
    (8 oz) plain flour and 3 teaspoons
    baking powder
$\frac{1}{4}$ teaspoon salt
75–100 g (3–4 oz) shredded suet
cold water to mix

Sieve the flour and salt together and rub in the suet lightly with the fingertips. Add just sufficient water to mix to a soft but not sticky dough, using a knife and your fingers. Turn on to a floured board and pat into a smooth ball. Use as required.

When a recipe says 225 g (8 oz) suet crust this means pastry which is made with 225 g (8 oz) flour plus the other ingredients.

Variation:
If preferred 225 g (8 oz) plain flour with 2 teaspoons baking powder may be used instead of self-raising flour. 50 g (2 oz) of the flour may be replaced by the same amount of fresh white breadcrumbs for a lighter and more spongy crust. This is sometimes liable to break if the pudding is turned out of the basin.

How to line a pudding basin with suet crust
1. Roll out suet crust thinly 10 cm (4 inches) larger all round than the top of the basin. Cut out a quarter.
2. Fold remaining pastry into three, place inside the greased basin and unfold carefully. Press pastry evenly all round basin, damp cut edges and press firmly together.
3. Fill with prepared mixture. Gather remaining quarter into a ball, roll out into a circle to fit top of basin and place on top of filling.
4. Trim lining pastry about 1.5 cm ($\frac{1}{2}$ inch) above lid, damp edge, fold over on to lid and press together.

Choux Pastry

75 g (3 oz) plain flour
25 g (1 oz) butter or margarine
150 ml ($\frac{1}{4}$ pint) water
2 eggs, beaten

This quantity makes 75 g (3 oz) pastry. Sift the flour onto a piece of greaseproof paper. Melt the fat in the water in a small saucepan over gentle heat. Do not allow the water to boil before the fat has melted as it will evaporate and reduce the quantity. Bring the water to the boil, remove pan from heat and tip in the flour all at once.

Beat with a wooden spoon until the dough is smooth. Return the pan to moderate heat and continue beating until the dough forms a ball and leaves the sides of the pan clean. Do not overheat or the dough will become oily.

Cool the dough slightly and start adding the beaten eggs, a spoonful at a time. Beat thoroughly between each addition. If the egg is added too quickly, the slack dough will not pipe well.

Rough Puff Pastry

225 g (8 oz) plain flour
pinch of salt
175 g (6 oz) butter and lard or
    margarine and lard
1 teaspoon lemon juice
cold water to mix

This quantity makes 225 g (8 oz) pastry.
Sift the flour and salt into a mixing
bowl. Cut the fat into cubes about 1½ cm
(¾ inch). Add the fat to the flour and toss
it lightly until it is well covered with
flour.

Add the lemon juice to the water and
stir it into the flour without breaking up
the lumps of fat and using just sufficient
to bind the ingredients into dough.

With floured fingers, gather the
dough into a ball and put it on a floured
board. Shape it into a rectangular brick
using hands and a rolling pin.

With a floured rolling pin and using
short jerky rolls, roll out the dough into
a rectangle about 1 cm (½ inch) thick.
Keep the edges and corners neat. Mark
the pastry across into 3 equal parts.

Fold up the bottom third, keeping
fingers inside and the thumbs on top of
the pastry, and seal the edges so you
have a little 'tent' full of air. Fold the
top third of pastry down and seal in the
same way.

Seal the edges with the rolling pin.
Give the pastry a quarter turn to the left
or right.

Repeat the rolling, folding in air and
turning, 3 to 4 times, until no streaks of
fat are visible in the dough. Keep the
rolling pin floured and clear of fat or it
will stick to the pastry. Chill the pastry
until it is cold and stiff before using.

Flaky Pastry

225 g (8 oz) plain flour
pinch of salt
75 g (3 oz) butter
75 g (3 oz) lard
1 teaspoon lemon juice
250 ml (8 fl oz) water

This quantity makes 225 g (8 oz) pastry.

Sift the flour and salt into a mixing
bowl. Blend the butter and lard into a
round then divide it into four. Rub one
quarter of the fat into the flour as for
Shortcrust (see right). Add the lemon
juice to the water and add sufficient to
bind into a soft but not sticky dough.

Gather the dough into a ball and
knead it lightly on a floured board. With
a floured rolling pin, roll out the dough
with short jerky strokes into a rectangle about 38 × 18 cm (15 × 7 inches).

Mark the rectangle across into three
equal parts. With a rounded knife, flake
the second quarter of fat evenly over the
top two-thirds of pastry, leaving a 1 cm
(½ inch) border.

With floured fingers, keeping thumbs
on top and fingers underneath, fold over
the bottom third of pastry and seal the
edges firmly to incorporate air.

Fold the top third of pastry down and
seal in air in the same way. Seal the
edges with the rolling pin and give the
dough a quarter turn to the left or right.

Flour the board and rolling pin and
roll out again into a rectangle. Mark
into three and flake the third quantity
of fat onto the top two-thirds of the
rectangle. Fold, seal and give a quarter
turn as before. Roll again and repeat
with last quantity of fat. Repeat without adding any fat.

When the pastry is made put it in a
polythene bag and chill it in the refrigerator for at least 30 minutes until it
is cool and firm. If the dough becomes
sticky during making, chill pastry between rolls until stiffened. Keep the
board and rolling pin clean and dry and
well floured to prevent sticking.

Plain Shortcrust

225 g (8 oz) plain flour
pinch of salt
100 g (4 oz) margarine or lard (or half
    and half)
cold water to mix

This quantity makes 225 g (8 oz) pastry.
Sift the flour and salt into a mixing
bowl. Cut up the fat into chunks, toss it
into the flour and rub it in with the tips
of the fingers. Lift your hands well
above the bowl to incorporate as much
air as possible.

When the mixture is the consistency
of breadcrumbs, shake the bowl so that
any lumps rise to the surface and rub
them in. Do not over-do the rubbing or
the dough will become sticky before the
water is added.

Mix in the cold water, a little at a
time, using a knife with a rounded blade
edge. When the dough is beginning to
bind, use the fingers of one hand to
gather the mixture together. Add more
water if it is too dry and crumbly.

Work the dough into a soft ball,
leaving the bowl clean and dry. The
dough can be used right away or put in a
cool place until required. If refrigerat-
ing or freezing, wrap the pastry in foil or
polythene to prevent it drying out.

Lightly flour the pastry board and
rolling pin. Knead the dough lightly
and shape it into a round for a round
dish, or oval for an oval dish. Roll out
with short jerky rolls away from yourself. A 'steamroller' action will roll out
the air bubbles. Move the pastry about
on the board to make sure it does not
stick, but never turn it upside down.

Basic Batter Mixture

100 g (4 oz) plain flour
pinch of salt
1 egg
300 ml ($\frac{1}{2}$ pint) milk

Sift the flour and salt into a mixing
bowl. Make a well in the centre and
drop in the egg.

Gradually add half the milk to the egg
and work the flour into the well, stirring with a wooden spoon so that the
flour falls in a thin film onto the liquid.

Whisk with a rotary beater until
smooth, then gradually whisk in the
remaining milk. Leave to stand for 30
minutes to allow the flour to swell.

* Yorkshire Puddings

Follow the recipe for Basic Batter Mixture (above). Brush individual muffin
tins with oil or melted fat and heat them
on top shelf of an oven (220°C, 425°F,
Gas Mark 7). Whisk the mixture well
and pour it into a jug. Half-fill the tins
and bake in the top of the oven for 20 to
30 minutes or until well risen, crisp and
golden. Serve immediately because they
toughen as they cool.

Light Continental Batter

100 g (4 oz) plain flour
pinch of salt
1 tablespoon vegetable oil
300 ml ($\frac{1}{2}$ pint) tepid water
1 egg white

Sift the flour and salt into a mixing
bowl. Add the oil to the tepid water and
blend it gradually into the flour as for
Basic Batter Mixture (above). Just
before using, whip the egg white
until stiff but not brittle. Whisk the
batter and fold in the egg white evenly.

Basic Coating Batter

100 g (4 oz) plain flour
pinch of salt
1 egg
150 ml (¼ pint) milk

Sift the flour and salt into a mixing bowl. Drop the egg into a well in the centre of the flour and blend in the milk as for Basic batter mixture (p. 363).

Steamed Suet Dumplings

100 g (4 oz) plain flour
1½ teaspoons baking powder
½ teaspoon salt
50 g (2 oz) shredded suet
cold water to mix

Sift the flour with the baking powder and salt. Mix in the suet thoroughly. Add sufficient cold water to make a soft but not sticky dough. On a floured board, shape the dough into a round and divide it into eight pieces. With floured fingers roll each piece into a ball. Drop into boiling salted water or stock, or place on a stew or casserole, cover and simmer gently for 15 minutes, until well risen and fluffy.

Variation:
Self-raising flour can be used instead of plain flour and baking powder. One tablespoon of chopped fresh parsley may be added to the dry ingredients.

* Roast Herb Dumplings

Follow the recipe for Steamed Suet Dumplings (above), adding to dry ingredients 1 tablespoon chopped fresh parsley and 1 tablespoon chopped fresh mint for lamb; lemon thyme for veal or chicken; sage or savory for pork or duck. If fresh herbs are not available use 1 teaspoon dried herbs. Mix and shape the dumplings and place them in hot fat round a roasting joint for 20 to 30 minutes before the end of the cooking time; until risen and golden brown. Drain on kitchen paper.

Finely chopped onion or grated lemon rind can be added to the dry ingredients for extra flavour.

Bouquet Garni

A small bunch of fresh herbs tied together, or dried herbs tied in a muslin bag, used for flavouring stocks, soups, sauces and casserole dishes. It is left to infuse, i.e. to steep in the cooking liquid to extract the flavour and then removed and discarded. Use a piece of string long enough to tie one end round the handle of the pan so it can easily be withdrawn when required. The basic mixture is a bay leaf, 2 or 3 sprigs of parsley (stalk and leaves) and thyme, but this can be varied or extended with a piece of celery stalk, a sprig of rosemary or marjoram, a crushed clove of garlic or a slice of orange or lemon rind.

Muesli

1 × 225 g (8 oz) packet cornflakes
1 packet of 12 whole wheat biscuits
450 g (1 lb) rolled oats
350 g (12 oz) light soft brown sugar, or to taste
350 g (12 oz) cut mixed nuts
225 g (8 oz) stoned dates, finely chopped
450 g (1 lb) seedless raisins
225 g (8 oz) dried milk powder

Put the cornflakes and wheat biscuits in a large bowl and crush finely with the end of a rolling pin. Stir in the remaining ingredients until evenly mixed, then transfer to an airtight container.
Makes about 24 servings

Chantilly Cream

150 ml (¼ pint) double cream
2 tablespoons single cream
few drops vanilla essence
2 teaspoons caster sugar

Whisk the cream with a fork until it
thickens, add the vanilla and sugar to
taste and continue whisking until soft
peaks form. Do not overbeat.

* Fluffy Whipped Cream

Follow the recipe for Chantilly cream
(above) with this change: whisk 1 egg
white until stiff but not dry and fold into
the Chantilly Cream. It 'stretches' the
cream twice as far and is delicious
served with both hot and cold puddings,
hot chocolate and iced coffee.

Pâtisserie Cream

2 egg yolks
1 egg white
50 g (2 oz) caster sugar
25 g (1 oz) plain flour, sieved
300 ml (½ pint) milk
¼ teaspoon vanilla essence
alternative flavourings:
lemon juice, sweet sherry, rum

Whisk the eggs and sugar together until
nearly white. Gradually stir in the flour
and then the milk. Pour into a small
saucepan and bring to the boil, simmering steadily. Simmer for 3–5 minutes; it
will not curdle. Flavour to taste with
vanilla, lemon, sherry or rum. Pour on
to a cold plate to cool and stir occasionally to prevent a skin forming. Use as
required.

INDEX

C

D

E

F

G

M

N

Q

R

T

V

XYZ

Illustrations by Russell Barnett